Psychological
Dimensions
of War

VIOLENCE, COOPERATION, PEACE

AN INTERNATIONAL SERIES

Editors: Francis A. Beer, *University of Colorado, Boulder*
and Ted Robert Gurr, *University of Maryland, College Park*

Violence, Cooperation, Peace: An International Series focuses on violent conflict and the dynamics of peaceful change within and among political communities. Studies in the series may include the perspectives and evidence of any of the social sciences or humanities, as well as applied fields such as conflict management. This international book series emphasizes systematic scholarship, in which theory and evidence are used to advance our general understanding of the processes of political violence and peace.

Volumes in the Series

Psychological Dimensions of War

Edited by
Betty Glad

VIOLENCE, COOPERATION, PEACE
AN INTERNATIONAL SERIES

 SAGE PUBLICATIONS
The International Professional Publishers
Newbury Park   London   New Delhi

Peace
U
22.3
, P77
1990
X

For information address:

SAGE Publications, Inc.
2455 Teller Road
Newbury Park, California 91320

SAGE Publications Ltd.
6 Bonhill Street
London EC2A 4PU
United Kingdom

SAGE Publications India Pvt. Ltd.
M-32 Market
Greater Kailash I
New Delhi 110 048 India

Printed in the United States of America

Library of Congress Cataloging-in-Publication Data

Main entry under title:

Psychological dimensions of war/edited by Betty Glad.
       p. cm. — (Violence, cooperation, peace)
   Includes bibliographical references and index.
   ISBN 0-8039-3940-X (C). — ISBN 0-8039-3941-8 (P)
    1. War — Psychological aspects. 2. Psychology. Military.
  3. Military history, Modern — 20th century. 4. Nuclear warfare.
  I. Glad, Betty. II. Series
  U22.3.P77 1990
  355'.001'9 — dc20
                                         90-8755
                                            CIP

FIRST PRINTING, 1990

Sage Production Editor: Astrid Virding

Contents

Acknowledgments

This work was inspired in some important ways by Hans J. Morgenthau. The realist framework he provided in his graduate courses at the University of Chicago caused me to look at the world in a new way. His sharp intelligence, moral sense and respect for even those students who disagreed with him gave me a view of what the academic world could be like. My own thinking, expressed to him at the time, that the realist framework should be revised in some way to take account of the non-rational aspects of international behavior, has evolved over time.

This particular work was first conceived shortly after the International Society for Political Psychology conference I chaired at Oxford University in 1983 on the topic "People, Politics, and War." Several persons at that conference were subsequently asked to write specific chapters within a broad framework provided them. Others have subsequently joined the project. I am grateful to all the contributors for what seems to me to be some really fine chapters, as well as their grace in bearing with me as we went through the editorial process.

Several other colleagues have made contributions to the sections in this work that I wrote. An earlier project on the phenomenon of the limiting process in conventional war was cut short by the untimely death of my potential collaborator and friend Ronald Bartel. Robert Jervis's foreign policy seminar at Columbia University between 1986-1988, provided a stimulating intellectual environment at a time when I was completing some of my chapters and writing the introductions to the various sections of the volume. Lloyd Etheridge gave Charles Taber and myself several useful suggestions for improving the chapter on the domino theory. Colleagues at the University of South Carolina aided in various ways. Hal Birch and James Roherty provided useful feedback on the chapters dealing with limited war. Janice Love, Jerel Rosati, Robert Thompson, and Harvey Starr brought relevant works to my attention that somehow had been overlooked.

The tedious research would never have been completed had I not been aided by several supportive and conscientious research assistants. At the beginning of the project Sumit Ganguly, Charles Taber, David Anslow, and Graham Warder did bibliographic searches. In the middle phases Maria Ocasio, Patricia Drudy, and Irma Ottenwalder did library searches and aided in the word processing. Christine Buttimer, Eric Hansen, and David Wilke began the process of checking footnotes. At the University of South Carolina, in the final phases of the project, Brian Whitmore, Lucille Narjoux, Cindy Dial, Kenneth Kitts, and James Murphy checked stray footnotes and aided in all the other tedious details requisite to getting a book into press. Murphy and Kitts volunteered to burn the midnight oil with me as the publisher's deadline approached. Heidi Meyers, Merle Levy, and Bonnie Donovan provided valuable editorial assistance along the way. The secretarial staffs at both the University of Illinois and the University of South Carolina have patiently typed, photocopied, and handled mail relevant to this volume. I am very indebted to all of them.

Perhaps most important, my niece Cheryl Glad Jensen and her two vital young children, Christina and Jason Stout, provided the incentive for undertaking this project and provided some of the joys along the way that enabled me to carry it through.

Political/Psychological Perspectives of War: An Overview

Conflict between human beings is inevitable. Men and women have material and political interests which, in a world of scarce resources and limited positions of power, will bring them into competition with each other.[1] War, however, is a specific form of conflict in which large groups of men take up arms against each other and do battle for certain ends.[2] Traditionally this use of force has been viewed as a rational means to an obvious end (i.e., the protection of national or other group interests in a broader political arena). Clyde Eagleton, for example, saw war as a "means for achieving an end, a weapon which can be used for good or for bad purposes." It has been used to "settle disputes, to uphold rights, to remedy wrongs; and these are sure functions which must be served."[3] Often war results in a change in territories and other concrete goods.[4] For Hans J. Morgenthau, wars were the ultimate means for regulating the balance of power system. Against would-be aggressors, status quo states are forced, from time to time, to form military alliances to protect their continued integrity and independence.[5]

To understand fully the processes of war, however, one has to examine the psychological components of human motivation. States, as we shall show in some detail, go to war for a variety of reasons which cannot be understood without reference to the cognitive processes, the ego-defensive characteristics, and the emotions of both decision makers and the people fighting them. Nor can we understand the problems leaders have in controlling and ending wars simply in terms of some rational calculation of national self-interests. Even Hans J. Morgenthau, whose classic work, *Politics Among Nations*, assumes that states act on the basis of self-interest, has admitted that psychological analysis might shed further light on how nations behave. "The contingent elements of personality, prejudice, and subjective preference, and of all the weaknesses of intellect and will which flesh is heir to, are bound to deflect foreign politics from their rational course." Although Morgenthau doubted the value of inquiry into the motives of individual statesmen, he thought it might be worthwhile to examine those group processes which so often undermine the rational pursuit of the national interest. "The possibility of constructing, as it were, a counter-theory of irrational politics, is worth exploring," he admitted.[6]

Actually, psychoanalysts have questioned this emphasis on the rationality of group behavior for some time. Freud's *Civilization and Its Discontents*, published in 1930, triggered a spate of psychoanalytically oriented works in the 1930s and 1940s which explored the darker motives behind human aggression and war.[7] For a short period after World War II, scholars inspired by the rise of fascism and techniques used in fighting World War II turned their attention to the effects of nationalism and ethnocentrism on group behavior, the factors promoting group cohesion or disintegration on the battlefield, the use of propaganda in manipulating target populations, and the social and psychological effects of the aerial bombardments of civilian populations. In exploring this phenomena, researchers placed considerable emphasis on emotions and the ego-defensive needs as crucial to most human behavior.[8]

From the mid-1960s up to the late 1970s, however, most psychologically oriented students of the foreign policy process focused on the role of cognition in the decisions which can lead to war and the techniques for making deterrence credible. Experimentally derived psychological findings and analogues to computers and information processing systems drove these discussions. Misperceptions and other problems in assessing external events were traced to the biases in the information processing system (unmotivated biases) rather than the defensive operations or the emotions of the individuals involved (motivated biases). Robert Jervis, for example, argued in his influential *Perception and Misperception in International Politics* that there was little evidence for the operation of wishful thinking in decision-making processes. When decision makers distort information, it is because they see what they expect to see, based on lessons learned earlier in their careers.[9] To a certain extent this emphasis on the mechanical aspects of information processing was due to trends in academic psychology. Social psychologists, earlier concerned with both the motivational and cognitive aspects of behavior, came to rely on a cognitive psychology which placed emphasis on the information processing approach, seeing human beings as faulty computers.[10]

Since the late 1970s, however, there has been a renewed interest in the role of affect on foreign policy decision making. Janis and Mann prepared the way when they argued in *Decisionmaking* (1977) that decisions makers in high-stress situations are apt to use several defensive avoidance techniques in an effort to reduce psychological stress.[11] Richard Ned Lebow, in his *Between Peace and War* (1981), applied both pure cognitive and affect models to several foreign policy decisions. Although he found both models had explanatory power, he concluded that certain kinds of data might be missed if one did not look at affect.[12] Robert Jervis and his colleagues in the *Psychology of Deterrence* (1985) have shown, through an analysis of several deterrence failures, that motivated as well as unmotivated biases can contribute to the misperceptions which can undermine the deterrence value of threats and thus contribute to the outbreak of war.[13] Even the cognitive psychologists, as Sorrentino and Higgins have recently shown, are bringing affect back into their models as a way of more fully explaining information processing by human beings.[14]

In tune with these recent trends, we will explore in this work both motivated (i.e., affect driven) and unmotivated (to fit prior schema) biases, and refer to findings from both academic and psychoanalytic psychology. The sheer mechanical problems an individual has in processing complex information will be noted, as well as the importance of group dynamics on the decision-making process. But one must also look at underlying needs if one wants to fully understand why decision makers tend to bolster certain alternatives over others, why they seek unanimity in the opinions of the members of a group, why they are inclined to overestimate the power and evil intent of their enemies. The *psychological dimension*, in short, is defined for the purposes of this book as including not only cognitive processes (e.g., predisposing images, perceptions and misperceptions, capacity for learning) and group dynamics, but also the deeper emotional needs or ego-defensive traits that undergird these processes.

We make no simple equation, it should be clear, of the psychological element in the policy process with the irrational. In many places, of course, psychological variables will be used to explain what went wrong. We will address questions such as: How nations might drift into wars that do not serve their interests; how leadership pathologies may contribute to this drift; and why decision makers do not consider all the most important alternatives in a crisis and ignore important information. But we also note that cognitive simplifications may serve positive ends, that emotions may have constructive as well as destructive results. Thus an understanding of how easy it is to distort information during a crisis might well promote conservative behavior which will serve values better in the long run. Emotional factors, too, may reinforce rational considerations, depending on the circumstances. Anxiety, as Holsti points out below, often inhibits the consideration of alternatives during a crisis. But realistic fear and an ability to empathize with an enemy may enhance rationality during a crisis, if it results in searching behavior to try to understand the concerns of the other side in an effort to find a mutually agreeable compromise.[15]

Another caveat should be issued at this time. Psychological explanation is not seen as an alternative to political explanation, but as a complementary form of analysis. Rather than creating false polarities, our goal is to explore the interaction between political and psychological factors. The assumption is that foreign policy motivation, generally, is determined by many different factors, at several different levels of analysis. Simplicity of explanation is lost, it is true, when one resorts to multi-causal analysis. But as Richard Cottam has noted, the ability to explain is enhanced.[16]

The decision to go to war, for example, can best be seen as a result of several interacting political and psychological factors. From the long-term perspective we can see that certain social and political structures—domestic and international— make wars more or less likely. Power relationships, alliance structures, forms of government, and the competition over scarce resources do influence decisions to go to war. Yet it should also be clear that psychological factors also are at work at this level. Nations would not go to war so often if the underlying makeup of homo sapiens made it psychologically impossible for them to kill each other in a grand scale. Is it, as Einstein suggested to Freud, that men have within them a latent "lust for hatred and destruction" which rather easily can be called into play by leaders in control of the schools and the mass media?[17] Or does this lust vary from culture to culture? To answer this question one must go beyond the psychological characteristics common to all human beings to an analysis of the cultural or national variations which make war more or less probable for a particular group of people.

The proximate causes of a particular war, moreover, are equally complex. At one level the immediate causes consist of the specific purposes which leaders think war will serve, the particular strategies they have adopted, their ability to process information and control events in times of crises. These topics have been the traditional concerns of political scientists and historians. But psychological factors may also be evident in the triggering events which lead to specific decisions to go into battle. Rational choice is apt to be limited in situations where choices have to be made between several competing fundamental values. Misperceptions of the enemy and of the actual threat to one's own nation and its place in the world can lead to either over-reactions or under-reactions, both of which are likely to increase the likelihood of war. Crises, too, are apt to evoke the deeper emotional needs of key leaders in ways which can exacerbate the crisis.[18]

The discussion in this volume will be organized around the various phases of the war processes. In Part I, the section titled Predisposing Factors will explore the biological, cultural, and related psychological motives predisposing human beings to go to war with each other. In the second section of Part I titled Decision Making and Proximate Factors, the proximate causes of war will be investigated. Topics covered include the difficulties that decision makers have in making rational choices and managing crises, as well as the impact of idiosyncratic personality characteristics on decisions to go to war. In Part II we will examine the processes associated with conventional wars. The impact of combat on leaders, fighters, and civilians will be explored — as well as the problems of maintaining control during limited wars, and the possibility of learning from them. In Part III the logical, political, psychological and value problems associated with contemporary American and Soviet nuclear strategies will be delineated. Recent experience with conventional war and natural disasters will be used to depict the potential problem in controlling and limiting the damage of nuclear wars. The volume ends with an exploration of the implications of social-psychological perspectives for limiting wars in the future.

The focus in this work will be on wars between states. The phenomena of civil strife and terrorism would involve us in topics such as the nature of national identifications and the conditions under which men rebel, which would take us beyond the bounds set forth in this project. Suggestions for reading more detailed analyses of the topics covered in this volume are provided in the notes accompanying each chapter. With the exception of the chapters by Steven Kull, all of the material in this work is being presented for the first time.

Notes

1. For the classic analyses of group conflicts see Kenneth Boulding, *Conflict and Defense* (New York: Harper and Row, 1962); Jessie Bernard, "Parties and Issues in Conflict," *Journal of Conflict Resolution*, I,2 (June 1957): 111-121; Lewis A. Coser, *The Functions of Social Conflict* (New York: Free Press, 1956); Elton B. McNeil, ed., *The Nature of Human Conflict* (Englewood Cliffs, NJ: Prentice-Hall, 1965).

2. Quincy Wright in his classic work *A Study of War* (Chicago: University of Chicago Press, 1942, vol. 1, 8) defines war more broadly as "violent contact of distinct but similar entities."

3. Clyde Eagleton, quoted in James E. Dougherty and Robert Pfaltzgraff, *Contending Theories of International Relations*, 2nd ed. (New York: Harper and Row, 1981), 329.

4. See Paul F. Diehl and Gary Goertz, "Territorial Changes and Militarized Conflict," *Journal of Conflict Resolution*, 32,1 (March 1988): 103-22.

5. Hans J. Morgenthau with Kenneth Thompson, *Politics Among Nations: The Struggle for Power and Peace*, 7th ed. (New York: Alfred A. Knopf, 1973), 187-188.

6. Morgenthau and Thompson, *Politics Among Nations*, 5-7.

7. Sigmund Freud, *Civilization and Its Discontents* (New York: Cape and Smith, 1930); Harold Lasswell, *World Politics and Personal Insecurity* (New York: McGraw-Hill, 1935); John Dollard, Neal E. Miller, Leonard W. Doob, O. H. Mowrer, Robert R. Sears, *Frustration and Aggression* (New Haven, CT: Yale University Press, 1939); R. E. Money Kryle, "The Development of War," *British Journal of Medical Psychiatry*, 16 (1937) and "The Psychology of Propaganda," *British Journal of Medical Psychology*, 19 (1941). For earlier works see Caroline Elizabeth Payne, *The Neuroses of Nations* (London: G. Allen and Urwin, 1925); George M. Stratton, *The Social Psychology of International Conflict* (New York: Appleton, 1929). For an overview of the early psychoanalytic literature and a contemporary statement see Franco Fornari, *Psychoanalysis of War*, trans. by Alenka Pfeifer (Bloomington: Indiana University Press, 1975).

8. See, for example, E. A. Shils and M. Janowitz's "Cohesion and Disintegration in the Wehrmacht in World War II," *Public Opinion Quarterly* 12, 2 (1948): 280-315; T. W. Adorno, E. Frenkel-Brunswik, E. Levinson, R. N. Sanford, *The Authoritarian Personality* (New York: Harper and Row, 1950); Alfred Stanton and Stewart Perry, eds., *Personality and Political Crisis* (Glencoe, Illinois: The Free Press, 1951); Irving Janis, *Air War and Emotional Stress* (New York: McGraw-Hill, 1951); Harold Lasswell, *National Security and Individual Freedom* (New York: McGraw-Hill, 1950); Herbert C. Kelman, *International Behavior: A Social-Psychological Analysis* (New York: Holt, Rinehart and Winston, 1965); Charlotte Beradt, *The Third Reich of Dreams* (University of Chicago Press, 1968). For an overview of the field of political psychology since 1945, see Betty Glad, "Political Psychology: Where Have We Been, Where Are We Going?" in a series edited by William Crotty on the subdisciplines of political science, to be published by Northwestern University Press, due out in 1991.

9. R. Jervis, *Perceptions and Misperception in International Politics* (Princeton, NJ: Princeton University Press, 1976), 249-57.

10. For the neglect of affect in cognitive psychology in the 1960s and 1970s see Richard M. Sorrentino and E. Tory Higgins, "Motivation and Cognition," in their *Handbook of Motivation and Cognition: Foundations of Social Behavior* (New York: Guilford Press, 1986), 1-8.

11. Irving Janis and L. Mann, *Decision Making: A Psychological Analysis of Conflict, Choice, and Commitment* (New York: Free Press, 1977).

12. Richard Ned Lebow, *Between Peace and War: The Nature of International Crisis* (Baltimore, MD: Johns Hopkins University Press, 1981).

13. Robert Jervis, R. N. Lebow, J. G. Stein, *Psychology and Deterrence* (Baltimore, MD: John Hopkins University Press, 1985).

14. Richard M. Sorrentino and E. Tory Higgins, "Motivation and Cognition," in their *Handbook of Motivation and Cognition*, 9-19. Robert Jervis, too, recently has noted the importance of studying affect

in order to understand such matters as nationalism and war in his "Notes on Cognition and Affect in International Politics," March 9, 1987 (mimeographed).

15. John Kennedy's concerns about a possible Soviet escalation of the Cuban missile crisis can be seen as a positive response in this light. See the recently published transcripts of his meeting with the Executive Committee of the National Security Council on October 27, 1962. David A. Welch and James G. Blight, "The Eleventh Hour of the Cuban Missile Crisis: An Introduction to the ExComm Transcripts," and "The Annotated October 27 Transcripts," *International Security*, 12, 3/4 (Spring, 1988) 4-92. For the impact of empathy and moral values on altruistic behavior see Samuel P. Oliner and Pearl M. Oliner, *The Altruistic Personality: Rescuers of Jews in Nazi Europe* (New York: Free Press, 1988).

16. Richard Cottam, *Foreign Policy Motivation: A General Theory and a Case Study* (Pittsburgh: University of Pittsburgh Press, 1977), 1-13.

17. Albert Einstein to Sigmund Freud, July 30, 1932, "Why War?" in Robert A. Goldwin, ed., *Readings in World Politics*, 2nd ed. (New York: Oxford University Press, 1970), 88.

18. Several other scholars have stressed the multi-causal nature of war, though they do not use the Aristotelian four-cause analysis tacit in the above discussion. For example, in *A Study of War*, Quincy Wright suggests that one can analyze war at the levels of technology, law, social-political structure, and cultural values. To explore the factors that inhibit the proclivities to go to war, see Werner Levi, "On the Causes of War and the Conditions of Peace," *Journal of Conflict Resolution*, IV, 4 (December 1960): 411-420. For a more recent statement on the complex relationship between power structures and national motivations to the propensity for international conflict, see Benjamin Most and Harvey Starr, "Polarity, Preponderance and Power Parity in the Generation of International Conflict," *International Interactions*, 13, 3 (1987): 255-62. Some power structures, as they note, do not allow for the possibility of attack, while others leave the option open. In the latter, strong motivations to attack may be the most important factor in the outbreak of war (242, 256-57).

PART I

Causes of War

A. Predisposing Factors: Introduction

The anarchic political system in which states operate plays a major role in sustaining the war system. In the competition for scarce resources nations have to depend on themselves to secure their interests. Without central institutions and norms to allocate resources and contain the struggle for power, they have to rely on their arms as the ultimate arbiter.[1] The frequency with which any particular nation goes to war, moreover, is related to its position in the international political structure. A nation's capabilities, alliances, and domestic political processes have all been shown by various scholars to have an impact on the number of wars in which it engages. Powerful states go to war more often than less powerful states, as Singer and Small have pointed out.[2] Possibly this is because they think they can use their power to secure tangible political interests.[3] War, too, may become more likely as a weaker power approaches equality with a dominant power, as Organski suggests.[4] Alliance formation, however, has had different effects on the nations involved, depending on the period being studied. The aggregation of alliances has been correlated inversely to the frequency, magnitude, and severity of war in the nineteenth century, but positively related to war in the twentieth century.[5]

A nation's strategic posture, too, may make war more likely. If a state has put most of its resources into offense, and that offense is seen as giving a great advantage to the nation that initially employs it, there is an incentive in crisis situations to preempt. In 1914, the commitments of Germany, France, and Russia to offensive strategies took decision making out of the hands of the civilians.[6] Each nation's war plans required early mobilization, and once mobilization had occurred, the incentives were to defend through preemptive attack.[7] These offensive war plans reinforced an imbalance in civil/military relations that enabled the military to maintain its considerable independence of civilian control and increased its influence over the political processes leading to war.[8] The move toward first-strike nuclear strategies by the United States and the USSR in the 1970s and early 1980s created similar incentives to preempt in a crisis. If either one of the superpowers did not fire its nuclear tipped missiles first, its own missiles could be disabled and therefore made useless. It is the potential enormity of the costs of actually resorting to those weapons which has placed constraints on such choices.[9]

In addition to these structural and strategic factors, domestic political and constitutional factors may influence a nation's proclivity for war. Domestic conflict, as William Graham Sumner suggested many years ago, may also motivate statesmen to focus on external enemies.[10] Anthropologists have argued that social cohesion can be promoted through focusing on external enemies.[11] Some scholars have suggested that this is true within the communist bloc as well as among artificially created groups.[12] The impact of domestic constitutional forms on the proclivity to go to war has been explored by several scholars. Liberal theorists, for example, have often argued that democracies are less likely to initiate war than authoritarian or totalitarian regimes.[13] Richard Pipes, the historian of imperial Russia, even suggested to a Reuters reporter that the Soviets will have to make a choice between reforming their type of government or "going to war."[14]

Yet, there is much that cannot be explained in terms of international or domestic political structures and rationally driven strategic choices. Powerful nations may start wars, even when it puts at great risk the group's most important values — its territory, the lives of its members, and their freedom. Even when these states win, they often lose more than they gain — the costs of the economic and political upheaval placing them in a weaker position than they would have otherwise been.[15] Partly these results may be seen as the unanticipated consequences of risky choices.[16] Yet we would also like to know why states, more than individuals, seem inclined to undertake risky choices. Indeed, as Paul Kennedy has recently pointed out, powerful states in the modern world system seem to have a proclivity toward imperial overreach — their global commitments creating a drain on their economies, undermining, even, their position in the world political system.[17] Nor is the relationship between domestic political factors and war always clear-cut. The assumption that war may be used to promote internal integration has been questioned by Geoffrey Blainey.[18] Nor is there a simple relationship, from any broad historical perspective, between the republican form of government, and the decision to go to war.[19] Nor does there appear to be any clear relationship, as Midlarsky has shown, between the degree of structural complexity and differentiation within a nation and its entrance into war. "The most traditional and/or 'primitive' society may have virtually the same probability of experiencing war as the most developed nations."[20]

Indeed, there are indications that people, in some ways, relish armed conflict. The "emptiness of the reason men verbalize for war," according to Donald Wells in *The War Myth*, "suggests that war does not rest on any rationally calculated objectives." After all, if people didn't like to fight, there are no good reasons why they should do so much of it."[21] Certainly wars often do meet certain emotional needs, as Steven Kull shows in "War and the Attraction to Destruction" (Chapter 2). Through an analysis of the legends, war hymns, and poems of diverse cultures — from the ancient Hebrews and worshippers of Kali to the men who helped to create the atom bomb — conflict and destruction have been fascinating, even attractive in some strange ways. Nor has the advance of civilization ended the human taste for violence. Indeed, Lewis Mumford suggests that Western culture in the twentieth century has embraced a split in the human psyche that makes violent eruptions likely. Freud and Jung, he charges, had begun the task of integrating these two sides of man, but others failed to pick up where they left off.[22]

Perhaps this proclivity toward violence can be explained in terms of human biological determinants. Sigmund Freud and Konrad Lorenz, as Leonard Berkowitz notes in "Biological Roots: Are Humans Inherently Violent?" (Chapter 1), traced human aggression back to drives and instincts respectively. Both men, moreover, called into question the liberal faith of the day: the assumption that as human beings became more civilized, wars would diminish and become more humane. For Freud, civilization contributed to the intensity of the destructive drives. As the requirements of civilization become stricter and the outlets for instinctual behavior are increasingly inhibited within the community, the potential for explosive outlet grows. Leaders, in such situations, can turn aggressive impulses outward, targeting individuals outside the group.[23] For Lorenz, the problem lies in technological development or weapons of mass destruction. When men were fighting only with their hands or primitive weapons, the casualties were not likely to have a deleterious impact on the species. But the modern weapons of mass destruction introduced for the first time the possibility that human aggression could threaten the very survival of humankind.[24]

Yet, the idea that human beings are motivated either by an instinct or a drive for aggression has not been affirmed by the experiments on human aggression done after World War II. As Leonard Berkowitz suggests in his chapter, there is no real evidence of a human instinct for aggression that must be expressed regardless of circumstances. Even when individuals act purposively to hurt others, he suggests, the response may best be understood as the consequences of a biologically influenced, latent disposition to attack in reaction to adverse stimuli. It is a disposition that can be modified by learning and masked by other tendencies.[25]

The rejection of a narrow interpretation of human aggression in terms of either instinct or a biologically determined drive, however, did not exhaust the array of possible psychological explanations. Indeed, somewhat more complex and derivative human needs may contribute to conflicts between groups. The human fascination with apocalypses, as Steven Kull suggests in "War and the Attraction to Destruction" is related to an image of destruction as a positive force for cleansing and renewal.[26] Wars are also the by-product, in some respects, of the need of human beings to find their identities in groups. Through these identifications, as Jerome Frank suggests, men and women often come to see those who differ from them as threatening. "An individual human life," he notes,

is a momentary flash of experience squeezed between two oblivions in a universe that appears indifferent to human existence, or at least gives no universally convincing sign of caring. Since the full recognition of one's utter insignificance is intolerable, everyone has some way of shielding himself from the awful truth. Most people accomplish this defense by identifying with some enduring and larger group and, beyond that, by viewing their lives as being in the service of some more or less permanent abstraction — freedom, democracy, communism.[27]

Given these basic emotional facts, the very existence of other polities professing different views is apt to be threatening to the individual. The existence of alternative ideologies suggests that one's own may be wrong. But to lose faith in one's own ideology is to strip life of its meaning, leading to a kind of psychological death. That is the reason battles to defend those ideologies are apt to be especially bitter.[28]

Pride is another important factor contributing to conflicts between groups. The nation, in addition to the meaning it gives to individual life, provides an outlet for narcissistic proclivities repressed in the individual's own interactions within the group. A person, ordinarily, cannot present himself as more beautiful, powerful, or moral than his or her fellow citizens. But a person can proudly engage with others in ceremonies suggesting that his or her country is the greatest, the best in the world, and that difference is due to its members.[29] Indeed, at the psychodynamic level, Vamik Volkan has suggested, human beings need outside groups against which they can define themselves, and as objects upon which they can dump all the dark, fearful, repressed sides of self. Through the processes of externalization and projection they cast out their inner devils, gaining thereby an identity with which they can live.[30]

The result of these various social psychological processes, in short, is that groups which differ from one's own are apt to be seen as the enemy — threatening and powerful in many ways, but also morally inferior. Each nation, each tribe, sees itself as the embodiment of peaceful longings and of virtue, while the other is the evil and aggressive one. Moreover, as the conflict with the enemy moves from ritualized conflict to actual battle, the enemy is dehumanized. Human beings, typically, need to see themselves as moral beings, and the result is that those to whom they do violence are apt to be seen as a less than human sub-species.[31] Not surprising, given these psychological characteristics of groups, one is apt to find symmetry — a kind of mirror imaging, as Urie Bronfenbrenner has called it — in the images opposing groups adopt in their characterizations of each other.[32] These images are maintained through the selective screening out of evidence that does not support the image of the enemy, or through the use of a double standard in interpretation.[33]

Once nations have gone to war, moreover, they each bring additional pressures on their citizens to conform to the dominant view. Under conditions of extreme threat, as D. J. Finlay, Ole Holsti, and R. R. Fagan have pointed out, all groups are inclined to see the enemy as the embodiment of evil, and they tolerate little domestic opposition to that perception.[34] On the battlefield soldiers are faced with the grim need to kill and the possibility of being killed. Authority systems and peer group incentives, as Anthony Kellett points out in Chapter 10, create incentives for them to do their duty. Civilians, too, will be pressured to support the war effort and they may engage in actions which are normally constrained; indeed, when prodded to do so by authorities they see as legitimate, they may punish fellow citizens who for one reason or another are seen as not supporting the war effort. This is especially apt to occur when the responsibility to administer pain is shared, as the famous experiments of Stanley Milgram suggest.[35] Internal changes in a group at war, moreover, may provide positive incentives to embrace the war. The enhanced cohesion of the group, the new occupational opportunities opened up to warriors and civilians alike provide positive gains for large sectors of the populace. The greater concern for minorities and the underprivileged which occurred during World War II, Ofer Zur argues, had a special appeal to women.[36]

Yet, to fully understand the psychological components predisposing human beings to fight each other, one must go beyond the political and psychological characteristics of men and women as a whole. Various human groupings vary in the meaning they give to wars. Whole civilizations may use wars as ways of dealing with basic existential problems. Neolithic warfare, Sue Mansfield argues, was governed by rituals designed to show human mastery over nature and provide outlets for the anger toward the dead parents one was obliged to honor. In feudal societies warriors embraced the heroic ideal as a means of feeling alive, of mastering death and loss through voluntarily confronting them.[37] Specific cultures also shape how aggression is expressed and influence the choice of targets. The actual expression of aggression against outsiders may be encouraged or inhibited, as various anthropologists have shown, depending on the group involved. The Pueblo Indians, as Clyde Kluckhohn has pointed out, almost never engaged in intensive armed conflict, while many Plains Indians engaged in battles almost routinely.[38]

The extent of sex role differentiation within different cultures may also influence their need to do battle, as Sir Geoffrey Gorer has suggested. The Arapesh of New Guinea, the Lepchas of Sikkim in the Himalayas and the Ituri of the Congo rain forest do not hurt or kill their neighbors, though they have the weapons to do so. They have been pushed around by others, it is true. But they have certain characteristics in common which give us a glimpse of a human possibility for transcending war. Each one of these groups manifest "an enormous gusto for concrete physical pleasures — eating, drinking, sex, laughter — and they all make very little distinction between the ideal characters of men and women, particularly that they have no ideal of brave, aggressive masculinity." Each, in short, sees sexual differences as interesting and enjoyable facts of life rather than heroic roles which must be achieved.[39] The importance of masculine imagery to male roles in war also has been noted by Mansfield. Arab soldiers facing sexually mixed Israeli combat units, for example, fought to the death rather than face the shame of being captured by women.[40]

More detailed images — of the role one's nation plays in the scheme of the world, of the nature of one's enemies, of the likely consequences of war — will also influence how a nation defines its interests, as well as the likelihood it will use force to secure those interests.[41] At times external threats may be framed in ways which encourage passive responses. The Aztec's willingness to respond forcefully to the Spanish incursions was hindered by their own mythology which foretold of the return of the God Quetzalcoatl who was tall, pale skinned, with long, dark hair and a beard.[42] In Great Britain in the 1930s, images of the destructive power of the new aerial warfare contributed to the widespread opposition of the British public to Governmental proposals for rearmament.[43] The United States in the mid-1930s was immobilized by the widespread public acceptance of the view presented in the Nye Committee Report that the United States had entered into World War I because munitions manufacturers had induced the country to provide unneutral arms and loans to the British and the French. American neutrality legislation, which from 1935 to 1939 barred American loans and the shipments of arms to any of the belligerents and thus the Allies, could not be amended to permit aid to the Allies until Hitler invaded Poland.[44]

At other times the way in which a nation frames the world will encourage military responses. Powerful nations, as Betty Glad and Charles S. Taber suggest in "Images, Learning, and the Decision to Use Force: The Domino Theory of the United States," in Chapter 3, are apt to see all changes to the system which protects their interests as threatening. Thus the U.S. decision to go to war in Vietnam, as they show in detail in their chapter, was not based on clear threats to American security, but on a metaphor rooted in misreadings of history and certain psychological and political assumptions which were never clearly examined. The limits of that view of the world, as well as the reasons for its adoption are explored in some detail.

Notes

1. See Hans J. Morgenthau, *Politics Among Nations: The Struggle for Power and Peace*, 5th ed. (New York: Alfred A. Knopf, 1973), 167-197; and Andrew Bard Schmookler, *The Parable of the Tribes: The Problem of Power in Social Evolution* (Berkeley: University of California Press, 1984), 329-330.

2. J. David Singer and Melvin Small, *The Wages of War, 1816-1954: A Statistical Handbook* (New York: Wiley, 1972), 258-287.

3. Jerome D. Frank, *Sanity and Survival: Psychological Aspects of War and Peace* (New York: Random House, 1967), 34-36.

4. A. F. K. Organski, *World Politics* (New York: Alfred A. Knopf, 1958), 371-389.

5. See J. David Singer and Melvin Small, "Alliance and the Onset of War, 1815-1945," in *Quantitative International Politics: Insights and Evidence,* ed. J. David Singer (New York: Free Press, 1968), 247-286.

6. Michael Howard, "Men Against Fire: Expectations of War in 1914," *International Security,* 9, 1 (Summer 1984): 41-57.

7. Stephen Van Evera, "The Cult of the Offensive and the Origins of the First World War," *International Security,* 9, 1 (Summer 1984): 58-107.

8. Jack Snyder, "Civil Military Relations and the Cult of the Offensive," *International Security,* 9, 1 (Summer 1984): 108-146.

9. Richard Ned Lebow, "Windows of Opportunity: Do States Jump Through Them?" *International Security,* 9, 1 (Summer 1984): 147-186.

10. William Graham Sumner, *War and Other Essays* (New Haven, CT: Yale University Press, 1911), 3-40. For the argument that American political leaders used entry into the Spanish American War and World War I to stamp out the reform movement in the United States see Walter Karp, *The Politics of War: The Story of Two Wars Which Altered Forever the Political Life of the American Republic (1890-1920)* (New York: Harper & Row, 1979).

11. See Clyde Kluckhohn, *Mirror for Man: A Survey of Human Behavior and Social Attitudes* (Greenwich, CT: Fawcett World Library, 1960), 173; Robert F. Murphy, "Intergroup Hostility and Social Cohesion," *American Anthropologist*, LIX, 6 (1957): 1018-1035; Frank, *Sanity and Survival*, 92-95.

12. P. T. Hoppman, "International Conflict and Cohesion in the Communist System," cited in Ralph White, *Psychology and the Prevention of Nuclear War* (New York: New York University Press, 1986), 299; and B. M. Bass and G. Dunteman, "Biases in the Evaluation of One's Own Group, Its Allies and Opponents," *Journal of Conflict Resolution*, 7, 1 (1963): 16-20.

13. For critique of this view see Kenneth N. Waltz, *Man, the State and War: A Theoretical Analysis* (New York: Columbia University Press, 1959), 16-41, 94-123.

14. Quoted in Jonathan Alter, "Reagan's Dr. Strangelove," *The Washington Monthly* (June 1981): 12.

15. For the argument that none of the nations initiating a major war in the twentieth century emerged as winners see John G. Stoessinger, *Why Nations Go to War* (New York: St. Martins, 1974), 219. However, J. David Singer and Melvin Small, *The Wages of War, 1816-1965: A Statistical Handbook* (New York: Wiley, 1972), 366-370, found that initiators did prove victorious in about two-thirds of wars examined. The differences between the studies may reside in the sample. Unlike Stoessinger, Singer and Small included nineteenth-century wars in their sample — a century in which wars were much less devastating than they later proved to be. The significance of even these early "wins" has been questioned by Norman Angell in *The Great Illusion: A Study of the Relation of Military Power to National Advantage* (New York: Putnam's, 1910), ix-xiii. Imperial conquests, he argued, do not pay off economically in the long run. For later work supporting this view see N. Peffert in "The Fallacy of Conquest," *International Conciliation* (New York: Carnegie Endowment for International Peace, No. 318, 1936), 119-159. He shows that German, Italian, and Japanese conquests in the twentieth century did not lead to substantial population movements outward to the conquered areas, despite claims that these areas were secured for that purpose. Indeed, as Richard Rosencrance suggests, the benefits of trade and cooperation greatly exceed that of military conquest and occupation; see *The Rise of the Trading State: Commerce and Conquest in the Modern World* (New York: Basic Books, 1986), 155-162. Evidence for this point of view is found in Valerie Bunce's "The Empire Strikes Back: The Transformation of the Eastern Bloc from a Soviet Asset to a Soviet Liability," *International Organization* 39, 1 (Winter 1985): 1-46. She argues that in the past 15 years the contribution of the Eastern bloc countries to the Soviet Union's economic growth, national security, and domestic political support has declined sharply. For a critique of these views see Geoffrey Blainey, *The Causes of War* (New York: Macmillan Free Press, 1973), 87-96; and J. H. Jones, *The Economics of War and Conquest* (London: King and Son, 1915), ix-15.

16. For literature on risky choices, see the introductory section on "Decision Making and Proximate Factors," this volume.

17. Paul Kennedy, *The Rise and Fall of the Great Powers: Economic Change and Military Conflict from 1500 to 2000* (New York: Random House, 1987), 392.

18. Geoffrey Blainey, *The Causes of War* (New York: Free Press, 1973), 71ff. See Raymond Tanter, "Dimensions of Conflict Behavior Within and Between Nations 1958-1960," *Journal of Conflict Resolution* X, 1 (March 1966): 41-64. But compare with Jonathan Wilkenfield, "Domestic and Foreign Conflict Behavior of Nations" In *Analyzing International Relations: A Multi-method Introduction,* eds. William D. Coplin and Charles W. Kegley, Jr. (New York: Praeger, 1975), 96-112.

19. For a critique of the liberal faith in the peaceful proclivities of democracies, see Kenneth N. Waltz in *Man, the State and War* (New York: Columbia University Press, 1959), 101-114.

20. Manus Midlarsky, *On War: Political Violence in the International System* (New York: Free Press, 1975), 177.

21. Donald A. Wells, *The War Myth* (New York: Pegasus, 1967), 16-177.

22. Lewis Mumford, "The Revolt of the Demons," *The New Yorker* (23 May 1964): 155-185.

23. Sigmund Freud, *Civilization and Its Discontents* (New York: Cape and Smith, 1930), 58-63, 69, 86-92.

24. Konrad Lorenz, *On Aggression* (New York: Harcourt, Brace, & World, 1966), 237-248.

25. For objections to the instinct theory of aggression from a neo-Freudian psychoanalytic perspective see Eric Fromm, "Man Would as Soon Flee as Fight," *Psychology Today* (23 August 1973): 35-45; and Frank, *Sanity and Survival*, 76-90. Fromm distinguishes between different types of aggression in terms of the motives involved. See his *The Anatomy of Human Destructiveness* (New York: Holt, Rinehart, & Winston, 1973), 185-267. For the view that aggression which is represented in the family will be displaced elsewhere and that authoritarian personalities are more inclined than others to displace, see Else Frenkel-Brunswik, "Intolerance of Ambiguity as an Emotional Perceptual Personality Variable," *Journal of Personality*, 18 (September 1949): 108-143; and T. W. Adorno, Else Frenkel-Brunswik, Daniel J. Levinson, and R. N. Sanford, *The Authoritarian Personality* (New York: Harper & Row, 1950), 384-389. See also Frieda L. Bornston and J. C. Coleman, "The Relationship Between Certain Parents' Attitudes Toward Child Rearing and the Direction of Aggression of their Young Adult Offspring," *Journal of Clinical Psychology*, 12 (1956): 41-44. The group scapegoated, as Betty Glad suggests in "Black and White Thinking in Ronald Reagan's Approach to Foreign Policy," *Political Psychology*, 4, 1 (Spring 1983): 33-76, is apt to be a group which the broader culture perceives negatively.

26. See also Spencer R. Weart, *Nuclear Fear: A History of Images* (Cambridge, MA: Harvard University Press, 1988).

27. Frank, *Sanity and Survival*, 109; for how shared values developed, see pp. 100-101.

28. Ibid., 131.

29. Fromm, *The Anatomy of Human Destructiveness*, 200-205. See also Frank, *Sanity and Survival*, 104-107.

30. Vamik D. Volkan, *The Need to Have Enemies and Allies* (Northvale, NJ: Jason Aronson, 1988), 18-19.

31. Ibid., 120-122.

32. Urie Bronfenbrenner, "The Mirror-Image in Soviet-American Relations: A Social-Psychologist's Report," *Journal of Social Issues*, XVII, 3 (1961): 45-56. The fact that two groups undergo similar social psychological processes, however, does not imply that the two competing parties are politically or morally equal, or that they bear equal responsibility for the outbreak of any given war. Hitler, for instance, really was bent on the physical destruction of the Jews, the conquest of Europe, and the replacement of democratic government with his own totalitarian form. Throughout the Cold War, the United States and the USSR had very different ideologies, strategies, and political processes. Daniel Frei, for example, argued that those who saw the USSR as beset by the same kinds of interest group competitions as the United States missed some important differences between the two systems. See his *Perceived Images* (Totowa, NJ: Rowman & Allanheld, 1986), 197-198.

33. Frank, *Sanity and Survival*, 124-129. For an important work empirically demonstrating the mirror imaging process between the Japanese and the Americans during World War II, see John W. Dower, *War Without Mercy: Race and Power in the Pacific War* (New York: Pantheon, 1986); for mirror imaging in public statements see William Eckhardt and Ralph White, "A Test of the Mirror-Image Hypothesis: Kennedy and Khruschev," *Journal of Conflict Resolution*, 1, 3 (September 1967): 325-332; Seweryn Bialer, "The Psychology of U.S.-Soviet Relations," *Political Psychology*, 6, 2 (1985): 263-273. For an experimental study showing that other groups are generally overvalued compared to one's own, and that competition enhances this differentiation, see Bernard M. Bass and George Dunteman, "Bias in the Evaluation of One's Own Group, Its Allies and Opponents," *Journal of Conflict Resolution*, VII, 1 (1963): 16-20.

34. See D. J. Finlay, Ole R. Holsti, and R. R. Fagan, *Enemies in Politics* (Chicago: Rand McNally, 1967), 25-96.

35. More than 90% of Milgram's subjects, if they shared the responsibility, would give the maximum shock, despite the screams and struggle of the confederate subject. Stanley Milgram,

"Behavioral Studies of Obedience," *Journal of Abnormal and Social Psychology*, 67 (1963): 371-378 and "Some Conditions of Obedience and Disobedience to Authority," *Human Relations*, 18 (1965): 57-76. For a general discussion of the conformity motive, see Fromm, *The Anatomy of Human Destructiveness*, 207.

36. Ofer Zur, *Men, Women and War: Gender Differences in Attitudes Toward War* (doctoral dissertation, Wright Institute, Berkeley), University Microfilm 3 1-475-874.

37. Sue Mansfield, *The Gestalts of War: An Inquiry Into Its Origins and Meanings as a Social Institution* (New York: Dial Press), 49-50, 108, 124-126, 235-136.

38. See Kluckhohn, *Mirror for Man*, 48. For the divergent American, Russian, and British attitudes toward compromise see Margaret Mead and Rhoda Metau, "The Anthropology of Human Conflict," in *The Nature of Human Conflict*, ed. Elton B. McNeil (Englewood Cliffs, NJ: Prentice Hall, 1965), 116-137.

39. Geoffrey Gorer, "Man Has No 'Killer' Instinct," *New York Times Magazine* (27 November 1966): 47-118, passim.

40. Sue Mansfield, *The Gestalts of War*, 214.

41. Herbert Kelman defines an image as "the organized representation of an object in an individual's cognitive system," in "Social-Psychological Approaches to the Study of International Relations," in *International Behavior: A Social-Psychological Analysis*, ed. Herbert C. Kelman (New York: Holt, Rinehart, & Winston, 1965), 3-39. Actually, what people often study when they talk about an "image" are the perceptions of several objects interacting within a field, the objects often having positive or negative value for the observer. That is the definition used in this work.

42. William H. Prescott, *History of the Conquest of Mexico*, John Foster Kirk ed., Vol. 1 (Philadelphia: J. B. Lippincott, 1873), 61.

43. Uri Bialer, *The Shadow of the Bomber: The Fear of Air Attack and British Politics 1932-1939* (London: Royal Historical Society, 1980), 150-160.

44. Betty Glad, *Key Pittman: The Tragedy of a Senate Insider* (New York: Columbia University Press, 1986), 271-273.

Chapter 1

Biological Roots: Are Humans Inherently Violent?

LEONARD BERKOWITZ

I. Traditional Instinct Conceptions

Analysts of war often describe the combatants' aggression as coolly calculated behavior carried out in the more or less rational pursuit of certain objectives. A good deal of the fighting can indeed be interpreted in these terms. However, these discussions all too frequently neglect the hatred that can also exist and the anger that can propel some of the violent actions. When do those emotions arise and why do they occur at all? More important, what part do they play in hostilities?

Delving into these same questions, Albert Einstein arranged a 1932 League of Nations forum on the topic, having decided no question was more crucial than whether there was "any way of delivering mankind from the menace of war." Suspecting that the answer could be found in human psychology, the eminent physicist invited Sigmund Freud's opinion. How is it, Einstein asked, that propaganda devices succeed so well in rousing men to war? Might it not be that people had within them a "lust for hatred and destruction" which ordinarily was latent but could be aroused and raised to "the power of a collective psychosis."[1]

The possibility that Einstein raised was very much in line with Freud's dark view of human nature. Freud believed that "an active instinct for hatred and destruction" resides in the depths of the human personality, and his response to Einstein spelled out his conception of the aggressive instinct.[2] It is worth summarizing Freud's thinking on this matter since his prestige has legitimated the idea of an aggressive instinct for many. Then, we will turn to another and more recent version of this doctrine, that of the Nobel Prize-winning, pioneering student of animal behavior, Konrad Lorenz.

As Freud saw it, all organic life sought the reduction of nervous excitation to the lowest possible level. Extending his belief that all pleasure-seeking is basically oriented toward the lessening of internal tension, he maintained that all living organisms essentially wanted to die, for to die was to be free from stimulation. However, Freud also realized that this peace could not be easily attained. Death is usually feared and consciously avoided rather than sought out. This is because the yearning for self-annihilation is opposed by the life instinct, Eros, causing the death urge to be deflected outward. As a consequence, instead of seeking their own death, people are supposedly impelled to attack others. Their search for inner peace presumably forces them to desire the active destruction of others. Moreover, according to Freud, whatever outward aggression people display, whether in fantasy or in open behavior, lessens their own internal drive to die. To apply this thesis to a specific case, we would say that Gandhi's abhorrence of all aggression necessarily required him to seek his own death.

Freud's conception of an innate drive to violence is very similar in important respects to the analysis offered by the eminent "father of ethology," Konrad Lorenz.[3] Along with Freud, Lorenz viewed motivation as fundamentally endogenous. Without positing an urge to die, he believed with Freud (a) that an instinct was basically an impulse to action, and (b) that this drive was generated spontaneously within the organism independently of experience. For both men, moreover, the aim of the behavior propelled by this primitive urge was the reduction of the inner excitation. Both theorists also maintained that a wide variety of substitute activities could provide this "energy discharge." Indeed, because of this similarity in their underlying ideas about instincts and motivation, a number of Freudians were drawn to ethology in the 1950s and 1960s, and Lorenz's work in particular was often cited in support of psychoanalytic formulations.[4]

Lorenz based his analysis of human aggression to a considerable extent on observations of fighting in birds and fish. Early ethologists had reported that the aggression exhibited by these species was largely unlearned and often took place without demonstrable stimulation. The higher vertebrates possessed much the same kind of unlearned drive to aggression, he insisted. "Man has inherited instincts, too," he wrote, "and the instinct to aggress is not a reactive one, but is a spontaneous activity within ourselves.[5]

It is important to recognize the motivational assumptions implicit in this theory. In Lorenz's energy model (to employ Hinde's characterization[6]), many socially significant behaviors, including aggression, are not primarily a reaction to some external event, but are impelled by spontaneously generated excitation within the relevant instinctive center in the nervous system. If the action occurred in response to a situational stimulus, according to Lorenz, this stimulus only "unlocked" inhibitory mechanisms within the nervous system, thereby releasing the instinctive behavior. Further minimizing the importance of external conditions, Lorenz held that releasing stimuli were not always necessary for the instinctive behavior to take place. He maintained that the action might "go off" by itself in "vacuum activity," merely because an excess of instinctive energy had accumulated within the particular instinctive center.

Lorenz believed that overt violence could explode in just this manner. In his 1966 book, *On Aggression*, written for a general audience, he argued that "it is the spontaneity of the [aggressive] instinct that makes it so dangerous."[7] Unless society furnishes its members with acceptable and safe ways to discharge the aggressive energy inexorably building up inside them, uncontrolled outbursts of violence are bound to occur. Civilized people today supposedly suffer from an insufficient release of their aggressive drive. As just one example of this thesis, Lorenz maintained that expeditions to distant corners of the world were often rent with serious dissension because the explorers lacked a suitable external target for their pent-up aggressive urges. Their isolation presumably kept them from reducing their aggressive drive in attacks on "strangers or people outside their own circle of friends." In such circumstances, according to Lorenz, "the man of perception finds an outlet by creeping out of the barracks (tent, igloo) and smashing a not too expensive object with as resounding a crash as the occasion merits."[8]

We can also get some of the flavor of Lorenzian theorizing in his discussion of how the aggressive drive can be diverted through evolution so that it serves nonviolent ends. Theorizing that particular action patterns have developed over the eons from earlier forms of behavior, Lorenz suggested that behaviors serving one purpose can undergo alteration in the course of evolution and come to have a different function. Despite this outward change, however, the drive motivating the original pattern presumably still powers this altered action. For Lorenz, the appeasement gestures or greeting ceremonies performed by animals and humans alike are a good example. Lorenz thought that the smile of greeting was initially a redirected threatening, and although this evolutionary newer action was spurred by a "transformed" aggressive motivation, it now served to unite people. Thus, Lorenz maintained, a diverted aggressive energy drives the social bonds that tie individuals together in affection and even love.

The psychoanalytic concept of sublimation also envisions a diversion of instinctive energy from one behavioral channel into another, although at the individual developmental level rather than over the course of evolution. As is well known, this idea tells us that people cannot only express but also gratify their primitive urges in socially acceptable ways. The surgeon presumably discharges his instinctive drive to violence in a socially desirable manner as he employs his surgical knife to save his patients' lives. And similarly, the aggressive force supposedly powers constructive problem solving and even intellectual attainment as we attempt to "sharpen" our wits, "attack" and "struggle with" our difficulties, and try to "master" our problems. From this perspective, aggression is not all bad but is actually necessary for optimal human development. Aggression theoretically is "the basis of intellectual achievement, of the attainment of independence, and even of the proper pride that enables a man to hold his head high among his fellows."[9]

II. Critique of the Traditional Conception

The preceding summary highlights some of the major features of traditional formulations of the aggressive instinct doctrine. Space does not permit a detailed examination of the empirical and theoretical shortcomings of these analyses, and all I can do here is comment on several of their flaws.[10]

DIFFERENT TYPES OF AGGRESSION

One major problem inherent in practically every version of the aggressive instinct idea is the assumption that all violent actions basically serve the same underlying purpose and are governed by the same biological mechanism — in other words, that there is one drive to aggression. In actuality, however, very few, if any, researchers now engaged in this field of study share this unitary conception, and they typically believe it is necessary to distinguish among different types of animal aggression. Indeed, on the basis of his review of the physiological evidence, Moyer proposed seven different categories: predatory, inter-male, fear-induced, irritable, territorial defense, maternal, and instrumental aggression. All of these involve the deliberate injury of another but they presumably have different neuroendocrine bases.[11]

Social psychological investigators do not make this many distinctions in their discussions of human aggression, but most of them do differentiate between two main types. All aggression, they typically say, is a deliberate attempt to injure or destroy someone (either physically or psychologically). However, they generally believe that it is at least necessary to distinguish between (a) instrumental (or incentive-motivated) aggression and (b) hostile (angry, irritable, annoyance-motivated, or aversively-stimulated) aggression.[12] In the former case the attempt to injure is carried out primarily to attain some nonaggressive goal. Thus a soldier might try to kill his enemy because he thinks this will help end the war or could save his own life. In the second type of aggression, the principal goal is to do injury. A very angry person usually wants to hurt the one who has offended him more than he desires other external rewards.

This chapter focuses primarily on the latter form of aggression, the aggression that arises from strong emotional arousal and is affected by a number of involuntary influences. The former, instrumental aggression, obviously is important and undoubtedly occurs frequently, but I will not say very much about it since this chapter is not intended to review the entire domain of aggression research.

Whatever the nature and number of types of aggression that should be established, all aggression clearly is not of one piece. They may all seek the injury of the target, but they are not all carried out for the same reasons and do not have the same neural and endocrine bases.

ENDOGENOUS OR REACTIVE? INNATE OR ACQUIRED?

I have referred several times now to yet another major problem with the traditional conception of an aggression instinct: the notion that the impulse to violence is spontaneously generated within the organism and is not produced as a reaction to external conditions. As was noted earlier, theorists holding this endogenous position basically say that the surrounding situation only affects aggression either by releasing or raising inhibitions against this behavior. Lorenz explicitly rejected the idea that aggression is primarily a response to something in the environment. Social scientists take this latter view, he said, because of a misguided optimism. Having a liberal belief in the perfectibility of man, they want to attribute social ills — including violence — to environmental flaws that might be remedied rather than to intractable human nature.

The emphasis on endogenously motivated aggression is closely tied to a de-emphasis of the role of learning and experience in aggression and social behavior generally. Although Lorenz at times acknowledged the impossibility of drawing a sharp distinction between what is innate and what is learned,[13] in his popular writings such as On Aggression he repeatedly minimized the way in which people can acquire aggressive tendencies through frustrations and other aversive experiences or by learning that aggression can produce favorable outcomes. Some other ethologists have taken a similar stance. Eibl-Eibesfeldt, for example, has argued that there is evidence that aggressive behavior can develop in humans independently of any training to be aggressive, and he also interpreted this evidence as confirming the existence of an innate and spontaneously generated drive. For him, neurophysiological research suggests that "human beings are subject to neurogenic fits of rage, produced by spontaneous firings of cells in the brain stem and temporal lobes."[14]

However, the evidence for the endogenous position is nowhere near as clear as these writers would have us believe. Take the neurophysiological findings just mentioned. These observations actually are of people suffering from some neurological disorder, and do not necessarily show that "normal" human beings also display these presumably spontaneous outbursts of violence. Moreover, other neurophysiological research indicates that brain damage often leads to heightened aggressiveness by enhancing the organism's responsiveness to aversive stimulation or other aggression-eliciting stimuli, and not by creating a spontaneous urge to attack someone or something.[15]

Perhaps even more damaging to the endogenous position are findings regarding the effects of isolation. As Hinde noted, Lorenz's energy model implies that organisms who are physically isolated and therefore cannot discharge their accumulating aggressive drive in attacks on a suitable target will become increasingly inclined to aggression. Some research has confirmed this expectation, Hinde reported, but other studies have not. Moreover, according to Hinde, even when isolation appears to promote aggression, "alternative types of explanation supported by hard data render hypothetical energy models unnecessary."[16] A study of isolation-induced aggression in mice is used as an illustration. The physical separation in this experiment led to greater fighting apparently because (a) the previously isolated animals had a greater tendency to initiate exploratory interactions with another individual, and (b) they were more reactive to stimulation from the other, perhaps because of a lowered threshold to stimulation of all sorts, so that the encounter readily escalated into an aggressive episode. Other animal investigators have also questioned Lorenz's contention that instinctive behavior can "go off" all by itself in seeming "vacuum activity" (to use the ethological term). In the critics' view, the supposedly spontaneous responses are frequently evoked by environmental stimuli rather than being driven out by internally generated excitation.[17] In general, then, as we learn more about the complex array of biological, environmental, and social influences that can influence behavior, the less adequate we find the simple energy models of motivation such as those propounded by Freud and Lorenz.

Almost 30 years ago, J. P. Scott, a widely respected scholar and researcher in the area of animal behavior, offered this conclusion regarding the traditional notion of an instinctive drive to destruction:

> There is no physiological evidence of any spontaneous stimulation for fighting arising within the body. This means that there is no need for fighting . . . apart from what happens in the external environment. . . . We can also conclude that there is no such thing as a simple "instinct for fighting" in the sense of an internal driving force which has to be satisfied. There is, however, an internal physiological mechanism which has only to be stimulated to produce fighting.[18]

Studies of animal and human aggression conducted in the years after Scott's statement only add further corroboration.

IMPRECISE USAGE

Whatever their motivational assumptions, popularizers of the traditional instinct doctrine are all too likely to employ the term "instinct" in a vague and imprecise manner. This is often true of Lorenz as well as his nonprofessional followers. In their communications to a general audience, they rarely, if ever, offer a precise definition of this concept, and critics have taken them to task for this failure.[19] Lorenz elsewhere has acknowledged this imprecision but has generally defended himself by saying he used the word only in a shorthand sense.[20] Nevertheless, it is difficult to excuse this vagueness as only shorthand. When ethologists communicate to their technically oriented peers, they generally speak of instincts, or better still, instinctive movements, as relatively stereotyped actions characteristic of a particular species that are initiated by fairly specific stimuli. This definition hardly applies to some of the human phenomena Lorenz has characterized as instinctive, such as the supposedly "instinctive need to be a member of a closely knit group fighting for common ideals."[21]

Indeed, because of the multiplicity of ways in which the term "instinct" is used and its resulting looseness, many specialists in the field of animal behavior refuse to use this word at all.[22] It is time to cast out the concept from professional discourse, in the social as well as the biological sciences, for its imprecision as well as for the erroneous ideas that generally accompany it.

ON THE SUPPOSED DIVERSION OF THE AGGRESSIVE DRIVE

As has often been noted, the traditional aggressive instinct formulation generally likens the organism to an energy reservoir or hydraulic system, and maintains
that the pent-up energy can be discharged through a great number of alternative
channels.[23] The psychoanalytic concepts of displacement and sublimation are
based on such an assumption, and essentially contend that accumulated instinctual
energy can be reduced in some substitute action, whether directed toward an
alternative target or through an alternative behavior. Psychoanalytically oriented
mental health workers and Lorenz ethologists have also followed this line of
thought in advocating sports as a safe outlet for pent-up aggressive drive. William
Menninger, one of the founders of the famous Menninger Clinic in Kansas, once
expressed this view when he wrote, "competitive games provide an unusually
satisfactory outlet for the instinctive aggressive drive," although he also suggested
that "sedentary intellectual competition," such as chess and checkers, could also
lead to a beneficial release of some degree.[24] Some of the instinctivists cited in this
chapter, such as Lorenz and Storr, have gone even further and have called for more
athletic competitions as a way to better international harmony. For Storr, "rivalry
between nations in sports can be nothing but good."[25]

It is easy to understand the popularity of this belief in the aggression-reducing
benefits of competitive games; among other things, people readily grasp the
metaphor of a reservoir of aggressive energy pressing for discharge, and they may
even think their own experience testifies to the "release" that can be obtained in
sports. However, this seeming fit between metaphor and experience is more
apparent than real, and largely arises from incomplete analyses. A growing body
of carefully collected evidence indicates that athletic competition does not necessarily lessen the chances of violence and may even increase the probability of
aggressive outbursts under some circumstances.[26]

Spectators do not always reduce their violent inclinations through watching the
players compete. Sports did not improve the relations between Czechs and Russians shortly after the Russians had suppressed the Czechs' attempt to liberalize
their government. In March 1969, when a Czech hockey team defeated the Russian
team in the world championship tournament, exuberant Czechoslovakian youths
ransacked the Prague offices of the Russian airline; instead of finding a release in
their victory, the excited men were sufficiently stirred up to attack the symbols of
those they hated. Many other incidents of a comparable nature in the United States
and elsewhere could also be cited.[27] Similarly, in his review of the effects of sports
on aggression, Goldstein[28] noted that "It is not difficult to find comparable
occurrences at boxing and soccer matches and hockey and football games throughout the world." In addition he quoted an observation made by Crook, a highly
regarded researcher of animal behavior, that "the behavior of crowds watching
conventionally" competitive sports often indicates the arousal of aggressive attitudes rather than their happy sublimation.[29]

If watching competitive games does not produce a "happy sublimation" of pent-up aggressive energy, why is it that so many people think that this does happen? The answer must be, in part, that they know they feel better after seeing an interesting game and might even be less aggressive at these times. However, if the spectators are less aggressive after an athletic contest than they otherwise would have been, this is probably not due to a discharge of energy from their hypothetical reservoir of aggressive drive but (a) to the pleasure they experienced in watching the contest so that they are in a good mood and not angry with anyone, and (b) to being so caught up by the contest that they temporarily forgot their troubles.

Second, we should also recognize that the players themselves are not necessarily less aggressive as a result of the competition. Indeed, a now substantial body of research demonstrates that competition is more likely to generate hostility toward the rivals than to produce a greater friendliness. The well-known "Robber's Cave" study conducted by Muzafer and Carolyn Sherif is only one example among many. Competition between two groups of boys led not only to verbal hostility but even to outbreaks of open violence.[30] Here too, there is no mystery about why this occurs: Competition is often frustrating. As the players compete against each other, they may be bothered by their inability to win the prize; resenting their rivals' efforts to block their victory, they may well become antagonistic toward them.

The idea that diverted aggressive energy empowers the individual's struggle for attainment and mastery also does not hold up under close examination. There is no good evidence that efforts to succeed at some task or to overcome one's problems are *generally* impelled by an urge to hurt someone (although, of course, a person's hostility toward his rival might intensify his efforts to win the competition). As a matter of fact, the hostility characteristically exhibited by those possessing a Type A personality indicates that these people do not reduce their aggressive tendencies in their intense drive to succeed.[31]

In sum, few theorists concerned with the realm of human motivation (except for proponents of orthodox psychoanalysis and Lorenzian ethology) now subscribe to the hydraulic-energy model. This formulation offers a metaphor that is easily understood but one that, nevertheless, is not in accord with the best evidence.

III. Policy Implications

If, as noted above, Lorenz could say that critics fault his conception because of a "misguided liberalism,[32] correspondingly it is also true that adherence to the traditional formulation tends to be associated with socio-political conservatism. And it is easy to see why. An innate aggressive drive of the kind envisioned by Freud and Lorenz cannot be abolished by social reforms or lessened by the alleviation of unpleasant conditions. For the instinctivists, humans are inherently dangerous and supposedly have to be controlled. Civilization and social order ultimately have to be based on force if not on diversionary circuses rather than on education and understanding.

Freud expressed just this position in his reply to Einstein. As Freud saw it, law was the might of the community. But more than this, law also was violence "ready to be directed against any individual who resists it." In his pessimism, Freud believed there was no use trying to eliminate people's aggressive urges. Society could only restrain them or, at best, divert their destructive impulses "to such an extent that they need not find expression in war."[33]

Lorenz's conservative picture of humankind extended beyond his conception of an innate drive to violence. As I noted above, he thought social scientists had a "mistaken" belief in human perfectibility and thus wanted to attribute social ills generally to environmental flaws which might be remedied rather than to intractable human nature. It is no use trying to alter society, he seemed to be saying. Human suffering should not be traced to society and its institutions but to the deficiencies in human make up — and these deficiencies will always be with us.

IV. An Alternative Conception of the Predisposition to Aggression: Latent Predispositions

The criticisms just voiced against the traditional instinct doctrine do not mean that I reject the possibility of genetic influences on behavior. Such a possibility has not been very popular in the social sciences in the past,[34] but it is now clear that humans have some built-in tendencies to react in particular ways to certain stimuli. Psychologists and other students of human behavior have shown, for example, that human babies have an inherent preference for certain kinds of stimuli and do not start with blank neural pages, so to speak, in learning to see and organize complex visual stimulation. Similarly, Barnett has pointed out,[35] human babies as well as young cats and rats are apt to retreat from the edge of a potentially dangerous cliff even though they have never experienced this kind of edge before. The mere sight of a "visual cliff" apparently activates withdrawal tendencies in these infants without past learning having taken place.

The lesson to be drawn from this and other evidence should be obvious: Proponents of the traditional instinct conception are not speaking for all biologists when they talk about a spontaneously generated drive to action. For all of his eminence as a pioneering student of animal behavior, Lorenz's insistence on endogenous motivation is not only not shared but is severely criticized by many other highly respected researchers.[36] We can admit the role of hereditary influences on human behavior without accepting the traditional instinctivists' view of how these influences operate.

The previously quoted statement of J. P. Scott[37] comes much closer to the contemporary consensus regarding biological dispositions to behavior. As Scott said, there is no "internal driving force which has to be satisfied. There is, however, *an internal physiological mechanism which has only to be stimulated to produce fighting*" (italics added). Two ideas are involved here: (a) Aggression is a reaction to external conditions and not to the product of a spontaneously generated drive, and (b) more generally, behavior occurs when "an internal physiological mechanism" is activated by appropriate stimulation.

This latter notion is the essence of the newer conceptions of "instinctive" tendencies in behavior. These tendencies, we might say at the risk of considerable oversimplification, are genetically determined dispositions to respond in a particular manner to certain stimuli.[38] They are latent; a readiness to respond, but not an active impetus to behavior. Thus, the infants in several mammalian species are apparently "programmed" to move back when they sight a visual cliff and, to take yet another example, human babies are genetically inclined to smile when they see a smiling face.

The organism's physiological condition greatly affects the degree to which the specific stimulus elicits the genetically "preprogrammed" response. Internal states can make the animal (or person) either more or less responsive to the environmental stimuli. Very often this happens because the physiological condition affects the organism's reactivity to the situational detail.[39] I have sometimes used an admittedly crude metaphor in trying to make all this more concrete. We might think of the instinctive disposition as being something like the internal wiring in a TV set. The set does not possess a "drive" to give off pictures. Rather, it has been "preprogrammed" to respond in certain ways (give off electrical signals that are used to construct images on the TV tube) to the appropriate environmental stimuli (signals from the TV station) when it is in an appropriate "physiological" state (i.e., when the electrical current is turned on).

V. The Frustration-Aggression Hypothesis and Aversively Stimulated Aggression

In contrast to the notion of endogenously produced aggression inherent in the traditional conceptions of instinctive aggression, the view taken here is that one major type of aggression — hostile or angry aggression — is largely a reaction to external events. As was just suggested, humans as well as other animal species may be biologically predisposed to respond in particular ways to these occurrences. Let us take a brief look at some of the conditions that can generate aggressive inclinations.

FRUSTRATION-ENGENDERED AGGRESSION

In 1939 John Dollard, Neal Miller, and their colleagues at Yale University published a now classic monograph offering two sweeping and interrelated theoretical propositions: (a) that frustrations give rise to an instigation to aggression, and (b) that all aggression could be traced to some prior frustration.[40] Research and analysis in the succeeding years indicate that the Yale formulation has considerable validity but, nonetheless, should be modified. For one thing, contrary to the second proposition, every aggressive action is not the product of an earlier thwarting; instrumental aggression carried out for some other purpose can be learned independently of frustrations. We should therefore confine ourselves to the first and primary idea. In employing this formulation, however, we have to be clear as to just what is meant by a frustration and also must realize that the hypothesis refers to aggressive inclinations rather than to open aggression.

The frustration-aggression hypothesis has been severely criticized, and current social-psychological discussions of aggression tend to give relatively little attention to thwartings as a major source of aggression.[41] In my view, many of these objections are ill-founded. Some rest on an unfortunate conception of a frustration as a deprivation (an inability to reach a goal that is generally desirable) whereas the original Yale formulation suggests that frustration exists only to the degree that the goal had been both wanted and expected. Dollard and his associates essentially conceived of a frustration as a barrier to the attainment of an anticipated goal.[42] We could say people are deprived if they do not own a car or a color TV set, since most members of our society tend to want these things; but we should only regard them as frustrated to the extent that they desire these objects and had been anticipating the pleasures the car and/or TV set would bring them. Then too, it is often argued that frustration instigates aggression only if that frustration is believed to be illegitimate or improper. In answering this contention, I suggest that an "improper" or unwarranted frustration usually is more apt to produce aggressive reactions than a supposedly legitimate thwarting because (a) people are less likely to restrain themselves in the former case (society defines their aggressive reactions as more appropriate) and (b) the frustrations when perceived as illegitimate are experienced as much more unpleasant.[43] The possibility of inhibited aggression highlights the point made just before: Frustrations do not necessarily give rise to overt aggression even when they block the satisfaction of strong desires; the aggressive inclinations are very likely to be restrained if the thwarted person believes any display of open hostility will be punished in some way, even if only by social disapproval.

DISPLACED HOSTILITY AND CHARACTERISTICS OF VICTIMS DRAWING ATTACKS

Of course, as the Yale group also recognized (explicitly in line with psychoanalytic theory), the inhibited instigation to aggression might be displaced in an attack upon a substitute target. A later analysis by Neal Dollard sought to account for the selection of the victim of displaced aggression through an insightful extension of the then dominant associationistic learning theory.[44] According to this formulation, the victim draws the attack not only because the thwarted aggressor believes it is safe to hurt this person, but also because the victim has a moderate degree of similarity to the frustrater (i.e., is associated with the frustrater).

I have extended the Miller-Dollard analysis of hostility displacement by suggesting that both negative and positive factors influence the extent to which innocent people are apt to be attacked by those who are inclined to be aggressive. Some persons evoke aggressive reactions because they are mentally connected with earlier frustraters in that they have similar emotional meaning for the aggressor, such as being disliked. The positive factors have to do with the rewards that are obtained from acting aggressively. In this case, aggressors choose victims for displaced hostility when they will be rewarded for attacking.[45]

All of this suggests that particular minority groups, such as blacks or Jews, serve man as scapegoats because their perceived qualities (in the minds of those who are ready to aggress) evoke hostile reactions from those who are emotionally upset at the time. More than being safe targets, they draw hostility because they basically remind the angry persons of other emotionally provoking occasions; and/or they are viewed as decidedly unpleasant; and/or the would-be aggressors think, that in the past, aggression against these groups has paid off in some way.[46]

AVERSIVELY STIMULATED AGGRESSION

Returning to the frustration aggression thesis, we may conclude that if we employ a theoretically adequate conception of frustration, recognize the possibility of restraints, and consider the suitability of the available targets, we can find a good deal of support for the basic frustration-aggression notion in published research with animals and human children and adults.[47] This supporting evidence does not necessarily mean, however, that it is the frustration in itself that engenders the aggression. In recent years I have suggested, along with a number of other psychologists, that thwartings give rise to aggressive inclinations because they are unpleasant occurrences that people usually attempt to avoid. From this point of view, the negative feelings produced by a negative state of affairs generate an inclination to strike out at an available target.[48] Frustrations lead to aggressive reactions not because a hope has been dashed but because these occurrences are unpleasant. The factors affecting the likelihood of an aggressive response to a thwarting probably operate by influencing the frustration's aversiveness.

Simplifying a very complex process, the present formulation holds that the negative affect generated by an aversive occurrence produces a number of behavioral inclinations — to fight and to flee — as well as several relatively primitive feelings, including anger and fear. A wide variety of conditions (including genetic influences, prior learning, and the perceived consequences of a particular action) determine the relative strengths of these different tendencies and feelings. Thus, a person might prefer to escape from the aversive situation because of his genetic endowment and/or prior learning but, nevertheless, the inclination to attack an appropriate available target is presumably present along with the urge to escape from the unpleasant event.

Because of the wide variety of animal species that exhibit aggressive reactions to a broad range of aversive conditions, it is my guess (as a working supposition) that a genetic predisposition is at the basis of this phenomenon. Humans, like many other animals, are predisposed to aggression when they are suffering. Learning obviously can strengthen or weaken this inclination, and it also can be augmented or countered by other situational influences. Furthermore, existing emotional and physiological conditions can raise or lower the probability of open aggression. Whatever the complications, it is through this "programming" that the "animal in us" is apt to be revealed; not through the operation of an innate endogenous drive to violence, but in our responses to the things that give us physical and psychological pain.

THE INTERACTION OF PERSISTING AND TEMPORARY INFLUENCES

Whatever open aggression occurs following an aversive event is probably the result of a variety of influences operating together, some arising from earlier experiences and learning and some from the immediate situation. Even when people are feeling bad because of their exposure to an unpleasant state of affairs, they are unlikely to attack someone else unless they believe their aggression will not be strongly punished and their inhibitions against aggression are weak at the time. Moreover, the likelihood of overt aggression is also affected by the degree to which these persons had suffered previously from aversive stimulation, the extent to which their aggressive behavior had been reinforced in the past, whatever values they hold justifying aggression in the particular circumstances, and whether the available target has the stimulus properties that evoke impulsive aggressive reactions.

This recognition of the multiplicity of factors affecting the display of violence highlights the oversimplified nature of traditional instinct ideas; human (and animal) behavior is far more complex than the traditional instinct doctrine would have us believe. Indeed, the same comment should also be directed towards any other formulation holding that violence is mainly the result of a single set of determinants. All aggression is not simply the product of frustrations or aversive stimulation; nor is it solely or even chiefly produced by prior learning or cultural values regarding aggression. How people act in a given situation is partly affected by the habits and values they have acquired in the past – but also by how aroused they are at the time, the characteristics of the available targets, and the perceived benefits and costs of behaving aggressively on that particular occasion.

VI. Why War?

It is now time to return to Einstein's question with which this chapter began: Why do wars arise? An easy response would be that they occur for a good many different reasons. Indeed, I would suggest that psychology of individual aggression probably tells us little about the development of international conflicts. Wars do not grow out of an urge for death and destruction inherent in human nature; nor are they greatly affected by a lifelong history of frustrations and/or exposure to aversive events that generate aggressive inclinations. Rather, I tend to agree with those analysts who view wars as stemming largely from rationalistic (although not necessarily intelligent) decisions based on the perception of conflicting goals, considerations of costs and benefits, and beliefs about the likelihood of the possible outcomes.

I do not want to rule out emotional factors altogether, however. They undoubtedly play some part in the equation, at least at times. But instead of stressing anger, I would indict pride as another major culprit.

Pride can be both subtle and pervasive and there are any number of ways that it can affect international relationships. While this is not the place to explore the intricacies of this complex phenomenon, a few observations might be in order based on recent social psychological research and theory regarding self-identity and self-aggrandizement. These matters surely have some role in patriotism and international rivalries and conflict.

It is not especially profound to say that persons often seek to heighten their self-worth, and that they frequently identify themselves with the groups to which they belong. What is noteworthy here is how readily and even automatically people align themselves with the groups around them and then try to enhance the value of these particular collectives in order to increase their own importance.

Much of the social psychological evidence we have here stems from research conducted in Europe following the pioneering studies of the British psychologist, Henri Tajfel.[49] In these experiments the participants were assigned to one of two temporary groups on the basis of exceedingly trivial criteria and then were asked to allocate resources to all of the individuals around them. The subjects typically favored people in their own group over those in the other group in dividing the available resources. This was true even when they were anonymous, could not learn how much any one person had given anyone else, would not benefit directly, and did not have any prior acquaintance with the others in the situation.

According to Tajfel and his colleagues, this ingroup favoritism is not the result of an inherent disposition to dislike those who are different, but grows out of a widespread desire to mark off one's identity in as favorable a manner as possible. People often want to distinguish themselves from others around them, and will employ their membership in a particular group as a way of doing this, especially if this is the only means available. In favoring those in their own group, they are helping to identify themselves by differentiating themselves from nongroup members and asserting the value of this self-identity.

If this argument is correct, we should not be surprised at how readily people proclaim the merits of the country to which they belong. Nationality is an important part of self-identity and, when people are dealing with foreigners, it serves their desire for uniqueness. By extolling the virtues of their country, they are essentially buttressing their own worth. Pride in country is to a considerable extent pride in self.

In the interests of world peace, some might hope to lessen this equation of one's self with one's nation; but, it is obviously difficult to sever self from country. Consider the British. Nowadays they do not proclaim their national virtues with anywhere near the intensity that this is done in the United States, and there seems to be much less insistence on patriotism in the United Kingdom than in the United States. Still, average Britishers feel better about themselves when people representing their country succeed in some difficult task (e.g., when their military forces defeated the Argentines in the Falkland Islands) and they feel something of a personal defeat when national representatives are humiliated. (A good many of my British acquaintances were greatly distressed and even personally shamed by the violent behavior of Liverpool soccer fans at the European Cup soccer games in 1985.) I am willing to bet that, to a greater or lesser degree, people of all nations are displeased when persons symbolizing their country suffer a physically or psychologically painful defeat. Blows to the national pride are individual humiliations as well.

The negative affect generated by these aversive occurrences can then be exacerbated and prolonged if the mass media and/or important personages in the country repeatedly bring up the national injury and heighten the sense of personal failure. The media and these leaders also can contribute to a lessening of whatever reluctance the public has to go to war (i.e., lowering their restraints against violence) by facilitating the interpretation of the aversive event as having been unjustifiably and intentionally produced by representatives of a disliked nation. It is generally agreed that the Hearst newspapers played this kind of role and helped bring on the Spanish-American War by the way their reporters covered the sinking of the U.S. Battleship Maine in the Havana Harbor. But, again, I must hasten to say that this type of process is by no means the major cause of war. International conflict, like many other human actions, is multiply determined.

Notes

1. Albert Einstein, "Why War?" [Letter to Professor Freud] (Geneva: International Institute of Intellectual Cooperation, League of Nations, 1933).

2. Also see Sigmund Freud, "Why War?" in *Collected Works* Vol. 16 (1933; London: Imago, 1950 reprint).

3. Lorenz, *On Aggression* (New York: Harcourt, Brace, & World, 1966).

4. For example, see Anthony Storr, *Human Aggression* (New York: Atheneum, 1968).

5. Cited by Dolf Zillmann in his *Hostility and Aggression* (Hillsdale, NJ: Erlbaum, 1979), 47. Eibl-Eibesfeldt, one of Lorenz's younger colleagues, has defended and extended Lorenz's notion of endogenously motivated aggression in a number of articles and books. See, for example, his chapter, "Phylogenetic Adaptation as Determinants of Aggressive Behavior in Man," in *Origins Of Aggression*, eds. Willard W. Hartup and Jan de Wit (New York: Mouton, 1978).

6. Robert A. Hinde, "Energy Models of Motivation," *Symposia of Society of Experimental Biology*, 14 (1960): 199-213.

7. Lorenz, *On Aggression*, 50.

8. Ibid., 55-56.

9. Storr, *Human Aggression*.

10. See Leonard Berkowitz, *Aggression: A Social Psychological Analysis* (New York: McGraw-Hill, 1962) for a discussion of Freud's idea of a "death instinct," and Dolf Zillmann, *Hostility and Aggression* for a more recent examination of this notion as well as of Lorenz's formulation. A

convenient compilation of critiques of the Lorenzian analysis can be found in Ashley Montagu, ed., *Man and Aggression*, 2nd ed. (New York: Oxford University Press, 1973). For summaries of research into animal behavior that are very different from Lorenz's, see Robert Hinde, *Ethology* (Oxford: Oxford University Press, 1982), and S. A. Barnett, *"Instinct" and "Intelligence,"* (London: MacGibbon & Kee, 1967).

11. See K. E. Moyer, *The Psychology of Aggression* (New York: Harper, 1976). A criticism of Moyer's classification can be found in F. A. Huntingford, "Analysis of the Motivational Processes Underlying Aggression in Animals," in *Analysis of Motivational Processes*, eds. F. M. Toates and T. R. Halliday (London: Academic Press, 1980). The interested reader will find important discussions of the classification of aggression in *Interdisciplinary Approaches to Aggression Research*, eds. Paul F. Brain and David Benton (Amsterdam/New York: Elsevier, 1981), and in Robert Hinde's chapter, "The Study of Aggression: Determinants, Consequences, Goals and Functions," in *Origins of Aggression*, eds. Hartup and de Wit.

12. See Zillmann, *Hostility and Aggression*, Chap. 5, and also Brendan G. Rule, "The Hostile and Instrumental Functions of Human Aggression," in *Origins of Aggression*, eds. Hartup and de Wit, for discussions of this difference. My chapter, "The Concept of Aggression," in Brain and Benton, eds., *Interdisciplinary Approaches to Aggression Research*, also examines the scientific status of these constructs.

13. For example, in a comment to the journalist, Joseph Alsop, quoted in my article, "Simple Views of Aggression," *American Scientist*, 57 (1969): 372-383, ethologists are now agreed that there is no justification for the sharp line between innate and learned behavior often drawn by advocates of the traditional instinct doctrine. Where these advocates have typically regarded instincts as genetically fixed action patterns, research has demonstrated that even such species-characteristic behavior patterns as songbird singing can be modified by experience. Barnett put it this way: "No behaviour, however stereotyped and species-characteristic, or however essential for survival, may any longer be regarded as a thing-in-itself, fixed by some form of predestination . . . every feature of behaviour is subject to the hazards of development." See Barnett, *"Instinct" and "Intelligence"*, 80.

14. See Eibl-Eibesfeldt, "Phylogenetic Adaptation as Determinants of Aggressive Behavior in Man," 47-48.

15. Some of the relevant evidence along these lines can be found in Pierre Karli, "Aggressive Behavior and its Brain Mechanisms (As Exemplified by an Experimental Analysis of the Rat's Mouse-Killing Behavior)," in *Origins of Aggression*, eds. Hartup and de Wit.

16. Hinde, "The Study of Aggression," in *Origins of Aggression*, eds. Hartup and de Wit, 9-10.

17. See Leonard Berkowitz, "Simple Views of Aggression."

18. John P. Scott, *Aggression* (Chicago: University of Chicago Press, 1958), 62.

19. See especially the chapters by Barnett and Schneirla in *Man and Aggression*, ed. Montagu.

20. In an interview with the journalist Joseph Alsop as quoted in Berkowitz, "Simple Views of Aggression."

21. In Lorenz, *On Aggression*.

22. The term does not appear in the index to Hinde's book, *Ethology*, while Barnett said the word is not used in any technical sense in his book, *"Instinct" and "Intelligence."*

23. See Berkowitz, *Aggression: A Social Psychological Analysis*; Hinde, "Energy Models of Motivation"; and Zillmann, *Hostility and Aggression*, for three somewhat different discussions of this hydraulic model in analyses of aggression.

24. William C. Menninger, "Recreation and Mental Health," *Recreation*, 42 (1948): 340-346.

25. Storr, *Human Aggression*, 132-133.

26. Some of this evidence is discussed in my article, "Sports, Competition, and Aggression," *The Physical Educator*, 30 (1973): 59-61. Also see R. G. Geen and M. G. Quanty, "The Catharsis of Aggression: An Evaluation of a Hypothesis," in *Advances in Experimental Social Psychology*, Vol. 10, ed. L. Berkowitz (New York: Academic Press, 1977), and J. H. Goldstein, *Aggression and Crimes of Violence* (New York: Oxford University Press, 1975).

27. E. T. Turner, "The Effects of Viewing College Football, Basketball and Wrestling on the Elicited Aggressive Responses of Male Spectators," *Medicine and Science in Sports*, 2 (1970): 100-105.

28. Goldstein, *Aggression and Crimes of Violence*, 47.

29. J. H. Crook, "The Nature and Function of Territorial Aggression," in *Man and Aggression*, ed. Montagu, 215.

30. M. Sherif, O. J. Harvey, W. R. White, and C. Sherif, *Intergroup Conflict and Cooperation: The Robber's Cave Experiment* (Norman: University of Oklahoma Book Exchange, 1961). More recent investigations confirming and extending the findings of Sherif et al., are discussed in the chapter on aggression in my text, *A Survey of Social Psychology*, 3d ed. (New York: Holt, Rinehart, & Winston, 1986).

31. This personality type is often discussed in the literature on behavioral medicine and health psychology. For one discussion on this syndrome see the chapter by Howard Leventhal, "Health Psychology," in L. Berkowitz, *A Survey of Social Psychology*.

32. Lorenz, *On Aggression*.

33. Freud, "Why War?"

34. Ashley Montagu expressed this widely held view in his introduction to the first edition of his book, *Man and Aggression*, when he held that "the notable thing about human behavior is that it is learned. Everything a human being does as such he has had to learn from other human beings."

35. Barnett, *"Instinct" and "Intelligence,"* 164.

36. See Montagu, *Man and Aggression*, and Hinde, "Energy Models of Motivation," in particular.

37. J. P. Scott, *Aggression*.

38. Much more comprehensive discussions of this newer theoretical approach to genetically influenced predispositions can be found in Barnett, *"Instinct" and "Intelligence,"* and Hinde, *Ethology*.

39. See the chapter on immediate causation in Hinde's book, *Ethology* for one discussion of this interaction between inner physiological conditions and external stimuli. The previously cited collection of chapters edited by Toates and Halliday, *Analysis of Motivational Processes*, offers a convenient summary of the research pointing to such an interaction even in the cases of food, hunger, and sex. On looking at the evidence, the editors of this latter book concluded, "All motivational systems are both internally and externally controlled" (p. 2).

40. J. Dollard, L. Doob, N. Miller, O. Mowrer, and R. Sears, *Frustration and Aggression* (New Haven, CT: Yale University Press, 1939).

41. See Zillmann, *Hostility and Aggression*. Many of the criticisms of the original 1939 formulation are considered at length in my 1962 book, *Aggression: A Social Psychological Analysis*.

42. This particular interpretation of the Yale group's differently worded formal definition of "frustration" is discussed in my article, "Whatever Happened to the Frustration-Aggression Hypothesis?" *American Behavioral Scientist*, 46 (1978): 299-310.

43. Ibid.

44. See the discussion of hostility displacement in Berkowitz, *Aggression: A Social Psychological Analysis* for a sympathetic treatment of the Miller-Dollard analysis. A less technical and also more up-to-date conception of hostility displacement can be found in the chapter on aggression in Berkowitz, *A Survey of Social Psychology*.

45. L. Berkowitz, "Some Determinants of Impulsive Aggression: Role of Mediated Associations with Reinforcements for Aggression," *Psychological Review*, 81 (1974): 165-176.

46. See my chapter on aggression, in Berkowitz, *A Survey of Social Psychology*, for a nontechnical but somewhat more complete discussion.

47. Leonard Berkowitz, "Frustration-Aggression Hypothesis: Examination and Reformulation," *Psychology Bulletin*, 106 (1989): 59-73. Also see Berkowitz, *Aggression: A Social Psychological Analysis*, and Berkowitz, *A Survey of Social Psychology*.

48. See L. Berkowitz, "Aversively Stimulated Aggression: Some Parallels and Differences in Research with Animals and Humans," *American Psychologist*, 38 (1983): 1135-1144. I present evidence in this article indicating that a remarkably wide variety of unpleasant conditions can give rise to aggressive tendencies.

49. H. Tajfel, "Experiments in Intergroup Discrimination," *Scientific American*, 223 (1970): 96-102.

Chapter 2

War and the Attraction to Destruction

STEVEN KULL

Since the threat of nuclear war impinges on every human's life, it is only natural that we should grope for some rational explanation for what has motivated humanity to create the capacity for its own destruction. Rational explanations, however, may not be adequate. All parties say they do not want a nuclear war and acknowledge that there would be no winners and probably very few survivors. Yet there is still a feeling that such a war could occur and preparation for it continues unabated.

While the possibility of nuclear war is a particularly vivid instance of the human potential for self-destruction there are also many instances apparent in the more limited, but still highly destructive, wars that have occurred. Throughout history soldiers have frequently gone into battle with great enthusiasm, knowing that they were jeopardizing their lives. They have volunteered for suicide missions and even competed for the privilege of doing so. Whole battalions have persevered in fighting to the death even when retreat was an available option.

The collective decision to go to war also can have self-destructive aspects to it. There are numerous instances of nations going to war in the face of impossible odds. Furthermore, even when the odds are favorable, the decision to go to war may be, arguably, self-destructive: as noted in other chapters, the benefits of winning a war are commonly outweighed by the costs.

Granted there are many possible explanations for such apparently self-destructive behavior. And most likely such behavior is influenced by numerous motivational factors. In this article I will explore the possibility that one of these factors is a more or less conscious attraction to destruction. In the first section I will examine evidence that humans are attracted to destruction and that this attraction can be observed in attitudes about war and nuclear weapons. In the second section I will explore the probability that the attraction to destruction is not fundamentally an attraction to biological death but to certain symbolic and archetypal processes.

AUTHOR'S NOTE: This is a revised version of an article that originally appeared as "Nuclear Arms and the Desire for World Destruction" in *Political Psychology,* 4, 3 (September 1983): 563-591. Reprinted with permission.

I. The Attraction to Destruction

THE ATTRACTION TO SELF-DESTRUCTION

Perhaps the most vivid evidence that humans can be attracted to destruction is the fact that humans, at times, do commit suicide and explicitly express a desire for death.

Indeed, suicide is considerably more common than most people recognize. According to official statistics (which generally are regarded as conservative) in the United States 1 out of 60 lives ends in suicide. This is a fairly typical rate and in some countries is several times higher. *Attempts* at suicide are vastly more frequent. It is generally estimated there are 8 to 10 times as many suicide attempts as there are successful suicides.

Besides overt suicidal acts, a wide range of self-destructive behavior has been characterized as "subintentional suicides." Some deaths by auto accidents, the abuse of drugs and alcohol, and even the persistent pursuit of a stressful life-style can be interpreted as an expression of some degree of self-destructive motivation.

In present-day culture, we almost automatically associate suicide with pathology and depression. Numerous examples, however, make it abundantly clear that many acts of self-destruction have been entirely unrelated to pathology or depression. In ancient Greece and Alexandria, a number of philosophers extolled the virtues of suicide as the only meaningful response to the human condition. Individuals were known to commit suicide at the end of their lectures or at the climax of sumptuous feasts. In ancient Rome, many Christians actively sought out the opportunity to be martyred as a means of ensuring entrance into heaven. This intentional martyrdom became such a problem that the church was compelled to take a drastic measure, making suicide the worst possible sin. Nevertheless, in the Middle Ages, a heretical sect, the Albigenses, practiced endura (suicide by fasting) as the most direct means of attaining unity with God. In the romantic era of the last century, following the publication of Goethe's *The Sorrows of Young Werther*, suicide became fashionable and reached epidemic proportions. In the early twentieth century, the Dadaists argued for suicide as a sublime artistic act. This idea has also appeared more recently in certain punk and New Wave art forms.

However it is achieved, the image of death holds a fascination and is often presented as an attractive condition. Death itself may be presented as a beautiful, seductive woman or as a blissful state, as in this selection from a poem of Walt Whitman's:

> Come lovely and soothing death
> Undulate round the world, serenely arriving, arriving
> In the day, or in the night, to all, to each
> Sooner or later delicate death.
>
> Prais'd be the fathomless universe
> For life and joy, and for the objects and knowledge curious

And for love, sweet love — but praise! praise! praise!
For the sure-enwinding arms of cool enfolding death . . .

Approach, strong deliveress,
When it is so, when thou hast taken them, I joyously sing the dead,
Lost in the loving floating ocean of thee,
Laved in the flood of thy bliss O death.

Even when the post-death state is not described in such positive terms, death can still hold attraction as a climactic fulfillment of one's life. To die in an exemplary fashion leaves behind a legacy that offers some degree of immortality. Nearly every culture glorifies those who willingly sacrifice their lives in the name of an abstract cause and presumably the appeal of this kind of death contributes to the motivation of young men to join dangerous military endeavors. In the Japanese Samurai code, it is explicitly stated that the way of the Samurai is "nothing but a path to death."[1]

One variant of the attraction to self-destruction that is particularly relevant to the subject of war is the attraction to dying together in group formation. The exhilarating comradery generated by the potential of imminent mutual death has been glorified by numerous writers in terms that approach the ecstatic and mystical. Dying together with others for a cause is widely vaunted as the most desirable form of death.

The glorification of this kind of death appears in numerous national anthems. The following verse from the national anthem of the Philippines portrays the pleasure of the "sons" of a country dying together as a pleasure that is of a higher order than a mystical, rapturous union with a maternal figure:

Beautiful land of love, O land of light,
In thine embrace 'tis rapture to lie.
But it is glory ever, when thou art wronged,
For us thy sons to suffer and die.

The following selection from the Prussian national anthem also uses family imagery, suggesting, in this case, a fusion with the father as well as one's country achieved through the act of dying in group formation:

I am a Prussian. Do you know my banner?
Its colors lead with black and white the way.
To die for freedom was my father's manner
That, you must note, my banner does convey.
Ne'er shall I be despairing
Like them I will be daring.

THE ATTRACTION TO WAR

Today it is no longer fashionable to be in favor of war, per se. But looking back beyond the last few decades, there is an abundance of cases in which war is explicitly glorified. Among the ancient Greeks, Pericles derided the unwillingness to go to war as a sign of spiritual decay. Thucydides saw war as building character. Hume, Bacon, Hegel, and Treitschke also saw war as building character and improving the health of nations. Peace was seen as leading to moral stagnation. Spencer saw war as necessary for the eugenics of mankind and Adam Smith called war the "noblest of arts."

In the early part of this century, the glorification of war almost reached religious proportions. Josiah Royce, in *The Philosophy of Loyalty*, writes:

> Let his elemental passion for conflict hereupon fuse with his love for his own countrymen into that fascinating and blood-thirsty form of humane but furious ecstasy which is the war-spirit.[2]

Von Bernhardi wrote, shortly before World War I:

> The efforts directed towards the abolition of war must not only be termed foolish, but absolutely immoral and must be stigmatized as unworthy of the human race. To what does the whole question amount? It is proposed to deprive men of the right and the possibility to sacrifice their highest material possessions, their physical life, for ideals, and thus to realize the highest moral unselfishness.[3]

No material gain from war is promised, rather the sacrifice of one's possessions and one's life is glorified as an end and an ideal in itself. In the 1930s such militaristic philosophies ultimately reached their zenith in Germany, Italy, and Japan. In Japan, the glorification of death in battle attained such heights that Japanese commanders had to actively discourage soldiers from sacrificing themselves.[4]

Finally the attraction to war, especially in cultures that abjure war, can be detected, arguably, in the attitudes that are attributed to groups perceived as an enemy. Enemies are frequently seen as having an atavistic desire for war. The psychological roots of this perception are suggested by the fact that the enemy's behavior, which is considered evidence of their warlike intentions, is frequently replicated by the party who fears them — though, of course, in the name of defensive measures. It can be argued that neither party really wants war and that war is primarily derived from a misperception of the other side's intentions. The fact that both sides regard it as so plausible that the other side has such militaristic aspirations, however, suggests that perhaps they exist somewhere deep in the psyches of both sides.

THE WORLD DESTRUCTIVE DEITY

In numerous cultures throughout the world there are images of deities with strong impulses to be cruel and even to destroy the world. Such images, being largely anthropomorphic in character, can be interpreted as reflecting deep-seated and often unconscious feelings held by individuals in those cultures.

In the Hindu system the primary destructive deity is a Shiva. Shiva is a complex god — at times playing a beneficent role, but for the most part, breaking down forms. He is known as "the Reabsorber," "He Who Takes Back," and the embodiment of "Super-Death." His son Skanda is the God of War. Zimmer writes:

> Shiva is . . . the swallower of time, swallower of all the ages, and cycles of ages. He reduces the phenomenal rhythm and whirlpool to nought, dissolving all things, all beings, all divinities, in the crystal pure, motion-less organization of Eternity . . . .[5]

Closely related to Shiva is the goddess Kali. She is depicted standing in a sea of blood from the children that she has destroyed, and sips their blood from a skull. Often, she is surrounded by flames that represent the conflagration that ends each world-period.

Perhaps the most vivid display of the bloodthirsty quality of a deity is in its demand for human sacrifices — a practice that appears in numerous cultures. In Hinduism, it is the goddess Camunda, a consort of Shiva, who demands such sacrifice. The following is a verse from the *Bhavabuti* repeated by priests at human sacrifices:

> Hail, hail! Camunda, mighty goddess, hail!
> I glorify thy sport, when in the dance
> That fills the court of Shiva with delight
> Thy God descending spurns the earthly globe.
> . . . the whirling talons rend
> The crescent on thy brow; from the torn orb
> The trickling nectar falls, and every skull
> That gems thy necklace laughs with horrid life.

Numerous stories in the Old Testament depict a God that is impulsive, wrathful, jealous, and prone to demand macabre tests of loyalty. He is called "a man of war" and "a jealous God" who not only "visits iniquity" on the unfaithful, but punishes their innocent progeny "unto the third and fourth generations." When he finds his creation unacceptable he destroys it in a massive flood. He shows infanticidal tendencies by asserting His right to demand the firstborn son in all cases, and in the case of Abraham, actually makes the demand, relenting only when Abraham has the knife at his son Isaac's throat.

In the New Testament, there is an increased emphasis on the loving aspect of God, even to the point of identifying God with love itself. However, this loving quality is not easily won: to realize it, God's son, Christ, must be sacrificed. Once again, the image of a god with infanticidal tendencies appears. Christ offers himself as a cathartic object to mollify these impulses. Furthermore, Christ must continually beseech God to restrain his harsh ways with his children. Carl Jung writes:

> Although Christ has complete confidence in his father and even feels at one with him, he cannot help inserting the cautious petition — and warning — into the Lord's Prayer: "Lead

us not into temptation, but deliver us from evil." God is asked not to entice us outright into doing evil, but rather to deliver us from it. The possibility that Yahweh, in spite of all the precautionary measures and in spite of his express intention to become the Summum Bonum, might yet revert to his former ways is not so remote that one need not keep one eye open for it. At any rate, Christ considers it appropriate to remind his father of his destructive inclinations towards mankind and to beg him to desist from them.[6]

Jung further suggests that the essential meaning of the incarnation in Christ is that God needs to have his destructive tendencies tempered by a humanizing experience. Such an experience would, hopefully, make God more compassionate and restrained.

With the story of the apocalypse in Revelations, however, the restraint of the deity is entirely lost. Here the wrath of God (also depicted as the "wrath of the Lamb," a symbol of the short-lived effort to be somewhat more kind) is released in a massive destruction of the human race, after which there are only 144,000 survivors. Among the many images of destruction is one of the "great winepress of the wrath of God . . . high as a horse's bridle, for one thousand six hundred stadia" in which humans are crushed.[7]

Beside the anthropomorphic images of deities, the desire for world destruction also can be projected onto the world or the universe itself. In this case, the world is seen as having a tendency to go through a periodic process of apocalyptic self-destruction followed by renewal. Mircea Eliade has described this as "the myth of the eternal return" and demonstrates its appearance in virtually all cultures.[8] A variety of systems map out elaborate frameworks covering millions of years with the periodic apocalyptic moments carefully and mathematically determined. Eliade also observed that more recently, as the concept of time has evolved from a cyclic concept to a more linear one, the image of the apocalypse has become less associated with a cyclic process and more with the image of a final end. This end is usually followed by some transformation into some other entirely different mode of being, though sometimes the image of an absolute end also appears.

WAR AND THE WORLD DESTRUCTIVE DEITY

One of the most stirring images used to incite the sacrifices of war is the image of a deity that wants the war. The choice to participate in the war is not presented primarily as a means to achieve personal gain, but rather as an opportunity to fuse one's self with this larger deity — the fusion being most fully achieved when there is a willingness to sacrifice one's life to fulfill the divine purposes.

Although the purposes of the deity may be presented as being ultimately beneficial in the human dimension, this is by no means always the case, and is often fairly incidental. The deity is often depicted as having a certain fanaticism and destructiveness that is oblivious to human suffering. Calls to battle do not necessarily emphasize the benefits of war as much as the idea that the intention of the deity transcends the question of human suffering, and that it would be better for all to die in the name of that intention than not to subordinate to it. For example, in the American Civil War song "The Battle Hymn of the Republic," the war itself is described not as a battle between groups, but as the "coming" of God in a style drawn from the apocalyptic imagery of Revelations:

> Mine eyes have seen the glory of the coming of the Lord;
> He is trampling out the vintage where the grapes of wrath are stored;
> He hath loosed the fateful lightening of His terrible swift sword
> His truth is marching on.

God is even quoted as intending to kill not only the enemy but also the soldiers themselves as an act of "Grace."

> I have read the fiery gospel writ in burnished rows of steel:
> "As ye deal with My contemners so with you My Grace shall deal."

In the final verse, the soldiers affirm not only their willingness to die but also their intention to die:

> In the beauties of the lilies Christ was born across the sea,
> With a glory in his bosom that transfigures you and me;
> As He died to make men holy, let us die to make men free
> While God is marching on.

The intentions of the deity toward war are not always clothed in the images of righteousness as they tend to be in Christian imagery. In Hindu literature, the deity is depicted as being in favor of war itself. One of the major Hindu texts, the *Mahabarata*, is a long epic poem describing a war between lines of descendants that ultimately results in the destruction of both sides. This war is directly encouraged by the deity, Krishna. In the most famous section of the *Mahabarata*, the "Bhagavad Gita," the leader of one side, Arjuna, begins to question the purpose of the war. Krishna appears promptly and insists that he must carry out the slaughter, reminding him that physical life is only temporal, and at the same time maligning his masculinity should he have a change of heart. There is no ambiguity about Krishna's desire to manifest himself through war. When he shows himself in his "glory," there are "marvelous and many uplifted weapons."

The fact that these wishes of the gods are harmful to humans is also recognized. In a section of the *Mahabarata* titled "The Tyranny of the Divinity," God is presented as a cruel parent acting out his own sadistic infanticidal tendencies through the medium of war:

Behold the power of illusion that hath been spread by God, who confounding with his illusion, maketh creatures slay their fellows . . . the Selfcreate Grandsire, Almighty God, spreading illusion slayeth his creatures by the instrumentality of his creatures, as one may break a piece of inert and senseless wood with wood, or stone with stone, or iron with iron! And the supreme Lord, according to his pleasure, sporteth with his creatures, exalting and destroying them like a child with his toy.[9]

The collective self-destructiveness of war appears not only in the imagery of an anthropomorphic deity, but also in the more impersonal images of totality going through a periodic or final apocalyptic destruction. These processes are sometimes depicted as intensifying the enmity between people, thus leading to wars that are disastrous to all parties. Here again, the pain and the suffering is not only simply attributed to human action; it is seen as the inevitable unfolding of the impersonal patterns of some larger entity.

NUCLEAR ARMS AND THE WORLD DESTRUCTIVE DEITY

There are reasons to believe that the attraction to world destruction plays a role in relation to nuclear weapons. At times the image of a world destructive deity is projected onto the bomb itself.

Oppenheimer, the father of the atomic bomb, when he observed the first atomic explosion, reported that his first thought was the quote from the "Bhagavad Gita" describing the god, Krishna:

> If the radiance of a thousand suns
> were to burst at once into the sky
> That would be like the splendor of the Mighty One . . .
> I am become death
> The shatterer of worlds.

Perhaps Oppenheimer was simply making a casual literary comparison. However, Lifton's study of the psychological dynamics operating in the group of scientists who developed and later promoted atomic weapons reveals that their attitude toward the bomb had a highly religious quality.[10] He uses the word "nuclearism" for this mentality, and describes it as follows:

Nuclearism is a secular religion, a total ideology in which "grace" and even "salvation" — the mastery of death and evil — are achieved through the power of a new technological deity. The deity is seen as capable not only of apocalyptic destruction but also of unlimited creation. And the nuclear believer or "nuclearist" allies himself with that power and feels compelled to expound on the virtues of his deity.[11]

Lifton goes on to examine how this "religion" spread to other politicians and diplomats who played a crucial role in establishing the U.S. government policy of stockpiling vast arsenals of atomic and nuclear weapons and openly resisting any treaties that would limit their development.

The image of the deity acting through nuclear weapons also appears in a number of fundamentalist Christian groups that interpret the Bible literally and find evidence that an apocalyptic destruction of the world is imminent. Many Biblical passages, including some attributed to Jesus, can be interpreted as meaning that the Second Coming will occur in this epoch. These passages indicate that the Second Coming will be preceded by wars and massive destruction. Old Testament descriptions can be used to elaborate this idea, as well. Some of these descriptions have an almost uncanny similarity to the events that would lead up to and result from a nuclear war. For example, Isaiah's vision of the apocalypse depicts a war in which all sides lose and which results in widespread damage to the ecology — a phenomenon that was certainly unknown in Isaiah's time:

> For the indignation of the Lord is upon all the nations, and his fury upon all their armies: He hath utterly destroyed them, He hath delivered them to the slaughter. . . . And the streams thereof shall be turned into pitch, and the dust thereof into brimstone, and the land thereof shall become burning pitch. It shall not be quenched night nor day; the smoke thereof shall go up forever: From generation to generation it shall lie waste; none shall pass through it for ever and ever.[12]

It is quite easy to transpose such images of the predicted apocalypse onto the imagery of nuclear war and conclude that God is actually preparing the apocalypse through the development of nuclear weapons. Some fundamentalists go so far as to advocate building nuclear weapons so as to expedite the day when the nuclear apocalypse will come.

II. The Meaning of Destruction

THE MEANING OF SELF-DESTRUCTION

What is it that attracts individuals to their own destruction? Freud theorized that the aim of the death instinct is toward actual biological death, consistent with the general entropic tendency of matter.[13] Using principles of the physical universe to explain subjective motivation is questionable. It may be useful, though, to use the dedifferentiating tendency of matter as a metaphor for the human attraction to "de-structure" the field of experience. But the subjective condition that is attractive need not be equated with biological death. The biological aspects of dying are nearly always perceived as extremely repugnant and frightening. However, as discussed above, the subjective condition that is imagined to be achieved through death is frequently seen as positive and desirable. Conflict, frustration, or alienation is dissolved or de-structured. No longer is there tension between the self and the environment but rather a peaceful unity.

Such de-structured states, however, are not necessarily an end point. Though they, at moments, may seem completely satisfying, once achieved they tend to eventually lead to a reemergence of a revitalized desire for structured activity. In other words, the attraction to destruction appears to be part of a larger archetypal process of death leading to rebirth — of destruction leading to renewal. More than simply a periodic repetition, each time destruction occurs certain structures of experience are permanently changed so that the renewal leads to the emergence of a newly altered form. The essence of the process is the achievement of transformation.

From this perspective, the effort to act out self-destructive impulses through the act of suicide can be interpreted as a tendency to "literalize" what is essentially a psychological process. Hillman, in a study of suicide, has argued that the suicidal patient is essentially seeking to radically alter or terminate his or her life as it has been.[14] Effective interventions with suicidal patients may involve finding ways for the patient to go through this self-destructive process other than the literal method of biological suicide. A study of patients who recovered from a severe suicidal episode found that most recovered patients had made some significant change in their life situation—something that could be interpreted as a "death" of an old self.[15]

This image of death as leading to a psychological transformative process appears in a variety of contexts. Various studies of primitive initiation rites point to the image of willfully inflicted death followed by rebirth as an almost universal characteristic.[16] The neophyte submits to a series of painful experiences that are meant to "kill" the "old self" as a means of realizing the "new self" who is then a more integrated part of the group. Perry's studies of acute schizophrenics illustrate the widespread imagery of death as a symbol of the psychotic break itself and the imagery of wholeness and integration as the conclusion of this process.[17] In artistic creativity the imagery of destruction as a transformative process also appears. The artist Kandinsky writes:

> Painting is a thundering collision of different worlds, intended to create a new world which is the work of art. Each work originates just as does the cosmos—through catastrophes which out of the chaotic din of instruments ultimately create a symphony, the music of the spheres.[18]

THE MEANING OF WORLD DESTRUCTION

The attraction to world destruction can also be interpreted as being part of an archetypal transformative process. Several anthropologists and psychologists, most notably Eliade, have examined certain rituals of world destruction that appear in numerous cultures.[19] The imagery of the ritual emphasizes the destruction of the old world as a necessary process for bringing in the new. There are roughly three aspects of the ritual: (a) the destruction of forms, (b) contact with the primordial transcendent level, and (c) the recreation of forms or rebirth.

The destruction of forms is characteristically enacted in widespread chaos. For a certain period, the normal laws of the society dissolve: there are orgies, servants play at being masters, kings are humiliated, and there is general frenzy and indulgence. Through ritual enactments, the world is drowned by floods or devoured by flames. Sometimes, there are acts of self-mutilation, or animal or human sacrifices. Groups of soldiers enact ritual combats of death and destruction. Eliade writes:

> The last days of the past year can be identified with the pre-Christian chaos . . . [they] mark the abolition of all norms and in their violence, to illustrate an overturning of values (e.g., exchange of condition between masters and slaves, women treated as courtesans), a general licence, an orgiastic modality of society, in a word, a reversion of all forms to indeterminate unity . . . and a return to the primordial unity, to the inauguration of a "nocturnal" regime in which limits, contours, distances are indiscernible.[20]

The shattering of forms makes possible a reconnection with a dimension that transcends mundane existence. This dimension is beyond time and the ritualized destruction constitutes what Eliade calls the "abolition of time." By breaking the structures of mundane time, one is able to experience the eternal realm, the source of all time, the unified ground from which all forms arise.

Finally, the experience of this "original" condition leads to the re-creation of time, form, and the world. The overall emphasis of the ritual is not simply to escape the structures of time, but to reenact what Eliade calls the entire "cosmogonic act." The effect of this process is one of regeneration, purification, and renewal. A prototype of the entire process can be found in the ritual of baptism, where the immersion in water (a symbolic death or dissolution) is followed by a re-emergence in a more purified form. The process of re-creating the world often entails a kind of struggle against the chaos of the formless which may be depicted as a battle of a deity against a dragon or sea monster. In some cases, this process is enacted through ritual combat where one group succeeds in subduing another. The chaos, symbolizing the original unstructured condition is now conquered and subdued in order to re-create the organized world. The ritual itself may include a formal re-establishment and re-instatement of ontological and legal structures.

The vestiges of such themes of world destruction still appear in modern society. The modern New Year's Eve party with its chaos, indulgence, atypical behavior, and images of the old year dying and the new year as a baby, show many of the earmarks of the original ritual form. The importance of destruction as an image of birth or origin is also indicated by the fact that three major countries of the modern world, the United States, USSR, and China, all see themselves as explicitly founded on a revolution, which is referred to in reverent, semi-religious terms and celebrated on a yearly basis. In the United States, this celebration is accompanied by explosions, fireworks, and in some cases re-enactment of some of the original battles of the revolution.

WAR AND THE ARCHETYPE OF WORLD DESTRUCTION

The question now arises whether war in general and the potential for nuclear war in particular can be understood in terms of the archetypal process of world destruction exemplified by primitive rituals.

It is a popular assumption that war is a fixed trait in human behavior. Numerous philosophers have described war as being the original or most natural human condition. However, the preponderance of archaeological and anthropological evidence suggests the contrary. The phenomenon of war seems to have emerged only fairly recently in human evolution. Wars as we know them (i.e., wars of conquest) only appeared approximately 7000 years ago. Before then, there were ritual wars, but even these only go back approximately 13,000 years. It was during that period (the Neolithic Period) the first weapons of war appeared, although the technology necessary for such weapons existed as far back as the Middle Pleistocene period (nearly 200,000 years ago).[21]

There are good reasons to believe that rituals of world destruction preceded the appearance of the first ritual wars. There is evidence that in the pre-Neolithic ages there were widespread rituals that involved themes of destruction, death, and rebirth.

It may be that the original ritual wars of the Neolithic period evolved out of rituals of destruction and renewal more than from the competition for resources. These wars closely followed the patterns of the ritual of world destruction. Highly formalized rules were followed and, usually, as soon as just one person was killed, both sides would make a hasty retreat. The essence of the war was the act of killing as a ritual act. As in the archetypal ritual of world destruction, the war represents a return to the original chaos, followed by the conquering of chaos, and the re-establishment of religious and legal structures — a re-enactment of the cosmogonic act of creation.[22]

Although the wars of civilized society have become increasingly associated with political and economic conquest, they are nonetheless still closely related to archetypal processes. The ostensible reasons for war continue to be bound up with collective symbolic and religious meanings. War is justified and valued as a transcendental test that leads to purification, renewal, and the prevalence of the good. As Gaster[23] and Bentzen[24] have suggested, war can be considered an "historification" of processes that are fundamentally more mythic and religious.

One can still observe many of the archetypal patterns found in primitive rituals of world destruction. The normal, established structures of living are dramatically disrupted and there is widespread destruction. For a period of time, events take on a heightened significance. The encounter with death, the potential for cultural collapse, the sense of the individual being swept up by collective forces, the potential for heroism and honor — all of these give war an aura of transcendence that is not afforded by the mundane character of normal living. Finally, with the end of the war, a new order is created that has a peculiar vitality. This is more than a simple release from the destructive effects of the war. The destruction itself seems to engender a new intensity, a regeneration, and a revitalization.

NUCLEAR ARMS AND THE ARCHETYPE OF WORLD DESTRUCTION

Numerous aspects of the nuclear arms phenomena also reflect key elements of the archetype of world destruction. First and foremost, the image of the exploding bomb is an exceedingly powerful, transcendental image, of which there are few in our highly secularized society. The image of the bomb implies not only destruction, but total annihilation and a return to the beginning.

Such associations can be found in the response of those who observed the first atomic explosions. The survivors of the Hiroshima explosion actually referred to the bomb as "the original child."[25] After the first atomic explosion of Alamogordo, William Lawrence described the experience as follows:

> On that moment hung eternity. Time stood still. Space contracted to a pinpoint. It was as though the earth had opened and the skies had split. One felt as though he had been privileged to witness the Birth of the World. . . . The big boom came about a hundred seconds after the great flash — the first cry of a newborn world.[26]

The attitudes expressed about the first atomic explosion also suggest this image can play a role as a symbol of world transformation. Henry Stimson, the Secretary of the War during the development of the bomb, expressed the view that the making of the atomic bomb "should not be considered simply in terms of military weapons, but a new relationship of man to the universe."[27] After the bombing of Hiroshima an article in the *New York Herald Tribune* said, "One forgets the effect on Japan or on the course of the war as one senses the foundations of one's own universe trembling."[28] President Truman, on hearing the news, exclaimed, "This is the greatest thing in history!"[29]

Apparently, the image of nuclear arms can be a powerful symbol for eliciting fundamental archetypal processes related to the image of world destruction. As Lifton and Olson write:

> Expressed boldly, there may be a need to destroy one's world for purposes of imagined rebirth, a need which lends itself either to suicidal obliteration or to transformation and regeneration. . . . Thus, nuclear weapons can achieve vivid symbolic representation in our minds precisely because of their promise of devastation.[30]

III. Deliteralizing Destruction

Although the attraction to destruction may be a powerful and pervasive force in the individual psyche and the behavior of nations, this is not meant to imply that humans must necessarily act it out in the literal dimension of physical violence and war or even the constant preparation for war. There are numerous individuals who are virtually never physically violent, and there are societies which have little violence and in which the concept of war is unknown. Obviously it is a vast question why some individuals and societies are more violent than others. There are reasons to believe, however, that a contributing variable is how effectively the individual and the society integrate the tendency to destruction with the polar tendency to stability and preservation.

Paradoxically it seems that violent behavior is most apt to occur when there is an identification with either the destructive or preservative pole. The most basic form of militarism can be characterized as an identification with the destructive principle. This phenomenon was described above as the desire for war and the almost mystical belief in the transformative power of war. Here the preservative impulse is suppressed in the heroism of self-sacrifice.

More common today is an identification with the principle of preservation; the tendency to identify with established structures and to regard their defense as intrinsically right and essential. The impulse to destruction is repressed and, instead, is projected onto the enemy who is seen as having such destructive zeal that it has little concern for preserving human life. For example both Americans and Soviets have had a tendency to view the other side as so compelled to destroy the opposing social system that they may accept the near total destruction of their own society. In response, both sides have at times considered initiating the use of military force preemptively even while recognizing that this would certainly lead to massive destruction to their own side. One can interpret that in this way the repressed and projected impulse to destructively pursue an ideological goal, asserts itself in the name of its opposite.

There have been a number of studies that lend support to the hypothesis that a tendency to identify with established structures and repress destructive/transformative processes correlates positively with support for the use of military force. Eckhardt found that militarism correlates with rigidity in cognitive processes, dogmatism, intolerance of ambiguity, lack of creativity, and an emphasis on law and order as a means of maintaining the status quo.[31] Benson found that Congressmen who saw religion primarily in terms of rigid, traditional, and absolute rules and who saw God as a restrictive force were far more prone to support high military spending than Congressmen who approached religion in a nontraditional fashion and saw God as difficult to define, as mysterious, or as essentially a process.[32]

On the social level it is also relevant that pluralistic democracies are much less apt to initiate wars than nations with fixed ideologies. Pluralistic democracies virtually never go to war with each other. Presumably by having institutions that can allow processes of change to occur internally there is less need to act out the archetype of destruction and renewal in the nation's external relations.

In summary a variable that may influence the tendency to act out the destructive principle in a violent fashion is the capacity to remain disidentified from both the zealous urge for destruction and the crystallized attachment to established structures. Identification with either tendency leads to polarization and a greater propensity for destruction to be manifested in an unmitigated form. Less prone to literally violent expression of the destructive principle are personal and social forms that embrace structure in a looser fashion and view personal and collective identity as being a *process* that includes an ongoing, or at least periodic, transformation.

Notes

1. J. Hara-Kari Seward, *Japanese Ritual Suicide* (Rutland, VT: C. E. Tuttle, 1968).

2. Josiah Royce, *The Philosophy of Loyalty* (New York: Macmillan, 1919), 39-40.

3. F. Von Bernhardi, *Germany and the Next War*, trans. A. H. Powdes (New York: Chas. A. Eron, 1914), 84.

4. Russell Spurr, *A Glorious Way to Die: The Kamikaze Misson of the Battleship Yamato April 1945* (New York: Newmarket, 1981).

5. Heinrich Zimmer, *Myths and Symbols in Indian Art and Civilization* (New York: Harper, 1946), 167.

6. Carl G. Jung, *Answer to Job*, trans. R. F. C. Hull (Princeton, NJ: Princeton University Press, 1969), 48-49.

7. Revelations 7: 4; Revelations 14: 19-20.

8. Mircea Eliade, *Cosmos and History: The Myth of the Eternal* (New York: Harper & Row, 1959).

9. "The Tyranny of the Divinity," *Mahabarata* (3:30).

10. Robert J. Lifton, *The Broken Connection* (New York: Simon & Schuster, 1979).

11. Lifton, *The Broken Connection*, 369.

12. Isaiah, 34: 2, 9, 10.

13. Sigmund Freud, *Beyond the Pleasure Principle* (New York: Bantam, 1959).

14. Erich Hillman, *Suicide and the Soul* (Zurich: Spring 1964).

15. L. M. Moss and D. M. Hamilton, "Psychotherapy of the Suicidal Patient," in *Clues to Suicide,* ed. E. S. Shneidman and N. L. Farberow (New York: McGraw-Hill, 1957).

16. Mircea Eliade, *Rites and Symbols and Initiation: The Mysteries of Birth and Rebirth* (New York: Harper & Row, 1965).

17. John Perry, *The Far Side of Madness* (Englewood Cliffs, NJ: Prentice-Hall, 1974).

18. V. Kadinsky, "Ruckblicke" [Reminiscences] in *Modern Artists on Art*, ed. R. I. Herbert (Englewood Cliffs, NJ: Prentice-Hall, 1964).

19. Mircea Eliade, *Cosmos and History*.

20. Ibid., 68-69.

21. Susan Mansfield, *The Gestalts of War: An Inquiry Into Its Origins and Meaning as a Social Institution* (New York: Dial Press, 1982).

22. Ibid.

23. T. H. Gaster, *Thespis: Ritual, Myth and Drama in the Ancient Near East* (Garden City, NY: Doubleday, 1961).

24. A. Bentzen, *King and Messiah* (London: Lutterworth, 1955).

25. Thomas Merton, *Original Child Bomb* (New York: New Directions, 1962).

26. William L. Lawrence, *Men and Atoms* (New York: Simon & Schuster, 1959).

27. Lifton, *The Broken Connection*, 336.

28. Ibid., 371.

29. Ibid., 371.

30. R. J. Lifton and E. Olson, "The Nuclear Age" in *Death: Current Perspectives,* ed. E. S. Shneidman (Palo Alto, CA: Mayfield, 1976), 102.

31. Eckhardt (1980).

32. Peter L. Benson, "Religion on Capitol Hill," in *Psychology Today* 15 (12): 46-57.

Chapter 3

Images, Learning, and the Decision to Use Force:
The Domino Theory of the United States

BETTY GLAD and CHARLES S. TABER

Walter Lippman once observed that people base their decisions on the "pictures in their heads." The real environment, as he saw it, is too complex, too transient, for direct knowledge. People are simply not equipped "to deal with so much subtlety, so much variety, so many permutations and combinations." To manage this world with some efficiency, they reconstruct it in their heads on a simpler model. The images they create enable the individual to distinguish important from unimportant data and to give it meaning. Images, in short, provide individuals with the maps without which they could not traverse the world.[1]

Some of these "maps" have important ramifications for decisions to go to war. The very definition of the nation's place in the world and of its interests and possible threats to it, we suggest in this chapter, is a function of culturally shared images. When decision makers see their nation as the center of a universe in which other peoples around them are properly tributary states, it has important implications for policy.[2] When leaders see their state as but one among several equals, operating within a shared civilization, that has different ramifications. Alliances can be formed and reformed to counter threats from challengers to the continued existence of that system, but victory will not be pursued to the point that the members themselves are destroyed.[3]

Even within a system in which there are shared values, states may perceive their roles somewhat differently, depending on their relative power and location. Major powers, for example, are apt to perceive themselves as guardians of the system. The American "domino theory," which we analyze here, is one example of what we call a system maintenance image.[4] An adaptation to the new role of America in the world political system after World War II, the domino theory expanded the definition of the U.S. national interest and envisaged threats to those interests in ways which were new to the American culture. Through an analysis of the premises of this theory, and the reasons for its adoption, one may gain insight into how such images influence America's decisions to go to war. One hypothesis we will also explore is that immediate and pressing domestic interests (political, bureaucratic, and psychological) influenced the very composition of those images and the nature of their application to particular cases. Generalizations along these lines are further developed in the study by Glad in Chapter 13, this volume.

Images, as we will show in this work, may be judged in terms of how well they map the relevant political terrain. People have persistent difficulty, as Walter Lippman noted, in securing "maps on which their own need, or someone else's need, has not sketched in the coast of Bohemia."[5] Yet we know that images differ from one another in their reliability as guides. Their effectiveness extends, as Lippman observed, "all the way from complete hallucination to the scientist's perfectly self-conscious use of a schematic model. . . ."[6]

Attempts to evaluate various images as policy guides, it is true, can present certain epistemological problems. An image can only be evaluated in terms of other images, Kenneth Boulding has suggested in his pathbreaking work, *The Image*. Tests such as the inner consistency of the elements of the image, the extent to which the image is shared by a broader public, the contribution of the image to the survival of the individuals holding them—all present problems in terms of some correspondent theory of truth.[7]

Yet images contain generalizations, often tacit, about the characteristics of empirical objects and the relationships between them. These generalizations may be submitted to several kinds of tests for verification. What are the logical relationships between the premises? Do the characterizations of the objects provided by a particular image overlook important data? Do the relationships they posit accord with the broader body of knowledge we have in the social sciences? Moreover, as Ernest May has shown, one can make rough approximations, as historians have traditionally done, about how well images drawn from historical lessons fit new situations.[8] This method of analysis gives rise to several questions. Were the original lessons based on a clear understanding of the conditions which made for success or failure in earlier operations? Have they been applied to new situations in ways which show a concern for both similarities and differences between the two cases?

One might even evaluate images in terms of the sophistication of the learning involved. Mere changes in ideas, or behavior, some have suggested, is an indicator that learning has taken place.[9] But most observers of foreign policy-making processes are not interested in what may be simple random activity. They are concerned with adaptive thought and behavior and define learning in terms that focus on the development of greater capabilities in an actor. At the simplest level, adaptation may consist of the repetition of behavior which has brought positive results in the past and the avoidance of behavior which has been punished. A higher order of learning, as Lloyd Etheredge suggests, is more interesting. Language, goal definition, and how experience is used to solve problems and develop new skills are the phenomena to be studied. Optimal strategies have been developed, it is assumed, when there is a match between the actor's images and the reality of the situation, and when skills have been acquired that enable him to achieve his goals.[10]

This higher learning is manifest in an increase in discrimination in approaching a problem. It requires, as Ernest May has suggested, a better understanding of history. One must know the conditions under which earlier policies succeeded or failed, and be able to differentiate the present case from earlier ones.[11] Subjectively, Etheredge points out, higher learning does not require a greater certainty in the actor about what he knows. To the contrary, it "can be observed as a shift from the too simple and too confident generalization — often boldly advanced and staunchly defended — to complex, integrated understandings grounded in realistic attention to detail."[12] At the highest level, learning is displayed through wisdom (the ability to approach problems in a way that integrates scientific knowledge), intuition (the ability to grasp what is going on in a specific situation), creativity (the ability to generate novel ideas which have value), and goal-implementing skills.[13] Decision makers, in short, are not simply tied to the past. Historical, scientific, and commonsense knowledge provides a basis for their thinking, but creative thought processes may lead to new ideas and new solutions to problems.

Judgment at this highest level, we suggest, was not a characteristic of the domino theory.[14] It did capture certain elements of the new realities with which the United States had to deal. But it also contained crude historical analogies, offered simplistic assumptions about the nature of human motivation, and suggested definitions of the nation's interests which did not differentiate between central and peripheral concerns. Reinforcing an American proclivity to overlook the relevance of concrete historical circumstances to the accomplishment of its goals, the domino theory also glossed over the possible negative side effects of undertaking efforts with a high probability of failure. Certainly it did not provide a sophisticated framework for understanding the costs and possible consequences of the American involvement in Vietnam.

*　　*　　*

The specific metaphor of falling dominoes did not animate discussions of U.S. foreign policy in the late 1940s. But the basic assumptions which that image would later so easily conjure up, had been embraced by American decision makers as early as the spring of 1946, when President Harry Truman asked the U.S. Congress for $400 million in military and economic assistance to counter communist pressure on the governments of Greece and Turkey. His concerns, as he expressed at the time, extended beyond these countries. "Collapse of free institutions and loss of independence would be disastrous not only for [Greece and Turkey] but for the world. Discouragement and possibly failure would quickly be the lot of neighboring peoples striving to maintain their freedom and independence."[15] In Dean Acheson's words, "like apples in a barrel infected by one rotten one, the corruption of Greece would infect Iran and all to the east."[16]

Versions of the domino theory were also evident in discussions of the Vietnam situation as early as April 1950. The Joint Chiefs of Staff thought the fall of Indochina to communism would lead "almost immediately [to] a dangerous condition with respect to the internal security of the Philippines, Malaya, and Indonesia" that "would contribute to their probable eventual fall." Japan, they argued, would be economically threatened by the loss of its remaining Asian markets and sources of raw materials.[17] Their concerns were echoed in a series of other secret administration policy papers.[18]

The fears of Washington policymakers seemed to have been substantiated in June 1950, when the North Korean armies crossed the 38th parallel. Washington viewed the move as Soviet inspired. As one State Department official put it, "the relationship between the Soviet Union and the North Koreans [was] the same as that between Walt Disney and Donald Duck."[19] The Soviet objective, as it was argued in one CIA memorandum, was to "undermine the position of the United States and the Western Powers throughout the Far East" and "test the firmness of U S resistance to Communist expansion."[20]

For Harry Truman, it was essential that America's response be tough and unambiguous. Margaret Truman recalls him saying, "*if we stand up to them like we did in Greece three years ago, they won't take any next steps* (emphasis added)."[21] Later in his *Memoirs* he wrote:

> Communism was acting in Korea *just as Hitler, Mussolini, and the Japanese had acted ten, fifteen, and twenty years earlier*. I felt certain that if South Korea was allowed to fall, Communist leaders would be emboldened to override nations closer to our own shores. If the communists were permitted to force their way into the Republic of Korea without opposition from the free world, *no small nation would have the courage to resist threats and aggression by stronger Communist neighbors*. If this was allowed to go unchallenged it would mean a third world war, just as similar incidents had brought on the second world war (emphasis added).[22]

After the attack on South Korea, the metaphor firmly took hold and the domino theory was widely accepted within the Washington foreign policy establishment. A CIA memorandum in December 1950 predicted disasters for Thailand, Malaya, Burma, Indonesia, and the Philippines should Indochina fall.[23] By 1952 State Department policymakers were assuming that communist military victories in Southeast Asia would exert increasing military, economic, and political pressure on the area's remaining non-communist countries and could induce the fall of the entire region to communism.[24]

The Eisenhower Administration was as concerned with the potential fall of Asian dominoes as its Democratic predecessor had been. In his first appearance before the Senate Foreign Relations Committee, Secretary of State John Foster Dulles argued that the loss of Indochina would result in the fall of all Southeast Asia, putting "Japan . . . in a very precarious situation."[25] President Dwight Eisenhower introduced the specific metaphor of "falling dominoes" in a 1954 press conference. America should support the French in Vietnam because of "what you would call the 'falling domino' principle," he said. "You have a row of dominoes set up, you knock over the first one, and what will happen to the last one is the certainty that it will go over very quickly."[26] Three days earlier, Eisenhower had written Winston Churchill that he did not see how "Thailand, Burma, and Indonesia could be kept out of Communist hands" if Indochina were allowed to fall. Japan might even topple under economic pressure, in which case the "threat to Malaya, Australia, and New Zealand would be direct."[27] While briefing John Kennedy shortly before leaving office, Eisenhower asserted that "Laos was the key to all Southeast Asia." If Kennedy could not forge a political settlement there, then he should "intervene unilaterally."[28]

Kennedy, however, needed little instruction, having already embraced the domino theory. In a speech before the American Friends of Vietnam in 1954, he saw the security of several Asian countries as being "threatened if the red tide of communism overflowed into Vietnam."[29] When asked about the domino theory during his presidency, Kennedy responded, "I believe it. I believe it."[30] His primary foreign policy advisers had similar views. Secretary of State Dean Rusk and Secretary of Defense Robert McNamara, on a fact-finding trip to Vietnam, reported that the loss of South Vietnam would lead Southeast Asia and Indonesia into a "complete accommodation with communism" and would "undermine the credibility of American commitments elsewhere."[31]

In 1961, Vice President Lyndon Johnson also argued that "we have to decide whether we are going to help these countries [in Southeast Asia] to the best of our ability or throw in the towel in the area and pull back our defenses to San Francisco."[32] As president, he likened North Vietnam to Nazi Germany and proclaimed that a retreat from Vietnam would eventually lead to battles in other countries and "on the beaches of Waikiki."[33] His Secretary of Defense, Robert McNamara, wrote him in a 1964 memorandum that the fall of South Vietnam to communism would have political consequences for countries as far away as India, Japan, Australia, and New Zealand.[34] Indeed, as late as November 1967, President Johnson's senior informal advisers on Vietnam — the "wise men" — were unanimous in their unqualified support of the concepts embraced in the domino theory and felt confident that American activities in Vietnam were "on the right track." This was despite the findings of Clark Clifford, on a visit to Southeast Asia prior to his appointment as Secretary of Defense, that the leaders in the region were unanimous in rejecting the validity of the domino theory.[35]

Two years later President Richard Nixon justified his refusal to withdraw from Vietnam in similar terms:

> Our defeat and humiliation in South Vietnam . . . would promote recklessness in the council of those great powers who have not yet abandoned their goals of world conquest. This would spark violence wherever our commitments help maintain the peace — in the Middle East, in Berlin, eventually even in the Western Hemisphere.[36]

For a short time after the end of the Vietnam war, the domino theory lost some of its power to shape American foreign policy decisions. The American experience in Vietnam led Richard Nixon, in his second term of office, as well as Gerald Ford and Jimmy Carter during their presidencies, to reconsider the advisability of direct military involvement in the defense of all non-communist regimes in the third world. Each of these three presidents, albeit with much ambivalence, was willing to consider the possibility that conflicts between the United States and the Soviet Union might be muted through the recognition, by diplomatic means, of the common interests of both countries in arms reduction and mutual security measures.[37]

In Ronald Reagan's first term as president of the United States, however, the domino theory regained its vitality in American decision-making circles. Repeatedly, in his early political career, Reagan argued in domino terms. The decision to limit the war in Korea, in Reagan's view, encouraged the communists to challenge in Laos, and the agreement to neutralize Laos in 1961 led to the communist challenge in Vietnam.[38] The 1980 Republican platform, which almost completely reflected Reagan's views, warned of "the Marxist Sandinista takeover of Nicaragua and the Marxist attempts to destabilize El Salvador, Guatemala, and Honduras."[39] As president, Reagan's policies toward the Sandinista government in Central America was based on the domino theory. Moreover, the incursion into Lebanon in 1982, was based on the premise, most clearly articulated by Alexander Haig, that the civil conflict there had its origins in the Soviet support of Syria and of its "oft-time agent, the PLO."[40]

Underlying Assumptions of the Domino Theory

For most of its proponents, the domino theory was a metaphor rather than a well-thought out explanation of the reasons why the fall of one area to communism would lead to the fall of others. Yet certain causal links were assumed. When they were explicitly stated, they were treated, for the most part, as self-evident truths. Rarely were they viewed at top policy-making levels as premises to be examined. These basic assumptions may be summarized as follows:

(1) An aggressor nation will challenge the status quo powers to peripheral, seemingly unimportant issues, testing their will to resist. Thus it was argued in a Security Council document of 30 March 1948 (NSC 7), that "the ultimate objective of Soviet directed world communism is the domination of the world. To this end, Soviet directed world communism employs against its victims, in opportunistic coordination, the complementary instruments of Soviet aggressive pressure from without and military revolutionary subversion from within."[41] The Soviet approach, said Dean Acheson after the Korean invasion, was to detect "weakness or disunity" and "exploit them."[42] If not challenged, they will advance more ambitious claims.[43] As Dean Rusk explained it:

Hitler could see that the Japanese militarists in Manchuria were not stopped. He saw that Mussolini was not stopped in Ethiopia. This encouraged him. Now, what happens here in Southeast Asia, if Peiping discovers that Hanoi can move without risk or can move with success? What further decisions are they going to make.[44]

(2) Standing up to the aggressor, however, would cause them to back down. Like schoolyard bullies who try to achieve their goals through intimidation, aggressors are assumed to have feet of clay. As Lyndon Johnson once said:

One thing is clear. Whether communist or fascist or simply a pistol-packing racketeer, the one thing a bully understands is force and the one thing he fears is courage. . . . I want peace. But human experience tells me that if I let a bully of my community make me travel the back streets to avoid a fight, I merely postpone the evil day. Soon he will chase me out of my house. Indeed, if you let a bully come into your front yard, the next day he'll be up on your porch, and the day after that he'll rape your wife in your own bed. But if you say to him at the start, "Now, just hold on, wait a minute," then he'll know he's dealing with a man of courage, someone who will stand up to him. And only then can you get along and find some peace again.[45]

(3) The United States, as the core power in the alliance of the free world, must stand up to the USSR to maintain the morale of its allies. If one nation is allowed to fall to Soviet inspired aggression without a firm response, other less powerful nations will lose faith in the will of the core power to protect them. As Lyndon Johnson saw it, the well-being of people around the globe rests on America's "abiding commitment to preserve and perpetuate the enduring values of mankind." To leave Vietnam would shake their confidence in the value of an American commitment and the "deep and flowing springs of moral duty" from which it emanates.[46] Should this occur, the less powerful members of the status quo alliance might accommodate themselves to the aggressor state rather than stand alone.

(4) Revolutionary communism is simply a form of Soviet expansionism. Proxies such as North Vietnam and Cuba serve as convenient conduits through which the Soviet Union can extend its influence through the spread of communism. This version of the domino theory often employs a disease metaphor. As W. W. Rostow proclaimed in a speech in 1961, "we are determined to help destroy this international disease, this guerrilla war designed, initiated, supplied, and led from outside an independent nation."[47] Communism, in short, is carried by revolutionary hosts to other nations like the spread of an epidemic. And because mere proximity to these agents makes a society vulnerable, one cannot take lightly the fall of even one country to communism. For if one country falls, several others will follow.

From this perspective, local conditions that make a nation susceptible to the revolutionary movement are seen as relatively unimportant. This is the assumption in Jeane Kirkpatrick's argument that revolutions are the result of the violence perpetuated by Marxist-inspired leaders as well as the failure of the United States to support the traditional leaders coming under attack. Nicaragua and Iran, for example, were solid allies of the United States until these regimes "became the object of a major attack by forces explicitly hostile to the United States." Local discontent with the repressive regimes of Somoza and the Shah, she assumes, were not the primary causes of the revolutionary ferment which developed in those countries.[48] Indeed, Western liberals err in interpreting "insurgency as evidence of widespread popular discontent and a will to democracy." Rather than meeting such insurgencies with calls for democratic reform, she concludes, U.S. policymakers should provide support for friendly dictators. That is preferable to running the risk of losing yet another country to communism.[49]

Reasons for the Adoption of the Domino Theory

There were several reasons for the adoption of the domino theory:

(1) Partly it was the result of the lessons political decision makers had drawn from their readings of history. Political leaders, as Tetlock has pointed out, are determined not to re-create the mistakes of the past.[50] Typical is Harry Truman's view that the "lessons of history" offer clear guides to "right principles" of action.[51]

History offers up many possible lessons, however, and the particular ones drawn will depend on a variety of factors. Often, learned images are based on dramatic and memorable events, occurring early in the decision maker's political life, which have had visible impact on the fortunes of the individual or his nation.[52] The adoption of the domino theory by American decision makers after World War II can be understood, partly, in these terms. Most of the men playing key roles in the formulation of American foreign policy after World War II experienced a very salient event — the Munich Conference — during the formative phase of their political or educational careers. Lyndon Johnson and Harry Truman were in the U.S. Congress at the time. John Kennedy, McGeorge and William Bundy, and Robert McNamara were in college. It seemed to them that Hitler was being encouraged in his aggressions by the failure of Great Britain and other status quo powers to offer resistance at Munich. The USSR, as they saw it, was now acting as Hitler once had and they were going to avoid, at all costs, the mistakes they thought Chamberlain had made at Munich.[53]

(2) The domino theory was also useful in that it provided American decision makers with a map explaining their new world. It not only provided a diagnosis of the threat the United States faced from the USSR, it also suggested simple prescriptions for dealing with that threat. Because the causes of revolutionary movements and local communist aggressions were to be found in the aggressive nature of international communism, there was little reason to look at the local causes of discontent or at the actual national interests of the USSR or China. Nor did one have to analyze the complex relations among the communist powers and their allies. A policy response was predetermined — the United States must take a hard-line stand against any expansion of communism. Moreover, the costs of that policy response were viewed as not being high because the communists are only testing the West. They would back down when they meet resistance.

(3) The domino theory also served immediate and pressing domestic political, organizational, and psychological interests. The notion that the Soviet Union was bent on the conquest of the world served the bureaucratic interests of decision makers in Washington. In the immediate postwar period several diplomats in the State Department—Joseph Grew, Loy Henderson, George Kennan, and James Dunne—viewed the Soviet moves in Eastern Europe as signs of unlimited imperial ambition. George Kennan's long telegram from Moscow on 22 February 1946, for example, argued that the inner dynamics of the Soviet system was the source of an appetite for expansionism that could only be contained by the firm application of counter pressure wherever it attempted to expand.[54] Given the United States's need to act at the time and the lack of clear data about what actually motivated Stalin, these assessments made as much sense as alternative interpretations suggesting that the Soviets were simply pursuing, in these acts, their traditional national interest or acting out of fear of the United States.[55]

The speed with which this view of Soviet motives was picked up and circulated throughout the government and the informed public, however, suggests that many top military and political leaders in the United States were predisposed, in terms of their own bureaucratic or personal interests, to embrace such an interpretation of Soviet motives. Secretary of the Navy James Forrestal, for example, circulated George Kennan's long telegram warning of Soviet expansionistic proclivities throughout the upper levels of the national security bureaucracy and sponsored Kennan for a position as the only civilian director of the newly established National War College.[56] Other Navy and Air Force officials, Ernest May suggests, found that circulating these views of the USSR would help them extract money from Congress for carriers and bombers.[57] By early 1946, the Joint Chiefs of Staff joined in. The immediacy of the Soviet threat, they argued, required consideration of increased military support for U.S. foreign policy goals. A focus on long-term military potential would "not be sufficient to avert disaster in another war."[58]

(4) The domino theory was also useful to political leaders in their attempts to win both congressional and public support for extending U.S. influence in parts of the world where it had not traditionally been active. The U.S. Congress and the general public had not been prepared in the immediate postwar era for military and economic commitment to areas of the world which seemed distant from traditional American concerns. The Truman administration, for example, had difficulties, initially, in selling its Turkish-Greek aid package to a Congress that was treating it as a "rather trivial issue." To win support for their proposals, the administration began to express the threat in apocalyptic terms. Dean Acheson, for example, portrayed the Soviet goals in the area as the encirclement of Turkey and the control of the eastern Mediterranean and Middle East in a threat "unparalleled since ancient times." Only then did the Congress and the public come together in a "national acceptance of world responsibility."[59]

(5) The alacrity with which the domino theory was embraced can also be understood in terms of broader proclivities in the American culture. Historically, Americans have been inclined to use abstract principles for guidance in their

foreign policy decision making. Through the nineteenth and early twentieth century, American policies towards Europe and Latin America were based on the two-sphere concept of the Monroe Doctrine; and for the first 50 years of the twentieth century American policies toward the Far East were based on the principles of the open door and the territorial integrity of China. The domino theory similarly provided an abstract, easily understood guide for action. The transformation of the Greek-Turkish aid program into a program for the defense of democracy around the world can be understood in these terms. As George Kennan observes in his *Memoirs*: "We like to find some general governing norm to which, in each instance, appeal can be taken, so that individual decisions may be made not on their particular merits but automatically, depending on whether the circumstances do or do not seem to fit the norm."[60]

(6) The domino theory also met the career and psychological needs of the new civilian strategists, as Hannah Arendt suggests, who by the time of the Vietnam War were dominating high-level decision making. Their objectives were intangibles, such as the maintenance of the United States's reputation as the mightiest nation in the world and the support of the morale of South Vietnam and other allies. At stake for the strategists was their image of U.S. omnipotence, their personal career successes, their identification with the power and prestige of the United States, and the abstract models they employed as guides to action. Divorced from the constraint of concrete strategic material or imperial objectives, Arendt argues, they felt no need to ground themselves in fact. Neither CIA reports nor the relevant historical background of Southeast Asia were important to them.

Not only did the decision-makers seem ignorant of all the well-known facts of the Chinese revolution and the decade-old rift between Moscow and Peking that preceded it, but "no one at the top knew or considered it important that the Vietnamese had been fighting foreign invaders for almost 2,000 years.[61]

Though these "problem solvers" were not strictly speaking domino theorists, they linked up with them.[62] Both groups of men encouraged systems of thought that undermined respect for limits and the search for facts. In the end, for both approaches, there were "no real aims, good or bad, that could limit and control sheer fantasy.[63]

Evaluation of the Validity of the Domino Theory

Certain aspects of the domino theory, we suggest, did accurately represent key features of the new world in which the United States found itself after World War II. As balance of power theorists have long realized, countervailing power is the only reliable method for limiting the ambition of potentially expansionistic foreign nations. "You may cover whole skins of parchment with limitations, but power alone can limit power," John Randolph pointed out many years ago.[64] National leaders, as political realists note, are often tempted to take for their countries what they can cheaply secure. But when faced by others with near equal power and the possibility of war, they will often back down. In those instances where they do not, other assessments have to be made. Diplomatic accommodation may be possible when their goals are limited. But when their objectives are directly counter to one's own basic interests, war may be the only remedy.[65] The United States acted in accord with these precepts when it countered Stalin's pressures against Turkey, Iran, and West Berlin in the immediate postwar period.[66]

The domino theory, however, went beyond these simple balance of power concerns in its core idea that even threats to apparently minor interests must be met with commitments to preserve the status quo. Because all interests are linked, one cannot distinguish between vital and more peripheral concerns. It is a view of the world that many larger status quo nations have embraced, though the images used may be of the spread of prairie fires or diseases rather than dominos.[67] Thus Athens during the Peloponnesian Wars in the fifth century B.C. gave the small island of Melos, a Spartan colony which had remained neutral in the early days of the wars, a choice between allying with Athens or being destroyed. Its continued neutrality, the Athenians argued, would encourage others to aspire toward a similar independence.[68] In more recent times, Great Britain's decision to use force to prevent Argentina from seizing the Falkland Islands was motivated, in part, by the concern that a passive response would ultimately lead to similar attacks on Gibraltar and other remaining outposts of the British Empire.[69]

Even challenges to economic norms have been countered in these terms. American decision makers in the late 1930s, for example, saw Latin American attempts to nationalize industries as a threat to the entire international legal structure supporting free enterprise. When Mexico nationalized oil properties in 1938, the State Department pushed for limited economic sanctions. If the United States acquiesced in an expropriation without appropriate compensation, Secretary of State Cordell Hull warned, "other nations would quickly follow suit."[70] After World War II, the U.S. Congress added the Hickenlooper Amendment to the Foreign Assistance Act of 1962 mandating the automatic cessation of economic aid to any country expropriating private property without speedy and adequate compensation. Otherwise, as one congressman warned, a veritable "prairie fire" of confiscation would lay waste to American property rights throughout the third world.[71]

There is some legitimacy to this linkage of interests. Nations have had legitimate concerns about the implications of any failures on their part to stand up to even minor threats to their interests or their influence in the future. Military and economic resources are worth little unless others are convinced they would be used to protect vital interests. "Goodwill, prestige, and saving face," as Robert Jervis notes, "are often not ephemeral goals pursued by politicians courting domestic support or foolish statesmen unappreciative of the vital role of power." They all use signals to convince others of what their future actions might be. Through actions which are mainly symbolic, they show that they are willing to make sacrifices for a goal. If they can convince others that in an emergency they will use their military or economic power, even when it is costly for them to do so, they may not even have to resort to that use.[72]

The credibility of contemporary nuclear deterrence doctrine is based on such considerations. After the Soviet explosion of its own atom bomb in 1949, American strategic experts became increasingly concerned about whether or not the United States could rationally back up its warnings that it might actually resort to the use of nuclear weapons.[73] Certainly, one could not make those judgments based on the past behavior of states.[74] To maintain the credibility of these deterrent threats, U.S. policymakers came to think that they had to cultivate a reputation for toughness. By defending nations at the periphery, the United States could send a message to the USSR that threats to more central interests would be met, if necessary, with a nuclear response. As Thomas Schelling said in 1966: "The main reason why we are committed in many of these places is that our threats are interdependent. Essentially we tell the Soviets that we have to react here because, if we did not, they would not believe us when we say that we will react there."[75]

Nuclear powers may also have to stand tough to assure *themselves* that they might actually resort to nuclear weapons under certain circumstances. Through the actual defense of lesser commitments, according to this argument, decision makers assure themselves that they have the resolve to actually employ nuclear weapons should a deterrent threat be called for.[76] Measured and appropriate responses to low- and middle-level threats to important values, in short, are seen as ways of reinforcing the beliefs of others and oneself that graver threats to central national interests would be met with a nuclear response.[77]

Problems in the Domino Theory

Although the domino theory does grasp certain aspects of the world which it purports to explain, it is far too simplistic in several ways. It does not distinguish between the motives of rational and non-rational aggressors or between those bent on unlimited imperialism and those committed to a limited expansionistic course out of more traditional national interests. Nor does it address the possibility of over-commitment and failure for those who define their interests so globally. Certainly, in its post-World War II manifestation, it has not paid sufficient attention to the complexity of the relationships among communist regimes. Moreover, it has glossed over the indigenous roots of revolutions and local wars, and the limitations of imitation and contagion of effects. The problem, in part, is that the domino theory is based on several questionable historical and psychological assumptions.

(1) *Misinterpretation of the Munich Conference.* The domino theory is rooted in a questionable interpretation of the Munich Conference, given what we now know about Adolf Hitler's personality, goals, and attitudes toward opponents. The German Führer was not testing the will of the Allies in 1938. Nor would he have been deterred from using force to achieve his goals. Shortly before the Munich

Conference, Hitler informed his generals that he had decided to use force to solve the Czech problem that fall.[78] His diplomatic maneuvers at Munich, as Williamson Murray indicates, were designed to isolate the Czechs so the German military could destroy them in a quick campaign.[79] Indeed, Hitler was disappointed that he had obtained the Sudetenland without a battle. As he later told Dr. Hjalmar Schacht, "that fellow [Chamberlain] has spoiled my entry into Prague."[80]

At the same time, Hitler saw even limited resistance to his designs as threatening and unfair. When Sir Horace Wilson, Chamberlain's close adviser during the Munich crisis, informed him of Czech opposition to his demands, Hitler responded with fury. Jumping to his feet, he shouted that the Germans were being treated like "niggers." Similarly, when he later heard that Winston Churchill, Duff Cooper, and Anthony Eden had condemned Chamberlain for signing the Munich accord, he bitterly attacked the "malevolent" threesome. In Hitler's eyes, the British were responsible for the crisis.[81]

Psychologically, Hitler needed war, as Robert Waite has argued. A deeply disturbed person, he had the political power to turn his private fantasies into public reality. Unchecked in his early political career, his vision became increasingly grandiose and he ultimately felt invincible. Driven by the need to avoid any hint of effeminacy, Hitler could not back down. He valued obstinacy as "an essential masculine trait and prided himself that he had it in abundance."[82] As General Alfred Jodl recalled, Hitler's military and political philosophy was expressed in countless tirades to the German General Staff: "that one had to stand or fall, that each voluntary step backwards was an evil in itself."[83]

The only way that Hitler might have been stopped in 1938 was through a military coup d'etat. At the time of the Munich Conference, certain high military officials were conspiring to remove him from office should the British and French intervene.[84] Their plans, however, had little chance of success. By the Munich Conference, Hitler had become commander-in-chief of the armed forces. His opponents in the military had shown no daring in the past and their plans were dangerously naive. An early plan, conceived by former chief of staff Ludwig Beck, would even have allowed Hitler to return to power. The conspirators assumed that they could force Hitler to forego his war plans and embrace domestic reforms such as freedom of expression.[85] Army chief of staff Franz Halder's plan, under which the conspirators were operating in September 1938, was to arrest Hitler and place him on trial. Most of the conspirators in both plans did not have direct command of troops. It is doubtful that the younger officer corps and the common soldiers, who thought Hitler a genius, would have followed their orders.[86]

This is not to suggest that Neville Chamberlain cannot be faulted for facilitating and legitimizing Hitler's seizure of the Sudetenland.[87] But the real issue at Munich was whether Great Britain should fight Hitler immediately or later on. Winston Churchill and H. R. Trevor-Roper thought it would have been best to have gone to war in 1938. By handing over a strategically important part of Czechoslovakia to Hitler, the Allies lost the greatest arsenal in central Europe and the opportunity for an early alliance with Russia against Hitler.[88] On the other hand, the delay in the war enabled the Royal Air Force to equip itself with the Hurricanes and Spitfires that enabled them to win the Battle of Britain. Hitler's subsequent seizure of the rest of Czechoslovakia and his attack on Poland also made his intentions clear even to isolationists in Great Britain and the United States, thereby unifying the people in those countries in the war effort against him when it came.[89]

(2) *Simplistic Views of Motives of the Enemy*. The domino theory is also based on a simplistic view of human motivation. For example, the American interpretations of North Vietnam's infiltration into South Vietnam as a Russian test of the United States reduced the nationalist goals of small nations to mere big-power plays on the world's political chessboard. Certainly it ignored fifty years of Vietnamese history and the role Ho Chi Minh had played as an anti-colonial nationalist.[90] In the 1920s he had been known as Nguyen Ai Quoc, or "Nguyen who loves its country" and his most impassioned essays dealt with the injustices of colonial rule. Indeed, in the 1930s, when confronted with a choice between his patriotism and the Comintern, Ho Chi Minh chose the former. When Moscow replaced him and the other leadership of Indochina's Communist Party (ICP), that party lost its popular support and virtually ceased to exist.[91]

The complexity of Soviet motivations was also misunderstood when American decision makers interpreted the Soviet intervention in Afghanistan in 1979 as the result of the failure of the United States to make its deterrence threats clear. There is little evidence, as Lebow and Cohen suggest, that the USSR invaded Afghanistan to challenge the United States or that American deterrence warnings, or lack thereof, were of central relevance to Russian decision makers. On the contrary, Lebow and Cohen argue, the Soviet Union was clearly more motivated by the political and military instability that seriously threatened its influence in Afghanistan, a country that had been in its sphere of influence for some time.[92]

This propensity of American decision makers to see the Soviet Union as simply responding to American moves was a manifestation, as Lebow and Cohen also point out, of a more general psychological tendency of any group of human beings to see themselves as the central point of reference for others—the "egocentric bias." Situational pressures unrelated to one's self that may contribute to an enemy's aggressive behavior (e.g., his strategic vulnerabilities) are ignored or de-emphasized. Steps they take which appear less aggressive or more favorable to one's own interests are explained in terms of external factors that compel that action. Thus, if the Soviet Union does not invade a country, it is because of the countervailing strength of the United States and its allies. Concessions they might make to secure an arms limitation agreement are not based on their desire for peace, but the result of the military "chips" the United States has secured against them.[93]

(3) *Problems with the Bully Metaphor*. Evaluation from academic psychology raises more general questions about the assumption that an aggressor will back down when challenged. On the contrary, bullies tend to react violently to the slightest threat. Violence-prone men, as Hans Toch suggests:

scan human contacts assiduously for the possibility of threatening implications. The actions of other people are eventually classified as either non-challenging (safe) or as challenging (requiring action). Because of the dreaded consequences of error, the scales are far from evenly weighted: with greater or lesser distortion, potentially harmless encounters become transmuted into "unprovoked" onslaughts by "vicious" bullies . . . [the other person's] response is likely to lead to violence because it usually feeds into the hypothesis that provides the aggressor's rationale for offensiveness.[94]

More generally, when a goal-oriented "organism" is prevented from reaching its goal, aggression may result. In the words of Leonard Berkowitz, "a frustrating event increases the probability that the thwarted organism will act aggressively soon afterward."[95] Where the frustrating event is identifiable and widely experienced by an entire society, an increase in the aggressiveness of both leaders and the people is the likely result. The American bombings over Vietnam had an effect along these lines. The lumber and rubber industries upon which many Vietnamese depended for a living were destroyed. Schrapnel and unexploded shells killed the Vietnamese who tried to cultivate their land. Mosquitoes bred in the bomb craters and malaria spread. Frustrated in their attempts to secure basic needs, many peasants came to view the United States as the enemy.[96] Thus it is no surprise that John McCone would report that the massive American bombings over North Vietnam, begun in the spring of 1965, seemed to stiffen Hanoi's resolve.[97] The saturation bombing in the free fire zones in South Vietnam actually gained new recruits for the Viet Cong and the Viet Minh.[98]

Threats, moreover, are apt to evoke counter threats, as Morton Deutsch and Robert Krauss have pointed out, even when concrete incentives suggest that backing down will bring more positive results.[99] Further, aggressive stances tend to be imitated, as Olle Holm has shown.[100] The mere introduction of weapons into the environment can increase the probability of an aggressive response to frustration.[101] Similar effects have been found when subjects are exposed to violent films or even slides of weapons before being thwarted in a simple task.[102] In short, the notion that a nation is testing its opponents with every expansion and that, like a bully, it will back down when countered, is seriously controverted by much of the research on aggression. In fact, standing up to aggressors may backfire and increase their aggressiveness.

(4) *Simplistic View of The Roots of Revolutions.* In attributing revolutionary movements to international communism, the domino theory also fails to discern the local roots of discontent and the various local conditions that can weaken a government. The simple epidemiological metaphor that is most often used suggests that the spread occurs throughout mere proximity — almost magically — like a disease through germs in the air or the spoiling of rotten apples in a barrel.

A more sophisticated epidemiological model would alert political observers to the local conditions that make a country susceptible to revolution and the possibility that those local governments can devise techniques to immunize themselves in certain important ways. Indeed, contemporary research in biology suggests that the process of infection can best be understood if the process is broken down into three elements: "an infecting micro-organism, a means of transmission of the organism from one host to another, *and a recipient host in which the organism can establish itself*" (emphasis added).[103]

Using such a model one will look beyond mere proximity to the carriers of "disease" to the susceptibilities of the potential target states. Indeed, certain students of the revolutionary process have already begun to move in this direction. Their suggestions are that the spread of revolution is likely only when the following three conditions are met: (1) The revolutionary ideas promise to meet important needs for the target society — to produce enjoyment, raise the standard of living, or produce other desirable consequences; (2) The target government in power is estranged from widely shared national goals, and a native insurgency movement is able to provide politically legitimate alternatives to that current government; and (3) The revolutionary ideas do not conflict with traditional values.[104]

From this perspective, the successes and failures of various counter insurgency operations after World War II can better be understood. Strong, reform-minded, indigenous governments were crucial to the defeat of communist movements in Greece and the Philippines, as Schaeffer has suggested. Indeed, the role of the U.S. government in these operations was minor compared to U.S. intervention in other cases.[105]

Vietnam, by way of contrast, was particularly vulnerable to revolutionary communism and not a very favorable place for the United States to test its counterinsurgency capabilities. Ho Chi Minh and the Vietnamese communists had led the fight against French attempts to reestablish their colonial regime in Indochina after World War II and their nationalist credentials were strong. Moreover, the Viet Minh Front was the only movement with a detailed program designed to meet the needs of the peasants. Their land policy, prior to 1954, was to lower rents and redistribute to the poorer peasants the land belonging to the French and those identified with them. After 1954, the land they broke up came only from absentee owners. "Rich and middle-class peasants were rarely dispossessed."[106]

All the American-backed governments that came to power in South Vietnam after the Geneva Agreements, in contrast, lacked both legitimacy and the will to make the necessary reforms.[107] Ngo Dinh Diem, who took over the reins of the Saigon government in October 1955, had never taken up arms against the French. Both his government and the others which followed his overthrow relied on army officers and bureaucrats who were strongly identified with the puppet Bao Dai regime.[108] These governments were unrepresentative of the people they governed in other ways as well. In a predominantly Buddhist society, their support came "from refugee Catholics and important elements of the church in the South: the Hoa Hao and Cao Dai sects, the Khmer ethnic minority, and cooperative factions of the Montagnard, or hill peoples." Within government circles, too, there were recurrent struggles for influence between northern refugee elements (mostly Catholic) and men from the Cochinchinese majority in the South.[109] The legitimacy of the Diem and subsequent governments in Saigon was further undermined by the extent of their identification with the United States. President Diem had been installed by America and his government survived on American aid. The several regimes that came to power after his overthrow and death increasingly assumed the appearance of American puppets and became more estranged from the concerns of most Vietnamese.[110]

(5) *The Credibility Problem.* The domino theory may even lead to policies that undermine the credibility of the deterrent threats it is supposed to maintain. When a great power cannot differentiate clearly between its central and marginal national security interests, it can dissipate its energies and resources. American involvement in the Vietnam War, for example, led to the neglect of important allies in areas strategically more important than Southeast Asia. Thus, when the Egyptian blockade of the Tiran Straits in the late spring of 1967 cut off Israeli access to the Red Sea, President Johnson, Secretary of State Dean Rusk, and Secretary of Defense Robert McNamara opposed sending direct military assistance to Israel. The feeling in the Administration, as Walter Laquer has noted, was that " 'one war is about all we can manage at a time. . . .' "[111] The Israelis were asked to show restraint while the United States worked out a diplomatic solution to break the blockade, including an effort to get the U.N. Security Council to sponsor an Aqaba Gulf Seas Users Conference to guarantee safe passage through the Gulf. A fait accompli of this sort, of course, could not be reversed by such measures, and under pressure from its own military bureaucracy the Israeli government decided to act on its own. On June 6, they attacked the Arab forces.[112]

An extreme angst about one's "credibility," moreover, can create an asymmetrical relationship with a client regime, limiting one's ability to influence that government to move toward economic and political reforms. An absolute commitment to such a regime is apt to give it an illusion of invulnerability, reinforcing insensitivities to the local political environment. Moreover, the client regime in such circumstances may be in a position to wrest arms and political concessions from its patron, through threats that if its demands are not met, it may well lose it's will to defend itself and might even defect to the enemy camp. The Shah of Iran, for example, turned the tables on the United States in such a way. Whenever Washington hesitated to meet his requests for additional arms sales, he would note that there are "many other sources in the world." He also was fond of reminding American leaders that a failure in Iran would undermine America's credibility in the world. "You look like a crippled giant. . . . [Iran] can hurt you as badly if not more than you can hurt us."[113]

This "crippled giant" phenomenon is most likely to become manifest, for the reasons suggested above, in any relationship in which a patron nation makes absolute commitments to an unpopular regime, especially when the major power commits itself to states in areas of the world peripheral to its own central national security interests. In making such commitments one creates a situation where one might have to accept a loss. The alternative — an escalation to a much higher force level — can create problems concerning the proportionality of means to ends. In either event the major power faces considerable loss of prestige. In choosing a backdown, it seems impotent. In choosing an escalation, it seems imprudent and reckless — not the kind of core power other states would like to rely on for the future of their own countries.

(6) *Exaggeration of the Domino Effect and Counterproductive Military Interventions.* The domino metaphor is also likely to overestimate the effect of revolutionary success in one nation on neighboring regimes and to miss the exact nature of the links that on occasion may create domino effects. As the more sophisticated epidemiological model outlined above suggests, one cannot understand the spread of the insurrectionary "disease" without looking at the particular vulnerabilities of specific regimes and the possibility of enhancing their "immune systems." The very fear of falling dominoes, as Robert Jervis has pointed out, may lead neighboring regimes to initiate new programs which restrict their spread.[114] Most nations of Southeast Asia, for example, were able to maintain their positions with certain moderate counter-measures despite the fall of Vietnam. Thailand established tighter border security to prevent the transmission of revolutionary ideas from adjacent countries. Malaysia joined that country in a bilateral pact to cooperate in border areas. Both governments also took more active measures by supporting counterrevolutionary Cambodian forces with material aid and sanctuary.[115]

Moreover, interventions to prevent the dominoes from falling are apt to have counterproductive results elsewhere. American political and military interventions in Southeast Asia, for example, contributed to the fall of Laos and Cambodia. Early U.S. reluctance to support a neutral, non-communist government in Laos contributed to the instability of that government. Prior to the American involvement in that country, the communists had practically no indigenous support. But David Halberstam notes, "with our money, our CIA men, and our control of the Royal Laotian Army, we had in fact systematically destroyed the neutralist government of [Prince] Souvanna, eventually forcing the neutralists to the side of the Communist Pathet Lao."[116] Souvanna Phouma himself indicated in a 1967 interview that the U.S. intervention in Vietnam would have benefited Laos only if Laotian territory had not become a battleground in the war, and if the United States had understood that Laos had to keep its unity and maneuverability to deal with both of its large neighbors.[117]

Even more dramatically, the American diplomatic and military intervention in Cambodia contributed to the spread of the Khmer Rouge. Prewar Cambodia, as Arnold Isaacs recalls, was a "peaceful, fertile place that offered its seven million people no great material well-being but the psychic security of tradition, religion, and a village life . . . tranquil and slow as the flow of the numberless muddy streams that nourished the great rivers. . . ."[118] When the Nixon government encouraged Lon Nol to take up arms against the communists in northwest Cambodia it took the first of a series of missteps. Lon Nol's troops proved to be ineffectual against the battle-hardened communists, and the Americans, who had been engaged in secret B-52 bombing raids against areas in which the communists provided sanctuary to the Viet Cong, were called in to bomb wider areas of the Cambodian countryside.[119] As the military situation on the ground deteriorated, the bombing increased. With the destruction of the countryside and the crops upon which the Cambodian way of life depended, starvation became rampant.[120] Relatively few in number before the fighting started, Cambodian communists grew rapidly in the face of the foreign challenge.[121] Indeed, popular support for the communists had grown so that when the Khmer Rouge took Phnom Penh in 1975, they were welcomed with parades and fireworks.[122]

By this time, however, the more moderate Vietnamese communists had been replaced in the fields by native Cambodian insurgents — the fanatical and vicious Khmer Rouge. This whole process had been fed by the American bombings of Cambodia and the separation of the Khmer people from their local communities. The shattering of village life and normality loosened the external constraints on behavior, and the psychological makeup of the Khmer people was such that many of them went out of control. As Isaacs notes:

> Khmer culture is one that traditionally permits little outward expression of hostility, and thus does not teach its people to control aggressive drives when customary restraints are abandoned. It is for that reason, perhaps that "smiling people" like the Khmer often turn savagely cruel when they do become violent. The phrase "running amok" was contributed to our language by the Malays, a people culturally akin to the Khmer and similarly nonaggressive: "Amok" is a Malay word for someone in the grip of uncontrollable bloodlust.[123]

Ironically, from the American perspective, the only major domino effect in the post World War II world took place within the Russian Empire. Developments in Eastern Europe at the time of this writing suggest that the epidemiological model delineated above does presage the circumstances under which revolutionary movements will spread. Each communist government in Eastern Europe was vulnerable in very important ways. Each country had a strong nationalist tradition, each government had originally been imposed on that country by the Soviet Union and each government had failed in some important ways to provide its populace with the material and non-material goods they sought. The expression of these tensions were checked for a period of time by the policies and overwhelming military capabilities of the USSR. Their interests in the area had never been peripheral and they had shown that they were prepared to use force to sustain regimes which they saw as friendly. It was only when the Soviet Union redefined its national interests to permit political diversity in the region and rejected interventionism as a policy, that the way was prepared for some groups in Eastern Europe to "test" the situation. When early challenges to the old line communist governments of Poland and Hungary were met with neither significant military resistance at home nor a Soviet military response, it was only a matter of time before other nations, similarly discontented, would move to change their governments.

Conclusions

Images of the nature of the world order and the position of one's own nation in that order, as we have seen, play a central role in how decision makers define their interests, the nature of the threats to those interests, and possible policy responses. The adoption of the domino theory by key decision makers in the United States, to the extent that it provided these decision makers with an extended definition of the nation's vital security interests and envisaged the need to meet any threats with a military response, played a major role in its decision to go to war in Korea in 1950 and Vietnam in the mid-1960s. The image was based on certain lessons growing out of the appeasement of Hitler at Munich prior to World War II and it reflects, to a certain extent, the interests of the United States as the dominant actor in the maintenance of an international system which served its interests. The alacrity with which the image was adopted, however, also was due to domestic bureaucratic and political interests, certain cultural proclivities, and the psychological investments of key decision makers.

The domino image, however, provided a poor guide for action. It misinterpreted in important ways the "lessons of Munich," failed to explore the validity of the psychological assumptions upon which it was based, was applied to concrete situations which it did not accurately describe, and exaggerated the effects of the fall of one regime to the fall of others. Further case studies might indicate whether or not the concern with domino theories of one sort or another and the presence of domestic political and psychological pressures to indiscriminately apply them might explain, at least in part, the proclivity of big powers, as contrasted to minor ones, to take the initiative in the use of force.

Notes

1. Walter Lippmann, *Public Opinion* (New York: Macmillan, 1929), 15-16. For a general study of the nature of images, see Kenneth E. Boulding, *The Image: Knowledge in Life and Society* (Ann Arbor: University of Michigan Press, 1956). For use of concepts from cognitive psychology and historical case studies to explore the formulation and consequences of images on foreign policy, see Robert Jervis, *The Logic of Images in International Relations* (Princeton, NJ: Princeton University Press, 1970); Robert Jervis, *Perception and Misperception in International Relations* (Princeton, NJ: Princeton University Press, 1976), 117-202, 239-253; John D. Steinbruner, *The Cybernetic Theory of Decision: New Dimensions of Political Analysis* (Princeton: The Princeton University Press, 1974); Robert Axelrod, ed., *Structure of Decision: The Cognitive Map of Political Elites* (Princeton: Princeton University Press, 1976); Phillip Tetlock and Charles B. McGuire, "Cognitive Perspectives on Foreign Policy," in *Psychology and the Prevention of Nuclear War*, ed. Ralph White, 265-266; Deborah Welch Larson, *Origins of Containment: A Psychological Explanation* (Princeton, NJ: Princeton University Press, 1985); Alexander George, "The Operational Code: A Neglected Approach to the Study of Political Leaders and Decision-Making," *International Studies Quarterly* (1969): 251-280. For works showing the impact of the world views of leaders on a nation's definition of policy goals, see Nathan Leites, *The Operational Code of the Politburo* (New York: Rand Corporation, 1951); Ole R. Holsti, "Cognitive Dynamics and Images of the Enemy," in *International Behavior: A Social-Psychological Analysis*, ed. Herbert C. Kelman (New York: Holt, Rinehart, & Winston, 1966), 43-334; Betty Glad, *Charles Evens*

Hughes and the Illusions of Innocence (Champaign: University of Illinois Press, 1966); L. Johnson, "Operational Code and the Prediction of Leadership Behavior: Senator Frank Church at Mid-Career," in *A Psychological Examination of Political Leaders,* eds. Margaret G. Hermann and Tom Milburn (New York: Free Press, 1977). For a recent analysis of complex images in U.S. foreign policy belief systems, see Charles S. Taber, *A Computational Model of U.S. Foreign Policy Belief Systems, 1949-1960* (unpublished doctoral dissertation, University of Illinois, 1990).

2. For an example of this point of view, see Norton Ginsberg, "On the Chinese Perception of a World Order," (manuscript, University of Chicago, February 1966).

3. For this perspective see Hans J. Morgenthau with Kenneth W. Thompson, *Politics Among Nations: The Struggle for Power and Peace,* 6th ed. (New York: Alfred A. Knopf, 1985), 198-217.

4. For our purposes, a system maintenance image is defined as a configuration of symbols that suggests a given regime is legitimate. The image may also have implications for the ways in which members of the system should act to maintain that system. Occasionally these images may be based on systematic analyses and therefore deserve the term "theory." Often, however, they are based on comparisons, often tacit, in which one event or situation is understood and experienced in terms of earlier events or situations. The domino theory, we suggest, was an image of this metaphorical sort. For the nature of metaphorical thinking and its relationship to similes and allegories see Colin M. Turbayne, *The Myth of Metaphor* (New Haven, CT: Yale University Press, 1962); George Lakoff and Mark Johnson, *Metaphors We Live By* (Chicago: University of Chicago Press, 1980). For use of metaphors in anti-terrorist language, see Kenneth S. Hicks, "Metaphors We Kill By: Metaphorical Construct in the Formulation and Justification of the United States Response to Terrorism" (unpublished paper, University of South Carolina).

5. Lippman, *Public Opinion,* 16.

6. Ibid., 15-16.

7. Boulding, *The Image: Knowledge in Life and Society,* 16.

8. Ernest May, *"Lessons" of the Past: The Use and Misuse of History in American Foreign Policy* (New York: Oxford University Press, 1973), ix-xiv. For a historical approach showing how a foreign policy decision maker developed his mind set, see Betty Glad, *Charles Evans Hughes and the Illusions of Innocence.*.

9. L. A. Falkowsi, *Psychological Models in International Politics* (Boulder, CO: Westview, 1979).

10. For a review of learning concepts relevant to this discussion, see Lloyd Etheredge and James Short, "Thinking About Government Learning," *Journal of Management Studies,* 20, 1 (1983): 46-47; and Charles S. Taber, "Learning and War," (paper presented to the 1986 Annual Meeting of the International Studies Association in Anaheim, California, 25-29 March).

11. May, *"Lessons" of the Past,* xi-xiv, 178-179.

12. Lloyd Etheredge, *Can Governments Learn? American Foreign Policy and Central American Revolutions* (New York: Pergamon, 1985), 143.

13. Etheredge and Short, "Thinking About Government Learning," 46-47.

14. Indeed, as Etheredge and Short suggest, this kind of creativity is rarely present in bureaucratic decision making; see "Thinking About Government Learning," 55.

15. "Special Message to Congress on Greece and Turkey: The Truman Doctrine," *Public Papers of the Presidents of the United States: Harry S Truman, 1947* (Washington, DC: Government Printing Office), 179.

16. Dean Acheson, *Present at the Creation: My Years in the State Department* (New York: Norton, 1969), 219.

17. Department of State, *Foreign Relations of the United States, 1950* 6: 780-781.

18. Department of State, *Foreign Relations of the United States, 1949* 7: 1128-1133. For details on a BDM Corporation report documenting the impact of the domino theory on decision making, see Larry Berman, *Planning a Tragedy: The Americanization of the War in Vietnam* (New York: Norton, 1982), 130-131. For a recent work documenting the hold the domino theory had over decision makers in the early phases of the Vietnam War, see William Conrad Gibbons, *The U.S. Government and the Vietnam War: Executive and Legislative Roles and Relationships,* Part I (Princeton, NJ: Princeton University Press, 1986), 67.

19. Edward Barret quoted in the *New York Times*, 26 June 1950.

20. Quoted in Rosemary Foot, *The Wrong War: American Policy and the Dimensions of the Korean Conflict, 1950-1953* (Ithaca, NY: Cornell University Press, 1985), 59.

21. Margaret Truman, *Harry S Truman* (New York: William Morrow, 1973), 461.

22. Harry S Truman, *Memoirs: Years of Trial and Hope* (Garden City, NY: Doubleday, 1956), 333.

23. Department of State, *Foreign Relations of the United States, 1950* 6: 962-963.

24. Department of State, *Foreign Relations of the United States, 1952-1954* 13: 82-89.

25. *Executive Sessions of the Senate Foreign Relations Commmittee, 1953* 5: 386.

26. "Presidential News Conference of April 7, 1954," *Public Papers of the Presidents of the United States: Dwight D. Eisenhower* (Washington, DC: Government Printing Office, 1954), 381-382.

27. Department of State, *Foreign Relations of the United States, 1952-1954* 13: 1239-1241. See also Dwight D. Eisenhower, *Mandate for Change* (Garden City, NY: Doubleday, 1963), 180-187. Eisenhower, however, wavered—sometimes resisting the implications of the domino theory that the United States should intervene militarily in the Vietnamese war. See Gibbons, *The U.S. Government and the Vietnam War*, 88, 201-202.

28. Arthur M. Schlesinger, Jr., *A Thousand Days: John F. Kennedy in the White House* (New York: Greenwich House, 1965), 163. See also David Halberstam, *The Best and the Brightest* (Greenwich, CT: Fawcett Crest, 1969), 109.

29. John Galloway, ed., *The Kennedys and Vietnam* (New York: Oxford University Press, 1974), 103.

30. Quoted in May, *"Lessons" of the Past*, 93.

31. *The Pentagon Papers* in *New York Times*, ed. (New York: Bantam, 1971), 150.

32. Quoted in Raymond Aron, *The Imperial Republic: The United States and the World, 1945-1973*, trans. Frank Jellnik (Cambridge, MA: Winthrop, 1974), 103.

33. Quoted in Stanley Karnow, *Vietnam: A History* (New York: Viking Press, 1983), 250. For other Johnson statements see *Public Papers: Lyndon B. Johnson, 1965*, 398-399. For a strategist's view of the domino theory, see Herman Kahn, *On Thermonuclear War* (Princeton, NJ: Princeton University Press, 1960).

34. Excerpts from the memorandum of 16 March 1964, *The Pentagon Papers* in *New York Times*, ed., 278.

35. Herbert Shandler, *The Unmaking of a President* (Princeton, NJ: Princeton University Press, 1977), 129-130.

36. Address at the White House, 3 November 1969, reprinted in *U.S. News and World Report* (11 November 1969).

37. But Zbigniew Brzezinski, Jimmy Carter's national security adviser, wrote in his memoirs that the Soviet intervention in Afghanistan was encouraged by an earlier lack of resolve on the part of the United States. "To me," he wrote, "it was a vindication of my concern that the Soviets would be emboldened by our lack of response over Ethiopia." See Zbigniew Brzezinski, *Power and Principle: Memoirs of the National Security Adviser, 1977-1981* (New York: Farrar, Strauss, & Giroux, 1983), 429.

38. See Betty Glad, "Black and White Thinking: Ronald Reagan's Approach to Foreign Policy," *Political Psychology*, 4,1 (Spring 1983): 33-76.

39. Walter Lafeber, *Inevitable Revolutions* (New York: Norton, 1984), 271.

40. See Betty Glad, "The United States' Ronald Reagan," in *Leadership and Negotiation in the Middle East*, eds. Barbara Kellerman and Jeffrey Rubin (New York: Praeger, 1988), 221.

41. Quoted in Thomas H. Etzold and John Lewis Gaddis, eds., *Containment: Documents on American Policy and Strategy, 1945-1950* (New York: Columbia University Press, 1978), 165.

42. Dean Acheson, *Department of State Bulletin* 22, 599 (20 March 1959): 427.

43. See Philip E. Tetlock, "Policy Makers' Images of International Conflict," *Journal of Social Issues*, 39, 1 (Spring 1983): 70.

44. Senate Committee on Foreign Relations, *Supplemental Foreign Assistance, Fiscal Year 1966, Vietnam* (89th Cong., 2nd sess., 1966): 596.

45. Quoted in Doris Kearns, *Lyndon Johnson and the American Dream* (New York: Harper & Row, 1976), 95. In fact, the bully metaphor was sometimes used in pre-World War II foreign policy

discussions. Thus Senator Key Pittman, the Chairman of the Senate Foreign Relations Committee in the 1930s, noting the Japanese expansions in the Pacific, argued that "the only way to stop an international bully is to present him with the possibility that you may use arms against him." See Betty Glad, *Key Pittman: Portrait of a Senate Insider* (New York: Columbia University Press, 1986), 259. For other harbingers of the domino theory in the late-1930s, see Robert Thompson, *The Road to Pearl Harbor* (New York: Simon & Schuster, forthcoming).

46. "Commencement Address at Catholic University," 6 June 1965, *Public Papers of the Presidents of the United States: Lyndon Johnson* (Washington, DC: Government Printing Office), 640-644.

47. Walt W. Rostow, "Countering Guerrilla Attack," *Army*, 12, 2 (September 1961): 53-57.

48. Jeane Kirkpatrick, *Dictatorships and Double Standards: Rationalism and Reason in Politics* (New York: Simon & Schuster, 1982), 25-26.

49. Ibid., 34.

50. Tetlock, "Policy Makers' Images of International Conflict," 76-77.

51. May, *"Lessons" of the Past*, 82.

52. Jervis, *Perception and Misperception*, 239-282.

53. For George Ball's early adherence to the domino theory see May, *"Lessons" of the Past*, 113.

54. Ibid., 23-28, 30.

55. For these alternative interpretations, see Gar Alperovitz, *Cold War Essays* (Garden City, NY: Doubleday, 1970), 35-50, and Betty Glad's "Dilemmas of Deterrence," this volume.

56. John C. Donovan, *The Cold Warriors: A Policy-Making Elite* (Lexington, MA: D.C. Heath, 1974), 60-61.

57. May, *"Lessons" of the Past*, 23-28, 30.

58. Ibid., 30.

59. Joseph M. Jones, *The Fifteen Weeks, February 21 –June 5, 1947* (New York: Viking, 1955), 138-141.

60. George F. Kennan, *Memoirs 1925-1950* (New York: Pantheon Books, 1967), 322.

61. Hannah Arendt, "Lying in Politics," *Crises of the Republic* (New York: Harcourt Brace Jovanovich, 1972), 31. Even when administration officials met with experts on Vietnam, they were apt to dismiss their judgments out of hand. For example, when Paul Kattenberg, head of the Interdepartmental Working Group on Vietnam, told top officials at a meeting on 31 August 1963 that the Diem regime had very little popular support, his views were simply dismissed. See Donovan, *The Cold Warriors*, 188-191.

62. Arendt, *Crises of the Republic*, 40-41.

63. Ibid., 38.

64. Quoted in William Cabell Bruce, *John Randolph of Roanoke*, Vol. 2 (New York: G. P. Putnam, 1922), 221.

65. See also Morgenthau with Thompson, *Politics Among Nations*, 77-82.

66. For a discussion of the United States's interest in breaking the Berlin blockade in these terms, see Alexander George and Richard Smoke, *Deterrence in American Foreign Policy: Theory and Practice* (New York: Columbia University Press, 1977), 117, 558-561.

67. For the use of the prairie fire metaphor, see Kenneth Rodman, *Sanctity Versus Sovereignty: The United States and the Nationalization of Natural Resource Investments* (New York: Columbia University Press, 1988), 47-48.

68. Richard Ned Lebow, "The Paranoia of the Powerful: Thucydides on World War III," XVI, 1, *PS* (Winter 1984): 11. For the argument that Athens really undertook this occupation as a prelude to the expansion of her empire, see William T. Bluhm, " 'Hubris and Aggression,' A Critique of Lebow's 'Paranoia of the Powerful': An Alternative Theory," XVI, 2, *PS* (Summer 1984): 586-591.

69. Richard Ned Lebow, "Miscalculations in the South Atlantic: The Origins of the Falklands War," in *Psychology and Deterrence*, eds. Robert Jervis, Richard Ned Lebow, and Janice Gross Stein (Baltimore, MD: Johns Hopkins University Press, 1985), 89-124.

70. Rodman, *Sanctity Versus Sovereignty*, 116.

71. Rodman, *Sanctity Versus Sovereignty*, 47-48. Administration officials opposed the Hickenlooper amendment as too rigid, preferring to approach each case in terms of the possible cost of

using sanctions to the overall policy goals of the United States. For details on the Hickenlooper Amendment and the Bolivian and Mexican expropriations and the American response, see Rodman, *Sanctity Versus Sovereignty*, 46-48, 103-107.

72. Robert Jervis, *The Logic of Images in International Relations* (Princeton, NJ: Princeton University Press, 1970), 7, 254-255.

73. See, for example, Bernard Brodie, *Strategy in the Missile Age* (Princeton, NJ: Princeton University Press, 1959), 147-172, Thomas Schelling and Morton Halperin, *Strategy and Arms Control* (New York: Twentieth Century Fund, 1961), 3; Klaus Knorr, *On the Uses of Military Power in the Nuclear Age* (Princeton, NJ: Princeton University Press, 1966), 87-95.

74. Patrick M. Morgan, "Saving Face for the Sake of Deterrence," in Jervis, Lebow, and Stein, eds., *Psychology and Deterrence*, 131.

75. Thomas Schelling, *Arms and Influence* (New Haven, CT: Yale University Press, 1966), 55.

76. See Patrick Morgan, "Saving Face for the Sake of Deterrence," 134-135.

77. Thus, had the United States not taken some sort of action when offensive Soviet missiles were placed in Cuba in 1962, it could be argued, there would have been some doubt in Moscow about the inclination of the United States to ever get involved in a situation where it might have to use nuclear weapons (George and Smoke, *Deterrence*, 466-472).

78. John Toland, *Adolf Hitler* (Garden City, NY: Doubleday, 1976), 464-465; Francis L. Loewenheim, *Peace or Appeasement? Hitler, Chamberlain, and the Munich Crisis* (Boston: Houghton Mifflin, 1965), 151; Walter Goerliz, *History of the German General Staff* (New York: Praeger, 1954), 309-311; Mathew Cooper, *The German Army: 1933-1945* (New York: Stein & Day, 1978), 77-103.

79. Williamson Murray, *The Change in the European Balance of Power, 1938-1939: The Path to Ruin* (Princeton, NJ: Princeton University Press, 1984), 204-205.

80. Quoted in John Wheeler-Bennett, *The Nemesis of Power* (New York: St. Martin's, 1964), 427.

81. Toland, *Adolph Hitler*, 495-498.

82. Robert Waite, *The Psychopathic God* (New York: Basic Books, 1977), 382, 396-397. Indeed, as Waite also points out in his chapter in this volume, both Hitler's language and some of the extraordinary strategic errors he made suggest that he also wanted to be destroyed. With Hitler's self-destructive impulses, it is clear that opposition from the British and French at Munich would not have made any long-term difference in his drive toward war.

83. Quoted in Percy Schraum, *Hitler: The Man and the Military Leader* (New York: Watts, 1971), 108, 110. Even in the face of Allied breakthroughs on both fronts in 1944, Hitler remained convinced that victory was possible through the exertion of his will.

84. Telford Taylor, *Munich: The Price of Peace* (Garden City, NY: Doubleday, 1979), 690; Toland, *Adolf Hitler*, 470-498.

85. Taylor, *Munich*, 691; Toland, *Adolph Hitler*, 640.

86. Murray, *The Change in the European Balance of Power*, 205, 736-767. Cooper, *The German Army*, 102; Goerliz, *History of the German General Staff*, 334; Hubert Ripka, *Munich: Before and After*, trans. Ida Sindelkova and Edgar P. Young (London: Victor Gollancz, 1939), 212-223; Winston Churchill, *The Second World War: The Gathering Storm* (Boston: Houghton Mifflin, 1948), 311-313.

87. Lowenheim, *Peace or Appeasement?*, 63.

88. Moreover, the Germans outproduced Great Britain and France by 300% in the arms race the next year. See H. R. Trevor-Roper, *Hitler's War Directives* (London: Sidgwick & Jackson, 1964), 156; and Churchill, *The Second World War: The Gathering Storm*, 305.

89. See Trevor-Roper, *Hitler's War Directives*, 155; Murray, *The Change in the European Balance of Power*, 214, 284-290. For additional information on the Munich crisis, see George F. Kennan, *From Prague After Munich: Diplomatic Papers, 1938-1940* (Princeton, NJ: Princeton University Press, 1968); Theodore Prochazla, Sr., *The Second Republic: The Disintegration of Post-Munich Czechoslovakia (October 1938—March 1939)* (New York: Columbia University Press, 1981); John W. Wheeler-Bennett, *Munich Prologue to Tragedy* (New York: Duell, Sloan, & Pearce, 1948).

90. Huynh Kim Khanh, *Vietnamese Communism, 1925-1945* (Ithaca, NY: Cornell University Press, 1982), 19-89. See also Stanley Karnow, *Vietnam: A History*, 126.

91. Khanh, *Vietnamese Communism*, 172, 184-188.

92. Richard Ned Lebow and Davis S. Cohen, "Afghanistan as Inkblot: The Carter Administration's Reaction to Soviet Intervention," (paper delivered at the Ninth Annual Scientific Meeting of the International Society of Political Psychology, Amsterdam, 29 June – 3 July 1986).

93. For further discussion of these perceptual characteristics, see Lee Ross and Craig A. Anderson, "Shortcomings in the Attribution Process: On the Origins and Maintenance of Erroneous Social Assessments," in *Judgment Under Uncertainty: Heuristic and Biases,* eds. Daniel Kahneman, Paul Slovic, and Amos Tversky (London: Cambridge University Press, 1982), 140-144. See also Susan T. Fiske and Shelley E. Taylor, *Social Cognition* (New York: Random House, 1984), 72-98.

94. Hans Toch, *Violent Men,* rev. ed. (Cambridge, MA: Schenkman, 1980), 185-186.

95. Leonard Berkowitz, *Roots of Aggression* (New York: Atherton, 1969), 2. For detailed discussion of the frustration-aggression hypothesis and revolutions, see Ted Robert Gurr, *Why Men Rebel* (Princeton, NJ: Princeton University Press, 1970), 33-39.

96. See Ralph White, "Misperception and Vietnam," *Journal of Social Issues,* 22 (Fall 1966): 24-26.

97. Memorandum from John A. McCone, 2 April 1965, *Pentagon Papers, New York Times,* ed., 440.

98. Betty Glad, "Toward a Policy of Realism: Prospects of a Negotiated Settlement in South Viet Nam," in "Viet Nam: The Alternatives for American Policy," ed. Reza Rezazadeh *Forum on Public Affairs, Unit Two* (Platteville, Wisconsin State University, 1965).

99. Morton Deutsch and Robert M. Krauss, "The Effect of Threat Upon Interpersonal Bargaining," *Journal of Abnormal and Social Psychology,* 61 (1960): 181-189.

100. Olle Holm, "Four Factors Affecting Perceived Aggressiveness," *Journal of Psychology,* 114 (July, 1983): 227-234.

101. Leonard Berkowitz and A. Lapage, "Weapons as Aggression-Eliciting Stimuli," *Journal of Personality and Social Psychology,* 7 (1967): 202-207.

102. J. Leyens, Leoncio Camino, and Teresa Cisneros, "Effects of Movie Violence on Aggression in a Field Setting as a Function of Group Dominance and Cohesion," *Journal of Personality and Social Psychology,* 32 (1975): 346-360.

103. Ian Taylor and John Knowelden, *Principles of Epidemiology,* 2nd ed. rev. (London: J. and A. Churchill, 1964), 107.

104. For discussion of the relationships of domestic political and cultural forms to the receptivity to foreign ideas, see Philip Laemmle, "Epidemiology of Domestic Military Intervention: Evaluation of Contagion as an Explanatory Concept," *Behavioral Science,* 22, 5 (September 1977): 327-333; David Klingman, "Temporal and Spatial Diffusion in the Comparative Analysis of Social Change," *American Political Science Review,* 74, 1 (March 1980): 123-136. See also Kenneth Boulding, *Conflict and Defense* (New York: Harper & Row, 1962), 123-144; also see Gurr, *Why Men Rebel,* 341-347.

105. D. Michael Schafer, *Deadly Paradigms: The Failure of U.S. Counterinsurgency Policy* (Princeton, NJ: Princeton University Press, 1988), 238-239.

106. Selig Harrison, *The Widening Gulf: Asian Nationalism and American Policy* (New York: Free Press, 1979), 92.

107. The old Vietnam National Party, for example, pledged to overthrow the feudal, capitalist, colonial regimes, but provided little doctrinal rationale for its activities. The Dai Viet, a dissident faction that left the Vietnam National party in 1939, at first offered only "national survival" as its doctrine. It later embraced anti-communism as its sole ideology and in the 1960s became the center of the opposition to Ho Chi Minh. See Harrison, *The Widening Gulf,* 88, 93-94.

108. Ibid., 104.

109. Ibid., 107, 112-113.

110. Ibid., 115-123.

111. Walter Laquer, *The Road to War: The Origins and Aftermath of the Arab-Israeli Conflict, 1967-68* (Baltimore, MD: Penguin, 1970), 211.

112. Ibid., 154-155, 166, 178-180, 189-190.

113. Bruce W. Jentleson, "American Commitments in the Third World: Theory vs. Practice, *International Organization,* 41, 4 (Autumn 1987): 667-704.

114. See Jervis's "Domino Beliefs and Strategic Behavior," to appear in Jack Snyder and Robert Jervis, eds., *Strategic Beliefs and Superpower Competition in the Asian Rimland* (manuscript, July 1987).

115. Thomas Wilborn, "The Soviet Union and ASEAN," in *The Soviet Union in the Third World* ed. Robert H. Donaldson (Boulder, CO: Westview), 281. For the argument that the Nicaraguan revolution is not likely to spread to the rest of Latin America in a domino-like process, and that even if it did it would be limited and represent no real threat to vital U.S. interests, see Jerome Slater, "Dominos in Central America," *International Security*, 12, 2 (Fall 1987): 105-134.

116. Halberstam, *The Best and the Brightest*, 110-111. For the critique that the United States never saw Laos as anything but a sideshow to its Vietnamese operations, see Arnold Isaacs, *Without Honor* (Baltimore, MD: Johns Hopkins University Press, 1983), 153-181.

117. Harrison, *The Widening Gulf*, 196.

118. Isaacs, *Without Honor*, 191-193, 289.

119. Ibid., 198. Earlier, in 1969, the United State's bombing of Vietcong sanctuaries in Cambodia had driven the Vietnamese communists even further into Cambodia, undermining the neutralist government. See Elizabeth Becker, *When the War Was Over: The Voice of Cambodia's Revolution and Its People* (New York: Simon & Schuster, 1986), 144-145.

120. Isaacs, *Without Honor*, 217-220, 225-226, 230-231.

121. Harrison, *The Widening Gulf*, 197; Isaacs, 220.

122. Isaacs, *Without Honor*, 280-281.

123. Ibid., 231. See also 232-233, 248-289. For the paranoia and the fantasies of the Khmer Rouge see James William Gibson, *The Perfect War: Technowar in Vietnam* (Boston: Atlantic Monthly Press, 1986), 166-169, 220-238.

Causes of War

B. Decision Making and Proximate Factors: Introduction

Thucydides argued more than 2,000 years ago that once nations enter into a crisis, events spin out of control and war becomes inevitable.[1] Most contemporary strategic and traditional foreign policy theorists on the contemporary scene have not been so pessimistic about the ability of statesmen to avoid war.[2] Decision makers, it is often assumed, will meet certain standards of rationality in the management of threats or the resort to force. As responsible actors they will survey various alternatives, face trade-offs directly, and choose the alternative that best serves the national interest.[3] Ordinarily this best alternative, as Anatol Rapoport shows in his "The Problem with Gains-Maximizing Strategies" (Chapter 4), can be determined logically. Through mathematical analyses, one can determine the strategies which would best maximize goals in every type of strategic situation.

Yet, actual foreign policy crisis decision making is much more complex than the logical models suggest. In prisoner's dilemma games, the best solution, as Rapoport also suggests, may require one to resort to ethical norms or subjective factors which reinforce trust.[4] Moreover, in situations where one has to deal with multiple values that cannot be easily ranked or compared, individuals are apt to simplify their choices by settling on single quantitative indicators. The arms race between the United States and the USSR today, he suggests, is an example of this adaptation.

The way the alternatives are framed, as Rapoport also notes, may also influence decision makers to choose alternatives other than the mathematically best one. Even when the probable gains (the payoffs multiplied by the probability of achieving them) are identical, individuals will choose differently, depending on whether or not the "gain" is seen as a possible gain from a given base line, or a loss from that base line. Elaborating on a similar theme, Amos Tversky and Daniel Kahneman have experimentally demonstrated in previously published work that statistically identical preferences may be reversed, depending on whether or not the probable outcome is viewed as a gain or a loss. People are averse to suffering losses from the status quo, often rejecting fair bets on the toss of a coin.[5] Indeed, people generally, in their everyday lives, are not good statisticians. As Kevin

McKean shows in his summary of the experimental literature, men and women have difficulties in understanding that in any series of random events an extraordinary happening is apt to be followed by one more ordinary. They make generalizations about the future based on a small sample of events they have observed. They overestimate the probability of vivid, imaginative events (such as accidents or murder as causes of death) and underestimate the probability of the more common and less dramatic events (such as death due to ordinary causes such as emphysema or a stroke).[6]

Organizational factors, too, may introduce factors other than the rational calculation of broader group interest into the decision-making process. Bureaucratic interests and standard operating procedures, as Graham Allison has shown, can influence the very definition of a nation's foreign policy objective and create special problems for the implementation of policy.[7] Moreover, the political interests, skills, and access to the relevant action channels of individual political leaders also play a role in the definition of policy. The skill with which an American president uses his key advisers can be crucial to winning bureaucratic support for the alternatives he prefers. President John Kennedy's establishment of the Executive Committee during the Cuban missile crisis, for example, facilitated the consideration of various alternatives open to the United States, and the subtle pressures he exerted on that committee to rally support behind the alternatives he came to prefer, headed off potential opposition to his policies in the foreign policy establishment.[8]

Factors related to the crisis situation itself, as Ole Holsti points out in "Crisis Management" in Chapter 5, further impede the ability of key decision makers to process relevant information and to generate alternative courses of action. Major values, by definition, are at stake and one must respond quickly to protect those interests in a situation of considerable ambiguity regarding both the intentions of the other side and its response to any actions one may take. The use of threats is apt to create defensive reactions in the party threatened, issuing in an interactive process in which fears and defensive reactions of each party are mutually reinforcing.[9] The emotional stress on national leaders in such situations is likely to be quite severe, further limiting the ability to make rational calculations.[10] To be able to act at all in such situations, relevant information is apt to be screened out of the process and the consideration of alternatives limited to one or two obvious courses of action. The interests and values of the enemy are likely to be misperceived, deterrent warnings regarded as bluffs, and the costs of favored courses of action underestimated. A double standard is apt to be used in the evaluation of the motives of the enemy. One's own aggressive behavior is likely to be attributed to external threats, while the aggressive behavior of the other side is perceived as the expression of its own essential characteristics.[11] In these and other ways, the decision makers are prone to buttress the choices to which they are predisposed.[12] Rational choice, in short, is undermined when one does not know the major alternatives in the game, and payoffs and costs associated with each.

Small group dynamics may reinforce proclivities to misperceive the situation. Self-censorship and direct group pressures are apt to induce group members to conform to prevailing views, thereby promoting illusions of invulnerability and feelings that the group is inherently moral. Irving Janis, in his book delineating this phenomenon, has documented several failures along these lines. The failure of U.S. officials at Pearl Harbor to heed signs that the base might be attacked was one clear, maladaptive response along these lines.[13] In other situations group think, by limiting the anxiety felt by members of the decision making group, may facilitate action. But if the dangers are not clearly seen, one can undertake enterprises with a high probability of failure. Jimmy Carter's decision in 1980 to undertake a rescue operation to free American hostages in Iran is a recent example of such an adaptation.[14]

The specific personality characteristics of highly placed individuals can also influence decision making, although the ways in which that personality impacts on the definition of national goals, depends on several factors. In constitutionally based polities the personality of the individual leader will have little impact, ordinarily, on the long-term objectives of the regime. Only in crises and other high stress situations, as Greenstein has noted, is the impact of his personality apt to be crucial.[15] In totalitarian regimes, however, one leader may so impress his values on a regime that his goals become the regime's goals. Adolph Hitler, as Robert G. L. Waite points out in "Leadership Pathologies: The Kaiser and the Führer and the Decisions for War in 1914 and 1939" (Chapter 6), shaped the German nation in a way that made war inevitable. In authoritarian regimes, by way of contrast, the personality of the leader is likely to influence the political process in a more limited way. The absence of strong leadership at the center, for example, may lead to policies of drift, with the specific results depending on the circumstances. Thus as Waite also shows, Kaiser Wilhelm, despite his last-minute apprehensions, was not strong enough to block the military policies which caused Germany to take the military offensives which opened hostilities in World War I. In other instances, the absence of leadership at the center has left a nation ill prepared to counter a would-be conqueror. After the kidnapping and execution of Montezuma, for example, the Aztecs were incapable of putting together a coordinated response to counter Cortés's invasion of their homeland.[16]

The leadership qualities which are most directly relevant to the outcome of a crisis, as the experimental and case study literature suggests, are as follows. Aggressive decision makers are more likely to embrace confrontational policies than nonaggressive leaders.[17] In some cases they may undertake symbolic actions that promote hatred of the enemy, amplifying the regressive proclivities in a people and promoting the externalization of internal conflicts through the legitimation of hate against an "evil" dehumanized other.[18] In prisoner' dilemma-type situations both high risk takers and persons intolerant of ambiguity are more likely than low risk takers or persons tolerant of ambiguity to choose competitive solutions which maximize their own gains. Persons high in test anxiety and defensiveness, moreover, are apt to respond to the failure of a high risk strategy by a heightened commitment to such a strategy, rather than opt for more conservative stances.[19] Leaders, too, may be influenced by considerations of their own self-worth in their diplomatic moves. When humiliated in bargaining games, as Brown's experimental work suggests, they are likely to retaliate, with severity, at considerable cost to themselves.[20]

Proclivities toward cognitive simplicity will reinforce situationally induced tendencies to misinterpret key signals during a crisis or unrealistically bolster a desired alternative. The U.S. support for the Israeli intervention in Lebanon in 1982 and its own subsequent entry into that conflict can partly be understood in terms of Ronald Reagan's tendency to see the world in black and white terms. Perceiving most conflicts in the world as Soviet induced, Reagan did not understand that the Lebanese civil war had indigenous roots and that the Israeli invasion could undermine the stable balance between Shiite, Christian, and Druse which had been the only basis for peace.[21]

The ability to function under conditions of stress, too, will differ from individual to individual. Leaders with good ego strength may be able to respond constructively and creatively to threats to their political order.[22] The defense mechanisms of other individuals, however, may break down, when their central values are threatened, with no obvious options to choose from. Overt anxiety reactions may follow, leaving the individual feeling helpless and uncertain, wavering between contradictory courses of actions, and searching out the opinions of others. In some cases, the individual may simply withdraw from the situation. After the Nazi attack on Russia, for example, Stalin was incapacitated for approximately two weeks. He had not only mis-estimated the situation when he signed the nonaggression pact with Hitler in 1939, but he had ignored warnings from the British, the Americans, and his own intelligence sources that an invasion was imminent.[23]

For some actors the phenomenon of what Freud called substantive (as opposed to process) irrationality may make means-ends calculations an impossibility. Hitler's unconscious needs to destroy and be destroyed can only be understood in these terms. For those dealing with such a leader, the best policy options are not at all clear. Resistance to their aggressions may simply feed into their need to destroy and be destroyed. Indeed, as Holsti has pointed out, elsewhere, deterrence threats are not likely to prove effective against a "nation lead by a trigger-happy paranoid, or by someone seeking personal or national self-destruction or martyrdom, or by decision makers willing to play a form of international Russian roulette . . ."[24]

What all this suggests is that rationality can only be approximated in most decision-making situations. When national leaders are faced with choices between major values in situations where they are subjected to organizational and political pressures as well as the constraints of time, their ability to weigh outcomes may be seriously impaired. During crises there is so much potential for misunderstanding, for the making of commitments from which backing down is difficult, that nations may drift into a war that they would not have chosen on simple means-ends calculations before the crisis arose. The best strategies for national leaders to follow may be similar to those chosen by so many individuals in their private lives. In the real world, where one has incomplete information about outcomes and probabilities and personality values are at stake, the avoidance of risky choices may be the best option to follow.[25]

Notes

1. Thucydides *History of the Peloponnesian War*, trans. Rex Warner (Harmondsworth, Middlessex: Penguin, 1972), Books 1 & 2, 124-136.

2. See, for example, Richard Ned Lebow's study of 26 crises, some of which did not end in war, *Between Peace and War: The Nature of International Crisis* (Baltimore, MD: Johns Hopkins University Press, 1981), 334-337.

3. For the classic realist perspective see Hans J. Morgenthau as revised by Kenneth W. Thompson, *Politics Among Nations: The Struggle for Power and Peace*, 6th ed. (New York: Alfred A. Knopf, 1985), 4-17. For a survey of the literature assuming that national interests are rationally determined, see Graham T. Allison, *Essence of Decision: Explaining the Cuban Missile Crisis* (Boston: Little, Brown, 1971), 10-38. For an overview of the broader decision-making literature, see Carol Barner-Barry and Robert Rosenwein, "Decision Making: The Quintessential Political Act," in *Psychological Perspectives on Politics* (Englewood Cliffs, NJ: Prentice-Hall, 1985), 237-269.

4. For the argument that cooperative solutions are apt to be more difficult to achieve when the players are nations or states, see Deborah Larson, "Game Theory and the Psychology of Reciprocity" (unpublished paper, Columbia University, 29 October 1986).

5. Amos Tversky and Daniel Kahneman, "The Framing of Decisions and the Psychology of Choice," *Science*, 211 (30 January 1981): 453-458; Daniel Kahneman and Amos Tversky, "Choices, Values, and Frames," *American Psychologist* (April 1984): 341-349.

6. Kevin McKean, "Decisions, Decisions, Decisions," *Discover* (June 1985): 23-31.

7. For the impact of standard operating procedures on both the Soviet Union and the United States during the Cuban missile crisis, see Allison, *Essence of Decision*, 67-184.

8. For Kennedy's desire to meet in some way the Soviet demand to get American missiles out of Turkey in exchange for the Soviet withdrawal of its missiles from Cuba, see David A. Welch and James G. Blight, "The Eleventh Hour of the Cuban Missile Crisis: An Introduction to the ExComm Transcripts," *International Security*, 12, 3 (Spring 1988): 4-92; and for Kennedy's diplomacy, outside ExComm, to make that trade a possibility see pp. 227-230. For Robert F. Kennedy's role in bringing about a consensus for the blockade option in the ExComm group, see Allison, *Essence of Decision*, 194, 207-209.

9. The arms race, as Lewis W. Richardson points out in *Statistics of Deadly Quarrels* (Pittsburgh, PA: Boxwood Press, 1960), is one example of this kind of interaction. See also Michael D. Wallace, "Arms Races and Escalation," *Journal of Conflict Resolution* (March 1979). In extreme cases, the interaction process may deteriorate into the phenomenon Morton Deutsch ("The Prevention of World War Three: A Psychological Perspective," *Political Psychology*, 4:1 [1983]: 3-31) has termed a "malignant process." The result may be self-fulfilling prophecies in which a gamesmanship orientation leads the players away from a concern for real values and into abstract conflicts over images of power. For an earlier study of the German decision to go to war in the summer of 1914 that suggests such processes were involved in the opening phases of World War I, see Robert C. North, "Perception and Action in the 1914 Crisis," *Journal of International Affairs*, 21, 1 (1967): 103-122. For the argument that the action/reaction pattern does not explain the U.S./Soviet arms race today, see Albert Wohlstetter, "Is There a Strategic Arms Race?" *Foreign Policy* (Summer 1974). For the argument that technological advances have been the most important catalyst of the arms race, see Ladd Hollist in "An Analysis of Arms Processes in the United States and the Soviet Union," *International Studies Quarterly* 21, 3 (September 1977): 503-528.

10. For the impact of physiological factors such as fatigue on the ability of decision makers to function under stress, see Thomas C. Wiegele, in "Decision-Making in an International Crisis: Biological Factors," *International Studies Quarterly* 17, 3 (September 1973): 295-335.

11. For further discussion of the fundamental attribution errors, as this is called, see Phillip Tetlock and Charles B. McGuire, "Cognitive Perspectives of Foreign War, 265-266. See also Ralph White, *Fearful Warriors* (New York: Free Press, 1984), 135-185.

12. For the differentiation between motivated and unmotivated biases and how they have influenced perceptions in actual deterrence situations, see Robert Jervis, Richard Ned Lebow, and Janice Gross Stein, *Psychology and Deterrence* (Baltimore, MD: Johns Hopkins University Press, 1985), 4, 24-27, 117-202, 203-232. For an elaboration on how motivated biases lead to defensive avoidance strategies see Irving L. Janis and Leon Mann, *Decision Making: A Psychological Analysis of Conflict, Choice and Commitment* (New York: Free Press, 1977), 87. For Pakistan's misperceptions of both Indian intentions and capabilities prior to their 1965 intervention in Kashmir, see Sumit Ganguly, "Deterrence Failure Revisited: The Indo-Pakistani Conflict of 1965," (paper presented at the meeting of the International Studies Association, University of Illinois, Urbana, 1985).

13. Irving Janis, *Victims of Groupthink: Psychological Studies of Policy Decisions and Fiascoes* (Boston, Houghton Mifflin, 1972), 50-100. For Janis's most recent work on this topic see "International Crisis Management in the Nuclear Age," in *Psychology and the Prevention of Nuclear War,* ed. Ralph White (New York: New York University Press, 1986), 381-396.

14. See Betty Glad, "Jimmy Carter's Handling of the Hostage Crisis," *International Political Science Quarterly,* 10, 1 (January 1989). For a somewhat more positive analysis of the impact of Carter's ideology and personality on his foreign policy, see Jerel A. Rosati, *The Carter Administration's Quest for Global Community: The Impact of Beliefs on Behavior* (University of South Carolina Press, 1987). For an analysis of problems of rationality in general of U.S. presidential foreign policymaking, see Alexander L. George, *Presidential Decision-Making in Foreign Policy: The Effective Use of Information and Advice* (Boulder, CO: Westview, 1980).

15. Fred Greenstein, "Objections to the Study of Personality and Politics," in *Personality and Politics* (Princeton, NJ: Princeton University Press, 1987), 33-62. Ideally, as Nicolo Machiavelli argued in *The Prince* (London, J. M. Dent & Sons, 1938, chaps. 18, 25, pp. 141-145, 203-207) the head of state should be one whose own nature allows him to respond as the situation requires. When the times call for it, he will be conservative and prudent, when not, he will be bold and take risks. A contemporary version of that view is found in Nathan Kogan and Michael A. Wallach's suggestion that the ideal foreign policy decision maker should be flexible enough to choose either conservative or risky strategies, depending on the circumstances. See their *Risk Taking: A Study in Cognition and Personality* (New York: Holt, Rinehart, & Winston, 1964), 211-214. Many people, as Machiavelli, Kogan, and Wallach note, are not capable of such flexibility, their own characters locking them into a narrower range of responses.

16. George C. Valliant, *Aztecs of Mexico* (Garden City, New York: Double Day, 1947), 234-254, passim. The problems of the Aztecs, as Valliant notes, were compounded by strategic views which were so different from the Europeans that they were unable to follow up on the victories they did achieve.

17. See, for example, Lloyd Etheridge, *A World of Men: The Private Sources of American Foreign Policy* (Cambridge: MIT Press, 1978).

18. Vamik D. Volkan, *The Need to Have Enemies and Allies* (London: Jason Aronson, 1988), 183-195.

19. N. Kogan and M. A. Wallach, *Risk Taking: A Study in Cognition and Personality* (New York: Holt, 1965), 155-158, 213; Jeffrey Z. Rubin and Bert R. Brown, *The Social Psychology of Bargaining and Negotiation* (New York: Academic Press, 1979), 177-178.

20. Bert Brown, "The Effects of Need to Maintain Face on Interpersonal Bargaining," *Journal of Experimental Social Psychology* 4 (1968): 107-122.

21. Betty Glad, "The United States' Ronald Reagan," in *Leadership and Negotiation in the Middle East,* eds. Barbara Kellerman and Jeffrey Rubin (New York: Praeger, 1988), 200-230; Robert Jervis, *Perception and Misperception in International Relations* (Princeton, NJ: Princeton University Press, 1976), 239-253. For an application of cognitive processing theories to the beginnings of the Cold War

from the U.S. perspective, see Deborah Welch Larson, *Origins of Containment: A Psychological Explanation* (Princeton, NJ: Princeton University Press, 1985). For a general critique of the tendency to use psychoanalytic interpretations of leaders to depreciate them, see Betty Glad, "Contributions of Psychobiography," in *Handbook of Political Psychology,* ed. Jeanne Knutson (San Francisco, Jossey-Bass, 1973), 296-321.

22. For an analysis of Mikhail Gorbachev in these terms, see Betty Glad, "The Psychological Sources of Gorbachev's Conduct," forthcoming.

23. Seweryn Bialer, ed., *Stalin and his Generals* (New York: Pegasus, 1969), 181; John Stoessinger, *Why Nations Go to War,* 4th ed. (New York: St. Martin's, 1985), 39-48. For the argument that most individuals may respond with erratic or passive behavior to situations in which the most important aspects of their trusted environment has broken down, see Harry Stack Sullivan, "Psychiatric Aspects of Morale," in *Personality and Political Crisis,* eds. Alfred H. Stanton and Stewart E. Perry (Glencoe, IL: Free Press, 1951), 44-60.

24. Ole Holsti, *Crisis, Escalation, War* (Montreal: McGill-Queens University Press, 1972), 8-9.

25. The very logic of strategic interactions, Zeev Maoz argues, may create incentives for rational statesmen to fight. Certain nonlogical processes (i.e., as described in attribution theory) may further contribute to this outcome. See Zeev Maoz, "The Para Bellum Paradox," in *The Paradoxes of War,* manuscript in preparation.

Chapter 4

The Problem with Gains-Maximizing Strategies

ANATOL RAPOPORT

The notion of a gains-maximizing strategy suggests that it is easy to define a "rational decision." Yet, it is not at all easy to make any formal definition of rationality "stick." Indeed, attempts to define the term lead to difficulties and paradoxes.

Gains-maximizing strategies do not necessarily imply an identification of rationality with greed. Gains can refer to anything, gain of self-respect, gain of respect of others, gain of knowledge, power, skills — whatever people aspire to or strive for whether for selfish or altruistic reasons. So the issue is not the morality of maximizing anything. The issue is clarity. Is it possible to define a gains-maximizing strategy unambiguously? Is it possible to display such a strategy in every concrete situation in a way that will make it intuitively acceptable? If not, where do ambiguities or ambivalences stem from? These are the questions to which this essay is addressed.

Instead of attempting to define rationality in general, let us begin with a definition of a more specific concept — that of a rational actor, trusting that the definition will find acceptance. "A rational actor is one who takes into account the consequences of his actions." This definition seems simple, yet it implies a great deal: for example, the ability to choose among actions, an awareness of consequences of each action, and the ability to order the consequences on a preference scale.

Intuitively, the meaning of scale of preference seems clear. Yet, a meaningful ordering on such a scale must satisfy certain conditions. For example, the reference relation must be *transitive*; that is, if an item O_1 is preferred to O_2 and O_2 to O_3, then one cannot show a preference of O_3 over O_1. We might hesitate to call a person who had such a cyclical preference rational.

Nevertheless, a more detailed examination of the circumstances in which the actor finds himself may well make a cyclical preference reasonable or at least understandable. This idea can be illustrated by the following somewhat facetious example.

Consider a man with three wives, W_1, W_2, and W_3. W_1, the senior wife, has certain priority claims. W_2 is intensely jealous of W_3, the favorite wife. When choosing between W_1 and W_2, the man must prefer W_1 (because of her privileged position). In the absence of W_1, the man must prefer W_2 over W_3, because of the former's intense jealousy. But in the absence of W_2, he can and does choose W_3 over W_1, who, secure in her seniority, is above jealousy.

The example illustrates how an apparently irrational decision rule can appear rational in the light of certain information. Because we can never be sure of having *all* the information about a particular situation, we see that it may at times be difficult to decide on the basis of some formal definition whether or not a decision is rational. This casts doubt on the definition.

If we bypass the problem posed by intransitivity of preferences and related obstacles in the way of ordering consequences of actions, then we can formulate the simplest rule of rational decision: order the consequences on a preference scale and choose the action that leads to the most preferred consequence. More generally, we can formulate a contingency plan that specifies which action will be chosen if that leading to the most preferred or to each most preferred in descending order consequence is blocked. If the preference scale reflects amounts of gain, we have a gains-maximizing scale.

Decision problems in real life are scarcely ever so simple. Complications stem from three sources: (1) the consequences of actions are not known with certainty; (2) several actors, whose objectives do not coincide in general are attempting to maximize their respective gains; and (3) the actor is trying to satisfy several objectives simultaneously. These three sets of circumstances define three principal branches of *normative decision theory*: the *theory of risk*, the *theory of games*, and *multiple criteria decision theory*.

Theory of Risk

The central concept in the theory of risk is that of the *expected gain* or the *moral expectation*, which arose in the first systematic studies of probability, that in turn were inspired by certain gambling problems.

A seventeenth-century gambler, Chevalier de Méré, once wrote a letter to Blaise Pascal, the eminent French mathematician, in which he raised a number of questions concerning games of chance and, in one instance, a problem concerning how to divide the stakes when a game is canceled. Specifically, suppose A and B play a game in which a fair coin is tossed. If it lands heads up, A gets a point; if tails, B gets a point. The player who accumulates 10 points first wins the stakes. Suppose now that the game has to be called off when A has obtained 5 points and B, 7 points. How should the stakes be divided between them? Player A might suggest division in the ratio 5:7, but B may object, because he needs only 3 additional points to win, whereas A needs 5. B might propose a ratio of the inverses, that is, 3:5 in B's favor. Note that this ratio gives him 5/8 (62.5%) of the stakes, whereas the ratio proposed by A gave him 7/12 (58.3%). Which procedure is more equitable?

Pascal's proposed solution of the problem introduced the concept of expected gain.[1] Consider the chances that A wins 10 points before B. This probability can be calculated in terms of the negative binomial distribution (the details of which need not concern us), which turns out to be 29/128. Accordingly, B's chance of winning the game at the time it is broken off is the complementary probability 99/128. According to this ratio, B should get 77.4% of the stakes, even more than he claimed on the basis of how many points each lacks.

More generally, the expected gain is a weighted sum of all possible gains associated with an action, where the weights are probabilities that the respective gains are realized. In de Méré's problem, the expected gains of A and B were calculated by multiplying the stakes by the sum of the probabilities of all sequences of events that would have led to a win by one or the other player.

The attractiveness of expected gain is enhanced by the Law of Large Numbers, which states that if the action is performed many times in the same context, the average gain per iteration will with high probability be very near the formally calculated expected gain. It is this same principle that enables insurance companies and gambling houses to make profits. Even though insurance companies must on occasions pay out large amounts, and gambling houses must pay large winnings to lucky players, in the long run their payments will be very near the total expected gain of the insured (or gamblers), which is calculated in advance to be negative. The corresponding positive sum will accrue to the company (or casino).

In short, the concept of expected gain permits us to extend the concept of rational decision to situations involving risks. However, to extend the concept from decisions under certainty to decisions involving risk, we must add new concepts: probability and *cardinal utility*.

In ordering actions, decisions, or outcomes under certainty, the actor needs to specify only the order of preference; he need not specify *by how much* he prefers one to another. For decisions under risk, however, preferences must be specified as numerical magnitudes; that is, a *cardinal scale* must be constructed, which may not be easy. For instance, when it comes to whiskey, I can say with assurance that I prefer rye to scotch to bourbon, and these preferences are reflected in my choices when offered a choice. I could also say that my preference for scotch over bourbon is considerably greater than my preference of rye over scotch (because I don't like bourbon at all), but I would hesitate to specify more precisely the ratio of these preference differences.

However, in order to analyze the expected gain of utility in decisions under risk, utilities of outcomes must be given on a scale that allows us to determine statistical expectations. An *interval scale* does this. The origin and the unit of an interval scale can be chosen arbitrarily, but once chosen, the utilities of all the outcomes in a given situation are numerically fixed.[2] Thus, an interval scale is one kind of cardinal scale. To calculate expected utility as a probability-weighted average of possibly realized utilities, the utilities must be given on at least an interval scale, because the operations used to calculate expected utilities presuppose a scale at least this strong.[3] Thus, if utilities are given on an interval scale, a rational decision can be defined as one that maximizes the expected utility of an outcome.

Determining a Cardinal Utility Scale

J. von Neumann and O. Morgenstern were the first to propose a method for establishing a cardinal utility scale.[4] To illustrate their method, suppose I am offered the following choice: (a) scotch, or (b) a lottery ticket that entitles me to either rye or bourbon, depending on whether a ticket labeled Rye or Bourbon is pulled out of a hat. I will naturally want to know how many bourbon tickets and how many rye tickets are in the hat, in order to estimate my chances of winning one or the other. If there are considerably more rye than bourbon tickets, I may take the chance and choose the lottery, which offers a high probability of winning my favorite drink. But if my chances of getting rye are small, I will prefer the certainty of scotch to the risk of getting bourbon. It stands to reason that for *some* proportion of the tickets, that is, for some probability of winning rye, I will be indifferent between scotch and the lottery. Suppose this probability is p, so that the probability of getting bourbon is $(1 - p)$. Recall that the origin and the unit of an interval scale can be arbitrarily chosen. Let us, therefore, assign utility 0 to bourbon (the least preferred) and 1 to rye (the most preferred). Our problem is to determine the utility of scotch, which, according to my declared preference, should be some number between 0 and 1. *If* we assume that my conception of rationality is associated with maximizing expected utility in risky situations, we can write

$$u(S) = pu(R) + (1 - p)u(B).$$

The left side of the equation represents the utility of scotch; the right side the expected utility of the lottery, being the weighted average of the utilities of rye and of bourbon, given that we have set $u(R) = 1$ and $u(B) = 0$, we see that p (which, being a probability, is a number between 0 and 1) turns out to be the utility of scotch.

Suppose now that my choice is broadened to include gin and that my preference for gin falls somewhere between scotch and bourbon. We can now use the same procedure to determine the utility I assign to gin by pitting gin against a lottery ticket involving rye and bourbon.

Note, however, that this method will work only if the utilities so determined exhibit certain consistencies: having determined the utilities of both scotch and of gin by pitting each against the rye-bourbon lottery, we ought to get the same utility value for gin by pitting it against a scotch-bourbon lottery. If I am indifferent between gin and a lottery that promises scotch with probability q and bourbon with probability $(1 - q)$, we can write

$$qu(S) + (1 - q)u(B) = u(G).$$

But we have already determined $u(S) = p$ and set $u(B) = 0$. Therefore we must have pq as the utility of gin, and this must be the same value we obtain by pitting gin against a rye-bourbon lottery. Such consistency is by no means guaranteed.

The above example shows that in principle a cardinal utility can be established even for qualitatively different alternatives. The task ought to be easier when alternatives can be naturally quantified, for example, amounts of money. We should not expect, of course, that the cardinal utility of an increase of money will be proportional to that increase. If we make such an assumption, the principle of maximizing expected gain leads immediately to grave difficulties, as demonstrated by the well-known St. Petersburg paradox.

The St. Petersburg Paradox

Daniel Bernoulli, a Swiss mathematician working in St. Petersburg in the middle of the eighteenth century, posed the following problem. Suppose one is offered a chance to play a game in which a fair coin is tossed until tails appears. When this happens, the player is paid 2^n units of money if n heads have preceded tails. Thus, if the first toss results in tails, $2^0 = 1$ unit is paid; if one heads precedes tails, $2^1 = 2$ units are paid, if two heads, $2^2 = 4$ units, and so on. The question posed by Bernoulli was how much the player should be willing to pay for playing this game. If the player refuses to play, his monetary gain will be zero.[5] If he plays, he will win at least one unit and probably more (if one or more heads precede tails.) To decide how much to pay, the player must calculate his expected gain and compare it with the amount he is asked to pay. If he wishes to maximize the net expected gain, he should be willing to pay any amount less than the expected gain of the gamble, for then his net gain will be positive, whereas if he refuses to play, his net gain will be zero.

The expected monetary gain of the St. Petersburg Paradox game is the probability-weighted average of all possible gains. For example, the probability of gaining 1 is 1/2, of gaining 2 is 1/4, of gaining 4 is 1/8. Multiplying the probabilities by the associated gains, we obtain

$$(1/2) + 2 \times (1/4) + 4 \times (1/8) + \ldots$$

Since the expected monetary gain exceeds any given number, the player should be willing to pay *any finite amount* for the privilege of playing the game. Because in all likelihood no one would consent to pay more than a few units, we must choose between concluding that no one is rational or else that maximization of expected monetary gain cannot be rational in all circumstances.

This finding led Bernoulli to postulate that utility of money increases with the amount of money at a decreasing rate. Specifically, he assumed that the utility of an increment of money is a logarithmic function of the increment, so that an increment from 1 to 10 units is worth as much as an increment from 10 to 100 units. Given the constant of proportionality in such a function, the amount that an expected utility maximizer should be willing to pay can be calculated: it will always be finite.

Is It Always Rational to Maximize Expected Utility?

The concept of utility has been a subject of spirited controversy among economists, psychologists, and philosophers. The details of these controversies need not concern us here. The questions, however, are relevant to this discussion. How can utilities assigned by an actor to objects, events, or conditions be measured? Is it always rational to attempt to maximize one's expected utility? Clearly, answers to the second question depend on answers to the first, but this interdependence of the two questions leads to further difficulty. We have seen that the determination of cardinal utility is made by observing choices in risky situations. But underlying this determination is the assumption that the rational actor will choose the alternative that yields the greater expected utility. In this way, the assumption of maximization of expected utility becomes tautological: expected utility is *defined* as that which is maximized.

This assumption that expected utility is always (tautologically) maximized is problematical, however, because the definition of utility based on risky choices requires certain consistencies of behavior that are by no means guaranteed. In this way, irrationality becomes associated with inconsistency and would supply the only basis for distinguishing rational from irrational behavior *if* the preference order of risky choices were the only way of establishing cardinal utilities. If, however, there are other methods of determining cardinal utilities independent of preference orders of risky choices, the question whether it is always "rational" to maximize expected utility can no longer be answered automatically (tautologically) in the affirmative.

The Allais Paradox

An energetic challenge to the view that rational choice in risky situations is always the one that maximizes expected utility was advanced by M. Allais.[6]

Suppose a person is asked to choose between two alternatives to two different situations, as shown in Table 4.1.

TABLE 4.1

Situation I	Choice A	$1,000,000
	Choice B	$5,000,000 with probability .10 or $1,000,000 with probability .89 or nothing with probability .01
Situation II	Choice C	$1,000,000 with probability .11 or nothing with probability .89
	Choice D	$5,000,000 with probability .10 or nothing with probability .90

Many persons have been observed to choose A in preference to B in situation I and D in preference to C in situation II. This behavior is easily seen to be inconsistent with the principle of maximizing expected utility *regardless* of what their utility for amounts of money may be. To see this, imagine a lottery with 100 tickets. In situation I, tickets 1-10 entitle the holder to $5,000,000, tickets 11-99 to $1,000,000, ticket number 100 to nothing. To choose B in situation I is to prefer a ticket in this lottery to $1,000,000. In situation II, choice C refers to a lottery in which tickets 1-11 entitle the holder to $1,000,000 and tickets 12-100 to nothing. Choice D refers to a lottery in which tickets 1-10 entitle a person to $5,000,000 and tickets 11-100 to nothing.

Now in situation I if a ticket numbered 11-99 is drawn, clearly the actor receives the same amount whether he chooses A or B. So the significant choice in situation I is between $5,000,000 with probability 10/11 or nothing with probability 1/11 versus $1,000,000 with certainty.

Turning to situation II, we note that the actor receives the same amount (nothing) however he chooses if a ticket numbered 1-89 is drawn. So the real choice in this situation is between $1,000,000 and a lottery promising $5,000,000 with probability 10/11 or nothing with probability 1/11. Thus, ignoring the cases where it does not matter how the actor chooses, the real choice in both situations is between exactly the same alternatives. Therefore if the actor prefers $1,000,000 for certain, he should choose A in situation I and C in situation II. If he would rather take his chances with the lottery, he should prefer B in situation I and D in situation II.

What shall we say about people who prefer A to B in situation I and D to C in situation II? We could, of course, say that they are "irrational," but by that we could only mean that their behavior is inconsistent with the principle of maximizing expected utility. In fact, some of these people, when their "inconsistency" is pointed out, change their preference to make it consistent with the principle. The late L. V. Savage, a foremost proponent of expected utility maximization, was among these. When the inconsistency of his choices was pointed out to him, he conceded that he chose "irrationality" and reversed his preference in situation II.

The maximization of expected utility is unassailable as a principle of rational decision — in short, if the definition of maximum expected utility is "that which is maximized by a rational decision maker." The principle can be challenged, however, if a way of measuring utility can be found that is "independent" of the assumption that it is maximized in rational choices under risk. Procedures for determining utility functions without resorting to offers of risky choices have indeed been proposed. They are similar to psychometric procedures used in determining subjectively perceived magnitudes (e.g., light intensities, tone frequencies, weights) as functions of objective magnitudes. These measurements can be regarded as meaningful only if certain consistency criteria are satisfied by the subjects. Thus, the same problem is raised as in deriving utility functions from preferences among risky choices. But until some evidence is obtained about which type of inconsistency is a greater obstacle to establishing a cardinal utility measure, the choice between the two methods must remain a matter of philosophical preference.

If the psychometric method of determining utility functions can be shown to be reasonably effective, maximization of expected utility need not be accepted as a principle of rational choice. Other principles can be advanced with equal justification. It should be noted that risk aversion or risk enjoyment are already incorporated in the determination of utility functions derived from references among risky choices, so that refinements in the form of considering higher moments of the probability distributions cannot be introduced into the principle of rational choice. The rejection of the maximization of expected utility by M. Allais and by the proponents of the "French School" associated with his name is based on the postulated existence of a cardinal utility measure that can be determined independently of observations of risky choices (for example, by psychometric methods.)

The maximization of expected gain seems especially justifiable in situations where a risky choice can be repeated many times, for then the Law of Large Numbers provides assurance that expected gain per choice will be with very large probability very nearly the actual gain per choice. In these situations it seems safe to maximize expected monetary gain (regardless of the utility of money), as insurance companies and gambling houses do.

The following example, however, shows that the opportunity to make many repeated risky choices can make a gamble with positive expected gain *less* attractive as the number of choices increases. Consider this gamble. A fair coin is tossed. If it lands heads, the gambler wins 1.6 times the amount bet; if tails, he loses what he bet. Thus, the expected gain of each unit bet is $(.5)(1.6) + (.5)(-1) = .30$. The gamble seems especially attractive if it can be repeated many times. However, there is always a possibility of going broke. To hedge against this, the gambler decides to bet one half of his capital each time. Assuming that money is infinitely divisible (fractions of a cent can be bet), ruin is excluded. Many will be surprised to learn that after 10,000 such bets, it is practically certain that the gambler will end up with less than what he started with. To see this, consider what can happen if he bets twice. There are three possibilities: (1) he wins both times; (2) he wins once, loses once; (3) he loses both times. The respective probabilities of these three cases are 1/4, 1/2, 1/4. If the gambler's initial capital is $1, he bets $.50 the first time. If he wins, his capital becomes $1.80, and he bets $.90 the second time. If he wins again, his capital becomes $.90 + $1.44 = $2.34.

If he wins the first time and loses the second time, he is left with $.90. It is easy to see that losing the first time and winning the second time leads to the same result.

If he loses both times, he is left with $.25. Thus, his expected capital after two plays will be

$$(.25)(2.34) + (.5)(.90) + (.25)(.25) = \$1.0975$$

Note, however, that the combined probabilities of the two cases when he ends up with less than he started with is .25 + .5 = .75, while the probability of ending up with more than he started with is only .25. It can be shown that as the number of gambles increases, although the *expected* size of his capital keeps increasing, the *probability* that he will end up with more than he started with gets progressively smaller. If he bets 10,000 times, the probability that he ends up with more than he started with becomes vanishingly small. Hence the Law of Large Numbers works *against* the gambler even if the expected gain is positive in the sense that the probability of ending up with a positive gain keeps decreasing. Under these circumstances it seems irrational to maximize expected gain.

Interpersonal Comparisons

Let us now examine another important issue having a direct bearing on the maximization principle, namely, interpersonal comparison of utilities. We will assume that utilities are measurable on a scale no stronger than the interval scale. As noted earlier, the point of origin and the unit of that scale can be chosen arbitrarily. Neither the zero nor the unit of a person's utility scale can be determined by observation. Then the conclusion is unavoidable that utilities of different persons cannot be compared. While it is always possible to infer that in acquiring some object, actor X gains x units of utility (once the unit of his scale has been chosen) and that by relinquishing the same object, actor Y loses y units of his utility (once *his* unit has been chosen), it is impossible to say whether X's gain is larger or smaller than Y's loss. It follows further that utility losses or gains of different persons cannot be meaningfully added. Thus, when Y gives up the object to X, it is impossible to say whether the algebraic sum of the respective utility changes (the "social gain," if you will) has been positive or negative.

Without some method of interpersonal comparison of utilities, no meaning can be ascribed to a "social welfare function," (i.e., some measure of an aggregate of individual utilities, which can be assumed to be maximized in a rational and humane society). Without such a social welfare function, Jeremy Bentham's principle, "the greatest good for the greatest number" falls by the wayside.

Yet it is obvious that in any society worthy of the name interpersonal comparison of utilities is implied in practically any social regulation. The prohibition of murder can be understood as reflecting the assumption that the disutility of getting killed is greater than the utility that a murderer derives from killing. Thus murder is associated with a net decrease of "social utility." Similarly, the graduated income tax is a reflection of the commonly held view that a unit of money means more to a poor man than to a rich man. In fact, if the diminishing marginal utility of money were the only consideration, one would have to conclude on the basis of interpersonal comparisons that equalization of assets and incomes would maximize the social welfare function (i.e., the sum of individual utilities). It is, of course, possible to argue that this interpretation of the social welfare function leaves out many other components that ought to be incorporated in it. By the same token, however, the standard of "rationality" implicit in the presumed behavior of *homo economicus* can also be seriously questioned. Nicholas Georgescu-Roegen writes:

> if this dogma [impossibility of interpersonal comparisons] is accepted, economics must reconcile itself to being a science (perhaps the only one) unable to recognize at least a modicum of standards in the phenomenal domain which it purports to study. Fortunately the dogma flies in the face of two irresistible forces: the faculty of man called empathy, without which "there is really no game which we can play at all whether in philosophy, literature, science, or family," and the hierarchy of wants.[7]

The two forces, it turns out, are closely linked. While it may be all but impossible to compare interpersonal utilities in the realm of luxuries (i.e., items that satisfy appetites rather than needs), denial of interpersonal comparisons in the realm of basic needs amounts in effect to a dismissal of any social ethos in which empathy plays any role. For instance, there may be "no objective justification for taxing those who have motor boats and using the money to help others buy hunting equipment."[8] Yet, most will agree that there is ample justification for taxing possessors of yachts to provide a minimum standard of nutrition and medical care for everyone.

Once we admit utilities associated with values other than "bundles of commodities" (the only utilities considered in classical economics), many instances of (1) apparently irrational behavior and (2) paradoxes generated by the theory of games are seen in a different light. Instances of the former are typically observed where certain rules of conduct other than maximization of utility increments in the exchange of commodities must be regarded as having "utility". Philanthropy and competition in giving something of greater value in the exchange of gifts are well-known examples. Instances of the latter necessitate a thorough reexamination of the very concept of "rationality." Resolutions of these apparent manifestations of irrationality and of the paradoxes can be sources of important insights.

Theory of Games

So far we have focused our attention on the single decision maker, choosing among alternatives available to him. To be sure, once the assumption of one-to-one correspondence between actions and outcomes is abandoned, the outcomes appear as no longer determined by the actor's choices alone. We can conceptualize another agent — Nature, who, by choosing among so-called "states of the world," also influences the outcomes. In fact, we can think of an outcome as a result of a joint choice, one by the actor, the other by Nature. Situations of this sort are sometimes called "games against Nature." These, however, are not yet genuine games. This is because although Nature can be regarded as another player in the sense of making choices, she does not have interests. She is neither benevolent nor malevolent toward the actor: she chooses among the "states of the world" without considering the utility of the resulting outcomes accruing either to herself or to the actor.

Once we assign utilities associated with the outcomes to the "other player," we are in another realm. The theory of games started as an analysis of so-called *games of strategy* — of which chess, poker, and tick-tack-toe are typical examples. Although games of this sort usually involve several moves, it has been shown that they can be collapsed into a set of single choices made simultaneously by the players. That is, each player chooses a *strategy* — a plan of action that specifies the move to be chosen in each situation that can possibly occur in the course of the game, when the player in question is to make the move. Logically, a decision of this sort involves no loss of flexibility, because all contingencies are already contained in the formulation of the strategy. One problem posed by the theory of games is to determine a strategy that can be reasonably recommended to each player as in some sense optimal.

Of course, because of the limitations of memory and of information-processing capacity of human beings, none but trivial games can be so reduced. Nevertheless, this way of defining a game of strategy has great conceptual value. It turns attention to the problem of defining an optimal strategy, which is no simple matter. Further, the depiction of a game in terms of strategies provides a model of real-life situations, where participants with conflicting interests can confine their attention to a choice among a manageable number of alternatives, so that the problem of dealing with superastronomical numbers of strategies need not be faced.

The simplest models of this sort are two-person games in which each of two players has a few available strategies. The model can be represented in the form of a matrix, whose rows designate the strategies available to one of the players, whom we shall call Row, and the columns represent the strategies available to the other player, whom we shall call Column.

Each cell of this matrix represents an outcome of the game, that is, the result of a simultaneous choice of strategy by each of the players. The entries in each cell may be conceived as pairs of numbers. The first is the *payoff* to Row, the second the payoff to Column. It is assumed that the payoffs are the respective utilities of the outcomes to Row and to Column.

COLUMN

	S_2	T_2	U_2	W_2
S_1	−1	2	−3	−8
T_1	0	5	−1	1
U_1	2	−3	−9	6

R
O
W

Figure 4.1. Two Person Zero Sum Game

The conceptually simplest two-person games are *constant-sum* games, in which the algebraic sum of the two payoffs in each cell is the same. This implies that the more one of the players wins, the less the other wins or the more the other loses. That is to say, in a two-person constant-sum game, the interests of the two players are diametrically opposed.

The utilities in two-person games are usually given on an interval scale. Since the zero and the unit of such a scale can be chosen arbitrarily, a constant-sum game can without loss of generality be represented as a zero-sum game, in which the sum of the payoffs in each outcome is zero. The terms constantsum and zero-sum can be used interchangeably.

Since in a zero-sum game, once the payoffs of one player have been given, those of the other are determined, only the payoffs of one player (by convention, Row's) have to be shown in the matrix. An example of a two-person zero-sum game is shown in Matrix 1 (see Figure 4.1).

In these game-theoretic models, the players are always assumed to be "rational" in the following sense: (1) each player strives to effect an outcome in which the payoff accruing to him (and to him alone) is maximized under the constraints of the situation; (2) each player assumes that the other is rational in the same sense.

The assumption that the other, like oneself, is rational defines the constraints of the situation. First, it attributes to the other the same goal that one pursues oneself, namely maximization of payoff. Second, one assumes that whatever one decides is the best strategy will be inferred by the other by the same reasoning, and that the other will act on that inference. In other words, there are limits on the extent to which one can keep one's choice of strategy secret.

Turning to Matrix 1 (Figure 4.1), suppose that Row thinks that U_1 is his best strategy (say because it contains the largest payoff, 6). If so, he must assume that Column has also inferred this, and since Column's interest is to *minimize* Row's payoff, Column will, acting on that inference, choose U_2, which awards Row his largest loss, −9. So U_1 cannot be Row's best strategy. A best strategy should be, if possible, one which remains best even if revealed to the opponent. Let us see what this strategy may be in the game represented by Matrix 1.

COLUMN

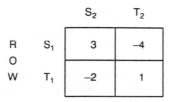

Figure 4.2. Asymmetric Button-Button Game

Associated with each strategy is the worst outcome that it may lead to. For instance, the worst outcome for Row associated with S_1 is a payoff of -8; the worst outcome associated with T_1 and U_1 respectively are payoffs -1 and -9. Of these three worst outcomes, -1 is preferable. If Row is guided by the *maximin principle* (choosing the strategy that contains the maximum of the minima), he should choose T_1. We see that this turns out to be the best strategy in the sense defined above. For if Row's choice is revealed to Column, Column, seeking to minimize Row's payoff will choose U_2. Then Row, attributing rationality to Column, can infer this choice and on the basis of this inference will still conclude that his best choice is T_1. Similar reasoning leads to the conclusion that U_2 is Column's best strategy.

Note that the outcome of the game arrived at in this manner awards to Row a payoff which is minimal in its row and maximal in its column. An outcome of this sort is called a *saddle point* of the game. It represents a sort of equilibrium in the sense that it awards to each player the best payoff that he can hope to get under the constraints of the situation, namely, diametrically opposed interests and rationality of both players. If a zero-sum game has several saddle points, then the choice of any strategy that contains a saddle point among its outcomes results in an outcome that is a saddle point. Moreover, the payoffs in all the saddle points are equal.

In some zero-sum games the maximin principle cannot be justified, because there are no saddle points. As an example, consider Matrix 2 (see Figure 4.2).

In this game, no payoff is simultaneously maximal in its column and minimal in its row. Let us see what the choice by Row of his maximin strategy, T_1, leads to.

Attributing rationality to Column, Row must deduce what Column would do, if Row's choice of T_1 were known to him. In that case, Column to minimize Row's payoff, would choose S_2. But if Column were to do this, Row would choose S_1. But if Column inferred this, he would choose T_2, which would make T_1 the better strategy for Row, and so on. Column's reasoning will also enter a perpetual cycle, so that the maximin principle does not lead to any stable conclusion. Whatever strategy seems best, the other seems better. Yet game theory shows a way out.

Recall the problem first encountered with regard to the alternatives in games against nature. This problem was resolved by introducing the concept of expected gain, that is, a probability-weighted average of the possible gains associated with each outcome. The optimal choice could be defined as the choice of the alternative that maximizes expected gain. In effect, the ambiguity was removed by extending the realm of possible gains to include expected gains. The determination of optimal strategies in two-person zero-sum games without saddle points is based on a similar idea. This time, however, it is the realm of available strategies that is extended. Specifically, assume that Row's available strategies, as defined by the game matrix, are R_1, R_2, ... R_n. Row can choose a *mixed strategy* $(x_1, x_2, ... x_n)$, where the x's add up to 1, by using a random device which determines strategy R_i with probability $x_i \geq 0$ $(i = 1, 2, ... n)$. Thus, it is not the uncertainty about the state of the world (as in games against nature) that provides the concept utilized in the new definition of optimal choice but rather the uncertainty deliberately introduced by the players in making their choices. The purpose of introducing this uncertainty is to deny to the opponent knowledge about one's actual choice.

The way this device operates can be seen most clearly in "Button-Button," the simplest two-person zero-sum game without a saddle point. Hider conceals a button in either hand, and Guesser tries to guess which. If Guesser guesses correctly, he wins a unit; if not, Hider wins a unit. It is intuitively clear that the optimal strategy for both Guesser and Hider is to guess (hide in) either hand with equal probability. If, however, the payoffs for guessing and/or the penalties for not guessing are not equal, it may be advantageous to Hider and/or Guesser to favor the one or the other hand.

Matrix 2 (Figure 4.2) illustrates the situation. Let Row be Guesser and Column Hider and let S stand for left hand, T for right. We see that if Row guesses correctly, he wins 3 units, if the button was in the left hand, but only 1 if it was in the right. If Row fails to guess correctly, Column wins 2 units if he hid the button in his left hand, 4 if in the right.

We will now show that Hider's optimal strategy, given the payoffs in Matrix 2, is to conceal the button in either hand with equal probability, but Guesser's optimal strategy is to guess the left hand with probability .3 and the right with probability .7. This follows from the circumstances that if Guesser uses the prescribed mixed strategy, his expected gain will be −.5 units regardless of where Hider hides the button. Similarly, it is easy to see that Hider's expected gain will be +.5 units regardless of how Guesser guesses, as long as the button is in either hand with equal probability.

Summarizing the results so far obtained from the analysis of two-person zero-sum games, we see that "maximization of gain" in this context should be understood as assurance of certain guaranteed minimal gains or expected gains, as the case may be. This interpretation of optimality or "rationality," if you will, is a consequence of the fact that in two-person zero-sum games, the co-player is an adversary in the strictest sense, and his rationality *as an adversary* makes the reasoning transparent—whatever helps self hurts other and vice versa. Three principles can be easily accepted as being in accord with the goal of maximizing expected gains in games against Nature and in two-person zero-sum games.

COLUMN

		C_2	D_2
R	C_1	0.0	−10, 10
O			
W	D_1	10, −10	−100, −100

Figure 4.3. Chicken Game

(1) *The Sure Thing Principle.* In a game against Nature the outcome depends on the alternative chosen by the actor and on the state of the world at the time. Complications arise when the actor prefers one alternative if one state of the world obtains and another if another state obtains. If, however, he stands to gain more by choosing the first alternative *regardless* of the state of the world, then this alternative is surely the choice. Such straight-forward decisions are said to be guided by the Sure Thing Principle. The same principle applies in a zero-sum game, where nature is replaced by an adversary.

(2) *The Maximim Principle.* A saddle point in a two-person zero-sum game, if it exists, awards to each player the best of the worst payoffs associated with each strategy, hence the maximin. If each player ascribes rationality to the other, the strategy containing the maximin is optimal for both.

(3) *The Equilibrium Principle.* If in a two-person zero-sum game neither player can improve his payoff by choosing another strategy, pure or mixed, while the other player does not change his strategy, these strategies are said to be in equilibrium against each other, and the resulting outcome is called an equilibrium. We have seen how the Equilibrium Principle gives meaning to optimal strategies in two-person zero-sum games even if they have no saddle points.

Variable Sum Games

Let us now see how these three principles fare in contexts that are not representable by zero-sum games. The first example will be a game nicknamed "Chicken." The original scenario of this game depicts two automobiles rushing toward a head-on collision. The driver who swerves to avoid collision, while the other driver stays on course, earns the epithet "Chicken" and loses the game. Recently it has been applied to nuclear deterrence theory, as Glad shows, below.

Assuming that each driver chooses between two strategies, "Swerve" and "Don't Swerve," the game can be represented by Matrix 3 (see Figure 4.3).

	C_2	D_2
C_1	1, 1	−10, 10
D_1	10, −10	−1, 1

Figure 4.4. Prisoner's Dilemma

"Swerve" is represented by strategy C (Chicken), "don't swerve" by D (Daring). The outcome C_1C_2 results if both swerve. Then neither player wins, but both live. In outcomes D_1C_2 and C_1D_2, the daring driver wins 10 units from the prudent one. If both "show resolve" (in the expectation that the other will yield), they crash (outcome D_1D_2). The large loss suffered by both drivers in that outcome is arbitrarily represented by the payoff −100.

Note that the Sure Thing Principle does not apply, since if the other driver swerves, it is advantageous to play the hero; but if the other does not swerve, it is disastrous to follow his example. Thus, what is the best choice depends on the other's choice.

The Maximin Principle dictates strategy C. Both swerve, and the outcome seems to be eminently reasonable. Note, however, that if each infers that the other infers that it is reasonable to swerve, each may think it is safe to stay on course and win. Thus, an apparently rational strategy turns out not to be optimal against itself (i.e., against an equally rational opponent).

As for equilibria, there are two conspicuous ones in this game, namely, D_1C_2 and C_1D_2. Of these, Row prefers D_1C_2 (in which he wins 10), while Column prefers C_1D_2 for the same reason. But if each player chooses the strategy that contains his preferred equilibrium, D_1D_2 results, which is not an equilibrium — besides being the worst outcome for both.

If mixed strategies are admitted, the game is seen to possess still another equilibrium. If each player chooses C with probability .9 and D with probability .1, then neither can improve his expected payoff, −1, by shifting away from this mixed strategy. For this reason, this pair of mixed strategies constitutes an equilibrium. The expected payoff guaranteed by it (−1) is better than the payoff guaranteed by the maximin strategy (−10), but it is less than the payoff that both can get if *both* use the maximin strategy, for then each gets 0.

We see that in situations of this sort, identifying "rationality" with maximization of gain can be beset with considerable ambiguity. Just how does one "maximize gain" in the Game of Chicken?

It might seem that the root of the difficulty is that the game has multiple equilibria or that the outcome suggested by prudence (C_1C_2) is not an equilibrium. That this is not necessarily the case is shown in the analysis of the game called prisoner's dilemma[10], depicted by Matrix 4 (see Figure 4.4). For the application of this game to the national security dilemma facing nuclear states, see Glad, below.

In this game, all three principles of rational decision dictate strategy D to both players. This strategy is optimal from the point of view of the Sure Thing Principle, since each player gets more by choosing D than by choosing C regardless of how the co-player chooses. The Maximin Principle dictates D, since by choosing D, each player avoids getting the worst payoff (−10). Moreover, outcome D_1D_2 is an equilibrium, because in shifting away from it, while the other player stays put, a player impairs his payoff. Finally, we see that D_1D_2 is the only equilibrium in this game.

But if the choice of D is rational, what has happened to the maximization of gain? To be sure, each player maximizes his own gain by choosing D rather than C. However, *both* players fail to maximize their gains, since by choosing D they get −1 each, whereas had they chosen C (i.e., had they *not* attempted to maximize their gains), they would have gotten +1 each.

For this reason, strategy C in prisoner's dilemma has been called the "cooperating" strategy and D the "defecting" strategy. The game is instructive in that it drives home the most important lesson about cooperation. It seems from the point of view of the individual that by not cooperating he maximizes his own payoff. And so he does, regardless of whether the other cooperates or not. Yet individually rational choices lead to collectively irrational ones. Collectively rational choices, on the other hand (C), although they seem to violate individual rationality, would have been more in accord with the players' individual interests.

Generalizations of the prisoner's dilemma situations to more than two players are depicted by so-called Tragedy of the Commons games. The original scenario of such games was suggested by G. Hardin.[11] The Commons is pasture land owned collectively by a community of farmers. It is in the interest of each farmer to add a cow to his herd grazing on that land. It seems innocuous to do so, since just one more cow has no discernible effect on the pasture. However, if every farmer reasons that way and adds a cow, the pasture may be overgrazed entailing losses for everyone. In our age, the oceans are analogous to Commons. Pursuit of individual interest by each country engaged in commercial fishing (maximizing the yield) can result in drastic depletion of the fish population, entailing losses for every one.

Multiple-Criteria Decision Making

All the foregoing examples were meant to illustrate the sort of problems that arise in connection with identifying maximization of individual gain with rationality. The problem of defining the maximum itself, however, was by-passed. It was assumed throughout that a utility measurable on an ordinal scale could be assigned to every outcome, and even though it was not always obvious whether a decision could be regarded as a gains-maximizing one, there was no difficulty in comparing the gains (utilities) and deciding which was the greater of the two or the greatest of the several.

In one example only, that of the man with three wives, ambivalence permeated the comparison of utilities. The situation appears to preclude a consistent ordering of utilities: W_1 preferred to W_2 preferred to W_3 preferred to W_1. A closer look at the situation reveals the source of the difficulty. In choosing among the wives, the man attempts to pursue two different goals: the satisfaction of his own preference and the defusing of W_2's jealousy.

In recent years, multiple criteria decision making has received a great deal of attention. Mathematicians see the problem as that of projecting a multidimensional preference space onto a single dimension. To be of use, the rule that assigns the utilities must be designed not just for a particular choice situation but for a whole class of choice situations, and it should be "reasonable," that is, have certain specified desirable properties.

For example, consider the choice situation in buying a car. I care about safety, fuel economy, and price. Say the choice is between cars C_1, C_2, and C_3. According to some criteria of safety, C_1 is the safest; C_2 travels farthest on a liter of fuel; C_3 is the cheapest. Which car do I prefer?

At least three different decision rules suggest themselves:

(1) Two of the criteria, price and fuel consumption are quantifiable in an obviously straightforward way. The third, safety, is not so easy to quantify. But in principle an index of safety could be constructed from accident statistics on the three cars. Given three indices characterizing each of three cars, the cars could be compared by assigning weights to the three indices and comparing the weighted averages — the "scores".

(2) Another way is to rank order the criteria according to their importance. Then if safety is the most important criterion, C_1 is the choice; if fuel economy, C_2; if price, C_3. This method exemplifies so-called lexicographic ordering.[12]

(3) Finally, we can rank order the items according to how they compare on the number of criteria on which they excel. This last method, however, may lead to cyclic preferences, as can be readily seen, if the rank orders of the three cars are (C_1, C_2, C_3) on safety; (C_2, C_3, C_1) on economy; and (C_3, C_1, C_2) on price. This is so because C_1 excels C_2 on two criteria (safety and price), C_2 excels C_3 on two (safety and economy), and C_3 excels C_1 on two (economy and price). So each car beats another "by majority vote," as it were, if criteria correspond to votes.

The intransitivity of preferences so engendered is called the Condorcet Paradox.[13]

Collective decision making arrived at by some aggregation of preferences of the individuals comprising the collective is an important instance of multicriteria decision making. Here the preference order of each individual for the alternatives (e.g., candidates, policies, priorities) is a criterion by which to judge the equality of the final decision. One would like, if possible, to satisfy every one's preferences. Generally, however, this is not possible. The problem of designing an aggregation rule which is in some sense "optimal" is essentially a fundamental problem of democratic decision: the problem of effecting "the greatest good for the greatest number."

A more modest task than that of finding an optimal aggregation rule is that of finding some acceptable rule. Kenneth Arrow attacked this problem by formulating certain desiderata that a social decision rule purporting to be democratic should satisfy.[14]

(1) *Independence of Individual Preference Orders.* Each individual should be free to express any preference order for the proffered candidates or alternatives independently of others' preference orders.

(2) *Non-Malevolence.* Suppose applying the rule results in alternative x being rated higher than y. Next, suppose that another vote is taken, whereby some voters rate x higher than before and none rate it lower, while the ratings of y remain unchanged. Then the aggregate rating of x should not be lower than that of y as a result of the second vote. In other words, the aggregate rating of an alternative should not be weakened if it is strengthened in the estimation of the voters.

(3) *Independence from Irrelevant Alternatives.* If, as a result of one vote, alternative x receives a higher rating than y, then the ranking should not be reversed as a result of another vote in which none of the individual preferences between the two alternatives have changed.

(4) *Citizens' Sovereignty.* It should be possible by *some* vote (e.g., a unanimous preference ordering) to effect any given aggregate ranking of alternatives.

(5) *Non-Dictatorship.* There should be no individual whose preferences always determine the aggregate ranking of alternatives.

If there are only two alternatives to choose from, these five criteria can be easily satisfied by various aggregation rules, for instance, by majority vote. If, however, the number of alternatives exceeds two, the above five desiderata are incompatible. They cannot all be satisfied. Thus, the search for an "optimal" aggregation rule is pointless: not even an acceptable rule can be found, if by an acceptable rule we mean one that satisfies the above five criteria.

Majority rule, for example, fails when the number of alternatives exceeds two, because intransitive majorities can arise, precluding a consistent social ranking of alternatives by applying majority rule in paired comparisons. The lexicographic ordering rule fails to satisfy the minimal criterion of democratic decision: the most important criterion becomes the preference order of the most important voter, who thereby becomes the dictator. There remains only the construction of an index, that is, a projection of several dimensions upon one. Once a single standard of value can be applied to all alternatives, maximization of gain comes into its own, for the index can provide an unambivalent order of preference.

The Ethical Dimension

If we are dealing with a single actor who must choose among alternatives differing on several dimensions, we might concede that the construction of an index is entirely up to him or her. In choosing among jobs, for example, we may feel it is the chooser's privilege to assign weights to salary, location, prospects, and so forth. If, however, the index involves aggregating preferences of several individuals, it acquires an ethical dimension — making interpersonal comparison of utilities. Indeed, even in decision situations involving a single actor, "hidden dimensions" of utility may raise serious, at times painful, dilemmas as the following examples will illustrate.

Imagine that a perfect vaccine against leukemia has been discovered. It prevents the disease with certainty. In rare instances, however, the vaccine is lethal. In terms of chances of dying within a given stretch of time, there is no question that the vaccine confers an advantage. Assume it reduces this chance by a factor of 10. Nevertheless, some would hesitate to call a parent irrational if he or she refuses to vaccinate a child.

Our next example relates to the gruesome practice of shooting hostages. During World War II, the Nazis took hostages in occupied countries and shot them in retaliation for acts of violence by the underground resistance. As a perverse act of cruelty, they would sometimes ask a mother of two sons taken hostage to indicate which of them was to be killed. In case the woman refused to name one, they would shoot both. Maximization of gain (here, minimization of loss) dictates naming one son. Yet it is, in a way, understandable why a mother faced with a choice of this sort would refuse to choose.

The "hidden dimension" in both of these examples is the *procedure*, which is taken into consideration along with the projected result (or the statistically expected result) of the choice. In the case of the vaccine, the question that looms is not only whether the child is to live or die but also about all the other features of the situation. The death of a child caused by the disease (which had previously killed many children) is not the same as the death of a child caused by a vaccine which *statistically* is supposed to (and does) save lives of children. The mother whose son, chosen by her, is shot must continue to live with the memory that it was she who ordained his death. The mother who refused to choose lost both sons but she is spared *this* tormenting memory. Of course she has another in its place — of *not* having saved the life of one. Somehow, however, sins of commission weigh more heavily in human conscience than sins of omission. (The same seems to be the case in the vaccine dilemma.) Surely, different people will feel differently about choices of this sort, and no one is qualified to judge them. Our purpose has been merely to show that "maximization of gain" is not a straightforward matter and that the difficulties often are rooted in the "hidden dimensions" of value.

Dilemmas imbedded in some non-zero-sum games can be interpreted in the same way. In prisoner's dilemma (Matrix 4), it is individually rational to choose D. If, however, one is motivated by the Kantian categorical imperative (act as you wish others would act), one must decide that C is "the right thing to do." This choice may bring the largest loss (if the other defects) but also the satisfaction, regardless of outcome, of having "done the right thing."

The same considerations apply to Tragedy of the Commons type situations. If every one else "does the right thing," taking advantage of it so as to maximize one's gain is not only profitable but can even be rationalized by pointing out that in a large population of players, the effect of one's defection is negligible. But this rationalization is convincing only if one judges one's defection by its isolated effect. The rationalization collapses in the light of the realization of what would happen if everyone used the same reasoning. Thus, the reward of cooperation in a Tragedy of the Commons situation is the awareness of having "done the right thing." The value is in the act itself, not in its consequences.

Many other situations come to mind in which the "bottom line" expressed as some formal index must be weighed against the procedure required to maximize gain. Passing for the purpose of dramatic illustration into the realm of fancy, imagine a serum that can save thousands of lives but can be obtained only by draining the blood of one living child. The maxim "the end justifies the means" flounders on the realization that what you get is not only the "end" but also the fact of having used the means and that the construction of a weighted index to combine the utilities of the ends and of the means is not to be lightly undertaken.

The Seductive Appeal of Maximization

Perhaps the most serious problem with the maximization of gain principle in real life situations is the known human propensity to search for certainty and for addictions of all kinds. Every decision situation is a source of tension. Arrival at a decision, especially when accompanied by a comfortable rationalization, resolves the tension. Quantitative indices are tension reducers par excellence. The easiest decisions are those based on comparison of quantities, when there is an a priori commitment to the largest (or smallest) quantity. Quantification precludes difficulties engendered by intransitive preferences or incomparable alternatives. Having an index of one's performance suggests at all times an objective assessment of "how one is doing." It also stimulates rational assessment of the relative values of alternative courses of action on the basis of comparing one-dimensional utility indices assigned to anticipated outcomes: Everything can be compared with everything else. Agonies of decision making in the face of incompatible goals are avoided. One might even speculate that "materialist" values, characterizing behavior patterns in the business world, may be less a reflection of greed than of the attraction of certainty. An unambivalent objective measure of "success" provides a shortcut in decision making, a justification of one's own decisions, and a basis for consensus, hence for efficient organization of cooperative effort.

The obverse side of quantification is its addiction-inducing potential. The ubiquitousness of universal standards of worth reflects people's attraction to one-dimensional indices. George F. Babbit, the prototype of the stolid businessman in Sinclair Lewis's novel, admires one building more than another because it is four stories taller. Performance indices are legitimate measures of prowess in competitive sports, because they provide objective measures of *competitive* excellence. Less fortunate is the pervasive use of such indices in areas where competition may denigrate rather than enhance excellence. Objective measures of competitive excellence cannot be applied seriously to quality in the arts, and indices referring to salaries of film stars, sales prices of paintings, sales volumes of books, and so forth are misleading. Measurement of popularity indices of political figures lead to similar problems. The value of such indices as measures of systemic influences of mass behavior is not in dispute. The less fortunate effect is the facile identification induced in the public mind of these indices with all measures of excellence: the salary of an actress with her talent, the magnificence of a painting with its sales price, the competence of a politician with his poll ratings.

In countries where hunger is chronic, obesity is often regarded as a sign of health. When I was a child, public weighing machines still proclaimed "Your weight indicates your health. Are you gaining or losing?" The implication in those days was that gaining weight is a sign of good health and losing weight of poor health. In our age, this superstition has disappeared at least in over-fed countries. The concept of optimal body weight related to age or height is taken for granted. But nothing analogous exists with respect to money. There is no concept of optimal income or optimal total worth. No one is urged to reduce either, say, in the interest of mental health. Only most recently have voices been raised urging the recognition of limits to growth. These are, however, confined to total global measures. The addiction to seeking to maximize personal income, the assets of a firm, or share of the market continue unabated where opportunities for pursuing these goals exist.

Clearly, the most obviously dangerous addiction to magnitude is in the area of "national security." Identification of "national security" with the destructive potential at one's disposal stems from the battle field model of international relations. It is natural to suppose that in battle the side with superior firepower wins the day. Of course, other considerations, both strategic and tactical; skills; morale; and so forth must also be taken into account. However, these other factors can be regarded as contributing to effective use of destructive power. By appropriately defining strength, one can say that the stronger of the adversaries emerges victorious, hence by extension wins the war, hence enhances "security."

That this is a delusion can be readily established by examining historical evidence, which does not so much refute as make meaningless the maxims of conventional wisdom about security through strength. The strongest nations have been victimized by war as much, if not more, than the weakest. One cannot argue convincingly that the United States or the Soviet Union are more secure from ravages of war than Costa Rica or Finland. Despite its problematic relationship to "national security," military potential remains the most widely accepted index of "security," mainly because it can be measured. It is not difficult to seduce people into believing that whatever grows is vigorous, healthy, and strong. To be sure, problems arise with regard to methods of comparing relative importance of the various components of the war machine. These problems, however, are just so much grist for the mill. Complexities encourage the development of "expertise." And since military expertise is based largely on detailed knowledge of weapons, logistics, and so forth — all of it "hard" knowledge spiked with facts and figures — this sort of expertise confers authority on the guardians of "national security," fixates their conception of it in the public mind, and firms the legitimacy of their concerns.

The addiction to quantification of destructive power exacerbates the arms race between the rival powers. The objective indices permit at all times the measurement of one's position vis-à-vis the adversary. Since one can never be "ahead" in all components of the war machine, there is never any lack of objectively supportable reasons for quantitative expansion and qualitative "improvement" of the means of total destruction.

The net effect is continued erosion of "security" if by security we mean immunity to devastation. On the contrary, it makes both sides increasingly vulnerable to complete devastation. The concept of "deterrence" obscures this absurdity and nurtures the addiction to gigantism and to the imperative of freewheeling technological sophistication of the war machine.

The Dissolution of Rationality

And so the concept of maximization of gain has run the full circle. We have seen that there is no fundamental trouble with the concept as long as a one-to-one correspondence can be established between actions and outcomes and as long as the outcomes can be ordered on a one-dimensional scale of preference. This concept was made more complex by the introduction of models of decision under risk, where the outcomes depend not only on the actor's choices but also on states of the world (Nature's "choices"). When an adversary replaced Nature as the agent outside the actor's control, zero-sum model rationality could still be incorporated into the decision model by ascribing rationality to the adversary. When the Other could be imagined to be only partly an adversary and partly a potential ally (variable sum games), game theory was revealed as a basis for a theory of conflict resolution as well as of strategic decisions. The multicriteria decision model suggested a rigorous approach to a theory of social choice.

These advances in sophisticated decision theory, however, have made no discernible impact on the decision processes driving the present arms race. Even the awareness of the adversary *as an adversary*, a fundamental condition of rational decision in competitive games, has been obscured in the pursuit of elusive total superiority (the U.S. fixation) or of "parity" (the Soviet fixation). The assumption always seems to persist that the next "advance" will bring one nearer the goal. The obvious response of the Other in kind is left out of consideration. The most reasonable conclusion is that the fetish of maximization of gain has uncoupled people's actions from their reason. Whatever "reasoning" goes on reflects a fixation on indices to be maximized to the total exclusion of awareness of consequences. The following excerpt is a typical example. The authors discuss various methods of cost-benefit analysis that can be used in allocating funds to various weapons systems. Of one such method they write:

> This criterion . . . takes into account not only the numbers of our offense bombers and missiles but also their operational effectiveness. . . . It is still, of course, an ambiguous criterion, and requires more precise definition. For example, what target system — population, industry, or military bases — should be used to keep score?[15]

We need only imagine the realities to which bland terms like "target system" and "keeping score" refer to appreciate the fixation on maximization of gain (more bang for a buck; more rubble for a ruble) in its most bizarre manifestation.

Notes

1. The emergence of the concept can be traced to the correspondence between the two leading mathematicians of seventeenth-century France, Blaise Pascal and Pierre de Fermat. The correspondence was published in 1657 in "De Rationalis in Ludo Alea" ("Ratiocination in Dice Games") by Christian Huygens, who gave the first rigorous definition of mathematical expectation, the concept underlying the idea of expected gain.

2. The best-known examples of interval scales are the commonly used temperature scales, Celsius and Fahrenheit, on which the zero point and the unit were chosen arbitrarily.

3. The strength of a scale is inversely related to the degree of arbitrariness with which numbers can be assigned to the magnitudes measured on it. For example, the ordinal scale is weak, because magnitudes x, y, and z in that order can be represented equally well by any three numbers in the same order of magnitudes. The interval scale is stronger, because in assigning numbers to magnitudes measured on it, ratios of differences must remain invariant. The stronger the scale, the more meaningful relations can be expressed between the magnitudes. For example, a ratio of temperatures is meaningless on the Celsius or on the Fahrenheit (interval) scale, but is meaningful on the Kelvin (ratio) scale.

4. See also, John Von Neumann and Oskar Morgenstern, *Theory of Games and Economic Behavior*, 2nd ed. (Princeton, NJ: Princeton University Press, 1947).

5. Daniel Bernoulli, "Specimen Theoriae Novae de Mensura Sortis," *Commentarii Academiae Scientarum Imperialis Petropolitanae, 1730-1731*, trans. Louise Summers *Econometrica*, 22 (1954): 23-26.

6. Maurice Allais, "The 1952 Allais Theory of Choice Involving Risk" in *Expected Utility Hypotheses and the Allais Paradox*, eds. M. Allais and O. Hagen (Dordrecht, The Netherlands: D. Reidel, 1979).

7. Nicholas Georgescu-Roegen, "Utility," in *International Encyclopedia of the Social Sciences*, Vol. 16, ed. D. L. Sills (New York: Macmillan & Free Press, 1968), 264.

8. Ibid.

9. Since Chicken is not a zero-sum game, payoffs to both players must be specified in each cell of the game matrix.

10. The often told scenario of prisoner's dilemma features two burglars under arrest. There is enough evidence to convict them of possession of stolen goods but not enough to convict them of breaking and entering. Conviction of the more serious crime can be obtained only if one, or both, confess. The prisoners are told that if both confess, their sentences will be somewhat reduced; if neither

confesses, they will be charged only with possession of stolen goods, which carries a considerably lighter sentence; if only one confesses, he will not be prosecuted (in consideration of his having turned Crown's evidence), while the other, convicted on the strength of the former's confession, will receive the maximum sentence.

The actual numerical utilities in this game are immaterial as long as they reflect the players' orders of preference for the four outcomes.

11. Garret J. Hardin, "The Tragedy of the Commons," *Science* 162 (1968): 1243-1248.

12. Lexicographic ordering is so named because it governs the arrangement of entries in a dictionary: first according to the first letter, then according to the second letter, and so on.

13. Marquis de Condorcet (1743-1794) was a French mathematician who, in an era of growing interest in democracy, became concerned with problems arising in designing voting procedures in accordance with principles of democratic decisions.

14. Arrow's famous Impossibility Theorem was first proved in his *Social Choice and Individual Values* (New York: Wiley, 1951).

15. Charles J. Hitch and Roland Neely McKean, "The Economics of Defense in the Nuclear Age," in *American National Security,* eds. Morton Berkowitz and P. G. Bock (New York: Free Press, 1965), 126.

Chapter 5

Crisis Management

OLE R. HOLSTI

"When the going gets tough, the tough get going" is a favorite aphorism of countless football coaches and Marine drill instructors. It also appears to be deeply embedded in the mind sets of many students and practitioners of foreign policy decision making. Although usually worded more elegantly, the essence of this proposition may be found in both theoretical treatises on international relations and in the memoirs of statesmen. According to this view, when the stakes in a situation are low and the costs of miscalculation are limited, various kinds of errors and nonrational elements may reduce the quality of decisions. But in a major crisis, when even national survival may be at issue, leaders and governments will rise to the challenge, performing at their best.

Nowhere is this proposition expressed as clearly as in the memoirs written by Richard Nixon some years before he assumed the presidency. He described crises as "mountaintop experiences" in which he often performed at his best: "Only then [in crises] does he discover all the latent strengths he never knew he had and which otherwise would have remained dormant." He added that:

> It has been my experience that, more often than not, taking a break is actually an escape from the rough, grinding discipline that is absolutely necessary for superior performance. Many times I have found that my best ideas have come when I thought I could not work for another minute and when I literally had to drive myself to finish the task before a deadline. Sleepless nights, to the extent that the body can take them, can stimulate creative mental activity.[1]

AUTHOR'S NOTE: Parts of this essay have drawn upon several previous publications: *Crisis, Escalation, War* (Montreal: McGill-Queens University Press, 1972); "Theories of Crisis Decision Making," in *Diplomacy*, ed. Paul Gordon Lauren (New York: Free Press, 1980): 99-136; "The Effects of Stress on the Performance of Foreign Policy-Makers," in *Political Science Annual* VI, ed. Cornelius P. Cotter (Indianapolis: Bobbs-Merrill, 1975), 255-319 (the latter coauthored by Alexander L. George); and "Crisis Decision Making," in *Behavior, Society, and Nuclear War* eds. Philip E. Tetlock et al. (New York: Oxford University Press, 1989), 8-84.

Others have appraised the effects of crisis on decision making in a similar vein, suggesting, for example that, "a decision maker may, in a crisis, be able to invent or work out easily and quickly what seems in normal times to both the 'academic' scholar and the layman to be hypothetical, unreal, complex or otherwise difficult," and, "routine experience may lead us imperceptibly to ignore a slowly changing or suddenly new reality, but we do sometimes rise to a challenge with heightened alertness and an increased sense of responsibility, especially on matters of great moment."[2]

Most theories of nuclear deterrence also presuppose rational and predictable decision processes, even during intense and protracted international crises. They assume that threats and ultimata will enhance calculation, control, and caution while inhibiting recklessness and risk taking. In short, these scholars and policy makers tend to be sanguine about the ability of policy makers to be creative when the situation requires it — and never is that requirement greater than during an intense international crisis.

These observations appear to confirm the conventional wisdom that in crisis decision making, necessity is indeed the mother of invention. Is there any reason to question the universal validity of that view? Although scenarios of decision-making malfunctions resulting in a nuclear war are limited to novels and movies, not all of the relevant evidence is totally reassuring. The recollections of those who have experienced intense and protracted crises suggest they may be marked at times by great skill in policy making, and at others by decision processes and outcomes that fail to meet even the most permissive standards of rationality. Some recall the "sense of elation that comes with crises,"[3] whereas others admit to serious shortcomings in their own performance during such situations. Dwight Eisenhower, for example, recalled, "You see a poor, rather stupid fellow behind a desk and you wonder why he couldn't do better than that [in crisis situations]. Unfortunately, that picture comes up too often."[4] Indeed, although the definitive history of the Watergate episode remains to be written, the evidence suggests that Nixon's performance during that culminating crisis of his presidency was at best erratic, certainly falling far short of his self-diagnosis.

But anecdotes do not provide a sufficient basis for addressing the issue. How *do* decision makers respond to the challenges and demands of crises? Does high motivation lead to more accurate perception of the situation and relevant actors, an enhanced ability for processing information, and an increased capacity for creative problem-solving? Or, is the capacity for coping with complex problems sometimes impaired, perhaps to the point suggested by Richard Neustadt's phrase, "the paranoid reaction characteristic of crisis behavior?"[5]

First, let us define the term, crisis. There are a number of definitions in use. However, several characteristics are common to most of them. Crises are marked by a severe threat to important values and time for responding to the threat is limited. There also is widespread agreement that these attributes of crisis — as well as several other aspects of the situation — give rise to stress among those who have to cope with it.[6]

To explore the relationship between crisis and the cognitive aspects of decision making, this essay will examine three diverse bodies of literature for insights and evidence. Various theories of international relations, foreign policy, and deterrence provide a rather varied set of answers. Psychologists, too, have generated substantial data on the question. Owing to important differences between the experimental laboratory and foreign offices, this evidence is better used as a source of insights and hypotheses than as direct answers to questions about the impact of stress on crisis decision making. To overcome these limitations, it is fortunate that we can also draw upon a growing body of systematic and comparative research on international crises. The concluding section of this chapter examines several approaches for improving performance in crisis management.

Theories of Foreign Policy Decision Making

It is useful to distinguish between four levels of analysis — the nation, bureaucratic organizations, decision-making groups, and the individual — because each tends to yield a somewhat different diagnosis about crisis decisions (see Table 5.1). As a rule, theories that focus on larger units (nations, organizations) are more optimistic about the impact of crisis on the quality of decision making than are those that deal with smaller ones (groups, individuals).

The traditional and still dominant "realist" theories usually incorporate the assumption that nation-states are best characterized as "unitary rational actors." Consequently, they attach relatively low explanatory power to cognitive aspects of decision making in crises. As the most useful perspective for understanding the relations between nations, realists assume that in an international system characterized by structural anarchy, policy makers are guided by the "national interest." They may at times miscalculate their interests, the resources available to various national actors, or the motives of adversaries. Worse, they may succumb to utopian or ideological thinking, or to the parochial values of domestic politics. But realist theories rarely distinguish between policy making in crises and other situations; when they do so, they tend to predict better performance in the former because of a reduced likelihood that irrelevant or inappropriate values will intrude into the calculations. Even when the outcome of a crisis is war, the explanation is one of calculated political choice. Michael Howard makes the point clearly: "Whatever may be the underlying causes of international conflict . . . wars begin with conscious and reasoned decisions based on the calculation, made by *both* parties, that they can achieve more by going to war than by remaining at peace."[7] The same point is made even more strongly by Theodore Abel in his treatise on war.[8]

Theories of deterrence are especially sanguine about the calculated aspects of decision making. Although there are several approaches to deterrence and none of them is free from controversy, most of them share two central propositions. First, foreign policy can best be characterized as a process of rational calculation. As Thomas Schelling has put it, the premise is "not just of intelligent behavior, but of behavior motivated by a conscious calculation of advantage, a calculation that in turn is based on an explicit and internally valid value system."[9] Second, as the stakes in a situation increase — for example, when a nation faces a major threat to core values, or perhaps even to its existence — policy processes will even more closely approximate the norms of calculated decision making. Conversely, deterrence — whether in criminal law or nuclear strategy — is of doubtful efficacy against madmen, the suicidal, or those who welcome martyrdom.

An organizational/bureaucratic perspective also tends to point to optimistic views about decision making in international crises. The central premise is that decision making in bureaucratic organizations is heavily constrained, and not only by the legal and formal norms that are intended to enhance the rational and eliminate the capricious aspects of bureaucratic behavior. Nevertheless, there is evidence that diagnoses of and prescriptions for the situation are often colored by parochial perspectives rooted in bureaucratic roles: "Where you stand depends on where you sit." Crises provide both the motivation and the means for reducing some of the more pathological aspects of normal bureaucratic behavior, including those arising from hierarchy, specialization, and centralization. Crises are likely to move the locus of decision making to the top of the organization where higher quality intelligence is available and broader, less parochial values may be invoked. Several analysts place special emphasis on the salutary effects of short decision time in reducing the opportunities for decision making by bargaining, incrementalism, lowest common denominator values, muddling through, and the like.[10] Thus, "it may be, paradoxically, that the model of means-ends rationality will be more closely approximated in an emergency when time for careful deliberation is limited."[11]

Yet, studies of actual international crises from an organizational perspective are not so sanguine. Allison's study of the Cuban missile crisis revealed a substantial number of malfunctions, especially in the implementation of some key decisions, including, but not limited to, removal of obsolete missiles in Turkey and grounding of weather-sampling flights near the Soviet Union.[12] As the President complained at the time, "There is always some son of a bitch who doesn't get the word." Perhaps equally sobering is the conclusion of Neustadt's analysis of two crises involving the United States and the United Kingdom. Despite sharing many political and cultural values, leaders of even those long-time friends significantly misperceived the other's interests and policy processes during the Suez and Skybolt missile crises.[13]

Groups, according to some studies, may often perform better than individuals in coping with complex tasks. Underlying this perspective are the premises that the group is not merely the sum of its members and that the dynamics of group interaction are likely to have a positive impact on both the substance and quality of decisions owing to diverse perspectives and talents, a division of labor, and high-quality substantive debates centering on diagnoses of the situation and prescriptions for coping with it. They may also provide decision makers with emotional and other types of support needed to deal with a stressful situation.[14]

TABLE 5.1: Four Perspectives on Crisis Decision Making

Conceptualization of decision making	Realism: Unitary rational actor	Decision making as the result of bargaining within bureaucratic organizations
Sources of theory, insight and evidence	Political science History Philosophy	Organization theory Sociology of bureaucracies Bureaucratic politics
Premises	Decisions guided by the national interest and the logic of an anarchical international system	Central organizational values are imperfectly internalized Organizational behavior is political behavior. Structure and SOPs affect substance and quality of decisions.
Constraints on rational decision making	Inadequate understanding of the national interest Miscalculation of resources or motives of rivals Utopian thinking Lack of prudence Intrusion of domestic politics	Imperfect information, resulting from centralization, hierarchy, specialization Organizational inertia Conflict between individual and organizational utilities Bureaucratic politics and bargaining dominate decision making
Prognosis: decisions made in crises versus "normal" situations	Tends to be higher, as impact of domestic politics, etc., is likely to be reduced.	Variable to higher, as higher quality information and superordinate values are likely to dominate parochial ones

Yet, groups are also vulnerable to such pathologies as "groupthink," in which concern for group solidarity supersedes effective performance of vital decision-making tasks. As a consequence, groups may be afflicted by unwarranted feelings of optimism and invulnerability, stereotyped images of adversaries, inattention to warnings, and powerful, if subtle, pressures against dissent.[15] Some also have suggested that groups are more prone to high-risk decisions, but evidence for this hypothesis is rather controversial.[16] Effective and imaginative leadership appears to be a necessary condition for averting some of the more deleterious aspects of group dynamics, but leaders themselves are not immune to high stress, and leadership performance appears to become more variable under such circumstances.[17] Thus, from the group perspective, the prognosis for decision making in crisis is mixed.

Individual approaches to decision making often emphasize the gap between the demands of the classical model of rational decision making and the substantial body of theory and evidence about various cognitive constraints that come into play even in relatively simple situations. Going beyond some of the earlier

TABLE 5.1: continued

Decision making as the product of group interaction	*Decision making as the result of individual choice*
Social psychology Sociology of small groups	Cognitive psychology Dynamic psychology
Most decisions made by elite groups. Group is different from the sum of its members. Group dynamics affect substance and quality of decisions.	Importance of subjective appraisal and cognitive processes.
Groups less effective for some decision-making tasks. Pressures for conformity Quality of leadership "Groupthink"	Cognitive limits on rationality Information processing distorted by cognitive consistency dynamics Individual differences on abilities related to decision making (e.g., problem-solving ability, tolerance of ambiguity, defensiveness and anxiety, information seeking). Cognitive dissonance (post-decision phase).
Variable to lower, depending heavily on the ability of leader to make use of the group, avoid "groupthink", etc.	Tends to be lower, as high stress tends to erode cognitive abilities

formulations that focused on various types of psychopathologies among political leaders (e.g., paranoia, authoritarianism), the emphasis in recent studies is on cognitive constraints that affect the decision making performance of "normal" rather than deviant subjects. Thus the universe of concern includes all leaders, not merely those who display evidence of clinical abnormalities (e.g., Hitler and Stalin).

The several relevant models share a concern for cognitive strategies for dealing with complexity, incomplete or contradictory information and, paradoxically, information overload. They variously characterize the decision maker as a problem solver, naive or intuitive scientists, cognitive balancer or dissonance avoider, information seeker, and cybernetic information processor.[18] Common to virtually all of these approaches is an interest in belief systems images of relevant actors (including self-images), perceptions, information processing, certain personality attributes (e.g., ability to tolerate ambiguity, cognitive complexity), and the impact that these may have on decision-making performance. A subject of special interest has been the impact of high stress — for example, that induced by an intense crisis — on cognitive performance. The next two sections will examine some evidence on this point from experimental research and studies of international crises.

Crisis, Stress, and Decision Making: Some Experimental Evidence

Before reviewing this literature, it is important to delineate a realistic rather than idealized, textbook model of rational decision making. Cognitive constraints on rationality include limits on the individual's capacity to receive, process, and assimilate information about the situation; an inability to generate the entire set of policy alternatives; fragmentary knowledge about the consequences of each option; and an inability to order preferences for all possible consequences on a single utility scale.[19] Because these constraints exist in all but the most trivial decision-making situations, it is not instructive to assess the impact of crises against a standard of synoptic rationality. A more modest and realistic set of criteria might include the ability to deal effectively with the following cognitive, information processing and management tasks:

- Define the main elements of the situation; for example, what is at stake
- Identify and consider adequately the major values, interests, and objectives to be fulfilled
- Search for and evaluate the major alternative courses of action
- Estimate the probable costs and risks, as well as the probable consequences, of various alternatives (and, as a corollary, distinguish the possible from the probable)
- Search for new information relevant to assessment of the options
- Maintain receptivity to new information, even that which calls into question the validity of preferred courses of action (and, as corollaries, discriminate between relevant and irrelevant information, resist premature cognitive closure, and tolerate ambiguity)
- Consider the problems that may arise in implementing various options
- Assess the situation from the perspective of other parties
- Resist both defensive procrastination and premature decisions
- Monitor feedback from a developing situation
- Make adjustments to meet real changes in the situation (and, as a corollary, distinguish real from apparent changes)[20]

A substantial body of theory and evidence suggests that intense and protracted crises may erode rather than enhance the ability to cope with these tasks. Figure 5.1 presents a series of hypotheses linking the defining attributes of crisis, first to stress and then to selected aspects of decision-making performance. These propositions are presented not as iron laws but as a checklist of points at which decision making may be vulnerable to the effects of stress.

The relevant psychological literature suggests that an important aspect of crises is that they are characterized by high stress for the individuals and organizations

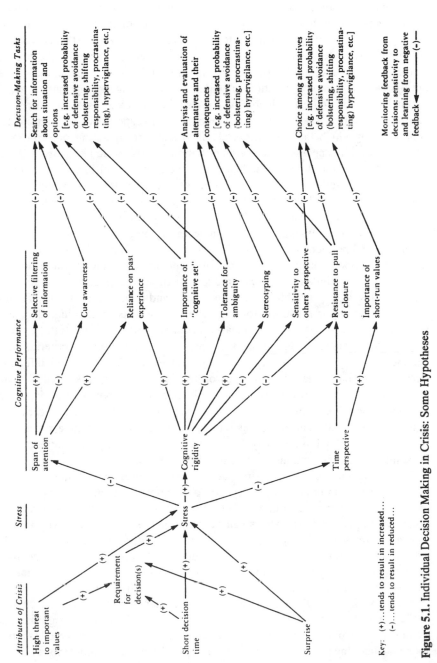

Figure 5.1. Individual Decision Making in Crisis: Some Hypotheses

involved. That a severe threat to important values is stress inducing requires little elaboration. The element of surprise may also be a contributing factor; there is evidence that unanticipated and novel situations are generally viewed as more threatening.[21] Finally, crises are often marked by intense work schedules, owing to the severity of the situation (high threat), the absence of established routines for dealing with them (surprise), and limited decision time. Lack of rest and diversion, combined with excessively long working hours, are likely to magnify the stresses in the situation. Moreover, crisis decisions are rarely if ever analogous to the familiar multiple-choice question in which the full range of options is neatly outlined. The theoretical universe of choices usually exceeds by a substantial margin the number that can or will be considered. Especially in unanticipated situations for which there are no established standard operating procedures or decision rules, it is necessary to search out and perhaps create alternatives. Thus, quite aside from the threat to be dealt with, the requirement of having to make decisions may itself be a significant source of stress, arising, for example, from efforts to cope with value complexity, cognitive constraints on rationality, role factors, small group dynamics, and bureaucratic politics.[22]

Some degree of stress is an integral and necessary precondition for individual or organizational problem solving; in its absence there is no motivation to act. Low levels of stress alert one to the existence of a situation requiring attention, and the need to increase vigilance and preparedness to cope with it. Increasing stress to moderate levels may heighten one's motivation and ability to find a satisfactory solution to the problem. Indeed, for some elementary tasks a rather high degree of stress may enhance performance, at least for limited periods of time. If the problem is qualitatively simple and performance is measured by quantitative criteria, stress can increase output. The primary concern here, however, is not with the effects of stress on persons engaged in manual or routine repetitive tasks, but with its consequences on the performance of officials in leadership positions during international crises. These are nearly always marked by complexity and uncertainty, and they usually demand responses which are judged by qualitative rather than quantitative criteria. It is precisely these qualitative aspects of performance that are most likely to suffer from intense and protracted stress.[23]

The preponderance of experimental evidence indicates that intense stress, although it may improve simple psychomotor output, impairs cognitive performance. The most general summarizing statement is that the relationship between cognitive performance and stress can be described as an "inverted U." Low to moderate stress may facilitate better performance but, according to most of the experimental evidence, high stress degrades it. Observational evidence from related field research (for example, studies of natural disasters, or performance in combat or other dangerous circumstances), and from analyses of foreign policy decision making — studies that are more directly relevant with respect to subjects, setting, and decision-making task, but often are considerably less rigorous and systematic — also tends to suggest that intense and protracted stress erodes rather than enhances the ability of individuals to cope with complex problems.[24]

Because the evidence is far too voluminous and complex to summarize in detail, only a few of the main findings are outlined below, with focus on three intervening variables: span of attention, cognitive rigidity, and time perspective.[25]

(1) Quite aside from the experience or anticipation of harm, the sources of stress in a decision-making situation may include task overload, information overload, and task or role conflicts. One way of coping is to narrow one's span of attention to a few aspects of the decision-making task.[26] This may be a functional strategy if it permits the executive to eliminate trivial distractions, filter out irrelevant information, and develop an agenda of priorities. However, these benefits may be balanced or even outweighed by a number of costs.

Attention to fewer cues can be helpful if only trivial and irrelevant ones are overlooked, but as stress increases, filtering is likely to be less discriminating. As a consequence important dimensions of the situation may escape scrutiny, conflict of values may be overlooked, and the range of perceived alternatives is likely to narrow, but not necessarily to the best ones. In these circumstances search activity tends to be dominated by past experience, the misapplication or overgeneralization of which is often a primary source of low-quality decisions.[27]

(2) There is also some evidence that persons experiencing intense stress tend to suffer increased cognitive rigidity, and erosion of general cognitive abilities, including creativity and the ability to cope with complexity. Charles Lindblom suggests that, "a serious emergency or crisis often transforms a policy analyst's perception (and sometimes galvanizes his energies) with the result that he gets a new grasp on his problem."[28] Yet the decision maker is likely to establish a dominant perception through which he interprets information, and to maintain it tenaciously in the face of information that might call for a reappraisal. Often this precept is a familiar one transferred from previous situations (for example, "lessons of history"), even though it may be inappropriate for the circumstances at hand. It is more likely to be characterized by stereotypes than by subtlety as the complexity of the psychological field is reduced. It is neither possible nor wise to change one's beliefs and theories each time some discrepant information is received but it is at least useful to be aware that evidence about an unfolding situation may be consistent with more than a single explanation. Tolerance for ambiguity is likely to suffer from high stress, with the result that conclusions will be drawn more quickly than is warranted by the evidence. Finally, caricatures of motivational structures may develop: the anxious become more anxious, the energetic become more energetic, the repressors become more repressive, and so on.[29]

(3) It has been observed that high-ranking foreign policy officials typically have a high discount rate, assigning high value to immediate achievements, and discounting heavily the value of those that might be realized in a more distant future. Both experimental and historical evidence indicate that high stress tends to result in a shorter time perspective and, as a consequence, a reduced resistance to premature closure.[30]

The consequences of these intervening variables for decision-making tasks may include some of the following:

(1) Search for information about the situation and alternative courses of action, while likely to become more active, also is apt to become more random and less productive. A loss of ability to make subtle discriminations often accompanies intense and protracted stress. As a result, search behavior may be adversely affected in several ways: other actors and their motives are likely to be stereotyped, and the situation itself may be defined in overly simple, one-dimensional terms — for example, that it is a zero-sum situation, or that everything is related to everything else. The ability to invent nonobvious solutions to complex problems may be impaired. As it becomes increasingly evident that optimal solutions are not readily at hand, there may be an increased tendency to persuade oneself that others (e.g., adversaries) are capable of finding a "way out" for all parties, and that their failure to do so is a sign of bad faith. Finally, complex problems are more likely to be defined by "what is already in" (e.g., the decision maker's beliefs, expectations, cognitive and emotional predispositions), and less by the "objective" attributes of the situation. In ambiguous situations or in circumstances of information overload one also may be more likely to screen information and to respond in terms of personal predispositions.[31]

(2) Analysis and evaluation may also be impaired by stress. The ability to identify side effects and unintended consequences of various policy options, especially of "preferred" options, is reduced.[32] That is, there is a tendency to overestimate the benefits of certain alternatives, and to overestimate the costs of others. As the propensities to apply "all or nothing" criteria to the assessment of policy options increases, decision makers may find themselves increasingly persuaded that a single policy will permit all values to be satisfied.

(3) In making choices, individuals vary widely in the decision rules they fall back on when faced with uncertainty, and in the types and degrees of error they are willing to tolerate. Cordell Hull relied upon a set of maxims from Jefferson and Gladstone, Harry S Truman tended to look for applicable lessons from history, and Calvin Coolidge attempted to avoid decisions ("sit down and keep still") in the expectation that many problems would disappear.[33] Other decision rules might include: In case of uncertainty, select policies that have brought success in the past; or, if in doubt, choose the option that will relieve the most proximate danger. When experiencing stress, decision makers are likely to cope by relying on familiar or readily available decision rules, probably employing increasingly crude and undifferentiated versions of them as stress increases. For example, they may find parallels between the present and previous situations and draw upon analogies that are based on superficial rather than fundamental similarities.[34]

(4) In circumstances of high stress there is an increased likelihood that the decision maker may fail to recognize adequately the existence of a conflict between utilities or to believe that a policy option that satisfies one important value will somehow also enable him to satisfy others. In this event motivational conflict and cognitive imbalances are overlooked or suppressed. On the other hand, if the decision maker does recognize the conflict over utilities and the probability that no available alternative will maximize or even satisfy all of them, then this will add

another source of stress to the decision process. This observation illustrates the point made earlier that stress may be created not only by the external situation (e.g., threat to important values), but also by the tasks associated with formulating a response to it.

(5) As stress increases, resistance to pressure for premature closure declines. In some cases any action may be seen preferable to prolonging a decision process that is itself a source of stress.[35] Concomitantly, priorities are likely to shift, with greater emphasis being placed on satisfaction of short-term values. In many circumstances this may be highly functional, but in others it may entail heavy long-term costs.

(6) Sensitivity to and learning from negative feedback about a developing situation may also be affected. Simple learning may be facilitated by stress, but complex learning is generally disrupted. The more difficult and distasteful the decision and the process leading up to it, the greater the tendency to engage in cognitive dissonance reduction through information processing that is biased in favor of evidence supporting the choice, and the lower the probability that the decision will be subject to dispassionate reexamination in the light of subsequent feedback.[36] Thus sensitivity to subtle cues, especially those that suggest the inadequacy of the original decision, tends to decline.

It is true, however, that individuals appear to differ rather widely in the ability to tolerate stress, the threshold at which it begins to impair performance, and strategies for coping with various types of stress. For example, anxious persons tend to suffer a great decrement in cognitive performance and those with experience in stressful situations may fare better.[37] But the personality and other correlates of performance under stress are at best imperfectly understood, and it is hazardous to predict from behavior under normal conditions, or even those of simulated stress. In this connection, Robert Kennedy's recollections of the Cuban missile crisis are worth noting.

> The strain and hours without sleep were beginning to take their toll. However, even many years later, those human weaknesses — impatience, fits of anger — are understandable. Each of us was being asked to make a recommendation which would affect the future of all mankind, a recommendation which, if wrong and if accepted, could mean the destruction of the human race. That kind of pressure does strange things to a human being, even to brilliant, self-confident, mature, experienced men. For some it brings out characteristics and strengths that perhaps they never knew they had, and for others the pressure is too overwhelming.[38]

This brief overview of experimental evidence is suggestive rather than exhaustive. Moreover, the emphasis has been on processes rather than on decision outputs and, just as we cannot assume that "good" processes will ensure high-quality decisions, we cannot assume that erratic processes will always result in low-quality decisions. But even if Figure 1 describes only some modal tendencies rather than unvarying responses to crisis, there is sufficient evidence to call into question the validity of the premise that we always rise to the occasion in crises. The evidence cited here suggests that the causalties of crises and the accompanying high stress may include the very abilities that are most vital for coping with such situations: to establish logical links between present actions and future goals; to search effectively for relevant policy options; to create appropriate responses to unexpected events; to communicate complex ideas; to deal effectively with abstractions; to perceive not only blacks and whites, but also to distinguish them from the many subtle shades of gray that fall in between; to distinguish valid analogies from false ones, and sense from nonsense; and, perhaps most important of all, to enter into the frame of references of others. With respect to these precious cognitive abilities, the law of supply and demand may sometimes operate in a perverse manner; as crisis increases the need for them, it may also diminish the supply.

The vast experimental literature to stress is suggestive, and it can serve as an important source of insights and hypotheses. For several reasons, however, it must be used with caution by the student of foreign policy decision making. Research ethics limit the range of stress-inducing stimuli that may be employed in the laboratory. The situation must of necessity be relatively benign and of short duration. Many studies limit themselves to a single type of stress in order to isolate the effects of the independent variable. The tasks undertaken by subjects who have been exposed to stressful stimuli have tended to be either psychomotor problems such as repairing field telephones or cognitive problems for which there is a clearly defined answer. Relatively few laboratory studies have involved more complicated cognitive processes or highly intellectualized tasks that often confront the policy maker. Subjects usually have been students, who differ by virtue of age and experience from political leaders. Finally, many experimental studies isolate the subject, rather than placing him into a context of groups or organizations, both of which may provide the political leader with supports and/or constraints in performing the required decision-making tasks.

In short, the ultimate test of relevance and validity is not how often one can replicate laboratory experiments on the consequences of stress for cognitive performance, but whether some of the same effects may be found in foreign offices and other venues of policy-making in crises.

Decision-Making in Crises: Comparative Studies

Fortunately, a growing body of comparative systematic research on actual international crises provides less precise but more directly relevant evidence. Before summarizing some of these studies, it may be worth examining research on two of the most dramatic crises of the twentieth century: that leading up to World War I in 1914 and the 1962 Cuban missile confrontation between the United States and the Soviet Union.

The events that gave rise to what is arguably the most consequential war in modern history — World War I — provide perhaps the most compelling evidence of misperceptions, inadequate information processing, and other cognitive malfunctions that significantly shaped the unfolding and outcome of a major international crisis. The state of military technology, European alliance commitments, the balance of power and threats to its stability, contingency plans of foreign and war offices, offensive military doctrines, historical enmities, economic competition, and imperial rivalries undoubtedly created a setting fraught with potential for conflict, and no adequate explanation of World War I can be blind to them. But even if these factors constituted a necessary background, they do not appear sufficient to explain the many decision-making malfunctions that characterized the July crisis. Among the more notable of these were misperceptions of other nations' interests, intentions, and likely responses to certain contingencies (e.g., the subjugation of Serbia); insensitivity to warnings; suppression, distortions, or rejection of information that called into question familiar premises; failures to see errors as the crisis developed; attribution of almost complete freedom of action to adversaries while insisting that virtually insurmountable barriers constrained one's own policy choices; and highly erratic behavior during the culminating hours of the crisis. Lebow's assessment that German policy during the crisis can best be understood in terms of "the cognitive closure of the German political system"[39] is very close to the mark.

The Cuban missile crisis — another frequently analyzed event — seems to have been characterized by higher quality decision processes.[40] American success in obtaining removal of the offensive missiles from Cuba without provoking a war has led many analysts to conclude that President Kennedy and his advisory group (the "ExComm") did so by avoiding some of the more catastrophic errors of their counterparts almost a half-century earlier. Indeed, some of them have noted that Kennedy had read and was influenced by Barbara Tuchman's *Guns of August*, a best-selling account of the misperceptions and miscalculations that characterized policy-making in European capitals during the summer of 1914. Specifically, Kennedy often is credited with creating a decision making environment that encouraged spirited debate on policy options; a sensitivity to likely Soviet perceptions, calculations and responses; a willingness to adopt a less violent strategy of coercive diplomacy in the first instance; some creative efforts to lengthen rather than constrict the time for the Kremlin to ponder its policies; and tight control over the deployment of the naval blockade and other military forces. Thus if 1914 often is described as the classic case of decision making malfunctions exacerbated by crisis-induced stress, the missile crisis is cited almost equally often as the textbook example of ways to avert some of the impediments to effective policy-making in high stress situations. However, recent evidence also indicates that decision processes during the missile crisis deviated in significant ways from the classical norms of analytical decision making. Robert McNamara's depiction of the process is worth noting: "There were deep differences of opinion among us, and very strong feelings about Cuba, and the fact is that we weren't going through an unemotional, orderly, and comprehensive analytical decision-making process."

Aside from underscoring the obvious point that crisis processes and outcomes may differ significantly, the evidence from 1914 and 1962 raises further questions about the relevance of explanations that focus on decision-making performance with an emphasis on information processing and other cognitive tasks.[41] Specifically, did changes in the international system between 1914 and 1962, resulting in different constraints and strategies for pursuing national interests, account for the different behavior in the two crises? Or, even if one accepts an interpretation that attaches substantial significance to the crisis-induced stress on decision making in 1914 — and many do not — was this a deviant case of limited theoretical and policy relevance? A somewhat similar argument could, of course, be developed with respect to the missile crisis.

Fortunately, it is not necessary to rely solely on evidence adduced from these two frequently studied cases. Recent years have witnessed the development of a rather substantial literature of systematic and comparative crisis studies, providing a base of evidence that goes well beyond the dramatic events of 1914 and 1962.

- Snyder and Diesing undertook a study of 16 crises, including five occurring prior to World War I, three during the interwar period, and eight since World War II. Their impressive research is impossible to summarize briefly, but a few findings of special relevance are worth citing. They found ample evidence of stereotyped thinking, restricted search for alternatives, and impaired ability to estimate the consequences of action, but unlike some students of crisis, they question whether these decision-making malfunctions can be traced to time pressures. Rather, "the cause must lie in some other stress-producing aspect, such as having to make difficult trade-offs between important values and high risks in a situation of considerable uncertainty."[42] Of special relevance is the finding that information processing during crises was generally rather poor, as only 40% of the messages between governments were correctly interpreted, with the remainder incorrectly interpreted (52%) or distorted in transmission (8%). Although they found that the accuracy of interpretation increased during the culminating stages of crises, incorrect information processing ranks high among the authors' tentative conclusions about the causes of war.[43]
- Drawing on his research on Israeli behavior during the crises of 1956, 1967, and 1970, Brecher found strong support for the hypotheses that time will be perceived as more salient, decision makers will become more concerned with the immediate rather than the distant future, and that they will perceive the range of alternatives open to themselves to be narrow.[44]
  On the other hand, a study of American decision making during the Berlin blockade, using the Brecher research design, found relatively few adverse consequences of the crisis. Despite manifestations of cognitive rigidity and fatigue. "The widely held assumption that high stress is necessarily dysfunctional finds little support in the Berlin case study."[45]
- Lebow's study of international crises also raises questions about the quality of decision making. His work is based on 26 cases, spanning the period between 1898 (Fashoda, Cuba) and 1962 (missiles in Cuba), ranging in duration from a week (Dogger Bank) to 311 days (Berlin Blockade), and resulting in a variety of outcomes — including war, both diplomatic victories and defeats for the initiator, and

compromise settlements. Using both cognitive and motivational models, and drawing upon the work of Robert Jervis and Irving Janis, respectively, he explains the often erratic behavior of policy makers in crises. They often pursued strategies based on unrealistic judgments of how their adversaries would respond. The expectation that opponents would back down was justified only in three of 14 "brinkmanship" crises, two of which involved Nazi Germany (Rhineland, Munich); the remainder of the cases resulted in war (5), compromise settlement (2), or the initiator being forced to back down (4).[46]

It may be worth noting that although Lebow's case studies and definition of crisis overlap substantially with those selected by Snyder and Diesing — nine of the crises appear in both studies — their interpretations of the evidence do not always coincide. For example, whereas Snyder and Diesing found that decision makers in crisis are often able to change their strategies in the face of new information about adversaries, Lebow concludes that "learning during a crisis is likely to be hindered by the same impediments that caused the initiator to misjudge his adversary's resolve in the first place."[47] Another of several important disagreements concerns the impact of time pressure. Snyder and Diesing indicate that the longer a crisis lasts the more likely it is to get out of control, but Lebow comes to the opposite conclusion.

- Smoke's analysis of escalation is also relevant for present purposes. It encompasses five case studies, including the Seven Years War, the Crimean War, the Austro-Prussian War, the Franco-Prussian War, and the Spanish Civil War. Escalation of conflict was accompanied by some of the same perceptual and cognitive consequences found in crisis studies, including a narrowing range of expectations and a sense of a closing future created by the adversary's actions. "The subjective future closes in faster than one anticipates it should because it is closing in for psychological, and not just objective, reasons."[48]

- Suedfeld, Tetlock, and their colleagues, in their crisis studies, focused on conceptual complexity in information processing. Conceptual complexity is defined as the ability to make accurate distinctions, the integration of large amounts of diverse information in making coherent judgments, flexibility, and high-quality information processing in stressful or information overload situations, whereas conceptual simplicity is characterized by simple responses, gross distinctions, rigidity, and restricted information usage. A standard scoring technique was used to code documentary materials from a wide range of crises (e.g., World War I, Cuban missile crisis, Morocco, Berlin Blockade, Korean War) as well as more extended periods of time centering on the Middle East and Soviet-American relations. Their findings reveal substantial, although not uniform, support for hypotheses linking crisis-induced stress to cognitive simplicity, on the one hand, and nonviolent conflict resolution to cognitive complexity on the other.[49]

Crisis Management in the Nuclear Age

Not surprisingly, the findings concerning decision-making performance in crises is somewhat mixed. Not all crises spin out of control owing to misperceptions, miscalculations, or other cognitive malfunctions. Although the period since World War II has witnessed repeated crises and many instances of deterrence failure, it has been relatively free of direct violence between the major powers. Several explanations have been offered.

- The existence of nuclear weapons has dramatically changed the payoffs for war. Thus, whatever the decision-making shortcomings that may occur in crises, the threat of nuclear war is such a dominating aspect of reality that any group of leaders short of the clinically-suicidal will be restrained, cautious, and calculating. The Cuban missile crisis, according to one analysis, demonstrated that "the possibility of irreparable harm" resulting from nuclear war "makes clear why neither Nikita Khrushchev nor John Kennedy behaved like the irrational juvenile delinquents who are sometimes presumed to occupy the seats of power today, strapped by their seatbelts in a carefree game of chicken."[50]
- Crises may serve as surrogates for war, offering means of effecting needed changes in the international system.[51] They may even give rise to more stable relations between adversaries. The period immediately following the missile crisis, which witnessed several major steps to stabilize relations between Washington and Moscow, is often cited as evidence.
- Because policy makers learn from their experiences, crises tend to become "routinized" and therefore less dangerous. "Output received from occurrences and situations in the international environment and from sequences of international interaction are processed by the advanced modernizing social organizations according to their perceived characteristics: if these outputs are recognized as familiar and expected experiences met repeatedly in the remembered past, they will be treated in a highly routine fashion." The participants gain experience in ways of coping with the environment and adversaries and, although threats and challenges may continue to characterize relations between parties, uncertainty is reduced. Thus, "repeated exposure to acute crises may reduce the probabilities of an outbreak of general war."[52]

No doubt there are important elements of truth in each of these propositions. Yet the suspicion lingers that even the experience of more than four decades without nuclear war does not establish conclusively that policy makers have now become immune to decision-making malfunctions that could result in an unwanted and unforeseen war. A recent biography reveals that five times during 1954 alone, President Eisenhower resisted substantial pressure from his advisers in the National Security Council, Joint Chiefs of Staff, and State Department to use nuclear weapons against China.[53] Interpreting this evidence is not unlike determining whether the glass is half empty or half full. Do we draw reassurance from Eisenhower's rejection of the advice, or do we ponder whether another leader, with less experience in military affairs or a different belief system, might have decided differently?

Such questions have provided an impetus for several proposals for rationalizing crisis management. The basic task, however, is far more easily described than accomplished: Protect one's most vital national interests without provoking war, through a skillful blend of coercion and accommodation. Prescriptive theories dealing with this matter span a broad range. Differences among them usually are rooted in varying images of the opponent, its probable responses to coercion and accommodation, and the primary threats against which one must guard.

(1) One position assumes that the adversary is a thoroughly rational actor whose policies reflect a careful calculation and appreciation of the opportunities and dangers in an emerging situation. The primary task of crisis management therefore is to communicate one's interests and demands as unambiguously as possible, while avoiding concessions, for those will merely encourage the opponent to make further demands. Accommodation misleads the adversary and postpones rather than avoids war. With a clear exposition of one's interests and an unconditional determination to protect them, the opponent will either be forced to back down (ending the crisis on favorable terms for oneself) or to escalate (thus exposing his lack of interest in resolving it on terms short of one's capitulation). Strategies of crisis management thus include "burning one's bridges" and other steps that will convey to adversaries an unambiguous signal of one's resolve and commitment.[54]

(2) A different approach to crisis management places emphasis not only on protecting one's primary interests but also on avoiding actions that might drive either side into a mutually undesirable process of escalation, ending in war. This view incorporates somewhat less heroic assumptions about either side's ability to overcome constraints on rational decision making, especially under the pressures of crisis. Instead of burning bridges, advocates recall with approval Sun Tzu's dictum, from *The Art of War*, that one should build golden bridges behind one's adversaries. Consequently, crisis management proposals deal with both decision processes and the substance of policies. Illustrating the former is an essay that directly addresses some disruptive manifestations of stress on decision making, with special emphasis on the following areas: fixation on only one reasonable option, simplification of the adversary and his limitations, physical fatigue, collapsed time perspective and neglect of future consequences, and excessive concurrence seeking. The essay suggests some indicators that may be used for monitoring decision processes as well as some possible prescriptions for coping with them.[55]

The Cuban missile crisis offers an excellent illustration of the difference between this and the previous approach. Several members of the ExComm, including Maxwell Taylor, Douglas Dillon, and Paul Nitze, were convinced that more forceful action such as an air attack on missile sites would not provoke a violent Soviet response. As Taylor put it, one need not fear such a response unless Nikita Khrushchev was "crazy and full of vodka," in which case "his colleagues in Moscow would take care of him." Dillon similarly dismissed the fear that conventional military action could lead to nuclear war as "preposterous." In contrast, Robert McNamara and Dean Rusk were far less confident that the Soviets would be forced to act with restraint because of overall American nuclear superiority and a conventional advantage in the Caribbean area. The former proposed "McNamara's Law": "It is impossible to predict with a high degree of confidence what the effects of the use of military force will be."[56] The essential difference between those two groups was thus in perceptions of Soviet leadership and decision processes.

(3) Crisis management prescriptions also deal with actions to reduce the incentives for the opponent — whose rationality may not be without limits in high-stress situations — to escalate or even launch a preemptive attack out of fear ("he who hesitates is lost"), miscalculation, or similar motives. For example, George emphasizes

> presidential control of military options, pauses in military operations to give the opponent time to assess the situation and to respond to proposals, military moves that constitute clear and appropriate demonstrations of one's resolve and limited crisis objectives, military moves closely coordinated with political-diplomatic actions and communications as part of an integrated strategy for persuading the opponent to alter his policy and behavior in the desired direction, confidence in the discriminating character as well as the effectiveness of military options, military moves that avoid motivating the opponent to escalate, and avoidance of impression of resort to large-scale warfare."[57]

(4) The relevant literature also includes prescriptive theories that deal more broadly with the various cognitive, bureaucratic, and other constraints of rationality in the decision-making process. Contributions of this type include the following:

- George has offered suggestions for improving the quality of information and advice available to top-ranking leaders through a system of "multiple advocacy."[58]
- Janis's analysis of high-quality decisions and fiascoes has led him to propose a number of steps to reduce the likelihood that decision groups will be afflicted by "groupthink."[59]
- Allison and Steinbruner deal with a number of suggestions for improving the quality of organizational decision making. For example, both discuss the limitations and possible dangers of the conventional premise that governments behave like unitary rational actors.[60]
- Drawing upon their detailed analyses of the missile crisis, Blight and Welch propose that further policy-relevant work must go beyond the cognitive aspects of decision making to give greater attention to such emotional factors as fear.[61]

Although there is some convergence in this literature — for example, on the importance of slowing the pace of events to relieve time pressure on policy makers — the entire effort has elicited some rather sharp critiques. One is that these prescriptions are banal and "about as useful as general advice to hospital room personnel — keep calm, have equipment ready, and make no premature diagnoses."[62] Another survey of the literature concludes that the results adduced from crisis research are deficient in several important respects: claims for crisis management prescriptions are insufficiently modest; much of the advice consists of epigrams that are, at best, little more sophisticated than common sense, and thus hardly merit extensive research and, at worst, are dangerously simplistic; many crisis situations are intractable and thus impervious to crisis management advice; and prescriptions are too heavily oriented to process.[63]

There is no doubt some validity to these points, but the criticism also seems to be based in part on a misunderstanding. Crisis research has been motivated less by naive aspirations to create cookbook recipes for coping with crises than by the hope that one might at least lay open to serious scrutiny, through rigorous research, some of the received truths that often underlie official thinking about deterrence, coercive diplomacy, crisis management, and other aspects of international affairs.

A somewhat different charge is that students of crisis are critical of the rational actor model of foreign policy, and yet they propose antidotes to decision-making failures based on precisely that model. The belief that crisis can be managed more effectively is described as a defense mechanism that policy-makers and social scientists have erected to protect themselves from anxiety about the consequences of nuclear war.[64]

This is not the place to speculate about the deeper motives of crisis management theorists or to engage in a thorough analysis of the "epigrams" they have offered. Perhaps the enterprise is indeed a delusion, but what is the alternative? There is surely no guarantee that systematic probes into cognitive, motivational, and other decision-making malfunctions will yield greater wisdom and ultimately enable us to better defuse crises. But is it a more dangerous delusion than reliance on the epigrams that so often guide foreign policies: the *para bellum* doctrine, the "domino theory," "the lessons of Munich," the "lessons of Vietnam" (of which there are many, often mutually exclusive versions), or the other, often unexamined axioms that have at times served as substitutes for analysis of foreign policy situations?[65]

In the final analysis, however, one criticism cannot easily be dismissed. Even far better crisis management theories than are presently available — or foreseeable — would be an inadequate basis on which to pin too many hopes. It is instructive to recall the point made by those who claimed responsibility for the effort to assassinate Prime Minister Thatcher and her cabinet in October 1984: "We failed this time, but *we* only have to be lucky *once.*" In nuclear crises, we only have to be unlucky once.

Crisis management, in short, is no substitute for crisis avoidance. Even decision making in the Cuban missile crisis, often depicted as a source of important lessons about sensitive and effective crisis management, has drawn some criticism, and not only from purveyors of a vulgar psycho-McCarthyism that has depicted Kennedy as bringing the world to the brink of nuclear holocaust as the direct result of deep-seated character or personality defects. Among thoughtful critiques from a cognitive perspective, those of Lebow and Snyder stand out.[66] They have questioned whether Kennedy permitted, much less encouraged, open debates in the ExComm, citing, for example, the derisive treatment accorded to UN Ambassador Stevenson, who proposed bargaining rather than coercive diplomacy to gain removal of the missiles from Cuba. Lebow depicts Kennedy's leadership as "promotional" rather than open. Snyder's conclusion is that, despite frequent depictions of the ExComm's decision processes as a model of openness and rationality, the President and his advisers perceived only the single option of a relentless policy based on coercion, rejecting any tradeoff of values. These are the characteristics of a cognitive rather than an analytical decision maker.[67]

But perhaps the most authoritative words of sobriety, addressed to those who may have become overly enthusiastic about adducing formulas for crisis management from the missile episode, came from President Kennedy himself. He remarked, some weeks after the crisis, "You can't have too many of those." That point is underscored by Robert McNamara. " 'Managing' crises is the wrong term; you don't 'manage' them because you *can't* 'manage' them. . . . And that holds whether or not you're talking about a nuclear crisis."[68]

Finally, the missile crisis — and many other crises as well — appears to have an important lesson for scholars about the inadequacy of structural realism and rational choice approaches as models for all seasons and all reasons. Any serious effort to understand crisis decision making and to improve our ability to cope with crises must also be able to deal with the nonrational elements of the policy process. We must, in short, incorporate political psychology as a central element, rather than as a residual category, into our analyses.

Notes

1. Richard M. Nixon, *Six Crises* (New York: Doubleday, 1960), xvi, 105.

2. Herman Kahn, *On Escalation: Metaphors and Scenarios* (New York: Praeger, 1965), 38; Albert Wohlstetter and Roberta Wohlstetter, "Controlling the Risks in Cuba," in *The Use of Force,* eds. Robert J. Art and Kenneth N. Waltz (Boston: Little, Brown, 1971), 263.

3. Chris Argyris, *Some Causes of Organizational Ineffectiveness Within the Department of State* (Washington: Center for International Systems Research, Department of State Publication 8180, 1967), 42.

4. Dwight D. Eisenhower, "Address to *Washington Post* Book and Author Lunch," quoted in *Palo Alto Times* (1 October 1965).

5. Richard E. Neustadt, *Alliance Politics* (New York: Columbia University Press, 1970), 116.

6. Charles F. Hermann, "Some Consequences of Crisis which Limit the Viability of Organizations," *Administrative Science Quarterly* 8 (1963): 61-82. This definition has achieved moderately wide acceptance among students of foreign policy crises, but some have criticized the inclusion of surprise as a part of the definition. Surprise is included in the present essay because, whether or not it is a necessary condition for a crisis, there is evidence that it exacerbates stress for decision makers. For further discussions of the term crisis, see Charles F. Hermann, *Crisis in Foreign Policy: A Simulation Analysis* (Indianapolis: Bobbs-Merrill, 1969); Charles F. Hermann, "International Crisis as a Situational Variable," in *International Politics and Foreign Policy*, rev. ed., ed. James N. Rosenau (New York: Free Press, 1969), 409-421; Charles F. Hermann, ed., *International Crisis: Insights from Behavioral Research* (New York: Free Press, 1972); James A. Robinson, "Crisis: An Appraisal of Concepts and Theories," in *International Crisis,* ed. Hermann (New York: Free Press, 1972); Kent Miller and Ira Iscoe, "The Concept of Crisis: Current Status and Mental Health Implications," *Human Organization* 22 (1963): 195-201; Glenn H. Snyder and Paul Diesing, *Conflict Among Nations: Bargaining, Decision Making and System Structure in International Crises* (Princeton, NJ: Princeton University Press, 1977); Richard W. Parker, "An Examination of Basic and Applied International Crisis Research," *International Studies Quarterly* 21 (1977): 225-246; Raymond Tanter, "Crisis Management: A Critical Review of Academic Literature," *Jerusalem Journal of International Relations* 2 (1975): 71-101; Richard G. Head, Frisco W. Short, and Robert C. McFarlane, *Crisis Resolution: Presidential Decision Making in the Mayaguez and Korean Confrontation* (Boulder, CO: Westview, 1978); Michael Brecher, Jonathan Wilkenfeld, and S. Moser, *Crisis in the Twentieth Century* (New York: Pergamon, 1988); Brecher and Wilkenfeld, *Crisis, Conflict and Instability* (New York: Pergamon, 1989); and Irving L. Janis, *Crucial Decisions: Leadership in Policy Making and Crisis Management* (New York: Free Press, 1989).

7. Michael Howard, *The Causes of War* (Cambridge, MA: Harvard University Press, 1983), 22.

8. Theodore Abel, "The Element of Decision in the Pattern of War," *American Sociological Review* VI (1941): 855. For excellent empirical studies of deterrence and deterrence failure, see Alexander L. George and Richard Smoke, *Deterrence in American Foreign Policy* (New York: Columbia University Press, 1974); Robert Jervis, Richard Ned Lebow and Janice G. Stein, *Psychology and Deterrence* (Baltimore, MD: Johns Hopkins Press, 1985); and Paul K. Huth, *Extended Deterrence and the Prevention of War* (New Haven, CT: Yale University Press, 1988).

9. Thomas C. Schelling, *The Strategy of Conflict* (New York: Oxford University Press, 1963), 4.

10. Harold Wilensky, *Organizational Intelligence: Knowledge and Policy in Government and Industry* (New York: Basic Books, 1967): 76-81, 175-179; and Theodore Lowi, *The End of Liberalism: Ideology, Policy, and the Crisis of Public Authority* (New York: Norton, 1969): 158-160.

11. Sidney Verba, "Assumptions of Rationality and Nonrationality in Models of the International System," *World Politics*, 14 (October 1961): 115.

12. Graham Allison, *Essence of Decision: Explaining the Cuban Missile Crisis* (Boston: Little, Brown, 1971).

13. Neustadt, *Alliance Politics*.

14. Joseph De Rivera, *The Psychological Dimension of Foreign Policy* (Columbus, OH: Merrill, 1968); Glenn D. Paige, *The Korean Decision* (New York: Free Press, 1968); Alexander L. George, "Adaptation to Stress in Political Decision-Making," in *Coping and Adaptation*, ed. G. V. Coelho, David A. Hamburg, and J. Adams (New York: Basic Books, 1974); Irving Janis, *Victims of Groupthink* (Boston: Houghton Mifflin, 1972); and Janis, *Groupthink* (Boston: Houghton Mifflin, 1982).

15. Janis, *Victims of Groupthink*; and Janis, *Groupthink*.

16. Compare, for example, Barry Schneider, "Danger and Opportunity" (unpublished doctoral dissertation) (Columbia University, 1974); and Alexander L. George, *Presidential Decisionmaking in Foreign Policy: The Effective Use of Information and Advice* (Boulder, CO: Westview, 1980), 97, and the literature cited there.

17. Paul E. Torrance, "Group Decision-Making and Disagreement," *Social Forces*, 35 (1957): 314-327; and Torrance, "A Theory of "Leadership and Interpersonal Behavior Under Stress," in *Leadership and Interpersonal Behavior*, eds. Luigi Petrullo and Bernard M. Bass (New York: Holt, Rinehart, & Winston, 1961), 100-117.

18. Among the many relevant works, see especially, Leon Festinger, *A Theory of Cognitive Dissonance* (Evanston, IL: Row, Peterson, 1957); Irving Janis and Leon Mann, *Decision-Making* (New York: Free Press, 1977); George, *Presidential Decisionmaking*; John Steinbruner, *The Cybernetic Theory of Decision* (Princeton, NJ: Princeton University Press, 1974); Robert Jervis, *Perception and Misperception in International Politics* (Princeton, NJ: Princeton University Press, 1976); Robert Axelrod, *The Structure of Decision* (Princeton, NJ: Princeton University Press, 1976); Ole R. Holsti, *Crisis, Escalation, War*; Richard Ned Lebow, *Between Peace and War* (Baltimore, MD: Johns Hopkins University Press, 1981); Richard Cottam, *Foreign Policy Motivation* (Pittsburgh: University of Pittsburgh Press, 1977); Ralph K. White, *Nobody Wanted War: Misperception in Vietnam and Other Wars* (New York: Doubleday/Anchor, 1970); White, *Fearful Warriors: A Psychological Profile of U.S.-Soviet Relations* (New York: Free Press, 1984); and Irving L. Janis, *Crucial Decisions: Leadership in Policy-Making and Crisis Management* (New York: Free Press, 1989).

19. James G. March and Herbert Simon, *Organizations* (New York: Wiley, 1958), 138.

20. Somewhat different lists appear in Patrick M. Morgan, *Deterrence: A Conceptual Analysis* (Beverly Hills, CA: Sage, 1977), 102-103; Janis and Mann, *Decision-Making*; and George, *Presidential Decisionmaking*, 10.

21. Sheldon J. Korchin and Seymour Levine, "Anxiety and Verbal Learning," *Journal of Abnormal and Social Psychology* 54 (1957): 234-240.

22. For a further elaboration of this point, see Alexander L. George, "Toward a More Soundly Based Foreign Policy: Making Better Use of Information," Appendix D, Vol. II, *Report of the Commission on the Organization of the Government for the Conduct of Foreign Policy* (Washington, DC: Government Printing Office, 1975), see especially pp. 17-53.

23. Alfred Lowe, "Individual Differences in Reaction to Failure: Modes of Coping with Anxiety and Interference Proneness," *Journal of Abnormal and Social Psychology* 62 (1961): 303-308; and Sara B. Kiesler, "Stress, Affiliation and Performance," *Journal of Experimental Research in Personality* I (1966): 227-235.

24. Sheldon J. Korchin et al., "Visual Discrimination and the Decision Process in Anxiety," *AMA Archive of Neurology and Psychiatry* 78 (1957): 424-438; Robert E. Murphy, "Effects of Threat of Shock, Distraction, and Task Design on Performance," *Journal of Experimental Psychology* 58 (1959): 134-141; Harold M. Schroeder, Michael J. Driver, and Siegfried Streufert, *Human Information Processing* (New York: Holt, Rinehart, & Winston, 1967); C. R. Anderson, "Coping Behavior as Intervening Mechanisms in the Inverted-U Stress-Performance Relationship," *Journal of Applied Psychology* 60 (1976): 30-34; R. R. Grinker and J. P. Spiegel, *Men Under Stress* (New York: McGraw-Hill, 1945); E. Paul Torrance, "A Theory of Leadership and Interpersonal Behavior Under Stress," in *Leadership and Interpersonal Behavior*, eds. Luigi Petrullo and Bernard M. Bass (New York: Holt, Rinehart, & Winston, 1961), 100-117; George W. Baker, and Dwight W. Chapman, eds., *Man and Society in Disaster* (New York: Basic Books, 1962); and A. D. Baddeley, "Selective Attention and Performance in Dangerous Environments," *British Journal of Psychology* 63 (1972): 537-546; Leo Postman and Jerome Bruner, "Perception Under Stress," *Psychological Review*, 55 (1948): 322; Richard S. Lazarus, James R. Averill, and Edward M. Opton, Jr., "The Assessment of Coping," in *Coping and Adaptation*; D. Krech and R. S. Crutchfield, quoted in Sheldon J. Korchin, "Anxiety and Cognition," in *Cognition: Theory, Research and Promise*, ed. Constance Sheerer, (New York: Harper & Row, 1964), 63; Thomas W. Milburn, "The Management of Crisis," in *International Crises: Insights from Behavioral Research*, ed. Charles F. Hermann (New York: Free Press, 1972), 265; and James Joll, *1914: The Unspoken Assumption* (London: Weidenfield and Nicolson, 1968), 6. The psychobiological effects of crisis and stress are discussed in Thomas C. Wiegele, "Models of Stress and Disturbances in Elite Political Behaviors: Psychological Variables and Political Decision-Making," in *Psychopathology and Political Leadership*, ed. Robert S. Robins (New Orleans: Tulane Studies in Political Science, 1977); Wiegele, "Decision Making in an International Crisis: Some Biological Factors," *International Studies Quarterly*, 17 (1973): 295-335; and Wiegele, *Leaders Under Stress: A Psychophysiological Analysis of International Crisis* (Durham, NC: Duke University Press, 1985).

25. More comprehensive summaries may be found in Richard S. Lazarus, James Deese, and Sonia F. Osler, "The Effects of Psychological Stress Upon Performance," *Psychological Bulletin* 49 (1952): 392-317; Fred E. Horvath, "Psychological Stress: A Review of Definitions and Experimental Research," in *General Systems: Yearbook of the Society for General Systems Research*, 4, eds. Ludwig von Bertalanffy and Anatol Rapoport (1959): 203-230; C. N. Coffer and M. H. Appley, *Motivation: Theory and Research* (New York: Wiley, 1964); Irving Janis and Howard Leventhal, "Human Reaction to Stress" in *Handbook of Personality Theory and Research* eds. Edgar F. Borgatta and William W. Lambert (Chicago: Rand McNally, 1968), 1041-1085; Lazarus, Averill and Opton, "The Assessment of Coping"; Holsti, *Crisis, Escalation, War*; Milburn, "The Management of Crisis"; Charles F. Hermann and Linda P. Brady, "Alternative Models of International Crisis Behavior" in *International Crisis*; Irving Janis, *Stress and Frustration* (New York: Harcourt Brace Jovanovich, 1973); and D. E. Broadbent, *Decision and Stress* (London: Academic Press, 1971).

26. James G. Miller, "Information Input Overload and Psychopathology," *American Journal of Psychiatry*, 66 (1960): 695; Miller, "Information Input Overload," in *Self-Organizing Systems*, eds. M. C. Yovits, G. T. Jacobi, and G. D. Goldstein (Washington, DC: Spartan Books, 1962), 61-78; Holsti, *Crisis, Escalation, War*, 104-118; A. D. Baddeley, "Selective Attention and Performance in Dangerous Environments," *British Journal of Psychology* 63 (1972): 537-546; Harry B. Williams, "Some Functions of Communication in Crisis Behavior," *Human Organization* 16 (1957): 15-19; and Hermann, "Some Consequences of Crisis which Limit the Viability of Organizations."

27. Broadbent, *Decision and Stress*, 16; Glenn D. Paige, *The Korean Decision* (New York: Free Press, 1968), 48; Milburn, "The Management of Crisis," 265; and Norman R. F. Maier, *Problem-Solving Discussions and Conferences* (New York: McGraw-Hill, 1963), 221.

28. Charles E. Lindblom. *The Policy-Making Process* (Englewood Cliffs, NJ: Prentice-Hall, 1968), 22.

29. Fredric B. Nalven, "Defense Preference and Perceptual Decision-Making," (unpublished doctoral dissertation) (Boston: Boston University, 1961), abstracted in Paul Wasserman and Fred S. Silander, *Decision-Making: An Annotated Bibliography, Supplement, 1958-1963* (Ithaca, NY: Cornell University, 1964), 78; Melvin Manis, *Cognitive Processes* (Belmont, CA: Wadsworth, 1966), 97-102; F. P. Kilpatrick, "Problems of Perception in Extreme Situations," in *Readings in Collective Behavior,* ed. Robert R. Evans (Chicago: Rand McNally, 1969), 169, 171; Ralph K. White and Ronald Lippitt, *Autocracy and Democracy: An Experimental Inquiry* (New York: Harper, 1960), 171; M. Brewster Smith, Jerome S. Bruner, and Robert W. White, *Opinions and Personality* (New York: Wiley, 1956); Robert Jervis, "Hypotheses on Misperception," *World Politics* 20 (1968): 454-479; Jervis, *Perception and Misperception*; C. D. Smock, "The Influence of Psychological Stress on the 'Intolerance of Ambiguity,' " *Journal of Abnormal and Social Psychology* 50 (1955): 177-182; and Milburn, "The Management of Crisis," 265.

30. Graham T. Allison and Morton H. Halperin, "Bureaucratic Politics: A Paradigm and Some Policy Implications," *World Politics* 24 (1972, supplement): 40-79; Holsti, *Crisis, Escalation, War,* 14-17, 119-142; Samuel T. Cohen and A. G. Mezey, "The Effects of Anxiety on Time Judgment and Time Experience in Normal Persons," *Journal of Neurology, Neurosurgery and Psychiatry* 24 (1961): 266-268; Harry B. Williams and Jeannette F. Rayner, "Emergency Medical Services in Disaster," *Medical Annals of the District of Columbia* 25 (1956): 655-662; Jonas Langer, Seymour Wapner, and Heinz Werner, "The Effects of Danger Upon the Experience of Time," *American Journal of Psychology* 74 (1961): 94-97; John Cohen, "Psychological Time," *Scientific American* 211 (November 1964): 116-124; George Usdansky and Loren J. Chapman, "Schizophrenic-Like Response in Normal Subjects under Time Pressure," *Journal of Abnormal and Social Psychology* 60 (1960): 143-146; Pauline N. Pepinsky and William B. Pavlik, "The Effects of Task Complexity and Time Pressure Upon Team Productivity," *Journal of Applied Psychology* 44 (1960): 34-38; N. H. Mackworth, and J. F. Mackworth, "Visual Search for Successive Decisions," *British Journal of Psychology* 40 (1958); Herbert G. Birch, "Motivational Factors in Insightful Problem-Solving," *Journal of Comparative Psychology* 37 (1945): 295-317; Bruner et al., *A Study of Thinking*; Peter Dubno, "Decision Time Characteristics of Leaders and Group Problem Solving Behavior," *Journal of Social Psychology* 59 (1963): 259-282; F. E. Horvath, "Psychological Stress"; and Donald R. Hoffeld and S. Carolyn Kent, "Decision Time and Information Use in Choice Situations," *Psychological Reports* 12 (1963): 68-70.

31. March and Simon, *Organizations*, 116; Milburn, "The Management of Crisis," 275; Holsti, *Crisis, Escalation, War,* 143-168; Jerome Bruner, cited in Louis C. Gawthrop, *Bureaucratic Behavior in the Executive Branch* (New York: Free Press, 1969), 113; Siegfried Streufert, Michael J. Driver, and Kenneth W. Haun, "Components of Response Rate in Complex Decision-Making," *Journal of Social Psychology* 3 (1967): 286-295; George A. Miller, "The Magical Number Seven Plus or Minus Two: Some Limits on Our Capacity for Processing Information," *Psychological Review* 63 (1956): 81-97; Karl E. Weick, "Processes of Ramification Among Cognitive Links," in *Theories of Cognitive Consistency* eds. Robert P. Abelson et al. (Chicago: Rand McNally, 1968), 516-517; and Jerome E. Singer, "Consistency as a Stimulus Processing Mechanism," in *Theories of Cognitive Consistency*, 337-342. The tendency to see events as linked to each other is illustrated by the events of October 1962. When news of China's invasion of India reached those who were grappling with the problem of Soviet missiles in Cuba, some of them initially assumed that the two events were linked as part of a worldwide assault on the non-communist world, even though by this time there was no shortage of evidence indicating a deep split between Moscow and Peking.

32. Milburn, "The Management of Crisis," 273.

33. Cordell Hull, *Memoirs* (New York: Macmillan, 1948), cited in George, "Adaptation to Stress"; and Richard Fenno, *The President's Cabinet* (Cambridge, MA: Harvard University Press, 1959), cited in George, "Adaptation to Stress."

34. Kilpatrick, "Problems of Perception," 171; White and Lippitt, *Autocracy and Democracy*, 171-173; and Milburn, "The Management of Crisis," 274. For historical evidence on the uses and misuses of the "lessons of history," see Ernest R. May, *"Lessons" of the Past: The Use and Misuse of History in American Foreign Policy* (New York: Oxford University Press, 1973); Robert Jervis,

Perception and Misperception in International Politics; and Richard E. Neustadt and Ernest R. May, *Thinking in Time: The Uses of History for Decision-Makers* (New York: Free Press, 1986).

35. On the basis of the "six crises" he experienced up to the 1960 election, Richard Nixon observed: ' Decisive action relieves the tension which builds up in a crisis. When the situation requires that an individual restrain himself from acting decisively over a long period, this can be the most wearing of all crises" (Nixon, *Six Crises*, 113).

36. This is one of the nonobvious predictions of cognitive dissonance theory that has been supported in repeated experiments. Festinger, *A Theory of Cognitive Dissonance*.

37. Nathan Kogan and Michael Wallach, *Risk-Taking: A Study in Cognition and Personality* (New York: Holt, Rinehart, & Winston, 1964); and Baddeley, "Selective Attention."

38. Robert F. Kennedy, *Thirteen Days* (New York: Norton, 1969), 22.

39. Lebow, *Between Peace and War*, 119.

40. Among the many studies are Allison, *Essence of Decision*; Lebow, *Between Peace and War*; Janis, *Groupthink*; Glenn H. Snyder and Paul Diesing, *Conflict Among Nations*; Alexander L. George, David K. Hall, and William W. Simons, *The Limits of Coercive Diplomacy* (Boston: Little, Brown, 1971); Holsti, *Crisis, Escalation, War*; Alexander L. George and Richard Smoke, *Deterrence in American Foreign Policy* (New York: Columbia University Press, 1974); Wohlstetter and Wohlstetter, "Controlling the Risks in Cuba"; Jack L. Snyder, "Rationality at the Brink: The Role of Cognitive Processes in Failures of Deterrence," *World Politics*, 30 (1978). 345-365; James A. Nathan, "The Missile Crisis: His Finest Hour Now," *World Politics*, 27 (1975): 256-281; Roberta Wohlstetter, "Cuba and Pearl Harbor," *Foreign Affairs*, 43 (1965): 691-707; Paul Anderson, "Decision Making by Objection and the Cuban Missile Crisis," *Administrative Science Quarterly*, 28 (1983): 201-222; and Fen Osler Hampson, "The Divided Decision-Maker: American Domestic Politics and the Cuban Crises," *International Security* 9 (1984-85): 130-165. Excluded from the very partial list are the many memoirs and journalistic accounts of the crisis. Since the studies cited above, transcripts of some ExComm deliberations have been published. Moreover, several conferences, including American and Soviet officials involved in the missile crisis, have been held. These materials are indispensable to any analysis of that crisis. See James G. Blight and David A. Welch, *On the Brink: Americans and Soviets Reexamine the Cuban Missile Crisis* (New York: Hill and Wang, 1989); James G. Blight, Joseph S. Nye, Jr., and David A. Welch, "The Cuban Missile Crisis Revisited," *Foreign Affairs* 66 (1987): 170-188; David A. Welch and James G. Blight, "An Introduction to the ExComm Transcripts," *International Security* 12 (1987-88): 5-29; White House, "Tapes and Minutes of the Cuban Missile Crisis," *International Security* 10 (1985): 164-203; McGeorge Bundy and James G. Blight, eds., "October 27, 1962: Transcripts of the Meetings of the ExComm," *International Security* 12 (1987-1988): 30-92; and Bruce J. Allyn, James G. Blight, and David A. Welch, "Essence of Revision: Moscow, Havana, and the Cuban Missile Crisis," *International Security* 14 (1989-90): 136-172. The McNamara quotation is from Blight and Welch, 51.

41. For a spirited debate on the relationship of process to outcome in crisis decision making, see G. M. Herek, Irving L. Janis, and Paul Huth, "Decision Making During International Crises: Is Quality of Process Related to Outcome?" *Journal of Conflict Resolution* 31 (1987): 203-226; a critique focused on the Cuban missile crisis by David A. Welch, "Crisis Decision Making Reconsidered," *Journal of Conflict Resolution* 33 (1989): 430-445; and a rejoinder by Herek, Janis, and Huth, "Quality of U.S. Decision Making During the Cuban Missile Crisis: Major Errors in Welch's Reassessment," *Journal of Conflict Resolution*, 33 (1989): 446-459.

42. Snyder and Diesing, *Conflict Among Nations*, 492.

43. Ibid., 316, 503.

44. Michael Brecher, "Research Findings and Theory-Building in Foreign Policy Behavior," in *Sage International Yearbook of Foreign Policy Studies*, Vol. II, ed. Patrick J. McGowan (Beverly Hills, CA: Sage, 1974), 71. See also Brecher, *Decisions in Crisis: Israel, 1967 and 1973* (Berkeley: University of California Press, 1980); Brecher, "State Behavior in International Crisis," *Journal of Conflict Resolution*, 23 (1979): 466-480; Brecher, "Toward a Theory of International Crisis Behavior," *International Studies Quarterly*, 21 (1977): 63-74; Brecher and Jonathan Wilkenfeld, "Crises in World Politics," *World Politics*, 34 (1982): 380-417; Brecher, Wilkenfeld, and S. Moser, *Crises in the*

Twentieth Century (New York: Pergamon, 1988); and Brecher and Wilkenfeld, *Crisis, Conflict and Instability* (New York: Pergamon, 1989).

45. Avi Shlaim, *The United States and the Berlin Blockade, 1948-1949* (Berkeley: University of California Press, 1983): 410.

46. Lebow, *Between Peace and War*, 271.

47. Ibid., 272.

48. Richard Smoke, *War: Controlling Escalation* (Cambridge, MA: Harvard University Press, 1977), 295.

49. Peter Suedfeld and Philip Tetlock, "Integrative Complexity of Communications in International Crises," *Journal of Conflict Resolution*, 21 (1977): 169-186; Suedfeld, Tetlock, and Carmenza Ramirez, "War, Peace, and Integrative Complexity," *Journal of Conflict Resolution*, 21 (1977): 427-441; Ariel Levi and Tetlock, "A Cognitive Analysis of Japan's 1941 Decision for War," *Journal of Conflict Resolution*, 24 (1980): 195-211; and Theodore D. Raphael, "Integrative Complexity Theory and Forecasting International Crises; Berlin 1946-1962," *Journal of Conflict Resolution*, 26 (1982): 423-450.

50. Wohlstetter and Wohlstetter, "Controlling the Risks in Cuba," 262-263.

51. Charles A. McClelland, "The Acute International Crisis," *World Politics*, 14 (1961): 182-204; Kenneth Waltz, "The Stability of a Bipolar World," *Daedalus*, 93 (1964): 883-884; Coral Bell, *Conventions of Crisis: A Study of Diplomatic Management* (London: Oxford University Press, 1971), 115-116, and Bell, "Decision-Makers and Crises," *International Journal*, 39 (1984): 324-336.

52. McClelland, "The Acute International Crisis," 199, 200. However, constant exposure to crises, especially simultaneous crises, may well result in a setting that is not conducive to rational decision making. On this point, see Wilensky, *Organizational Intelligence*.

53. Stephen Ambrose. *Eisenhower: The President* (New York: Simon & Schuster, 1984), 229-230.

54. Schelling, *The Strategy of Conflict* is a classic study. Less subtle and far more ideological is: Robert Strausz-Hupé et al., *Protracted Conflict* (New York: Harper, 1959); there are many other publications that crudely equate crisis management with the intestinal fortitude to coerce the adversary into submission.

55. Margaret G. Hermann and Charles F. Hermann, "Maintaining the Quality of Decision-Making in Foreign Policy Crises: A Proposal," Appendix D. Vol. II, *Report of the Commission on the Organization of the Government for the Conduct of Foreign Policy* (Washington, DC: Government Printing Office, 1975), 124-136.

56. Blight and Welch. *On the Brink*, 100-101, 154, 155, 161, 169, 170, 179, 194, 216.

57. George, *Presidential Decisionmaking*, 246. For a further discussion of the potential tensions between political and military factors in crisis management, see George, "Crisis Management: The Interaction of Political and Military Considerations," *Survival*, 26 (September/October 1984): 223-234. Other useful discussions of crisis management may be found in Phil Williams, *Crisis Management* (New York: Wiley, 1976); Coral Bell, *The Conventions of Crisis*; and William Langer Ury and Richard Smoke, *Beyond the Hotline: Controlling a Nuclear Crisis* (Cambridge, MA: Harvard Law School, 1984).

58. Alexander L. George, "The Case of Multiple Advocacy in Making Foreign Policy," *American Political Science Review*, 66 (1972): 751-785, 791-795.

59. Janis, *Victims of Groupthink*; and Janis, *Groupthink*.

60. Allison, *Essence of Decision*; John Steinbruner, "Beyond Rational Deterrence: The Struggle for New Conceptions," *World Politics*, 28 (January, 1976): 223-245; and Robert Jervis, Richard N. Lebow, and Janice G. Stein, *Psychology and Deterrence* (Baltimore, MD: Johns Hopkins Press, 1985).

61. Blight and Welch, *On the Brink*, 131.

62. Paul Schroeder, quoted in Arthur N. Gilbert and Paul Gordon Lauren, "Crisis Management: An Assessment and Critique," *Journal of Conflict Resolution*, 24 (1980): 657.

63. Gilbert and Lauren, "Crisis Management." For a somewhat different appraisal, see Ole R. Holsti, "Historians, Social Scientists, and Crisis Management," *Journal of Conflict Resolution* 24 (1980): 665-682.

64. Lebow, *Between Peace and War*: 298. See also Lebow, *Nuclear Crisis Management: A Dangerous Illusion* (Ithaca, NY: Cornell University Press, 1987).

65. See, for example, Ernest R. May, The Nature of Foreign Policy: The Calculated Versus the Axiomatic," *Daedalus* 91 (1962): 653-667; and May, *"Lessons" of the Past*.

66. Lebow, *Between Peace and War*; and Snyder, "Rationality at the Brink."

67. Like many earlier conclusions about the missile crisis, these are subject to revision in the light of evidence made available since 1987. Many of Kennedy's admirers and critics appear to have overstated the analytical aspects of the process in pre-1987 writings.

68. Blight and Welch, *On the Brink*: 100-101.

Chapter 6

Leadership Pathologies: The Kaiser and the Führer and the Decisions for War in 1914 and 1939

ROBERT G. L. WAITE

> *Warum hat Deutschland den Krieg begrüsst und sich zu ihm bekannt, als er*
> *hereinbrach? Weil es den Bringer seines dritten Reiches in ihm erkannte . . .*
> *die Synthese von Macht und Geist*

—THOMAS MANN, April 1915[1]

Any discussion of the role that personality played in Germany's decisions to go to war in 1914 and 1939 must involve both history and psychology. But therein lies a rub: for those who seek to apply psychology to history often claim too much; those historians who spurn psychology claim too little for it.

My own view can be quickly stated: psychology can help us to reach a deeper understanding of the past, but that is all it can do. No more should be claimed for it — and no less. It is a useful supplement to historical analysis, not a substitute for it. As with economic or political analysis, psychology is — in St. Thomas' distinction — necessary, but not sufficient.

What Thucydides concluded about the causes of the Peloponnesian Wars of the fifth century B.C. is true of both world wars of the twentieth century: they too were due to "the interplay of Man and Circumstances." We need to keep both sides of this important historical equation in mind. We are all indebted to Marx, B. F. Skinner, and other "structuralists" and "social environmentalists" for showing us the importance of external circumstance. We should join them in viewing events "from the outside." But we are also beholden to Freud, Erik Erikson, Heinz Kohut, and all those "personalists" who remind us that history is about people — human beings not only of flesh and blood but of emotions, fantasies and irrational convictions. People are a part of our historical data. And since they are, psychologists can help us to understand their emotions and the reasons for their actions.

We need to look at historical events — in our case, decisions for war — from both the outside and the inside; we must study both Circumstance and the Man.

* * *

First, let us consider the man, Kaiser Wilhelm II of Hohenzollern. His personality is important to our inquiry because the constitution of Imperial Germany made him the ultimate political authority. He, and he alone, made the final decision for war; he was the supreme commander of his armed forces. And beyond the constitution he practiced what was known as *Kommandogewalt*: power of command that by-passed parliamentary control.[2] He made all appointments from generals to diplomats, judges to professors. The Kaiser was "The All Highest," *Der Allerhöchste*.

Wilhelm liked it that way. And so did the German people. Thomas Mann and Max Weber hailed the power of the Kaiser. Paul de la Garde proclaimed that "only the pure, strong will of a single man can help us . . .;"[3] In 1913 Friedrich Meinecke said that "We Germans . . . want a *Führer* for the nation, one with whom we will go through fire."[4] Indeed throughout the nineteenth century, so widespread was the longing for a "New Caesar" and "Führer" that a historical monograph was devoted to the subject,[5] and a popular book of 1897 noted the national "longing for an overwhelming personality . . . a true master."[6]

Here we confront a central problem of Wilhelm's reign which has proven troublesome to all his biographers: the contrast between Wilhelm's promise and his performance. On all counts, the promise seemed brilliant. Never, since Frederick the Great, had a German prince shown so much talent. Wilhelm had a quick and retentive mind; he impressed archaeologists, linguists, and engineers with his intelligence. He wanted to be the greatest ruler of German history. And the imperial constitution supported his aspirations; it called for an absolute monarch of immense political power. Moreover, his people hailed the promise. He fit his times. In a luminous essay, Thomas Kohut has shown how Kaiser and people served as each others' mirror-image, each reflecting the others' aspirations for integration and glory.[7] As Walter Rathenau noted in 1919, "Never has an epoch with greater justification appropriated the name of its monarch."[8] It was indeed Wilhelmian. One may doubt if ever in history a person of such talent and ambition had been dealt such good cards.

Yet rarely have cards been so badly played. Why he failed so abjectly could be the complex and fascinating theme of an extensive book; in this essay we must limit ourselves to those personality traits which have a direct bearing on his decision to go to war.

First we should note that Wilhelm must rank among the most conspicuous exhibitionists of history: constantly he felt the need to parade his power. He inscribed bibles in the Potsdam Garrison Church, "I walk among you as your God."[9] President Theodore Roosevelt was surprised to see how high he sat at his desk. It was because saddles had been mounted behind the Kaiser's desks in Berlin, Korfu, and in exile in Doorn. One of the many Latin epigrams he wrote to hone his excellent Latin and to publicize his political thinking appears in his own handwriting beneath the heroic portrait he presented to the Ministry of Public Works in Berlin: *Sic volo, sic jubeo* [You do what I like].[10]

Yet behind these psychic defenses cowered an anxious, childlike person who was constantly afraid of falling apart. A contemporary described him well:

> Behind the image of master . . . one can sense . . . dependent childishness. Here is a person who needs to be sheltered, who needs reassuring arms to protect him from forces . . . which are pulling him asunder. . . . He is a being who is torn apart [*eine zerrissene Natur*].[11]

He was indeed torn apart. Any issue that required a choice between alternatives made him positively ill. So he usually ran away. Perhaps he hated to make decisions because he was himself so profoundly confused, impelled in so many different directions, torn into so many different selves. Symptomatic of his *Zerrissenheit*, his inner disjointedness, was his sexual confusion. At times he could appear soft, sentimental, aesthetic. He was drawn to Philipp Eulenburg and his homosexual friends of the Liebenberg Circle who entertained themselves gaily in sexually explicit pranks, skits, and dances, and performed on at least one occasion in women's clothing.

Yet outside this entourage it was important to Wilhelm to cover his inner confusion and deny his sexual ambivalences in displays that were "public caricatures of public masculinity."[12] His ambivalence was shown in little mannerisms — such as the way he shook hands. To prepare for an introduction, he would turn his heavy rings inward. If a man were presented, he would often extend two fingers. But if it were a woman, particularly an English woman, he would sometimes crush her hand in the cruel grip of his powerful right hand. As she stifled a cry of pain his eyes would flash and he would remark jocularly in English, "A bit of the celebrated mailed fist, what?"[13] His definition of the ideal man is worth noting: "A person of crystalline character, that is to say of remorseless severity. [*unerbittliche Strenge*]."[14] And that is the way he fancied himself. A sign in a photographer's shop in Berlin in 1913 advertised "267 heroic poses of the Emperor, all different."[15] But since no photograph could do justice to his grandiose self-idealization, he gave detailed instructions for a portrait to be painted in which he appears as Mars, god of war and apotheosis of power,[16] an image consistent with his fantasy that he was a special agent of God, answerable to Him alone, and sent on earth to rule the entire world.[17]

Yet there were other traits that bespeak a profound sense of insecurity. He could never really trust another person. Indeed an admirer concluded that "this one word, 'mistrust,' illumines the innermost nature of the Kaiser, it is the key to his . . . character."[18] Wilhelm told his valet that he could not confide in anyone — not even his wife. "With her," he said, "I've got to dissemble, as I do with everybody else."[19] The Kaiser was constantly on guard, ready to spring to the defense of his vulnerable self. His American dentist remembered him once saying, " 'Fix my teeth well,

Davis, . . . so that I can bite. There are lots of people I would like to bite!' He snapped his jaws together."[20]

So much, for the moment, about the Man. Let us turn to Circumstance, those external pressures that bore on the decision for war in August 1914.

* * *

Within Germany, the ruling elites looked apprehensively at the growth of socialism and saw it as a menace to the entire political, social, and economic structure of the German Empire. Apprehension was intensified by the last prewar elections to the Reichstag in 1912, which dealt a shattering defeat to the parties of the establishment and made the Socialists the largest party in Germany. In 1912 one out of three Germans had voted for the Marxist party. The spectre of revolution and social upheaval seemed to loom over Germany.[21]

A realistic assessment of the so-called "Socialist Peril" must conclude, however, that revolution was really not imminent; this reformist, patriotic socialist movement was not bent on overturning the Wilhelmian establishment. Certainly Trotsky was not impressed with the revolutionary zeal of the German workers. "They'll never seize a railway station," he said in disgust, "unless they have purchased a *Bahnsteigkarte*" [railway platform ticket].

But in the lives of men and nations, what people believe to be true is more operative than what is objectively true. The Kaiser and his entourage *believed* that Germany stood on the very brink of socialist revolution. With obsessive rigidity they were determined to make no concessions and to prepare for the worst. Thus there grew in court and military circles the temptation to think of war as a solution to domestic turmoil — real or imagined. Just as German liberalism had been swept aside in the 1860s by the triumphant march of military victories and national unification, so now it was felt that a smashingly successful war would rally national support behind Kaiser and country and engulf socialism in a rising tide of patriotic fervor.

A second force bearing directly on the decision for war in 1914 was the power and influence of the German army, so exalted since the *Blitzkrieg* victories that had proven Bismarck correct in his self-fulfilling prophecy which has become a credo of Imperial Germany: "Great problems are solved not by resolutions and majority votes but by Iron and Blood."

The Kaiser's Germany was a militarist state. Repetition of that fact does not diminish its importance. Mirabeau's famous *mot* of the eighteenth century gained increasing validity in the twentieth: "Prussia is not a state that has an Army; it is an Army that has a state." In his massive study of German militarism, Gerhard Ritter noted that "in the West, the army was a sort of necessary evil, but here [in Germany] it formed the highest pride of the nation."[22] The attitude of many German intellectuals was expressed by Werner Sombart who looked about him in 1914, found militarism everywhere, and pronounced it good: "German militarism" he said, "is the most complete synthesis of Potsdam and Weimar. It is Beethoven in the trenches."[23]

Of specific importance to Germany's decision for war was the military establishment's carefully developed Schlieffen Plan. It was devoutly believed that with this plan Germany could defeat the enemies that she imagined were encircling her and establish dominion over the Continent. Two *Blitzkriege* were planned: first France would be quickly smashed, then the full weight of German arms would be hurled against slowly mobilizing Russia. The war would be over in a few months. But everything depended on this one plan; it was the only one the Germans had. It should be noted that the Schlieffen Plan gave no thought to defensive war. This was calculated aggression through two peremptory military strikes. Speed was of the essence. But now, in 1914, the Kaiser and his generals believed that the Russian military reforms, announced in 1913, had greatly increased the "Russian Menace." They noted anxiously that new Russian railroad lines were being built to the German frontier and that another 500,000 men were to be added to the immense Russian army. German military planners put great pressure on the Kaiser to strike before Russia was ready.[24]

Hypernationalism was another force bearing down on Germany in 1914. Of course Germany had no monopoly on strident patriotism in the decade preceding World War I. Jingoism is an English word; chauvinism is French. But in no country did so many people from so many walks of life support so aggressive a nationalism, urging Germany to achieve her manifest destiny in a *Drang nach Osten* against Russia and a *Drang nach Western* against France, Belgium, and England.

These two forces, militarism and overbearing nationalism, engendered an attitude that has been called "collective megalomania" [*kollektiver Grossenwahn*]: the conviction that Germany was invincible, that its matchless army could accomplish grandiose war aims. A thoughtful German historian has written that the most fatal expression of German militant nationalism was found "in the irrational exaggeration of its power; in an almost mystical faith in its own invincibility. The chief source and carrier of that myth was the army. The conviction was expressed in army circles that Germany could take on all three Entente powers at once."[25]

Another conviction that influenced Germany's decision for war was the widespread belief, shared by the Kaiser, that the Fatherland was encircled by hostile enemies: that France, Russia, and England were conspiring to launch an attack on Germany. This belief had no basis in fact. None of these countries intended to start an aggressive war against Germany. Russia was struggling to recover from the national trauma of its defeat by Japan and subsequent revolution; England was beset by labor unrest, and the threat of civil war in Ireland; France was torn between the political right and left with the right trying to blunt leftist antiwar criticism by an openly nonbelligerent stance. (The French government actually *pulled back* their troops 10 km from the German frontier on August 1, 1914, thereby dangerously exposing the important Briey basin to German attack.[26])

The Kaiser and his advisers, however, were convinced that their country was encircled by enemies bent on attacking Germany and thwarting its destiny to impose its will on Europe and the world. They spoke apprehensively, for example, of the *englische Gefahr* [the English peril] and seriously believed that Britain, without declaration of war or advance warning, was about to "Copenhagen" Germany's new navy, just as Nelson had blown up the Danish fleet in 1801 while it lay at anchor.

It is not enough to dismiss German hysteria as a calculated ploy to drum up support for increasing army and naval expenditures, although surely it had that consequence. Nor is it enough to throw up one's historical hands in despair and exclaim "What a strange and incomprehensible self-deception lay in this word *Gefahr*!" As Jonathan Steinberg has written, "What makes the Copenhagen complex so puzzling . . . is that it began to influence German policy before the Germans had a fleet worth 'Copenhagening.' Why should Britain risk international opprobrium and dangers of major war to destroy six or seven old tubs?"[27] It made no sense. But it was believed.

These irrational fears were rooted in the remarkable ambivalence which both the German people and their half-English Emperor felt toward England. England was, at the same time, admired and despised. In this and in many other ways Wilhelm reflected with fidelity the attitudes of his countrymen. Indeed he not only shared their ambivalence, he was its leading exponent. He wanted to be the complete English country gentlemen in tweeds and gaiters, and at the same time the Prussian officer in his many regimental uniforms — one side of him "conspiring to frustrate the other and neither completely succeeding."[28]

The navy was of special importance to him, for it was his personal means of compelling respect from his English mother whom he both admired and distrusted. His new navy would force her to respect him;[29] no longer could the English tell him what to do or bar his way to overseas domination and *Weltpolitik*. But now the British were about to destroy his shiny new ships and frustrate his plans. And they were talking of slowing down the naval race. Wilhelm perceived this latter goal was just another English trick to limit his power and continue British domination over him. He would have none of it. The intensity of his feelings about "his" navy and his personal identification with it are clear:

> England can only act that way as long as we don't have a fleet that can command their respect . . . I was the one who planned and forged a navy as my weapon. How, where and when I plan to deploy it is absolutely my affair alone . . . everyone else has to be silent and obey. Bare your teeth! That's the only way to get along with England . . . That's what you always have to do with England.[30]

Wilhelm, who had said that "one cannot have enough hatred for England,"[31] awarded a special commendation to the author of the "Hate Song," so popular in Germany on the eve of war. One verse goes:

Hate by water and hate by land
Hate of the heart and hate of the hand
We love as one, we hate as one,
We have but one foe alone: England.

There were, however, other foes. Russia, on the East was a menace. Of this the Kaiser seemed convinced.[32] The German Chancellor, Bethmann-Hollweg agreed with him and wrote in one of his gloomy moods, "The future belongs to Russia, which grows and grows, looming above us as an increasingly terrifying nightmare." When his son talked about planting trees on the family estate, Bethmann shook his head saying that the Russians would be taking over the land in a few years. There was only one ray of hope: Russia would not be ready for war until 1917 or 1918.[33] The army was right: since war was inevitable, it was better to fight it now. As the Chief of the General Staff put it in 1912: "The sooner the better."[34]

France threatened from the West. Despite all evidence to the contrary, the Kaiser and his entourage managed to persuade themselves that at any minute the French would launch an offensive along the Meuse.[35]

In actual fact, Germany, incomparably the strongest military and industrial power on the continent, was in no danger from attack. But the more important historical fact is that the Germany who made policy decisions *believed* their country was menaced by simultaneous invasion from east and west. Sometimes the problem for historians is not to find evidence to support an assertion so much as it is to formulate assertions that do justice to the peculiarities of the evidence. Consider the curious memorandum of the famous Count Schlieffen who looked at Germany in the glory days of 1909 and saw nothing but impending disaster:

Enemies on all sides! . . . An endeavour is afoot to bring all these Powers together for a concerted attack on [us]. At the given moment the doors are to be opened, the drawbridge let down, and the million-strong armies let loose, raving and destroying across the Vosges, the Meuse, the Königsau, the Niemen, the Bug and even the Isonzo and the Tyrolean Alps. The danger seems gigantic.

In 1912 he reaffirmed his apprehensions: "Germany's neighbors were lying in wait for their unprotected, weaker adversary who was entirely on his own.[36] By 1914, the consequences of these fears were to be ominous, for as Fritz Stern has reminded us, "It is naive and excessively rationalistic to suppose that aggression must spring from lust of conquest. Fear, too, impels aggressive action."[37] By July 14 the Kaiser and his advisers were afraid; they became convinced that the only way to rid themselves of this fear was to smash encircling enemies through "preventive war."

Another powerful, if perplexing emotion helped precipitate war in 1914. Many influential Germans shared the Kaiser's conviction that the Fatherland was somehow *fated* to go to war in order to fulfill its historical destiny. As Wilhelm told the Austrian Ambassador to Berlin, it was not enough for Germany to control Europe, he was driven by Destiny to fulfill a greater mission: to dominate "the entire world."[38] The Chancellor of Germany asserted that "The question is not whether we want to or not . . . we *can't do anything other* than carry on *Weltpolitik*."[39] And the Chief of the Imperial General Staff asserted that the Great War was ordained by Fate and World Historic Forces; "This war," he wrote in November 1914, "was a *necessity* [*Notwendigkeit*] dictated by world historical development . . . which gives to each nation a special task to fulfill. . . ."[40]

Those Germans who spoke most about their Destiny were not exultant about it; they were depressed. Consider the attitude of Kurt Riezler, Chancellor Bethmann-Hollweg's chief adviser and confidant who may have been "the most sophisticated of German thinkers and politicians in the age of Weltpolitik,"[41] but was certainly one of the most peculiar. Driven by the conviction that Germany was condemned to strive after the unattainable, he stood on its head Bismarck's dictum: "Politics is the art of the possible." Not so, said Riezler. "Politics is the striving after the *impossible*," he insisted in his influential book of arresting title, *The Necessity of the Impossible* [*Die Erforderlichkeit des Unmöglichen: Prolegomena zur einer Theorie der Politik*, Munich, 1912].

Wilhelm, too, dreamed the impossible dream and set unattainable goals for himself and his empire. He confided to an intimate:

> I have long ago made my program of *how* I wanted to be German Kaiser, how I conceived of the German Kaiser: deep into the most distant jungles of other parts of the world, everyone should know the voice of the German Kaiser. *Nothing* should occur on this earth without having first heard him. His word must have its weight placed on every scale. . . . Also domestically the word of the Kaiser should be *everything*.[42]

Here is a 20th-century political version of the 19th-century German Romantics' compulsion to "strive for infinitude" [*Streben nach Unentlichkeit*]. Such a destiny ineluctably thrust world domination upon Germany and filled Riezler and his superiors with apprehension. Even in the heady days of August 1914, amid smashing German military triumphs, Riezler wrote uneasily of "the difficulty for the German to accustom himself to the mien of world dominance which we *must* wear after victory."[43]

The Chief of the General Staff and the Kaiser shared his pessimism. Moltke found no pleasure, no reassurance, in a gigantic parade of overwhelming military power:

> Behind this gaudy frivolity grins the gorgon head of war which hangs over us. . . . No action on our part can change our course; there is no turning back. . . . It becomes worse and worse. We all live under this dread force which kills all joy of accomplishment. One can scarcely begin anything without hearing the inner voice saying "Wither? It is all in vain!"[44]

Someone who saw the Kaiser during the first days of August 1914 said he looked as if life had left his body: "Here was a man . . . who had some premonition of impending disaster."[45]

Dread of the future was not confined to Moltke and the Kaiser. Historians of Germany need to notice the strange fascination with catastrophe felt by many German intellectuals across time. One of them, the liberal journalist Karl Ossietzky, described his friends as "fanciers of every catastrophe, gourmets of international misfortune"; Franz Werfel (who later took his own life) described himself and his colleagues as "insignificant stokers of the fires of Hell in which Humanity now is roasting"; and Thomas Mann, in his essay on *Friedrich und die grosse Koalition*, wrote that the true measure of Frederick's greatness lay not in his military triumphs but in his capacity to contemplate "his own destruction [*Untergang*] as well as that of others."

This penchant for destruction was reinforced by a curious infatuation with disease and death. A literary critic has written, "There is in Germany a body of opinion . . . popularized by many of the most prominent literary figures of the last century, to the effect that disease is more than something to be done away with; that it is a fascinating phenomenon and . . . that it may be one of the distinguishing marks of genius."[46] His assertion can be readily documented. It will be recalled that Hans Castrop's self-realization on the Magic Mountain comes through contact with disease and death; Goethe's Wilhelm Meister's first awakening comes after a hemorrhage; Novalis asks "Could disease not be a means of higher synthesis?" and reaches a peculiar conclusion: "The more agonizing the pain, the higher the pleasure that lurks within it [*Je fürchterlicher der Schmerz, desto hoher die darin verbogene Lust*]. . . . Illness, along with death, is to be numbered among human pleasures."

Heine too praised "creative illness," saying "I believe that by suffering even animals could be made human."[47] Among humans, death was exalted in the German military tradition. Army regulations called for a "corpse-like obedience" [*Kadavergehorsam*]; members both of the Kaiser's elite Hussars and Hitler's special SS bore on their headdress the skull and bones of the Death's Head.

Admittedly, these reflections on a possible German penchant for destruction, disease, and death are speculative. What can be asserted with confidence, however, is that there was a remarkable *Zerrissenheit* in Germany on the eve of World War I. Like their Kaiser, the Germans seemed torn between exultant power and assertions of invincibility on one hand, and pessimism and a fatalistic acceptance of impending catastrophe on the other. This contradiction may have been the basis of a starker and more ominous duality: the emotional instability of the Kaiser was coupled with immense military and industrial power. It was a lethal combination.

* * *

We now turn to the part played by Wilhelm's personal pathology in the coming of World War I. Let us begin in 1908 when the Kaiser had two harrowing experiences that were to affect his mental state on the eve of War. In the autumn of 1908 he gave the English newspaper, *Daily Telegraph*, permission to publish an astonishing interview he had granted to a certain Colonel Stuart-Wortley.

In the interview, Wilhelm exclaimed, "You English are mad! Mad as March hares!" This was because they distrusted him and misunderstood his intentions. Unlike the majority of Germans, he personally liked the English and only wanted to be their friends. As proof of friendship, he said that during the Boer War he had received an anxious letter from his beloved grandmother, Queen Victoria, who was afraid that Britain was being defeated. Wilhelm hurried to her aid by personally drawing up the battle plan which subsequently defeated the Boers. The plan, Wilhelm insisted, had been approved by his own General Staff; copies could be seen in the Royal Archives in Windsor. The Kaiser also confided that when the Boer War was at its height, France and Russia had wanted him to join them against England in order to "humble her into the dust." The Kaiser gallantly refused. Furthermore, he declared, England had no reason to fear the German Navy. It was not designed to attack England but to "protect our ambitions . . . in the outermost seas of the world." England should welcome such a powerful fleet and form an alliance with him to control the Pacific Ocean and beat back the "Yellow Peril" of the Japanese.[48] Before its publication, Wilhelm had written to Colonel Stuart-Wortley saying that he had read the proposed draft of the interview carefully and was much pleased with it.[49]

For reasons that are passing strange, the Kaiser seems to have believed that his remarks would lead to friendlier relations with England and enhance his image as a far-seeing statesman with a firm grasp of international affairs. The results were the opposite. Indeed if he had deliberately contrived to infuriate everyone he mentioned — British, Germans, Japanese, French, Russians, and Chinese — he could scarcely have been more successful.

In Great Britain neither the press nor the army took kindly to the suggestion that the Queen could not trust her own army to develop military plans for the Boer War. (Despite Wilhelm's assertions, his plans cannot be found in the Royal Archives at Windsor Castle.) Nor were the English reassured by the Kaiser's dreams of global naval power, or by his suggestion that England and Germany should join naval forces to confront Japan, which had recently become an ally of Britain. Russia and France were disturbed by the Kaiser's public statements about their alleged intentions against England. Japan and China did not view with equanimity the Kaiser's remarks about protecting civilization from the "Yellow Peril".

It was in Germany, however, that the interview did the most damage to Wilhelm's image. The German people, who were very much pro-Boer, were dismayed to learn that their Kaiser, by his own admission, had plotted with England to defeat the gallant and beleaguered Boers and had even called on the German army to help crush them. Germans talked openly of the Kaiser's "treachery."[50] Generals von Moltke and Schlieffen both flatly denied that they had ever been consulted about the Kaiser's military plans for the British in South Africa. (No such plans can be found in the archives of the German army.) The Kaiser's conduct during the affair caused members of his entourage to express concern about his sanity. One confided to a friend that she feared the Kaiser's "brain was giving way."[51] The immensely influential Baron von Holstein in the Foreign

Office wrote to his cousin: "It is obvious that if the Kaiser continues to indulge his tongue, the conduct of foreign policy is impossible."[52]

For the first time in German history, in press and parliament, representatives of all political parties mounted a sustained attack on their ruler. Serious questions were raised about the Kaiser's mental health. The whole incident made Wilhelm appear irresponsible, deceitful, unbalanced, and — most damaging of all — ridiculous. The leading German humor magazine carried a cartoon suggesting that a muzzle would be a useful addition to the Kaiser's elaborate equipage.[53]

The Kaiser did not follow that suggestion. In subsequent interviews with the respected American journalist and ordained minister, William Bayard Hale, and with American congressmen, he said that England was ruled by a bunch of "ninnies"; that war with England was "inevitable"; and that the United States should join Germany in punishing England for "treason against the white race." Together the two powers could crush England and smash the "Yellow Peril." The Japanese, he said, "are devils . . . who are sowing seeds of sedition and treachery in every quarter." He also said that Japan's victory over Russia only proved the decadence of Russia: "Those Russians were not fit to fight. . . . My God, I wish my battalions could have a chance at 'em [the Japanese]. We'd have made short work of it!"[54]

Meanwhile, throughout the entire "Daily Telegraph Crisis," the Kaiser was undergoing another experience which further undermined his public image of masculine assertiveness. His most intimate associate and closest advisor, "Phili" Eulenburg, who called the Kaiser "My Darling and My Beloved," was indicted for homosexuality.[55] The trial, replete with demeaning and sordid testimony, dragged on month after month. In imperial Germany, with its exaltation of "manly virtues," homosexuality was perhaps the most heinous accusation that could be brought against a man. It was deeply disturbing to the nation that their Kaiser's most intimate associates of the Liebenberg Circle were practicing homosexuals.

The trial was a public scandal and a personal trauma for Wilhelm. He felt a compelling need to reaffirm his masculinity and to suppress public (as well as personal) questions about his own sexual preferences. To prove his masculinity he had to appear tough, unyielding, arrogantly belligerent. To make concessions, to negotiate and to compromise, was to display feminine weakness. The suggestion, for example, that Germany seek some accommodation with Russia was dismissed out of hand as "equivalent to 'self-castration.' " [Selbstentmannung]. The use of this word, Fritz Stern has suggested, may well be "an unconscious allusion . . . to frequent charges of civilian effeminacy."[56]

A public test of Wilhelm's assertions of masculinity came during the international crisis over Agadir in 1912, when manly patriots of the army pressed for a showdown with France. Wilhelm waffled and backed down. Nationalist German newspapers consequently wrote scathing editorials calling the Supreme War Lord "Guillaume le Timid" and asking pointedly if Germans had become "a race of women."[57]

To Wilhelm the innuendo was intolerable. It again raised public and personal doubts about his capacity to make "manly" decisions. He felt that he *must* be decisive. But he was not a decisive person. In anxious bewilderment, he told an associate, "Don't you see, I am what I am! I can't change!"[58] But at least he would *appear* decisive. Thus from 1912 to 1914 Wilhelm's memoranda and public statements grew even more bombastic as he joined his countrymen in what has been called "compensatory belligerency."[59]

The real showdown came in 1914 after Sarajevo. Wilhelm was confronted with the most important decision of his career. And once again he was tortured by *Zerrissenheit*. One side of Wilhelm called for war, another for peace. As the Christian leader who would bring peace to all mankind, Wilhelm could reflect on the folly of war and ask, "What has become of the so-called World Empires? Alexander the Great, Napoleon I, all the great war heroes have swum in blood and suppressed the people who . . . rose against them and brought their empires to naught."[60] This Wilhelm, when he read the Serbian reply to Austria's ultimatum, sighed with relief and wrote in the margin: "A brilliant achievement! . . . all reason for war is gone. . . ."[61]

Yet this same Wilhelm trumpeted power, shook the mailed fist, and said he wanted to see French corpses piled up like cordwood, six feet high.[62] Once again two parts of this deeply disjointed person were vying for mastery in the choice between peace and war.

Two things moved him to war: the concatenation of military, social, and diplomatic pressures; the lifelong pressure from within to appear manly and decisive. The more he asserted his manliness and the more he posed as his own ideal of "remorseless severity," the more he was drawn to a military decision.

One sentence of a conversation with Alfred Krupp during the July Crisis of 1914 is particularly revealing. Apparently recalling the ridicule he had suffered when he refused to fight France in 1912, he told Krupp, "This time I won't cave in!" Krupp later recalled that it was "almost pathetic" to see how his Kaiser tried to prove that he was not a weakling. Three times Wilhelm repeated the sentence with deepening voice and mounting fervor: *Diesmal falle Ich nicht um!*"[63]

But once the war had started and the Schlieffen Plan had been set inexorably in motion another Wilhelm rose to assert himself. On August 1, 1914, he tried to stop the German armies that were already advancing on the Western Front. Moltke and the General Staff, driven to distraction by their "Supreme War Lord's" dithering interference, managed to get his orders countermanded. The war went on.[64]

*   *   *

In considering the part Hitler's psychopathology played in launching World War II, one finds again the interplay of external circumstance and personal psychology.

The circumstance of historical continuum connecting the two wars is striking. The German people never accepted either the peace settlement of 1918 or the new democracy. When Hitler promised to destroy both the "Treaty of Shame" and the

"Government of Weimar traitors," he won wide support across the social spectrum, as a careful statistical analysis of "who voted for Hitler" has shown.[65]

The army, which had been so decisive in setting German policy during the Empire, continued to do so under the Republic. The attitude and the specific program of the army were most succinctly expressed in a little-noticed memorandum to the Chancellor written on September 11, 1922 by the commander of the Republic's army, General Hans von Seeckt. In it Seeckt demanded the remilitarization of Germany in defiance of the Versailles settlement: "The man who still lives in the days of Versailles and maintains that Germany has permanently renounced all 'imperialist and military aims' . . . is not fit to represent German interests." Seeckt called for a national revival of military spirit and preparation for war: "The stupid cry of 'no more war' " must be stifled. Like Meinecke in 1913, Seeckt in 1922 longed for a new "Führer" whom "the German people will follow in the struggle for their existence." That existence, he insisted, could only be assured by war: "the task is to prepare the people for this battle . . . it will *not* be the duty of our leading statesmen to keep Germany out of war . . . but to come in on the right side with all possible strength."[66]

German war aims prior to both world wars also show a remarkable continuity. This was particularly true with regard to eastern Europe. Hitler's demand for a *Drang nach Osten*, the subjugation of Poland, and German *Lebensraum* had all been on the agenda of the Pan-Germans in the 1890s and the September Program of 1914. Even the cadence and rhythm of the call for German domination was preserved through the years: *Das Heilige Römische Reich Deutscher Nation* of the First Reich became the *Mitteleuropaisches Reich Deutscher Nation* of the Second and the *Grossgermanisches Reich Deutscher Nation* of the Third Reich. It is true that plans for Poland set forth during the Empire and Republic were not as brutal as Hitler's. No one spoke of exterminating Jews and Poles. Still, the conclusion of a specialized study seems justified. "The way to racial expansion had been shown to National Socialist Germany. . . ."[67]

General Seeckt's plan for Poland in 1922 is particularly noteworthy because it is the one Hitler would follow twenty years later: wipe Poland from the map by partitioning it between the Soviet Union and Germany. Seeckt's prose is crisp and very clear:

> With Poland we come now to the core of the Eastern problem. The existence of Poland is intolerable [*unerträglich*] and incompatible with Germany's vital interests. It must disappear and will do so through its own inner weakness and through Russia — with our help.[68]

With regard to Russia, however, the war aims of Kaiser and Führer differed sharply. True, both agreed that it was necessary to defeat Russia. But Hitler, unlike Wilhelm, planned the annihilation of the Russian people. Recently a member of the *Militärgeschichtliches Forschungsamt* [Research Center for Military History] at Freiburg has written an important article with the arresting title, "Der andere

Holocaust" [The Other Holocaust] which demonstrates that when Hitler said he would "annihilate the Judeobolsheviks" he meant precisely that: the systematic extinction [*Ausrottung*] of the Russian people. Hitler's draconian plans had the active support of the Army, the Foreign Office, and leading industrialists.[69]

Wilhelm's Germany was a militarist state. It became more so under Hitler when the ideology of *Kampf* permeated society. "Battle-thinking" was the ideal of education from primary school to university. Elementary school teachers were enjoined to inculcate *wehrgeistige Erziehung* [militaristic attitudes], and they attempted to do so even in homework assignments. In an arithmetic class, for instance, children wrestled with this problem: "A machine-gun mows down an enemy reconnaissance unit. Of a total of 250 shots, 20 hit the enemy solders. express this figure in percentages."[70] At the university level, Martin Heidegger, probably the most influential Germany philosopher of the twentieth century, hailed Nazism as the culmination of German cultural history, the fulfillment of Thomas Mann's dream of 1915: a Third Reich uniting Spirit and Power. In his inaugural address as rector of the University of Freiburg in May 1933, Heidegger called for action and battle: "Not theses and ideas are the laws of your being! . . . The Führer himself, and he alone, is Germany's reality and law today and in the future." In that spirit Heidegger dedicated himself, his colleagues and his students to one united "battle community" [*Kampfgemeinschaft*].[71] The Nazis, delighted with this ringing endorsement of their program, distributed thousands of copies of Heidegger's speech, and saw to it that his name and picture appeared in the official *Führer-Lexikon* of the party.[72] Heidegger raised no objections.

Domestic social and economic pressures also influenced the decision for war in 1939, as they had done in 1914. During the Third Reich, "the jungle of competing and overlapping economic organizations and internal tensions," a noted social historian has written, contributed directly to Hitler's decision for war. So insistent were these pressures that "the only solution open to his regime was more dictatorship and more rearmament, then expansion, then war and terror, then plunder and enslavement. . . . A war for the plunder of manpower and materials lay square in the dreadful logic of German economic development."[73] Wolfgang Sauer, another student of Germany's economic condition on the eve of war, puts the matter more succinctly: "Hitler's economic policies could not possibly have been fulfilled without war."[74]

* * *

These historical circumstances — and others left undiscussed here — were surely important to the onset of war in 1939. But Hitler's personality was of primary importance.

Kaiser and Führer had strikingly similar personality traits. Both had been physically and emotionally abused as children. Young Wilhelm had suffered under the care of his well-meaning but incredibly insensitive mother who, in her determination to heal his incurably atrophied left arm, personally supervised treatments of excruciating pain and futility.[75] Hitler was battered by his brutal father while his ineffective mother cowered and failed to intervene. As children, both had watched sibling rivals die protracted and ugly deaths. As survivors, both felt they were especially chosen for heroic missions. Both felt isolated and alone. Basically distrustful, each abandoned his closest friend.

As adults, both remained immature, incapable of emotional or intellectual growth, childlike in their tastes. The Kaiser entertained his guests by making funny faces, chasing them around his yacht or playfully spanking their behinds;[76] the Führer played practical jokes and liked to see how fast he could undress and jump into bed. The Kaiser's favorite poem was Kipling's "If." He memorized it, translated it into German, and hung it on his study wall. The Führer's favorite reading was Karl May's wild West stories; his favorite movies were *Snow White and the Seven Dwarfs* and *King Kong*.[77] Both rulers were compulsive talkers who bored captive audiences with monologues and lapidary pronouncements on every conceivable subject. To read memoirs of the Kaiser's conversations is not unlike reading the Führer's interminable soliloquies as recorded in his so-called *Tischgespräche*. "The Kaiser," someone has said, "approached every problem with an open mouth."[78] Both were driven personalities, *zerrissene Naturen*. Although both could feel shame and embarrassment, neither seemed capable of feeling guilty.[79] Any fault was always someone else's. Both rulers were the personification of the nation, each giving his name to an era: The Second Reich was "Wilhelmian," the Third Reich was called "Hitler's Germany." Both used triumphant ceremonial occasions in an effort to achieve personal integration and affirmation from the masses.[80] In both men, grandiose assertions of power and infallibility served as defenses against feelings of inadequacy and fears of homosexuality.

Both announced, in remarkably similar phrases, that they were the instruments of God — thereby seeking to borrow from the Almighty the confidence they lacked in themselves. In a speech in Königsberg of 1910, the Kaiser said, "Deeming myself the instrument of the Lord, I go my way without regard for the views and opinions of the day.[81] In Munich in 1936, the Führer proclaimed, "I go the way that Providence has dictated to me with all the assurance of a sleepwalker. Neither threats nor warnings will divert me from my path.[82] Both believed that they were chosen by God/Providence/Destiny to rule the world.

But there were politically crucial differences. As an actor Hitler was convincing: he came across as the Führer. Wilhelm came across as a *poseur*. There was also a vast difference in sheer political ability. Like Wilhelm, Hitler had difficulty making up his mind, but once he had done so he drove relentlessly, ruthlessly, and effectively toward his goal. The Kaiser dithered. The Führer had uncanny *Fingerspitzengefühl* — the capacity to sense the mood and the needs of another person or a vast audience and respond brilliantly to those needs. The Kaiser seemed impervious to the needs of others or to "the rabble beneath me." The Führer won over opposition; the Kaiser alienated supporters.[83]

Their personal differences affected their political careers; and their careers, in turn affected their psychic development. They became rulers of Germany in very different ways. Wilhelm had not sought the position; he had been born into it. Hitler, the school dropout and derelict, had forged his own way to the top; he and he alone created both the myth and the reality of the Führer. The protean Wilhelm kept trying to shape himself to fit different images of the Kaiser which he imagined others expected him to fulfill; Hitler created a world after his own image, shaping others to fulfill his personal needs. Wilhelm posed as various Kaisers; Hitler *was* the Führer.

Being their country's ruler affected the two men differently and had vastly different political consequences. Wilhelm's psychic problems grew more severe after he became Kaiser and the dangers of personal disintegration increased. By contrast, the position of Führer gave Hitler an ideal opportunity — so disastrous for mankind — to sate his cravings for power, aggression, and domination. Hitler's conviction that he was Germany's instrument of Destiny drove him with an intensity that brooked no opposition and inspired such faith that thousands of Germans, hungering and thirsting after leadership, hailed him as Messiah. He projected power. Wilhelm projected indecision. In short, the Führer's psychopathology was for a time a political asset; the Kaiser's was a political liability throughout his reign.[84]

There is another contrast of direct concern to this study. World War II was indeed "Hitler's War"; World War I was not, in any meaningful way, Wilhelm's. He had not caused it; only part of him had wanted it; he did not direct it. From the very outset his orders were countermanded or ignored, and he forfeited military and political control to his generals. But Hitler hanged disaffected generals on meat hooks and watched colored films of piano wire tightening around their necks.

There was a historic difference between the two men in words and deeds. With the Kaiser the two were often separated. He talked about exterminating the political opposition, shooting prisoners of war, burning English cities to the ground. But that was only talk. With the Führer, there was a terrifying coherence between talk and action. The horror of Hitler was this: he practiced what he preached, he did what he said he would do. Indeed as Elie Wiesel has commented bitterly, "Hitler was the only one who kept his promises to the Jewish people."[85]

Given the nature of Hitler's personality and the circumstances he created in the Third Reich — and given the acquiescence of Western appeasers and the cooperation of the Soviet Union — World War II was probably inevitable. Without war the Third Reich made no sense. Thus it was only technically true that World War II began with the invasion of Poland in September 1939. It had really begun as soon as Hitler came to power in January 1933. From the very beginning, his Germany required war. Hitler needed it for his Reich, but he also needed if for himself. "I am totally convinced," he said, "that this war does not differ one hair's breath from the battle I fought within myself . . . the resolve to strike was always in me" [*war immer in mir*].[86] To fulfill that personal need he militarized a nation and led it to war. The war was not, as some revisionists prefer to believe, somehow forced upon a reluctant Hitler. It was in his bones and guts and psyche; it was the very *raison d'être* of his Reich.

There was another personal reason why Hitler wanted war in 1938 or 1939. His mother had died of cancer before she was 50 and Hitler feared — against all medical evidence — that he too was dying of cancer. This obsession prompted him in 1938 to draw up his personal will and, on several occasions in 1939, to muse about the catastrophic consequences his death would have on a Germany suddenly deprived of his commanding genius. Besides, as he said, he much preferred to wage war at the age of 50 (in 1939) when he was still energetic enough to enjoy it.[87]

The psychopathology that had aided Hitler in attaining and consolidating power became his nemesis during the war. How often he had proclaimed that as the instrument of God he was infallible, that he could not fail. But he protested too much. He kept taking risks to prove his infallibility. He gambled at impossible odds in order to dispel all doubt and to prove his invincible power. "You know," he said, "I am like a wanderer who must cross an abyss on the edge of a knife. But I *must*, I *must* cross."[88]

To say that Hitler was "insatiable" is not hyperbole. He was just that. He could not be satiated, he could not stop: "We shall attack, and it is immaterial whether we go 10 or 1,000 kilometers beyond the present lines. For whatever we gain, it will always be the starting point for new battles . . . *I just can't help myself*' [*Ich kann halt nicht anders*].[89] His very real accomplishments were never enough: not the absorption of Austria; nor the Munich agreement; not the victory over Poland, the Low Countries, and Norway; not the fall of France; not the establishment of a Greater German Reich more extensive than the Empires of Charlemagne or Napoleon. They could never be enough because, as Norbert Bromberg has noted in his penetrating study of Hitler's psychopathology, they could give only temporary relief. The internal drives continued. Caught in a psychological trap, Hitler kept on trying to prove the unprovable: that he was everything his image of unconquerable infallibility claimed him to be.[90]

Hitler's psychic needs led him to make decisions that would lead to his downfall: the invasion of the Soviet Union, the declaration of war against the United States, and the massacre of the Jews of Europe. From a traditional historical perspective, all three were irrational, unnecessary, and self-defeating.

As Alan Bullock has pointed out, there was no compelling military, economic, or strategic reason for invading Russia. In June 1941 Hitler was allied with Stalin who was trying to appease him by shipping immense quantities of raw materials to Germany. Moreover, at that time Hitler already controlled a huge land mass stretching from the English Channel to the plains of Poland, from Norway to the Pyrenees. Who could deny him his Greater German Reich? Surely not battered and beleaguered England, who stood alone against him.[91] Nevertheless, Hitler felt compelled to attack.

In mid-December 1941, when the German invasion was halted in the blizzards before Moscow, and the Red Army was counter-attacking along the Eastern front, Hitler, without consulting his foreign office or his military advisors, suddenly declared war on the United States. He thereby assured that America's industrial and military power would now be directed against Germany rather than against Japan.

Historians of German-American and Russian-German relations have quite rightly called Hitler's decision "irrational."[92] Viewed politically and militarily, it was indeed.

Hitler's hunger for impossible victories against impossible odds, however, could not be sated even by simultaneously warring against the Soviet Union and the United States. To his mind there was an enemy more worthy of his historic mettle. He must annihilate the Jews. Quite apart from the horrendous human consequences, Hitler's decision made no political or economic or strategic sense. The Jews had never been a political threat to Hitler's Reich and they were a clear cultural and economic asset. Yet at a time when reason dictated that Hitler should have concentrated all national energies on defending his Reich from the Soviet armies attacking from the East and the Allies from the West, he gave the orders that diverted hundreds of trains and billions of hours to the enormous logistical task of collecting, "processing," killing, and disposing of millions of innocent people who had been no threat to him or his Reich. The Holocaust contributed significantly to his defeat. It, too, was "irrational."

* * *

The decision for war in 1914 and again in 1939 was determined by the interplay of circumstance and pathological personality. But the circumstances were different, and so were the personalities of the Kaiser and the Führer. And these personal psychological differences determined the extent to which each was able to master his circumstances.

In the Kaiser's Germany, war was not inevitable. There were, it is true, domestic pressures which produced a climate favorable to war. But Imperial Germany was not beset by those economic tensions and crises which, within the Third Reich, could find resolution only through wars of conquest.

Moreover, Wilhelm was not in control of circumstances to the extent Hitler was. He possessed neither the ability nor the effective power wielded by the Führer. Although the Kaiser's political power was great, his position was defined by tradition, and his actions were curtailed by important political and social restraints. Prussian aristocrats, to take one example, looked warily at his claims of absolute power and recalled the old trans-Elbian jingle:

Und der König absolut —
Wenn er unsern Willen tut.[93]

His personality also limited his capacity to act with firmness of purpose and sense of direction. He was a mercurial dilettante with no clear plans for war — or indeed for anything else. Bismarck had compared him to a toy balloon that is let loose in the air: he drifted about unpredictably, erratically, and ineffectively with no particular destination in mind.

The limits of Wilhelm's personal influence are seen most clearly in the part he played in drawing up the strategic plans for war. In theory, the Kaiser as "Supreme War Lord" was responsible for all military decisions. But in practice it was the

German General Staff that did the planning for World War I, and their strategic plan had a decisive bearing on the decision to go to war. Trusting neither Wilhelm's military judgment nor his discretion, General Moltke and his staff worked out their modifications of the Schlieffen Plan without consulting the Kaiser. They were able to do so because temperamentally Wilhelm lacked the attention span and the *sitzfleisch* to endure long planning sessions which he found unbearably tedious.

One historical result of all this was the fateful decision to attack France by invading neutral Belgium. This decision, which brought the British Empire into the war, was made without the Kaiser's knowledge. This extraordinary fact was confirmed by Moltke during a conversation in 1921 with the noted anthroposophist and Goethe scholar, Rudolf Steiner, which shows clearly the extent and the arrogance of military power in Imperial Germany:

> How was it, I asked, that a war Minister could maintain in the Reichstag that the plan for the invasion of Belgium did not exist? "This Minister," Moltke replied, "did not know of my plan, but the Chancellor was informed." And the Kaiser? I asked. "No way!" answered Moltke. "He was too talkative and indiscreet. He would have blabbed it to the entire world."[94]

In August 1914, Wilhelm II, as Emperor and Supreme War Lord of Germany, signed the documents that launched World War I. But he had not done so because he had a clear plan for the war or because he was the master of circumstances leading to its outbreak. He had not acted so much as he had been acted upon by a combination of forces that he was unable or unwilling to master: insistent psychological pressures and the relentless logic of a disastrous strategic plan for war over which he had abandoned control.[95]

In contrast to Wilhelm, Adolf Hitler was a fanatic ideologue with obsessions about space, time, and racial purity. He knew with single-minded intensity exactly what he wanted from war, and he never deviated from his purpose. At a bare minimum, he wanted to dominate the continent and conquer a vast expanse of land in central and eastern Europe. This Greater Reich of the German Nation was to be populated by racially pure Aryans. (Hence the Führer Awards for female fecundity and frenetic efforts to increase racially desirable stock.) Lesser breeds were to serve as slaves or be sterilized or annihilated. During peacetime Hitler had experimented with "euthanasia" and the sterilization of thousands of people he considered "unworthy," but only conquest on a vast scale would provide him with the opportunity to carry out the mass sterilization and the genocide that his plans required.[96]

Hitler knew well that his master plan for an enormously expanded German Reich could never be achieved without war. That was fine with him. For war was not a last resort; it was his first choice, indeed the only way to get what he wanted.

Unlike the Kaiser, the Führer was personally responsible for drawing up the strategic plans and supervising their execution. He planned first to smash France and England and then to turn against his ally, the Soviet Union. He had looked forward to war in 1938 during the Czech crisis and felt thwarted by Chamberlain and the Munich Accord. Next time, he thundered, "no son of a bitch" [*schweinehund*] was going to deprive him of his war.[97]

There was no secret about Hitler's intentions. His plans for *Lebensraum* in the East and racial "purification" had been stated explicitly in *Mein Kampf* and were commonplaces of Nazi propaganda. In an important speech of November 10, 1938, Hitler told a hundred journalists that he was determined to go to war and that it was their duty to prepare the German people for war. Any statements he had made about peace were purely for political purposes.[98] In February 1938 and again in August 1939 he explained to army officers why it was necessary to go to war in the West against England and France in order to achieve dominion in the East.[99] The conquest of Poland was merely a preliminary to fulfilling his ambition of conquering the Soviet Union.

Hitler was able to indulge his personal fantasies about war, conquest and genocide because he controlled the power of a modern militarized state dedicated to those ends. Hitler had created that state and he alone determined policy for it. Thus it was the Führer who was in very truth what the Kaiser only claimed to be: "The All-Highest."

In 1939, war came again to the world because one man, Adolf Hitler, lusted for it and mastered the circumstances which could bring it about. His personal pathology required war, for war was always within him. Despite his bellicose blustering, war was not within the Kaiser. Notice the different behavior of the two men after giving the orders that plunged their countries — and the world — into war.

In August 1914, Wilhelm signed the orders for war and was immediately appalled by what he had done. He tried to back out and then, distraught and sleepless, spent anxious hours seeking solace in prayer. An associate said that he had never seen the Kaiser look so disturbed and tragic: "Here was a man whose whole world had collapsed."[100]

On August 31, 1939, after signing Order No. 1 which would send the *Wehrmacht* crashing into Poland the next morning, Hitler was "in a state of euphoria all day." He had a very good night's sleep.[101]

Wilhelm loved to dress up and play soldier in any one of his 250 uniforms, have himself photographed in 267 heroic poses, and painted as the very incarnation of War. But he didn't really mean it. Hitler did.

Notes

    1. Why did Germany hail the War and embrace it when it broke out? Because it recognized in it the bringer of its Third Reich . . . the synthesis of Power and Spirit. ("An die Redaktion des *Svenska Dagbladet* (Stockholm) April, 1915, in *Gesammelte Werke*, 13 vols. (Frankfurt/M., 1974), XIII, 551. Also reprinted as Anhang to *Friedrich und die Grosse Koalition* (Berlin, 1915). I am indebted to Adolf Gasser and Edson Chick for directing me to this quotation. This essay has profited greatly from helpful criticisms made by my colleagues, Thomas A. Kohut and Fred H. Stocking.

2. Manfred Messerschmidt, "Die Armee in Staat und Gesellschaft: die Bismarckzeit," and Wilhelm Deist, "Die Armee in Staat und Gesellschaft: 1890-1914," in Michael Stürmer, ed., *Das Kaiserliche Deutschland: Politik und Gesellschaft: 1870-1918* (Düsseldorf, 1970).

3. Elisabeth Fehrenbach, *Wandlungen des deutschen Kaisergedankens, 1871-1918* (Munich, 1969), 158, 200-206; Fritz Stern, *The Politics of Cultural Despair: A Study in the Rise of Germanic Ideology* (Berkeley, 1961), 49; Wolfgang Mommsen, *Max Weber und die deutsche Politik: 1890-1920* (Tubingen, 1959), 45, 53-58, 79-80.

4. As quoted in Fehrenbach, *Kaisergedanken*, 91.

5. Friedrich Gunolf, *Caesar im neunzehnten Jahrhundert* (Berlin, 1926).

6. Otto Mittelstadt, *Vor der Fluth: Sechs Briefe zur Politik der Gegenwart* (Leipzig, 1897), as quoted in Friedrich Zipfel, "Kritik der deutschen Oeffentlichkeit an der Person und an der Monarchie Wilhelms II bis zur Ausbruch des Weltkrieges," (unpublished Ph.D. dissertation, Free University of Berlin, 1952), 47.

7. "Mirror Image of the Nation: An Investigation of Kaiser Wilhelm II's Leadership of the Germans," in Charles B. Strozier and Daniel Offer, eds., *The Leader: Psychohistorical Essays* (New York, 1985).

8. Walter Rathenau, *Der Kaiser: eine Betrachtung* (Berlin, 1919 and reedition, 1923).

9. Lady Norah Bentinck, *The Ex-Kaiser in Exile* (London, 1921).

10. Graf Ernst Reventlow, *Von Potsdam nach Berlin* (Berlin, 1940), 398; Asa Don Dickinson, ed., *The Kaiser, A Book about the Most Interesting Man in Europe* (New York, 1914), 116-168.

11. Rathenau, *Kaiser*, 27.

12. The phrase is Isabel Hull's. See her splendid study, *The Entourage of Kaiser Wilhelm II: 1888-1918* (Cambridge, 1982).

13. Anne Topham, *Chronicles of the Prussian Court* (London, 1926), 15.

14. Quoted by Hull, *Entourage*, 177.

15. Henry W. Fischer, ed., *The Private Lives of William II and His Consort*, 3 vols. (New York, 1909), I, 69.

16. A reproduction of the portrait appears in Dickinson, *The Kaiser*, 19.

17. There are many statements to this effect. See E. F. Benson, *The Kaiser and his English Relations* (London, 1936), 51, 126; Lotha Freiherr Hugo von Spitzemberg, ed., *Das Tagebuch der Baronin Spitzemberg* (Gottingen, 1960), 297-298; Sir Sidney Lee, *King Edward VII* (London, 1925), who quotes a letter of the Kaiser of 30 December 1901 to Edward VII, 135-136, 15.

18. Paul Liman, *Der Kaiser: Ein Charackterbild Kaiser Wilhelms II* (Leipzig, 1909), 138-139.

19. Captain Sigurd von Ilseman, *Der Kaiser in Holland*, 2 vols. (Munich, 1967 1969), II, entry for 20 September 1935.

20. Arthur N. Davis, *The Kaiser I Knew: My Fourteen Years with the Kaiser* (London, 1918), 57.

21. Dirk Stegmann, *Die Erben Bismarcks, Pateien und Verbände in der Spätphase des Wilhelminischen Deutschlands: 1897-1918* (Köln, 1970), 105 ff, 277 ff, 293 as cited by Adolf Gasser, "Der deutsche Hegemonialkreig von 1914," in Imanuel Geiss and Bernd Jurgen Wendt, eds., *Deutschland in der Weltpolitik des 19. und 20. Jahrhunderts* (Dusseldorf, 1974), 323; Wilhelm Deist in Stürmer, ed., *Kaiserliche Deutschland*, 319, and Volker R. Berghahn, "Flottenrüstung und Machtgefüge" in same volume, 393.

22. *Staatskunst und Kriegshandwerk: Das Problem des 'Militarismus'; in Deutschland*, 4 vols. (Munich, 1965 –), II, 117.

23. As quoted in *Die Zeit*, 24 August 1984 in a feature article on the 70th anniversary of Germany's invasion of Belgium drawing its title from the statement of Moltke justifying the shooting of Belgium civilians: *"Wer sich uns in den Weg stellt . . ."* [Whoever stands in our way . . .].

24. See Fritz Fischer, *Germany's Aims in the First World War* (New York, 1967), *The War of Illusions* (New York, 1975); and Imanuel Geiss, ed., *July 1914: The Outbreak of the First World War: Selected Documents* (New York, 1967), and his earlier *Julikrise und Kriegsausbruch, 1914*, 2 vols. (Hannover, 1963).

25. Gasser in Geiss, "Deutsche Hegemonialkrieg," 326.

26. Arno J. Mayer, "Domestic Causes of the First World War" in Leonard Krieger and Fritz Stern, eds., *The Responsibility of Power: Historical Essays in Honor of Hajo Holborn* (New York, 1968), 297, and conversations with my colleagues, Dudley W. R. Bahlman, John M. Hyde, and William G. Wagner.

27. Jonathan Steinberg, "The Copenhagen Complex," *The Journal of Contemporary History*, I, 3 (July 1966): 43.

28. Michael Balfour, *The Kaiser and His Times* (London: Pelican, 1975), 83-85.

29. Thomas A. Kohut, "Kaiser Wilhelm II and his Parents," in John C. G. Röhl and Nicolaus Sombart, eds., *Kaiser Wilhelm II: New Interpretations* (Cambridge, 1982), 84-85. See also Golo Mann, "Wilhelm II" in *Archiv der Weltgeschichte*, Karl Dietrich Bracher, ed. (München, 1964), 12.

30. Lydia Franke, *Die Randbemerkungen Wilhelms II. in den Akten der Auswärtigen Politik als historische und psychologische Quelle* (Leipzig, 1934), 127, 130, 141.

31. Lamar Cecil, "History as Family Chronicle: Wilhelm II and the Dynastic Roots of the Anglo-German Antagonism," in Rohl, ed., *New Interpretations*, 101.

32. On this issue, as in others, the Kaiser was of two minds. He expressed his fear of Russian attack many times, but he also told the Austrian ambassador to Berlin on July 5, 1914 that "Russia at the present time was in no way prepared for war." Quoted by Geiss, *July Crisis*, 77.

33. Konrad H. Jarausch, "The Illusion of Limited War: Chancellor Bethmann-Hollweg's Calculated Risk, July 1914," in *Central European History*, Vol. II, No. 1 (March 1969): 58.

34. In the War Council of December 8, Moltke said, *Ich halte einen Krieg fü)r unvermeidlich und je eher, desto besser."* as quoted in Gasser, "Hegemonialkrieg," in Geiss, *Deutschland in der Weltpolitik*, 312.

35. See statements by Moltke, Bethmann-Hollweg, and Jagow in *Deutsche Dokumente* numbers 788, 790, 791 reprinted in Geiss, *July Crisis*.

36. Moltke's memoranda of 1909 and 1912 in Gerhard Ritter, *The Schlieffen Plan: Critique of a Myth* (New York: 1958), 101-102.

37. "Bethmann-Hollweg and the War: The Limits of Responsibility" in Krieger and Stern, eds., *Responsibility of Power*, 268.

38. Quoted in Paul Kennedy, "The Kaiser and German Weltpolitik: Reflections on Wilhelm II's place in the Making of Foreign Policy," in Röhl, ed., *New Interpretations*, 158.

39. Chancellor Bülow, *Nachlass*, draft speech, Bundesarchiv Koblenz, quoted in Kennedy, ibid., 149 (emphasis added).

40. Generaloberst Helmuth von Moltke, *Erinnerungen, Briefe, Dokumente 1877-1916*, Eliza von Moltke, ed. (Stuttgart, 1922), 14. "Necessity" was a favorite word of the German General Staff. Thus in an important memorandum of 1913, Moltke noted that in implementing the Schlieffen Plan it "is not pleasant" [*angenehm*] to begin the war by violating the neutrality of a neighboring state. But it was necessary [*notwnedig*]" because "it is our only chance for quick success." Ritter, *Staatskunst und Kriegs-handwerk*, II, 270-271.

41. Geiss, *July Crisis*, 369.

42. "Ein Zwiegesprach," Eulenberg Papers, Bundesarchiv, Koblenz, Vol. 74 quoted in Kohut, "Mirror-Image," 217 (italics in original).

43. Riezler diary entry of 21 August 1914 in Stern, "Bethmann-Hollweg and the War," 273. (Italics in original.)

44. Moltke, *Erinnerungen*, 338.

45. Balfour, *Kaiser*, 358.

46. Hermann John Weigand, *Magic Mountain* (Chapel Hill, NC: Duke University Press, 1964), 45.

47. Ibid., 40-42.

48. The German translation of this interview is given in full in Johannes Hohlfeld, ed., *Dokumente der deutschen Politik und Geschichte von 1848 bis zur Gegenwart*, Band II, "Das Zeitalter Wilhelms II, 1980-1918," (Berlin, 1951); see also *Die grosse Politik der europaischen Kabinette, 1871-1914*, Vol. 24, Anlage, 170-174.

49. Letter to Colonel Stuart-Wortley, October, N.D., 1908, Miscellaneous Manuscripts, Bodleian Library, Oxford.

50. See Dispatch from Germany, *New York World*, November 1, 1908.

51. Princess Marie Radziwell, *This Was Germany: An Observer at the Court of Berlin: Letters of Princess Marie Radziwell to General Di Robilant*, ed. and trans., Cyril Spencer Fox (London, 1937), 52-53. See also R. Vierhaus, ed., *Das Tagebuch der Baronin Spitzemberg* (Gottingen, 1960), 513.

52. Letter of November 6, 1908 in Helmuth Rogge, ed., *Friedrich von Holstein: Lebensbekenntnis in Briefen an eine Frau* (Berlin, 1932), 324-325.

53. The muzzle cartoon appeared in *Simplicissimus*, 28 December 1908.

54. See the articles by Hale's son, William Harlan Hale, "Thus Spoke the Kaiser: The Lost Interview Which Solves an International Mystery," *The Atlantic Monthly*, 1, 153 (May and June, 1934): 513-523, 696-705. The younger Hale was badly mistaken, however, in thinking that the full text of the interview was not known to foreign governments. It had not been "lost." The German, British, Japanese, French — and presumably the Russian — foreign offices all had copies of the full text and were deeply disturbed by it. (See Ralph R. Menning and Carol Bresnahan Menning, " 'Baseless Allegations': Wilhelm II and the Hale Interview of 1908," *Central European History*, Vol. VXI, Number 4 (December 1983): 368-397. The Kaiser had granted Hale permission to publish the interview and it was slated to appear in the *Century Magazine* in November 1908 — at the very time international fires were being set by the Kaiser's inflammatory *Daily Telegraph* interview.

55. The question of the Kaiser's sexual preferences remains open. Two historians who have studied the matter carefully conclude that while it is clear that Eulenburg was a practicing homosexual who fell in love with Wilhelm, Wilhelm's relationship to Eulenburg is less certain. He was very much attracted to him, but it is unlikely that he had physical relations with Eulenburg, or with any other male. [John C. G. Rohl, ed., *Philipp Eulenburgs politische Korrespondenz*, 2 vols. (Boppard am Rhein, 1976, Introduction; and conversation with Röhl at Sussex, January, 1982; see also Hill, *Entourage*, 64, 69, 70, 111]. I would conclude that Wilhelm was not an overt homosexual, but that he felt the need to defend against persistent homosexual tendencies by public displays of masculine power.

56. *Responsibility of Power*, 267.

57. Fischer, *War of Illusions*, 83.

58. Wilhelm, as quoted by Lawrence Wilson, *The Incredible Kaiser: A Portrait of William II* (New York, 1963), 91.

59. Hull, *Entourage*, 262-265.

60. Otto Hammann, *Um den Kaiser* (Berlin, 1919), 93-94.

61. Immanuel Geiss, "The Crisis of July 1914" in *Journal of Contemporary History*, I (1966): 86.

62. Admiral Müller's diary entry of 30 August 1914 begins, "The Kaiser, as he has often done recently — positively revels in blood: 'Pile the corpses 6 ft. high . . .' "Georg Alexander von Müller, *The Kaiser and His Court the Diaries, Notebooks and Letters of the Chief of the Naval Cabinet, 1914-1918*, Walter Gorlitz, ed. (London, 1961).

63. Volker Berghahn's translation for the quote "This time I won't chicken out!," seems anachronistic. (*Germany and the Approach to War* (London, 1973), 193). The phrase can also be rendered, "This time I won't give in" or "This time I won't collapse." It is important to emphasize that the decision which led directly to the First World War was made personally by the Kaiser without prior consultation with military or civilian advisors. Of the vast literature on the "July Crisis," see especially Luigi Albertini's magisterial work, *The Origins of the War of 1914*, translated and edited by Isabella M. Massey, 3 vols. (London, 1953), the second volume of which is devoted entirely to "The Crisis of July 1914." For a German view, see Imanuel Geiss' studies, previously cited at note 26. A recent American history of the period concludes that of the major events leading to the war, Wilhelm's decision on 5 July was the crucial one: "All the other actions to the fatal end followed like a chain reaction." Bernadotte W. Schmidt and Harold Vedeler, *The World in Crucible, 1914-1919* (New York, 1984), 8.

64. Fischer, *War Aims*, 86-87 and Moltke, *Erinnerungen*, 19-20.

65. Richard F. Hamilton, *Who Voted for Hitler?* (Princeton, N.J., 1982).

66. The full text of this important memorandum can be found in *Der Monat*, November 1948: "Der Seeckt-Plan: aus unveröffentlichten Dokumenten. Neues Tatsachenmaterial über die geheime Zusammenarbeit zwischen Reichswehr und Sowjet-Armee," 43-58. Translated excerpts are given in John Wheeler-Bennett, *Nemesis of Power: The German Army 1918-1945* (London, 1953), 136-138.

67. Imanuel Geiss, *Der polnische Grenzstreifen, 1914-1918: Ein Beitrag zur deutschen Kriegszielpolitik im Ersten Weltkrieg* (Hamburg, 1960), 5, 105, 108, 149.

68. "Der Seeckt-Plan," *Monat* November 1948.

69. Rolf-Dieter Müller, "Der Andere Holocaust: Der Krieg gegen die Sovietunion," *Die Zeit*, Nr 27 (8 July 1988).

70. William Ebenstein, *The Nazi State* (New York, 1943) in Robert G. L. Waite, *Hitler and Nazi Germany* (New York, 1969), 77, see also Christa Kamenetsky, *The Cultural Policy of National Socialism* (Athens, Ohio, 1984).

71. Martin Heidegger, *Die Selbtsbehauptung der deutschen Universitäten* (Breslau, 1933).

72. *Das deutsche Führer-Lexikon* (Berlin, 1934), 180.

73. T. W. Mason, "Some Origins of the Second World War," in *Past and Present* (December 1964), reprinted in Esmonde M. Robertson, ed., *The Origins of the Second World War* (London, 1971), 124-125.

74. Wolfgang Sauer, "Die Mobilmachung der Gewalt," in Karl Dietrich Bracher, Wolfgang Sauer, and Gerhard Schulz, *Die nationalzozialistische Machtergreifung: Studien zur Einrichtung des totalitären Herrschaftssystems in Deutschland* (Cologne, 1960), 751-752.

75. Wilhelm's mother describes the treatments in letters to her mother, Queen Victoria. See especially letters of 11 August 1859, 12 December 1859, 14 May 1861, 21 April 1863 and 28 April 1863 (Royal Archives, Windsor Castle). Treatments included immobilizing the good arm; placing the head in pulleys and harnesses to pull it straight; putting the arm in still-warm entrails of rabbits; using electricity to shock it into life. In later life, the Kaiser remembered bitterly that the amateurish efforts to cure him had no results "save excruciating pain." (*My Early Life*, New York, 1926), 26.

76. The Diaries of Admiral Philip W. Cumas, British Naval Attaché to Germany, 1906-1908 (Imperial War Museum, London, Microfilm); *Daisy Princess of Pless by Herself*, Desmond Chapman-Huston, ed. (London, 1928), 259; Henri de Noussanne, *The Kaiser as He Is* (New York, 1905), 118.

77. Robert G. L. Waite, *Psychopathic God: Adolf Hitler* (New York, 1977), 8-14.

78. To my knowledge the first to use this delightful epigram was Michael Balfour. But when I complimented him on it he said that it had not originated with him, and did not know where it had come from. Sounds very much like one of Adlai Stevenson's comments.

79. Norbert Bromberg has persuaded me that I was mistaken, in the *Psychopathic God*, in assigning guilt feelings to Hitler. See his persuasive discussion in *Hitler's Psychopathology* (New York, 1983), 259-269.

80. See Thomas Kohut, "Kaiser Wilhelm II and the Attempt to Achieve Personal and National Integration through Ceremonial." (unpublished paper)

81. *Reden* as quoted in Zipfel, "Kritik der deutschen Oeffentlichkeit," 158.

82. Max Domarus, ed., *Hitler: Reden und Proklamationen, 1932-1945* (Munich, 1965), 606.

83. Wilhelm's proclivity for alienating the very people he should have cultivated was extraordinary. Only a few indications can be given here. He needed close rapport with his generals; he embarrassed them publicly on maneuvers, he insulted them during his interminable games of skat by accusing them of cheating; he announced that their historic heroes, Bismarck and the elder von Moltke, were "lackeys and pygmies." He called the proud Imperial Princes "my vassals." He said that his loyal and long-suffering Chancellor, Bethmann-Hollweg, was "ripe for the sanatorium." He told his Naval Cabinet that he was fed up with their questions. "To hell with it, I am the All-Highest War Lord, I do not decide, I simply command." He told the German Socialists, the largest party in the country, that they were "unworthy to bear the name of German." He said that Socialist representatives should be hauled out of the Reichstag and shot. He announced to startled members of the Foreign office that "you diplomats have messed your pants, the entire Wilhelmstrasse stinks of shit."

84. Historians of Wilhelmian Germany debate at length about the extent of the Kaiser's effective political power: was there or was there not a "Personal Government?" For a valuable essay on this subject see John C. G. Röhl's Introduction to the volume he and Nicolaus Sombart edited, *Kaiser Wilhelm II: New Interpretations* (Cambridge, 1982). Thomas Kohut has made an important distinction

and concludes that Wilhelm was effective as a symbolic leader of Germany but a failure as a political leader. See his "Mirror Image," in *The Leader*, 22.

85. As quoted by Alvin Rosenfeld, International Scholars' Conference on the Holocaust, Indiana University, Bloomington, Indiana, November 5, 1980.

86. Domarus, ed. *Reden*, 1422-1423; Waite, *Psychopathic God*, 386-388. For an authoritative discussion of Hitler's war plans, see the first volume of a multivolume study, *Das deutsche Reich und der Zweite Weltkrieg*, being produced by the Research Center for Military History, Freiburg under the general editorialship of Manfred Messerschmidt. Volume one is entitled *Ursachen und und Vorausetzungen der Deutschen Kriegspolitik*, by Wilhelm Deist, Manfred Messerschmidt, Hans-Erich Volkmann, and Wolframm Wette (Stuttgart, 1979).

87. A photostatic copy of his handwritten will, dated May 2, 1938, may be found in Library of Congress, Manuscript Division, Ac.11590, Box 791. For his comments in 1939 about imminent death see as examples, *Documents in German Foreign Policy*, Series D. (Washington, D.C., 1956), 7: 201-202; Baldur von Schirach interview in *Stern* magazine, September 1967; and Domarus, *Reden und Proklamationen*, 1426-1427.

88. Domarus, *Reden*, 476.

89. Ibid., 470-471.

90. Bromberg, *Hitler's Psychopathology* 168, 184-185, 318.

91. Alan Bullock, "Hitler and the Origins of the Second World War," in *British Academy for the Promotion of Historical, Philosophical and Philological Studies Proceedings*, 53 (London, 1963), 259-287.

92. Albert Seaton, *The Russo-German War, 1941-1945* (New York, 1971), 214. See also James B. Compton, *The Swastika and the Eagle: Hitler, the United States, and the Origins of World War II* (Boston, 1967), xiii, 236.

93. The lines may be rendered:
We want a king with total sway —
If he will let us have our way.

94. Adolf Gasser, "Der deutsche Hegemonialkrieg von 1914," *Deutschland in der Weltpolitik des 19. und 20. Jahrhunderts*, Imanuel Geiss and Bernd Jurgen Wendt, eds. (Düsseldorf, 1974), 319. Chancellor Bethmann-Hollweg approved of the violation of Belgium neutrality because, though regrettable, it was "necessary." A student of English foreign policy on the eve of the War has concluded with high irony that it took "the sublime genius of the German General Staff" to bring England into the war against Germany. Paul Kennedy, *The Rise of Anglo-German Antagonism: 1860-1914* (London, 1980), 458-459.

95. Self-imposed limitations on his own power were continued after the war started. Walter Goetz, "Kaiser Wilhelm II. und die deutsche Geschichtschreibung," *Historische Zeitschrift*, 179 (1955), 37. Having surrendered his power to the Generals, Wilhelm then sulked and complained petulantly that they never consulted him. Admiral Georg Alexander von Müller, *Der Kaiser: Aufzeichnungen des Chefs des Marinekabinetts . . . über die Aera Wilhelms II*, Walter Görlitz, ed. (Berlin, 1965), 42. As the war progressed, the Kaiser gave up more and more political authority. His oft-repeated comment, "The Supreme Command considers it necessary . . .," identified correctly the basis for all military and — increasingly — for major political and economic decisions. By 1916, Germany had become a military dictatorship under generals Hindenburg and Ludendorff, with Kaiser Wilhelm reduced to endorsing their decisions. The extent of his abandonment of political power is perhaps best expressed in his admonition to Prince Max of Baden when he appointed him to the Chancellorship in October 1918: "You have not come here," he said, "to make trouble for the High Command." (Quoted by Golo Mann, "Wilhelm II", *Archiv der Weltgeschichte*, Karl Dietrich Bracher, ed. (Munich, 1964), 16.

96. Gerhard L. Weinberg, *The Foreign Policy of Hitler's Germany: Starting World War II, 1937-1939* (Chicago and London, 1980), 27, 451, 653, 657-58. See also Müller's article, "Der andere Holocaust," cited in Endnote 69.

97. Weinberg, *Starting World War II*, 463, 466.

98. For the text of the speech and critical comment see Wilhelm Treue, "Rede vor der deutschen Presse (10 November 1938)", *Vierteljahrshefte für Zeitgeschichte*, V. No. 2 (April, 1958), 175-191.

99. Nuremberg Document #798, PS, *Trial of the Major War Criminals*, 26: 338-339 and Weinberg, 558-562, 582.

100. Another intimate reported that Wilhelm could "be found in tears in corners of churches all over the Rhineland praying for hours together." See Balfour, *The Kaiser*, 358.

101. William L. Shirer, *20th Century Journey: The Nightmare Years: 1930-1940* (New York, 1984), 440.

PART II

Conventional War/Processes:
Introduction

A variety of psychological factors contribute to the problems governmental leaders have in managing contemporary limited wars. The need to limit the weapons used and the kinds of targets struck are apt to be countered by battlefield and domestic political concerns which reinforce psychological incentives to escalate, as Betty Glad and J. Philipp Rosenberg show in "Limited War. A Framework for Analysis" in Chapter 7. The specific difficulties American decision makers had in containing the Korean conflict is delineated in a second essay, "Tacit Bargaining Under Fire: The Korean War."

Once in a war, decision makers are also apt to be motivated to keeping it going out of a need to justify their earlier decisions. Thomas Milburn and Daniel J. Christie, employing cognitive dissonance theory, make this case in "Effort Justification as a Motive for Continuing War: The Vietnam Case." Drawing from historical materials and the experimental literature in social psychology, they show how many Americans, both leaders and the public, became increasingly committed to the Vietnam war as a consequence of the time and attention they gave to the project. The ability of individuals to confront the rising costs of the war and reconsider the whole enterprise, as Milburn and Christie also show, was influenced by the extent of their original involvement in the decision to go to war and their individual personalities.

The problems of contemporary warfare, however, cannot be understood by focusing exclusively on decision makers. Before 1914, traditional studies of battle concentrated on leaders and the outcomes of their battles. The men in uniform, it was simply assumed, would do their duty. A few historians — mainly of the French revolution — did note that some warriors performed with greater élan than others.[1] But the complex interaction between organizational factors, battlefield conditions, and human motivation to explain combat behavior did not become a major concern of scholars until recently. Today we know that despite their attitudes toward war in the abstract, men have to be trained and psychologically reinforced to fight and possibly die on the battlefield. In "The Soldier in Battle: Motivation and Behavioral Aspects of the Combat Experience," Anthony Kellett summarizes most of what is known today about this topic.[2]

Civilians, too, suffer psychologically in most contemporary wars. The very purpose of aerial bombardment, as George H. Quester argues in "The Psychological Effects of Bombing on Civilian Populations: Wars of the Past," is to undermine enemy morale. Public responses to the bombings, however, depend on a variety of factors such as the victims' distance from the bombings and the effectiveness of their own governments in providing outside assistance after the attack. Governmental leaders, given their personal commitments and political needs, may be less likely than civilians to consider surrender as a response to the bombing.[3]

Widespread public and elite attitudes may also make it difficult, as Paul R. Pillar argues in "Ending Limited War: The Psychological Dynamics of the Termination Process" (Chapter 12), to end any war which does not simply result in the complete demoralizing and/or disarming of one of the parties. Psychological shifts, he points out, must occur in a nation during a war if a negotiated settlement is to succeed. Perceptions of the enemy must change so that common ground can be found with that enemy, unsatisfied parties must relinquish their search for scapegoats, revenge, or redemption, and both sides must avoid the temptation to go for a big return for a low marginal cost.[4]

Nations, presumably, come out of a war having learned something in the process. Participants in high-cost wars might rethink their strategies and try to avoid situations which lead to such costly encounters. Yet, as Glad points out in "Limited War and Learning: The American Experience" in Chapter 13, the historical evidence suggests that the particular lessons drawn will vary, influenced by the political, war, American political leaders learned, under the sword of the nuclear Damocles, how to keep a local conventional war from getting out of hand. These broader lessons, however, were neglected by American decision makers in the beginning phases of the Vietnam war, as they fastened on the political costs of losing new areas to communism. After the Vietnam war, many American military leaders rejected the whole limited war idea. Committed to traditional military doctrine, they held to the view that one must fight to win in armed combat, and that unless one has clear congressional and public support for that objective, the United States should not enter into battle.

Notes

1. See John A. Lynn, *The Bayonets of the Republic: Motivation and Tactics in the Army of Revolutionary France, 1791-94* (Urbana: University of Illinois Press, 1984), 282.

2. The malaria and hepatitis picked up by American and English troops in North Africa and Italy contributed to the postponement of the D-Day invasion and delayed Allied advances into Germany, Ralph C. Greene argues in "The Undisclosed Depleting Epidemics in the European Theater of Operations During World War II," (unpublished paper, 1986); see also Greene, "The Epidemics that Delayed D-Day," *MD* (June 1986): 57. In addition to the sources cited by Anthony Kellett in Chapter 10, see James G. Hunt and John D. Blair, eds., *Leadership on the Future Battlefield* (Washington, DC: Pergamon-Brassey's International Defense Publishers, 1985). For a general history of the related issue of psychological warfare, with which we do not specifically deal in this volume, see David Owen, *Battle*

of Wits: A History of Psychology and Deception in Modern Warfare (New York: Crane, Russak, 1979); and Peter Watson, *War on the Mind* (New York: Basic Books), 1978.

3. Lord Cherwell's personality, for example, influenced the British decision in World War II to concentrate its bombing on working class neighborhoods, as Hugh Berrington has shown in "When Does Personality Make a Difference: Lord Cherwell and the Area Bombing of Germany," *International Political Science Review*, 10, 1 (June 1989).

4. The literature on how wars end is quite limited. Aside from Paul R. Pillar's *Negotiating Peace* (Princeton, NJ: Princeton University Press, 1983), major books and special journal editions include "How Wars End", ed. William T. R. Fox, *Annals of the American Academy of Political and Social Science*, 392 (November 1970); Fred C. Ikle, *Every War Must End* (New York: Columbia University Press, 1971); Nissan Oren, ed., *Termination of Wars* (Jerusalem: The Magnes Press, The Hebrew University, 1982); and Berenice Carroll, ed., "How Wars End: An Analysis of Some Current Hypotheses," *Journal of Peace Research*, 4 (1969): 295-320. Paul Kecskemeti's *Strategic Surrender* (Stanford: Stanford University Press, 1958), deals with surrender between major powers. Drawing on the World War II experiences, he shows that nations gave up when their armies and command structure were still intact. Their decisions were based on projections of obvious trends indicating that, over time, their relative situation would only get worse. For how nuclear wars might end see Clark C. Abt, *A Strategy for Terminating a Nuclear War* (Boulder: Westview, 1985); Paul Bracken, "War Termination," in *Managing Nuclear Operations*, eds. Ashton Carter, John Steinbruner, and Charles Zaket (Washington: Brookings Institution, 1987).

Chapter 7

Limited War: The Political Framework

BETTY GLAD and J. PHILIPP ROSENBERG

Recent experience with total war has obscured a long prior history of more limited encounters.[1] The very notion of war as a rational instrument of policy, as von Clausewitz wrote in the early 19th century, presupposes that armed conflicts would be limited by the nature of the political ends sought. "The political design is the object, while war is the means, and the means can never be thought of apart from the object."[2] Indeed, "the great majority of all international wars," as Robert Osgood notes "have been fought for ends far short of domination or annihilation, and by means far short of the complete destruction of the enemy's armed forces or his society."[3]

The nature of earlier limits were most evident in the modern state system in the wars of the 18th century. Ordinarily, the combatants in these wars maintained the distinction between the armed forces and the civilian populations and respected the boundaries of neutral nations. These limits were in part the result of the ethos of the period. Wars were fought for limited territorial or dynastic ends. They were no longer perceived as moral crusades, as the religious conflicts of the 16th and 17th centuries had been.[4] Material factors sustained these limits, as Osgood points out. The firepower that one belligerent could bring to bear against another was limited, and there were few economic and demographic resources which could be mobilized for military purposes. Constraints on the application of coercive force were closely tied to problems in recruiting and financing an army, as well as in the refusal of many fighters to see their activity as anything other than commercial employment.[5] In short, the moral climate and the material limits of the time, as Jordan and Taylor have pointed out, limited the intensity, the geographic scope, and the strategic objectives of war.[6]

Limited wars today — at least those in which the major powers have a substantial interest — differ in several respects from this earlier phenomenon. Restraints are not apt to be based on traditional notions of who the fighters are, of which targets are acceptable, and which geographical boundaries define the arena of conflict. Furthermore, there are no tangible and obvious limits to the arms and supplies available for military use. Limitations of such wars often requires a conscious

Interest Ratios

Power Ratios	A > B	A = B	A < B
A > B	1) A Wins	2) A Wins	3) ?
A = B	4) A Wins	5) ?	6) B Wins
A < B	7) ?	8) B Wins	9) B Wins

Figure 7.1. Possible Outcomes of Various Limited Types of War

decision not to employ military force in the most effective manner possible. The most powerful weapons in one's arsenal may not be used, obvious targets may be declared off limits, and unneutral aid by a third party to the other side may have to be ignored. Based upon a conscious hobbling of one's existing military capabilities, these limits seem to be more arbitrary, less "natural" than those honored in the 18th century. As a result, these limits are often difficult to maintain, and a substantial domestic debate may arise over the wisdom of their retention.

Strategic theorists are agreed upon the importance of most of the above. But there are differences among them in the exact definitions of limited war they would employ. Some have emphasized the primary importance of limited objectives. Thus, Osgood has written that "the decisive limitations upon war are the objectives of war."[7] Similarly, David Rees has described limited war as "political war par-excellence, in that purely military considerations are excluded."[8] But Bernard Brodie has suggested that the essential aspect of contemporary limited war is to be found in the deliberate restraint on the use of force. It is rooted in a prior desire to keep the war limited. One speaks of a limited war, he has written, "in a sense that connotes a deliberate hobbling of a tremendous power that is already mobilized and that must in any case be maintained at a very high pitch of effectiveness for the sake only of inducing the enemy to hobble himself to a like degree."[9]

Actually, if we look at the full array of possibilities, we can see that contemporary wars may be limited by the importance of the interests involved, the capabilities of the actual and potential belligerents and their concerns for avoiding a larger war. Several of the possible relationships, in terms of conventional wars, may be expressed diagrammatically, as we see in the figure above.

In some instances, as Figure 7.1 suggests, a short, conventional military undertaking may resolve the issue at hand. This is the case (cells 1, 9) when one nation has both a greater interest at stake and a greater military capability than its adversary. Contemporary examples would include the United States intervention in Grenada in 1983 and the Soviet intervention in Hungary in 1956. Even in the instances in which one nation has overall an approximate equality in capabilities with an adversary (cells 4, 6) it is likely to prevail if it has a much clearer and stronger interest in the outcome of the conflict. The conflict between the United States and the USSR over the emplacement of Soviet missiles in Cuba in 1962 is an example of this sort. The United States had the greatest stake in the immediate issues at hand, and the Soviet Union backed down, albeit with some face-saving outs.

At the other extreme (cell 5) is the case where both adversaries are relatively equal in terms of the interests involved and their relevant capabilities. In this instance, a quick and decisive outcome is unlikely, particularly if neither side possesses weapons of mass destruction with which they could escalate the conflict. The Iran-Iraq war, which lasted from 1980 to 1988 and killed nearly one million people, is a contemporary example of this kind of conflict.[10]

Some of the wars noted in this figure may involve a nearly total effort (in terms of the goals and the mobilization of available weapons, people, and resources) in the pursuit of centrally important national goals on the part of one of the parties. The possibility noted in cell 5 is the one kind of engagement in which this is true of both belligerents. But all the wars noted above are limited to the extent that nuclear weapons are not employed and many major powers remain out of the conflict. Certain problems will arise, it should be noted, in situations where the possibility of escalation exists (e.g., the introduction of new kinds of weapons or the entrance of new parties into the conflict.) Take the situation noted in cells 4 and 6, above. If the nation with the greater interest in the outcome of a conflict at one level decides in the course of the conflict that it can obtain even more than it had envisaged at the beginning of the conflict, its adversary may be required to redefine the situation. Finding that it has new interests being challenged, that adversary is likely to escalate its commitment to the situation. The result is that the conflict moves from the type shown in cell 4 or 6, to that shown in cell 5. Two powers with equal interests and capabilities are now joined in battle, with results less clearly determinate than they had been earlier.

To illustrate the above point, one might look at the Cuban missile crisis. Had the United States used its first victory over the USSR to demand new concessions in Berlin or Eastern Europe, a broader conflict could have resulted. If two nuclear powers were to find themselves in this kind of situation, they would face the real possibility of a drift into nuclear war. Competition in risk taking could lead to a kind of chicken game in which neither side backs down. It is the realization of this possibility that provides the major motivation for both sides to avoid such a situation, or to get out of it as soon as they can. Even in situations where one belligerent has nuclear weapons and the other does not, the fear of escalation may serve to contain the conflict. If the nonnuclear power has a strong ally, the nuclear power has an incentive to keep its behavior constrained so that the other will have no motives to enter into the fray. During the Korean War, as we shall see, the United States was reluctant to take the war to mainland China out of fear that its Soviet ally might directly enter into the battle.

Especially problematical, in terms of defining and predicting what the end of the war might look like, are those cases (cells 3, 7) in which asymmetries in capabilities are offset by crosscutting asymmetries in interests. The American operation in Vietnam was subjected to such cross-pressures, and the course of that war should be instructive as to some of the problems the more powerful country is apt to face in such a situation. The initial U.S. assumption was that as the militarily superior power, it could gradually increase its efforts against the Vietcong and the North Vietnamese to the point that they would be reasonable and agree to some sort of compromise. What the United States failed to anticipate was that for the enemy this was not a limited war in which mutual constraints would be observed and some compromise worked out at the end.[11] For the North Vietnamese the war was fought for a purpose central to their aspirations and needs (i.e. national unification) and they would be willing to bear a very high level of pain to achieve their goals. Eventually, the United States had to increase its commitments to Vietnam to the point that the military and economic costs of the war seemed incommensurate with the American interests at stake and many Americans began to challenge its purported objectives.[12] Eventually, the morality of the entire endeavor came under serious question. As Robert McNamara noted on May 19, 1967, "The picture of the world's greatest superpower killing or seriously injuring 1,000 noncombatants a week, while trying to pound a tiny backward nation into submission on a issue whose merits are hotly debated, is not a pretty one."[13] These concerns, when combined with apprehensions that the Chinese might intervene if the United States escalated further, led the United States to freeze its operations at a medium level of violence.[14] The result was a military stalemate, for a long period of time, at a higher level of violence.[15]

It is these asymmetrical wars in which one or both parties possess nuclear weapons (or have allies who might employ them on their behalf) that are most likely to present the problem of finding boundaries of the sort mentioned above. The value of Brodie's definition of limited war is that it focuses our attention on the most crucial variables in these types of contemporary limited wars. While it is the discovery and maintenance of the limits which keeps the war limited, this process requires a great deal more than the simple will to avoid mutual destruction. Bargaining of some sort must take place to discover boundaries to the conflict. But negotiating in wartime is apt to be especially difficult, with emotions running high, diplomatic relations nonexistent, and other normal communication channels clogged. The alternative, ordinarily, is a form of tacit bargaining. Intentions are signaled through statements and moves, and the goal is the coordination of actions around certain salient solutions.

These salient solutions include phenomena such as prevailing historical boundaries, rivers, or mountains important to the defense of each; equity in the form of a return to the status quo antebellum; or a 50-50 division of disputed goods. All are obvious points at which the opponents may meet for their mutual benefit, without either losing face.[16] Qualitative differences between weapons may also provide prominent boundaries for mutual limitation and restraint.[17] The most significant limit on warfare since the end of World War II has been found in the refusal to use biological or nuclear weapons. Initially the value of these weapons as markers was to be found in the incentives not to employ them because of the massive and indiscriminate damage they could cause. But even if these weapons were to be refined so that their destructive capabilities could be better controlled, they retain their importance as symbols. It is so difficult to reach understanding concerning conflict limitations during actual hostilities that traditions of nonuse of certain kinds of weapons may be the one limit combatants can settle upon. An additional reason for maintaining the nuclear "boundary" has been delineated by John Thomas. Soviet strategic thought up to the middle 1980s had been based on the assumption that nuclear war must be total.[18] In this regard, an initial use of strategic nuclear weapons by the United States could have been interpreted by the USSR as a decision for all-out war.

Once limits have been reached in tacit bargaining, there is an incentive to maintain them. Both sides have had to identify, separately but simultaneously, boundaries for the conflict which make sense to the other; and success on the first try may be essential to any understanding. Because these mutually acceptable limits are so difficult to find, the fear is that if one gives up one set of understandings, no other alternatives may be found.

Yet, military and domestic political pressures to cross these boundaries are apt to build up in the course of war. The nature of the limiting process may not be understood by many people within each nation, and domestic military, political, and psychological pressures to escalate can become very strong.[19] A variety of battlefield situations, too, are apt to provide incentives to escalate, as Glad and Rosenberg point out, below, in "Bargaining Under Fire."[20] But escalation, as Richard Smoke has indicated, is a risky business. Escalating powers often are insensitive to the concerns of their opponent and they may well threaten new interests of the other side without realizing it.[21] Military superiority at one level of violence, moreover, may not be present at other levels of violence. It has been argued, for example, that the United States could have secured a better outcome in the Korean war had it used its overall conventional superiority against the Chinese forces in Manchuria. Had the USSR entered into that conflict as a consequence of the American escalation, as Glad and Rosenberg note, below, the United States would have had to face an unpleasant choice between a possible military defeat or the escalation of the war to the nuclear level, where it did have superiority.

The successful management of most types of limited wars, as the forthcoming suggests, demands a great deal of its decision makers. It requires an extraordinary degree of rationality and self-control in a situation where subjective factors inevitably play a central role. In the typical wars of the 18th century, traditional notions of what one does in battle and what constitutes a win or loss provided a framework for national leaders against which they could check their progress. In the prototypic limited war today, the very definition of how war is to be fought and what a successful ending might be has to be worked out de novo. To maintain control of the war, under these circumstances, a clear vision of the enemy's goals, capabilities, and ability to receive messages must be maintained and difficult choices squarely faced.

Leaders will have serious problems in meeting these conditions. Objectivity regarding one's enemy is difficult under any circumstance. But when a war drags on, without any clear end in sight, decision makers are apt to contemplate escalations without seriously considering how their actions might legitimately threaten the other side. Moreover, as Glad and Rosenberg show, below, the need to adhere to certain apparently arbitrary limits to keep the war limited is apt to be countered by strong domestic political pressures to escalate the war. To avoid the cognitive dissonance and anxiety that such choices provoke, national leaders may well choose the domestically rewarding or psychologically rewarding alternative, downplaying the probability that their pursuit will have negative consequences in terms of the conduct of the war.

The termination of limited wars, too, is likely to fall short of some rational standard. Only those conflicts in which one nation has greater capabilities and more important interests at stake than its adversary are apt to be short and have clear markers (i.e., conventional military victory) which will define when the war is over. Certain other kinds of conflicts may go on for a very long time and require an extraordinary diplomatic skill for even a cessation of hostilities. In those cases in which nations of nearly equal capability are competing over matters which each consider of vital importance, the natural result is apt to be some sort of stalemate. Mutual exhaustion may provide the motive for an end to such wars. The Iran-Iraq war is an example of this kind of ending. Often in such situations, as Paul Seabury has suggested, "the substantial issues are not even for the moment resolved. . . ." The first three Middle East wars of 1945-48, 1956, 1967, and the Laotian Truce of 1961 he sees as examples of such endings.[22]

In asymmetrical wars there is not even one most likely outcome. The party with greater capabilities in reserve, for example, may use those capabilities to bring things to a head.[23] Several Americans pressured the United States government to undertake operations along these lines both during both the Korean and Vietnam wars.[24] Alternatively, the more powerful combatant may decide that its interests do not justify the costs of remaining in the war and choose to leave the field of battle. This is how the Vietnam War ended for the United States, although the retreat was covered by a face-saving compromise.[25] Another possibility is that both sides may stop short of their maximum objectives, and end the conflict through a compromise which gives each side part of what it wants. This is how the Korean War ended (though Seabury placed it in the above category).[26]

Solutions which require compromise or retreat, however, are psychologically very difficult to work out. Leaders are apt to respond to prolonged competition over important goals with the feeling that their self-esteem is on the line. The other actor, then, is the one who must back down. These responses are apt to be especially strong for men who see themselves as powerful members of a hardball culture where concession is viewed as weak.[27] The difficulty of settling for any termination point short of victory is apt to be compounded by the widely shared psychological hurdles in the public as a whole. People who have suffered a great deal and who have become personally committed to specific national goals are apt to view any compromise, whether unilateral or mutual, as a betrayal. Anything short of a traditional victory is viewed as an act of defeat or submission.[28] In short, any end to a limited war short of victory requires important psychological shifts in both leaders and mass publics. The nature of these shifts and some of the difficulties in making them are delineated in detail by Paul Pillar in "Ending Limited War" in this section.

Notes

1. Charles A. Logfren, "How New is Limited War?" *Military Review*, XLVIII, 7 (July, 1967): 66-123.

2. Karl von Clausewitz quoted in Robert Osgood, *Limited War: The Challenge to American Strategy* (Chicago: University of Chicago Press, 1957), 23.

3. Robert E. Osgood, "Limited War," in *International Encyclopedia of the Social Sciences*, Vol. 9, ed. David Silk (New York: Macmillan and Free Press, 1968), 302.

4. Ibid., 302-303.

5. Osgood, *Limited War*, 64-66, 78-80.

6. Amos A. Jordan and William J. Taylor, Jr., *American National Security: Policy and Process* (Baltimore, MD: Johns Hopkins University Press, 1981), 250-251.

7. Osgood, *Limited War*, 4; see also 2-3, 15, 20-21, and 237-251.

8. David Rees, *Korea: The Limited War* (New York: St. Martin's, 1964), xvi.

9. Bernard Brodie, *Strategy in the Missile Age* (Princeton, NJ: Princeton University Press, 1959), 311. For general discussion, see 309-314.

10. Shaul Bakash, "History of Modern Iran," *Encyclopedia Americana* (Danbury, CT: Grolier), 15, 386.

11. See Jordan and Taylor, *American National Security*, 264-265.

12. James William Gibson, *The Perfect War: Technowar in Vietnam* (Boston: Atlantic Monthly Press, 1986), 96-97.

13. Mike Gravel, *Pentagon Papers: The Defense Department History of United States Decisionmaking on Vietnam*, 4 vols. (Boston: Beacon, 1971), IV: 171-172. For problems in fighting counterinsurgency warfare, see Eqbal Ahmad, "The Theory and Fallacies of Counterinsurgency," *Nation* (August, 1971): 70-85. For a discussion of the legality of the U.S. policies of destroying hamlets harboring the Vietcong, see Telford Taylor, *Nuremberg and Vietnam: An American Tragedy* (Chicago: Quadrangle Books, 1970), 144-148. For the application of traditional just war doctrine to contemporary warfare, see "Dilemmas of Deterrence," this volume.

14. For the political battles in 1968 to reverse the escalatory process, see Townsend Hoopes, *The Limits of Intervention: An Inside Account of How the Johnson Policy of Escalation in Vietnam Was Revised* (New York: David McKay, 1969), 97-116.

15. For these types of endings see William T. R. Fox, "The Causes of Peace and Conditions of War," in *The Annals of the American Academy* 392 (November 1970): 1-13; and Andrew Mack, "Why Big Nations Lose Small Wars: The Politics of Asymmetric Conflict," *World Politics*, 27, 2 (January, 1975): 175-200.

16. Osgood, *Limited War*, 10.

17. See Thomas Schelling, *The Strategy of Conflict* (Cambridge, MA: Harvard University Press, 1960), 64-68.

18. Bernard Brodie, *Strategy in the Missile Age*, 305-330; Klaus Knorr, *On the Uses of Military Power* (Princeton, NJ: Princeton University Press, 1966), 92-100; Schelling, *The Strategy of Conflict*, 259-263.

19. John R. Thomas, *Limited Nuclear War in Soviet Strategic Thinking,"* *Orbis*, X, 1 (Spring, 1966): 184-212.

20. For a criticism of the gradual escalation policies toward Vietnam see John A. McCone, "Memorandum of April 2, 1965," Document 97 in "The Pentagon Papers", *New York Times* ed. (New York: Bantam, 1971), 440.

21. For the view that threats to escalate can be rationally employed by nations possessing military superiority within a certain range of the metaphorical escalation ladder, see Herman Kahn, *On Escalation: Metaphors and Scenarios* (New York: Praeger, 1965), 37-51, 216-229, 290; and Colin Gray and Keith Payne, "Victory Is Possible," *Foreign Policy*, 39 (Summer 1980): 14-27.

22. Richard Smoke, *War: Controlling Escalation* (Cambridge, MA: Harvard University Press, 1977), 23-30.

23. Paul Seabury, "Provisionality and Finality," in Fox, *The Annals of the American Academy* 392 (November 1970): 96-104. For the dynamics of ending large conventional wars between major powers, see Paul Kecskemeti, *Strategic Surrender: The Politics of Victory and Defeat* (New York: Atheneum, 1964), especially 5-23. For an application of his concepts to nuclear war and the need for finding artificial limitations, ibid., 249-258.

24. See Larry Berman, *Planning a Tragedy: The Americanization of the War in Vietnam* (New York: Norton, 1982), 143; and Admiral U. S. Grant Sharp, "We Could Have Won in Vietnam Long Ago," *Reader's Digest* (May 1971): 118-123.

25. For the negotiations leading to the Vietnam truce signed in January 1973, and the view that this truce was but a marker in the continuing battle for the control of Vietnam, see Allan E. Goodman, *The Lost Peace: America's Search for a Negotiated Settlement of the Vietnam War* (Stanford, CA: Hoover Institution Press, 1978), 100-180. For the fall of South Vietnam in 1975, see Alan Dawson, *55 Days: The Fall of South Vietnam* (Englewood Cliffs, NJ: Prentice-Hall, 1977).

26. The dispute over repatriation of prisoners of war held up negotiations for about a year, and eventually a vast number of North Koreans and Chinese prisoners refused repatriation. During the last four months of the war, approximately 200,000 UN and communist soldiers were battle casualties. From Bevin Alexander, *Korea: The First War We Lost* (New York: Hippocrene Books, 1986), 482-483.

27. For a description of "hardball" style, see Lloyd Etheredge, *Can Governments Learn? American Foreign Policy and Central American Revolutions* (Elmsford, NJ: Pergamon, 1985), 146-157, 169, fn.71.

28. Oftentimes this results in a search for scapegoats. See, for example, General William C. Westmoreland's suggestion that the mass media contributed to the psychological victory the Vietcong attained in the United States after the TET offensive in his *A Soldier Reports* (Garden City, NJ: Doubleday, 1976), 321-328, 354-359.

Chapter 8

Bargaining Under Fire: Limit Setting and Maintenance During the Korean War

BETTY GLAD and PHILIPP ROSENBERG

A case study of the Korean War delineates the difficulties in discovering and maintaining limits during a conventional war. Certain boundaries were discovered in that war, and some were maintained. A close look at the decision-making process, however, shows how fragile those limits were. Battlefield-situational, and domestic political forces — as well as the accompanying underestimations of the enemy's interests and capabilities — contributed to and reinforced psychological pressures to escalate the war.

I. Salient Solutions to the Problem of Limits

Certain geographic boundaries provided the most obvious limits of the conflict. The 38th parallel, which had originally been used to facilitate the surrender of Japanese troops, had become an internationally recognized boundary with the establishment of separate Korean governments. When the North Korean armies crossed that boundary in June 1950, the United States and the United Nations Security Council interpreted the violation as a clear act of aggression and were determined to push the aggressor back to the parallel. The subsequent decision of the U.S./UN forces, in the fall of 1950, to cross that boundary, was a signal to the Chinese that the U.S./UN forces were no longer willing to settle for the status quo antebellum. Later, when it became clear that neither side could win the war without a possible escalation of the conflict beyond tolerable limits, the 38th parallel became the armistice line between the two sides. On the basis of this compromise, the war was brought to a close. Unlike the 38th parallel, one qualitative boundary was maintained throughout the war. United Nations ground troops stopped at the Yalu river, and Chinese bases on the Manchurian side of the river were not bombed. In return, the Chinese restricted their bombing of the UN forces from air bases within China. The United States, too, was able to operate out of air force and navy bases in Japan which were left intact.

The war also was limited qualitatively in terms of its participants. The United States decided not to accept the Nationalist Chinese offer of troops, and the USSR refrained from direct participation in the war. Weapons limitations — such as the moratorium on the usage upon both poison gas and nuclear weapons — were also observed.

There were target limitations even in the Korean peninsula proper, although these were asymmetrical in some respect and changed during the course of the war. The United States, for example, bombed North Korea, but the North Koreans did almost no bombing south of the 38th parallel. Prior to the Chinese entrance into the conflict, Americans refrained from bombing the bridges over the Yalu river, key links in the main supply routes for North Korean troops. After the Chinese entry into the war, the United States bombed these bridges. But even then American pilots were instructed to avoid flying over Chinese territory on their approaches to the bridges. The Chinese, for their part, limited their bombing of American positions in Korea. When their MIGS first appeared in action on 1 November 1950, the Chinese made no move to attack United Nations troops fighting in the Korean peninsula.

II. Motivation for Limits

The above limits were unilaterally discovered, asymmetrical to some extent, and were based on self-restraint.[1] They reflected, however, each side's fear of what the other side might do. Thus American restraint, especially in the early phases of the war, was motivated by the fear of Soviet entry into the war. Truman himself sent Stalin a personal note on 27 June 1950 assuring him that the U.S. goal in Korea was simply the restoration of the status quo antebellum.[2] The decision later not to expand the war against mainland China, Dean Acheson testified in Senate Hearings, was based on the concern that Moscow would honor its treaty obligation with China under the Sino-Soviet Pact signed in February 1950. "Even if the treaty did not exist," he said, "China is the Soviet Union's largest and most important satellite. Russian self-interest in the Far East and the necessity of maintaining prestige in the Communist sphere made it difficult to see how the Soviet Union could ignore a direct attack upon the Chinese mainland."[3] Such a counter escalation by the USSR, it was feared, would have been very costly. With Russian air and ground superiority in the area, the United States could have been expelled from Korea, and the Chinese mainland successfully defended.[4] In these circumstances the United States would have had no option but to accept a disastrous loss or escalate elsewhere.

Pressures from America's allies created additional incentives for self-limitation. On the eve of Truman's meeting with General MacArthur at Wake Island in mid-October 1950, the British Foreign Secretary Ernest Bevin bluntly suggested that the President give categorical instruction to MacArthur not to take action outside Korea without his express orders. In early November, an administration decision giving MacArthur the right of hot pursuit of Chinese planes into Manchuria and against Chinese planes attacking UN troops in Korea was reversed after all 13 U.S. allies vehemently objected to the decision. When Truman, in a press conference on November 30, suggested that nuclear weapons might be used against Chinese troops, the British prime minister, Clement Attlee, hurried to Washington to make sure that the British were consulted in any such decision. Indeed, Attlee urged the United States to negotiate with the Chinese, even if it meant falling back to the earlier objective of containing at the 38th parallel.[5] Later in the spring of 1951, when the United States considered a blockade of the entire China coast, the British, French, and other European political leaders expressed their opposition to this widening of the war. Even the new Churchill government, more inclined to support American initiatives in the war than the Labor government had been, opposed the blockade. The action could only be effective, they argued, if it included the Russian port of Dairen and Port Arthur, but that might prompt Russian entry into the conflict.[6]

Particular strategic and tactical considerations reinforced some of these limits. Key figures in the administration feared that if the United States attacked Chinese forces in Manchuria, the Chinese could bring their air force against crowded and vulnerable airports in Korea and Japan. The decision not to use nuclear weapons was partly due to the feeling that the use of these weapons would not be decisive in Korea. Simulations of the United States nuclear strikes (Operation Hudson Harbor) in the fall of 1951, for example, showed many difficulties in the timely identification of large masses of ground troops against which they could be meaningfully used.[7]

None of the above limitations would have persisted, however, if they had not served the mutual interests of the parties involved. Although they were asymmetrical in some respects, the particular limits reached made it possible to contain the conflict to the Korean soil in a way that permitted something like an equal test of strength in the area. The U.S. decision not to go beyond the Yalu boundary enabled China to put its men in Korea. China's decision not to bomb the major entry points of UN supplies enabled the United States to fight a conventional war within Korea. Proof that the United States saw its bombing limitations as dependent on the self-restraint of the Chinese is evident in the authority given MacArthur to bomb airfields and other bases in Manchuria and Central China should the Chinese launch major air attacks on U.S./UN troops inside Korea.[8] MacArthur's successor, General Matthew Ridgeway, asked for and was given similar authority.

III. Motives to Escalate: Battlefield Incentives

Even when limits are in the interests of all parties to a conflict, they often are very difficult to find and maintain. Several different kinds of pressures to escalate are apt to be present. First, and probably most obvious, are the battlefield incentives for the expansion of goals. The importance of these factors at several different phases of the Korean war should make this clear.

When the United States entered into the Korean War in late June 1950, its objective was simply to push the North Koreans back to the 38th parallel and restore the status quo antebellum. But battlefield successes led the United States to expand its objectives. At the time of the Inchon landing on September 15, the Joint Chiefs of Staff authorized General MacArthur to take action requisite to push the North Koreans back north of the 38th parallel and to destroy their forces.[9] With the success of that landing, U.S./UN troops previously bottled up at Pusan on the tip of the Korean peninsula swept North. On October 1, as South Korean forces crossed the parallel, General MacArthur demanded the complete surrender of the North Korean armies. A week later the United Nations approved a resolution which would enable the UN to establish "a unified, independent and democratic government in the sovereign state of Korea," and U.S. troops crossed over the line. Dean Acheson, who had initially proposed that U.S./UN troops only go up to the 38th parallel, had changed his mind shortly after the Inchon landing and he shepherded the resolution through the United Nations General Assembly.[10]

Washington's approval of the decision to move north of the 38th parallel was guarded in several respects. In their messages to MacArthur on September 15 and September 27, the Joint Chiefs of Staff had authorized action across the 38th parallel only on the condition that China and/or the Soviet Union showed no signs of intervening. To reassure the Chinese that a united Korea under UN auspices would not constitute a threat to them, the latter order specified that only South Korean troops be used in the provinces bordering on Manchuria or the USSR. A 15-mile buffer zone south of the Yalu would be established, within which non-Korean troops could not operate; and South Korean military personnel were not to hold top occupation posts north of the 38th parallel. The United States also refrained from bombing within a two-mile buffer zone along the Yalu and the hydroelectric plants located near the border which served the needs of Manchuria.[11]

But with the success of his troops in North Korea, MacArthur was able to ignore the conditions placed on his advances by Washington. In late October, the General ordered the U.S. 8th Army and the X Corp to move into the northeast Korean province bordering China and the Soviet Union. A month later MacArthur ordered what he characterized as a final "clean-up" operation, moving the full X Corp and the Eighth Army toward the Yalu in a classic pincer movement. Their orders were to go up to the bank of the river.

Somewhat paradoxically, the subsequent American retreat provided another kind of motivation for escalation of another kind. The Chinese had crossed the Yalu river in mid-October and by the end of the first week in November, had mauled the ROK First and Sixth Divisions and destroyed the 3rd battalion of the US 8th Cavalry.[12] On November 26, two days after MacArthur announced an end to the war offensive, the Chinese began their massive counteroffensive in the Yalu valley.

On November 30 and December 1, the U.S./UN troops suffered 11,000 casualties alone.[13] By December 5, communist forces had retaken the North Korean capital of Pyongyang. The American retreat, the longest in U.S. history, ended on January 20, some 50 miles south of the 38th parallel near Wonju. In June 1951, the battle lines were stabilized near the 38th parallel, after two other Chinese offensives had been turned back and the United States had been able to gain some ground.[14] The result was a war, which at the level it had been fought, seemed to offer no possible termination point.

Frustrated by the apparent stalemate, the United States at the end of August 1950, initiated "Operation Strangle," a major air interdiction campaign. Almost a year later, when it became apparent that this air campaign was not changing the battlefield situation, the United States undertook a massive bombardment of North Korea's cities and the Yalu power plants, as well as military targets. Chinese supply lines in North Korea were wiped out, civilian centers were devastated. Washington had even accepted the probability that a few bombs might fall on the Chinese side of the Yalu River.[15]

In the spring of 1953, when the armistice talks seemed to have reached a dead end, the Eisenhower administration considered other escalations which would have transformed the nature of the war. On 20 May 1953, the Joint Chiefs recommended that preparations be made for possible air and naval attacks against Communist communication lines in China and Manchuria, a naval blockade of the China coast, and the use of the Chinese nationalist forces in diversionary operations. Little opposition to the plan was expressed and Eisenhower himself announced that if circumstances dictated an expanded effort in Korea, this plan was the most likely to be employed. At this time the United States and the United Nations undertook the destruction of irrigation dams and rice fields in Korea as a means of increasing unrest in the countryside.[16]

American policy leaders at the time were even considering the possible use of atomic weapons. At a National Security Council meeting in February 1953, Dulles argued that the distinction between atomic and conventional weapons should be broken down and that it was the Soviet Union that had been trying to sell the idea that atomic weapons were in a category of their own. At the same meeting President Eisenhower suggested that the United States should consider the use of tactical nuclear weapons in the neutralized Kaeson zone. In March, Eisenhower and Dulles were "in complete agreement that somehow or other the tabu which surrounds the use of atomic weapons would have to be destroyed." The Joint Chiefs, too, in their 20 May 1953 proposals to the NSC, suggesting that strategic and tactical atomic bombs might be used to obtain "maximum surprise and maximum impact on the enemy, both military and psychologically." Eventually, nuclear weapons were incorporated into U.S./UN plans for military operations should the armistice talks fail. Atomic missiles were moved to Okinawa in Spring 1953, and Dulles subsequently confirmed that it had been the intention of the United States to use these weapons against Korea and China. Eisenhower himself subsequently noted in the spring of 1955 that he did not see why nuclear weapons, when used on strictly military targets, should be treated differently from a "bullet, or anything else."[17]

IV. Motives for Escalation: Domestic Military and Political Pressures?

Pressures by American military leaders were partly responsible for the U.S. decisions to escalate in response to the foregoing battlefield incentives. As early as July 1950, MacArthur confided to the visiting Army Chief of Staff General J. Lawton Collins his desire to carry the war into North Korea.[18] Later he sought out public support for his battles against what he viewed as unnatural constraints dictated from Washington. In a speech before the Veterans of Foreign Wars read on 28 August 1950, he criticized the Administration's policy of neutralizing Formosa. The Island, he argued, is the fulcrum of the American defense perimeter in the island chain bordering the Asian mainland."[19]

After MacArthur had crossed the 38th parallel, he presented the administration with fait accomplis, as suggested above. His decision in late October to use any and all ground troops in the drive into the northeast province bordering China and the USSR ran contrary to the express orders of the Joint Chiefs of Staff that non-Korean ground forces not be used on the Manchurian border.[20] His November 6 order to bomb the bridges of the Yalu was made before he had Washington's approval. Only after the General warned the president that not to bomb would result in a "calamity of major proportions," did the latter reluctantly agree that MacArthur could bomb the bridges spanning the Yalu up to the middle of the river.[21] The general's decision in late November to move his troops right up to the banks of the Yalu was in direct opposition to the suggestions of the Joint Chiefs of Staff that he halt his offensive on the high ground commanding the Yalu Valley. He had to destroy all enemy forces south of Korea's northern boundary, he explained. It was essential to the restoration of unity and peace to all of Korea.[22] Even in late November and early December, as his troops fell back under the Chinese assault, he continued his campaign to escalate the war. Messages were sent to the *New York Times*, *U.S. News and World Report*, *United Press*, and other news media justifying his policies and suggesting that the U.S./UN setback was due to the restrictions placed upon him by Washington.[23]

By the spring of 1951, MacArthur was openly challenging the authority of the president to define the goals of the war, as well as orders sent out on December 6 to clear all policy statements with Washington. On March 24 he undercut the president's attempts to begin negotiations with the Chinese by publicly calling for the surrender of Chinese forces. If he could carry the attack to China's "coastal areas and interior bases," he proclaimed, she would collapse.[24] Several days later, on April 5, a letter he had written the Republican Minority Leader in the House, Joseph Martin, was read on the floor of the House. In that letter MacArthur questioned the Administration's whole limited policy. There is "no substitute for victory in war," he proclaimed.[25]

Yet, MacArthur was not the only military man who wanted to expand the war. While Truman was president, it is true, the Joint Chiefs of Staff supported him in an attempt to keep the war limited.[26] Yet senior officers with command responsibilities in Korea battled against the restraints placed on their operations. On 27 May 1952, for example, General Mark Clark proposed that two nationalist divisions be sent immediately to join his troops. In October 1952, he urged a major drive north to the waist of Korea, supported by air and naval attacks on China. He even suggested that nuclear weapons might be used. The only exceptions to this line of thought by ground force commanders were Matthew Ridgeway and Maxwell Taylor.[27]

American politicians, too, made it difficult for the president to keep the war limited. Since the spring of 1950, Republican critics had been proclaiming that the Democratic administration had "lost" China, and that its policies, generally, had been "appeasement" in the face of communist advances. Secretary of State Dean Acheson was seen as the architect of these policies, an exemplar of what the senators saw as an arrogant, effete Eastern seaboard elite.[28] Even General George Marshall, who replaced Louis Johnson as Secretary of Defense in the fall of 1950, was subjected to a brutal nomination process in which several Republican members of the Senate charged him with being soft on Communism. William Jenner of Indiana, for example, accused Marshall of being a front for a "vicious sell-out."[29] Indeed, the Administration's Asian policy became a key issue in the 1950 Congressional elections. Senator Robert Taft blamed the North Korean invasion on the Truman Administration's China policy and Acheson's speech of January 1950, in which Acheson had stated that Korea was not within the defense perimeter of the United States.[30] As U.S./UN troops approached the 38th parallel in September 1950, Senator William Knowland charged that failure to cross the parallel would constitute appeasement of Russia.[31] Later, after MacArthur had been relieved of his command, Senator Robert Taft, Congressman Joseph Martin, and other Republican leaders discussed the possibility of impeaching the president. Senator Taft described any possible truce at the 38th parallel as "appeasement."[32]

These military and congressional pressures to escalate the war were reinforced by public pressures. Polls taken between August 1951 and November 1952 showed that a majority of the American people (55% to 60%) favored the bombing of Communist supply bases inside China. During this same period of time public support for American aide to Nationalist Chinese for the express purpose of attacking the People's Republic of China ranged from 56% to 59%. In May 1952, 53% agreed with the option presented in a Roper poll to "stop fooling around and do whatever is necessary to knock the Communists out of Korea once and for all," compared with only 13% who supported the pullout option. The president, himself, as a consequence of his resistance to the pressures for escalation suffered a loss of popularity by several percentage points.[33]

These difficulties, in both elite circles and within the American public, with the way the Truman administration limited the war were partly the result of broader cultural patterns. Americans had long seen their wars as moral crusades, as Robert Osgood and Robert Tucker have pointed out.[34] This attitude was evident even in the views of the American Ambassador to the UN, Warren Austin, who declared at the beginning of the Korean War that "the United Nations must see that the people of Korea attain complete individual and political freedom." Similar sentiments were expressed by Phillip Jessup in a CBS interview.[35] President Truman, himself, had reiterated, on September 1, the commitment made several years earlier in the Cairo declaration that the Koreans "have a right to be free, independent and united."[36]

Compromise in such situations becomes morally questionable. Victory must be the goal in battle, and field commanders should be allowed to use their best weapons and go to enemy bases to assure that end. This was the view of MacArthur and the group of army officers around him.[37] The General himself later charged that the Korean War had introduced "a new concept into military operations — the concept of appeasement, the concept that when you use force you can limit that force."[38] The Republican leaders of the Senate and many other Americans agreed with this assessment of the situation.[39]

V. Motives for Escalation: Psychological

MISPERCEPTIONS OF THE ENEMY AND OTHER EGO-DEFENSIVE ADAPTATIONS

When the Administration made its original decision to cross the 38th parallel, there was good reason to believe that the Chinese would respond militarily to American attempts to overthrow the North Korean regime. A threat was made on 25 September 1950, when the Acting Chief of Staff of the People's Liberation Army told K. M. Panikkar, the Indian Ambassador to Peking, that the Chinese would not "sit back with folded hands and let the Americans come up to the border." On October 3, the Chinese foreign minister, Chou En-lai, in a late night meeting with Panikkar, made the threat explicit. "American intervention into North Korea would encounter Chinese resistance." On October 8, Mao Tse-tung called on Chinese "volunteers" to "resist the attacks of U.S. imperialism." On October 10, three days after the first U.S. troops crossed the parallel, the Chinese Foreign Ministry issued another warning that "the Chinese people cannot stand idly by with regard to such a serious situation created by the invasion of Korea."[40]

These warnings, moreover, were accompanied by military steps which should have reinforced their credibility. In September, China sent fresh troops to Manchuria — a fact noted by both the Far Eastern Command and the CIA. In late October, Chinese combat forces were South of the Yalu — another fact the Far Eastern Command reported to Washington. Although the American intelligence agencies underestimated the actual Chinese strength, the information should have given prudent men cause for alarm.[41]

American decision makers at this point were caught on the horns of a dilemma. MacArthur's successes at Inchon, the pressures from Congressional leaders and the public, and the forthcoming Congressional elections all created a domestic political imperative to move ahead. If American decision makers did not order U.S./UN troops across the 38th parallel, it would be politically disastrous at home. On the other hand if China, as a consequence of that move, did intervene, the United States could find itself bogged down in a militarily unexpeditious enterprise, possibly even a much broader war.

To avoid the internal conflicts and the anxiety of having to choose between two pain-inducing alternatives open to them at this time, American decision makers opted for several ego-defensive devices people are inclined to use in such no-win situations.[42] They shifted much of the responsibility for the calculations of the risks of moving ahead to MacArthur. In an eyes only cable to him on September 30, General Marshall had said, "We want you to feel unhampered tactically and strategically to proceed north of the 38th parallel." An October 9 directive gave him the authority to continue operations, should the Chinese intervene "as long as, in your judgment, action by forces under your control offers a reasonable chance of success."[43]

When MacArthur failed to show the kind of prudence they urged upon him, the president and other leaders in Washington were guilty of procrastination, failing for some time to directly confront him. At a meeting on November 21, for example, top officials from State and Defense agreed not to change MacArthur's orders or otherwise limit his discretion to do what he saw as militarily necessary.[44] Even after his press barrage critiquing the restraints Washington had placed upon him, Washington only resorted, on December 6, to a general order to overseas military commanders and diplomats to clear all but routine statements with the appropriate departments and to refrain from direct communication on such matters with the publicity media.[45]

It took two clear acts of insubordination for Washington to finally confront MacArthur directly. His public threat, on March 24, to take the war to China was met with a direct order, sent to him personally, to clear all policy statements with Washington. When his letter to Joseph Martin was read on the floor of the House, the President finally confronted the impossible situation and decided that MacArthur had to be recalled. Two days earlier, Secretary of Defense George Marshall, after reading through a recount of MacArthur activities, had come to the conclusion that he should have been recalled two years earlier.[46]

The cost to the president of this decision was as severe, at least in the short term, as he and others must have feared. He was booed at Griffith Stadium in his first public appearance after the dismissal. Resolutions passed in the Illinois, California, and Florida legislatures and various city councils condemned his action. Telegrams pouring into the White House after the dismissal ran 20 to 1 against his decision. Republican leaders noted to the press that they had discussed the "question of impeachments. . . ."[47] Public opinion polls published in April showed that large majorities of the public — from 66% (AIPO) to 58% (NORC) — disapproved of the dismissal.[48]

In addition to procrastination and the delegation of decision-making authority, decision makers screened data in ways which would buttress the politically preferred option. The messengers bringing the Chinese deterrent threats to Washington were depreciated and their signals dismissed as bluff. President Truman, for example, dealt with one deterrent threat by depreciating the messenger. "Mr. Panikker had in the past played the game of the Chinese Communists fairly regularly," Truman wrote in his memoirs, "so that his statement could not be taken as that of an impartial observer."[49] Acheson thought the Chinese were engaged in a "poker game," and although there was a risk in crossing the 38th parallel, there would be a greater risk in "showing hesitation and timidity." Moreover since the UN forces were already advancing, he thought it too late to stop this process.[50] Even after the entry of Chinese volunteers into Korea in October, misinterpretations persisted. When the Chinese broke off all contact along the battle front in early November to give the United States time to back off, it was seen as a sign that China was only willing to engage in a token symbolic resistance and would therefore not intervene in full force.[51]

Groupthink was promoted through the exclusion from the inner decision-making circles of individuals who raised troubling questions about the general direction of the war. In the Far Eastern Command General MacArthur surrounded himself with like-minded individuals who screened information in ways that supported his policy preferences. In Washington, George Kennan, Paul Nitze, and others in the Policy Planning Council in the State Department who took the Chinese warnings seriously were never invited to brief Truman's advisory group or given the opportunity to develop their views in depth.[52]

Intelligence reports, too, were framed so as to support the preferred option. Major General Charles Willoughby, MacArthur's chief of intelligence, persistently underestimated Chinese strength in Korea, despite complaints from field commanders and others on the spot that his estimates were too low. MacArthur himself framed the reports he sent on to Washington with his own benign interpretations. On November 1, for example, he attributed stiffened opposition in battle to a decision by the North Koreans to make a last-ditch stand, rather than to the presence of two or possibly three Chinese regiments in the field. In early October, an Eighth Army report giving accurate descriptions of Chinese positions along the Yalu never was forwarded to Washington.[53]

Prevailing images of the Chinese that suggested they neither would nor could enter into the war were sustained through selective filtering of relevant data, and various rationalizations. Since the turn of the century America had supported the territorial integrity of China and the open door for trade policies, and had engaged in missionary, medical, and relief work in that country. Given this earlier history, many people in Washington saw themselves as strong and generous patrons and simply assumed that the Chinese viewed them in the same way. They appreciated all that the Americans had done for them, it was assumed, and would understand that the Americans had no aggressive designs towards them.[54] To maintain these prior images, the significance of the victory of the communist revolutionaries in China for the traditional U.S.-Chinese relationship, was downplayed. Communism simply was seen as an alien ideology imposed upon the Chinese by a few leaders and their Russian supporters. Eventually, it was assumed, they would find the Russian yoke onerous and throw it off. Certainly the Chinese would not intervene in Korea to protect what were essentially Russian interests.[55]

Geopolitical arguments, too, were employed to allay any potential concerns that the Chinese would really see the American presence in North Korea as a threat to their interests. Acheson, for example, thought it would be "sheer madness" for China to enter the war, when her greatest problem was with the Soviet domination from the north. By October 1950 the CIA endorsed this view, suggesting the Chinese would not accept Soviet aid necessary to fight a war against the United States because it would increase Soviet influence in Manchuria.[56] China, too, was perceived as being too militarily weak to mount an effective response. A Joint Intelligence Committee report of July 6, for example, concluded that the hit-and-run guerrilla tactics in which the PLA was experienced were not adequate to meet "a well trained force with high morale equipped with modern weapons and possessing the will and the skill to use those weapons."[57] At Wake Island on October 15 MacArthur assured Truman that if the Chinese tried to get down to Pyongyang, "there would be the greatest slaughter."[58] Omar Bradley, Dean Rusk, Philip Jessup, and other top officials at the meeting concurred.[59]

Chinese domestic considerations also were seen as working against Chinese involvement. The Chinese army, the Joint Intelligence Committee reported in early July 1950, was needed to maintain internal stability in North China and elsewhere. As a consequence, the Chinese would not be able to redeploy large forces on the North Korean border. Indeed, the entire domestic program and economy of the PRC would be jeopardized by such a move, according to a CIA memo of October 12. It would encourage anti-Communist forces in China to the point that "the regime's very existence would be endangered." The report concluded that despite the threats made by Chou En-lai, the troop movements to Manchuria, and propaganda charges of atrocities and border violations, "there are no convincing indications of an actual Chinese Communist intention to resort to full-scale intervention in Korea."[60]

Sometimes these perceptions of the Chinese were sustained through trend thinking. Because the Chinese had not entered the war at the beginning, they never would. Their best opportunity to intervene had been the previous July, it was argued, when UN forces were desperately defending the Pusan perimeters. With 200,000 troops massed on the North Korean border, they had outnumbered UN forces by about two to one. Within a ten-day march from the South, they could have had a decisive impact.[61] The possibility that the Chinese might view an American presence on their Manchurian boundary as a national security threat and therefore be more prepared to take costly risks was not seriously considered by those who held this view. This is a common error in affairs such as these. Past outcomes are often not seen as the consequence of several underlying causes, some of which might no longer be operative.[62]

There was a potential in the later phases of the war for similar mistakes about Soviet responses to new American escalations. Moscow had not responded aggressively to the American escalation in North Korean, the choice of bombing targets near the Russian border, and the stray American bombs that sometimes touched them. They also sought to play, on occasion, the role of peacemaker between the United States and North Korea.[63] This moderation, however, was perceived by some American experts simply as a reaction forced on them by American power, not a choice they had made. The United States counselor to Moscow, Walworth Barbour, saw the "amiable side of Soviet countenance" as the "forced smile of an exposed scoundrel." Soviet moderation, he continued, was not the sign of any change of heart, but the "early ephemeral fruits of the policy of containment and building areas of strength."[64]

Trend thinking was also evident in the assumption that because that country had not entered the war early, it would not do so in the future. "Moscow," as one intelligence estimate blandly noted, continues "to limit its own role in the Korean War and has not sought to use the war as an excuse for initiating broader hostilities."[65] Another intelligence report used by the NSC Planning Board assumed that the United States could undertake a major escalation of the war without too great a cost. If the U.S./UN forces destroyed industrial complexes through aerial bombardment, the USSR might "be willing to sacrifice some of their interests in Korea to obtain a cessation of hostilities." It was possible, the report admitted, that if these air attacks were combined with a new American thrust into North Korea, the USSR might introduce Soviet ground forces into Korea. But even in that event, the USSR would leave it to the U.S/UN forces to interpret whether or not the Soviet response was an act of war.[66]

Fortunately, President Truman, the Joint Chiefs of Staff, and the policy planning staff in the State Department were more sensitive than some of the intelligence agencies to the possibility that American escalations of war outside the Korean peninsula could bring the USSR into the war. Fear of a potential Russian retaliation, as we have seen, was a major motive for the initial decision to confine the war to the Korean peninsula.[67] When the Eisenhower administration, in the late spring of 1953, finally threatened a major escalation against the Chinese mainland, the Chinese backed down and an armistice was signed. The United States would never know what the USSR would have done had the United States actually implemented that threat.

IMPACT OF INDIVIDUAL PERSONALITIES

The idiosyncratic personality traits of a few key decision makers also fueled the pressures for escalation.[68] MacArthur's differences with his superiors in Washington over the limitations placed on his operations seem to have been grounded, in part, in his desire for a fight with the Chinese. At a meeting with General Ridgeway in August 1950, he discounted the view that the Chinese might intervene in Korea. But he added, "I pray nightly that they will — would get down on my knees" to have a chance to fight them.[69] MacArthur's later statement torpedoing the first Truman peace initiative, John Spanier suggests, was really an attempt to take the war to China proper in an effort to destroy, once and for all, their potential for expansion in Asia.[70] Truman himself would later observe that MacArthur's attempts to take the war to the Chinese mainland were not due to any illusions that the communists would not escalate in return. Rather, Truman contemplated, MacArthur, unlike himself, "was ready to risk general war."[71]

The General's feelings of infallibility were also relevant to the strategically disastrous decision he made in late November 1950 to separate his forces in the final drive up the Yalu. The General had been a risk taker throughout his military career and his luck in these earlier decisions had no doubt reinforced his feelings that he could not fail.[72] In this instance, as in the past, he simply dismissed the concerns of other military men. When the Joint Chiefs of Staff raised serious questions about the advisability of that operation on strictly military grounds, MacArthur dismissed their views as irrelevant, given their distance from the battlefield. Surrounded by aides who shared his views of his own powers, his intelligence reports supported his desire to move forward. When it began to become apparent that this undertaking would be less successful than his earlier ventures, MacArthur and his top aides refused to deal with that data. For example, Major General Oliver Smith (the commander of the First Marine Division) was ignored when he complained to General Edward Almond (the commanding general of the X Army Corp and MacArthur's Chief of Staff) that his troops were too strung out.[73]

This enormous self-confidence, moreover, was a factor in MacArthur's ability to intimidate his superiors in Washington. The President and Joint Chiefs had gone along with MacArthur in part, because they believed that battlefield commanders should be able to make decisions based on facts on the ground. As Truman later explained to Richard Neustadt, a president has to back up the field commanders he has picked: "That's the only way a military organization can work."[74] There were political reasons, too. MacArthur had also made it clear that he would publicly denounce any attempt to keep him from reaching the Yalu as an act of appeasement. As Acheson later noted, it would have been better militarily to have taken a stand, as the Chiefs had proposed, at the Pyongyang-Wonson line to the south. But "that would have meant a fight with MacArthur, charges by him that they had undermined his victory . . . and his relief under arguable circumstances."[75]

Yet, the failure of MacArthur's superiors to confront him directly also was the result of the awe he inspired in them. The president, in his meeting with MacArthur at Wake Island, did not confront him with their differences over the conduct of the war, and he told reporters afterwards that MacArthur was "one of America's greatest soldier-statesmen."[76] After MacArthur's dazzling success at Inchon, the members of the Joint Chiefs lost confidence in their judgments that might run counter to his. Admiral Sherman was so impressed that he later admitted that he wished he had MacArthur's self-confidence.[77] Indeed, in the Pentagon, as Ridgeway later noted, there was "almost a superstitious awe of this larger-than-life military figure who had been so often right when everyone else had been wrong. . . ."[78] Even Dean Acheson, who was put off by MacArthur's arrogance, decided it was someone else's responsibility to deal with him.[79] As he later confessed, he felt an "uneasy respect" for the "sorcerer" of Inchon.[80]

The desire for a fight with the Chinese was not confined to the General. John Foster Dulles, too, on several occasions, said and did things that suggest he wanted to beat the Chinese, rather than strike a deal with them. In March 1953, when speech writer Emmet Hughes asked him if he would be glad or sorry if the Communists were to accept tomorrow a compromise resolution forwarded by India, he responded, "We'd be sorry. *I don't think we can get much out of a Korean settlement until we have shown —before all Asia —our clear superiority by giving the Chinese one hell of a licking"* (emphasis in original).[81] Dulles subsequently made suggestions that, had they been heeded by President Eisenhower, could have stalled the peace process. Thus at a meeting of the NSC on 8 April 1953, Dulles suggested that the United States consider going back on provisions in the armistice agreed to earlier. It was "now quite possible to secure a much more satisfactory settlement in Korea rather than a mere armistice at the 38th parallel." His preference, which he had expressed to journalists at a dinner party two days earlier, would have been to reopen the talks to secure a division at the waist of Korea, rather than the 38th parallel. Later that month he expressed his views that the talks would prove to be a "booby trap," enabling a communist build-up to the disadvantage of the United States.[82] Later Dulles made it clear that he valued high-risk strategies as a way of maximizing American interests. "The ability to get to the verge without getting into the war is a necessary art," he observed. "We [the United States] had walked to the brink, and we looked it in the face."[83]

SUNK COSTS AND CHANGING VALUES

The pressures for escalation in certain phases of the Korean War cannot be understood without reference to the phenomenon of psychological entrapment. Whenever individuals find themselves in prolonged conflicts in which one or both sides have invested much, they are apt to get "locked into a self-perpetuating cycle of attempts to regain or justify . . . past losses."[84] In the process, their motives change and they seek new values not articulated at the beginning of their competitive interactions.

Experimental research centering around the dollar auction game is instructive along these lines.[85] In games where individuals make unrecoverable bids to buy a dollar, there are usually two natural quitting points to the game. The first is the value of the prize — the most rational conclusion from an economic cost-benefit standpoint. The second marker is the expenditure of 50% of the player's resources, an amount that in these experimental games was always larger than the value of the prize. Once this second threshold is crossed, few players stop short of expending all of their resources.[86] Underlying these shifts in the costs the players were willing to bear were shifts in motivations. From a desire for profit, players moved to a desire to regain money already invested, to a desire to beat the opponent. As the motivation shifted from economics to interpersonal goals, the perception of the opponent became increasingly important. In post test questionnaires, subjects often attributed the escalation to the active bidding of the other party, seeing themselves as only a passive follower.[87]

The players concern with his own prestige plays an important role in this phenomenon. Entrapment, as Rubin, Brockner, Small-Weil, and Nathanson have shown, is likely to exert a more powerful effect under social conditions when the need to appear tough and unyielding in the eyes of one's opponent is exacerbated through competition.[88] Subjects who perceive themselves to have been humiliated by their opponent are prone to retaliate with greater severity than those who were similarly exploited but who didn't perceive themselves as such. This retaliation occurs even though it requires sacrificing positive outcomes. In some instances the concern about the loss of face becomes so central that it "swamps" the importance of the tangible issues at stake.[89] Added to this is the widely held belief that quitting is an undesirable trait, indicating a lack of courage or willingness to persist.[90]

Limited wars, we suggest, may place participants into situations remarkably similar to the auction game. Once a belligerent has invested significant nonrecoverable resources in its attempt to win its original goal, the nature of its goals are apt to change. Values in these circumstances will shift from what may have been concrete, realizable goals such as territorial gain to amorphous objectives such as "winning," or the maintenance of the national prestige and self-worth of the decision makers involved.

The definition of American goals in certain phases of the Korean war can be understood in these terms.[91] Once the United States had publicly committed itself to the unification of Korea, it had a sunk cost which would not permit a retreat. A backdown at that time, as Alexander George and Richard Smoke suggest, would have meant a serious loss of prestige.[92] Even when it became clear that the Chinese had begun to infiltrate Korea, practically every American decision maker thought the United States should move ahead as a means of probing Chinese intentions. Even John Paton Davies, who feared China might have aggressive intentions, thought it would be humiliating for the United States to fall back to a defensive position at that time. It "would be interpreted by the Kremlin and Peiping as a precipitate retreat inviting bold exploitation."[93]

As the war and the armistice talks dragged on, the U.S. investment in terms of money, time, and prestige increased. Eventually, the United States was willing to risk general war for the sake of a point of national honor. In January 1952, the United States decided that there would be no concession on the issue of voluntary repatriation of prisoners, and the talks were deadlocked over the issue. In late May 1953, with the war dragging on and communists still refusing to accept the principle of the voluntary repatriation of prisoners, the Eisenhower Administration raised the stakes with an ultimatum. The other side would have to agree to the United Nation's final terms or the talks would be broken off. At another level, Secretary of State Dulles informed Nehru on a visit to New Delhi in late May 1953 that if the fighting had to be resumed, the United States would go all out to win and would restrict neither its efforts or its weapons.[94] In effect, President Eisenhower had chosen to make a threat of a larger war, rather than giving into the Communist demands on the issue of repatriation of prisoners.[95]

Sunk costs, in short, played a significant role in the American determination not to back down after it had crossed the 38th parallel and in the escalations in the final phases of the war. Moving from its initial position in January 1950 that Korea was not of prime strategic importance to its interests, the United States had come to the point where it was delivering ultimatums that might have been very costly to implement, risking as it were a general war in the Far East so as to salvage its honor. It was a response not altogether unusual, given the dynamics of such interactive processes.

VI. Conclusion

The Korean war shows some of the difficulties in controlling limited war in the nuclear age. In the process of that war America's top political and military leaders came to understand that any encounter in which the major powers have even potentially important interests at stake must be limited through tacit bargaining and the ability and willingness to find qualitative boundaries and quantitative limits to that encounter. Moreover, most of these leaders came to understand that the objective of such wars could only be not to lose; "winning" had become an inappropriate and dangerous goal. These understandings, however, were acquired with difficulty, against many countervailing forces. Battlefield victories, as well as battlefield stalemates, created incentives to escalate the war. These were reinforced by domestic military and political pressures, which in turn were motivated by ideological and psychological factors apt to be endemic in conflict of this sort. The decision makers who came to resist these pressures, as President Truman did after the initial crossing of the 38th parallel, are likely to do so at great political cost to themselves.

What the American case suggests is that limited war in the present age is based on a sophisticated doctrine, not likely to be embraced by military leaders trained to win or by men on the battlefield who might be sacrificed, or by politicians and people back home who have not been trained in strategic theory. Once these deadly competitions begin, decision makers are under great pressure to respond to these escalatory pressures, and under these circumstances they are prone to misperceive the intentions and capabilities of the enemy. Aside from the cognitive biases due to outdated perceptual screens, they are apt to be motivated by psychological defenses which enable them to act in apparently effective ways by minimizing the potential costs of escalation. Some leaders may resist these forces, though it is not at all clear that such leaders will be in a position of command. Many are inclined to project their private aggressions and fears onto the situation. Moreover, as the costs of the war mount, national goals are apt to change. Eventually, as the entrapment literature and the Korean experience both suggest, concrete limited objectives are apt to be replaced by concerns over national honor and self-esteem, with all the problems those motives present for finding a way out of the situation.

Notes

1. Morton H. Halperin, *Limited War in the Nuclear Age* (New York: Wiley, 1963), 56.

2. Walter Lafeber, *America, Russia, and the Cold War, 1945-1966* (New York: Wiley, 1967), 99.

3. Rosemary Foot, *The Wrong War: American Policy and the Dimensions of the Korean Conflict, 1950-1953* (Ithaca, NY: Cornell University Press, 1985), 137.

4. Ibid., 136.

5. David Rees, *Korea: The Limited War* (New York: St. Martin's, 1964), 167-171; Foot, *The Wrong War*, 85, 94. For an overview of allied pressures for limitations on the United States, see Dennis Stairs, *The Diplomacy of Constraint* (Toronto: University of Toronto Press, 1974).

6. Foot, *Wrong War*, 155.

7. Ibid., 117, 155.

8. Ibid., 141.

9. Rees, *Korea*, 99-100.

10. Ronald F. Bartel, *Attitudes Toward Limited War: An Analysis of Elite and Public Opinion During the Korean Conflict* (doctoral dissertation, University of Illinois, 1970), 67; see also, Rees, *Korea*, 100-102; David S. McLellan, *Dean Acheson: The State Department Years* (New York: Dodd, Mead, 1976), 285, 9-27.

11. Rees, *Korea*, 103; Bartel, "Attitudes Toward Limited War," 43, 73; Halperin, *Limited War*, 51-53; McLellan, *Dean Acheson*, 285.

12. James McGovern, *To the Yalu* (New York: William Morrow, 1972), 48-66.

13. Foot, *Wrong War*, 101.

14. Rees, *Korea*, 178-195, 243-264.

15. Bartel, *Attitudes Toward Limited War*, 46; Foot, *Wrong War*, 178.

16. Ibid., 208-209.

17. Quotes from Foot, *Wrong War*, 208, 213. For other arguments that U.S. threats were serious, see Ronald J. Caridi, *The Korean War and American Politics: The Republican Party as a Case Study* (Philadelphia: University of Pennsylvania Press, 1968), 272; Fred I. Greenstein, *The Hidden-Hand Presidency* (New York: Basic Books, 1982), 62.

18. Rees, *Korea*, 98.

19. John W. Spanier, *The Truman-MacArthur Controversy and the Korean War* (New York: Norton, 1965), 73-74.

20. Trumbull Higgins, *Korea and the Fall of MacArthur* (New York: Oxford University Press, 1960), 64-65; Spanier, *The Truman-MacArthur Controversy*, 123.

21. McGovern, *To the Yalu*, 75,233; see also J. H. Kalicki, *The Pattern of Sino-American Crisis: Political-Military Interactions in the 1950s* (New York: Cambridge University Press, 1975), 63.

22. McGovern, *To the Yalu*, 104, 12-13, 34.

23. Spanier, *The Truman-MacArthur Controversy*, 149-151.

24. Ibid., 200-201; Higgins, *Korea and the Fall of McArthur*, 108-109.

25. McGovern, *To the Yalu*, 170-178; Spanier, *The Truman-MacArthur Controversy*, 203-204.

26. General Omar Bradley, Chairman of the Joint Chiefs of Staff; General J. Lawton Collins, Army Chief of Staff; and General Hoyt Vandenburg, Air Force Chief of Staff, were all protegés of General Marshall, serving with him in the European Theater of Operations in World War II. Along with Admiral

Forrest P. Sherman, Chief of Naval Operations, who had served in the Pacific, they were all pragmatists, as defined by Morris Janowitz. See his *The Professional Soldier: A Social and Political Portrait* (Glencoe, IL: Free Press, 1960), 283-321. See also Irving L. Janis, *Victims of Groupthink* (Boston: Houghton Mifflin, 1972), 53.

27. Foot, *Wrong War*, 177, 184; Rees, *Korea*, xv.

28. Rees, *Korea*, 60-61.

29. Lebow, *Between Peace and War*, 175.

30. Rees, *Korea*, 65.

31. Ibid., 100.

32. Foot, *Wrong War*, 156-157.

33. For aid to Nationalists, see Leonard Kuznitz, *Public Opinion and Foreign Policy* (Wesport, CT: Greenwood Press, 1989), 157-158. Other poll data from John E. Mueller, *War, Presidents, and Public Opinion* (New York: Wiley, 1973), 78, 103, 227.

34. Osgood, *Limited War*, 33-34; Robert W. Tucker, *The Just War: A Study in Contemporary American Doctrine* (Baltimore, MD: Johns Hopkins Press, 1960), 74-93. Tucker argues that Americans evaluate the justice of a war in terms of its origins and purpose. The whole notion of commensurability of means and ends is foreign to the American experience.

35. Bartel, *Attitudes Toward Limited War*, 65-55.

36. Walter Lafeber, *America, Russia, and the Cold War, 1945-1971*, 2nd ed. rev. (New York: Wiley, 1972), 108.

37. Janowitz, *The Professional Soldier*, 294-296, 308-311.

38. Robert McClintock, *The Meaning of Limited War* (Boston: Houghton Mifflin, 1967), 44.

39. Caridi, *The Korean War*, 111-112.

40. Quotes from McGovern, *To the Yalu*, 10-11; see also Foot, *Wrong War*, 79.

41. Lebow, *Between Peace and War*, 157-164, passim.

42. For the original description of these adaptations in a policy-making context, see Irving L. Janis and Leon Mann, *Decision Making* (New York: Free Press, 1977), 81-106.

43. McGovern, *To the Yalu*, 12-13.

44. Richard Ned Lebow, *Between Peace and War: The Nature of International Crisis* (Baltimore, MD: Johns Hopkins University Press, 1981), 183; See also McGovern, *To the Yalu*, 78.

45. They did reject, however, his proposals which would have expanded the wars to the Chinese mainland. See Spanier, *The Truman-MacArthur Controversy*, 140, 150-151; Rees, *Korea*, 179-181; Foot, *Wrong War*, 114.

46. Higgins, *Korea and the Fall of MacArthur*, 110-118.

47. Spanier, *The Truman-MacArthur Controversy*, 211-212; William Manchester, *The Glory and the Dream: A Narrative History of America, 1932-72* (New York: Bantam, 1975), 561-562.

48. Mueller, *War, Presidents, and Public Opinion*, 229. The acronyms AIPO and NORIC stand for American Institute of Public Opinion and National Opinion Research Center.

49. Harry S Truman, *Memoirs: Years of Trial and Hope*, vol. 2 (Garden City, NY: Doubleday, 1956), 362.

50. Foot, *Wrong War*, 79.

51. See McGovern, *To the Yalu*, 86-91; Foot, *Wrong War*, 88-91; Higgins, *Korea and the Fall of MacArthur*, 67-75.

52. See Irving L. Janis, *Victims of Groupthink*, 62-64.

53. Lebow, *Between Peace and War*, 158-159, 162-163.

54. Ibid., 205-207.

55. Lebow, *Between Peace and War*, 207, 227. For a general review of the literature on U.S. misperceptions of China during the Korean War, see Lebow, *Between Peace and War*, 148-228.

56. Foot, *Wrong War*, 81.

57. Foot, *Wrong War*, 81. See also Foot, *Wrong War*, 86-87; McGovern, *To the Yalu*, 85-87; Lebow, *Between Peace and War*, 180-181.

58. Rees, *Korea*, 119.

59. Foot, *Wrong War*, 78.

60. Ibid., 80-81.

61. Ibid., 79-80.

62. For general discussion of this kind of misinterpretation, see Jervis, *Perception and Misperception*, 227-228.

63. A Soviet plane was shot down on September 4, in bad weather over the Yellow Sea and American planes strafed a Russian aerodome by mistake in October 1950. For the mild Soviet response to these events and their peace feelers throughout the war, see Foot, *Wrong War*, 76-77.

64. Ibid., 77.

65. Ibid., 225.

66. Ibid., 225-226.

67. Ibid., 225-226.

68. See Fred Greenstein, "The Impact of Personality on Politics" in his *Personality and Politics* (Chicago: Markham Publishing, 1969), 33-62.

69. Foot, *Wrong War*, 85.

70. Spanier, *The Truman-MacArthur Controversy*, 201.

71. Truman, *Memoirs*, 415-416.

72. For MacArthur's personal courage and earlier military risk taking, see Lebow, *Between Peace and War*, 155-156, and note 20. For his boldness in opposing presidents, see McGovern, *To the Yalu*, 21-26. For the insecurities that undergirded this grandiosity, see Joseph De Rivera, *Psychological Dimensions of Foreign Policy* (Columbus, OH: Charles E. Merrill, 1968), 247-257.

73. The division was saved from possible destruction only because Smith, on his own responsibility, ordered his men to drag their heels, to stop work on two airstrips and stockpile supplies along the routes of their advance (Lebow, *Between Peace and War*, 161).

74. Rees, *Korea*, 151.

75. Dean Acheson, *Present at the Creation: My Years in the State Department* (New York: Norton, 1969), 468.

76. McGovern, *To the Yalu*, 8. The President's own background and personality reinforced his reactions to MacArthur. He typically responded to feelings of insecurity by acting "tough," as Ernest May has suggested. See *"Lessons" of the Past: The Use and Misuse of History in American Foreign Policy* (London: Oxford University Press, 1973), 75. That was the capacity he eventually tapped when he relieved MacArthur of his command. For an excellent psychobiographic study, see Alonzo Hamby, "An American Democrat: Toward an Understanding of the Personality of Harry S Truman" (Ohio University, manuscript, 1989).

77. Lebow, *Between Peace and War*, 155, 179.

78. McGovern, *To the Yalu*, 97.

79. McLellan, *Dean Acheson*, 284.

80. Dean Acheson, *Present at the Creation* (New York: Norton, 1969), 467.

81. Foot, *Wrong War*, 212.

82. Ibid., 210-211.

83. Quoted in James Shepley, "How Dulles Averted War," *Life* (16 January 1956), 79.

84. Allen I. Teger, Mary Cary, Aaron Katcher, and Jay Hills, *Too Much Invested to Quit* (Elmsford, NY: Pergamon, 1980), 2. For further discussion of entrapment, see Bert Brown, "The Effects of Need to Maintain Face on Interpersonal Bargaining," *Journal of Experimental Psychology* 4 (1968): 107-122: Bert R. Brown, "Face Saving and Face Restoration in Negotiation" in *Negotiations: Social-Psychology Perspectives* ed. Daniel Druckman (Beverly Hills, CA: Sage, 1977), 275-299; Joel Brockner, Jeffrey Z. Rubin, and Elaine Lang, "Face-Saving and Entrapment," *Journal of Experimental Social Psychology*, 17 (1981): 68-79; Russell J. Leng, "When Will They Ever Learn?" *Journal of Conflict Resolution* 27, 3 (1983): 379-419; Jeffrey Z. Rubin and Bert Brown, *The Social Psychology of Bargaining and Negotiations* (New York: Academic Press, 1975); and Richard Tropper, "The Consequences of Investment in the Process of Conflict," *Journal of Conflict Resolution* 16, 1 (March, 1972): 97-98.

85. Teger, *Too Much Invested*, 24-25, 34, 92. In the original classroom version of this game, a dollar was auctioned off to the highest bidder. Thus if the highest bid was 90 cents, the winning bidder would make a 10-cent profit. The next to last bidder, however, has to also pay his bid without getting anything

in return. In all 40 runs of this version of the dollar auction, the winning bid exceeded the $1 prize. When put in dyads, the majority of people quit as the bidding approached the value of the prize. However, when the bidding passed the value of the prize, it continued, for the most part, until virtually all the resources of both parties were gone. This was true whether the players played with points (90%) or money (83%). See the chapter by Paul Pillar, this volume, for another usage of this auction game.

86. These threshold findings, incidentally, support Schelling's contentions that players in bargaining situations seek symbolic limits. The concept of fair price, or 50% of one's resources has always played a symbolic role in bargaining situations.

87. Teger, *Too Much Invested*, 92. This last result helps to explain one of the findings of the Stanford Studies on the origins of World War I that the nations on each side of the conflict saw themselves as simply responding to the provocative cuts of the other side. See Ole R. Holsti, Robert C. North, and Richard A. Brody, "Perceptions and Actions in the 1914 Crisis," in J. David Singer, ed., *Quantitative International Politics* (New York: Free Press, 1968), 123-58.

88. Jeffrey Rubin, Joel Brockner, Susan Small-Weil, and Sinaia Nathanson, "Factors Affecting Entry into Psychological Traps," *Journal of Conflict Resolution*, 24, 3(1980), 424.

89. Brown, "Effects," 107; "Face Saving," 275.

90. Teger et al., *Too Much Invested*, 2.

91. For details showing the change in American goals before the war began and afterwards, see Rees, *Korea*, 132-36.

92. Alexander L. George and Richard Smoke, *Deterrence in American Foreign Policy: Theory and Practice* (New York: Columbia University Press, 1974), 191. For a review of the literature dealing with misperception in the Korean war, see Lebow, *Between Peace and War*, 148-228.

93. Foot, *Wrong War*, 97-99.

94. J. H. Kaliki, *The Pattern of Sino-American Crises: Political-Military Interactions in the 1950s* (New York: Cambridge University Press, 1975), 81; Foot, *Wrong War*, 230. Earlier in April, a "discreet threat" was made that in the absence of satisfactory progress, nuclear weapons would be used. See Dwight D. Eisenhower, *The White House Years: Mandate for Change; 1953-56.* (Garden City, NY: Doubleday, 1963), 181. Barry Blechman and Robert Power argue that there is no evidence that the United States made explicit threats to use such weapons, and that such interpretations ignore important factors in the ending of the war such as the death of Stalin, the fear of conventional attacks against mainland China and Formosa, and the inconclusive nature of the war. See their "What in the Name of God Is Strategic Superiority," *Political Science Quarterly*, 97 (1982-83): 589-602.

95. Nations in which wars take place may have more intense interests in victory than powerful allies that come to their aid and, as a consequence, they may make it difficult for their more powerful allies to work out a compromise. The South Koreans created certain problems for the United States along these lines. On June 18, 1953, after the communist negotiators had accepted the U.S. position on prisoners of war, Syngman Rhee released over 25,000 prisoners of war from South Korean camps. This precipitate action almost undermined the peace talks. South Korean support for the truce was obtained only after the United States agreed to provide long-term military assistance to guarantee the security of that country, and after an attack by Chinese Communist forces virtually wiped out the two ROK divisions. [See Rosemary Foot, *The Wrong War: American Policy and the Dimensions of the Korean Conflict* (Ithaca, NY: Cornell University Press, 1985), 230-31; and T. R. Fehrenbach, *The Fight for Korea: 1950 to the Pueblo Incident* (New York: Grosset and Dunlap, 1969), 112-14].

Chapter 9

The Psychological Effects of Bombing on Civilian Populations: Wars of the Past

GEORGE H. QUESTER

One of the great legends of the twentieth-century military analysis is that civilian populations have not been cowed by aerial bombardment, but rather have simply been driven to rally behind their government, defying the opposing air force to inflict more damage.

This is how we remember the responses of the British to the 1940 Luftwaffe Blitz over London, with the voice of Edward R. Murrow reporting a magnificent popular resolve back to the United States.[1] This is also what is often alleged to have been the findings of the United States Strategic Bombing Survey (USSBS) — a set of careful studies of the responses of the Germans and the Japanese to the conventional bombings of their cities, prior to the final attacks on Hiroshima and Nagasaki.[2] And this is what has been conjectured to be the impact of the U.S. Air Force bombings of the North during the Vietnam War, as the tremendous investment in such aerial attack is deemed fruitless at best, and possibly counterproductive.

Yet the United States Strategic Bombing Survey has unfortunately been referred to much more often than it has been read. David Halberstam, in *The Best and the Brightest* referred to "the U.S. Strategic Bombing Survey . . . which proved conclusively that the strategic bombing had not worked; on the contrary, it had intensified the will of the German population to resist (as it would in Vietnam, binding the population to the Hanoi regime)."[3] Actually, the opposite conclusion was presented in the Survey's *Summary Report* for Europe,[4] and its specific Report 64b on *The Effects of Strategic Bombing on German Morale*,[5] and then in the *Summary Report* on the air offensive in the Pacific,[6] and the specific Report on Japanese morale.[7]

Indeed, common sense suggests that ordinary people would not be so able to shrug off the destruction of their homes and cities, or so inclined to redouble their commitment to their nation's war efforts under such circumstances. In the face of man-made disasters, exceeding the worst of the natural disasters, might not the ordinary person lose some of his willingness to persist in the endurance contest of a war? And might he not be inclined to direct some of the resentment and blame at his own government, rather than channeling all of this toward the enemy?

One therefore has to be very careful about summaries of the "lessons" of World War II bombardment. What caused Japan to surrender? If the atomic bombings were not needed because Japan was about to surrender in any event, would such a surrender have occurred without the kinds of ordinary bombings demonstrated at Tokyo? While Hitler would not have been willing to surrender as a way of terminating Allied air attacks, he had tried at the outset of World War II to dissuade Britain and France from launching a bombing exchange. And the German military officers who tried to assassinate Hitler surely were in part motivated by the devastation being inflicted on Germany by the bombings, bombings which might be terminated if a truce could be negotiated with Britain and the United States after Hitler had been killed.

We will thus be searching here for patterns of human motivation, patterns which will tell us something about individual human beings and the societal relationships which bind them together, in the face of bombardment. We are searching for clues about how such individuals, societies, and governments might respond under any similar patterns of conventional bombing attacks in the future.

In so doing, we have to be willing to cross-examine, and move past, any myths which have been a part of our memories of World War II. Instead we will have to watch for the workings of the more rational calculus affecting individuals and governments, and also for attenuations of rationality here.

Predictions and Observed Realities of World War II

Studies of the impact of bombing in World War II have not totally contradicted the image of pluck under such pressure, but they have certainly not supported it so strongly either.[8] We have indications that the British government was quite worried throughout the Blitz about the willingness of Londoners to put up with it. Public opinion data, moreover, is mixed on whether such Londoners were consumed with a hatred for the Germans and a desire for revenge, or instead resentment of their own government. The latter could occur because of the less than totally effective air raid arrangements, or perhaps simply out of a tendency to blame one's government for seemingly man-made misfortunes.

What is most interesting and remarkable about the Londoners in 1940 is not some kind of stoic resistance, or their commitment to their government and to the prosecution of the war, but how these Londoners behaved so much more bravely than the Londoners of World War I.

The German air raids of World War I had been conducted by Zeppelin airships, and then by biplanes, delivering bomb totals which were a tiny fraction of what was to be delivered in the next war. Overall, they delivered a total of 225 tons of bombs, a minuscule quantity as compared with even a single air raid in World War II. The number of people killed came to about 1,300.[9] Typically, not more than one town house in a block was destroyed.

Yet the impact of these early air raids were considerable. Ordinary Londoners fought to get into subway stations, and assaulted Royal Flying Corps officers in the street for alleged failures to do their duty; some even demanded the closing of factories when an enemy air raid was imminent, for fear that the lights of such a factory might attract the enemy's bombardment.[10]

After 1918, speculations about the future impact of any aerial bombardment of civilian populations were pessimistic — a reaction to these responses of the British, and the likelihood that future air raids would be able to carry larger bomb loads, and perhaps incendiary bombs and poison gas. Giulio Douhet, the Italian theorist of air warfare, had visited London during World War I as a liaison officer, and some of his predictions about the horrendous impact of future air war were derived from the impressions of these visits.

> Here is what would be likely to happen to the center of the city within a radius of about 250 meters: Within a few minutes some 20 tons of high explosive, incendiary, and gas bombs would rain down. First would come explosions, then fires, then deadly gases floating on the surface and preventing any approach to the stricken area. As the hours passed and night advanced, the fires would spread while poison gas paralyzed all life. By the following day the life of the city would be suspended; and if it happened to be a junction on some important artery of communication traffic would be suspended.

> What could happen to a single city in a single day could also happen to ten, twenty, fifty cities. And since news travels fast, even without telegraph, telephone, or radio, what, I ask you, would be the effect upon civilians of other cities, not yet stricken but equally subject to bombing attacks? What civil or military authority could keep order, public services functioning, and production going under such a threat? And even if a semblance of order was maintained and some work done, would not the sight of a single enemy plane be enough to stampede the population into panic? In short, normal life would be impossible in this constant nightmare of imminent death and destruction. And if on the second day another ten, twenty, or fifty cities were bombed, who would keep all those lost, panic-stricken people from fleeing to the open countryside to escape this terror from the air?[11]

Or the similarly staggering predictions of J. F. C. Fuller:

> I believe that, in future warfare, great cities, such as London, will be attacked from the air, and that a fleet of 500 aeroplanes each carrying 500 ten-pound bombs of, let us suppose, mustard gas, might cause 200,000 minor casualties and throw the whole city into panic within half an hour of their arrival. Picture, if you can, what the result will be: London for several days will be one vast raving Bedlam, the hospitals will be stormed, traffic will cease, the homeless will shriek for help, the city will be in pandemonium. What of the government at Westminster? It will be swept away by an avalanche of terror.

Then will the enemy dictate his terms, which will be grasped at like a straw by a drowning man. Thus may a war be won in forty-eight hours and the losses of the winning side may be actually nil![12]

Other British writers, including various Royal Air Force planners and some civilian officials, foresaw similar disasters, and predictions of horrendous air attacks also reached the public in Germany after World War I, and in Japan, France, and Italy.

When World War II came, the sheer destructiveness of the air raids was indeed far greater than World War I, and the disruption of ordinary life, the eradication of landmarks and neighborhoods, could have been expected to produce a great deal of depression, and unorganized and purposeless behavior.

This did not really occur, however. Compared to what British planners had feared, the public responses of 1940 and 1941 were surprisingly controlled. Bombed much more heavily than in World War I, the inhabitants of London did not this time protest or riot, and did not demand that peace be made with Hitler.[13]

Wherever bomber raids occurred — in Germany, Japan, and Russia as well as Great Britain — the incidences of panic and looting were markedly less than had been feared. Similarly less were incidences of psychiatric disorders traceable in any way to air raids. Here the incidence was not only less than predicted; there was indeed no noticeable increase from peace to war, from the months before the air raids to the period after.[14]

When explaining this relative lack of panic in World War II, as compared to World War I, one must look at several factors. The societies of World War II were generally more dominated by police, Germany having obviously moved very far in this direction between the wars, but with even Britain having become ready to tolerate greater suspensions of ordinary civil liberties and individual freedoms. Some of this greater capacity for state domination has to be allowed to explain the greater order which ensued.

More important, the air war was not as bad as expected. It had been widely anticipated that poison gas would be used, directed against cities and civilian populations, definitely incapacitating government agencies, killing people huddling in shelters.[15] Yet during the World War II air attacks, no such use of gas occurred, due to a complicated limited war exchange of restraints which still does not lend itself to easy explanation.[16] Part of the explanation for this mutual restraint was that each side was imputing to the other a slightly greater capacity than existed in reality, and a greater capacity than it could count on for itself. The Germans, in particular, exaggerated how far along the United States and Britain were likely to be in the development of deadly gases, extrapolating from the materials that the Allies were purchasing in neutral countries (often purchasing simply to keep the Germans from getting them).

But another part of this mutual nonuse of poison gas was probably due to more modest calculations on each side about the ease with which such weaponry could in fact be brought to bear. In retrospect, it certainly does not seem likely that it was only this avoidance of gas that kept multi-city disasters from being realized in World War II. Could the Royal Air Force and the Eighth Air Force have devastated a larger number of German cities in a single evening, if only they had not felt constrained from using gas? The winds had often turned out to be the under-analyzed factor in the earlier extrapolations of potency for such chemical weaponry. Given that the peak of success in an incendiary attack was to achieve a firestorm — a miniature hurricane caused by the intense fires ignited in the middle of a city — it hardly follows that the poison gas would have made all the difference (at least not the chemical weaponry that was available to the powers in the years from 1939 to 1945).

Any toughness of the British popular response may be very much attributed to initial expectations that the air war would be much more severe than it was, a multiple of what actually occurred in World War II. A more general proposition may thus be forwarded here: bad events which are nonetheless a pleasant surprise as compared with even worse events may help a population cope. The aerial attacks of World War I basically were a total surprise, since very few Englishmen had anticipated this kind of warfare. "The Blitz" of World War II was not nearly as much of a surprise. Indeed its magnitude was somewhat of a surprise in reverse.

At the risk of making too much of this comparison of expectations and actual occurrences (analogous in a minor way to how we respond to a snowstorm of six inches when 12 inches had been predicted), it is clear that it played an important role in the bombing impacts that we have studied most closely.[17] Where Allied air attacks against the German population were less destructive than anticipated, the impact was not such as to destroy morale. Where the attacks lived up to, or exceeded expectations, amid the prospect that such attacks would continue until Germany was defeated or surrendered, the impact on morale was more decidedly negative.[18]

Thus the Allied bombing of Dresden did undermine morale. Some 1,600 acres of the city were destroyed in a single 14-hour period (while 600 acres of London was destroyed in the entire war).[19] More than 75,000 people were killed. Having escaped most of the air offensive for much of the war, Dresden was correspondingly underprepared for the air attack that came. It had just ingested a large flow of refugees from the Russian ground force advance. A peacetime population of 630,000 had swollen to more than a million people, because of the influx of refugees from the East.

More generally, no one on the German side was prepared for the phenomenon of fire storms, such as occurred at Dresden, Hamburg, and Kassel in 1943. One of the most important aspects of the air-bombings of German cities was the disruption of communications lines within and through such cities, so that fire fighting could not be coordinated, and Luftwaffe interceptors could not get instructions as to which bomber stream to attack.[20]

Yet even here the damage was not quite as extensive as had been predicted before 1939. There was no way for the Royal Air Force or the U.S. Army Air force, or the two of them working together, to impose this kind of punishment on more than one German city at a time. Moreover, the resilience of German organizational systems and communications systems was indeed remarkable. When Hamburg was subjected to such severe attack, personnel and resources were moved in from other German cities, with the clear message thus that the rest of Germany was coming to the stricken city's aid. Discovering that other cities are still intact might produce some jealous and invidious comparison; but it also provides a framework of normalcy to which one could turn in retreat.

Goebbels's organization even attempted to use the Dresden bombings to improve morale. If the Allies were already so close to victory, and still were devastating German cities, how much more miserably would they treat the German population after it had surrendered?[21]

When subsequent bombings were less destructive, morale improved. David Irving suggests that the failure of a March, 1945, air raid on Chemnitz to match the results achieved at Dresden may have had this effect.[22]

Despite any negative effects of the Allied bombings on German morale, they played a less significant role in that country's surrender. There were surely many Germans, as the U.S. Strategic Bombing Survey found, who looked forward to an end to the war; but Hitler would not capitulate to terminate the Allied bombings, and the mass of Germans had no means of forcing Hitler to do so.

The American bombing of the Japanese, however, played a more significant role in their surrender. Moral critics of this use of atomic bombs sometimes argue that it was totally unnecessary, since the Japanese were allegedly on the brink of capitulating in any event. This latter possibility is difficult to prove, but if it is true, the prior question must then be posed of what it was that would have made the Japanese so ready to give in. The physical misery due to the naval blockade, and the conventional bombings of Japanese cities, are the only factors that might have motivated such a surrender, for otherwise the Japanese military command looked ready to mount a defense of the home islands into 1946 and 1947 and well beyond.[23]

Some 300 B-29's on Tokyo did more damage than the single B-29 dropping a nuclear weapon on Hiroshima, and then the next on Nagasaki. More than 100,000 people were killed in a single night's attack, more than would be killed in either of the nuclear bombings.[24] Still, the Japanese military resisted surrender. Even in 1945, several Japanese Generals were predicting that the casualties imposed on American invasion forces could be pushed high enough to induce Washington to settle for a compromise peace.[25]

The drops of nuclear bombs over Hiroshima and Nagasaki added the element of surprise which brought about the surrender. They did not destroy the government. Indeed if a conventional or nuclear attack on Tokyo would have killed the Emperor or "decapitated" the Japanese command structure, it would have been much more difficult to achieve a surrender in 1945. Rather, the Japanese were *persuaded* to *decide* to surrender. The apparent ease of the nuclear attacks impressed the Japanese decision makers, by their own accounts after the war,[26] and enabled the Emperor to intervene and order a surrender.

Extrapolations After 1945

We do not have any data for the U.S. bombings of Vietnam (or of North Korea) which is remotely as detailed or as complete as that offered by the first-hand observations of the bombings of Britain, or by the post-surrender USSBS studies of Germany and Japan.

The tendency is to extrapolate to these cases the alleged lessons from earlier instances. Critics of the American participation in the Vietnam War were thus very inclined to argue that history proved that no one could ever be bombed into a willingness to surrender, and/or that such bombings always drove the bombed people into a greater loyalty to their government and its cause. Moreover, it was argued by critics of the bombings that these were Asian peoples, less dependent on urbanization or on creature comforts, and thus perhaps more inured to hardship; these were also societies governed by Communist regimes, with whatever stoicism and solidarity this might produce.

One important confusion here stems from the U.S. official government policy statements explaining such bombing attacks. It is extremely rare for a government to admit that it is deliberately bombing to impose hardship on the enemy's civilian population. For fear of alienating world opinion, or for fear of future war crimes trials, euphemisms are applied that military targets are being aimed at when cities are struck, so that the destruction of civilian residences and civilian lives is merely inadvertent collateral damage.

The real explanation for the leveling of Tokyo in 1945 was not the official one, that the Japanese had cleverly dispersed a great deal of their military weapons production to small shops scattered across the residential districts, but it was rather a desire to make life miserable for the Japanese, and thus perhaps to put their government into the mood to consider a surrender.[27] If the bombing of Tokyo did not cripple Japanese war production as much as was advertised, this did not make the air raids a failure, for they must be judged in terms of this unadmitted strategy.

In Vietnam, too, there was a discrepancy between the stated and actual goals. The official explanation of U.S. air attacks in Vietnam was that it was intended to hamper the movement of supplies down the Ho Chi Minh trail to South Vietnam. The real, if unadmitted, reason for U.S. air attacks was more probably to make life miserable in the North, to make the population resentful of and rebellious against the Hanoi regime, or to make Hanoi less eager to press on with the war, as the costs of continuing the assault in the South had risen.[28] If the bombings of North Vietnam did not physically preclude the flow of munitions toward the South, this did not make these air raids a failure either, for they must be judged in terms of whether they could discourage a continued and expanded Communist offensive.[29]

In Vietnam, it is very unlikely that the population rallied behind the Hanoi regime every time American fighter-bombers or B-52s appeared overhead, or that the Hanoi regime thus welcomed such air raids as a timely morale-booster. Indeed the patterns of North Vietnamese bargaining behavior show that Hanoi very much wished to terminate and fend off the bombings, and that the Communist regime was ready to make concessions when further bombings were threatened.

Nixon and Kissinger threatened in 1972 that any escalation of fighting would lead to a resumption of the B-52 attacks on North Vietnam.[30] The final Communist assault on the South came only after Watergate had begun, and after Congressional actions had effectively prevented Nixon from resuming any air raids on the North;[31] shifting away from guerrilla tactics (which had effectively kept Saigon from inflicting a defeat on the Vietcong, but in turn might never have given Hanoi a victory), North Vietnam now felt it could resort to an outright conventional armored warfare offensive.

The Pace of Escalation

Some very different questions have been posed about the target policies on the pace at which the U.S. bombings of Vietnam were introduced, and their psychological and social results.

The bombings of North Vietnam were managed much more carefully than the escalations into the bombing campaigns of World War II. The tonnages of bombs used in the entire Vietnam War exceeded the totals dropped in World War II. But the aiming of such bombs was always more careful than had been the pattern in 1944 and 1945, and was never as blatantly an "area attack" as the RAF incendiary raids on German cities. Within the pattern of the above constraints, the United States progressed from the Rolling Thunder attacks of the 1965-1968 period, to Linebacker I in May of 1972, and then Linebacker II in December of 1972, progressively escalating the damage done to items of great value to Hanoi's civilian economy, in a measured but significant enhancement of the countervalue aspects of the attacks. The Linebacker II bombing raids are still very plausibly the reason Hanoi agreed to a truce.[32]

The reason for this policy was that the United States had to be concerned about what the Soviet Union or China might do with their nuclear arsenals. It seems very important that Moscow and Beijing both sense a limit to the war, a limit by which they would feel themselves secure against air attack and open-ended escalation. Any sudden application of the U.S. conventional potential over North Vietnam might have been too psychologically jarring for these nuclear-equipped Communist states, jumping over firebreaks and prior limits to the war. The introduction of U.S. air attacks was thus gradual and punctuated by numerous pauses.

Critics of this process of limitation vary in their sophistication. Some simply dismiss the entire need for such moderation, by which one is forced to fight "with one hand behind his back," reflecting a traditional attitude which refuses to see the implications of the over-arching thermonuclear balance. Others admit the need for mutual restraints holding back the highest levels of destructiveness (the American bombings of an ally of the Soviets and the Chinese could surely not be *guaranteed* against risks of counter-escalation, since these bombings had not been so precedented in the past). But they still note that a very high price was paid, in that the

North Vietnamese regime and people were thereby able to adjust gradually to the air attacks, suffering less than they would have with a more sudden escalation.[33]

To bomb an enemy target heavily is typically demoralizing to that enemy's government and people. To be less able or less willing to bomb the same targets a week or a month later, because defenses have stiffened, or because the attacking side is running out of spare parts or ammunition, or because of demonstrations in Washington, might conversely buck up the morale of the side being attacked.

The U.S. ability to bomb targets in North Vietnam or North Korea was always somewhat in question, because of the constantly shifting and improving technology of air defenses, and because the American public and government would be averse to heavy losses in air raids. The endurance contest war is, therefore, rarely just an issue of how long the bombed public can endure, but is normally also determined by how long the bombing country can persist.

Damage Assessments: Proclivities for Exaggeration or Understatement

The major instances of civilian exposure to aerial attack since World War II have come with the U.S. air raids on North Korea during the Korean War, and air raids on North Vietnam during the Vietnam War. In these cases, the totality of government controls has stood in the way of any kind of sampling of victim responses and victim attitudes such as we have been discussing here.

Despite such shortages of data, however, there have been no shortages of speculation and theorizing, much of it again falling back on the assumption of the inherent unproductive nature of all aerial bombardment alleged to have been discovered during World War II. The time may come when we get to know more of the trends in popular reactions to the bombings of North Vietnam, and the trends in government plans and responses to such bombardments. Yet the odds are against the Communist side every giving out any frank accounting of the disutility it was suffering, or any thoughts Hanoi might have been entertaining of compromise or surrender.

It is clear, nevertheless, that the total damage inflicted by the U.S. Air Force raids on North Vietnam was considerably less per bomb dropped than in comparable raids in World War II, with much of the credit perhaps belonging to the care with which bombs were aimed in the attacks on Hanoi and Haiphong. Official statements from Hanoi complained about the Linebacker II air raids, but claimed only a total of some 1,600 people were killed in the attacks.[34]

Some observers argue that the damage was so limited due to North Vietnamese civil defense preparations, rather than to American restraint and care. But it is more likely that the North Vietnamese authorities and the Americans had a shared interest here (given the prospects of much more serious escalation) in keeping the lid on the punishment that was being inflicted, even while a certain amount of punishment was being doled out. Could it be that Hanoi understated the casualties inflicted, cooperating with the U.S. Air Force not just in protecting some people against air attack, but also in covering up the more wanton consequences of such attack?

Any government undergoing bombing will face a similar dilemma, of whether to overstate or to understate the intensity of the other side's attack. For purposes of directing the condemnation of world opinion at one's adversary, overstating the attack may make more sense. For purposes of convincing one's adversary that one will not give in first, that one can bear up under the strain, understating the damage suffered may make more sense, consistent with the need to pretend to shrug off the worst the enemy can do.

The propaganda agencies of any regime will regard it as their challenge to make the best possible use of an enemy's air attacks. In the bombings of World War II, the victims' government typically would overstate the degree of countervalue punishment it had received. The Dutch government stated that 30,000 people had been killed in the Luftwaffe bombing of Rotterdam, rather than the more correct figure of 980.[35] A subtle and sophisticated mechanism employed in Germany by Goebbels's organization was to spread rumors magnifying the number of casualties in an Allied attack — with subsequent "official" corrections in a way that left ordinary Germans feeling that things were not so bad.[36] At times damage to a city was exaggerated where Allied bombers had indeed missed their target — in hopes that subsequent air raids on the same city would be held back.[37]

Returning to the thinking of the attackers, their goal might of course be to fine-tune their bombardment, hitting targets which no one could condemn, but which nonetheless were valuable to the opposing regime, valuable enough to induce thoughts of conciliation. Killing civilians in North Vietnam was thus less appropriate from an American point of view than destroying cement plants, because the Hanoi regime had ambitious plans for construction which could be frustrated by such attacks, and because the outside world would be less morally engaged and horrified by this kind of attack.

Hitting only military targets has always been a way of avoiding world condemnation, but attacking the purest of military targets has also always involved some countervalue impact, in the wounding or killing of some of the young men that constituted the enemy's military capability. To the extent that the aim of a military campaign is to impose pain on the other side, an artillery barrage along the front lines (as along the Suez Canal in 1970), or an exchange of insurgent and counter-insurgent attacks (as in Vietnam) thus brings many of the same thoughts and governmental decisions into play as the exchange of bombing attacks against cities. The difference comes in the way one reaches the morale of civilians at home — by letters that their sons have been wounded or killed, or by bombs hitting their homes directly — with the resulting differences in morale, panic, disgruntlement, and desire for revenge.

Governments Versus Populations

There may be some important differences in how governments or ordinary civilians respond to such bombardments. Ernest May has offered an analysis of bombing campaigns suggesting that incumbent governments are normally not driven toward surrender or compromise by such punishment, even if populations or alternative government leaders might be. Rather they are induced all the more to stick it out, as part of the endurance contest that wars often become.[38] A certain kind of logical or psychological syndrome comes to work in governments which depend at all on popular support: the suffering already undergone becomes a sunk cost which must be compensated for by some ultimate victory, or else the ruler will have too much to explain and to account for.

Air warfare in particular is apt to become an endurance contest, seeing who can endure suffering the longest. While air raids often are rationalized as counterforce attempts to defeat an enemy, typically they are intended to inflict suffering on an enemy's valued items, his cities, and his people, so as to create the wish to sue for peace. When two sides then engage in such attacks, the war becomes a betting contest of who will have to give up first. If one is on the verge of asking for peace, but the other side is also, would one not be foolish to surrender today, rather than holding out a little longer and having the enemy surrender next week? This is especially so if we are the rulers of a country which has already suffered air raids, and has been wondering whether there will be any fruits of victory to make up for all this damage.

For the leaders of a country in such a contest their entire future may be at stake. When engaged in such a contest it is best to fool and blind one's self, trying to ignore and forget the immediate suffering. Whoever is best at repressing such unpleasantness on his own side will have the best chance of winning the contest. At the extreme, the contest could produce the kinds of behavior exhibited by Adolf Hitler after 1942, who blotted out all reports of damage to German cities, or reports of the loss of panzer divisions.

Some ordinary citizens may feel inclined to join their leaders in this exercise. Others, with no career stake in victory, but with a stronger personal stake in a termination of the war, will lean in the opposite direction. Some secondary government officials will join with the leader in the endurance contest. But other officials may feel less responsible for any surrender or truce that did not produce gains of victory sufficient to cover the sunk costs already paid; and some might be inclined to depose the current government, even using the failure of the war as a reason for this change.

One can hardly generalize here to suggest that incumbent governments never cut their losses. Yet incumbents will generally be more likely to stick it out than their opposition or potential rivals for power, or their citizens. The syndrome is somewhat comparable to that of the investment in a great public works project which has come to be costing much more than was originally estimated. If the project is halted halfway to completion, it reflects badly on the government officials who launched it. If it is once completed, its magnificence may lead taxpayers to forget how much more it cost. Again the government officials involved will have very rational reasons to cultivate a certain irrationality, and a sentiment of "damn the torpedoes, full speed ahead."

Impact on Motives Versus Impact on Rationality

We have two distinct impacts of aerial attack to consider here. First, the sudden loss of a home or a loved one changes reality for the attacked individuals. It changes the opportunities that are available, as well as the individual's preferences which will be relevant to future decisions. How these opportunities are changed, and how these preferences are changed (these are the "opportunities curves" and "indifference curves" of basic economic theory) is not always so obvious, however, and does not always work in the same direction. Much may depend on whether additional air raids are to be expected, or whether the individual still has a large (and threatened) vested interest in urban life, or whether he has already lost most of what he cares about. Much will similarly depend on the opportunities available for revenge, and even on the objective need for revenge.

Second, the chaos accompanying an air raid, and the trauma afterwards, may substantially reduce the ability of ordinary citizens, as well as of national leaders, to understand what the remaining opportunities are. All of us make life decisions somewhat imperfectly, by the purer standards of the rationality of relating means to ends. We most likely would make such life decisions even less well in the atmosphere of an exchange of air raids. After even a mild earthquake in Los Angeles, school psychologists reported for more than a year afterward that children showed signs of having been upset by the experience, with a slightly negative impact on schoolwork, and on other social activities.

An increase in major psychiatric disorders (e.g., the incidence of suicide) would be an imperfect indicator of broader depression or psychological upset. Yet there has been no clear increase in major psychiatric disorders recorded after the outbreaks of war, or after the outbreaks of bombing.[39] Indeed there have even been instances where the suicide rate dropped with the outbreak of war. One might explain this in terms of people who had suffered an intense anomie in peacetime, and suddenly found a role for their lives, in defending their country against a new enemy. More generally, it might well be that severe psychological disorders, such as those requiring hospitalization or causing suicide, are so unrelated to reality that they cannot be used as indicators of how society copes with bad news.

Bombing campaigns might more reliably be assumed to increase stress. But "stress" is also a concept with some complications. Does danger, and a greater demand for our attentiveness and for the rendering of important decisions, necessarily lead to psychological breakdowns, or to an attenuation of our ability to perform tasks and make decisions? The experience of World War II offers some cases where civilian populations remained disciplined and productive under enormous pressure. For example, the population of Leningrad produced war materials for the many months of the German siege.[40] But there were cases where such populations were far more listless and unproductive even after the causes of the immediate stress were over (e.g., Germany and Japan for the first year or two of the occupations after the surrenders of World War II).[41] The latter had no bombs or shells to dodge, and no sounds of explosions ringing in their ears, and still got less accomplished.

All of this, however tentatively, suggests that civilian behavior under the stress of war depends on many variables. When life is hard, but the course of the war is turning around, people may rally behind the cause, even while dodging bombs. When a war has been lost, and the currency of the nation is inflated and valueless, such people may conversely not find it worthwhile to turn their energies toward much of anything.

We thus have some findings. Nobody likes to be bombed. Nobody likes to lose a war, either. People do not like to be unpleasantly surprised. Incumbents like to remain in office, and ordinary people respond to disasters in complicated ways. The question is what we are to make of all of this, where a future war could expand on so many dimensions.

Notes

1. On the British experience during World War II, see Richard M. Titmuss, *Problems of Social Policy: History of the Second World War, United Kingdom Civil Series* (London: H. M. Stationery Office, 1950).

2. *United States Strategic Bombing Survey*, 321 Volumes (Washington, DC: Government Printing Office, 1945-47).

3. David Halberstam, *The Best and the Brightest* (New York: Random House, 1972), 162.

4. *The United States Strategic Bombing Survey: Summary Report (European War)* (Washington, DC: Government Printing Office, 1946).

5. *The United States Strategic Bombing Survey: The Effects of Strategic Bombing on German Morale* (Washington, DC: Government Printing Office, 1946).

6. *The United States Strategic Bombing Survey: Summary Report (Pacific War)* (Washington, DC: Government Printing Office, 1946).

7. *The United States Strategic Bombing Survey: The Effects of Strategic Bombing on Japanese Morale* (Washington, DC: Government Printing Office, 1946).

8. The most important surveys of our experience with bombing are: Fred Charles Ikle, *The Social Impact of Bomb Destruction* (Norman: University of Oklahoma Press, 1958); Irving L. Janis, *Air War and Emotional Stress* (New York: McGraw-Hill, 1951); Terence H. O'Brien, *Civil Defence: History of the Second World War, United Kingdom Civil Series* (London: H.M. Stationery Office, 1955); Constantine Fitzgibbon, *The Winter of the Bombs* (New York: Norton, 1957); Max Seydewitz, *Civil Life in Wartime Germany* (New York: Viking, 1945); and Titmuss, *Problems of Social Policy.*

9. L. E. O. Charleton, *War Over England* (London: Longmans, Green, 1936), 53-67, 80, 97-98.

10. For an account of the panic caused in these early air raids, see H. A. Jones, *The War in the Air*, Vol. V (Oxford: Clarendon, 1935), 7.

11. Giulio Douhet, *The Command of the Air* (New York: Coward-McCann, 1942), 58.

12. J. F. C. Fuller, *The Reformation of War* (New York: E. P. Dutton, 1923), 150.

13. See Fitzgibbon, *The Winter of the Bombs.*

14. Titmuss, *Problems of Social Policy*, 338-341.

15. For predictions assuming the use of gas in air raids on cities, see Storm Jameson, ed., *Challenge to Death* (New York: E. P. Dutton, 1935).

16. A more extensive survey of the explanations of the restraints on chemical warfare can be found in John Ellis Van Courtland Moon, "Chemical Weapons and Deterrence: The World War II Experience," *International Security*, 8, 4 (Spring 1984): 3-35.

17. For a related discussion, see Irving L. Janis, "Psychological Effects of Warnings," in *Man and Society in Disaster*, eds. G. W. Baker and D. W. Chapman (New York: Basic Books, 1962), 55-92.

18. See David Irving, *The Destruction of Dresden* (New York: Holt, Rinehart, & Winston, 1964), 154-155.

19. Ibid.

20. Ibid., 144-145.

21. Ibid., 216.

22. Ibid., 158.

23. On the Japanese decision to surrender, see Herbert Feis, *The Atomic Bomb and the End of World War II*, rev. ed. (Princeton, NJ: Princeton University Press, 1966); R. J. C. Butow, *Japan's Decision to Surrender* (Palo Alto, CA: Stanford University Press, 1954); and Paul Kecskemeti, *Strategic Surrender* (Palo Alto, CA: Stanford University Press, 1958).

24. Wesley Craven and James Lea Cate, *The Army Air Forces in World War II,* Vol. V (Chicago: University of Chicago Press, 1953), 609-614.

25. Feis, *The Atomic Bomb and the End of World War II.*

26. See Edward Zuckerman, *The Day After World War III* (New York: Viking, 1984), p. 70; and Feis, *The Atomic Bomb and the End of World War II.*, 199.

27. The reasoning behind the patterns of bombing of Japanese cities is laid out in Craven and Cate, *The Army Air Forces in World War II*, 609-625.

28. See Robert L. Gallucci, *Neither Peace Nor Honor* (Baltimore, MD: Johns Hopkins University Press, 1975), 54-57.

29. For a useful overview of the uses (counterforce and countervalue) to which aerial bombardment has been put, basically agreeing with the interpretation presented here of the bombings of North Vietnam, see M. J. Armitage and R. A. Mason, *Air Power in the Nuclear Age* (Urbana: University of Illinois Press, 1983).

30. For some further analysis of the mixed impact of the aerial bombardments in Vietnam, see W. Scott Thompson and Donaldson D. Frizzell, eds., *The Lessons of Vietnam* (New York: Crane Russak, 1977), 125-172.

31. See Guenter Lewy, *America in Vietnam* (New York: Oxford University Press, 1978), 410-415.

32. Ibid., 410-417.

33. Ibid., 393-394.

34. Ibid., 413.

35. Irving, *The Destruction of Dresden*, 25.

36. Ibid., 207.

37. Ibid., 216.

38. Ernest R. May, *"Lessons" of the Past* (New York: Oxford University Press, 1973), Chapter V.

39. See Janis, "Psychological Effects of Warnings," in *Man and Society in Disaster,*, Chapter 5, and Titmuss, *Problems of Social Policy*, Chapter XVII.

40. On the Soviet accomplishments during the siege, see Leon Goure, *The Siege of Leningrad* (Berkeley: University of California Press, 1962) and Harrison Salisbury, *The 900 Days: The Siege of Leningrad* (New York: Harper & Row, 1969).

41. On the postwar German and Japanese malaise, see Jack Hirshleifer, *Disaster and Recover: A Historical Survey* (Santa Monica, CA: RAND Corporation, RM-3079, 1963).

Chapter *10*

The Soldier in Battle: Motivational and Behavioral Aspects of the Combat Experience

ANTHONY KELLETT

> *"No man wants to die; what induces him to risk his life bravely?"*
>
> — FIELD-MARSHAL EARL WAVELL

Until the twentieth century, relatively little thought seems to have been given to the role played by human factors in war. Although some commanders (Napoleon among them) clearly recognized the importance of motivation and morale, for the most part senior officers appear to have taken the battlefield performance of their soldiers largely for granted. More than a century ago a French colonel, Charles Ardant du Picq, wrote that morale was "rarely taken into account."[1] Archibald Wavell, an officer who attended the British Staff College in 1909-1910, later recalled that even as recently as that year insufficient emphasis was placed "on the factor of morale, or how to induce it and maintain it."[2]

In psychological terms, as in so many other respects, World War I was a watershed in military thinking. Although the concept of mass armies was not entirely new, for the first time war touched the lives of almost everyone in most of the belligerent nations (approximately 65 million men were mobilized, many of them under compulsion). Thus there developed in the public an awareness of, and interest in, the human experience of war. The professional interest of staffs also had been aroused, as was evident in the 1922 Enquiry into Shell Shock (in Britain). Some of the (hitherto largely unanticipated) features of the war, including the incidence of mutiny in several armies, challenged existing assumptions about combat behavior and encouraged a closer examination of behavioral issues. Nonetheless, it was not until World War II that academic developments (notably the use

AUTHOR'S NOTE: The views expressed are the author's, and do not necessarily reflect those of the Canadian Department of National Defence.

of survey techniques) and military interest coalesced to produce a wide-ranging study of motivation, morale, and behavior in battle.

Military research into the human factors has continued with varying intensity since World War II, and has largely revolved around the wartime "discovery" of the primary group. The research effort of the Korean War, which produced the "Fighter Factor" studies, was not repeated during the Vietnam War. However, since that war there has been a considerable, and sometimes controversial, retrospective examination of its behavioral aspects, and the recent Arab-Israeli wars (1973 and 1982) have further stimulated interest in the role of psychological factors in war.

This study examines soldier behavior in battle and the motivations that influence that behavior, both thematically and cross-culturally. The perspective is largely historical, although findings from the social sciences are also included. The focus is organizational in that the article is primarily concerned with mission-oriented behavior. Nonetheless, examples of deviation from organizational norms will be examined in terms of what they indicate about the relationship of individuals and small groups to the larger organization and its objectives, and because these examples illuminate the balance between duty and defection, fight and flight, against which a soldier's motivations are weighed.

I. Combat Preparation

It is extremely rare for a soldier to enter battle without preparation of any sort, but there is considerable variation in the degree and usefulness of the preparation men do receive. As will be seen, however well-prepared the soldier, battle normally comes as a shock to him.

Training. Training is the major part of a soldier's practical and psychological preparation for battle. Its purpose is to replace civilian with military attitudes; to familiarize the new soldier with weapons, tactics and fieldcraft; and to give him some sense of the noise and confusion of actual combat. Such training is intended not only to teach basic military skills and to propagate the values, sentiments, attitudes, and social traditions of the unit and of the armed services, but also to develop a homogeneous and cohesive community. An American academic who served during World War II summarized the effects of the basic training he underwent in the following terms: "The recruit is no longer an individual, with the right of personal choices, alternatives and decisions. Instead, he is, in informal army usage, 'a body.' This 'body' must be trained to act without question or hesitation to institutional stimuli. The loss of choice and initiative develops in him a sense of dependency on the institution for decisions."[3]

Before 1914, military training consisted largely of discipline and drills whose purpose was to ensure unity of action, to produce a predictable response, and to counter fear. Although the essence of training has changed, some automatic drills, such as "hitting the dirt" or "freezing" continue to be utilized, not only because they offer useful tactical guidelines and build up teamwork, but also because they help to counteract fear and facilitate a rapid response to enemy action. Since late in World War I, emphasis has been placed increasingly on familiarization training, which is intended to prepare the soldier to face the operational and psychological realities of the modern battlefield. It attempts to reproduce, as closely as possible, the sights, sounds, confusion, and even some of the danger of actual combat. In 1942 a British psychiatrist in North Africa found that combat soldiers strongly believed that "battle inoculation" (as such training was then called) was a most important part of the training of replacements and should be given to all troops before their first action. Officers interviewed by him claimed that, as a result of battle inoculation, they had been well prepared for their first experience of battle and were the steadier for it.[4]

One of the most valuable assets that training can confer on a soldier is confidence, not only in his own military skills and stamina, but also in his weapons and equipment. It has been the Israeli experience that company morale correlates significantly with personal morale and that the components of the latter include confidence in the soldier's own military skills, in his weapons, and in himself.[5] A British psychiatrist who served in the Falklands noted that the paratroopers had lower rates of battle shock than other British troops because they maintained their level of training, kept busy and fit, and were psychologically prepared.[6]

Cohesion. In addition to military training, armies also prepare their soldiers for combat by promoting cohesion. There is a type of cohesion (primary group cohesion) that is quite largely defined by social and situational factors and which can be expressed in ways antithetical to the organization. The type of cohesion that is approved and promoted by the military hierarchy is termed "esprit de corps," denoting the common spirit existing in the members of a group and inspiring enthusiasm, devotion, and strong regard for the honor of the group. In peacetime, and in particular in the context of the regimental system characteristic of many Commonwealth armies, the military authorities tend to promote long unit service and unit-oriented training which are thought to develop such esprit.

The role played by unit pride will be examined below, but it is relevant here to note that often regimental spirit not only supplies a more mission-oriented cohesion than does the operation of small group dynamics, but relies less on situational factors. The value of a preexisting cohesion, built up in peacetime, was demonstrated at the battle of Neuve Chapelle (1915) and at the defense of Calais (1940), and by the Israeli 7th Armored Brigade in the fighting on the Golan Heights in 1973. The Israelis, for whom time is of critical importance in the opening hours of any conflict, are convinced of the value of such preexisting cohesion.[7]

Mental Preparation. Another aspect of the process of battle preparation is mental preparation. Modern combat is more continuous, and in many ways more surprising, than was warfare in the age of Frederick the Great and Napoleon. Inevitably, the inexperienced soldier attempts to visualize what combat will be like, but there is a potential for demoralization if the battle, when it occurs, differs from the soldier's mental image of it. Thus physical preparation must be accompanied by psychological preparation, which is to a considerable extent accomplished by familiarization training. But it is also met by other means, among them the dissemination of information and discussion. Providing soldiers with as much information as possible (compatible with security) about the purpose of the fighting and the combat situation is particularly important, given the pervasive uncertainty, the "fog of war," associated with battle.

A wide gap between the mental preparation of British and Argentinian troops was evident in the Falklands War. The accounts of Argentinian conscripts are full of shock, unreality, and surprise. A soldier of the 7th Infantry Regiment told an interviewer: "They didn't prepare us mentally. . . . Where were we going? We didn't even know what they were fighting for."[8] On the other hand, the long Atlantic voyage was used to good effect by the British troops. On board the *Norland* the chaplain of the 2nd Battalion, the Parachute Regiment, led discussion sessions with each section (nine men) in turn, encouraging the soldiers openly to talk about their fears.[9] These sessions apparently proved helpful, not only in allowing the men to come to terms with their fears but also in building group bonds. Similar attempts at mental preparation were made aboard the *Queen Elizabeth II*, among the men of 5th Infantry Brigade.

Du Picq warned against expecting peacetime training responses from soldiers in combat, arguing that the contrast between the battlefield and the conditions of peacetime service was so great that morale would inevitably be adversely affected in the first phases of battle.[10] More recently, Lieutenant-General Charles Foulkes claimed that after four years of hard training his 2nd Canadian Division was initially no match for battle-experienced German troops in Normandy; he felt that it was two months before the division reached its full combat potential.[11] Most commentators, men with combat experience and analysts alike, point to the initial surprise of combat for inexperienced troops. After describing the initiate's approach to the front line, during which friendly equipment and troops mostly disappeared from view (unlike in training), S.L.A. Marshall wrote of the soldiers' bewilderment: "Here is surprise of a kind which no one had taught them to guard against. . . . Where are the targets? . . . How long will it be until the forces opposite begin to expose themselves and one's own forces will rally around the tactical ideas which training had taught them would prove useful? There is none present to tell the rifleman or his comrades that this *is* normal."[12]

However, the first experience of battle does not always contrast shockingly with the soldier's mental image of it, especially when imagination has been allied to realistic training, accurate information, and familiarity with the more credible literary and movie depictions of combat. An American infantry officer described his first action in Vietnam in 1970 as "a textbook situation" that conformed to his expectations.[13] Similarly, a British gunner, describing the "fog of war" problems in the Falklands, commented: "Certainly, events were more confusing than on any exercise. Despite that, the feeling persisted that one was still training. When the cease-fire was reported, the spontaneous cry went up all over the battlefield, 'Endex!' [end of exercise]."[14]

II. Combat

The motivations that, at a distance from actual combat, propel a soldier in its direction often differ substantially from those that sustain him during battle. Motivational changes result not only from the surprises frequently engendered by combat, which encourage a reexamination of the balance between motivations and risk, but also from the greatly increased importance of situational factors. Likewise, and for the duration of the actual fighting, hitherto relatively salient motivations (such as ideological convictions) may decline in significance, while remaining important in the context of the overall campaign. As Marshall wrote, "All values are interpreted in terms of the battlefield itself."[15]

Organizational Structure and Commitment. Historically, armies have always been divided into units varying greatly in size. The Roman Legion was divided into cohorts, centuries, and eight-man *contubernia*, whereas the smallest component of Frederick the Great's army was the seven-man *kameradschaft*. These subunits were essentially intended to meet administrative requirements, such as messing and tent accommodation. The development of breech-loading weapons in the late nineteenth century enforced dispersion on the battlefield, and the need to retain control over widely deployed men ultimately led the Germans to place tactical emphasis on the section-sized group of approximately 12 men during World War I;[16] by World War II the section and squad had become an intrinsic element in the organization of British and American combat units. The miniaturization of tactical units has continued since World War II, in that subsections are gaining in importance in an era of low intensity operations, in Northern Ireland and elsewhere. It will be seen that there have been roughly parallel reductions in the size of the social support group, from the company to "buddies," during the twentieth century. The rough parallelism between trends in organizational structure and group dynamics does suggest the influence of tactical factors on social bonding.

The behavior of primary groups quite often diverges from organizational norms, and therefore armies have long sought to promote loyalty to an entity larger than the soldier's immediate group. Some of the means used to develop organizational commitment (notably in the form of esprit de corps) in peacetime have been noted. As the British army has demonstrated, in the limited wars fought by it since the end of national service in 1960, units founded upon the regimental system are generally able to translate the ethos of that system from a garrison to a campaign environment with relatively few problems,[17] and esprit de corps channels primary group efforts in the direction dictated by the mission. However, in total wars a rapid expansion of manpower, limited training resources, and replacement problems make it more difficult to indoctrinate men into unit values and to maintain cohesion at the battalion level.

Discipline. Before 1914 armies laid a great deal of emphasis on formal discipline, both in garrison and in combat. The two world wars produced a greater emphasis on self-discipline, a transformation that can be attributed in part to the influx into the armies of great numbers of civilians from diverse social backgrounds, in part to the increasing dispersion of units on the battlefield, and in part to the social pressures applied by the group.

Although modern combat practice encourages each soldier to do his bit willingly, he is constantly aware that the military authorities have many ways of ensuring at least apparent compliance. Extremely punitive forms of discipline were widely used on the Russian front during World War II, and German accounts of the later stages of the war indicate that draconian disciplinary methods instilled fear in many of the German troops and materially discouraged desertion.[18] Even in the armies of the Western Allies a certain degree of coercion helped to ensure that the soldier remained in the front line. In "The American Soldier: Combat and Its Aftermath," Samuel A. Stouffer and his colleagues concluded that "the best single predictor of combat behavior is the simple fact of institutionalized role: knowing that a man is a solder rather than a civilian. The soldier role is a vehicle for getting a man into the position in which he has to fight or take the institutionally sanctioned consequences."[19]

While the external forms of discipline (dress and deportment) tend to be relaxed on active service, those units that reassert the more formal aspects of discipline when they are rotated out of the line for a rest period tend to benefit from the experience. Field-Marshal Sir William Slim wrote of the Burma campaign that "it was our experience in a tough school that the best fighting units, in the long run, were not necessarily those with the most advertised reputations, but those who, when they came out of battle, at once resumed a more formal discipline and appearance."[20] One principle of patient management for the immediate stage of battle shock is to treat casualties as soldiers, not as hospital patients, in a military environment reasonably close to the front line. Thus it is possible that the reassertion of formal discipline in rear areas to some degree constitutes the application (however unwittingly) to battle-weary units of the therapy generally proven effective with individuals.

Rewards. In addition to the use of discipline to discourage defection from the combat role, armies use a variety of positive inducements such as promotions, medals, and other forms of recognition to reward effective combat behavior. Before the twentieth century medals were rarely awarded, but their use has been institutionalized during the present century, and the attitudes of many soldiers have to some extent been influenced, negatively as well as positively, by the practice.

Medals may also be used to reinforce a latent role structure among combat soldiers. A study of Medal of Honor awards in the Vietnam War concluded that officers were awarded medals for "war winning" acts, enlisted men for "soldier saving" ones. The authors argued that these orientations were indicative of a latent role structure that involved the propagation of the military ethic among officers and the promotion of primary group loyalties among enlisted ranks.[21]

Yet awards policies can also have negative effects. A British soldier in World War I wrote:

> I have known good men eat their hearts out through want of recognition. How petty this sounds. Yet a ribbon is the only prize in war for the ordinary soldier. It is the outward visible proof to bring home to his people that he has done his job well. And, say what you may, a man's prowess will be assessed by the number of his ribbons.[22]

In their critique of American combat leadership in Vietnam, Gabriel and Savage claimed that some of the army's awards policies were so inane that they undermined morale, instead of stimulating it.[23]

But in the final analysis public recognition is a matter of equal concern for soldiers in combat because it both legitimates what they are doing and conveys approval for their efforts. (A divisional commander in Vietnam claimed that "an aggressive awards policy" was instrumental in developing high morale in his division.)[24] Even though the effects of popular applause tend to be short-lived, a lack of public recognition can have a long-term and detrimental influence on soldier attitudes. In both world wars there were armies that called themselves forgotten. Slim commanded one of them, and he recorded that "this feeling of neglect . . . had sunk deep. There was a good deal of bitterness in the army."[25]

Personnel Practices. During World War II it came to be recognized that introducing replacements into their combat units immediately before or even during battle, without giving them a chance to become socially integrated, increased the risk of psychiatric breakdown. However, manpower problems made it difficult to integrate replacements into their units only when the latter were out of the line, and in a sample of American infantrymen in Italy in 1945, more than 50% of the replacements had gone into combat within two days of joining their units.[26]

American researchers found during World War II that the lack of any near-term personal goals (notably the definite prospect of an end to the fighting) had negative repercussions for morale. The rotation of frontline troops to areas well removed from the fighting was tried by the United States Army on a small scale late in World War II, and a fixed combat tour was introduced during the Korean War. However, it was not until the Vietnam War that rotation was strongly linked with motivation and behavior.

In Vietnam enlisted men generally had to serve in frontline units for 12 months, officers for six. This policy was detrimental to stability and to the relations between officers and enlisted ranks, and it encouraged an individualistic perspective of the war. It also tended to impose a pattern of behavior and attitudes: during the initial period in the combat zone the soldier would display "apprehensive enthusiasm;" the middle period would be one of resignation, but despite a state of chronic depression, the soldier would be at his most effective during this time; and during the final period (the last month), he tended to show signs of "anxious apprehension" or "short-timer's fever," which was characterized by a notable decline in his efficiency and in his willingness to engage in offensive operations.[27] However, the effect on morale of the rotation policy was not wholly negative, and an American psychiatrist in Vietnam wrote: "The setting of a personal time limit has clearly done much to dispel the feeling of hopelessness which soldiers complained of in other wars."[28] The policy also probably contributed to a lowering of the rate of psychiatric casualties.

BATTLEFIELD ENVIRONMENT

One of the more surprising, and potentially demoralizing, features of battle is the sense of isolation it frequently engenders. Marshall described the novitiate's mental picture of battle as one of excitement and danger, and the warmth of group support, as well as lines of men and machines extending as far as the eye can see: "But it doesn't work out that way. Instead, he finds himself suddenly almost alone in his hour of greatest danger."[29] Noise on an unanticipated scale can be another surprising characteristic of combat; one purpose of familiarization training is to accustom soldiers to high volumes of sound, particularly because inexperienced soldiers often equate noise with lethality. The introduction of new and undreamed-of enemy weapons can be highly demoralizing. The first use of gas against French trenches (1915), of tanks against German trenches (1916), and of dive-bombers against French and British troops (1940) led on each occasion to widespread panic among the unsuspecting defenders.

The motivations and behavior of the combat soldier also are affected by physical conditions. During a World War II hospital stay, an American officer reflected on the miseries his men would be enduring: "I knew for certain that the worst part of the war was not the shooting or the shelling, although that had been bad enough — but the weather, snow, sleet and rain, and the prolonged physical misery which accompanied them."[30]

One of the most evident hardships of campaigning is fatigue. Intense emotional strain, deficient caloric intake, loss of sleep, strenuous physical exertion, and unfavorable weather can all contribute to fatigue. Naturally fatigue can have highly detrimental effects on combat performance, particularly, perhaps, on that of commanders. Research findings indicate that the negative effects of acute sleep deprivation on the performances of persons in mentally demanding jobs are greater than those of persons in physically demanding jobs. Good motivation and social support can counteract some of the effects of fatigue, but technological advances (such as night vision devices) now permit operations to be conducted on a more continuous basis than in the past, which reinforces the negative potential of exhaustion.

Adverse climate and terrain conditions can be as debilitating as fatigue; a Canadian officer who served in both world wars titled his autobiography *General Mud*, because in his experience mud was so pervasive and depressing a feature of war.[31] Equally, almost any type of terrain can have a negative psychological impact on men unfamiliar with it. Finally, armies are said to march on their stomachs, and the quantity, quality, and type of rations provided the soldier can significantly affect his outlook. The commander of one of Wingate's Chindit columns in Burma (1944) called a lack of food "the biggest single assault on morale."[32]

Although physical discomfort may be a more immediate influence on a soldier's motivation than danger for much of the time in the combat zone, the prospect of the latter is rarely far away. The awareness of danger is brought home to the soldier by the activities of the enemy and by the sight of casualties. Although danger and risk can be homogenized and generalized before battle, in combat certain enemy weapons evoke particular psychological reactions. A number of studies examined weapons' effects in World War II, and all concluded that psychological factors such as noise, lack of warning, and vulnerability were important in augmenting the physical effects of enemy weapons. Artillery and high explosives evoked the strongest reactions; psychiatrists found that indirect fire was a major source of psychiatric breakdown.

Obviously, casualties frequently are the most visible and forceful manifestations of danger. Survey data from World War II indicate that men whose companies had suffered heavy casualties, who had seen one of their best friends killed in action, and who had witnessed enemy atrocities, reported many more fear symptoms than soldiers who had not been subjected to such stresses.[33] Psychiatrists also found a significant correlation between being wounded and a subsequent psychiatric breakdown when the victim returned to his unit.[34]

In addition to the psychological consequences, casualties also have a bearing on cohesion. Primary groups are most heavily affected by casualties, and the turbulence they cause is reinforced by the problem of integrating replacements. Casualties also threaten the sense of group support and protection.

The quality and accessibility of medical care has an important bearing on the morale of the entire unit, not only on that of those who are wounded. Describing the predicament of a group of surrounded American paratroopers in Normandy, Marshall claimed that they were particularly affected by the shortage of medical supplies: "Men were dying whose lives could have been saved. The other men knew it, and for infantry, there is no other personal torment, no blow to group morale, to compare with this."[35] The Israelis, who have traditionally set great store by the rapid evacuation of both dead and wounded, have found that delays in evacuating the wounded could have negative effects on the other members of the unit.

LEADERSHIP

A striking feature of battle is the tendency toward confusion and paralysis which often occurs when a unit first comes under fire, and it is especially difficult to get soldiers to move once they have gone to ground. In such circumstances, leadership, or simply action of any sort, can exert a powerful influence, particularly since in threatening situations people tend to copy the behavior of others.

One of the most pervasive forms of leadership is example. One survey conducted in 1944 asked American infantrymen to assess which leadership practices were most evident in officers who had done a particularly good job of helping their men to feel confident in a tough or frightening situation. Leadership by example and personal courage were mentioned by 31%; 25% were encouraged by means of pep talks, jokes, and information; 23% mentioned the demonstration of concern for the men's safety and welfare; and 5% noted friendliness and informality on the part of the officers.[36] The Israelis have always set high store by exemplary leadership. Of the 781 fatalities incurred by the Israelis in the 1967 war, almost half were officers, leading one analyst to observe: "There is no doubt that the fact that so many commanders, proportionately, fell in battle had a salutary effect on the morale of the troops. . . . Improvised interviews on the army radio network gave eloquent confirmation to the soldiers' conviction that . . . they were not being asked to give their lives for something for which the commander would not give his own."[37]

Persuasive as leadership by example can be, not everyone in a group or unit will necessarily follow the lead of the more decided soldiers, and undoubtedly the extent of the response is influenced by the personality and the actions of the leader, as well as by such factors as the situation and the cohesiveness of the group. One characteristic that will encourage trust and emulation is professional competence; thus a skillful commander can confer a feeling of security on his men. E. B. Sledge, a Marine private who fought in the Pacific, was powerfully affected by the death of his company commander, who "represented stability and direction in a world of violence. . . . We felt forlorn and lost . . . to all of us the loss of our company commander at Peleliu was like losing a parent we depended upon for security."[38] (Sledge dedicated his war memoirs to the "beloved company commander of K/3/5.")

INDIVIDUAL MOTIVATION

Self-Esteem. Self-esteem plays an important role in combat motivation; it influences the soldier's relationship with his peers and his attitudes toward his unit, duty, discipline, and his mission. Marshall thought that most men are unwilling to take extraordinary risks, but are equally unwilling to be considered the least worthy among those present.[39] In a survey conducted shortly after World War II, 90% of the American enlisted men interviewed expressed the belief that soldiers are greatly concerned with the opinion in which they are held by other enlisted men in their units.[40]

The satisfaction of a man's desire for self-esteem can demand high levels of commitment. Jeffrey Williams, the historian of Princess Patricia's Canadian Light Infantry, who served with the regiment in Korea, wrote:

> There was not a man . . . who did not firmly believe that the Patricias were the best soldiers in the Canadian Brigade. . . . He knew too, that any action fought by the Regiment was watched and discussed by every other unit of the Brigade as well as by the British, Australians, New Zealanders and Indians of the Division. It mattered greatly to him what they thought of the Patricias.[41]

This concern for reputation seems to be particularly strongly felt by regular soldiers, for whom it is axiomatic that "The professional soldier always fights."[42] Many of the British soldiers in the Falklands seem to have been motivated by a desire both to test and to assert their professionalism.

However, many soldiers satisfy their need for self-esteem with much lower levels of organizational commitment. In the later stages of the Korean War, when a stalemate had effectively been reached, the armistice negotiations at Panmunjon seemed to the soldiers to have a greater bearing on the outcome of the war than did the efforts of the United Nations forces, and thus there was a reduced willingness to take risks. This situation led a psychologist to comment that "When social approval is possible without all-out effort, it is little wonder that there was less than a total commitment in . . . attitude."[43]

Describing the weak resistance of some British units during the German spring offensive of 1918, Middlebrook concluded: "The real limit of a Western soldier's resistance is the point at which he feels his individual honor has been satisfied."[44]

Primary Group Support. The primary group is an important and immediate source of motivation on the battlefield, and even self-discipline has a social basis, as du Picq recognized:

> What makes the soldier capable of obedience and direction in action is the sense of discipline. This includes: respect for and confidence in his chiefs; confidence in his comrades and fear of their reproaches, and retaliation if he abandons them in danger; his desire to go where others do without trembling more than they.[45]

Modern analysts have echoed du Picq's words. Marshall, for example, wrote: "I hold it to be one of the simplest truths of war that the thing which enables an infantry soldier to keep going with his weapons is the near presence or presumed presence of a comrade."[46] Stouffer argued that the primary group set and enforced group standards of behavior, and supported the individual in stresses that he would otherwise have found insupportable.[47] On the basis of the post-combat interviews he conducted, Gal concluded that the three principal factors influencing the Israeli soldiers' willingness to fight were group cohesion, leadership, and self-preservation. He argued that membership in a group encouraged soldiers to fight to protect their friends, out of a strong sense of reciprocal obligation, and also to preserve the honor of the unit.[48] When a soldier is on his own he loses not only the moral support of the group, but also the need to keep up an appearance of control. Men who have difficulty assimilating into primary groups have been shown to be more likely to suffer psychiatric breakdown or to desert than men who integrate easily.[49]

Primary group cohesion derives to a considerable extent from the psychological and physical protection conferred by the group. The desire for moral support produces a tendency for soldiers to bunch together in the open, despite orders and training to the contrary. Describing a World War I attack, an Australian noncommissioned officer commented that "it is strange how men creep together for protection. Soon, instead of four paces interval between the men, we came down to lying alongside each other, and no motioning could make them move apart."[50]

Support relationships can vary in size and nature. The tactical situation, dispersion, and a new rotation policy may have made the squad less salient for the American soldier in Korea than for his World War II predecessor. A sociologist found that during the Korean War "buddy" relationships were an important source of support and developed in situations of stress that provided opportunities for the offering or acceptance of help.[51] It appears that although primary groups still operated at a squad level in Vietnam (fragging was a group phenomenon), the rotation system gave the American soldier an essentially individualistic perspective, and group ties were pragmatic and situational responses to imminent danger, rather than "some kind of semimystical bond of comradeship."[52]

Given the frequently pragmatic basis of primary group bonding, it is not surprising that group cohesion can sometimes work against army goals. A fairly widespread live-and-let-live system developed on the Western Front in World War I, and in the Korean War it was found that primary groups sometimes assimilated their officers into patterns of behavior that were subversive of organizational goals.[53] In a study of American soldiers during the Vietnam War, one analyst argued that "where primary-group solidarity existed, more often than not it served to foster and reinforce *dissent* from the goals of the military organization and to organize *refusal* to perform according to institutional norms."[54]

Legitimacy. If group cohesion is to be directed into the channels desired by the military authorities, adherence to a social system wider than the group, and a consequent legitimation of the soldier's role, must be established. Where the group's own goals (e.g., survival) are accorded greater legitimacy than the demands of military authority, combat refusal, fragging, and similar responses may result. In an analysis of the Vietnam War, Charles Moskos found that for primary groups to maintain the soldier in his combat role, "there must be an acceptance, if not of the specific purposes of the war, then at least of the broader rectitude of the social system of which the soldier is a member."[55] He noted that once antiwar sentiment gained momentum in the United States, there was a corresponding drop in troop morale in Vietnam.

Colonel Reuven Gal, an Israeli psychologist, conducted hundreds of post-combat interviews after the 1973 and 1982 wars. He found that the legitimacy of their country's war aims was important for Israeli soldiers, and that in the 1982 Lebanon War, unlike in previous wars, a consensus about Israel's aims was lacking. Gal concluded that commanders play an important mediating role in establishing legitimacy, in part because they translate broader war aims into unit goals. Thus units where the troops had high confidence in their leaders generally had no legitimacy problems, and vice versa.[56]

Ideology. Political rather than military ideals often are influential in bringing the individual into combat, but tend to lose some of their significance in actual battle. A survey of veterans of the Abraham Lincoln Battalion, Americans whose participation in the Spanish Civil War was largely a function of political belief, found that in battle the soldier was too busy to be much influenced by ideological concerns; instead, "Ideology functions *before* battle, to get the man in; and *after* battle by blocking thoughts of escape."[57]

However, a highly committed minority can influence the behavior of other, less committed soldiers. Shils and Janowitz found that among German units in World War II the hard core of dedicated Nazis in each group and unit, although a relatively small proportion, made a significant contribution to the stability and military effectiveness of the primary group, and, by minimizing the probability of divisive political discussions, deferred the onset of defeatism.[58]

Unit Cohesion. Cohesion at the unit level has the effect of enhancing and compounding primary group cohesion and of harnessing it to the pursuit of organizational goals.

Different armies have different approaches to the promotion of unit cohesion. Most Commonwealth armies use variants of the regimental system. The influence of regimental pride on combat behavior is demonstrated by the exhortation of a British officer just before a World War II battle, when he told his men: "We've got to win our battles, whatever the cost, so that people will say 'They were worthy descendants of the 32nd' and that's saying a hell of a lot."[59]

The extent of regimental commitment may well be lower in new battalions raised in wartime than in regular battalions because such commitment is to a considerable degree a function of time. But in both types of units the behavior of even those men in whom regimental pride does not strike a responsive chord may be influenced by the behavior of individuals or small numbers of dedicated men, because of the importance of example and modeling in combat. If individuals provide leadership at the prompting of regimental loyalty, those who follow them are being indirectly influenced by the regimental ideal. For example, Slim described an attack by British troops at Gallipoli (1915) that was on the verge of collapse when a private ran forward, roaring "Heads up to the Warwicks! Show the blighters your cap badges!" The men nearest him plunged forward again, followed by the rest of the line, and the enemy trench was taken. Slim, who was an officer in the battalion, remarked that as a result of the private's initiative, the men "remembered their Regiment."[60]

Members of armies that are not characterized by the regimental system have other forms of organizational identification. Esprit can develop in most successful and cohesive bodies, both military and nonmilitary. American soldiers often identify with organizations larger than a regiment, such as Patton's Third Army or the 1st Infantry Division, perhaps because they are more stable and long-lived than are regiments. (Regimental insignia were rarely used in World War II). American soldiers also have often demonstrated identification at the company level (as Stouffer recognized), but it has not invariably conduced to effectiveness. For example, it was found in World War II that "pride in outfit and other aspects of intragroup bonds could be maintained at a high level without any corresponding tendency for the men to acquiesce with enthusiasm to the demands that the Army made on them."[61] Stouffer's study added that pride in outfit did contribute to cohesion, if not markedly so to aggression.

The cohesion and esprit of German units were evident during World War II, yet these units were often cobbled together in crises from men who were strangers to each other and to their officers, and it has been suggested that the true spirit of the German soldiers was esprit d'armée.[62] The Israelis consider unit cohesion to be critical to battlefield success. Israeli identification centers largely on the company, but some is also accorded to the brigade, on which much of the limited military symbology of the Israeli Defense Force is based.

Professional pride is yet another variant of unit pride, denoting a similar concern for corporate reputation. Such an attitude is particularly noteworthy of distinctive or elite units, such as the French Foreign Legion or special forces.

COMBAT BEHAVIOR

Courage and Fear. Some men do appear to enjoy the experience of war, regarding it as an adventure and relishing the heightened sense of awareness often induced by danger. Philip Caputo, for example, enlisted in the Marines in the mid-1960s "to find in a commonplace world a chance to live heroically."[63]

Such men may play a valuable role in enhancing combat effectiveness, their aggression taking the fight to the enemy — the U.S. Army Air Force discovered that fewer than 1% of its military pilots accounted for roughly 30% to 40% of the enemy aircraft destroyed in the air during World War II.[64] Aggressive individuals often provide the leadership that evokes emulation. However, at the junior rank level, the hero may not contribute much to cohesion. In Korea, men who were regarded as heroes could not integrate easily with their fellow soldiers because they appeared to be thinking first of themselves, and only secondarily of other members of the group, and they also tended to place a burden of example on their comrades.[65]

Most men, however, feel fear in battle. In a 1944 survey of wounded American veterans, 65% of the men admitted to having had at least one experience in combat in which they were unable to perform adequately because of intense fear.[66] The nature of fear seems to change with experience, from a fear of displaying cowardice to one of being killed or wounded. An important factor in the experience of fear is the degree of control felt by the individual in a particular situation; it was found that during World War II troops who expressed a high degree of self-confidence before combat were more likely to perform with relatively little fear during battle.[67] Fear also is modified by social factors, particularly by isolation or, conversely, by group support.

Courage, as Lord Moran recognized during World War I, is "willpower," a resolve not to quit and an act of renunciation which must be made not once but many times. He suggested that courage is an expendable resource which diminishes as the soldier's moral props, especially his comrades, are removed.[68] The view that courage is more the management of fear than the overt display of gallantry and aggression has gained wide currency in the present century. An American study of the psychological effects of different enemy weapons found, incidentally, that demonstrably brave soldiers (medal winners) were more likely than less obviously brave men to report an increase in their fears as the battle progressed.[69] Furthermore, heroic behavior has situational as well as psychological roots. Gal's investigation of heroism among Israeli soldiers in the 1973 war indicated that heroism tended to occur in conditions of intense combat, often in circumstances of saving others, and good leadership and strong unit cohesion were associated with heroic acts.[70]

Imitation can be an extremely important influence on an individual's reactions to threatening situations. In a survey of American veterans in Italy in 1944, 70% claimed to have reacted negatively to seeing a comrade break down, and half of the total sample added that it increased their susceptibility to fear.[71] Panic is sometimes the result of imitation. It normally results from surprise, from uncertainty, or from a feeling that the individual is facing imminent entrapment, necessitating a rapid escape. Marshall was called upon to investigate several panics. He concluded that each one was precipitated by a minor event, such as one or two men running to the rear without explanation; other men followed because they did not understand the reason for the sudden movement.[72]

Although panic and desertion are relatively rare, soldiers may remain in the front line without actually fighting. Du Picq wrote that it was a common error to assume that all the men present on the battlefield actually fought: "At a distance, numbers of troops . . . may be impressive, but close up they are reduced to fifty to twenty-five percent who really fight."[73] In World War II Marshall found that even in close-fought infantry actions only 15% to 25% of the men in a company would fire their weapons in an average stern day's action.[74]

Self-Preservation. The instinct of self-preservation can persuade a soldier to fight, or at least to remain in the front line, if he is convinced that he has little moral, social, legal, or physical alternative. As Stouffer and his colleagues noted, self-preservation is not a sufficient motive for persistence in combat, but in combination with other factors it becomes a major element in combat motivation.[75] Gal noted that most of the Israelis whom he interviewed indicated that survival was the main reason why they fought.[76]

Experience. The contribution of combat experience to motivation and behavior is a more complex one than the movie stereotype of hard-bitten veterans coaxing the green replacements would suggest. The performance curve associated with the rotation policy in Vietnam has been noted. It indicated that the soldier was most effective during the middle months of his tour and was likely to succumb to short-timer's fever as his tour drew to a close. This finding conforms roughly to the World War II experience, although the onset of both effectiveness and exhaustion may have occurred earlier in the latter conflict, when peak efficiency was probably reached within 3 weeks, and fairly pronounced symptoms of battle fatigue appeared after 6 weeks.[77] However, increased experience did build confidence, enabling soldiers to distinguish between the sounds of different weapons and to use ground more effectively. Nonetheless, some of these hard-won skills eventually deteriorated.

By contrast, the tyro tends to be less aware of his vulnerability and to feel a certain sense of immunity and even of "apprehensive enthusiasm" (unintegrated replacements are, of course, peculiarly susceptible to breakdown). In April 1944 the rifle companies of the American 8th Division were surveyed to determine the men's willingness to enter combat. It was found that nonveteran privates expressed greater willingness to go into action than did veteran privates.[78]

Breakdown Due to Stress. Battle stress decreases combat effectiveness and promotes psychiatric breakdown. Based on past experience, Chermol has predicted that at least one psychiatric casualty will occur for every four battle casualties during the initial 30-day period of a future high-intensity conventional war.[79] A high incidence of psychiatric casualties is naturally a source of concern for commanders. But Canadian commanding officers in Italy during World War II were told that battle exhaustion was their responsibility, and if it occurred in a coming action, "it would be taken as a reflection upon the ability of these officers."[80]

"Psychiatric casualties" include battle shock and battle fatigue cases. Whereas battle fatigue usually develops after weeks or months of moderate combat, battle shock, which is an emotional reaction to combat stress, can occur after hours or days of intense combat. In the 1973 and 1982 Mideast wars psychiatric casualties among Israeli soldiers generally took the form of battle shock.

Numerous factors contribute to psychiatric breakdown. The most critical is fear. Shortly after the end of World War II two American psychiatrists contended that "the key to an understanding of the psychiatric problem is the simple fact that the danger of being killed or maimed imposes a strain so great that it causes men to break down."[81] All soldiers are at risk, and the longer the individual stays in combat, the greater is the chance that he will become a casualty. The Israelis have found that the greater the intensity of battle (as reflected in the number of battle casualties), the greater will be the number and proportion of battle fatigue casualties, and the more rapid the onset of fatigue. Israeli psychologists have also found that age (notably the 26-30 group), prior or ongoing personal stress such as pregnancy, birth or death in the family, recent marriage, or financial problems, poor education, low motivation, low intelligence, being a reservist, being of low rank, and being from a support unit correlated with breakdown.[82]

Overall, psychological breakdown appears to be closely related to broader social factors. During World War II, a British psychiatrist found startling differences in rates of breakdown between apparently similar battalions that were fighting under similar conditions, and he attributed the higher rates to "poor leadership, poor team spirit, and poor training in the past."[83] In the 1973 war it was found that Israeli soldiers from units with good leadership and good unit cohesion, and who had stable personal and family lives, were less likely than other soldiers to suffer breakdown. Good company morale in the 1982 war also appeared to protect soldiers from breakdown.[84]

A variety of means is used to reduce the impact of stress on combat effectiveness. Screening procedures have proven useful in identifying individuals with predispositions to breakdown. When breakdown does occur, forward treatment has proved effective in returning a significant number of men with battle fatigue or shock to duty. The principles underlying forward treatment are immediacy (rapid response), proximity (treating casualties near the front), and expectancy (treating them as soldiers rather than patients). Soldiers in the acute stage of shock are treated in the rear, by abreaction. To facilitate the return to duty of the men undergoing forward treatment during the Lebanon War, the Israelis arranged to have comrades from their units pick them up. Among these Israelis treated forward in 1982, 75% were sent back to their units within 72 hours; a few relapsed, and others failed to reach their units for administrative reasons, leaving a net of 60% who returned to duty,[85] a rate roughly similar to that experienced by the British in World War II.[86]

III. Conclusion

The record of modern Western armies shows that most soldiers will fight when called upon to do so, usually without notable enthusiasm, but equally without widespread or persistent defection. The soldier's approach to battle, from depot to front line, is normally an incremental process, at each stage of which defection would represent an extreme step. Arrival in the combat zone frequently comes almost as a surprise,[87] but once he is there, the soldier has little alternative but to stay, under the combined influence of social pressure, discipline, physical compulsion, and the demands of self-preservation. Although a majority of combat soldiers are probably not intensely committed to their assigned missions, those men who are more aggressive or committed will disproportionately influence the performance of their units by their example. The suggestibility of most soldiers to strongly defined actions (whether a charge or a panic flight) gives added significance to the presence and the motivations of the committed (or disaffected) minority.

It is unlikely that any single motivator will appeal to all combat soldiers equally for any length of time, although there will be some consensus about such goals as "ending the task." Normally motivations will vary not only from soldier to soldier, but also, for each individual, from situation to situation. The motivations that sustain a soldier in combat often differ substantially from those that originally actuated him. The sheer immediacy of combat naturally reinterprets the soldier's values and motivations.

There does seem to be a distinction between the attitudes and motivations of career soldiers and those of individuals who serve for the duration. Combat motivation in career soldiers has tended to reflect organizational influences, and to a large degree derives from such factors as self-selection, forceful socialization, formal discipline, long unit service, professional pride, and adherence to organizational values. Short-service soldiers have shown themselves more likely to be influenced in their combat behavior by primary group allegiance, self-discipline, ideology, and their own preservice experiences and attitudes (as well as the attitudes of the home population).

Despite differential levels of commitment, and a varied susceptibility to policies designed to enhance motivation and morale, much can be done to sustain the soldier's preparedness to engage in battle. By contrast, negative results can flow from indifference to motivational considerations as Merrill's Marauders discovered at Stilwell's hands in Burma in 1944.[88] Describing his philosophy of command, Field-Marshal Montgomery concluded: "If the approach to the human factor is cold and impersonal, then you achieve nothing."[89]

Notes

1. Charles Ardant du Picq, *Battle Studies*, 8th ed. (Harrisburg, PA: The Military Service Publishing Company, 1947), 109.

2. John Connell, *Wavell, Scholar and Soldier* (London: Collins, 1964), 63.

3. John Ellis, *The Sharp End: The Fighting Man in World War II* (New York: Scribner, 1980), 14.

4. Robert H. Ahrenfeldt, *Psychiatry in the British Army in the Second World War* (London: Routledge & Kegan Paul, 1958), 203-204.

5. Gregory Lucas Belenky, C. Frederick Tyner, and Frank J. Sodetz, *Israeli Battle Shock Casualties: 1973 and 1982*, Report WRAIR NP-83-4 (Washington, DC: Walter Reed Army Institute of Research, Division of Neuropsychiatry, August 1983), 20.

6. Polly Toynbee, "We Indoctrinate Them — Otherwise They Wouldn't Fight," *Manchester Guardian Weekly* 127, no. 20 (November 1982):5.

7. Craig G. Rennie, *Military Motivation and the Regimental System in the Israeli Army*, Project Report No. PR258 (Ottawa: Operational Research and Analysis Establishment, October 1984), 54-55.

8. Daniel Kon, *Los Chicos de la Guerra: The Boys of the War* (Sevenoaks: New English Library, 1983), 15.

9. Max Arthur, *Above All, Courage. The Falklands Front Line: First-Hand Accounts* (London: Sidgwick & Jackson, 1985), 141-142.

10. Du Picq, *Battle Studies*, 118.

11. C. P. Stacey, *Six Years of War: The Army in Canada, Britain and the Pacific* (Ottawa: Queen's Printer and Controller of Stationery, 1955), 253.

12. S. L. A. Marshall, *Men Against Fire* (New York: William Morrow, 1946), 47.

13. Richard Holmes, *Firing Line* (London: Jonathan Cape, 1985), 72.

14. Jonathan Bailey, "Training for War: The Falklands 1982," *Military Review* LXIII, no. 9 (September 1983): 70.

15. Marshall, *Men Against Fire*, 161.

16. John A. English, *A Perspective on Infantry* (New York: Praeger, 1981), 19.

17. Colin Mitchell, *Having Been a Soldier* (London: Hamish Hamilton, 1969).

18. Guy Sajer, *The Forgotten Soldier* (New York: Ballantine, 1972).

19. Samuel A. Stouffer et al., *The American Soldier: Combat and its Aftermath, Studies in Social Psychology in World War II*, Vol. 2 (Princeton, NJ: Princeton University Press, 1949), 101.

20. William Slim, *Defeat into Victory* (London: Transworld Publishers, 1971), 459-460.

21. Joseph A. Blake and Suellen Butler, "The Medal of Honor, Combat Orientations and Latent Role Structure in the United States Military," *The Sociological Quarterly*, 17, 4 (Autumn 1976).

22. Denis Winter, *Death's Men: Soldiers of the Great War* (Harmondsworth: Penguin, 1979), 189-190.

23. Richard A. Gabriel and Paul L. Savage, *Crisis in Command: Mismanagement in the Army* (New York: Hill & Wang, 1978), 14-16.

24. Julian J. Ewell, "High Morale in Combat," *Military Review* LXII, 6 (June 1982): 26.

25. Slim, *Defeat into Victory*, 163-164.

26. Ellis, *The Sharp End*, 337.

27. Peter Watson, *War on the Mind: The Military Uses and Abuses of Psychology* (London: Hutchinson, 1978), 227-230.

28. Peter G. Bourne, *Men, Stress, and Vietnam* (Boston: Little, Brown, 1970), 75.

29. Marshall, *Men Against Fire*, 47.

30. Ellis, *The Sharp End*, 23.

31. E. L. M. Burns, *General Mud* (Toronto: Clarke, Irwin, 1970), 22.

32. Bernard Fergusson, *The Wild Green Earth* (London and Glasgow: Collins Fontana Books, 1956), 171.

33. Stouffer, *The American Soldier*, 80-82.

34. Dr. A. E. Moll, personal communication, 1980.

35. S. L. A. Marshall, *Night Drop: The American Airborne Invasion of Normandy* (New York: Jove, 1984), 126.

36. Stouffer, *The American Soldier*, 125.

37. Samuel Rolbant, *The Israeli Soldier. Profile of an Army* (South Brunswick: Thomas Yoseloff, 1970), 176.

38. E. B. Sledge, *With the Old Breed at Peleliu and Okinawa* (New York: Bantam, 1983), 141-142.

39. Marshall, *Men Against Fire*, 149.

40. Alexander L. George. "Primary Groups, Organization, and Military Performance" in *Handbook of Military Institutions,* ed. Roger W. Little (Beverly Hills, CA: Sage, 1971), 309.

41. Jeffrey Williams, *Princess Patricia's Canadian Light Infantry* (London: Leo Cooper, 1972), 78.

42. Morris Janowitz, *The Professional Soldier. A Social and Political Portrait* (New York: Free Press, 1964), 215.

43. H. F. Wood, *Strange Battleground: The Operations in Korea and Their Effects on the Defence Policy of Canada* (Ottawa: Queen's Printer, 1966), 181.

44. Martin Middlebrook, *The Kaiser's Battle: 21 March 1918: The First Day of the German Spring Offensive* (Harmondsworth: Penguin, 1983), 335-336.

45. Du Picq, *Battle Studies*, 122.

46. Marshall, *Men Against Fire*, 42.

47. Stouffer, *The American Soldier*, 130-131.

48. Colonel Reuven Gal, *Combat Stress, Morale and Commitment*, lecture presented at Collège militaire royal du Saint-Jean (Canada), 8 March 1984.

49. Larry H. Ingraham and Frederick J. Manning, "Psychiatric Battle Casualties: The Missing Column in a War Without Replacements," *Military Review* LX, 8 (August 1980): 27; Stouffer, *The American Soldier*, 278; Edward A. Shils and Morris Janowitz. "Cohesion and Disintegration in the Wehrmacht in World War II," *Public Opinion Quarterly* 12 (Summer 1948): 285.

50. Holmes, *Firing Line*, 159.

51. Roger W. Little, "Buddy Relations and Combat Performance" in *The New Military: Changing Patterns of Organization*, ed. Morris Janowitz (New York: Russell Sage, 1964), 199.

52. Charles C. Moskos, Jr., "The American Combat Soldier in Vietnam," *The Journal of Social Issues* 31, 4 (1975): 27, 37.

53. Little, "Buddy Relations," 213.

54. Sam C. Sarkesian, ed., *Combat Effectiveness: Cohesion, Stress, and the Volunteer Military* (Beverly Hills, CA: Sage, 1980), 257.

55. George, "Primary Groups," 307.

56. Gal, *Combat Stress*.

57. John Dollard, *Fear in Battle* (Washington, DC: The Infantry Journal, 1944), 42.

58. Shils and Janowitz, "Cohesion and Disintegration," 286-287.

59. F. M. Richardson, *Fighting Spirit: A Study of Psychological Factors in War* (London: Leo Cooper, 1978), 22. It is interesting to note that numerical regimental titles were abolished in the British infantry in 1881.

60. William Slim, *Courage, and Other Broadcasts* (London: Cassell, 1959), 85-86.

61. Stouffer, *The American Soldier*, 140. While the Stouffer study noted that the only survey items in the area of unit pride related to the respondents' pride in their company, the omission of more extensive questions in the realm of unit identification is in itself significant in what otherwise was generally an exhaustive and detailed investigation of combat soldier attitudes.

62. Shelford Bidwell and Dominick Graham, *Fire-Power: British Army Weapons and Theories of War 1904-1945* (London: George Allen and Unwin, 1982), 216.

63. Philip Caputo, *A Rumor of War* (New York: Ballantine, 1978), 5.

64. Morris Janowitz and Roger W. Little, eds., *Sociology and the Military Establishment*, 3rd ed. (Beverly Hills, CA: Sage, 1974), 57.

65. Little, "Buddy Relations," 203.

66. Stouffer, *The American Soldier*, 201-202.

67. Ibid., 224-225.

68. Lord Moran, *The Anatomy of Courage*, 2nd ed. (London: Constable, 1966), 154-155.

69. Cited in Watson, *War on the Mind*, 215-216.

70. Belenky, Tyner, and Sodetz, *Israeli Battle Shock Casualties*, 6-8.

71. Stouffer, *The American Soldier*, 208-209.

72. Marshall, *Men Against Fire*, 146.

73. Du Picq, *Battle Studies*, 131-132.

74. Marshall, *Men Against Fire*, 56.

75. Stouffer, *The American Soldier*, 169.

76. Gal, *Combat Stress*.

77. Ellis, *The Sharp End*, 250.

78. Stouffer, *The American Soldier*, 23-34.

79. Brian H. Chermol, "Psychiatric Casualties in Combat," *Military Review* LXII, 7 (July 1983): 28.

80. W. R. Feasby, ed., *Official History of the Canadian Medical Services 1939-1945*, Vol. 2 (Ottawa: Queen's Printer and Controller of Stationery, 1953), 68.

81. Ingraham and Manning, "Psychiatric Battle Casualties," 23.

82. Belenky, Tyner, and Sodetz, *Israeli Battle Shock Casualties*, 19.

83. Ahrenfeldt, *Psychiatry in the British Army*, 207.

84. Gregory L. Belenky, Shabtai Noy, and Zahava Solomon, "Battle Stress: The Israeli Experience," *Military Review* LXV, 7 (July 1985): 32.

85. Belenky, Tyner, and Sodetz, *Israeli Battle Shock Casualties*, 16.

86. Ahrenfeldt, *Psychiatry in the British Army*, 163-195.

87. R. L. Crimp, *The Diary of a Desert Rat* (London: Pan Books, 1974), 10.

88. The Marauders' historian cited several examples suggesting indifference on Stilwell's part towards the only American infantry unit in his command. Stilwell declined to inspect the regiment when opportunity offered, failed to confer any gallantry awards or make promotions, and pushed the men beyond their physical limits. The unit's combat record was a fine one, but its deactivation was probably hastened by the theater commander's neglect of morale issues. See Charlton Ogburn, Jr., *The Marauders* (Greenwich, CT: Fawcett Publications, 1964), 88, 238-239, 242, 259.

89. Viscount Montgomery, *Memoirs* (London: Fontana Books, 1960), 83.

Chapter 11

Effort Justification as a Motive for Continuing War: The Vietnam Case

THOMAS W. MILBURN and DANIEL J. CHRISTIE

The American Goals in Vietnam

As early as 1950 the United States began to underwrite the French position in Vietnam as a way of securing its commitment to the defense of Europe and as a way of protecting important natural resources and supplies in the area. Early in the American involvement the domino theory was also applied to Vietnam. The triumph of Communism there was perceived by every administration from Eisenhower on as a threat to U.S. interests throughout the world. Not just Vietnam was at stake but the entire free world.[1]

In the early years of the Vietnam war, before the United States got directly involved, the United States felt there were important gains to be made from having solid, steadfast, and durable allies in Southeast Asia: Although fear of the Communist threat in that area had declined markedly from the days before Sukarno's fall or from the period before Mao's Cultural Revolution, many Americans would have rested more easily if the Chinese and the Soviets had abandoned plans to expand their political claims or influences there. Moreover, American support of the French effort in Indochina had been viewed as necessary for strategic reasons in that its loss to Communism would mean the loss of vital raw materials and of millions of people to the West.[2]

More significant in the long run, American leaders regarded U.S. actions in Asia in domino theory terms, that is, standing up to aggression here would deter Soviet or Chinese attempts to expand their power or influence elsewhere. In short, important potential benefits for the United States included punishing Communist aggressors and containing Communist power and influence. The domino theory saw any conflict with the Communists as a test of American national resolve and capability.

The United States had become directly involved in Vietnam in 1955, when U.S. advisors took over the training of South Vietnam military forces and later that same year assisted Diem in becoming president. By 1958 the guerrilla war of the

Vietcong forces against the South Vietnamese government had increased significantly. Diem's policies in the early 1960s and the political instability of the country following his death in 1962 led the United States to get more directly involved politically and militarily. Berman has argued that American complicity in the removal of Diem somehow seemed to tie the United States to all future regimes and that our continuing interference in those regimes heightened our commitment and involvement.

In 1962 President Kennedy increased the number of American military advisors in Vietnam from 685 to 3,200, and, in 1962 to 11,300. By 1963 American forces in Vietnam numbered 16,500 and by 1964, 25,300. At the end of that year U.S. forces had recorded 400 deaths and 2,600 casualties.

By the end of 1965, the United States had 184,300 troops in Vietnam, an eight-fold increase from 1964. But in 1965 there also were dramatic changes in U.S. policy. President Johnson initiated bombing of North Vietnam on February 7. On March 28, the People's Republic of China issued a warning to the United States that the Chinese would provide support to the North Vietnamese if it were requested. On April 17, 1965, 15,000 persons demonstrated in Washington against the war. The number of U.S. forces in Vietnam continued to increase in 1966, more than doubling by the end of the year to 389,400. The use of B-52s to increase the intensity of our bombing started on April 12, 1966. By October 1967, 40% of U.S. combat-ready divisions, 50% of our tactical air power, and at least a third of U.S. naval strength (i.e., 480,000 Americans) were fighting on the Southeast Asian peninsula. The number of Americans killed in action (a total of 6,500 from 1960-1966) was nearing 9,000 (plus 60,000 wounded) for 1967 alone.[3]

The economic cost to the United States of this limited war also was enormous. American commitments to Vietnam had begun in 1950, when Truman authorized 15 million dollars in military aid to help France prevent the Chinese Communists from expanding into Indochina. Later, as France continued the war with the Vietminh, more funds were given to the effort. By the end of 1963, American assistance to South Vietnam was costing 400 million dollars annually. Between 1965, when the first American combat unit arrived in Vietnam, and 1973, when the last American soldier left there, the cost was more than 120 billion dollars. President Johnson's reluctance to increase taxes or to impose economic controls in order to pay for the war led to inflation which was later to be compounded by the Arab oil embargo of 1973. American costs also included the vast sums of inflated money that were required to rebuild the American military establishment after the war.

The ultimate cost in American lives amounted to nearly 58,000 persons who either died in the war zone or were missing in action. Data on the incidence and prevalence of psychological disorders suffered by Vietnam veterans who returned home and were met by indifference or hostility are still being compiled.

Application of the Effort Justification Hypothesis

A number of empirical studies have explored the "effort justification" hypothesis as an explanation for the repetition of behavior patterns that yield outcomes which are more costly than beneficial. In what follows, we review some of the empirical evidence which makes it clear that the expenditure of effort increases the value placed upon the end sought, as well as resistance to learning a new response. We might, therefore, predict that in prolonged conflicts, those who expend the most effort to achieve some ends would be the most apt to escalate the value of the ends sought.

Effort justification may be viewed within the broader framework of cognitive dissonance theory.[4] In Festinger's original formulation of the theory, the term *cognition* meant any knowledge, opinion, or belief about the environment, about oneself, or about one's behavior. When aspects of such cognitions are psychologically inconsistent, dissonance is aroused, and the organism is motivated to reduce the dissonance. Dissonance reduction may be accomplished by employing one or more of the following strategies: (a) redefining the situation, (b) adding new cognitions or modifying existing ones so that the ratio of inconsistent to consistent cognitions is decreased, (c) enhancing the attractiveness of the chosen alternative relative to the unchosen one, (d) selectively attending to and processing information that supports the decision, or (e) denying discrepant cognitions.

In short, effort justification is one strategy for reducing cognitive dissonance; that is, if one has expended a great deal of energy toward an outcome, then one must value that outcome. In other words, if I have knowledge that I have invested much of my time or energy in a project, particularly in a project that has not done well, I need to put in more effort to protect and to justify the effort I have already made and thereby reduce dissonance. If I have expended effort, I assume that it is for a worthwhile cause. Otherwise, I have behaved stupidly or exercised poor judgment.

One can see some of these proclivities in both public and elite reactions to U.S. commitments to Vietnam. As this country got militarily involved in Vietnam, the value placed on those efforts escalated, as well as the willingness to bear their costs. This is clearest with the American public. Initially the nation, as a whole, had little interest in Vietnam. In the Spring of 1964, one poll indicated that 63% of Americans paid little or no attention to Vietnam, and in June 1964, the University of Michigan Survey Research Center (SRC) found that 25% of its respondents reported that they had heard nothing of the fighting in Vietnam. Even after the Gulf of Tonkin incident in August 1964, the Michigan SRC found that 32% of the sample were paying no attention to the war in Vietnam.

But as the United States got ever more involved, people followed. Popular support for the war rose considerably during the last half of 1965 and remained high into 1966, even though American casualties had risen. Successive Harris polls found, however, that the percentage of Americans expecting a long war had increased from 54% in 1965 to 72% by mid-1966.

This made it increasingly difficult for the government even to consider leaving Vietnam. Senator Eugene McCarthy, who ran for the Democratic party nomination in 1968 on the promise of peace in Vietnam, has stated that one of the more important questions he had to face from the public was how he could justify the large loss of lives in the war if we were to pull out of Vietnam immediately. In abstract terms it would be hard to escalate the value of Vietnam beyond the domino theory, which antedated the escalation of the American presence there in 1965 to 1968. An unthinking acceptance of the theory was characteristic of most policy-makers in the 1950s and 1960s.[5] But presidents would differ on how much they were willing to pay for trying to keep the dominoes from falling. We should expect that the principles of effort justification would be the most potent during the second Johnson administration, after the commitments to military intervention in Vietnam had been made and the costs of the enterprise had begun to mount.

Eisenhower in 1954 rejected recommendations from some of his military advisors that the United States intervene militarily in Vietnam to save the French. Despite his adherence to the domino theory, he was not willing to risk direct military intervention at the cost of Congressional opposition and a possible military quagmire in Southeast Asia. Though Kennedy sent advisors to Vietnam, his approach seemed to be one of doing the minimum necessary to prevent the Communists from winning at the time, and some advisors suggest he was trying to keep his options open until after the 1964 campaign.

Under Johnson, however, increasing levels of commitment to direct military involvement in Vietnam were made. And as the cost of the enterprise began to mount, so did the commitment and the willingness to bear further costs. The vast sums of men, material, and money the Johnson administration poured into Vietnam has been outlined above. Soon, Johnson would be forced to sacrifice for the war the liberal domestic reforms, which initially had been his greatest concern. And his policies toward Europe, Latin America and Africa suffered as a consequence of the involvement. Ultimately he would forfeit his office and damage the presidential campaign of his hand-picked successor, Hubert Humphrey, rather than admit he was wrong.

Returning to some empirical studies, there is evidence that effort justification may be generalized to other tasks. Human subjects who are required to expend a high degree of effort on a preliminary set of tasks exhibit greater persistence on subsequent tasks than do subjects who are not required to exert a high level of effort.[6] Higher rates of response on a task have even been found in animals that were required to exert high effort on a preliminary task.[7] Similarly, research with clinical populations indicates that the number of performances required for reinforcement of one behavior (e.g., list learning) affects subsequent effort expended on other tasks requiring instrumental behavior; the direction of the relationship is positive — greater effort on task A is associated with greater effort on Task B.[8] What the studies by Eisenberger and his colleagues suggest is that the expenditure of a high degree of effort for the successful performance of an instrumental act may become a generalized component of instrumental behavior. The effects of effort are to increase persistence across a variety of tasks and behaviors for both human and animal subjects.

Still other research findings suggest that effort contributes to the rigidity of learned responses and may also decrease the rate of the learning of new responses.[9] Difficult new responses take longer to learn and are extinguished more slowly. In experiments concerning the results of effort, subjects tend to retain habits involving hard work longer than those involving less work.[10] However, effort without any reward, where reinforcement has occurred earlier, sometimes decreases time for unlearning.[11] Most important, the strongest and most frequently reported effect of effort is that of increasing the perceived worth of that for which one labors.[12]

The increasing costs of the Vietnam war were evident in the expenditure of time and energy of the president. Indeed, Johnson spent more of his own time on matters associated with the Vietnam problem than on any other — reportedly a day a week according to Rostow (personal communication, 1966).

In addition to the president, certain high-level U.S. specialists — McGeorge Bundy, Walt Rostow — spent many more hours on Southeast Asia than their job titles and functions would suggest. W. W. Rostow devoted most of his time to Vietnam. Both McGeorge Bundy and his brother Bill were deeply involved in the war and efforts to expand U.S. involvement. It was as if Southeast Asia had come to represent much of the cold war itself. Lives, money, and time are precious to Americans, and we spent all lavishly in Vietnam. We could not afford to lose.[13]

Furthermore, within the Johnson administration, individuals would differ in their evaluations of the war — depending on the direction of their initial commitments, the effort they expended, their personal responsibilities and emotional independence from the opinion of others in their immediate environment. To some extent we can rank order decision makers on each of these variables. The most committed, perhaps, were the members of the Joint Chiefs of Staff. They had made a commitment to winning the war, early in the discussion of U.S. policy toward Vietnam. During its course they would be willing to do everything possible to win the war, arguing at various times that the United States should invade the North, or totally disrupt Vietnamese society by bombing the dikes by which the rice culture was maintained.[14]

Next to them was President Johnson. Not only did he devote much of his time to the war, he had made his choices most freely. It was his war. And it is clear that he took responsibility for the war. Hence, shortly after the President became aware that Senator Fulbright (a close friend, fellow southerner, and Chair of the Senate Foreign Relations Committee) was opposed to escalation in Vietnam, President Johnson made the point that while he listened to everyone he could, he — not his advisors — had to take responsibility for deciding the policy.[15] It is not surprising that President Johnson showed the counterintuitive, nonrational, effort-justification effect. Under such circumstances, it is easy to see how he could have ignored the *dictum populi* in New York clothing industry concerning why one should lower prices and reduce inventory when the market began to do poorly. "Your first losses are your smallest ones." Yet, unlike the Joint Chiefs of Staff, Johnson also had broader domestic political concerns and was determined to escalate only to the highest level the public would bear without increasing public resistance. Gelb and Betts argue that the decision-making system "worked" in that it did what it was supposed to do. The aim of each president was to prevent the loss of Vietnam to Communism. They did not expect a victory in the classic sense of a decisive defeat of the enemy, but they did hope that the results of their efforts would be to prevent a communist win. American policies did prevent that loss for 25 years. Yet, as Gelb and Betts have to admit, it did not work in terms of achieving a long-term success in the area, nor did it prevent leaders from being willing to take serious risks, to engage in wishful thinking, and to commit the fatal error of letting hope override expectation.[16]

Aides such as W. W. Rostow and McGeorge Bundy, who had advised President Johnson on policies at the time the original commitments were made and shared his political interests, were close to him in their perspectives on the war. Other individuals, psychologically or politically independent of the president, were less inclined to value the war effort. Townsend Hoopes, for example, prided himself on his independence of thought and had no major responsibility for the original commitments to fight in Vietnam. By 1965 he was having grave doubts about the war and later would make extensive efforts to persuade McNamara that the United States should act to cut losses there.[17] George Ball had never favored a major investment of American energy and manpower in Southeast Asia, and on this and other occasions would show the emotional independence which enabled him to take unpopular stands with his colleagues. Personal characteristics and the failure to invest effort in the direction of the rest of the administration were the reason he failed to show the effect. Clark Clifford had an independent base as a high-powered lawyer in the business world, and earlier, as an informal advisor to the president, had raised questions about the wisdom of U.S. escalation in Vietnam.[18] As Secretary of Defense after McNamara's forced resignation, he would remain more open to facts indicating that the war was going badly and be able to announce to the president in the spring of 1968 that the war was unwinnable.

Other findings on the results of effort help explain how the commitment to escalation during a conflict could persist so long. Johnson and Steiner report that effort appears to increase the rigidity of a set of expectations.[19] Arrowood and Ross, and Yaryau and Festinger report that actual or anticipated high effort increases estimates of the probability of a preferred and desired future event, perhaps an operational definition of optimism.[20] The way they define a situation seems to attenuate or augment the intensity of experiences that people suffer or enjoy. Not only repression but also enhancement occurs. These results must be contrasted with learning as it ordinarily occurs in which we value more that which provides the larger payoff.

As the experimental work shows, the actual expenditure of effort will cause greater optimism about its effects. Extrapolating to the Vietnamese situation, escalation — one could predict — would be accompanied by an increased optimism regarding the results of such increased effort; and there were indications of this development. Thus, during the escalation of the Vietnam war, Johnson persisted in seeing the light at the end of the tunnel. McNamara, at least until the latter part of 1967, seized upon the body counts to prove to himself that the war was going well. McGeorge Bundy seems to have been excessively optimistic with regard to what U.S. military resources could achieve.[21] General Westmoreland exuded optimism throughout his stint as head of the U.S. forces in Vietnam. Indeed, he, Admiral Sharp, W. W. Rostow, and others who had so completely vested themselves in the Vietnam experience would later argue that the United States could have won only if it had gone all out in its efforts.

This optimism was buttressed by the administration's reliance on body counts as estimates of how things were going. It was perhaps an objective measure (though subject to an optimistic reporting bias that meant it lacked reliability and validity). But, the North Vietnamese did not have comparable utility schedules. And thus Ho Chi Minh could argue that the ratio of Vietnamese to American deaths could be 10 to 1 and the Vietnamese still would win. In short, the principle of effort justification suggests that where effort is considerable, probabilities concerning outcomes will be estimated as more favorable.

A more finely grained analysis of the attitudes of policymakers dealing with Vietnam shows swings from gloom to elation in the aftermath of each escalation. Although the long-term trend was one of pessimism, short-term increases in optimism occurred immediately following the introduction of new programs by each successive president.[22] Optimism was high in 1951, when American liaison teams made their way to Tonkin to join a failing French effort. The pessimism of late 1964 gave way increasingly, as Daniel Ellsberg points out, to "buoyant hopes by 1967 of a military victory, just as it had in the past." The initial responses of the Vietcong to each one of these escalations further encouraged the shift to unbounded optimism. "After suffering initial setbacks, they would lie low for an extended period, gather data, analyze experience, develop, test, and adapt new strategies, then plan and prepare carefully before launching them."[23] One can graphically conceptualize the fluctuations in optimism as a recurrent sawtooth with U.S. action, rather than concrete results, causing the initial acceleration of each successive line.

Seven years after publication of *A Theory of Cognitive Dissonance*, Festinger described a series of studies that further clarified the original theory and made a distinction between pre- and post-decisional periods. It was suggested that the more difficulty a person had in making a decision, the greater would be his tendency to justify the decision in the post-decisional period. Post-decisional processes result in an upward reevaluation of the chosen alternative and/or a downward reevaluation of the rejected alternative.[24] One possible cognitive strategy that could be employed to justify or reevaluate a particular decision would be to avoid dissonant information and seek consonant information.[25] Generally, the results of research indicate that under certain conditions, decision makers are likely to engage in selective exposure strategies.[26]

In the case of decisions regarding the Vietnam war, cognitive discord and emotional discomfort could be avoided by decision makers selectively processing information that supported their efforts vis-à-vis Vietnam. The Joint Chiefs, for example, when arguing for an all-out bombing campaign in 1965, discounted the possibility that the Chinese might actively enter into the war. Johnson himself seems to have stage-managed these discussions about escalating the war in 1965 so as to place himself in the middle between the views of the hawkish Joint Chiefs of Staff and the dovish George Ball. Views were presented that he really did not attend to, having made his decisions in advance of the meetings where these alternatives were presented.[27] Indeed, the president seems to have rationalized the escalation of the war on the ground that additional action would shorten the conflict.[28] As the war continued, he increasingly surrounded himself with Congressional loyalists like Senators Fred Harris of Oklahoma and Gale McGee of Wyoming. Similarly, after Clark Clifford replaced Robert McNamara as Secretary of Defense and began his maneuvers to steer Johnson away from further escalation, the president began to ignore Clifford and to consult with him only infrequently.[29] The president had a similar reaction to Senator Fulbright and Vice President Humphrey when their opposition became apparent.[30]

Groupthink was also employed during the escalation phase of the Vietnam war. When a policy-making group becomes highly cohesive, as Janis (1972) points out, views become homogeneous, thus making it very likely that all of the members will continue to support decisions to which the group has become committed. The result is action that members of the group would have avoided, had each made the decision individually. In Vietnam, Janis suggests, critical judgments were suspended and faulty decision made by policymakers because of social psychological processes.[31] Critics of the war within the administration were sometimes used to give the appearance that all the options were considered, but their views were downgraded in one way or another.[32] Sometimes they were removed from the inner circle. McNamara was kicked upstairs to the World Bank when he began to question the war. The president himself often ran National Security Council meetings to produce concurrence with his views. As Cooper describes them:

> The President, in due course, would announce his decision and then poll everyone in the room — Council members, their assistants, and members of the White House and NCS staffs. "Mr. Secretary, do you agree with the decision?" "Yes, Mr. President." "Mr. X, do you agree?" "I agree, Mr. President." During the process I would frequently fall into a Walter Mitty-like fantasy: When my turn came I would rise to my feet slowly, look around the room and then directly at the President, and say very quietly and emphatically, "Mr. President, gentlemen, I most definitely do not agree." But I was removed from my trance when I heard the President's voice, saying "Mr. Cooper, do you agree?" And out would come a "Yes, Mr. President, I agree."[33]

In short, there is evidence that policy makers employed a variety of well-documented psychological processes for reducing dissonance. Based on the evidence presented above, we would speculate that the processes used included rationalization, selective exposure to information, and group cohesion.

At this point we would like to elaborate on the reasons why a president is apt to experience the impact of effort justification for policies inherited from his predecessors. As Zimbardo notes, the notion of inherited commitment best describes the predicament of newly elected presidents.

> Although volition in decision making is an important determinant of dissonance, it is not a necessary condition because dissonance (like relatives) can be inherited. Responsibility for *maintaining*, rather than initiating, a given decision can be inherited in a given role and can create dissonance to the degree that the individual takes his self-definition from his role behavior and a vital part of that role involves keeping commitments.[34]

Once the nation has become committed to a policy, each president knows that failure to adhere to it may lead to many undesirable outcomes: social criticism, loss of self-esteem, humiliation, and others.[35] Moreover, each president's recommendations for increasing expenditures to sustain the commitments and his awareness of costs reinforce his personal responsibility. This phenomenon was evident in the views of several U.S. presidents that "it would be a bad year to lose in Southeast Asia," and that it would be undesirable to be "the first U.S. president to lose a war."[36] For Johnson between 1965 and 1968 not wanting to lose the war was the major objective that led to increasing force levels.

The personal responsibility felt by President Johnson is described by Cooper.[37] The public, as he saw it, could not understand why the United States was unable either to win a war against a small and weak military power, or to disengage itself from it. One result of this was that the president and his principal advisors felt they had to take personal charge of the war if only to vindicate themselves. Numerous fact-finding trips to Saigon by high-level officials attest to these concerns. The emphasis on quantifying the results of the war effort and securing progress reports from the field were symptomatic of both the anxiety and the need by high-level officials to feel they were taking actions that would succeed.

Personally and politically, Johnson invested so much in the enterprise that he could not admit error. As Kearns explains it:

> He could admit to a mistake — although not easily — after a legislative failure, and learn from it. But mistakes could not be admitted in a situation like Vietnam, where the effort was defined solely by a goal and where failure, therefore, was a challenge to the rightness of belief, to some integrity of self, which must be even more fiercely defended when under attack.[38]

Ultimately the commitment cost Johnson the very political support he had worked so hard to sustain. Again, Kearns:

> Johnson's belief that no Democratic President could survive the loss of South Vietnam to the Communists was based on the assessment, then generally accepted, that the Demo-

crats were particularly vulnerable at home to the charge of being soft on Communism abroad. But what were the dangers the Democrats faced at Home? Certainly the American people, regarding strength of will as a virtue and unaccustomed to defeat, were likely to be angry and troubled by a Communist takeover in Vietnam. However, at least before the escalations of 1965, it was not an American war, and a Communist victory would be viewed as a defeat for the "Free World," but probably not as the defeat—far more serious—of American military force. And, in the end, after paying a huge and bloody price, the American people seemed hardly to care when Communist forces moved into Saigon. The principal constraint, then, was not the extent of current public concern about Vietnam. It was fear that political opponents might be able to blame a Communist advance on weakness of American will, and successfully convince people of the administration's "softness" toward Communism.[39]

De-Escalation and Effort Justification

A particularly thorny problem for the principle of effort justification is explaining why any war would end. That is, if effort increases one's resolve to continue an endeavor, what theoretical constructs can be brought to bear on the problem of some sort of "stop mechanism?" Surely, the total amount of effort expended would continue to increase as war continued to be waged.

As noted earlier, the principle of effort justification also suggests that the effects of effort generalize to other tasks, increasing persistence across a variety of behaviors. Commitments made in Washington reinforced, and were reinforced by, the battlefield experience. Intuitively, it is true, there was good reason for Americans to increase their persistence on the battlefield. As Colonel Harry G. Summers, Jr., an instructor at the Army War College, has pointed out: the United States won many tactical victories, though it suffered a strategic failure in Vietnam. Paradoxically, as the experimental literature suggests, intermittent reinforcement (i.e., winning some battles periodically) might have resulted in greater persistence than winning all the battles. Summers is reported to have told a North Vietnamese colonel after the war. "You know, you never defeated us on the battlefield," to which his counterpart replied, "That may be so, but it is also irrelevant."[40] What the North Vietnamese officer must have had in mind was the classic guerrilla warfare doctrine which makes traditional battles between armed forces a peripheral concern. The significance of the Tet offensive was not that it improved the military situation of the Communist Vietnamese forces, but that it belied the assurances of political and military leaders in the United States that an end to the war was just around the corner.

Public opinion was another factor that played into the decision to de-escalate. With respect to public opinion, the difference between logical inconsistency and personal responsibility would seem to be relevant. Recent theoretical formulations contend that dissonance is aroused in human beings only when they are responsible for producing some undesirable consequence, that is, when the self is involved. Such ego-defense offers one explanation why an expenditure of effort would lead to attitude change.[41] It is possible that under some conditions both a general desire for dissonance reduction and ego-defensive effects may operate together.[42] As Greenwald and Ronis have noted, experiments should be carefully designed to avoid confounding ego-defensive effects with cognitive inconsistency effects so that each may be evaluated in terms of its contribution to attitude change.[43]

One hypothesis to consider then is that a president might continue to justify effort despite logical or cognitive inconsistency because of his personal responsibility. But American citizens would be compelled to justify effort primarily on the basis of avoiding cognitive inconsistency. Not directly responsible for the war, they would be able to experience dissonance earlier than the president. Relative to the Vietnam situation these dissonant events included mounting casualties, rising taxes, knowledge of political corruption in South Vietnam, uncertainties with regard to South Vietnam's desire for our continued occupation, vague objectives, no solution in sight, and the vivid portrayal of the war on television. With less ego-involvement in outcomes than government officials, large sectors of the public would strive to restore a balance in their lives by pressuring the government to get out of Vietnam. Indeed, the divergence between Johnson's views and public opinion was evident in the strong negative reactions he received to a speech in Minneapolis which reaffirmed his resolve to win in Vietnam. By March of 1968, the prevailing view of the public was not winning. Instead, the question was how to get out of the war.[44]

We recognize that the effect postulated by the effort justification hypothesis (i.e., the acceleration or persistence of effort) does not overwhelm all contrary stimuli, nor does it ordinarily continue indefinitely. Effort simply persists longer than it would have without choice (and choice over time equals commitment) and effort. Acceleration of effort sometimes is explained as an extinction burst: given that it is not reinforced by success, a quick withdrawal occurs. Hence, the persuasiveness of Clark Clifford, along with the countervailing forces of TET and public opinion, all seem to have been significant factors in the decision to de-escalate.

It is also important to note that the effect of effort justification does not go on forever, even for decision makers. One may value activities or products more as a function of having chosen to engage in them and having invested relatively more effort in them than in other enterprises, but scarcely *infinitely* more. The irrationality associated with decisions with which one identifies does not continue indefinitely; rather this serves as a hindrance to rational assessment of the costs and the probabilities of success related to past choice. It simply slows down the process and leads one to act less sensibly than would otherwise have been the case.

This was apparent in the decision to get out of Vietnam. Slowly various decision makers began to realize that the war was not winnable in terms of the time and cost U.S. citizens would tolerate. By 1967, for example, McNamara raises some questions about the premises on which decisions had been made. Hoopes describes McNamara's defection from the ranks as follows:

A definitive expression of his doubt, and the one which set him explicitly at odds with the Senate hawks, the military leaders, and (as it turned out) the President, was his statement before the Stennis Committee on August 25, 1967, on the pivotal issue of the air war against North Vietnam. . . . McNamara said in effect that, unless the United States shifted to an indiscriminate bombing campaign aimed at annihilating the population of North Vietnam, the air war against the North could not be expected to accomplish more than "to continue to put a high price tag on North Vietnam's continued aggression." He saw nothing in the record to indicate that Hanoi "can be bombed to the negotiating table."[45]

Not everyone is equally susceptible to the effects of effort and choice, as the above review of the literature suggests. A number of studies cited suggest that the effect is ego-defensive, that it is self-protective of one's decisions and their results. Moreover, as Zimbardo has reported, persons higher on a need for the social approval of others appear more susceptible to the effect. Conversely, persons who are particularly independent show less inclination to justify their efforts.[46]

Clark Clifford, who in early 1968 replaced Secretary of Defense Robert Mc-Namara, was highly influential in Johnson's decision to de-escalate. Clifford could look upon the war quite dispassionately since he was not a key player in the decision to escalate U.S. involvement. Indeed, two years earlier, Clifford had preferred to maintain his law practice and remain independent rather than take a cabinet position that the president offered him.

Clifford began to have some doubts about U.S. involvement in 1967 when he went on a fact finding mission in Asia and learned that leaders of various governments did not share the U.S. government's view that the domino theory applied to Vietnam and neighboring countries. After becoming Secretary of Defense, Clifford would find himself confronted by evidence that could only be accommodated by completely reframing the problem put before him. Specifically, rather than searching for means to meet the military's request for more troops, fundamental questions about the interests of the United States began to emerge, leading him to conclude that it was in the interest of the country to get out of Vietnam.[47]

Even the president eventually opted out of the situation. Unable to see any way of winning the war without enormous costs to his domestic programs and political support, Johnson decided in the Spring of 1968 to call a halt to the bombing north of the 20th parallel and not to seek another term as president. His decision, however, did not lead him to the clear conclusion that he should reverse his policies. Rather, his decision not to seek reelection may be viewed as an attempt to resolve dissonant cognitions. As Doris Kearns has pointed out, his actions were designed to bring the North Vietnamese to the negotiating table and, ultimately, if that did not work, to lay the groundwork for further escalation. Personally, it was a way of temporarily de-escalating without a loss of self-esteem.[48]

So it was that in finally offering an end to the air war against the North, Johnson was not forced to see himself as a coward running away from Vietnam. To the contrary, he convinced himself that he was the same man of courage determined to save South Vietnam, daring a new initiative in a continuing course. And, by coupling this initiative with a withdrawal from the presidential race, he made sure that it would not be read as a political trick. *In short, "the presidential rule that 'this is a bad year for me to lose Vietnam to Communism' " continued to influence Johnson to the very end.*[49]

Conclusion

Our intent has been to argue that the American effort in Southeast Asia may plausibly be regarded as a factor in having kept us there, even as the costs mounted to levels not originally anticipated. The large effort made in that conflict helped shape our values and subsequent behavior, making it increasingly difficult to even consider the possibility of rapid de-escalation or withdrawal. As mentioned above, not everyone involved showed the effects of effort justification. There were significant individual differences on that variable. The members of the Joint Chiefs of Staff and Lyndon Johnson, for instance, showed the effect strongly, as did the Bundys. It seems that those who came to oppose the war as the costs increased were relatively removed from personal responsibility for the war and/or had personalities which made them less susceptible to the effort justification effect over the long run. Their independence and limited needs for social approval from authority figures reduced their vulnerability.

We are aware that it is always risky to import theoretical notions and empirical findings from an already established body of research, and in some instances doubtlessly we have used hypotheses and extrapolated raw research findings beyond their intended limits. However, the principle of effort justification and related constructs derived from dissonance and self-theory would seem to be sufficiently robust to apply to the Vietnam war in particular, with possibly broader implications for protracted engagements by states in general.[50]

Notes

1. L. Berman, *Planning a Tragedy: The Americanization of the War in Vietnam* (New York: Norton, 1983), 9, 10, 131-132.

2. L. G. Gelb and R. K. Betts, *The Irony of Vietnam: The System Worked* (Washington, DC: The Brookings Institution, 1979).

3. T. Hoopes, *The Limits of Intervention* (New York: David McKay, 1973).

4. L. Festinger, *Theory of Cognitive Dissonance* (Stanford, CA: Stanford University Press, 1957).

5. Berman, *Planning a Tragedy*, 132.

6. R. Eisenberger and F. A. Masterson, "Required High Effort Increases Subsequent Persistence and Reduces Cheating," *Journal of Personality and Social Psychology*, 44, 3 (1983): 593-599.

7. R. Eisenberger, W. A. Heirdt, M. Hamdi, S. Zimet, and G. Bruckmeir, "Transfer of Persistence Across Behaviors," *Journal of Experimental Psychology: Human Learning and Memory*, 5, 5 (1979):

522-530; R. Eisenberger, J. Carlson, M. Guile, and N. Shapiro, "Transfer of Effort Across Behaviors," *Learning and Motivation*, 10 (1979): 188-197.

8. Ibid.

9. J. Capehart, W. Viney, and I. M. Huliska, "The Effect of Effort Upon Extinction," *Journal of Comparative and Physiological Psychology*, 51 (1958): 505-507; G. Collier and D. A. Levitsky, "Operant Running as a Function of Deprivation and Effort," *Journal of Comparative and Physiological Psychology*, 66 (1968): 522-523; R. L. Solomon, "Effort and Extinction Rate: A Confirmation," *Journal of Comparative and Physiological Psychology*, 41 (1948): 93-100.

10. E. G. Aiken, "The Effort Variable in the Acquisition, Extinction and Spontaneous Recovery of an Instrumental Response," *Journal of Experimental Psychology*, 53 (1957): 47-51; T. Grusee and G. Bower, "Response Effort and the Frustration Hypothesis," *Journal of Comparative and Physiological Psychology*, 60 (1965): 128-130; D. Lawrence and L. Festinger, *Deterrents and Reinforcement: The Psychology of Insufficient Reward* (Stanford, CA: Stanford University Press, 1962).

11. Capehart et al., "The Effect of Effort Upon Extinction," 505-507; Solomon, "Effort and Extinction Rate"; J. L. Maatsch, M. Adelman, and R. M. Denny, "Effort and Resistance to Extinction of the Bar-Pressing Response," *Journal of Comparative and Physiological Psychology*, 47 (1954): 47-50; T. Stachnik, "The Role of Response Effort in Extinction," *Psychonomic Science*, 9 (1967): 517-518; D. Quartermain, "Effect of Effort on Resistance to Extinction of Bar-Pressing Response," *Quarterly Journal of Experimental Psychology*, 17 (1965): 63-64.

12. E. Aronson and J. Mills, "The Effect of Severity of Initiation on Liking for a Group," *Journal of Applied Social Psychology*, 59 (1959): 177-181; I. Child, "Children's Preference for Goals Easy or Difficult to Obtain," *Psychological Monographs*, 60 (1946): 1-31; A. R. Cohen, "Communication Discrepancy and Attitude Change: A Dissonance Theory Approach," *Journal of Personality*, 27 (1959): 386 396; H. Freedman, R. M. Tarpy, and P. Komelski, "The Preference of Rats for a More Difficult Task," *Psychonomic Science*, 13 (1968): 157-158; H. B. Gerard and G. C. Mathewson, "The Effects of Severity of Initiation on Liking for a Group: A Replication," *Journal of Experimental Social Psychology*, 2 (1966): 278-287; M. Lewis, "The Effects of Effort on Value: An Exploratory Study of Children," *Child Development*, 35 (1964): 1337-1432; M. Lewis, "Effect of Effort on Choice: Value of a Secondary Reinforcer," *Psychological Reports*, 16 (1965): 557-560; M. Lewis, "Psychological Effect of Effort," *Psychological Bulletin*, 64 (1965): 183-190; D. E. Linder, J. Cooper and R. A. Wicklund, "Pre-Exposure Persuasion as a Result of Commitment to Pre-Exposure Effort," *Journal of Experimental Social Psychology*, 4 (1968): 470-482; T. M. Ostrom, "Physical Effort and Attitude Change," *American Psychologist*, 21 (1966): 692. (Abstract) Paper presented at American Psychological Association Convention, New York, September 1966 (also memo, Ohio State University, 1966); D. O. Sears, "Social Anxiety, Opinion Structure, and Opinion Change," *Journal of Personality and Social Psychology*, 7 (1967): 142-151; R. A. Wicklund, J. Cooper, and D. E. Linder, "Effects of Expected Effort on Attitude Change Prior to Exposure," *Journal of Experimental Social Psychology*, 3 (1967): 416-428; P. G. Zimbardo, *The Cognitive Control of Motivation: The Consequences of Choice and Dissonance* (Glenview, IL: Scott, Foresman, 1969).

13. Berman, *Planning a Tragedy*.

14. Ibid.

15. David M. Barrett, "The Mythologies Surrounding Lyndon Johnson, His Advisers, and the 1965 Decision to Escalate the Vietnam War," *Political Science Quarterly*, 103, 4 (1988): 637-663.

16. Gelb and Betts, *The Irony of Vietnam*.

17. Hoopes, *The Limits of Intervention*.

18. D. Halberstam, *The Best and the Brightest* (New York: Random House, 1972).

19. H. Johnson and I. D. Steiner, "Effort and Subjective Probability," *Journal of Personality and Social Psychology*, 1 (1965): 365-368.

20. A. J. Arrowood and L. Ross, "Anticipated Effort and Subjective Probability," *Journal of Personality and Social Psychology*, 4 (1966): 57-64; R. B. Yaryau and L. Festinger, "Preparatory Action and Belief in the Probably Occurrence of Future Events," *Journal of Applied Social Psychology*, 63 (1961): 603-606.

21. Berman, *Planning a Tragedy*.

22. D. Ellsberg, *Papers on the War* (New York: Simon & Schuster, 1972).

23. Ibid., 119-120.

24. L. Festinger, *Conflict, Decision, and Dissonance* (Stanford, CA: Stanford University Press, 1964); R. A. Wicklund and J. W. Brehm, *Perspectives on Cognitive Dissonance* (Hillsdale, NJ: Erlbaum, 1976).

25. Festinger, *Theory of Cognitive Dissonance*.

26. J. L. Cotton and R. A. Heiser, "Selective Exposure to Information and Cognitive Dissonance," *Journal of Personality*, 14 (1980); 518-527; D. Frey and R. A. Wicklund, "A Clarification of Selective Exposure: The Impact of Choice," *Journal of Experimental Social Psychology*, 14 (1978): 132-139; J. Mills, "Avoidance of Dissonance Information," *Journal of Personality and Social Psychology*, 2 (1965): 589-593.

27. Berman, *Planning a Tragedy*.

28. C. L. Cooper, *The Lost Crusade: America in Vietnam* (New York: Dodd, Mead, 1970).

29. S. Karnow, *Vietnam: A History* (New York: Viking, 1983).

30. Barrett, "The Mythologies Surrounding Lyndon Johnson."

31. I. L. Janis and L. Mann, *Decision Making* (New York: Free Press, 1977).

32. Berman, *Planning a Tragedy*; Halberstam, *The Best and the Brightest*.

33. Cooper, *The Lost Crusade*, 223.

34. Zimbardo, *The Cognitive Control of Motivation*, 278.

35. Janis and Mann, *Decision Making*.

36. Gelb and Betts, *The Irony of Vietnam*, 224.

37. Cooper, *The Lost Crusade*.

38. D. Kearns, *Lyndon Johnson and the American Dream* (New York: Harper and Row, 1976), 257.

39. Ibid., 258-259.

40. Approximately 2,000 French army soldiers and 8,000 Vietnminh died at Dienbienphu. Prior to the battle, Ho Chi Minh exclaimed that the French could kill 10 of his men for every one Frenchman and even at those odds, the French would lose and he would win. At Khesanh, at least 10,000 Communists were killed; fewer than 500 U.S. marines were killed in action. See Karnow, *Vietnam*, 17.

41. Wicklund, "Effects of Expected Effort," 416-428.

42. See R. A. Wicklund and J. W. Brehm, *Perspectives on Cognitive Dissonance* (Hillsdale, NJ: Erlbaum, 1976), 416-428.

43. A. G. Greenwald and D. L. Ronis, "Twenty Years of Cognitive Dissonance: Case Study of the Evolution of a Theory," *Psychological Review*, 85 (1978): 53-57.

44. Robert Schandler, *The Unmaking of a President* (Princeton, NJ: Princeton University Press, 1977).

45. Hoopes, *The Limits of Intervention*, 86-87; Hoopes goes on, stating: "[McNamara's] case rested essentially on a finding that North Vietnam, although a primitive agricultural society offering few industrial and military targets, possessed nonetheless a highly diversified transportation system. It had a capacity to import 14,000 tons per day, but was in fact importing only 5,800 tons. Of this, the remarkably small sum of under 100 tons per day was all that was needed to sustain NVN and Vietcong forces in the South. He argued that this requirement in the South was too small in relation to the capacity of the system to permit belief that we could, by bombing, prevent North Vietnam from sustaining combat operations at the 1967 level. In reading this conclusion he assumed the continued willingness of Russia and China to maintain a steady flow of military and war-supporting equipment, and the continued tenacity of the people of North Vietnam who "are accustomed to discipline and are no strangers to deprivation and to death."

46. P. G. Zimbardo, "The Effect of Effort and Improvisation of Self-Persuasion Produced by Role-Playing," *Journal of Experimental Social Psychology*, 1 (1965): 103-120.

47. Schandler, *The Unmaking of a President*.

48. Kearns, *Lyndon Johnson and the American Dream*.

49. Ellsberg, *Papers on the War*, 49.

50. Here is another example of the phenomenon we have discussed: Edward I of England, asked to mediate a conflict between two claimants to the throne of Scotland, obliged by arranging for a group of French scholars to work on the problem. They concluded in favor of the rival to Robert the Bruce, the less popular of the two candidates. Having invested in his "solution," Edward eventually sent two different expeditionary forces to Scotland in increasingly heavy-handed efforts to impose his preferred outcome. His efforts grew larger and produced a conflict between the two countries that persisted for several hundred years and was resolved only when James VI of Scotland became James I of England.

Chapter 12

Ending Limited War: The Psychological Dynamics of the Termination Process

PAUL R. PILLAR

As the preceding chapters of this book have shown, limited war often is not a straightforward, entirely rational, collective pursuit of national goals through military means. Individual goals become entwined with national ones, and the stress of warfare often evokes nonrational responses on the part of leaders, military commanders, and civilian populations. These factors may pose especially acute problems near the end of a war, when a wartime government's calculations of ends and means becomes more complicated and the need for rational decision making is all the greater. It is near the end of a war that a government must decide what kind of postwar world is desirable and attainable and must orchestrate its diplomatic and military moves to achieve its desired end.

This chapter examines the psychological mechanisms that commonly affect efforts to end limited wars. It assesses the particular responses that are most often seen in the final phase of a war and the impediments these responses pose to the peacemaker. Finally, it offers some conclusions regarding the overall effect of the terms and of the timing of peace settlements.

Three particular aspects of the terminal phase of limited wars have psychological implications that commonly affect both how the belligerents continue to wage the war and how they make peace.

First, the approach of peace forces people at war to change their perception of the enemy. No longer simply an object of hatred or a target of military operations, the enemy must now be thought of as a partner in a difficult search for an acceptable and workable settlement. For this search to be successful, the enemy's goals and sensitivities must be given greater attention — and greater legitimacy — than they are apt to have received earlier in the conflict.

AUTHOR'S NOTE: The views expressed in this chapter are those of the author and not necessarily those of the Central Intelligence Agency or the U.S. Government.

Second, the cumulative effects of combat on the will and rationality of the belligerents tend to be more apparent near the end of a war than earlier. Indeed, the expectation of peace may lead people at war, buoyed by the belief that their pain and suffering will soon be over, to support even more painful measures in a last-ditch effort to obtain their objectives.

Third, the imminence of peace brings into sharp and often disconcerting focus the relationship between costs incurred and results obtained. It sometimes confronts belligerents with peace terms that are disappointing in comparison with the effort they expended and that may have negative political consequences at home. The prospect of peace also forces leaders and people at war to form new images of the postwar world and of their own places in it.

These three aspects are present to some degree in all wars except the few that end with the outright extermination, forcible subjugation, or expulsion from contested territory of one of the belligerents. War is inherently an extreme measure, and to many people it always will seem inappropriate to wage it for purposes that are not extreme. The more that the terms of settlement fall short of the enemy's unconditional surrender, the more psychologically jarring they are apt to be.

Images of the Enemy

Warfare often gives rise to popular perceptions of the enemy that are even more distorted, tendentious, and simplistic than the images that people of different nations normally hold of each other. A major war may generate waves of emotion that embody a view of the enemy as evil incarnate. Allied public perceptions of Germany during World War I, for example, came to include an image of a malevolent "Boche" and led to moves to eliminate all association with anything German, such as the names of some cities. Lesser conflicts carry less emotion, although there is still a tendency to perceive the enemy's leadership — and sometimes the whole opposing nation — as more irredeemably wicked than they actually are, or than they would be perceived as being in the absence of a war. The public exaggerates the conflict of interest between the opponents, largely because this response makes it easier to accept the sacrifices that the war entails.

Governments generally find this distortion of public perception useful in waging war. It is easier to raise armies, money, and morale if a conflict is viewed as a struggle between good and evil rather than as an effort to obtain a marginally better set of peace terms. Thus, governments often encourage the distortion by overstating the differences between the objectives of the opposing nations and understating the diplomatic opportunities for resolving the conflict. This approach may offer the added benefits of conveying an image of determination to the enemy and discouraging that enemy from playing upon divisions within one's own country. Extreme anti-Germanism during World War I probably had these benefits for the Allies, whose coalition was otherwise shaky and whose appetite for war certainly lessened as the carnage continued.

Although the manipulation of perceptions may help to sustain the war effort, it inhibits the making of peace. Whether or not leaders come to believe their own rhetoric about the incorrigibility of the enemy, they are apt to find it difficult to talk about a peace settlement, much less to take steps toward reaching one, without undermining the will to fight that may still be needed to attain advantageous peace terms. Moreover, bellicose statements may cause the enemy leadership to underestimate the opportunities for a peace settlement and to be dissuaded from trying to reach one.

The latter problem arose less often before the advent of modern communications, when politicians and generals could make inspirational speeches to their followers with little risk their remarks would be heard, and interpreted, by the enemy. Now, however, leaders are apt to exploit the global reach of the media by using a speech or interview ostensibly addressed to a domestic audience to send a message to a foreign government. Aware of this possibility, governments at war examine all of the enemy leaders' statements for clues of their intentions. They cannot afford to dismiss bellicose statements as merely internal propaganda that implies nothing about diplomatic opportunities.

The diplomatic costs of manipulating images of the enemy and of the stakes in a conflict are most apparent when the belligerents must cope with low morale in their ranks, because often this is when they make the kind of hard-line statements that may convince the enemy there is little immediate hope for peace. For example, in the Algerian war for independence, both sides had serious morale problems among their troops. The bellicose declarations that the insurgents' government-in-exile issued to boost the sagging spirits of guerrillas in the field tended to contradict the conciliatory line it was taking in secret diplomatic initiatives. As such, the declarations undermined the credibility and effectiveness of those initiatives.[1] On the French side, President de Gaulle faced serious discontent in the army among officers who opposed any compromise with the rebels. In early 1960 (after six years of war) de Gaulle toured military installations in Algeria and placated the dissident officers with such statements as "France will not depart," and "There will be no Dienbienphu in Algeria." His words infuriated the rebel leaders, who postponed any further peace initiatives.[2] An armistice was not reached until two years later. That even such a master of ambiguity as de Gaulle could not please one audience without provoking another demonstrates the difficulty involved.

To discover whether or not the enemy is willing to reach a mutually acceptable compromise and to overcome the distrust that accompanies the distorted perceptions each side holds of the other generally requires a special kind of peace overture. Direct, high-level contacts can most quickly remove distrust, but they risk being perceived as a sign of weakness and a "suing for peace." Ambiguous, low-level contacts entail less risk in this regard but have less credibility. The best agent for a peace initiative is one who is known to have access to his government's leaders and can convey their intentions accurately, but who holds no official position and thus can be disavowed if necessary.

This kind of agent has frequently been used during limited wars to probe an opponent's desire to make peace. In the Algerian conflict, de Gaulle used Georges Pompidou, at the time a private citizen but also de Gaulle's personal friend, to make the initial secret contacts with rebel representatives.[3] During the Korean War, George Kennan, who was on leave from the State Department, played a similar role by meeting with Soviet representatives to confirm Moscow's desire for an armistice.[4] And in the prenegotiation phase of the Vietnam War, the Johnson Administration once used Henry Kissinger, a professor whose consulting work had given him access to the leadership in Washington, to explore the intentions of the North Vietnamese.

Misperceptions of the enemy's intentions are by no means dispelled once peace talks begin. The negotiation itself is often a clumsy process in which the belligerents only gradually discover what terms would be acceptable to each side and whether or not the enemy sincerely seeks a settlement at all.[5] The process may be hindered by disagreements over the importance of particular concessions. Experimentation has shown a tendency for subjects in the laboratory to minimize major concessions made by the opponent and to underestimate the opponent's concession rate when it is greater than the subject's.[6] This kind of misperception can compound distrust, as concessions go unreciprocated and hopes for an early peace are not realized.

Rationality and the Costs of War

The simplest explanation of why any limited war ends is that the belligerents decide the costs of the war exceed the anticipated benefits of continuing it. (That both sides should *decide* to terminate the conflict — rather than one or the other being forcibly and completely subdued — is part of what makes the war limited.) Yet it does not follow that an increase in a belligerent's costs *always* inclines it more toward peace. The effect sometimes is the opposite, with higher costs seemingly leading a belligerent to demand stiffer terms for peace.

For example, a perfectly rational decision maker, not prone to misperceptions or psychological defense mechanisms, might conclude that the military operations that caused the increased costs bring new objectives within reach, making it appropriate to levy demands that were not contemplated when the war began. Soviet Foreign Minister Molotov called this the "logic of war" when he explained the expansion of the USSR's demands during its unexpectedly difficult war against Finland in 1939-40. The Soviets found they could not secure their initial objectives without a major effort to crush the Finnish forces, an effort that opened new goals to the Red Army.

Other reasons stem from the bargaining process by which the belligerents hope to end a conflict that is costly to them both.[7] The enemy's costs are as important to each side's bargaining position as its own costs. Escalation of a war usually entails higher costs to both sides. It may be rational for a belligerent whose suffering has increased to demand harsher terms, because the other side's suffering has increased too.

Thus the rational actor may find himself making the seemingly irrational decision to continue a war that already has cost far more than the worth to him of either his original objectives or any other benefits he still hopes to gain. The costs that matter to him are the future (i.e., marginal) costs, not those already sustained. His past suffering is irreversible; only future military operations are subject to his decisions. At the same time, the probability that he will receive the desired benefits (i.e., the enemy's acceptance of favorable peace terms) may depend on the course of the entire war. In some limited wars, the process of weakening the enemy and breaking his will is one in which the effects of violence are at least partly cumulative. From this perspective, past efforts in the war are an investment, and the perceived probability of obtaining a high return after only a small additional effort may be relatively high. This evidently became the perspective of the Iraqi leadership once their war with Iran developed into a far longer struggle that they could have imagined when they first invaded Iran in 1980. In the latter part of the Iran-Iraq war — long after Baghdad had been forced to discard some of its original ambitious aims — the Iraqis were sustained by the belief that the cumulative effect of their air attacks on Iranian resources and morale would eventually force Tehran to give up the struggle. In retrospect, that belief was correct.

Moreover, in some wars the military operations being contemplated may entail only a small additional cost, but the anticipated benefit may be a key concession, such as who controls a contested territory. Expected benefits may be high compared to expected costs, not only because of a high perceived probability that the enemy will concede but also because of the high value of the anticipated concession. In the case of Iraq, the anticipated Iranian concession was very important indeed: namely, Tehran's abandonment of its goal of toppling the Iraqi regime of President Saddam Husayn. This situation is similar to the experimental procedure called the "both pay auction,"[8] described by Glad and Rosenberg above.

The disparities between military costs and diplomatic responses become even greater, however, when wartime leaders respond to costs irrationally. A common perceptual distortion is the tendency to regard past costs as an investment even when the effects of violence on the enemy are not cumulative. Lincoln expressed the underlying sentiment in his address at Gettysburg: "that from these honored dead we take increased devotion to that cause. . . . We here highly resolve that these dead shall not have died in vain." To think otherwise goes against some of our most basic emotions about human life.

To misperceive bloodshed as having brought one closer to an acceptable peace agreement when it really has not, however, may set back the chances for peace. The misperception may lead decision makers to miscalculate both the efficacy of further military operations and the need to compromise in reaching a peace settlement. The impact that casualties, destruction, and blockades had on the Confederacy during the Civil War was probably cumulative (making a part of

Lincoln's statement — about the dead not having died in vain — rational as well as inspirational). But in the Vietnam War, for example, it is questionable whether U.S. military operations sapped North Vietnamese strength rapidly enough for the effect on Hanoi's determination to be truly cumulative.

A related tendency is the upward reevaluation of wartime objectives in response to mounting costs. The mechanism involved, as described by Milburn and Christie, above, is the need to reduce cognitive dissonance.[9] The greater the perceived benefits of particular peace terms, the less the discomfort over the costs incurring in winning those terms. In addition, as war costs increase, there develops an unwillingness to back down under pressure, in order to avoid damage to one's self-esteem. Many experimental studies have demonstrated that this response is a common attribute of bargaining behavior, whether the pressure takes the form of punishment or merely threats to inflict punishment.[10] Similar behavior often has been observed when one state tries to pressure another. As an 18th-century observer of diplomacy wrote: "Menaces always do harm to negotiation, and they frequently push one party to extremities to which they would not have resorted without provocation. It is well known that injured vanity frequently drives men into choices which a sober estimate of their own interests would lead them to avoid."[11]

Sometimes this refusal to withdraw under pressure may involve an entirely rational concern for preserving a reputation for not yielding to force and thus for enhancing one's ability to drive a hard bargain in future conflicts.[12] But often it stems in part from injured vanity, in the sense that an individual leader has come to identify the war effort with his own self-esteem.[13]

A more general reason for irrational behavior in the face of rising war costs is the stress it produces and the resulting diminution of leaders' perceptual and cognitive capabilities.[14] The impact of such a reduction of capabilities on wartime decisions varies widely. At one extreme is a shattering of will (such as that exhibited by General Ludendorff and the German high command at the end of World War I) together with an inability to recognize and to exploit fully one's remaining assets. It is more common in limited wars, however, for the impairment of cognitive capabilities to promote rigid adherence to earlier political demands and a continuation of unsuccessful military policies. In other words, the reduced ability to process new information tends to perpetuate misconceptions about the enemy's will, resources, and objectives that were held when the conflict began.

Partly because of this rigidity, a sudden or dramatic military event is often required to evoke the political decisions necessary for a peace settlement. A major military failure with highly visible costs will have a direct impact on top leaders without having been filtered through, and possibly distorted by, a bureaucracy.[15] Moreover, a battle or campaign can be what Robert Jervis has called an index — an action that tests what the opposing forces are capable of winning or losing in the future.[16] The test is most conclusive, and thus most likely to lead to the opening of peace talks or to a peace agreement, if a belligerent makes a determined effort under the most favorable circumstances and still suffers a setback.

The fall of Dienbienphu, for example, was important in persuading the French to end their Indochina war, partly because French commanders had chosen the area as a good location for a showdown and had garrisoned it with elite paratroopers and Foreign Legionnaires. Similarly, the final Chinese offensive in the Korean War in May 1951 and the Communist offensive in Vietnam in the spring of 1972, because they both were maximum efforts that demonstrated the limits of the attacker's capabilities, were indexes that led the attackers to revise their expectations and to become willing to negotiate or to make new concessions.

Accepting an Imperfect Peace

Detailed plans for peace settlements and how to negotiate them seldom are laid out far in advance of actual peace talks. In the Korean War, for example, U.S. aims fluctuated with the movement of the front line up and down the Korean peninsula, and what were to become the stickiest issues in the negotiations — such as repatriation of prisoners — did not seem particularly important until after the talks with the Communists were under way. During the Vietnam War, the Johnson administration spent much time and effort considering what might bring the North Vietnamese to the conference table, but very little on what would happen once they got there.[17] It is thus usually only near the end of a war, as proposed settlements are formulated and placed on the negotiating table, that belligerents squarely face the problems of reconciling the sacrifices and the bloodshed with a decision to accept an outcome short of "victory."

The inability to come to terms psychologically with a compromise peace settlement may lead to any or all of these responses:

- *Scapegoating.* The failure to achieve "victory" might be blamed on the pusillanimity of civilian leaders, the ineptitude of military commanders, the opportunism of the political opposition, or the perfidy of allies. Each of these participants may place responsibility on any of the others. Scapegoating in this context is a psychological defense mechanism as well as a strategy to salvage one's reputation or to reap political advantage. One of the clearest examples of scapegoating were the accusations that Hitler and the Nazis directed against the German leadership in World War I for allowing the humiliation at Versailles.
- *Revenge.* The desire to have another go at the same opponent under future, more favorable circumstances may stem less from the harshness of the terms that the opponent imposed than from dissatisfaction that the terms do not accurately reflect their respective military capabilities. For example, German revanchism was less apparent after the unconditional surrender in World War II than after World War I, which was limited in that the Germans signed an armistice when their military resources were still far from exhausted.
- *Redemption.* Nagging thoughts of unrealized potential and "what might have been" may create a desire to redeem one's honor or reputation through battle with *any* opponent, not necessarily the previous one. This response has probably characterized

the attitudes of many Americans to the Vietnam War and has helped to provide public support for such subsequent military operations as the interventions in Grenada and Panama.

Such difficulties may be found at any of several levels in a war-making state: the individual leader, the military, and the population at large. The individual wartime leader often acquires a personal stake in the outcome of the war, psychologically as well as politically. Whatever the issues that caused the conflict, the leader may come to see it as "his" (or her) war and to view the outcome as a measure of personal worth. If this is a rational concern for one's reputation and prestige, and thus for one's political prospects, it may or may not impede a peace settlement. Depending on the climate of public opinion, an earlier peace with less favorable terms may be more politically beneficial than a continuation of the war in pursuit of better terms. But an irrational identification of self with state, in which the leader regards attacks on his armies as personal attacks on himself, is likely to mean missed opportunities for a settlement. The leader may resist a compromise that would be in the national interest but would not avenge the personal humiliation the enemy had inflicted on him earlier in the war.

Lyndon Johnson and the Vietnam War provide an example of a leader who assumed this kind of personal, psychological stake in a war. Doris Kearns has described how Johnson came to regard the war as a challenge to his own integrity and how his adherence to his policies stemmed in part from his insecurity in managing foreign affairs. Because he was less certain how to accomplish his goals in international affairs than in domestic politics, Johnson felt all the more the need to be certain that his goals were correct. His resistance to changing his policies toward Vietnam stiffened further when Robert Kennedy — whom Johnson disliked almost obsessively — started to oppose those policies openly.[18]

The military establishment may acquire a corporate stake in a war that is similar to a leader's personal investment in the conflict. In each case, self-esteem — either institutional or individual — is in jeopardy. For the armed forces, however, the upholding of self-esteem depends on the military rather than the political outcome. Military planners and commanders are not merely cogs in a government decision making machine that measures success and failure in terms of political outcomes. If they were, they would regard their own military efforts in good Clausewitzian fashion as merely means to accomplish political ends. In practice, most military leaders judge the success of a war at least partly in terms of how events on the battlefield prove the *military* effectiveness of their armies.

Armed forces thus have an institutional bias against an inherent aspect of limited war — namely, initiating and terminating military operations on the basis of political criteria. As a result, the military may experience either of two frustrations: being used against a militarily unvanquishable enemy (fighting a war "we could not win"); or being subject to restrictions intended to avoid escalation into a larger conflict (fighting a war "we were not allowed to win").

Scapegoating is one possible response by military leaders to such frustrations, with civilian leaders being accused of back stabbing or other actions that allegedly undermined the war effort. Another response is to seek redemption in a new war. For the French army, for example, the Algerian War seemed to be an opportunity to redeem itself for failures in Indochina. The Algerian insurrection broke out less than four months after the Geneva Accords that established a truce in Indochina, and the goal of "no Dienbienphu in Algeria" had strong personal meaning for many French officers. The belief that civilian leaders were taking away the opportunity for redemption underlay the involvement of military officers in the insurrection and terrorism aimed at blocking the Evian agreements, which granted independence to Algeria.

For the civilian population, reputation and self-esteem generally are not factors in responding to the termination of a limited war. The public usually has at least as much difficulty as the military leadership, however, in accepting an imperfect peace. Except for the well-informed elite, there is commonly little understanding of the limitations to military force and of its relationship to diplomacy. Public opinion is expressed more in terms of "winning" and "losing" than in terms of negotiating more rather than less favorable peace terms. In most cases, public opinion will be less refined, less measured, and less patient than official policy. There may be as much opposition from those who want to escalate the military effort to "win" the war as from those who believe it was a mistake to get involved in the first place. Some — including much of the opposition in the United States during the Vietnam War — have viewed either escalation or precipitate withdrawal as preferable to a compromise settlement achieved through limited military means.

Public opposition to a peace settlement may stem from an inordinate focus on past military successes and a failure to understand future military problems. This was true, for example, of the Japanese public during the Russo-Japanese War of 1904-1905, in which Japanese forces scored a series of brilliant victories but, by the time the peace conference at Portsmouth opened, faced the prospect of being outmanned and outgunned by the larger Russian Empire. The Japanese government understood these prospects and signed a peace agreement that reflected this understanding. In Tokyo, however, riots broke out when the bitterly disappointing terms of settlement were announced.[19]

It is more common for joy over a prospective peace to overshadow dissatisfaction with specific peace terms. Ironically, however, the public's craving for peace may force a government to prolong the war to avoid problems associated with the public's lack of understanding of how military force is related to diplomacy. If a cease-fire is established before a comprehensive settlement is negotiated, the *threat* of renewing the war provides the only remaining leverage to support the negotiating effort. Lack of public support for a renewed war may make this threat incredible. Resuming a war, in short, may be less politically feasible than continuing one already underway. That decision makers realize this is one reason most modern limited wars end with a cease-fire agreement that incorporates a political settlement, or at least as much of a political settlement as can be achieved. In the

Korean War, for example, the American commander of the UN forces, General Mark Clark, and other U.S. defense officials persuaded President Truman to reject a recommendation by the State Department to defer to a post-armistice negotiation the difficult issue of what to do with the Chinese and North Korean prisoners who refused repatriation. The U.S. military leaders feared, with good reason, that any armistice would give rise to a bring-the-boys-home sentiment on the part of the American public, thus eroding the UN forces' military posture in Korea. The Communist forces, meanwhile, no doubt would have strengthened their own positions, and the issue of repatriation might never have been settled satisfactorily.

In the absence of "victory," the public may choose as scapegoats either the politicians who were responsible for involvement in the war or those who made the peace. In some cases, there may be a renewed sense of dedication to achieve goals not yet attained, driven by a desire for revenge or redemption, as well as by the motives that led to those goals in the first place. With major powers, however, the most profound public response is likely to be a lowering of national confidence, as previous assumptions about what is attainable are called into question.

The response of the American public to the Vietnam War is the clearest recent example of a postwar crisis. Many Americans blamed civilian leaders, however, for what were perceived to be unreasonable restraints on the military, or for putting the military in a war that could not have been "won" anyway.[20] The conduct of the Vietnam War was particularly difficult for the public to understand, not only because the results seemed incommensurate with the costs but because a counter-insurgency aimed at attrition of the enemy's resources and will tends not to yield results that are clear and immediate. Military forces were used to inflict casualties and to take hills that later were abandoned, rather than to move a frontline across a map. Vietnam thus demonstrated acutely the problem of inadequate public comprehension and support that is present to some degree in all limited wars.

Conclusion

How important, overall, are psychological factors in the termination of limited wars? The impact that these factors (whether they pertain to leaders, military officers, or civilian populations) have on military and diplomatic events during the final stages of a conflict depend in large part on the political and decision making structures of the belligerents. Public sentiment clearly is not as independent or important a variable in a totalitarian state as in a democracy. Similarly, the political influence of senior military officers varies widely from state to state. The personal idiosyncrasies of the top leader will have a more apparent impact on policy in an autocracy than in a constitutional government, in which the leader's behavior is checked by other political actors. It is thus difficult to generalize about the extent to which divergence from a rational actor model affects the course of wars.

To the extent that nonrational behavior affects peacemaking, it usually hinders the process. Peace settlements generally take more time and resources to achieve than they would if the belligerents were rational actors. The process of bargaining during a limited war involves two parties who begin with divergent perceptions and expectations and eventually develop enough of a common outlook to make a settlement. The divergence of perceptions and expectations is due partly to incomplete information about such factors as the enemy's motivations and each side's relative strength. One of the purposes of bargaining, and thus of limited warfare, is to fill these information gaps.[21] The divergence may also be due, however, to the tendency by one or both belligerents not to process fully and effectively the information already available — that is, not to calculate rationally. Unlike the gaps in information, this tendency will not necessarily be corrected by waging war. Indeed, we have seen several ways in which warfare itself encourages irrational decision making.

Psychological distortions probably have less effect on the terms of settlement than on the speed or difficulty with which these terms are negotiated. Peace agreements depend more on the underlying interests, motivations, and military strengths and weaknesses than on the misperceptions, defense mechanisms, and other cognitive imperfections of decision makers. Decision makers must either take account of the strategic facts of a given limited war situation or be subject to challenge from those who do, whether the challengers be the enemy or elements within the decision maker's own camp. The process of challenge and correction typically is slow and imperfect, and more blood is spilled as a result, but the final political outcome tends to be similar to what rational decision makers could have achieved, albeit more quickly.

Notes

1. Phillippe Tripier, *Autopsie de la Guerre d'Algérie* (Paris: Editions France-Empire, 1972), 286-90.

2. Dorothy Pickles, *Algeria and France* (New York: Praeger, 1963), 72-73; Anthony Hartley, *Gaullism* (New York: Outerbridge and Dienstfrey, 1971), 173-75.

3. Merry Bromberger, *Le Destin Secret de Georges Pompidou* (Paris: Fayard, 1965), 182-84.

4. George F. Kennan, *Memoirs, Volume 2: 1950-1963* (Boston: Little, Brown, 1972), 36.

5. Paul R. Pillar, *Negotiating Peace: War Termination as a Bargaining Process* (Princeton, NJ: Princeton University Press, 1983), 90-143.

6. Andrew H. Michener et al., "Factors Affecting Concession Rate and Threat Usage in Bilateral Conflict," *Sociometry* 38 (March 1975): 62-80.

7. See Pillar, *Negotiating Peace.*

8. Richard Tropper, "The Consequences of Investment in the Process of Conflict," *Journal of Conflict Resolution* 16 (March 1972): 97-98.

9. Leon Festinger, *A Theory of Cognitive Dissonance* (Stanford, CA: Stanford University Press, 1957).

10. Morton Deutsch and Robert M. Krauss, "Studies of Interpersonal Bargaining," *Journal of Conflict Resolution* 6 (March 1962): 52-76; Morton Deutsch et al., "Strategies of Inducing Cooperation: An Experimental Study," *Journal of Conflict Resolution* 11 (September 1967): 345-60; Barry R. Schlenker et al., "Compliance to Threats as a Function of the Wording of the Threat and the Exploitativeness of the Threatener," *Sociometry* 33 (December 1970): 394-408.

11. Francois de Callières, *On the Manner of Negotiating with Princes*, trans. A. F. Whyte (Notre Dame, IN: University of Notre Dame Press, 1963), 125.

12. J. David Singer, "Inter-Nation Influence: A Formal Model," *American Political Science Review* 57 (June 1963): 430; Glenn H. Snyder and Paul Diesing, *Conflict Among Nations* (Princeton, NJ: Princeton University Press, 1977), 187-88.

13. Jack Sawyer and Harold Guetzkow, "Bargaining and Negotiation in International Relations," in Herbert C. Kelman, ed., *International Behavior* (New York: Holt, Rinehart and Winston, 1965), 484.

14. Dean G. Pruitt, "Definition of the Situation as a Determinant in International Action," in Kelman, *International Behavior*, 395-96; Ole Holsti, *Crisis Escalation War* (Montreal: McGill-Queens University Press, 1972), 12-13; Richard Smoke, *War: Controlling Escalation* (Cambridge, MA: Harvard University Press, 1977), 286-89.

15. Graham T. Allison, *Essence of Decision* (Boston: Little, Brown, 1971), 85, 262.

16. Robert Jervis, *The Logic of Images in International Relations* (Princeton, NJ: Princeton University Press, 1970), 18, 30-31.

17. *The Pentagon Papers*, Sen. Gravel edition (Boston: Beacon Press, 1971), vol. 3, 225-28, 238-39.

18. Doris Kearns, *Lyndon Johnson and the American Dream* (New York: Harper and Row, 1976), 256-59.

19. Shumpei Okamoto, *The Japanese Oligarchy and the Russo-Japanese War* (New York: Columbia University Press, 1970), 207-14.

20. See Myra MacPherson, *Long Time Passing: Vietnam and the Haunted Generation* (Garden City, NY: Doubleday, 1984), 59.

21. R. Harrison Wagner, "On the Unification of Two-Person Bargaining Theory," *Journal of Conflict Resolution* 23 (March 1979), 71-101.

Chapter 13

Limited War and Learning: The American Experience

BETTY GLAD

The nature of the lessons that American decision makers extracted from the Korean and Vietnam wars is our concern in this chapter. Toward this end we will examine American military policies after the Korean War, the themes decision makers employed when they were becoming involved in the Vietnam War and how they thought it should be fought, as well as later evaluations of what they did. Several factors, as we shall see, influenced the ways in which these lessons were articulated and how they were applied or not applied to new historical settings. Domestic political and bureaucratic interests and psychological needs all played a key role in the very framing of the lessons learned, as well as the selection, out of a whole repertoire of lessons possible, of the ones that seemed most relevant to the case at hand. The level of learning involved, too, also varied. In several instances the adaptations mainly consisted of determinations to repeat successful experiences and avoid those that were not. More complex and sophisticated learning, however, also took place.[1]

During the course of the Korean war, as suggested above, complex, higher level learning had taken place. After their initial mistakes in sending U.S./UN forces across 38th parallel and their failures to control MacArthur as he split his forces in the ill-begotten drive toward the Yalu, American political leaders showed an extraordinary ability to adapt to the situation in which they found themselves. Indeed their learning went beyond a mere application of lessons drawn from the past, for there was little in the past that was directly relevant to the situation at hand. Thus administration leaders came to understand that wars in which major powers had important interests at stake had to be fought in accord with certain qualitative limits, many of them tacitly negotiated, apparently arbitrary, to keep the violence within tolerable bounds. These understandings were worked out under fire, not always evenly, in response to specific factors (i.e., the U.S./UN successes and failures on the battlefield, political pressures at home and from allies, and the fear of a broader war). These new understandings replaced older ideas, which had gained currency in America, that in war one should apply the maximum force at one's disposal, targeting the weakest or most crucial forces and commercial centers on the other side.[2]

The learning that had the most immediate impact on American policy shortly after the Korean war, however, was mostly of the simpler stimulus-response type. The Korean war had created deep and painful political decisions within the United States. Once it had been terminated, the Eisenhower administration wished to avoid similar troubling divisions by relying on the conventional forces of its allies to withstand local aggression, assisting indigenous forces in the building of their own local positions of strength. The threat of nuclear retaliation, at times and places chosen by the United States, was to provide a kind of ultimate protection against the success of any local aggression.[3]

When American decision makers first made their commitments to intervene militarily in South Vietnam, they drew their lessons from conflicts other than the Korean war. The domino theory, rooted in the assumption that World War II could have been avoided if the Allies had but stood up to Hitler at Munich, was the architectonic image at this time — framing and limiting lessons derived from other experiences. Thus Ho Chi Minh's attempts to unify North Vietnam were seen as a Russian challenge to the West that the United States had to respond to with force, both as a means of checking the expansionist objectives of the USSR and maintaining one's own credibility as an ally. Recollections of the political costs Truman had suffered as a consequence of the fall of China to communism reinforced the interventionist bent. One could not let another area of the world fall to communism, without serious domestic political repercussions. As Secretary of State Dean Rusk and Secretary of Defense Robert MacArthur told President John Kennedy, the "loss of South Vietnam would stimulate bitter domestic controversy in the United States and would be seized upon by the extreme elements to divide the country and harass the Administration."[4] When Johnson became president, he, too, was concerned that a divisive debate about the loss of Vietnam "would be even more destructive to our national life than the argument over China had been."[5] Predisposed to intervention in South Vietnam on the basis of both the domino theory and these domestic political lessons, American decision makers sought out other experiences to buttress their choices. When members of the new Kennedy administration first considered direct intervention in Vietnam, they drew their lessons primarily from the Philippine operations against the Huks and the British operation in Malaysia. Small, specially trained military units had been effective in each of these counterinsurgency operations, reinforcing the feeling that the United States could succeed in similar operations in South Vietnam. Kennedy himself saw the campaign in the Philippines as a model for Vietnam. He was predisposed, in Arthur Schlesinger, Jr.'s words to back "tough, counter guerrilla action, generous provision for amnesty, real and sweeping reforms."[6]

References to the Korean war were avoided at this time, possibly because of the particular lessons the military had taken away from that enterprise. The Joint Chiefs of Staff at the time thought it would be a mistake to get bogged down in any new limited land wars in Asia (according to Roger Hillsman, head of the State Department Bureau of Intelligence and Research). White House officials did not want to undermine the enthusiasm of the army high command for the proposed military operations in Vietnam by reminding them of their concerns along these lines.[7]

It was not until the Johnson administration conducted its debates in 1964-65 over the U.S. policy toward Vietnam that explicit references to the Korean War were made.[8] The emphasis in those discussions, however, was on those aspects of the Korean operation which buttressed their desire to escalate the American commitment to Vietnam. The United States had acted with honor in Korea, using force to deter communist aggression, and it should do so again. Thus President Johnson noted that "the challenge we face in southeast Asia today is the same challenge that we have faced with courage and we have met with strength . . . in Greece and Turkey, in Berlin and Korea."[9] A major exception was George Ball, who noted several differences between the Korean and the proposed Vietnamese operations. The U.S. military commitment in Korea was approved by the United Nations and had the support of many other nations, as he noted. Moreover, the aggressor was clearly external and had crossed a boundary; and the government to which the United States was giving aide was clearly stable.[10]

Once the United States was committed to the war in Vietnam, various strategic "lessons" were drawn from the Korean experience on how to fight it. But the lessons depended on who the decision maker was and what he wanted to accomplish. The civilians who managed the war saw the need to limit the ground operations to South Vietnam and to show control in the selection of bombing targets in North Vietnam. Their strategic choice was a gradual escalation of the air war against North Vietnam, somewhat similar to the escalation of the air war against North Korea. The assumption, made explicit in Schelling's description of the tactic of compliance, was that if one could gradually increase the pain to the North Vietnamese to the point were the cost to them would exceed the possible gains from continuing their operations, they would cease hostilities.[11] These measures had the additional advantage that they would suffice to prevent the final loss of South Vietnam, while keeping the U.S. commitments below the level that would have created massive opposition to the war at home.[12]

Many top military leaders and a few civilian strategists, however, embraced a perspective very similar to General MacArthur's during the Korean War. They felt that the limitations on bombing Manchuria had impeded victory in Korea, and they questioned the whole concept of sanctuary.[13] The Joint Chiefs of Staff, for example, wanted to hit North Vietnam hard and fast, and go for key targets such as Haiphong Harbor early.[14] A top civilian adviser, W. W. Rostow, had prepared the way intellectually for the American bombings of Cambodia and the later ground interventions into that country arguing, in an article published in 1961, that one could not permit sanctuaries in counterinsurgency warfare.[15] In a subsequent memorandum titled "Victory and Defeat in Guerrilla Wars: The Case of South Vietnam," he argued that the United States could win the war by keeping the bombing pressure on North Vietnam and checking the Vietcong on the ground in the South. The goal was to convince Hanoi that its bargaining position would worsen over time.[16]

Both groups, in their emphasis on the effectiveness of firepower in the conduct of that operation, overlooked some of the differences between the two wars. The bombing of North Korea had been effective because the targets were the identifiable armies of the North Koreans and Chinese and some of the structures that supported them. But in South Vietnam the enemies were men who did not wear uniforms; and they hid at night and lived off the countryside and friendly populatior.s. The United States might have engaged in classic counterinsurgency operations of the sort the British used in Malaysia, but that would have involved more Americans in ground warfare and taken a long time — a cost the U.S. government and people did not seem willing to bear. The bombing attacks on entire communities in South Vietnam (i.e., the scorched earth policy undertaken in 1966) killed Vietcong and their supporters, it is true. But it was so indiscriminate it created new recruits for the other side, too. Moreover, in obliterating the distinction between combatants and noncombatants, which has traditionally regulated wars in an attempt to mitigate its human cost, the bombing raised doubts in certain sectors of the American people, that were not present during the Korean War.[17] The air war over North Vietnam, too, as a coercive strategy left much to be desired. As Wallace Thies has shown, President Johnson and has advisers were never able to fine-tune that campaign to support their diplomatic initiatives, due to factors beyond their control.[18] The attack on North Vietnamese sanctuaries in Cambodia in 1970 was the ultimate failure. It not only failed in its goal of finding and destroying a nerve center for guerrilla operations in South Vietnam, it upset a fragile balance in that country and contributed to the communist movement westward which would ultimately lead to the fall of that country to the Khmer Rouge.[19]

After the Vietnam war various segments of the American populace drew quite different lessons from that conflict. The liberal critics, as Richard Falk has noted, saw the war as a misapplication of the containment doctrine to a part of the world to which it was not really relevant and that it was a war in which the United States lost all sense of the need for the proportionality of ends to needs. Another group, embracing the Nixon doctrine, saw the war as the result of certain strategic choices it had made. Although the United States has global responsibilities and must play an important role in opposing the spread of communism, it should shift more of the burden to local governments. The radical position, which Falk himself forwarded, was that the whole intervention was based on false moral and geopolitical assumptions: China constituted no real threat to the area and under such circumstances there was no real moral or legal justification for aiding a repressive regime. Many military men and the political right in the United States preferred another option described by Falk: the United States had simply not put sufficient resources into the war to win.[20]

By the mid-1980s several military strategists were still rejecting the basic idea that constraints must be placed on conventional wars in which both of the major powers have an interest. They argued that the United States had won most of its battles in Vietnam, and that the U.S. defeat was due to political constraints and poor strategic planning.[21] The most influential argument along these lines was made in Colonel Harry Summers's *On Strategy*. The United States failed in Vietnam, he argues, because it did not make an all-out effort. The President should have asked Congress for a declaration of war, rallied the American people around the cause, and met the North Vietnam regular forces on the battlefield, possibly even taking the war into North Vietnam. Strategically, the United States should have sealed off the DMZ line through Laos up to Thailand so that the U.S./UN troops could isolate and attack North Vietnamese forces, increased the interdiction bombing of North Vietnamese forces and supply lines in the area, and blockaded all North Vietnamese ports. A major U.S. naval presence in the Gulf of Tonkin would have presented North Vietnam with the tacit threat against its very existence. The United States should even have refrained from statements that it would not use nuclear weapons as a part of that threat.[22]

Summers explicitly drew details from the Korean experience in making some of these strategic recommendations. Yet he fails to see some of the similarities in the limits placed on both operations, and the reasons for these limitations. The failure to blockade the ports of the enemy was in both instances based on the fear that interference with Soviet shipping could bring them more directly into the conflict. Moreover, in his recommendation that the United States should have sought conventional battlefield victories in Vietnam, Summers failed to see some important differences in the nature of the fighting forces involved in the two wars. In Korea the enemy employed regular units in relatively open terrain. In South Vietnam the North Vietnamese were not engaged in a conventional war against the South. Save for the major offensives launched in 1968, 1972, and 1975, the North Vietnamese fought a war without front lines. U.S. troops had to hunt down small units in jungles where there were few natural barriers.[23]

Indeed, Summers's assessments of the American strategic errors in Vietnam overlook the extent to which the United States actually pursued some of the policies he recommends, and it fails to take account of factors that limited the realistic choices open to American commanders. The United States did not deploy most of its troops in the pursuit of elusive guerrillas throughout the entire countryside. Rather they were used to keep roads open, protect their own logistical bases, and to meet large enemy units in the relatively unpopulated sections of Vietnam.[24] Interdiction bombing was tried and did not work, as McNamara testified before the Senate Armed Service Committee in 1967.[25] Proposals to seal off the entire South Vietnamese land frontier were rejected because they were seen as militarily unfeasible. The frontier extended for over 900 miles and would have required, as Westmoreland points out, "many millions of troops" to defend.[26]

Summers also fails to address fundamental issues about the relations of means to ends. Although he nods in the direction of the Clausewitzian doctrine that political ends must determine the means by which a war is fought, he does not really go into the details of what an American victory might have meant in terms of the political ends achieved. Could the Republic of Vietnam have established a lasting national structure, as he suggests? There is little to justify that optimistic assessment, as Gary Hess points out. "After all, opposition to the Saigon government was not a creation of North Vietnam, and the eventual manipulation and exploitation of the Vietcong by Hanoi should not obscure the southern origins of the insurgency."[27] And what would the North Vietnamese do after their defeat? Could they not simply wait to continue the war at a later date? To guarantee against this possibility, would a U.S. military presence in South Vietnam have been required for an indeterminate length of time?

Most important, Summers overlooks lessons from the Korean operation on how wars are kept limited. The People's Republic of China had entered the war in Korea when the United States, ignoring Chinese concerns and interests, plunged toward the Yalu. If the United States had invaded North Vietnam, would not the Chinese and Russians have been similarly tempted to intervene more directly in that war? The potential impact of a long and costly military operation on the United States, itself, is another matter that Summers left unexplored. Would the president really be able to mobilize public support for a possibly costly operation in an area of the world where there is no clear and pressing threat to the United States? The response of the public to the Korean and Vietnamese operations suggest not. Support for both wars, as John Mueller has shown, fell off as the wars dragged on and battle casualties rose.[28] Indeed the consensus in the American decision making elite for an active, interventionist role in the world was destroyed during the Vietnam War, and Americans as a whole came out of that war less inclined to support any American interventions abroad.[29]

The perspective expressed in Summers's work has broad support in the American military establishment. The book was written while Summers was a member of the faculty of the U.S. Army War College, as part of an Army project to discover what went wrong in the Vietnam War. Its wide use as a text in high-level military institutions—at the U.S. Army War College, the Army Command and General Staff College, and the Marine Corps Amphibious Warfare School—suggests that its arguments have resonance in the military establishment.[30]

This does not mean that high-level military men are more likely than civilian advisers to recommend that the United States undertake new military endeavors. Once committed to an operation, however, they are more apt to recommend aggressive solutions. As Richard Betts has shown in his study of several key national security decisions in recent American history, the Chairman of the JCS, the Army Chief of Staff, the Chief of Naval Operations, and the Air Force Chief of Staff opted for more aggressive military options than their civilian counterparts 67% of the time. The Commandant of the Marine Corps recommended more aggressive solutions in 100% of the cases studied. Field and theater commanders, regardless of service, opted for more aggressive military options than civilian advisers in 90% of the cases studied.[31] Typical of this attitude is the statement of General George S. Brown, Chairman of the Joint Chiefs of Staff in the Ford Administration. The United States could intervene if the Soviet Union were to trigger off an Angola type war in the Middle East, he argued, only if there was a "total commitment" and a "total mobilization" of the American people and government.[32]

This reluctance of the military to accept a limited war doctrine is understandable, given the duties they must perform. Putting men's lives at risk in situations where there is no commitment to use all the weapons in one's arsenal is bound to be frustrating for those who most directly pay the price. New weapons, too, are tempting. Like other professionals, military leaders are apt to want to try out the new devices, the new strategies they have built and discussed. Most important, as Betts has documented, they feel they need tangible goals by which to evaluate their success and a measure of autonomy in the practice of their profession.[33] Battlefield and political goals which fluctuate or are unclear are bound to frustrate those who can only define their goals in such terms. Indeed, Kinnard's survey of Army generals who had commanded troops in Vietnam showed that 68% of those polled thought that the objectives of the Vietnam War were either not as clear as they might have been or that the objectives needed rethinking. Most of the officers, 91%, thought that definition of objectives was one aspect of the Vietnam War that needed the most improvement.[34]

Yet views which require that the United States go all out to win in any military operation it undertakes can place the United States in a situation where it either does nothing when its interests are challenged, or responds in ways which increase the possibility of general war. With Hobson choices such as these, the results may well be no response. If the United States can only use military force when the whole nation is mobilized and all the relevant weapons targeted upon the objective, it is not likely that it will choose that alternative. The military option will only be used against small states in the U.S. sphere of influence where victory is a foregone conclusion, as in Grenada in 1983. In other circumstances, fear that intervention in a local situation could escalate into a major confrontation between the United States and the USSR could immobilize the nation.

What all this suggests is that learning from one war to the next—whether the goal is to prevent, win, or control conflicts in which one might enter—is apt to be uneven. Many Americans came out of the Korean and Vietnamese wars aware of both the need to keep conventional encounters limited and of the difficulties in maintaining those controls. But there are many who have not learned how dangerous the demand for victory in limited wars might be, especially when big power interests are involved. Adhering to an earlier American tradition, they fail to see how the new technology has fundamentally changed even the nature of local wars. As von Clausewitz noted a long time ago, under conditions

> of battle, the best laid plans of men are apt to go awry. Here the fog prevents the enemy from being discovered in time, a battery from firing at the right moment, a report from reaching the General; there the rain prevents a battalion from arriving at the right time, because instead of for three it had to march perhaps eight hours.[35]

In the contemporary era these problems are compounded beyond anything von Clausewitz ever considered. The call for victory, in such circumstances is apt to unleash a cycle of actions and counter-reactions in which each side resorts to the tempting weapons it has held in reserve. With nuclear weapons and intercontinental ballistic missiles in their arsenals, the end result may well be damage to both sides so severe that there remains no rational relationship between the goals sought and the price paid for the accomplishment of those goals.

Notes

1. For a review of learning concepts relevant to this discussion, in addition to the essay by Betty Glad and Charles Taber, "Images, Learning," above, see Lloyd S. Etheredge and James Short, "Thinking About Government Learning," *Journal of Management Studies*, 20, 1 (1983): 41-58. For a review of the concepts of learning employed by various psychologists, see Charles S. Taber, "Learning and War," paper presented to the 1986 Annual Meeting of the International Studies Association in Anaheim, California, 25-29, March, 1-7; for the use of history in the learning process, see Ernest May, *"Lessons" of the Past: The Use and Misuse of History in American Foreign Policy* (New York: Oxford University Press, 1973).

2. In addition to the members of the Joint Chiefs of Staff, only a few military leaders accepted these new perceptions of limited war. For one of these exceptions, see Matthew Ridgeway, *The Korean War* (Garden City, NY: Doubleday, 1967), 243-48.

3. By the late 1950s, however, some decision makers and strategic theorists were arguing that the United States should prepare for a broader array of strategic alternatives so that they would not have to resort to nuclear weapons to sever lesser interests. Eisenhower's commitments to the defense of Quemoy and Matsu in 1955 and the intervention in Lebanon in 1958 were early moves in this direction. President Kennedy's embrace of the strategy of graduated response propounded to him by General Maxwell Taylor was the ultimate elaboration of the framework.

4. Robert S. McNamara and Dean Rusk, "Memorandum for the President," 11 November 1961, in *Pentagon Papers: The Defense Department History of United States Decisionmaking in Vietnam*, 4 vols., ed. Mike Gravel (Boston: Beacon, 1971), II: 111.

5. Lyndon B. Johnson, *The Vantage Point: Perspectives on the Presidency* (New York: Holt, Rinehart, & Winston, 1971), 152.

6. Arthur Schlesinger, Jr., *A Thousand Days: John F. Kennedy in the White House* (Boston: Houghton Mifflin, 1965), 540-41. A few advisors, it is true, saw important differences between these earlier examples and the case at hand. In 1961, Lyman L. Lemnitzer, Chairman of the Joint Chiefs of Staff, for example, noted that the Malayan borders were more controllable than those of Vietnam, and the rebels there had been racially identifiable. Moreover, he warned, it took nearly 12 years to defeat the Malay insurgents, who were weaker than those in South Vietnam. "Memorandum to General Taylor," 12 October 1961, in *Pentagon Papers*, II: 650-661. The difficulties the French had in Vietnam also were noted by John Kenneth Galbraith, the U.S. ambassador to India. See May, *"Lessons" of the Past*, 95.

7. May, *"Lessons" of the Past*, 96-97. Despite their reservations, the Joint Chiefs of Staff informed Kennedy in 1961 that 40,000 troops could clean up the Vietcong threat; if there were North Vietnamese and Chinese intervention, 128,000 more troops would be needed. "Concept for Intervention in Viet-Nam," 11 October 1961, paper drafted by U. Alexis Johnson, in *The Pentagon Papers, New York Times*, ed. (New York: Bantam, 1971), 139.

8. May, *"Lessons" of the Past*, 109-110.

9. Ibid., 107-108.

10. Ibid., 109-110.

11. Thomas Schelling, *Arms and Influence* (New Haven, CT: Yale University Press, 1966), 69-78, 84-86, 174-176. For the slow squeeze bombardment policies relative to Vietnam which reflected this theory, see May, *"Lessons" of the Past*, 106-107.

12. Leslie H. Gelb with Richard Betts, *The Irony of Vietnam: The System Worked* (Washington, DC: Brookings Institution, 1979), 1-6.

13. David Rees, *Korea: The Limited War* (New York: St. Martin's, 1964), xiv-xv.

14. Neil Sheehan, ed., "The Covert War and Tonkin Gulf," *The Pentagon Papers* (New York: Quadrangle Books 1971), 244-278.

15. Walt W. Rostow, "Countering Guerrilla Attack," *Army*, 12, 2 (September 1961): 53-57.

16. Gravel, *Pentagon Papers*, III: 381-382.

17. Colonel Robert Thompson, who was in charge of the British operation in Malaysia, criticized the U.S. enterprise in Vietnam for its emphasis on immediate results and the indiscriminate use of firepower. See his *No Exit from Vietnam* (New York: David Mckay, 1970), 100-103, 124-126, 134-138. For the difficulties the United States had in dealing with the local political factors, see Zeb H. Bradford, "US Tactics in Vietnam," *Military Review*, LII, 2 (9 February 1972): 63-76. For a critique of the U.S. scorched earth policies, see Betty Glad, "Toward a Policy of Realism: Prospects of a Negotiated Settlement in South Viet Nam," in *Viet Nam: The Alternatives for American Policy: Forum on Public Affairs, Unit Two* ed. Reza Rezazadeh (Platteville: Wisconsin State University, 1965). For the critique that the costs of the war were incommensurate with the interests at stake and therefore morally problematical, see Arthur Schlesinger, Jr., "Vietnam and the End of the Age of Superpowers," *Harpers*, 238, 1426 (March 1969): 41-49. Lt. General W. R. Peers's inquiry into the My Lai massacre for the Army concluded that many officers knew about the massacre without reporting it. The Army War College in a subsequent study found that the distortion of official reports was widespread amongst officers, a deviation from professional standards. From James William Gibson, *The Perfect War: Technowar in Vietnam* (Boston: Atlantic Monthly Press, 1986), 440-442.

18. Wallace J. Thies, *When Governments Collide: Coercion and Diplomacy in the Vietnam Conflict, 1964-68* (Berkeley: University of California Press, 1980), 4-5, 12-15, 143-209.

19. For the consequences of the U.S. bombings of Cambodia, see Stanley Karnow, *Vietnam: The War Nobody Won* (New York: Foreign Policy Association, 1983), 591-592; Elizabeth Becker, *When the War Was Over* (New York: Simon & Schuster, 1986), 34; Gibson, *The Perfect War*, 409-410.

20. Richard Falk, "What We Should Learn from Vietnam," *Foreign Policy*, 1 (Winter 1970-1971): 98-114. Falk places Stanley Hoffmann, Townsend Hoopes (Deputy Assistant Secretary of Defense for International Security Affairs and Under Secretary of the Air Force from 1965-1969), and former ambassador Edwin Reischauer in the liberal school. He places Henry Kissinger, William Rogers, and Melvin Laird in the Nixon doctrine school. See also Richard Pfeffer, ed., *No More Vietnams? The War and the Future of American Foreign Policy* (New York: Harper & Row, 1968), 203-216.

21. See for example, S. L. A. Marshall, "Thoughts on Vietnam," in *The Lessons of Vietnam*, eds. W. Scott Thompson and Donaldson D. Frizzell (New York: Crane, Russak, 1977), 46-55. For overviews of these arguments, see Gelb, *The Irony of Vietnam*, 354-359; Gibson, *The Perfect War*, 445-451; Michael Maclear, *The Ten Thousand Day War: Vietnam, 1945-1975* (New York: St. Martin's, 1981), 354-356. For other perspectives, see Michael P. Sullivan, *The Vietnam War: A Study in the Making of American Policy* (Lexington: University of Kentucky Press, 1985), 152-186; Richard A. Hunt and Richard H. Schultz, Jr., eds., *Lessons From an Unconventional War: Reassessing U.S. Strategies for Future Conflicts* (Elmsford, NY: Pergamon, 1982).

22. Harry G. Summers, Jr., *On Strategy: A Critical Analysis of the Vietnam War* (Novato, CA: Presidio Press, 1982), especially 181-195. For a similar argument, see Bruce Palmer, Jr., *The 25-Year War: America's Military Role in Vietnam* (Lexington: University Press of Kentucky, 1984), especially 189-210. For support for Summer's view that the Tet offensive had devastated Vietcong forces in South Vietnam, see Stanley Karnow, *Vietnam: A History* (New York: Viking, 1983), 523-545. For the argument that the Phoenix program was successful, see Guenter Lewy, *America in Vietnam: Illusion, Myth, and Reality* (New York: Oxford University Press, 1978), 279-285.

23. For the nature of the ground war, see Hunt and Schultz, *Lessons From an Unconventional War*.

24. William Westmoreland, *A Soldier's Report* (Garden City, NY: Doubleday, 1976), 144-149.

25. See David Halberstam, *The Best and the Brightest*, paperback ed. (Greenwich, CT: Fawcett Publications, 1972), 782-783.

26. See Westmoreland, *A Soldier's Report*, 147. For an overall critique of Summer's strategic proposals, see Gibson, *The Perfect War*, 450. For a somewhat more favorable review, see Gary R. Hess, "The Military Perspective on Strategy in Vietnam: Harry G. Summer's *On Strategy* and Bruce Palmer's *The 25-Year War*," *Diplomatic History* (Winter 1980): 91-106.

27. Hess, "The Military Perspective on Strategy in Vietnam," 105.

28. See John E. Mueller, *War, Presidents, and Public Opinion* (New York: Wiley, 1973), 59-63.

29. For the impact of war on foreign policy elites, see Ole Holsti and James Rosenau, "Vietnam, Consensus, and the Belief Systems of American Leaders," *World Politics*, 32, 1 (October 1979): 1-56. For longer term impact on American policies, see Richard A. Falk, "Intervention and National Liberation," in *Intervention in World Politics* ed. Hedley Bull (New York: Oxford University Press, 1984), 119-133; Rosalyn Higgins, "Intervention and International Law," in Bull, *Intervention in World Politics*, 29-44; James N. Rosenau, "Foreign Interventions as Adaptive Behavior," in *Law and Civil War in the Modern World* ed. John Norton Moore (Baltimore, MD: Johns Hopkins University Press, 1974), 129-151; Sam Sarkesian, "Revolutions and the Limits of Military Power: The Haunting Specter of Vietnam," *Social Science Quarterly*, 56 (1976): 673-688; and Richard Smoke, "Analytic Dimensions of Intervention Decision," in *The Limits of Military Intervention*, ed. Ellen P. Stern (Beverly Hills, CA: Sage, 1977), 29-44.

30. John Lynn, "Learning From the Last War: An Essay on the New Military Critique of the Vietnam Conflict," (mimeographed paper, University of Illinois, 1986).

31. Richard K. Betts, *Soldiers, Statesmen, and Cold War Crises* (Cambridge, MA: Harvard University Press, 1977), 12-15, 215-221.

32. "What General Brown Really Said," *US News & World Report*, 81 (1 November 1976): 63-64.

33. Betts, *Soldiers, Statesmen, and Cold War Crises*, 9-15.

34. See Douglas Kinnard, *The War Managers* (Hanover, NH: University Press of New England, 1977), 169, 175-178. For an earlier study showing how differences in organizational role and personal alliances can influence which lessons are learned from war, see Morris Janowitz, *The Professional Soldier* (Glencoe, IL: The Free Press, 1960), vi-vii, 227-241, 283-301. For an example of the "pragmatist" approach, with its acceptance of the doctrines of limited war, see Ridgeway, *The Korean War*, vi-vii, 11-12, 153, 228-229, 245.

35. Anatol Rapoport, ed., *Clausewitz on War* (New York: Penguin, 1968), 165.

PART III

Nuclear War

Chapter 14

Dilemmas of Deterrence: Rational and Nonrational Perspectives

BETTY GLAD

"Thus far the chief purpose of our military establishment has been to win wars. From now on its chief purpose must be to avert them." This was Bernard Brodie's view of how nuclear weapons had changed the nature of contemporary war. In his pathbreaking *The Absolute Weapon: Atomic Power and World Order*, published at the dawn of the nuclear age, he argued that once the United States lost its monopoly on atomic weapons, these weapons could only function as a deterrent to attack. The only sensible strategy in such circumstances would be the development of a capacity to retaliate with a devastating effect against any nation undertaking a first strike against the US.[1] Twenty years later Klaus Knorr questioned the utility of nuclear weapons in a slightly different vein. The utility of one's weapons is directly related to the values of using them and inversely related to the costs one suffers as a consequence of using them (Utility = $\text{Value}^1 + V^2 + V^n / \text{Cost}^1 + C^2 + C^n$). Because nuclear weapons are so destructive, he suggested, they are apt to have no direct utility for those who possess them.[2]

Some strategic theorists suggested that to get around this basic paradox one could emphasize the threat value of nuclear weapons, rather than their actual usage. For those threats to be effective, however, three conditions had to be met, as Kauffman noted back in 1954: (1) the deterring power would have to have the capabilities to enforce its threat; (2) the punishments, if delivered, would inflict a burdensome cost upon the adversary; and (3) the threat would have to be credible (i.e., the adversary would have to believe that the deterring party was really prepared to implement the threat).[3]

This third condition was the one that presented a problem for the major powers. The use of nuclear weapons against an adversary that could retaliate in kind could be so costly that it raised serious questions about whether or not a nation, at the moment of truth, would actually resort to their use. To deal with this credibility problem, American strategic theorists have several techniques for making the resort to nuclear weapons appear more likely, should deterrence fail. Their recommendations may be summarized as follows:

(1) Decision makers should build up their reputations as risk takers in lower level encounters. If they are themselves willing to suffer net losses to deliver on threats at this level, then their opponents will assume that they will act in the same way in major encounters.[4] "Self-mutilation" in the first phase of a two-stage game, as Barry O'Neil has shown, may pay off in the second phase.[5]

(2) Decision makers also may increase the credibility of their threats by placing themselves in situations where it is no longer possible for them to choose a nonretaliatory response. By publicly staking their reputations on following through on a threat, or by placing their own troops on the front line where they would be the victims of any attempt to change the status quo, they would create an emotional climate in which they would have to respond.[6] Kennedy resorted to such tactics during the Cuban missile crisis. When he went public with explicit threats to stop Soviet ships if they did not pull out their offensive missiles from Cuba, it became politically difficult for him to back off from the implementation of his threats should they not succeed.[7] Programmed retaliatory responses against preselected targets in the event of a first strike of a particular magnitude would be another way of making a response nearly automatic. If the chief executive is killed, decision making devolves to lower authorities who are prepared to act in programmed ways. Steven Brams and Marc Kilgour have called this a probabilistic doomsday machine, and shown how it could enhance deterrence.[8]

(3) The credibility of one's threats may be enhanced, too, if the costs of carrying them out are perceived as less costly. Conventional graduated deterrence, which recognizes that nuclear weapons are not apt to be used for the pursuit of more peripheral interests, is one adaptation along these lines.[9] Certain nuclear war fighting strategies (labeled minimalist in this discussion), by making the resort to nuclear retaliation appear to be less disastrous than previously considered to be, may have a similar effect. Counterforce targeting, the protection of command and control mechanisms, and the development of tactical nuclear weapons are measures along these lines. By increasing the probability that one might actually use the nuclear option in this way, the credibility of deterrent threats is thereby enhanced.[10]

(4) One may also attempt to increase the credibility of nuclear threats by upgrading the values that can be achieved through their use. Some nuclear strategists (called "maximalists" for this discussion) argued that something comparable to the traditional victory in war could be secured through the development and possible usage of a superior first strike counterforce capability. Colin Gray and Keith Payne, for example, have argued in "Victory Is Possible," that the United States should target key Soviet institutions and leadership cadres vital to their recovery after a nuclear strike. Short-term Soviet recovery must be denied so they cannot "win," while U.S. defenses must be developed so the United States can recover quickly. The destruction of the then Soviet government and the establishment of a democratic government was the political objective which was seen as

COLUMN

	Cooperate	Do Not Cooperate
Cooperate	(3,3) Compromise 2	(2,4) Column "Wins" Row "Loses" 3
Do Not Cooperate	(4,2) Row "Wins" Column "Loses" 1	(1,1) Disaster War 4

R
O
W

Figure 14.1. Chicken Game

justifying these means.[11] Even if the United States does not resort to war, as Richard Pipes, Robert Jastrow, and others have argued, the mere demonstration that one has a nuclear war winning capability can be put to good diplomatic use. If a nation could potentially win a nuclear exchange, then the weapons can be used successfully to extract political concessions from the other side.[12]

(5) The credibility of a nation's nuclear deterrence threats, however, is still apt to be greatest, as George and Smoke point out, when central national interests are at stake and that fact is clear to the other side. Whether or not one will actually follow through against a challenger depends ultimately on the importance of the values that are being threatened and the costs one is willing to pay to protect those values. Knowing this, opponents are more likely to pay attention to "strategic, political, economic, and ideological factors determining the nature and magnitude of those interests than to rhetorical and other signaling devices the defending power may employ to enhance credibility."[13]

The logic of some of the strategies, suggested above, can be made clearer through the use of game theory. The nuclear war winning strategies are modeled on the "chicken game." Two players, "Row" and "Column," can choose either to cooperate or not to cooperate, leading to the four possible outcomes given in Figure 14.1. The number given first in each quadrant is the payoff for Row, with 4 the best. Only outcomes (2,4) and (4,2) are Nash equilibriums—positions from which neither player would have an incentive unilaterally to depart, because he would do worse if he did. If Row, for example, could be the first to move from (3,3) to (4,2) — by preempting or using threats to lock itself into the win situation — the other has no choice but to settle for that square. Retaliation would push the player to (1,1) which would be less advantageous to each. The numbers at the bottom of each square are the preferred options for Row. Column's preferred strategies differ only in that the preferred strategy would be (2,4) in the upper

COLUMN

	Cooperate	Do Not Cooperate
R Cooperate	3/3	1/4
O		
W Do Not Cooperate	4/1	2/2

Figure 14.2. Prisoner's Dilemma Game

right-hand quadrant and that the third choice would be (4,2) in the lower left-hand quadrant.

The stable deterrence strategy follows a variation of the chicken game.[14] Row can be induced to forego an aggressive strategy which would maximize the gains it might secure if Column can commit itself in advance to a retaliatory move. If Row then attacks and Column responds, both parties wind up in box (1,1) the worst possible choice for each. Confronted with this possible scenario, Row is deterred from opting for the first strike alternative, settling instead for the mutually cooperative solution. For this policy to work, of course, Column would have to employ some of the strategies noted above for locking itself into a course which it would not choose, if it had to make its choice after Row had attacked. Only by making its responses automatic in some way can it gain sufficient credibility for its threat to retaliate to convince Row that a first strike would not pay.

The nuclear security dilemma, which presents certain grave problems for crisis stability, can be better modeled with a prisoner's dilemma game (see Figure 14.2).

It should be apparent from Figure 14.2 that if Row and Column have invested their efforts into building first strike weapons, and if those weapons are vulnerable to being destroyed by a first strike from the other side, their mutually best option, in the long run, would be to cooperate. Both sides wind up in the top left-hand quadrant, the second best outcome for each player. But this is not a stable outcome. If one adversary should respond to the short-term advantages of a unilateral attack, the other side has no alternative but to counterattack (moving the outcomes to 2/2 in the lower right-hand quadrant). The worst outcome for Column would be to wait for Row to take out all its weapons, leaving Column defenseless (4/1 in the lower left-hand quadrant). It is this fear — that the adversary might get greedy and opt for the noncooperative strategy — that creates incentives for both players to go for the attack, or noncooperative option. As a result, both parties wind up with a result worse than that they could have secured through mutual cooperation.

Maximalist war fighting strategies, oriented as they are toward first strike capabilities and the destruction of the weapons and the defenses of the other side, are apt to place one in situations such as these. If both sides try to develop war winning potential, the eventual result is likely to be an actual resort to the uses of those weapons. Under conditions of tensions and uncertainty, each nation is apt to decide that it is "better to use them, than lose them."

The Potential for Misperceptions

In modeling these classic deterrence games one assumes a certain rationality in both of the adversaries. Threats must be heard, commitments understood, the possible alternatives known. Each player must also know what his own values are (at least in ordinal terms) relative to his adversary, and both sides must remain sufficiently cool at the time of crisis that they can continue to engage in an analysis of the benefits and costs of the alternatives open to them.

The data from the historical record suggests that the actual decision making, particularly in crises, often falls short of this rational standard. Deterrent threats at the conventional war level have often failed to achieve their goals in the past.[15] The actual capabilities players will bring to bear in a concrete local situation are hard to predict in advance and states have made many mistakes along these lines in the past. Moreover, the relationship of means to ends is often very complex. Even strategic and local military superiority does not guarantee that one will actually achieve the outcomes envisioned, as Bruce Russett's study of 17 cases between 1935 and 1961 suggests.[16] Threats, moreover are apt to increase anxiety and rigidity in the enemy, limiting the number of options they will actually consider. Moreover, the values assigned to various outcomes may change in the course of the exchange. When national self-esteem is on the line, as we have seen, decision makers are apt to upgrade the importance of "winning" whatever the nature of the substantive values originally at stake.

Warning signals often are ignored or misperceived in such situations. Partly the cause inheres in the situation. The noise in the system may make it difficult to separate important from unimportant information. Decision makers are apt to be faced with either an information overload or an information vacuum regarding the intentions of the other side, as Holsti has noted. The very nature of cognitive processing can add to the problems. To avoid information overload, human beings will simplify incoming data to fit images they have of the situation based on earlier experience. Evidence will be interpreted to conform with the wisdom of established policy: data that clearly does not fit with policy rationale will be seen as exceptional or special cases, and contradictory data will be ignored. Difficult value tradeoffs will not be squarely faced and the preferred options will be upgraded relative to the ones foregone.[17]

The potential for misperception, as Janis and Mann argue, is apt to be increased by the deeper emotions that conflicts evoke. When confronted with difficult tradeoffs, decision makers tend to utilize some form of defensive avoidance in an attempt to avoid anxiety. Thus they may procrastinate, deny responsibility for a decision, or bolster the least objectionable alternative.[18] The need to feel competent and moral, too, can reinforce proclivities to see the enemy as the source of all evil and to assume he will do the worst.[19]

In situations where central values are threatened and no option seems desirable, these defense mechanisms may no longer work. Overt anxiety reactions may follow, leaving the individual feeling helpless and causing him to waiver between contradictory courses of action, or in some cases to simply withdraw from the situation. After the Nazi attack on Russia, as we have seen, Stalin was incapacitated for approximately two weeks. On occasion, the phenomenon of what Freud called substantive irrationalities may make means-ends calculations an impossibility. The presence of unconscious desires in a player may lead him into choices which even he does not understand. For those dealing with such actors, the policy options are not at all clear, as Glad and Taber point out above. Deterrent threats will not have predictable results.

Irrationalities in the processing of information were at work in the U.S. response to the Chinese threat to intervene in the Korean War, as we have seen. This proclivity to misinterpret signals also has been evident in the decision making processes in several other cultures. Chinese restraint in the contested area of Ladakh in 1961 – 1962, for example, was misinterpreted by Jawharlal Nehru, Krishna Menon, and their military advisors as an indication of Chinese weakness rather than a sign of their self-restraint. As a result, the Indians tried to occupy as much of the disputed territory as possible which led to the hostilities they had not expected.[20] The Egyptian decision to attack Israel in 1973 was also influenced by wishful thinking. Feeling that diplomatic deadlock over the Canal had to be broken somehow, and that their relative position would deteriorate over time, decision makers in Cairo simply assumed that their military planners could come up with a plan that would somehow compensate for their military inferiority.[21] The Falkland Islands war, too, was the result in part of a misperception. The Argentinians clearly saw the Malvinas as a part of their national territory and thought it unlikely that the British would try to reimpose their colonial rule.[22]

The problems that Western scholars have had in interpreting the motives underlying Soviet nuclear strategic choices through most of the post-World War II period suggest that similar misperceptions may have been operative in superpower relations on the contemporary scene. The Soviet military buildup and their resort to first-strike weapons and strategies in the 1960s and 1970s were seen by some scholars as clear evidence of their goals for world domination.[23] Their expansionistic proclivities, Richard Pipes argued in 1981, were rooted in the Russian historical experience and Marxist doctrine. Elite decision making was based on the Clausewitzian doctrine that war is a continuation of politics by other means. The shakiness of the regime at home led the ruling elite to embrace a large military as a buttress to their position at home. Robert Bathurst, Richard Lowenthal, and Fritz Ermath have expressed similar views.[24]

From this perspective, American leaders who embraced detente as a sign that the USSR has changed were seen as naive. Detente for the Soviet Union, Pipes argued, was simply a "tactical adaptation" in an attempt to neutralize the American nuclear threat so that they could shift the world balance of power through subversion and ideological warfare.[25] Benjaim Lambeth saw the Soviet commitment to nuclear parity as but a "transitory and permissive springboard for testing Western resolve. . . ."[26] Bathhurst even saw those who wondered about what Soviet objectives might be, as Jimmy Carter did in 1980, as guilty of naive foolishness. It was similar to Roosevelt's illusions that an appeal to Stalin's sense of noblesse oblige would enable both countries to work together for democracy and peace.[27]

Other Western scholars have made radically different interpretations of Soviet behavior in the post-World War II period. Basically they saw the USSR as a nation-state concerned with its own security, opting for a strategy which made sense to its leaders, given their recent national experience.[28] Soviet policies right after World War II reflected the opportunities for low-cost expansionism. Their emphasis on nuclear war fighting strategies, Erickson argued, was simply a form of deterrence. Should an assault from the United States appear imminent, the USSR was prepared to preempt. The emphasis they placed on victory in such an exchange, he argued, was based on the need to maintain the morale of the Soviet military and the people.[29]

Even Gorbachev's foreign policy initiatives have been subjected to diverse interpretations. In 1987, Dimitri Simes saw the Soviet leader as employing a smarter, more creative approach to the Soviet Union's old zero-sum game with the United States in which "any gain for Washington is automatically a loss for Moscow." To respond properly to Gorbachev, he suggested, the "United States must distinguish between the merely pragmatic, vigorous and sophisticated Soviet policy" to one that would be "truly more benign."[30] But the tests he set up for truly benign behavior required quite extreme renunciations by the USSR. That country would have to come to terms with their technological and economic limitations and abandon, as a practical foreign policy goal, the aspiration of "being a global equal of — to say nothing of being superior to — the United States."[31]

Other scholars saw Gorbachev's initiatives as opening up whole new opportunities for big power cooperation. Matthew Evangelista, for example, saw his arms reduction campaign as not simply a reaction to Soviet economic difficulties or to the American military buildup. Previous Soviet leaders faced similar problems, but responded quite differently. Gorbachev's seriousness was evident in the substance of proposals he made and some of the personal risks he ran in pursuing his course.[32] Michael MccGwire also saw Gorbachev and his political allies as having real concerns about the possibility of nuclear war. Washington's assertions that its SDI program was for the purpose of stabilizing deterrence and hence in the best interests of the Soviet Union were not taken seriously in Moscow. Indeed, MccGwire suggests that a major barrier to the achievement of the limitation of nuclear weapons has been the American reluctance to give up its worst case assumptions of Soviet motives.[33]

There were serious problems, as Rick Hermann has suggested, in devising empirical tests which would definitely prove one view of the Soviet Union as superior to another.[34] In a situation in which there was much potentially relevant information that could be organized in different ways, diverse views were bound to flourish.

Yet there is considerable evidence that certain critics of the USSR have overlooked important data suggesting that the country's leaders have shown restraint at key points, prior even to their key concession to the West in the late 1980s.[35]

Thus in the mid-1960s, when China was embroiled in their cultural revolution, the USSR did not take Sinkiang. Nor did they take advantage of the U.S. preoccupation with Indochina to extend their influence over Iran.[36] It is also quite clear that key American decision makers and strategists have overestimated Soviet capabilities at several different times in the postwar period. Thus in 1950, NSC 69, drafted under the direction of Paul Nitze, proclaimed a bomber gap. By 1959, however, it was clear that the United States led the USSR in bombers by about 2 to 1. In 1959, there was an assumed missile gap, provoked by the launching of Sputnik in 1957. Estimates that the USSR would have 3,000 intercontinental ballistic missiles (ICBMs) were somewhat above the mere 40 they actually were able to develop by that time. The antiballistic missile (ABM) gap of 1963-67 also was exaggerated, as was the window of vulnerability which was said to exist in the early 1980s. The latter, which assumed that the Soviets could undertake a first strike against American land-based missiles, wiping out the U.S. ability to respond against their weapons, was explicitly denied by the Scowcroft Commission.[37]

There also has been considerable evidence of mirror images in recent U.S.-USSR relations. The Soviet view of the United States throughout most of the post-World War II period has been very similar to the U.S. view of the Soviet Union, as Urie Bronfenbrenner pointed out some time ago. Each saw the other as the aggressor and inherently untrustworthy. The people were seen as being exploited by the government and not really sympathetic to it.[38] Frei's more recent study of Soviet and American official opinion of the motives of each other suggests that the image of the other as the aggressor persisted into the late 1980s.[39] The U.S. response to Soviet first-strike policies with first-strike policies of its own convinced Soviet leaders that the United States was planning aggressive warfare against the USSR.[40] Even the supposed conflict between doves and hawks in Soviet ruling circles was a form of mirror imaging, Frei suggested — an inappropriate projection of the American experience onto a totally different political system.

Misperceptions: Policy Relevance

The consequences of these various perceptions of the Soviet Union for American nuclear policies may be briefly summarized as follows. Those who emphasized the inherently expansionist nature of the Soviet Union often came to the conclusion that the United States would be faced at some time in the future with a zero-sum situation in which it would have to destroy or be destroyed. War fighting strategies in which the United States could win or prevail made the most sense to these individuals. Those who interpreted Soviet behavior in traditional national security and balance of power terms were more likely to assume a commonality of interest between the USSR and the United States and the possibility in the long run for stable deterrence (as defined by the chicken game), as well as the possibility of

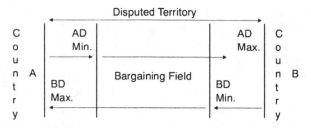

Figure 14.3. Bargaining Field

cooperative interactions best modeled by the mutually best resolution of the prisoner's dilemma.

Regardless of the position taken as to the ultimate nature of the Soviet goals, it should be clear that the very existence of such widely different interpretations of the goals and values of a potential enemy raise serious questions about the value of some of the commitment strategies described above. Demonstrating one's risk taking proclivities and freezing oneself into locked positions can be used to enhance deterrence — up to a point.[41] In real-life bargaining situations, however, one does not know the maximum concessions the other side is prepared to make to avoid the cost of war. Indeed, once one is committed to a position from which retreat is difficult or impossible, one is apt to rationalize that choice and to underestimate the values of the opponent. The result could be a war which is to the advantage of neither side. Figure 14.3 illustrates this point.

In Figure 14.3, A's and B's demands (D_{max}) represent their aspirations, whereas their minimum demands (D_{min}) represent what they would settle for rather than fight. The bargaining field is the shaded area between the D_{min} of each side. A deal within these limits would be considered better than a fight to both sides. If A, for example, could move first or freeze itself through some other mechanism at the point AD_{max} it could maximize the gain to itself and still have a deal. The problem is, as the psychological literature suggests, that A often does not know the BD_{min} point. If A moves to AD_{max} (past B's minimum point) due to misperceptions of B's values or a willful ignoring of B's deterrent threat, the result will be a war which is to the advantage of neither side. Both parties have lost.

Nuclear war fighting strategies, too, tend to be based on scenarios which overestimate the extent to which any adversary can control its weapons and populace and can resist pressures to escalate once war begins. The political, strategic, technological, and psychological barriers to the maintenance of middle range counterforce nuclear exchanges, delineated by Peter Sedereberg, below, are mostly ignored. Nuclear war fighting strategies that suggest one might win (i.e., "prevail") in such exchanges raise even more serious problems. Disabling strikes against the command and control capabilities of the other side, which these strategies require, could very well lead to a spasm response from the potential victim. If there are no leadership cadres with whom one can negotiate, if the remaining top officials are unable to communicate with their field commanders and assess what has happened to them, then the other side may have no option but to respond blindly.

Indeed, the whole idea of "winning" any kind of general nuclear war ignores the significance that modern weapons pose for the relationship of means to ends. As early as World War I, as Bernard Brodie has pointed out, the concrete political and military objectives of war were being replaced by the goal of making the enemy "cry uncle."[42] "Prevailing" in a nuclear war (i.e., having more unused weapons, or suffering less damage than the enemy) may be the nuclear war counterpart of this preoccupation with the submission of one's opponent, rather than the positive goals one might achieve. Certainly the data provided by Katz in his analysis of the probable consequences of nuclear war, below, suggests this is so. In addition to the immediate and direct damage, which would be enormous even in limited counter-force wars, the synergistic effects would spread the devastation from one sector of life to another, from one region to others, like a ripple throughout the entire system. What is a victory worth if one's country has been devastated and millions of people killed in the process? Perhaps the whole idea that nations can meaningfully engage in nuclear war simply is an attempt, as Jervis has suggested, to repeal the nuclear revolution.[43]

Confronting some of the dilemmas outlined above, several American strategists have argued that nuclear weapons are useful as a psychological tool. The United States must match the USSR, weapon for weapon and doctrine for doctrine, as a means of showing that it is committed to preserving its influence in the world. If the Soviets are going for a first-strike winning capability, it has been argued, then so should the United States. If the USSR has an inflated military budget, so should the United States. In line with this kind of thinking, the Scowcroft Commission, for example, recommended in its report to President Reagan the deployment of an American first strike weapon, the MX, as a sign of American resolve and a bargaining tool. It did this despite its finding that there was no "window of vulnerability" through which the USSR could deliver a crippling strike blow against the United States.[44] From this perspective, the balance of power is assessed through numerical balance sheets rather than through an assessment of the real technological capabilities of each player. If America's allies perceive the United States as falling behind the USSR, they may lose faith in its policies. Statistics — money spent on weapons, megatonnage, and so forth — all influence how others perceive the arms race, forcing the United States to keep up with the USSR. In short, the perception that one is keeping up with the other side is crucial to one's international reputation and prestige.

Certain paradoxes, however, are evident in this approach. In its effort to match Soviet military outlays, the U.S. government resorted to tactics which undermined the very goals which the matching was supposed to serve. To justify demands for larger military budgets, the Defense Department talked of Soviet nuclear superiority. But this kind of talk, as Steven Kull points out, below, undermined the very objective of the race — that is, the maintenance of the image that the United States is really number one for America's allies and the public. In Kull's view the American public supported the arms race, not because of any of these reasons, but for psychological reassurance. Keeping up with the Russians, somehow enabled the American people to live with the threat.

Moral Dilemmas

The possibility of massive nuclear retaliation has buttressed deterrence through-out much of the post-World War II epoch and done so without either side ever having to deliver on its threats. The possibility, however, is that in the long run this deterrence is likely to fail. Statistical models of the situation show that even if the probability of war is low in any one year, if that probability remains constant over several years, war at some time is highly likely.[45] Applying this logic to the possibility of nuclear war, Bradford Lyttle notes that even if the daily chance of one missile being launched is only one in 100,000,000 the probability that such an event will occur in 50 years is more than 50%. Douglas Lackey argues that there is a one in 100 chance of nuclear war in the next 40 years. These approaches all simplify the situation, as Joseph Nye points out, to the extent that they assume a constant probability over the years. Yet Nye's argument, that the probabilities are apt to get lower over time is based on a best-case analysis of several trends and a desire to keep our spirits up by not letting our imagination be "captured solely by images of imminent nuclear holocaust or by cynical views of the immutability of our dependence on nuclear weapons."[46]

Various groups have responded to the possibility of a nuclear holocaust in different ways. Some Christian fundamentalists have taken the stance described by Steven Kull above. Nuclear war is seen as inevitable and ultimately good in the final defeat of evil, the final scourge which will issue in the return of Jesus to this earth and the millennium. The appropriate attitude, as Hall Lindsey has suggested in his work forwarding this view is acceptance: "As history races towards this moment are you afraid or looking with hope for deliverance?"[47] Other Christians have argued that nuclear war would be so void of any redeeming quality that it must be avoided at all costs and that the only way to do that is to engage in nuclear disarmament.[48]

The Conference of American Catholic Bishops in their pastoral letter published in 1983 took a position different from both of the above. Unlike the fundamentalists, they make a presumption against war and view the commitment to the Christian faith as requiring action to prevent a nuclear holocaust. At stake is the whole of God's creation:

> In the nuclear arsenals of the United States or the Soviet Union alone, there exists a capacity to do something no other age could imagine: We can threaten the entire planet. . . . Every sinful act is a confrontation of the creature and the creator. Today the

destructive potential of the nuclear powers threatens the human person, the civilization we have slowly constructed, and even the created order itself.[49]

Employing traditional just war doctrine, they conclude that nuclear weapons by their very nature are so destructive that a moral nation would never directly target civilians nor use those weapons in attacks on military installations near civilian centers where the collateral damage would be massive. Unlike the nuclear disarmers, however, they make some concessions to traditional nuclear deterrence doctrine. As an interim measure, nations might threaten retaliation against a first strike by an enemy, provided that the collateral damage done would be contained as much as possible.[50]

Moral and legal philosophers such as Paul Ramsey and James Turner Johnson, and strategists such as Arnold Wohlstetter and Fred Ikle have also condemned countervalue targeting in just war terms and have argued that morally you cannot threaten to do what you cannot carry out in practice should your threats fail. Yet they differ from the disarmers and the Catholic bishops in their view that nuclear weapons can be used in ways which will meet the terms of traditional just war doctrine. This can be achieved if one targets military objectives only and engages in damage limitation strategies generally. Moreover, most adherents to this policy argue that pledges to engage in no first use of nuclear weapons would be counterproductive. The threat that one might escalate to the nuclear level in a conventional war is seen as an essential ingredient deterring conventional wars. The fact that one can actually deliver on threats to employ nuclear weapons, it is assumed, enhances deterrence. The result is that defense of the nation is achieved and the likelihood that one may have to actually resort to the use of nuclear weapons in minimized.[51]

The Christian Fundamentalists, as the above suggests, is the only group that has clearly opted for nuclear war as an alternative one must accept. Each one of the other alternative positions issues in paradoxes. The stances of the radical nuclear disarmers reduces the probability of a nuclear holocaust. But their policies, as the counterforce proponents argue, undermines deterrence. Nuclear disarmament, if it is unilateral, leaves the disarmed nation at the mercy of a potential aggressor. Even the resort to conventional defense is problematical, for it leaves the other side with the option of escalating unilaterally to the nuclear level.[52] Even if one retains nuclear weapons, the ability to deter a would-be aggressor would be undermined to the extent that one's threats to use them appear to be based on bluff. Moreover, the announcement, in advance, that one will not resort to first use of such weapons could increase the likelihood of a conventional war between the major powers.[53]

The counterforce option does not really resolve the paradoxes central to the nuclear age. First, it makes deterrence both more and less effective. To the extent that it increases the probability that threats will be implemented if deterrence fails, it enhances deterrence and thus decreases the possibility that one has to deliver on those threats. But to the extent that the nuclear retaliation is "conventionalized," the challenger is more likely to run the risk of not backing down in the face of threats. Countervalue threats, after all, had deterrence value because the potential damage was so great that it made up for the relatively low probability that one might actually implement such threats.[54] Moreover, once a deterrence breakdown has occurred, a nuclear response, shorn of its terror, is more likely. The damage might be less severe than that envisaged in a major countervalue attack. But what if the "collateral damage" turns out to be massive? One cannot avoid the moral problems presented by such possibilities, as the Catholic bishops have argued in a recent update of their pastoral letter on nuclear deterrence, by refusing to address the actual probable consequences of such a war.[55]

Moreover, what if the course of the war cannot be controlled in terms of just war considerations? Indeed, the assumption that decision makers, in the heat of a destructive battle, would continue to assess their retaliatory moves in terms of just war doctrine flies in the face of the only history we have regarding the actual use of nuclear weapons. American decision makers near the end of World War II chose to drop over Hiroshima and Nagasaki the only two nuclear bombs which have ever been dropped in part because there were relatively untouched workers' homes around the military targets that would be destroyed.[56] Countervalue strikes, in short, were chosen as the best way to end the war quickly and decisively. Contemporary decapitation strategies, which several counterforce proponents have embraced, present especially serious problems for maintaining such limits.[57] In blinding an adversary one could trigger off a spasm response from that adversary, thereby undermining any possibility of a commensurate relationship between means and ends. Counterforce wars, in short, may in fact be conducted in ways which make it impossible to meet the central principle of the traditional just war doctrine that the means used must remain significantly and proportionately related to the ends sought.

Perhaps the greatest weakness of the counterforce strategy is that it erases the distinction between offensive and defensive capabilities. To be able to survive a first strike from the other side with weapons which are able to do serious damage to the weapons of the other side, one must have many weapons and they must be accurate. But that capability may give the nation which possesses it the ability to strike first. If proponents of maximalist war fighting strategies should come to power in a nation possessing those capacities, they may well be tempted to undertake a massive, disabling nuclear strike against their opponents in an attempt to achieve a final victory over them. What would justify such an attack? What if the United States, for example, had the chance to destroy the Russian government? Would the result, as Colin Gray suggests, justify the damage done in such a strike? That kind of goal has never been seen as a legitimate cause for initiating war in the past. Is the destruction of a government one finds morally obnoxious a goal we would like to make legitimate now? How many millions of Russians could be killed for an objective for which they had not been consulted? How many millions of Americans may be legitimately sacrificed to that goal? Given the extensive nature of the damage done to both the United States and the USSR, would the United States in fact be able to guarantee that a democratic government, friendly to the United States, would replace the destroyed government?[58]

What the above suggests is that there is no strategic option, short of embracing the nuclear holocaust as a transforming experience, that one can choose without being presented with some very difficult value tradeoffs and some fundamental dilemmas. Alternatives which force one to choose between evils are anxiety producing, as we have seen, and are apt to lead to psychological defenses. It is not surprising, than, to discover that supporters of most of the above strategic alternatives have attempted to bolster their preferred option. Some proponents of mutual assured destruction (MAD) have taken refuge in the assumption that the threat of nuclear retaliation is so terrible that one does not have to really confront the possibility that in some circumstance, one actually may have to deliver on that threat. Counterforce proponents work from a best-case scenario, and some of them come close to what G. E. M. Anscombe has called "double think about double effect." Paul Ramsey, for example, has argued that disproportionate threats do enhance deterrence and may be relied upon just so long as the damage envisaged is collateral (i.e., unintentional). Even countervalue threats are legitimate, just so long as the threats are tacit, that is, based on the *possession* of countervalue weapons and the *appearance* one might use them in a retaliatory strike. Indeed, he even admits that threats disproportionate at one level (i.e., in terms of a particular target at hand) may be proportionate at another level (i.e., in terms of enhancing the possibility of world peace).[59]

In short, the basic dilemma — of how one can serve the two fundamental and opposing values of self-defense and the avoidance of a nuclear holocaust — permits no clear fix. Perhaps the Bishop's answer — a compromise shrouded in a purposive ambiguity — is the best one can do under the circumstances.[60] In opting for the retention of the counterforce threat, all the while expressing their deep fears that counterforce strikes in practice could not be sufficiently limited and controlled to meet the test of proportionality, the Bishops try to serve both of the contradictory objectives noted above. To deter a nuclear first strike against itself, a nation may maintain the threat of a limited nuclear second strike. To avoid a too facile resort to these weapons, however, one must not treat them as the normal and controlled means for serving national policy.[61] For nuclear bombs are different from earlier weapons and their usage is likely to have consequences which outstrip any good they might serve. Indeed, it is the recognition of the fact that the nuclear dilemma allows no satisfactory solution that provides the key to what must be done in the future. The superpowers must strive for the mutual reductions of nuclear arms and the reduction of political tensions. That is best hope for avoiding nuclear war in the long run.[62]

Notes

1. Bernard Brodie, ed., "The Weapon," in *The Absolute Weapon: Atomic Power and World Order* (New York: Harcourt, Brace, 1946), 76.

2. Klaus Knorr, *On the Use of Military Power in the Nuclear Age* (Princeton, NJ: Princeton University Press, 1966), 9, 82-87.

3. William W. Kaufmann, *Requirements of Deterrence* (Princeton, NJ: Princeton Center of International Studies, 1954), 7.

4. Thomas Schelling, *The Strategy of Conflict* (Cambridge, MA: Harvard University Press, 1980), 180-203. The original version of this book appeared in 1960. For a more recent explication of this point of view, see Robert Jervis, *The Illogic of American Nuclear Strategy* (Ithaca, NY: Cornell University Press, 1984), 135, 140-144.

5. Barry O'Neill, "Game Theory and the Study of the Deterrence of War," (paper prepared for the Research Workshop on Deterrence, National Research Council/National Academy of Sciences, Washington, DC, November 1986).

6. Schelling, *Strategy of Conflict*, 119-150, 190-199.

7. Graham T. Allison, *Essence of Decision: Explaining the Cuban Missile Crisis* (Boston: Little, Brown, 1971), 218-230.

8. Steven Brams and D. Marc Kilgour, "Is Nuclear Deterrence Rational?" *PS* XIX, 3 (Summer 1986): 645-650.

9. For the flexible response doctrine, see Maxwell Taylor, *The Uncertain Trumpet* (New York: Harper and Row, 1960), 5-7, 57-62, 130-164.

10. The phrase "minimalists" as used here should not be confused with minimal deterrence, which argues that if one has enough nuclear weapons to ride out an attack from the other side and to retaliate in ways that do damage to their central values that is sufficient for deterrence. See Herman Kahn, *Thinking About the Unthinkable in the 1980's* (New York: Simon and Schuster, 1984), 41-42.

11. Colin S. Gray and Keith Payne, "Victory Is Possible," *Foreign Policy*, 39 (Summer 1980): 14-27.

12. See Richard Pipes, "Strategic Superiority," *New York Times* (6 February 1977); and Robert Jastrow, "Why Strategic Superiority Matters," *Commentary* (March 1983), 27-32.

13. Alexander George and Richard Smoke, *Deterrence in American Foreign Policy: Theory and Practice* (New York: Columbia University Press, 1974), 560-561.

14. For an elaboration of this argument, see Steven Brams and D. Marc Kilgour, "Is Nuclear Deterrence Rational?" *PS*, XIX, 3 (Summer 1986): 645-650.

15. See Richard Ned Lebow, *Between Peace and War: The Nature of International Crisis* (Baltimore, MD: Johns Hopkins University Press, 1981), 57-95; and Lebow, "Conclusions" in Robert Jervis, Richard Ned Lebow, and Janice Gross Stein, *Psychology and Deterrence* (Baltimore, MD: Johns Hopkins University Press, 1985), 203-211.

16. Bruce Russett, "The Calculus of Deterrence," *Journal of Conflict Resolution*, VII, 2 (June 1963): 98-109.

17. See Robert Jervis, *Perception and Misperception in International Politics* (Princeton, NJ: Princeton University Press, 1976), 117-202; Phillip Tetlock and Charles McGuire, "Cognitive Perspectives on Foreign Policy," in *Psychology and the Prevention of Nuclear War*, ed. Ralph White (New York: New York University Press, 1986), 255-257; Lebow, *Between Peace and War*, 102-118.

18. Irving Janis and Leon Mann, *Decision Making* (New York: Free Press, 1977), 87.

19. Ralph White, *Fearful Warriors* (New York: Free Press, 1984), 136-287. For the possibility that this way of viewing the enemy will lead to malignant social processes, see Morton Deutsch, "The Prevention of World War Three: A Psychological Perspective," *Political Psychology*, 4, 1 (1983): 3-31.

20. Lebow, *Between Peace and War*, 188-192.

21. Janice Gross Stein, "Calculation, Miscalculation and Conventional Deterrence: The View from Cairo," in Jervis et al., *Psychology and Deterrence*, 34-60.

22. Richard Ned Lebow, "Miscalculation in the South Atlantic: Origins of the Falkland War," in Jervis et al., *Psychology and Deterrence*, 116. The British, employing their own version of the domino theory, however, saw that threat as having implications for Gibraltar and other outposts of their empire. Ibid., 115-17.

23. For an overview of Soviet strategies during this period, see David Holloway, *The Soviet Union and the Arms Race* (New Haven, CT: Yale University Press, 1983); Benjamin S. Lambeth, "How to Think About Soviet Military Doctrine," in *Soviet Strategy*, eds. John Baylis and Gerald Segal (London: Croom Helm, 1981), 114-117; Raymond C. Garthoff, "Mutual Deterrence, Parity and Strategic Arms

Limitation in Soviet Policy" in *Soviet Military Thinking,* ed. Derek Leebaert (London: George Allen and Unwin, 1981).

24. Richard Pipes, *U.S.-Soviet Relations in the Era of Detente* (Boulder, CO: Westview, 1981), 136, 154, 172-176; Robert Bathurst, "Two Languages of War," in *Soviet Military Thinking,* 31; Fritz W. Ermath, "Contrasts in American and Soviet Strategic Thought," in *Soviet Military Thinking,* 66-67; Richard Lowenthal, "Dealing with Soviet Global Power," *Encounter* (June 1978); 90. For views of American officials, generally, see Daniel Frei, *Perceived Images* (Totowa, NJ: Rowman & Allanheld, 1986), 185-225.

25. Pipes, *U.S.-Soviet Relations,* 53-54, 81, 100-101, 175.

26. Benjamin S. Lambeth, "The Political Potential of Soviet Equivalence," in *Strategy and Nuclear Deterrence,* ed. Steven E. Miller (Princeton, NJ: Princeton University Press, 1984), 258.

27. Bathurst, "Two Languages of War," 40. For a similar statement on Jimmy Carter's purported naiveté, see Pipes, *U.S.-Soviet Relations,* 171-172: see aslo George Breslauer's "Why Detente Failed," in *Managing U.S.-Soviet Rivalry,* ed. Alexander George (Boulder, CO: Westview, 1983), 319-340.

28. See Marshall Shulman, "What the Russians Really Want" in *Psychology and the Prevention of Nuclear War,* 55-70, especially 58, 60.

29. John Erickson, "Soviet View of Deterrence: A General Survey," in *The Soviet Union: Security Policies and Constraints,* ed. Jonathan Alford (New York: St. Martin's Press for International Institute for Strategic Studies, 1985), 136-145.

30. Dimitri K. Simes, "Gorbachev: A New Foreign Policy?" *Foreign Affairs,* 65:3 (Fall 1987): 478, 491.

31. Ibid., 499.

32. Matthew Evangelista, "Gorbachev's Disarmament Campaign: The New Soviet Approach to Security," *World Policy Journal,* III, 4 (Fall 1986): 571.

33. Michael MccGwire, "Soviet Military Objectives," *World Policy Journal,* III, 4 (Fall 1986): 668-695.

34. Richard K. Hermann, "American Perceptions of Soviet Foreign Policy: Reconsidering Three Competing Perspectives," *Political Psychology,* 6, 3 (Fall 1985): 375-411.

35. Of course some persons can be shown to be rigid in their commitments to negative images of the USSR, refusing to process new information that might raise questions about their view of that enemy. For an analysis of John Foster Dulles along these lines, see David J. Finlay, Ole R. Holsti, and Richard R. Fagen, *Enemies in Politics* (Chicago: Rand McNally, 1967), 25-96; see also Betty Glad, "Black and White Thinking: Ronald Reagan's Approach to Foreign Policy," *Political Psychology,* 4, 1 (Spring 1983): 33-76.

36. MccGwire, "Soviet Military Objectives," 682-683. As MccGwire also points out, the Soviet military buildup in the 1960s and early 1970s occurred mainly in the Far Eastern theater and had largely ceased by the end of the 1970s.

37. The window of vulnerability argument assumed that a Soviet first strike would do such damage to American land-based missiles that it would leave the American president with no choice but massive retaliation or doing nothing. For a somewhat sympathetic discussion of the window of vulnerability concept and a critique of the "bolt out of the blue" scenario, see Kahn, *Thinking About the Unthinkable,,* 125-127, 130-134.

38. Urie Bronfenbrenner, "The Mirror Image in Soviet-American Relations," in *Psychology and the Prevention of Nuclear War,* 71-81.

39. Daniel Frei, *Perceived Images,* 200, 41-78, 125-159.

40. Robert Jervis, "The Deterrence Deadlock: Is there a Way Out?" in Jervis et al., *Psychology and Deterrence,* 201-202.

41. For examples of commitment strategies, see Schelling, *The Strategy of Conflict,* 119-150, 190-199.

42. Brodie, *Strategy in the Missile Age,* 61-70. For pressures to escalate in war, see also Richard Smoke, *War: Controlling Escalation* (Cambridge, MA: Harvard University Press, 1979), 432-451, 24.

43. Robert Jervis, *The Illogic of American Nuclear Strategy* (Ithaca, NY: Cornell University Press, 1984), 147ff. For his critique of the attempt to build counterforce capabilities so that one can "prevail" at each level of possible encounter with the USSR, see ibid., 126-144, 131-134.

44. Scowcroft Commission on Strategic Force, *Survival* (July-August 1983): 177-186.

45. The probability of at least one unfortunate event occurring in a series of trials is equal to $1 - (1 - p)^n$. Thus, if we flip a coin 10 times, the chance of seeing tails at least once is 99.9%.

46. For Lyttle and Lackey citations and Nye's critique, see Joseph S. Nye, Jr., "The Long-Term Future of Deterrence," in *The Nuclear Reader: Strategies, Weapons, and War*, 2d ed., eds. Charles W. Kegley and Eugene R. Wittkopf (New York: St Martin's, 1989), 81-89. For another probability argument, see Rudolf Avenhaus, Steve J. Brams, John Fichtner, and D. Marc Kilgour, "The Probability of Nuclear War," manuscript, n.d.

47. Hall Lindsey with C. C. Carlson, *The Late Great Planet Earth* (Grand Rapids, MI: Zondervan, 1977).

48. See W. Stein, ed., *Nuclear Weapons and the Christian Conscience* (London: Merlin, 1961); George F. Kennan, "A Christian View of the Arms Race" in *The Ethics of Nuclear War and Nuclear Deterrence*, ed. James P. Sterba (Belmont, CA: Wadsworth, 1985), 122-126. Susan Moller Okin, "Taking the Bishops Seriously," *World Politics*, 36, 4 (July 1984): 527-54; Howard Davis, ed., *Ethics and Defense* (Oxford: Basil Blackwell, 1986), 1-20.

49. National Conference of Catholic Bishops, *The Challenge of Peace: God's Promise and Our Response: A Pastoral Letter on War and Peace* (3 May 1983), 39-40.

50. Ibid., 26-34, 46-50. See also Jim Castelli, *The Bishops and the Bomb* (New York: Doubleday, 1983), 185-276. For a discussion of the intellectual context in which the report was developed, see J. Bryan Hehir, "The Context of the Moral-Strategic Debate and the Contribution of the U.S. Catholic Bishops," (manuscript, Center of International Studies at Princeton University, April 1984). For another Catholic perspective on the just war doctrine, see William V. O'Brien, "Just-War Theory" in James P. Sterba, *The Ethics of Nuclear War and Nuclear Deterrence*. For a survey of the views of various religious denominations, see Janice Love "From Pacifism to Apocalyptic Visions: Religious Organizations' Perspectives on the Morality of Deterrence," in *After the Cold War: The Uncertain Moral Status of Nuclear Deterrence*, eds. Jonathon Davidson, Charles W. Kegley, Jr., and Kenneth L. Schwab, forthcoming.

51. For these arguments see Paul Ramsey, *War and the Christian Conscience* (Durham NC: Duke University Press, 1961), 231-324; Paul Ramsey, *The Just War: Formulation and Political Responsibility* (New York: Scribner's, 1968); James Turner Johnson, *Can Modern War Be Just?* (New Haven, CT: Yale University Press, 1984), 25-29, 84-85; Albert Wohlstetter, "Bishops, Statesmen, and Other Strategists on the Bombing of Innocents," in *The Nuclear Reader: Strategy, Weapons, War*, eds. Charles W. Kegley, Jr. and Eugene Wittkopf (New York: St. Martin's, 1985), 58-76; Herman Kahn, *Thinking About the Unthinkable*, 211-214. For Ikle's views, see Lawrence Freedman, *The Evolution of Nuclear Strategy* (New York: St Martin's, 1981), 348-350.

52. For critique of the unilateral nuclear disarmers by several British theologians, see Francis Bridger, ed., *The Cross and the Bomb: Christian Ethics and the Nuclear Debate* (London: Mowbray, 1983).

53. For a critique from a Catholic "realist" position that the bishops did not really address how one might meet evil threats such as those emanating from USSR, see William V. O'Brian, "A Christian Peace Perspective," in Judith A. Dwyer, SSJ, *The Catholic Bishops and Nuclear War: A Critique and Analysis of the Pastoral "The Challenge of Peace"* (Washington, DC: Georgetown University Press, 1984), 37-63. For a critique of the no first use doctrine and the nuclear freeze, see Charles Krauthammer, "On Nuclear Morality," in James P. Sterba, *The Ethics of Nuclear War and Nuclear Deterrence*.

54. Deterrence, in other words, equals the probability of implementation of threat x damage done if threat is implemented. To make this point more clear, look at the chicken game (Figure 14.1). When Column's absolute costs of winding up in box 4 are very high as compared to the gains from a possible win in box 3 (e.g., minus 100,000,000 as compared to plus 10,000) one is less apt to run the risk that a retaliatory threat is a bluff.

55. National Conference of Catholic Bishops: *Building Peace: A Pastoral Reflection on the Response to "The Challenge of Peace"* and *A Report on the Challenge of Peace and Policy Development 1983-88*, by the Ad Hoc Committee on the Moral Evaluation of Deterrence (Washington, DC: Catholic Conference of Bishops, June 1988), 67-68.

56. Walter S. Schoenberger, *Decision of Destiny* (Columbus: Ohio University Press, 1969), 127; Gar Alperovitz, *Atomic Diplomacy: Hiroshima and Potsdam: The Use of the Atomic Bomb and the American Confrontation with Soviet Power* (New York: Simon & Schuster, 1965), 115. Even the definition of what is moral may change if we adopt situational ethics, making allowance for the pressures for conformity which press upon individuals when making decisions in a group. For this argument see Ferdinand Schoeman, "Social Psychology and Assessments of Moral Judgment," (unpublished manuscript, Philosophy Department, University of South Carolina, Columbia, October 1989).

57. See, for example, Barry R. Schneider, "Invitation to a Nuclear Beheading," in *The Nuclear War Reader: Strategy, Weapons, War,* 2nd ed., eds. Charles W. Kegley, Jr. and Eugene R. Wittkopf (New York: St. Martin's, 1989).

58. The American Catholic Bishops reject even the morality of plans for extended counterforce nuclear exchanges or for "prevailing in a nuclear war." *The Challenge of Peace,* 58-59, and *Building Peace,* 39-40.

59. For quote and detailed critique of Ramsey's work, see Michael Walzer, *Just and Unjust Wars: A Moral Argument With Historical Illustrations* (New York: Basic Books, 1977), 279, 269-283.

60. In the 1988 update of their pastoral letter, the Catholic Bishops recognize an inherent tension between these two goals and make it clear that their ambiguity on this point in intentional. See *Building Peace,* 35. Judith Dwyer, *The Challenge of Peace and the Morality of Using Nuclear Weapons,* 8-9, argued that this also was the case with their 1983 statement.

61. National Conference of Catholic Bishops, *Building Peace,* 37.

62. The Catholic bishops did not gloss over moral differences between the United States and the USSR in their 1983 statement. They simply did not demonize them. See *The Challenge to Peace,* 76-84. For their detailed critique of several destabilizing strategies in their 1988 statement, see *Building Peace,* 43-77, esp. 60-62, 70.

Chapter 15

The Role of Perceptions in the Nuclear Arms Race

STEVEN KULL

Through the 1960s, American strategic policy was focused on building and maintaining retaliatory forces capable of surviving an all-out Soviet attack. During the 1960s Washington accomplished this task. Each superpower remained vulnerable to attack from the other. Each retained adequate survivable nuclear forces to retaliate in the event of an attack. Since then, new ideas have emerged that call for building weapons beyond these requirements of retaliation. One of the most persistent theories, arguably most responsible for the continuing arms race, is a version of perception theory.

Perception theory, a phrase applied to nuclear weapons issues by strategic analyst Arthur Macy Cox in his 1976 book *The Dynamics of Detente*, argues that building weapons beyond the requirements of deterrence can achieve important psychological objectives. It argues that important audiences misperceive the military relationship between the superpowers apparently largely because of a widespread illusion that nuclear weapons are not fundamentally different from conventional weapons. But, strikingly, perception theorists today do not favor trying to correct these misperceptions by dispelling this illusion. Instead, they propose playing along with the illusion by building weapons that create desired perceptions even when the weapons are not militarily necessary.

A primary concern of perception theory is a question as old as the arms race itself: "Who's ahead?" Perception theorists readily agree that in a real military sense — in the event of war — such comparisons are not important, given greatly redundant arsenals. They do not contest the fact of overkill. But they do insist that such comparisons have political and psychological consequences that outweigh military considerations. The perception of U.S. strategic inferiority by Soviet or other world leaders or even by the American public, they contend, might lead to developments that would weaken American security.

EDITOR'S NOTE: This chapter is a slightly edited version of "Nuclear Nonsense" which originally appeared in *Foreign Policy*, 58 (Spring 1985): 28-52. Reprinted with permission from *Foreign Policy* 58 (Spring 1985). Copyright 1985 by the Carnegie Endowment for International Peace.

Perception theory then takes another step. Not only does it claim that key audiences believe incorrectly that the question "Who's ahead?" is important, it also asserts that these audiences gauge "Who's ahead?" incorrectly, focusing naively on misleading numerical comparisons.

As a result, perception theory argues that the United States cannot simply focus on the relationship between the number of survivable American warheads and Soviet targets. The United States should also be concerned with the comparisons of the gross number of weapons on each side. Apparently, perception theory seeks to respond to the false belief that American weapons effectively cancel out Soviet weapons the same way a sword or more troops can offset their counterparts.

A later variation of perception theory proposes playing along with the illusion of conventionality in yet another and perhaps even more dangerous way. Some American leaders and strategists fear that the Soviets might be entertaining the illusion that nuclear war, like conventional war, can be limited and even meaningfully won. Again, perception theory proposes playing along with the illusion by recommending that the United States try, through its weapons procurements and by devising war fighting strategies, to create the perception that a nuclear war can be limited and even meaningfully won.

The assumption that this widespread illusion of conventionality does in fact exist is dubious, though not entirely farfetched. The most questionable aspect of perception theory, however, is its proposal that in order to create false impressions, the United States should play along with the illusion by building militarily unnecessary weapons according to mistaken parameters. The theory even proposes actively promoting the illusion at times — a course of action wrought with ironic contradictions.

Perception theory originally grew out of the idea that the Soviets believed in it. By the mid-1970s, the Soviets surpassed the United States in combined totals of intercontinental missiles (ICBMs) and submarine-launched ballistic missiles (SLBMs). This build-up created some uneasiness. Some analysts feared that the Soviets were trying to build enough weapons to gain the capability for a disarming first strike. But this seemed highly doubtful given the maintenance of U.S. assured destruction capabilities. More sophisticated audiences speculated that the Soviets might seek political advantages by acquiring more weapons than the United States.

The dominant sentiment, however, was a sentiment not to race the Soviets but to put a cap to superpower arsenals, which led to the first Strategic Arms Limitations Talks (SALT). In the spirit of detente, the principles of equality and equal security were established to guide the negotiations. Yet because American negotiators were interested in real military capabilities, gaining precise numerical equality in all strategic areas was not a high priority. As a result, the 1972 interim agreement accepted Soviet numerical advantages in ICBMs and SLBMs because from a military point of view this asymmetry was more than offset by the much larger U.S. advantage in bombers and by American technological superiority.

Nevertheless, uneasiness persisted. The SALT talks had endorsed, to a degree, the importance of equality. The news media were consequently full of numerical comparisons suggesting that the U.S. arsenal was inferior, and Senate critics jumped on the issue. During ratification hearings nearly all analysts agreed that from a military point of view the accord benefited the United States. Some specialists, however, warned that the treaty's terms could create worldwide an image of the Soviet Union on the rise and could prompt allies to accommodate Soviet wishes during crises and in daily diplomacy. SALT I was approved but only after the Senate included an amendment, written by the late Washington Democrat Henry Jackson, that requested "the President to seek a future treaty that, inter alia, would not limit the United States to levels of intercontinental strategic forces inferior to the limits for the Soviet Union."

This measure's passage represented a crucial shift. Hitherto, the American defense posture had been at least ostensibly rooted in military reality. Traditional deterrence theory recognized the importance of perceptions in nuclear matters but primarily stressed the need for an adversary to recognize correctly American retaliatory capabilities and intentions. But the Jackson amendment demanded equality regardless of its military relevance. From this point perceptional priorities began to drive weapons procurement in a manner increasingly independent of real military considerations.

Tenets of Perception Theory

In 1972, during the SALT I debate, the Georgetown University Center for Strategic and International Studies (CSIS) released a report by strategist Edward Luttwak, *The Strategic Balance*, that articulated the key tenets of perception theory. Luttwak recognized that a near "consensus of strategic experts would undoubtedly answer that the United States has in fact conceded nothing" of military significance in the SALT I treaty. Yet such thinking, he argued, "totally discounted" the "prestige effects deriving from the possessions of strategic weapons" that are "psychologically by far the most impressive of all instruments of power." He claimed that "with informed public opinion the world over" there is "definite awareness that one side or the other has more. And 'more' is widely regarded as implying greater power."

Luttwak recognized not only that this balance is essentially a misdirected measure of political power but also that the balance is incorrectly assessed, writing: "Outside the narrow circle of the technical experts the balance of strategic power is not measured in operational terms. Gross numbers and crude qualitative factors provide only the indices of strategic power which are widely recognized." Rather than decrying the inevitable arms race that arises from this distorted perspective, however, he argued that the arms race is a "natural manifestation of political conflict."

This last conclusion is the core of perception theory: the "natural" response to misperceptions of the strategic balance is not an effort to correct them but an attempt to compete in this realm of perception by means of an ongoing arms race.

Such thinking quickly moved into policy circles. Former Secretary of Defense James Schlesinger enshrined the tenets of perception theory as official U.S. policy in his annual reports to Congress for fiscal years 1975 and 1976. Schlesinger began the fiscal 1975 report by expressing concern about the improvements the Soviets had made in their nuclear arsenal during the 1960s, and he called for appropriate U.S. countermeasures. He recognized that this situation did not create an immediate military threat because the Soviet Union did not and could not hope to be able to launch a disarming first strike. But he added that "there must be essential equivalence between the strategic forces of the United States and the USSR — an equivalence perceived not only by ourselves, but by the Soviet Union and third audiences as well."

Schlesinger's elaboration of this concern drew on the key ideas of perception theory. He wrote that there is "an important relationship between the political relationship of many leaders of other nations and what they perceive the strategic nuclear balance to be." Rather than correctly perceiving this balance, he said, many leaders "react to the static measures of relative force size, number of warheads, equivalent megatonnage, and so forth." He concluded, therefore, that "to the degree that we wish to influence the perception of others, we must take appropriate steps (by their lights) in the design of strategic forces." In other words, Schlesinger proposed that the United States adapt the design of its nuclear arsenal to the mistaken perceptual habits of these leaders rather than help them adapt their perceptual habits to reality.

Meanwhile, CSIS analysts were adding new twists to perception theory. In the 1975 study *World Power Assessment*, CSIS Executive Director Ray Cline argued that "a growing and innovative arsenal will be perceived as more powerful than one which is static — even if the latter still retains an advantage in purely technical terms."

This argument is explained by concern over the fact that as the Soviet Union strove to catch up with the United States, it was improving its arsenal at a faster rate. Even though in absolute terms the United States was still ahead, the fact that its forces were growing more slowly than the Soviets' could be perceptually problematic, and presumably would need to be remedied. Similarly, Luttwak has argued that in the realm of perceptions, "time is discounted." He continued: "The most direct consequence of discounting time is that in determining perceptions of military capabilities the impact of rates of change may equal or outweigh the impact of current capabilities."

To deal with such perceptual complexities, Luttwak proposed that the United States carry out perceptual impact analyses, with an eye to "enhancing the images of power they generate." He even argued that a cosmetic restructuring of American ground units to make them appear larger in number should not be ruled out. Luttwak reiterated: "Objective reality, whatever that may be, is simply irrelevant; only the subjective phenomena of perception and value-judgment count."[1]

Evidently, even these subtleties of perception theory influenced policymakers. In 1976 a group of hard-line defense analysts convened by the CIA reported that new accounting methods showed that the Soviets were spending twice the percent-age of their gross national product on defense as previously estimated. This percentage was also much higher than that of the U.S. defense budget. No new information emerged about the weaponry itself, only that it had cost the Soviets much more than had been thought. Nevertheless, a shrill alarm was sounded: Because Moscow appeared to be spending more on the military than Washington was, the United States should catch up by increasing its defense budget.

After Schlesinger left the Pentagon, perception theory remained a major ratio-nale for weapons deployment. In his fiscal 1978 report to Congress, Schlesinger's successor at the Pentagon, Donald Rumsfeld, recognized that not even the Soviet ICBM build-up posed the threat of a disarming first strike. But like Schlesinger and other believers in perception theory, he feared the dangerous international miscalculations these asymmetries might produce. Rather than attempting to clarify that asymmetrics do not necessarily constitute a military threat, however, he called for "actions to create the necessary perception of equivalence."

Despite President Jimmy Carter's public recognition that the U.S. arsenal far exceeded the requirements of deterrence, his secretary of defense, Harold Brown, also cited the basic principles of perception theory. Brown wrote in his fiscal 1979 report to Congress, "The United States and its allies must be free from any coercion and intimidation that could result from perceptions of an overall imbalance or particular asymmetries in nuclear forces." Further: "Insistence on essential equiv-alence guards against any danger that the Soviets might be seen as superior — even if the perception is not technically justified."

Naturally, as perceptions became increasingly important in Pentagon planning, attention turned to whether weapon procurements were having the desired percep-tual effect on important audiences. To find out, the Department of Defense sponsored several studies that in 1978 were published in a book entitled *Interna-tional Perceptions of the Superpower Military Balance.* Focusing on audiences in Europe, Japan, the Middle East, the Soviet Union, and the United States, the studies found much evidence that contradicted the assumptions of perception theory. But, adding yet another twist in the logic of perception theory, the authors were able to justify the theory and the weapons procurement once again.

One key question the studies addressed was whether "perceivers tend to think in terms of numerical comparisons of superpower military strength." Based on a variety of evidence the resulting volume concluded that "it is generally felt that both sides have more than enough." The researchers found that some groups even stated directly it is "moot to ask, 'Who is ahead?' in a situation of mutual nuclear overkill." Perhaps most important, the authors found virtually no evidence to support the idea that America's allies favored greater "accommodations with the Soviets" in response to perceived shifts in some balances away from U.S. favor." The authors also observed that Soviet officials have recognized that superiority had no real value in the face of mutual assured destruction and that "parity is not the issue at hand."

Yet the authors argued implicitly that it is still important to build arms in light of international perceptions. They suggested that although America's allies and the Soviet Union apparently attach no military importance to the strategic balance in an environment of overkill and do not consider themselves to be affected by whatever shifts they perceive in the balance, some countries nevertheless keep a close eye on the balance and look for signs of U.S. resolve to maintain it. These countries do so because they mistakenly believe that other key audiences regard the balance as militarily significant — even though these countries consider that belief to be wrong.

The argument strongly suggested that in international power relations, perceptions of the superpower military balance are the coinage of international affairs even though all the key parties involved seem to recognize that the coins are counterfeit. The situation resembles nothing so much as a drawing-room comedy. All of the key characters know a certain secret — that strategic asymmetries are militarily irrelevant in an age of overkill — but they think that because others do not know the secret they act as if they do not know the secret either. A farcical quality emerges as all the characters, more or less unconsciously, collude to establish a norm of behavior based on a failure to recognize the secret. What is particularly striking, though, is that when the main character — in this case the Defense Department — is informed that, in fact, everybody knows the secret, it stiffens its resolve to maintain the charade.

Is Victory Possible?

In reality the dynamic is probably more complex than in this drawing-room comedy. At senior levels in particular there is evidence that some U.S. officials do not really believe in the military value of the weapons they call for even though they present their arguments in the context of certain war fighting scenarios.

Nevertheless they argue, in a variant of perception theory, that the Soviets' capability to gain an advantage in such implausible scenarios may create serious political problems for the United States. These officials are not satisfied with having a retaliatory capacity effective enough to deter a rational Soviet leader. Instead, they call on the United States to offset the potential Soviet advantage by gaining the capability to end the scenario in an equal or even superior position.

One particularly prominent example is found in an article that Special Adviser to the President and Secretary of State on Arms Control Matters Paul Nitze wrote for *Foreign Affairs* in 1976. The scenario that concerned Nitze was one in which the Soviets would make a major counterforce strike against the United States, followed by an American counterforce retaliation. Nitze was concerned that "the Soviets could, by initiating such an exchange, increase the ratio" of the advantage they held at the start of the exchange in throw-weight (a missile's capacity to lift material into space).

Nitze was not putting forth the absurd proposition that the Soviets might launch an attack simply to improve their throw-weight ratio. Nor was he arguing that this Soviet throw-weight edge might represent a real disarming first-strike capability. He acknowledged that even after such a strike the remaining American weapons would still "be conducive to continued effective deterrence even if the ratios are unfavorable." Instead, Nitze believed that the Soviets were pursuing a "*theoretical* war-winning capability" and that the Soviets would "consider themselves duty bound by Soviet doctrine to exploit fully that strategic advantage" (emphasis added).

Nitze's argument seemed to focus primarily on the potential effects of intrawar imbalances on third audiences or perhaps even on the United States. Gradually, though, another argument emerged that focused on the effects that such potential imbalances might have on Soviet willingness actually to initiate a war. This concern was fanned by several articles that presented evidence that the Soviets did in fact believe it was possible to win a nuclear war.

A variant of perception theory soon emerged in response to this concern. Harold Brown expressed concern in his 1981 report to Congress that the Soviets might be entertaining thoughts that a nuclear war could be won even though "these leaders should know by now, as we learned some years ago, that a war-winning strategy . . . has no serious prospect of success." He argued that the United States must "counter" Soviet developments lest Moscow "succumb" to this "illusion." This response went beyond weapons procurement and included developing strategies for winning limited nuclear war by controlling the process of escalation. Yet it seems that Brown did not really believe such a strategy was realistic. He wrote: "In adopting and implementing this policy we have no more illusions than our predecessors that a nuclear war could be closely and surgically controlled." Apparently the purpose of the policy was simply to make a desired perceptual impact.

Other analysts went even further and argued that it is indeed possible to win even a longer nuclear war. Strategic analysts Colin Gray and Keith Payne boldly argued in an article in *Foreign Policy* in 1980 that "Victory is Possible" and that therefore the United States should have a "victory strategy" that "would contemplate the destruction of Soviet political authority and the emergence of a postwar world order compatible with Western values."

A victory strategy became the equivocal American position after Ronald Reagan became president. The classified version of the 1982 defense guidance statement reportedly called for plans to prevail not only in a limited nuclear war but also in a protracted conflict in which the United States would aim to "decapitate" the leadership of the Soviet Union. In his fiscal 1984 report to Congress, Defense Secretary Caspar Weinberger wrote that "should deterrence fail, our strategy is to restore peace on favorable terms. In responding to an enemy attack we must defeat the attack."

Even those American analysts who seemed to believe most strongly that a nuclear war could be won now appear to have been following a form of perception theory. In their article, Gray and Payne offered extremely little in the way of explanation of how an all-out nuclear war could be won. The only scenario they described was a traditional limited-war scenario in which intrawar deterrence principles would operate. Instead, their primary argument was that simply having a victory strategy would buttress deterrence. They argued that the Soviet leaders would be "impressed by a plausible American victory strategy" and that this would have "the desired deterrent effect."

As perception theory insinuated itself into defense thinking, the efforts to rationalize it became fewer. Weinberger's reports to Congress generally skipped the circuitous perception theory arguments made by his predecessors. Typical is his simple assertion, in his fiscal 1984 report, that "the critical point in deterring war and preventing aggression is maintaining a balance of forces." Weinberger's next sentence, however, reveals a new basis for supporting this statement: "History has shown us all too often that conflicts occur when one state believes it has a sufficiently greater military capability than another and attempts to exploit that superior strength through intimidation or conflict with that weaker state."

Weinberger and other Reagan administration officials were drawing on the traditional concept of the balance of power in international relations. This concept has been applied widely to numerous historical situations in which conventional military imbalances, such as those in Europe during the late 1930s, played an important role in precipitating war.

Yet applying this concept to nuclear superpower relations, especially in an age of mutual overkill, is questionable. In conventional conflicts the outcome of a battle can often be predicted by comparing such factors as numerical troop strengths of opposing sides. In a nuclear war fought by greatly redundant arsenals, the weapons of both sides can inflict cataclysmic damage regardless of force levels.

Perception theory seems to have played a large part in creating this confusion. Perception theory argued that the nuclear balance was politically relevant because people mistakenly believed it was militarily relevant. But from the start, these fine distinctions were blurred, and many strategists and political leaders alike simply asserted that the nuclear balance is intrinsically important, just as a prenuclear conventional balance was. In other words, it appears that perception theory led many to believe in the illusion that it had so carefully described. The balance itself, not retaliatory nuclear capability, was portrayed as somehow preventing war. Thus Reagan said in a May 10, 1984, address, "As long as we maintain the strategic balance . . . *then* we can count on the basic prudence of the Soviet leaders to avoid [nuclear war]" (emphasis added). British Prime Minister Margaret Thatcher told the House of Commons, "The principle is a balance in order to deter."[2]

The most dangerous form of this thinking is the belief that balancing one weapon with a similar weapon somehow creates a defense against the first weapon or prevents its usage. Commenting on the Soviet SS-20 missiles, Reagan said that "the only answer to these systems is a comparable threat to Soviet threats." He did not explain, however, why a comparable threat is the best answer, much less the "only answer."

The MX and INF Controversies

No strategic controversies have better demonstrated the importance of perception theory than those over the MX (missile experimental) and intermediate-range nuclear forces (INFs) in Europe. The most persistent rationale for the MX was that it was needed to offset the growing theoretical vulnerability of America's land-based deterrent. MX advocates initially claimed, among other things, that the missile did offer the important military benefit of decreasing the vulnerability of U.S. counterforce weapons and making the Soviets think harder before striking first. By surviving a Soviet knockout attempt, the MX would give a president the classic counterforce option of retaliating against Soviet military targets and would create the possibility that nuclear war could be stopped before attacks on population centers began.

The Report of the President's Commission on Strategic Forces (the Scowcroft Commission), however, clearly rejected this argument. The commission concluded that the MX could not be protected. Thus, virtually the entire military rationale for the MX collapsed. If the Soviets were to launch a first strike, those missiles would be among the first targets hit. The commissioners further deemphasized the missile's military value by tacitly affirming that without it the United States still had adequate retaliatory capability.

And yet the commissioners concluded that the MX should be built nonetheless. They argued that the Soviet counterforce superiority constituted a "serious imbalance" that "must be redressed promptly." They recognized that "in a world in which the balance of strategic nuclear forces could be isolated from [political considerations], a nuclear imbalance would have little importance." But with an air of philosophical regret they supported building the MX because "the overall perception of strategic imbalance . . . has been reasonably regarded as destabilizing and as a weakness in the overall fabric of deterrence." They based their view, in other words, on perception theory.

The deployment of Pershing IIs and ground-launched cruise missiles (GLCMs) in Western Europe also was heavily influenced by perception theory. Indeed, in 1977, the West German Chancellor Helmut Schmidt called for new deployments in Europe in response to the placement of Soviet SS-20s aimed at Europe. In a critical speech in London he said, "SALT neutralizes [the superpowers'] strategic nuclear capabilities. In Europe, this magnifies the significance of the disparities between East and West."

Apparently his logic was derived from the perception theory principle that a missile on one side politically cancels out, or using Schmidt's word, "neutralizes," a missile on the other side. Thus the SS-20s allegedly constituted a major new threat to Europe. But from a military point of view this was clearly not the case. Even under the worst possible scenarios the United States would still have thousands of forward based and central strategic weapons with which to strike the kinds of targets for which the SS-20s were designed.

Some important military rationales for INF deployments have been advanced. But as Robert Jervis pointed out in his 1984 study, *The Illogic of American Nuclear Strategy*, the two dominant rationales not only suffer intrinsic problems but also directly contradict each other. One rationale argued that placing missiles in Western Europe would more closely couple U.S. strategic forces to Western Europe's defense because a Soviet invasion would supposedly force Washington to use its nuclear missiles or lose them, thus ensuring escalation to a strategic exchange. At the same time INF proponents claimed that the missiles were needed so that, should the Soviets strike Europe with intermediate-range missiles, NATO would have the option of retaliating in kind. Perhaps then the conflict might stay limited to Europe. But this idea directly contradicted the first rationale that sought to make escalation to a strategic exchange more certain.

Perception theory, however, offered a rationale that seemed to have fewer problems and gradually it became dominant. Former Defense Secretary Robert McNamara, in a 1983 article in *Newsweek*, supported the INF deployments saying, "There is no military requirement for NATO to deploy the Pershing IIs and cruise missiles. . . . The Europeans are operating on a misperception, but as long as it is held, it must be treated as a reality." Apparently this kind of thinking was shared by State Department officials. When Richard Burt, Assistant Secretary of State for European and Canadian affairs, was told that Pershing II deployment might have to be delayed because of continuing technical problems, he reportedly said, "We don't care if the goddamn things work or not. After all, that doesn't matter unless there's a war. What we care about is getting them in."[3]

Maintaining Illusions

Perhaps the most striking and questionable feature of perception theory is its recommendation for dealing with the supposedly widespread illusion that nuclear and conventional weapons are not fundamentally different. The idea that the illusion should be actively dispelled seems never to be seriously considered. Instead, perception theorists propose that the informed elite not caught up in the illusion should play along with the illusion as if it were real. They sometimes suggest that the illusion must be protected or even actively promoted.

Playing along, however, creates some curious problems. The illusion holds that there is a military requirement for more nuclear weapons. Therefore, the task of the military establishment is a real, business-as-usual military task and not a psychological one. Perception theory calls for the military to carry on in a manner consistent with the illusion in order to create the impression that the United States is moving forward in the arms competition and meaningfully increasing its force effectiveness. Yet as perception theorists have pointed out, frequently the military preoccupation with real force effectiveness leads to weapons procurement decisions that undermine some of the desired effects of perception theory.

A recent example is provided by the furor over the fact that the overall megatonnage and throw-weight of the U.S. arsenal is lower than the Soviets'. Perception theorists have worried about the perceptual impact of this imbalance and have pressed for correcting it. What is rarely mentioned is that in the past the American arsenal boasted three times its present megatonnage. Megatonnage was reduced because it made good military sense to shift to smaller, more accurate missiles as American technological progress afforded this option.

The problem stems not from faulty communication within the system but from a built-in contradiction in the logic of perception theory. To make the right perceptual impact the military must act as if it believes it is building nuclear arms for traditional military purposes. This leads the military to make decisions like the one to reduce megatonnage in light of improvements in accuracy. But when the military makes weapons procurement decisions consistent with the role perception theory wants it to play, it frequently builds weapons that do not make the right perceptual impact. One can only speculate how many billions of dollars have been spent as the vast defense establishment has loped its way through the endless circles of this logic.

Despite the problems inherent in trying to go along with the illusion, perception theorists have gone to extraordinary lengths to protect it. Supposedly one political problem that perception theory addresses is that the masses and political leaders are caught in the illusion that asymmetries between the superpower arsenals make a real difference for security. The knowledge that this is an illusion is limited to an elite who must perform what Luttwak calls "perceptual manipulations" upon the masses.

So how have perception theorists responded now that large segments of the masses have broken out of this illusion? What have they done when the argument that more nuclear weapons are militarily useless has become the stuff of slogans, picket signs, and bumper stickers? Have they welcomed this general enlightenment? Quite the contrary. Instead, they have mounted a countercampaign to offset what they depicted as a dangerous effort to enlighten the rest of the public.

Interestingly, one of the most common epithets hurled at nuclear activists is that they are naive, not incorrect, in their claims that more nuclear weapons are useless. This seems to imply that the truly intelligent thing to do is not to try to undermine this widely held illusion but rather to quietly join the ranks of the elite who wisely manipulate perceptions within the context of this illusion.

At times, perception theorists go further and even actively promote the illusion. Some defense analysts and certain government officials have played a major role in promoting the idea not only that the military balance is important but also that the American arsenal is dangerously inferior to the Soviet Unions'. It was noted in the previously mentioned Defense Department-sponsored study of international perceptions that American spokesmen and publications played a major role in shaping perceptions in Soviet and NATO audiences. But the authors observed that "the tendency of many U.S. spokesmen (particularly government officials at budget time) to emphasize Soviet strengths and U.S. weaknesses often had a negative impact on the perceived U.S. standing."

This behavior seems to contradict completely a key principle of perception theory, namely, that what is supremely important for deterrence and for all aspects of American foreign policy is that the United States be perceived by all people of the world as strong and ever capable of launching unacceptably destructive retaliatory attacks. Logically, to maintain this perception, government officials should brag publicly about the extraordinary power and invincibility of the American deterrent, buttressing their claims, of course, by extensive documentation. Presenting the United States as weak and vulnerable should be anathema. The peculiar logic of perception theory, however, has led the defense establishment to do just that.

Schlesinger sought to explain this apparent contradiction. He conceded in an August 1981 *Time* article that this emphasis on American weakness "is a self-inflicted wound," but he went on to say that "one of the penalties of a democracy is that we have to call public attention to the problem in order to get the necessary remedies."

As Arthur May Cox noted in his book *Russian Roulette*, this kind of thinking has led to a Catch-22. The original problem that needs to be remedied, according to perception theory, is the perception of inadequacy, not inadequate weaponry. The purpose of new weaponry is to modify this perception. But in order to galvanize support for expenditures that are meant to modify this misperception, the misperception is intentionally enhanced. Remedying the problem thus requires making the problem worse.

The variant of perception theory that calls for a victory strategy runs into the same problem. According to this idea, to make the desired perceptual impact, one that intimidates and deters adversaries and reassures allies, officials must project the image of believing that a nuclear war can be won. At the same time, to maintain the support needed to acquire the weaponry necessary to project this belief, officials must be on good terms with the public. Yet the public becomes uncomfortable when officials talk about winning nuclear wars. Therefore, it is necessary to explicitly disavow that "victory is possible." In short, government officials must create the perception domestically that they believe a nuclear war cannot be won because this is the only way they can obtain the support necessary to build the weapons needed to create the perception globally that they believe a nuclear war can be won.

But what is the alternative to a perception theory saddled with these problems of logic? The answer may be as simple as stating that the emperor has no clothes. Even if perception theorists are entirely correct in claiming that key audiences are caught up in the illusion that the strategic balance is critical or that a nuclear war can be won, it does not necessarily follow that the best response is to enter into this illusion and compete within it. It is possible to play it straight and effectively work to dispel the illusion.

This would require an active effort to inform all key audiences about the real nature of nuclear weapons, the irrelevance of most asymmetries in the strategic balance in a mutual overkill environment, and the impossibility of winning a nuclear war. Such an effort, of course, would easily be buttressed by a simple presentation of facts. Most important, though, U.S. weapons procurement and strategy for selecting targets would be adjusted to these realities. Only these concrete adjustments would give American assertions of these realities any genuine credibility.

If the Soviets attempted to gain political advantages by continuing their build-up unilaterally, the United States would respond not by matching the build-up--except to counteract any real military threats to American retaliatory capabilities--but rather by dispelling any notions that the Soviets were gaining any real military advantage. American restraint and realism would, of course, give this assertion real credibility. Restraint also would put the United States in a strong position to turn world public opinion against such Soviet efforts and could ultimately produce political benefits for America.

Space permits listing only a few key components of a realistic weapons procurement policy. First, the focus would move away from comparing numbers of weapons on each side and instead would center on the number of survivable American warheads in relation to the number of meaningful Soviet targets. The required number might change if the Soviet developments significantly reduced the number of American warheads that could survive a first strike. The American response, however, would emphasize the capability to threaten Soviet targets rather than replicating Soviet weapons.

Second, the strategies for target selection that the procured weapons would support would be based only on plausible scenarios, which are difficult, but not impossible, to define. This standard will permit strategic debaters to clash over the merits of highly flexible counterforce doctrines that tend to lower the nuclear threshold versus assured-destruction-based doctrines that seek to raise it. But the standard would not permit arguing for the necessity of maximum flexibility within the context of extraordinarily implausible scenarios. Nor would it accept arguments for a victory strategy based on scenarios that only an irrational adversary could regard as plausible. As has been frequently noted, deterrence can never be counted on to defend against an irrational adversary. Even if the Soviet Union is simply attempting to gain political advantage by appearing more irrational than America, America need not and should not follow suit. Further, eschewing a victory strategy and introducing corresponding appropriate restraint in U.S. weapons procurement would add credibility to the effort to dissipate any lingering illusions the public might be holding about issues like nuclear victory.

This playing-it-straight approach is less apt than perception theory to drive the arms race on its current dangerous course. The preoccupation with maintaining perceptions of strategic equality between the United States and the Soviet Union seems unexceptionable, but it has become an engine of the nuclear competition. This effect can arise from a genuine failure to understand how the adversary assesses the balance, which leads each side into an endless game of catch-up. But it probably arises more often from an effort to be "more equal" than the adversary. By framing an issue in terms of indexes in which one's own side is inferior and simultaneously ignoring indexes in which it is superior, superiority can be pursued in the name of equality.

Indeed, by placing such a premium on the military balance, perception theory actually hands the Soviets an advantage. It effectively validates the idea that the key arena for superpower competition is one in which the Soviets compete particularly well.

Finally, perception theory ultimately promotes the Soviet war-winning ideas that the United States has correctly identified as dangerous. Perception theorists claim that the best response to Soviet belief in war-winning is to project the same belief in the form of a victory strategy and corresponding weapons procurements. If the purpose of American actions is to disabuse the Soviets of this mistaken belief, the United States should not give the idea greater credence by espousing a victory strategy itself. If anything, this course of action is more likely to reinforce mistaken Soviet beliefs and thereby increase the danger perception theorists want to counteract. A more logical approach would be to state firmly and unambiguously that a nuclear war cannot be won and to make the American arsenal and strategies for picking targets consistent with this belief.

A Quick Fix

But why, if the logic is so dubious, the costs so high, and the benefits so questionable, does the United States play along with the illusion and continue the arms race?

Many suggested answers to these questions stress the sheer momentum of the arms race, the defense establishment's opposition to any letup, and the financial interests of defense industry contractors. Other theories point to the presence, in the Pentagon and especially among Reagan appointees, of an influential group of hard-liners who still hope to win the arms race and somehow bring about the end of the Soviet system. While these ideas offer some insight, none explains why the country as a whole continues to support the arms race.

Perception theory suggests that the public supports the arms race because it does not understand the reality of nuclear weapons. Apparently, however, the public does grasp nuclear realities. In a Public Agenda Foundation poll published in September 1984, 90% of respondents agreed that "we and the Soviets now have enough nuclear weapons to blow each other up many times over"; 89% agreed that there can be no winner in an all-out nuclear war"; and 83% agreed that even "a limited nuclear war is nonsense."

At the same time 71% of those polled agreed that the United States should continue to develop "new and better nuclear weapons." Why does the public continue to support an arms race it knows is pointless, and leaders who obviously obfuscate the realities of nuclear weapons?

Perhaps the answer is this: Americans hope to get relief from the overarching and terrible fact that they face an extraordinary threat to their survival and there is nothing they can do about it. If the Soviets should decide that they want to destroy the United States, they can do so in a matter of minutes. America can make counterthreats, but in the final analysis, there is no reliable defense against nuclear weapons. Psychologists have found that when people face a threat to which they cannot effectively respond, they tend to generate the illusion that there is some meaningful action they can take to reduce the threat. This can lead to certain kinds of irrational thinking in which they believe the threat to be counteracted by actions that do not reduce the threat or that sometimes even exacerbate it. At times, a vague rationality spurs these actions—for example, repeating an action that at one time did, or in other circumstances would, actually reduce the threat.

The American public may be hooked on the quick fix of illusory security that arms building provides. Every report that the Soviets have increased the size of their arsenal makes it almost inconceivable for the United States not to "do something"—especially since in the past, building more weapons did increase a country's security. Moreover, the enormity of the effort to match the Soviets gives it a certain credibility and, like the "big lie" makes it easier for each person to believe that someone, someplace, must truly understand the point of this excessive arms building. At the same time, however, it appears that Americans do know, at some level, that building more arms is not really enhancing their security. Expanding nuclear arsenals at best only makes them feel that this is so.

Thus perhaps the arms race has not been foisted on a passive American public. Perhaps the defense establishment has actually responded to a subtle mandate to obfuscate the reality of American vulnerability. Perhaps the defense that Americans wish the Pentagon to maintain is less a military defense against foreign aggressors than a psychological defense against an awareness that they have not yet assimilated.

Of course, if this awareness should take root, the implications would be profound. It could well lead to a greater realization that nuclear weapons, by making the major countries so vulnerable to each other, have altered the systematic features of geopolitical reality. What is required, then, is no less than a reconsideration of the role of force in international relations. The extent to which Americans and others avoid the awareness of this vulnerability suggests real apprehension about the changes this realization would entail. There are no simple solutions and no one can blindly claim that the future will be better. Consequently, eschewing the ineffective placebo of reflexive arms building may create some anxiety. But perhaps, by finally swallowing the medicine of vulnerability, humanity will at least greet the future having removed some of these veils of self-deception from its eyes.

Notes

1. Edward Luttwak, "Perceptions of Military Force and U.S. Policy," in Luttwak, *Strategy and Politics: Collected Essays* (New Brunswick, NJ: Transaction Books, 1980), 54-60.

2. In Strobe Talbott, *Deadly Gambits* (New York: Alfred A. Knopf, 1984), 172-173.

3. Ibid., 187.

Chapter 16

The Psychological Effects of Bombing on Civilian
Populations: Unlimited and Other Future Wars

GEORGE H. QUESTER

As we speculate about grisly futures, we must look at the attacks on civilians which have already occurred (i.e. high explosive and incendiary bombs), at those which were anticipated but then withheld on the basis of a curious mutual restraint (chemical warfare), and then also at those of which we have had only the smallest of foretastes (the use of nuclear weapons, which now would vastly exceed the explosive power of the A-bombs dropped on Hiroshima and Nagasaki). It is relatively easy to discuss the impact of attacks in which all mutual restraints are erased. Rather than simply being subject to depression, the people bombed might well then be subject to freezing and starvation, where the initial blast and fire had not taken their lives.

Civil defense in all these circumstances is apt to be much less successful than the efforts of World War II, or the civil defense operations we have seen within the United States in the aftermath of hurricanes, floods, and tornadoes.[1] Hurricanes and tornadoes never strike the entire country in a single night, and floods always leave intact the high ground. Hiroshima was the only Japanese city to be struck with an atomic bomb on August 6, 1945 and Nagasaki was the only city so struck on August 9. For any future nuclear war, the lessons extracted from the performances of bombed populations in World War II might thus tempt us to anticipate a better outcome than will actually occur.[2]

Yet, it is by no means certain that the next assault on cities in this world will include all the worst of these forms of attack. The logic of mutual restraint is now very powerful, as each side senses an interest in maintaining the other side's interest in practicing restraints, and thus practices restraints of its own. High-explosive bombs and incendiaries may come into use again, with greater restraints than one saw in World War II. As noted, U.S. B-52s over Vietnam carried bomb loads greatly exceeding those of World War II, but these bombings were far more carefully aimed and orchestrated. Chemical weapons may come into use, but not over urban areas where such use would be too obvious in the court of world opinion. Nuclear weapons may come into use, but might still be employed in less than all-out attacks, as only some cities were destroyed, or only targets away from cities were attacked.

Any rational considerations in a bombing exchange thus have to entail some vested interest in the future. Someone who has been killed has no future. Someone who has undergone such enormous personal losses that he does not care anymore has no future. Those who are making decisions in any war will have to take this into account, whether the war remains conventional, or has crossed the line to introduce nuclear weapons. The target planner on each side has acquired means of holding destructive potential in reserve, on board submarines if nowhere else. Only if such destruction can be threatened, but has not yet been inflicted, can it be harnessed for political purposes, as the termination of wars and the outlines of future peace are being negotiated.

This retention of a reserve of destruction, yet to be inflicted, took care of itself during World War II, as no one was ever capable of destroying all the cities of the other side in a single day. Even at Hiroshima and Nagasaki, the nuclear weapons available to the United States were limited. Nagasaki basically exhausted the U.S. stockpile, as the next bomb might not have been available for several weeks — the United States was bluffing in suggesting a pace of "one nuclear attack every three days."

To discuss possibilities of a "limited nuclear war" is typically to invite a great deal of ridicule.[3] Advocates of planning for such a war, as part of strengthening the American political position for some future crisis, are often accused of underestimating the side effects of any use of nuclear weapons, or of overrating the calmness and precision with which such weapons can be controlled and directed, once they have come into use.

Yet my intent here is not to advocate such an introduction of nuclear weapons, or to argue that escalation can be reliably controlled. The premise instead is that it is *not* automatically or inevitably true that such a limited use would lead to all-out nuclear war; any predictions about the impact of future aerial attacks must consider and accept *some* probability that nuclear weapons would be hitting only designated targets and not others.

Perhaps the use of nuclear weapons would be kept confined to some geographically limited arena of fighting (one nightmare of Eastern and Western Europeans is that such weapons would come into use only in Germany and Poland, and not the United States or the USSR). Perhaps they would be fired at the homelands of the two superpowers, but only at the opposing strategic nuclear forces, as each side makes an effort to go counterforce and disarm the other.

The collateral damage and side effects of such a war would still be horrendous. Estimates that the American civilian casualties in such a limited Soviet nuclear attack would be "only" 800,000 seem to be very unrealistic with tens of millions being much more plausible. Yet the difference between 10 million and 80 million is also hardly trivial, and this difference (apart from how it affects our values in life) could also translate into major differences in the psychological impact on the survivors.

The survivors would realize that a disaster had befallen their country and the globe. Even limited use of nuclear weapons will introduce one side effect which has not been experienced in warfare to date, radioactive fallout, forcing ordinary people to take shelter in basements for days and weeks, cut off from contact with friends and neighbors, cut off from fresh food and contact with the outside world. At the same time some such survivors will wonder why their own city did not get destroyed more directly in the thermonuclear exchange. Does this mean that the other side is short of ammunition? Or is the adversary desperately intent on trying to win a counterforce exchange, and correspondingly intent on minimizing the unnecessary countervalue exchange for the meantime? What have our missiles done to their side in the interim?

Nothing is beyond imagination for the nuclear war scenario,[4] with most of our imagination necessarily having to sink into greater pessimism here. Yet it is not beyond belief that some versions of a limited nuclear war could again lead to "less bad news than expected," with whatever this entails for countering panic or depression, or for the stiffening commitments to one's own government, for looking forward to victory, etc.

As in the London Blitz, we must contrast the objective change with the subjective surprise. The world is suddenly more chaotic and confusing, with all of one's normal habits and patterns of movement and communication and recreation being disrupted. Yet what if the ensuing disaster is of lesser magnitude than it was expected to be? To what extent does the latter impact outweigh and counteract the former?

The "Irrationality" of Retaliation

Much has been written about the illogic of revenge where a nuclear war is concerned. If an adversary has destroyed most of our cities in a nuclear missile attack, when good could it do our country to destroy most of his cities? The survivors will only have their lot worsened by a retaliatory response, forfeiting any help they might have received from the other side.

Indeed retaliation is generally not a rational act. By the execution of a "threat" we punish our adversary, but at a loss for ourselves as well. The threat is thus something that we will execute only because we said we would.

Let us illustrate the difference within an ordinary neighborhood situation. If a neighbor several times failed to appear when it was his turn to drive for a carpool, we might simply discontinue the carpool because his irresponsibility made him a bad partner. This is *not* the response we have labeled a "threat" or retaliation, because it is a response that makes perfect sense; the response is simply protecting one's own interests in terms of apparent probabilities, rather than "cutting off one's nose to spite one's face."

If we instead decided to punish our neighbor's irresponsibility by terminating our participation in his bridge club, this might also "teach him a lesson." But it would be more than a simple natural response on our part; it would rather be an additional sacrifice of our own interest, to ensure that his interest was damaged.

Such moves of spite are often made to seem childish and silly even in ordinary life. Yet such retaliation can make perfect sense in ordinary life, if the reputation for such retaliation induces other people to stick more closely to their obligations. We quit the bridge club so that other people will realize that we are not to be trifled with. If someone capriciously fails to deliver what he promised, we strike back, for otherwise this offender or other observers might conclude that we will be handy victims for anyone's caprice. Actions which cost one in the short run thus can make sense for broader purposes in the long run.

Threats work best, of course, when they never have to be executed, when their mere potential steers other parties in the direction we desire; for then we have the enhanced behavior of others, and still have no actual costs to bear. (We are leaving undiscussed for the moment the psychological disutility imposed on others by the mere contemplation of what we have been threatening.) Threats work terribly if they are made too often in situations where they are apt to be challenged. Threats work fairly well when they have to be executed only every once in a while, serving as a timely reminder that we intend to require certain behavior of others.

The rationality of executing threats thus relates very much to repeated encounters, as "the lesson" taught in the execution of a threat may produce more acceptable behavior from others in many rounds for the future. The problem with all-out nuclear war is that there may not be any significant people left on the other side to learn such lessons, and there may also be no one on our side to benefit from having taught such lessons.

However much sense it may make to pronounce a threat for purposes of deterrence (for example, "if you destroy my cities, I will destroy yours," or "if you seize control of West Berlin, we will destroy your cities"), the logic of going through with such threats, should deterrence fail, is far less clear. It may make sense to kick someone who has kicked us on the street. It may under almost any circumstance make little or no sense to devastate the Soviet Union.

Where logic does not apply, does psychology bring any important force to bear? Where someone has hurt us we may also be guided by an elementary emotional need for revenge. We "feel better" when we "get even," and very few of us spend much time asking *why* we feel better. Is it simply because we have so many times gone through the more explicit ends-oriented logic of the need to "teach lessons," so that our immediate craving for "revenge" as an end in itself is merely a conditioned reflex? Will this reflex persist, even where the revenge no longer will work as the means to any more material or longer term end? Will some be so demoralized that they no longer even care for revenge?

The data from the World War II bombings of London and other cities is suggestive. Several studies noted that those who had suffered a close personal loss, or had undergone a very near miss, were less inclined to demand revenge; they were more inclined to be numb and purposeless about the entire exchange, or resentful of all others and resentful of their own government. The demand for revenge, on the other hand, was often greater away from the portions of cities that had been hit hardest.[5] People who had suffered a distant miss (seeing enemy bombs strike more than a half mile away) were more inclined to continue the struggle of wills, the endurance contest of spiteful impositions of pain.

Leaders, too, motivated by the prospect of future interactions in international contests, motivated also (as noted above) by a special interest that their tenure in office might depend on the entire nation's "coming out ahead," would typically be more in the mood to stick it out, and hit back.

Yet it is possible that in nuclear exchanges even the leaders would find the East-West conflict had lost much of its significance, once a substantial amount of nuclear destruction had been suffered on one side or both. Concerns about being reelected might fade after a missile salvo had made it impossible for anyone to leave their fallout shelters on the next scheduled election day. When deterrence has failed, one must now decide whether to devastate a great number of cities on the other side "to get even." If the president of the United States were to respond as the survivors of the London Blitz, or of the fire bombings of Dresden or Tokyo, or of Hiroshima and Nagasaki responded, it is not so certain that revenge will be such a predominant motive.

Discussions of this topic normally draw the analyst to a different part of the picture, pertaining to communications and perceptions, rather than values and motivations. Communications could be so disrupted by a nuclear attack that no one feels in touch with what is happening. This could simply be a cybernetic overload, in the sheer chaos of the aftermath of such an attack. Perhaps a clever use of nuclear warheads would disrupt all the electronic communications links on one side or the other. Or perhaps the impact of grief, on all high-level officials, would make them incapable of rendering any decisions in any direction.

The social scientists may be able to make something out of this paradox, by which the ultimate in aggression against us might vitiate our reasons for getting even. Happily for world peace, no briefer in the Politburo will be able to offer a plausible or air-tight case that the American motivation for revenge would be totally lacking. Revenge will remain a very *possible* driving force, given all of what applied in the normal life of the day before. Such revenge can never be excluded, and deterrence indeed depends on it not being excluded.[6]

We must thus still rely on an instinct for revenge, even if we cannot put our finger on what its exact logical nature and basis might be. Since 1949, we have worried about a nuclear war mainly if one side or the other were to feel capable of a counterforce attack so devastating and accurate that its victims were *incapable* of hitting back with nuclear warheads of their own. We have not found ourselves worrying very much that one side or the other would simply go countervalue in its first strike, aiming to taking all the purpose out of life for the victims, so that they would somehow be *disinclined* to hit back with their nuclear warheads.

As we try to compare the impact of nuclear war with the earlier bombings from which we draw lessons, the most important fact remains that the nuclear devastation will be very much greater than anything experienced, thus making all inferences from the past perilous. The bombed populations of World War II were indeed surprisingly plucky, as compared to what had been predicted, and were largely willing to hit back and continue the war. But this was because World War II bombings were surprisingly tame. World War III bombings may be surprisingly catastrophic. All in all, as noted, this opens some important academic questions about the linkages of deterrence. We can all pray that these questions remain academic.

Notes

1. A discussion of the social responses to natural disasters can be found in H. E. Moore, *Tornadoes Over Texas* (Austin: University of Texas Press, 1958).

2. On the changes introduced with the nuclear factor, see Lester Grinspoon, "Fallout Shelters and the Unacceptability of Disquieting Facts" and Robert Jay Lifton, "Psychological Effects of the Atomic Bomb at Hiroshima" in *The Threat of Impending Disaster*, eds. George H. Grosser, Henry Wechsler, and Milton Greenblatt (Cambridge: MIT Press, 1964), 117-130, 152-193.

3. A very skeptical interpretation of the chances for keeping any nuclear war limited can be found in Louis Rene Beres, *Mimicking Sisyphus: America's Countervailing Nuclear Strategy* (Lexington, MA: Lexington Books, 1983).

4. For a well-developed argument that nuclear wars might be less bad than our worst expectations, see Herman Kahn, *On Thermonuclear War* (Princeton, NJ: Princeton University Press, 1960). For a more recent, and more pessimistic view, see Office of Technology Assessment, *The Effects of Nuclear War* (Washington, DC: Government Printing Office, 1979).

5. See Irving L. Janis, "Psychological Effects of Warnings" in *Man and Society in Disaster*, eds. G. W. Baker and D. W. Chapman (New York: Basic Books, 1962), 103-109, 127-137.

6. On the threat that leaves something to chance, see Thomas C. Schelling, *The Strategy of Conflict* (Cambridge, MA: Harvard University Press, 1960), 187-203.

Chapter 17

Away from Goodness: Problems of Control in Nuclear War

PETER C. SEDERBERG

Roger Boisjoly, the Morton Thiokol engineer who warned against launching the Challenger space shuttle in cold weather fearing the seals on the rocket boosters might fail, testified his superiors demanded that he produce the technical data supporting his contention. He replied he had no quantitative evidence, but he knew that the cold temperatures represented a move "away from goodness." Similarly, when we speculate on the operational, political, and psychological conditions that would characterize a nuclear war, we enter a realm of largely data-free analysis. Yet most analysts would concur with the judgment that the decision making environment would definitely be moving away from goodness.

Somewhat paradoxically, however, the absence of data obscures our recognition of uncertainty.[1] Without the discipline imposed by observation, conclusions will largely be determined by assumptions, and the range of assumptions made about the nature of a hypothetical nuclear war is essentially indefinite. The severity of the problems of control in a nuclear war depend particularly on both the intensity of the presumed war and the meaning of control. Once these have been specified, a commentator can derive reasonably persuasive conclusions about the control problem.

While it may be impossible to avoid a degree of circular reasoning, in this essay we attempt to mitigate it, first, by taking the control problem seriously; that is, we do not resolve it by definition. Second, the problems of control we identify are considered tendencies which intensify as the nuclear exchanges become more severe.

I. Control for What?

The objectives of control (conventionally denoted as C^3I, command, control, communications, and intelligence) can be defined in several ways, but two of them are not especially interesting. The first of these might be termed *managing Armageddon*. Specifically, the control task in this situation means that retaliation be assured against a major countervalue, counterforce, or countercommand strike from the other side. None of these would be particularly "limited," in that the targets would number in the hundreds, if not thousands, and the immediate casualties in the millions.[2]

The control problem in this extreme case involves designing a system capable of carrying out severe retaliation even if it is directly attacked or is disrupted by the effects of thousands of nuclear explosions. The broad consensus seems to be that control for assured destruction is robust; that is, we have a sufficiently invulnerable, "dumb" capability.[3] No rational adversary could count on being able to decapitate or declaw our nuclear forces sufficiently to avoid an unacceptable risk of unacceptable damage.

The capacity to retaliate after suffering a major nuclear strike, to be sure, fails to resolve the additional question of whether it would be prudent or moral to do so. We can persuasively argue that retaliation would only make a calamitous situation even worse. In addition, designing a system to carry out severe retaliation even as its capacity to coordinate and control surviving nuclear forces is disappearing (a so-called "fail-deadly" system) might well increase the risk of unintended escalation. Finally, the very catastrophic character of a major nuclear exchange may make it the most unlikely variation of what we hope is the generally remote possibility of nuclear war.

The second uninteresting nuclear control situation is that of *managing peripheral nuclear war*. If we assume a nuclear exchange "sufficiently" small and remote from the core interests of the nuclear superpowers, the distinctive control problems obviously diminish.[4] Essentially, the problem of nuclear war control is "conventionalized" in a number of ways: The nuclear devices used are small and accurate, thus blurring the distinction between nuclear and conventional weapons. The strategic and tactical context is usually construed in conventional terms. Finally, the geographic location of the exchange is generally assumed to be far from the superpowers' backyards.

In such a war, the control problems approximate those in a conventional conflict. Successful control demands an intelligent, but not necessarily invulnerable, control system. While the provision of a smart, if vulnerable, control system may present problems (as evident in the American operation in Grenada), it does not present the challenge of providing for a nuclear control system that is both invulnerable and smart.

The most serious problems of control exist in nuclear wars that lie between these two extremes; that is, a nuclear war between the superpowers that has not been definitionally relegated to either the conventional or the catastrophic. Specifically, we need to deal with a major military conflict that involves nuclear strikes against core interests (essentially, though not entirely, homeland targets). Under these admittedly underspecified conditions, what factors militate against escalation control? What undermines control for *politically meaningful war limitation*?

A politically meaningful limited nuclear war, as Arthur Katz notes elsewhere in this volume, is one that leaves the political, as well as the economic and social, structures of the adversaries essentially intact. Those who draw distinctions between a nuclear war that promptly kills "only" 25 million Americans, as opposed to 100 million, or who talk assuredly of the survival of the human species, even if the societies of the Northern hemisphere might be devastated, are not speaking in politically meaningful terms. Rather, they are dealing in a different realm of the amount of biomass destroyed. This may be significant, but, after some point, not to the states involved in a nuclear war. From the perspective of the German state, World War II was not meaningfully limited in its consequences, in that the regime was destroyed and the national territory dismembered.

Ian Clark argues that limitation entails two interrelated missions: First, the impact of the war must be limited so that the economic, social, and political structures of the contenders are not utterly destroyed. Second, the war must be terminated before one or both sides are utterly exhausted.[5] Given current super-power capabilities, this means a meaningfully limited nuclear war must be substantially less severe than the one the arsenals make possible.

Great power limited nuclear war requires that the participants consciously "hobble" their efforts, in contrast with prior centuries where limited conflict often emerged from the inherent limits on the power of the contestants.[6] Unfortunately, nuclear weapons "are inherently un-Clauswitzian: they resist disciplined use or service to political purposes. Their violence is too vast and too indiscriminate to serve wartime political aims."[7]

II. Problems of Control

Historical, political, strategic, technical-operational, and psychological factors appear to subvert efforts to control both consequences and duration of a nuclear war.

HISTORICAL PROBLEMS

Historically, our experience with great power wars of the 20th century is not encouraging. Granted the difficulty in generalizing from a case or two; nonetheless, the available evidence suggests that the trends are in the wrong direction. "Big power wars," Thomas Powers observes, "are violent out of all proportion to their goals, are fought to the bitter end, and engage in levels of gratuitous destruction."[8] Strategies of total war, which predate the destruction of nuclear weapons, essentially eliminate the distinction between combatants and noncombatants. The wartime objective of unconditional surrender further erodes limits on war's destructiveness and undercuts the possibility for a successful process of war termination short of the exhaustion of one or both parties.

Those who trust that a great power nuclear war would be meaningfully limited must explain why it would be exempt from the experience of the two previous world wars of this century. One possible contention might be the presumed benefits of the "crystal ball" effect; that is, contemporary leaders are apt to have a clear idea of the destructive consequences of war. Those who sowed war in August 1914 expected one both short and sweet; not the bitter harvest they eventually reaped. Current leadership would presumably not be so deluded.

We should, however, be cautious about underestimating the human capacity for delusion; after all, the sobering experience of the First World War did not prevent the Second. In any case, the efficacy of the crystal ball effect would seem most relevant *before* a war starts, not after the powers are well into it. Limited nuclear war doctrines, Desmond Ball argues, tend to ignore the probable historical origins of a possible exchange:

> A strategic nuclear strike by the United States or the Soviet Union against targets in the other's heartland — no matter how limited, precise, or controlled it might be — is most unlikely to be the first move in any conflict between them. Rather it is likely to follow a period of large-scale military action, probably involving substantial use of tactical nuclear weapons, in an area of vital interest to both adversaries, and during which the dynamics of escalation have already been set in motion.[9]

To these observations, we must add that the period leading up to the initiation of hostilities would most likely be extraordinarily poisoned, and probably paranoid.

POLITICAL PROBLEMS

Discussions of limited nuclear war, in addition to being ahistorical, often seem apolitical as well. Constraining and terminating a limited nuclear war involve some obvious political problems. Perhaps the most fundamental, though often overlooked, concerns the application of the principle of *pacta sunt servanda*.[10] An "agreed battle" must be fought according to certain mutually, if tacitly, recognized rules. This begs the question of how such a "pact" emerges. Formal prewar agreements as to how nuclear war ought to be conducted, though not inconceivable, stretch credulity. Tacit rules might emerge from prewar signaling or intrawar behavior (for example, we avoid their cities or political leadership in the hopes of reciprocity).[11]

Such intrawar communication, obviously, would tend to be rather crude. Consequently, the political leadership of both countries would be confronted with the dilemma of whether to keep the faith with an enemy who is pounding them with nuclear weapons, though not in an entirely indiscriminate fashion. Even if so inclined, how should the national command interpret ambiguous attacks or (possibly) accidental violations? Perhaps most fundamentally, why should such good faith be recovered during a war, when it would obviously have been lost before it?

We must also attend to the possible political and institutional contexts within which such assessments will be made. Apart from the operational and psychological problems discussed below, the leadership may find itself buffeted by significant political and military pressures.[12] Admittedly, a plausible outcome of a limited nuclear exchange might well be a widespread demand for an immediate cessation of hostilities. On the other hand, political pressure might build to escalate in order to recover "sunk costs." The costs that matter most to decision makers, as Pillar argues, are likely to be the marginal ones of the next step, not those already sustained.[13]

In addition, the institutional character of military organizations may not be conducive to meaningful limitation. Ball observes:

> The control of escalation requires extreme decisional flexibility: decision-makers must be able to adapt rapidly to changing situations and assessments, and must have the freedom to reverse direction as the unfolding of events dictates; their decisions must be presented clearly and coherently, leaving no room for misinterpretation either by subordinates charged with implementation or by the adversary leadership. These are not attitudes that are generally found in large national security establishments.[14]

Finally, the demands of attempting to negotiate deescalation and termination while fighting a limited nuclear war would place, if anything, even more strains on the political (and operational) capacity of the national command than those required to control escalation. A fundamental asymmetry exists in that it takes only one side to escalate but both must work to deescalate and terminate a conflict: "For deescalation to work," Paul Bracken writes, "both sides must consciously play the game. But for there to be a game there must be shared understanding and a level of internal political coherence."[15] Bracken concludes, "the theory of war termination presumes a level of behavior that is frequently uncharacteristic of governments."[16]

STRATEGIC PROBLEMS

In order to fight a meaningfully limited nuclear war, both sides must have plausible (and compatible) strategies for limiting the impact of nuclear combat and for ending the conflict before the point of collapse. While considerable thought and debate have gone into these problems, neither side appears to possess coherent strategic solutions to these two problems.

An initial paradox arises once one or both sides have convinced themselves that limited homeland nuclear war is possible. Specifically, by making nuclear war appear more feasible, does it make it more probable? Ironically, even if one side believes that limited nuclear conflict is a delusion, if they perceive that their adversary accepts its feasibility, the pressure on the agnostic side to preempt in a crisis will probably increase.

Limited war strategies become more plausible when clear boundaries exist to hinder escalation. In the past, geographic barriers often have provided these. The ability of today's superpowers to project military power transcends all geographic barriers, making them, in William Bunge's phrase, the "most intimate neighbors ever."[17] Their respective capitals are only minutes from each other.

Limited nuclear war eliminates one major remaining saliency, that between conventional and nuclear weapons. As Thomas Schelling has understated, " 'No nuclears' is simple and unambiguous, 'some nuclears' would be more complicated."[18] Logically, once strategic nuclear weapons have been used, the final strategic barrier has been breached, because nothing else remains to be withheld.[19] Any remnant of limitation would depend on the far more ambiguous interpretation of target selection and the size of the attack.

The existing American Single Integrated Operational Plan (SIOP), however, still identifies thousands of targets, which though not including population "per se," covers a range of military, political, and economic targets that would necessarily entail massive "collateral" damage.[20] One option that still remains is targeting the control structure of the enemy, a strategic move that will virtually eliminate the possibility for *deliberate* control. Indeed, the notion that effective deterrence of the Soviet Union rests on threatening what they value most, whether defined as political control or military power, undermines the notion of limited nuclear war.[21] After all, if a military attack threatens the core values of the ruling sectors, then it can no longer be considered meaningfully limited.

Counterforce strategies also raise certain difficulties. Perhaps the foremost would be that a full-scale, strategic counterforce attack, even if it were an unlikely bolt-from-the-blue, would neither be meaningfully limited from the perspective of its victim nor would it be able to insure that its initiator would be able to escape acceptable damage. A more restricted counterforce attack, involving only a portion of the target's forces, would most likely lead to a "worst-case" interpretation, as its victim would most likely view the attack as a precursor to more comprehensive strikes.

Since each side must have limited nuclear war strategies for there to be even a remote possibility for a successful limitation, the Soviet strategic position becomes of special importance. While a number of commentators argue that the Soviets have an interest in limitation and plan to avoid the utter destruction of their adversary, some serious doubts about likely Soviet action during a nuclear exchange must be admitted.[22] Stephen Meyer contends that

once one moves to nuclear strikes on the homeland, Soviet abilities to discern the scale and purpose of the attack decrease rapidly. Thus the Soviet's strategic culture and history are likely to be the primary determinants of their immediate reactions. Everything in the Soviet experience points to the assumption that the attack has a single strategic purpose: to destroy the Soviet state. Why else initiate nuclear exchanges?[23]

Meyer also raises another important caveat: the distinction between strategic *preference* and strategic *action*.[24] Neither side prefers their worst-case strategic option of massive attack to render their adversary incapable of waging further war, but once a strategic nuclear exchange has begun, escalatory dynamics might well push both of them in this direction. Bracken's analysis of command and control suggests that American and Soviet control systems might be considered parts of one huge, interacting system. Reciprocal alerts might well be mutually reinforcing, as each side assumes the other plans the worst (again recall the probable historical and political context of escalation). Once hostilities break out, the interactions "would be extraordinarily intense. . . . Multiple equilibrium tendencies would still exist, but more and more of them would lead to some form of all-out escalation once a few nuclears fly when both commands are on full alert."[25]

If strategies to control the destructiveness of a nuclear exchange seem underdeveloped and unconvincing, strategies of war termination are, if anything, even more flawed. Successful termination, first of all, presumes successful control of damage. If this has exceeded meaningful limits, then termination becomes rather moot. Moreover, Bracken observes that war termination concepts have not been successfully institutionalized. "Military organizations train on going up the nuclear alert ladder and carrying out their primary missions. There seems to be not nearly as much practice or attention given to deescalating a conflict, and going back down the alerting ladder."[26]

TECHNICAL-OPERATIONAL PROBLEMS

To have even minimum credibility, strategies of control and termination, as noted above, must be convincingly integrated with operational systems capable of carrying them out. Whatever the nature of strategic intention, the operational capability to control escalation and terminate a nuclear war at some meaningful point appears largely absent. Despite the investment of billions of dollars in this country over the past decade, serious doubts remain about the control system's technical capacity. In this area, Carter concludes that "trying to design a single system to be both survivable and flexible too easily results in a system that is neither."[27]

Perhaps the most fundamental operational dilemma is a variant of the "foolproof vs. bomb-proof" dilemma.[28] A foolproof control system attempts to limit damage and duration after a nuclear exchange has begun through tight control over all forces. If even one missile submarine, on either side, does not receive a cease-fire order, efforts to terminate hostilities could be effectively sabotaged.[29] Unfortunately, the capacity to control potential "fools" from going off on their own appears to require a very smart and, inevitably, vulnerable control system. Such a system either risks decapitation or deadly failure.

The multitude of technical problems encountered in the effort to "harden" control systems have been extensively surveyed elsewhere.[30] More important, perhaps, are the more qualitative dimensions of the technical task. First among these is the magnitude of the operational challenge. The conduct of a limited nuclear war requires a system capable of carrying out tasks of attack characterization, damage assessment, internal and external communication, and deescalation in a considerably compressed real time context and under unprecedented operational stress.

Purported solutions to these nuclear control problems are more susceptible to error and uncertainty than those devised for the control of conventional forces. Carter identifies several reasons why this must be the case.[31] First, nuclear forces cannot conduct the realistic exercises common in the conventional arena. Second, we have no historical experience of nuclear war from which to learn. Third, only a small or peripheral nuclear war would provide opportunity to learn from events. Fourth, in nuclear war "big things depend on little things"; that is, predicted effects depend on warning times differences of minutes, accuracies measured in tens of meters, or minor variations in error at each stage of the control process. Paradoxically, efforts to identify and compensate for probable areas of uncertainty and error might insure that the ones actually encountered will be different.

Accurate, centralized assessment is the crucial requirement for continued control: "The idea of stability in nuclear war, that an initial attack will not lead to a quantum jump to all-out escalation, depends on the ability of each side to calculate what it can do and what can be done to it."[32] Accurate assessment of capability and intention is difficult enough in peacetime when all the relevant organizations and technologies are presumably functioning optimally. In a limited nuclear war, the demands of assessment would increase dramatically at the same time the system would be degraded in unpredictable ways.

Marginally degraded systems do not necessarily lead to only marginal reductions in effectiveness; they could qualitatively transform the overall capability to control the war. For example, if the national command loses control over some forces, then even if termination is desired, pressure could build to fire the forces still under control, "on the grounds that the Soviets will inevitably empty their remaining arsenal if attacked by the isolated forces. . . . Given all the alternatives it seems best to destroy as much of the inevitable Soviet return strike as possible."[33]

Disrupted communications and control, therefore, place intrawar decision makers in both countries in a classic prisoner's dilemma, with little time or opportunity to learn cooperation from repeated games. More importantly, degraded control has to afflict only one participant to undermine deliberate limitation and termination, because both sides must be in control of their forces for the war to be assuredly limited.

In short, the qualitative dimensions of nuclear operations have contributed to a growing gap between the demands of increasingly complex strategies and the control structure to carry them out. Bracken suggests the gap exists not simply because the control system has not been built, but rather "because no one has any idea how to build it."[34]

PSYCHOLOGICAL PROBLEMS

Finally, the burden of controlling escalation in a nuclear war and bringing it to some end short of exhaustion will fall upon fallible and frail human beings. The possible psychological strain of nuclear war and its effects on decision makers can only be dimly anticipated from the clinical and historical profiles of crisis behavior. Clearly, though, the psychological climate is likely to be far worse than anything previously encountered. One issue here, as George Quester notes, is whether human beings can be "hardened" sufficiently to function appropriately in such circumstances.[35]

The essential psychological problem of nuclear war is that decision makers will be trapped in a "crazy social process," that is, one "increasingly dangerous and costly to the participants and from which the participants see no way of extricating themselves without leaving themselves vulnerable to an unacceptable loss in a value central to their self-identities or self-esteem."[36] A limited nuclear war where the choices appear to be the acceptance of terrible loss, perhaps even surrender, or the continuation of the exchange would seem to be the paradigmatic case of a crazy social process.

Complicating the terrible dilemmas facing the authorities in each country would be a "fog of war" of unprecedented density. Ball believes it would be highly unlikely that the situation to which the decision makers "believe themselves to be responding will in fact correspond very closely to the true situation, or that there will be a high degree of shared perception between the respective adversary leaderships."[37]

The essays by Glad and Rosenberg, Pillar, and Holsti in this volume suggest a variety of psychological problems that could arise to complicate efforts to control a limited nuclear war. Just as increasing demands on the technical-operational system coincide with its rapidly degrading capability, so would the demands on leaders be increasing just as events conspire to subvert their psychological equilibrium.

While some evidence suggests that moderate stress may enhance performance, severe stress would likely erode cognitive capabilities and bring psychologically dysfunctional characteristics to the fore. Holsti hypothesizes that severe crises are likely to increase cognitive rigidity, lower tolerance for ambiguity, intensify selective filtration of information, discourage the search for alternatives, reinforce the effects of stereotypes, reinforce the rush to premature closure, and impair the ability to comprehend the adversary's perspective.[38] Theories of limited nuclear war which assume rational decision makers operating in a context of near perfect information and control appear naive when contrasted with the probable decision making environment.

Finally, efforts to end a nuclear war place additional psychological demands on any decision makers still alive.[39] First, the image of the enemy must shift radically. The country that has inflicted the millions of casualties likely in even a very limited war must now be seen as a potential peace partner. Misperceptions of the enemy must be dispelled. Sunk costs must be accepted without any "adequate" compensation. Original war aims might have to be abandoned. Finally, leaders would have to face the political consequences of having led their country into calamity and having little to show for it.

III. Implications for the Design of Nuclear Forces

None of the foregoing analysis proves that a nuclear war involving strikes to the respective homelands cannot be kept within meaningful limits. After all, fortuitous factors could intrude: the weapons might not work or political leaders might draw back from the abyss before they lose control. Ironically, those who advocate "worst-case" analysis before the war breaks out sometimes seem to make "best-case" assumptions about how it will be conducted. Simple prudence seems to dictate that we admit that conditions during a nuclear war would represent a significant move away from goodness with respect to the systems of control. Perhaps some radical rethinking of strategy and restructuring of control systems need to be undertaken to keep this retreat from goodness from becoming a rout.

The preponderance of available evidence and analysis suggests that the hypothetical middle rungs of the escalation ladder may well be so slippery as not to exist, and the attempt to devise a system to climb them is, therefore, dangerous or futile. Ball concludes his 1981 analysis with the observation that, "control of a nuclear exchange would become difficult to maintain after several tens of strategic nuclear weapons had been used, even where deliberate attacks on command-and-control capabilities were avoided."[40] Despite the resources sunk into control systems since then, the situation has not been convincingly altered. What is more, we *can never know* whether the control problem has been successfully addressed, short of a nuclear war, and assuming it has may well be more dangerous than assuming it remains unchanged.

We should, then, follow Ashton Carter's advice and consider strategic control as involving two distinct systems. The first would be the smart, but necessarily vulnerable, system required for conventional warfare, as well as those extremely limited nuclear exchanges that fall below the "Ball threshold." The other would be the sufficiently invulnerable, but necessarily dumb, system capable of retaliating against a major nuclear attack. The clear recognition that an attack sufficient to decapitate the smart system would run the risk of activating the relatively invulnerable one, should serve to protect both.

The resolution of the control problem into a "dual-capable" system also suggests a need to reassess the relevance of our increasingly baroque strategic doctrine and the arsenal developed to carry it out. Most of the strategic thought and many of the weapons developed over the past two decades have been designed to fight nuclear wars of the "middle rungs." If these rungs do not exist in any meaningful sense, then these doctrines and weapons are redundant and dangerous. Perhaps by fully recognizing the problems of control,we will finally confront the frailty of our faith in nuclear-based security.

Notes

1. Ashton B. Carter, "Sources of Error and Uncertainty," in *Managing Nuclear Operations,* eds. Ashton B. Carter, John D. Steinbruner, and Charles A. Zraket (Washington, DC: Brookings Institution 1987), 617-618.

2. The literature discussing the possible effects of different nuclear exchanges is vast. For a review of many of these effects see Arthur M. Katz, "The Effects of Nuclear War," in this volume. Other recent studies that consider the impact of attacks that are less than the extreme "spasm" exchange are Ashton B. Carter, "Assessing Command System Vulnerability," in *Managing Nuclear Operations,* 555-610; William H. Daugherty et al., "The Consequences of 'Limited' Nuclear Attacks on the United States," *International Security,* 10 (Spring 1986): 3-45; Bennett Ramberg, "Targeting Nuclear Energy," in *Strategic Nuclear Targeting,* eds. Desmond Ball and Jeffrey Richelson (Ithaca, NY: Cornell University Press, 1986), 250-266; and Frank von Hipple et al., "Civilian Casualties from Counterforce Attacks," *Scientific American,* 259 (September 1988): 36-42.

3. Ashton B. Carter, "Command, Control, and Communications," [address at the MIT/Harvard Summer Program on Nuclear Weapons and Arms Control] (29 June 1988). See also Carter, "Assessing Command System Vulnerability," 555-610; and Michael Salman, Kevin J. Sullivan, and Stephen Van Evera, "Analysis or Propaganda? Measuring American Strategic Nuclear Capability, 1969-1988" in *Nuclear Arguments; Understanding the Strategic Nuclear Arms and Arms Control Debates,* eds. Lynn Eden and Steven E. Miller (Ithaca, NY: Cornell University Press, 1989), 172-263.

4. See, for example, Albert Wohlstetter and Richard Brody, "Continuing Control as a Requirement for Deterring," in *Managing Nuclear Operations,* 142-196. For an interesting psychological analysis of the tendency to conventionalize nuclear war see Steven Kull, *Minds at War: Nuclear Reality and the Inner Conflicts of Defense Policymakers* (New York: Basic books, 1988).

5. Ian Clark, *Limited Nuclear War* (Princeton, NJ: Princeton University Press, 1982), 36.

6. See Betty Glad and J. Phillip Rosenberg, "Limited War: The Political Framework," in this volume.

7. Salman, Sullivan, and Van Evera, "Analysis or Propaganda?", 233.

8. Thomas Powers, *Thinking About the Next War* (New York: Alfred A. Knopf, 1982), 47-48.

9. Desmond Ball, *Can Nuclear War Be Controlled?* Adelphi Paper #169 (London: International Institute of Strategic Studies, Autumn 1981), 36.

10. Clark, *Limited Nuclear War,* 59-61; 192-196.

11. For discussions of such signaling see Colin S. Gray, "Targeting Problems for Central War," and George H. Quester, "War Termination and Nuclear Targeting Strategy," both in *Strategic Nuclear Targeting,* 171-193, 285-311; see also Wohlstetter and Brody, "Continuing Control as a Requirement for Deterring."

12. See Betty Glad and Jerry Rosenberg, "Bargaining Under Fire: Limit Setting and Maintenance During the Korean War," and Paul R. Pillar, "Ending Limited War: The Psychological Dynamics of the Termination Process," in this volume.

13. Ibid.

14. Ball, *Can Nuclear War Be Controlled,* 36.

15. Paul Bracken, "War Termination," in *Managing Nuclear Operations,* 208.

16. Ibid., 208-209.

17. William Bunge, *Nuclear War Atlas* (New York: Basil Blackwell, 1988), 94.

18. Thomas Schelling, *Arms and Influence* (New Haven, CT: Yale University Press, 1966), 132.

19. Clark, *Limited Nuclear War,* 81.

20. Desmond Ball, "The Development of the SIOP, 1960-1983," in *Strategic Nuclear Targeting*, 57-84. For a report of recent revisions underway see Robert C. Toth, "U.S. Shifts Nuclear Response Strategy," *Los Angeles Times*, Sunday, 23 July 1989, A1 ff.

21. For a discussion of this and other problems with the current countervailing strategy see Robert Jervis, *The Illogic of American Nuclear Strategy* (Ithaca, NY: Cornell University Press, 1984).

22. See Wohlstetter and Brody, "Continuing Control as a Requirement for Deterring," 142-196 and Gray, "Targeting Problems for Central War," 171-193.

23. Stephen M. Meyer, "Soviet Nuclear Operations," in *Managing Nuclear Operations*, 528.

24. Ibid., 529-531.

25. Paul Bracken, *The Command and Control of Nuclear Forces* (New Haven, CT: Yale University Press, 1983), 224.

26. Bracken, "War Termination," 213.

27. Carter, "Assessing Command System Vulnerability," 558.

28. See Nigel Calder, *Nuclear Nightmares: An Investigation into Possible Wars* (New York: Viking, 1979), 84-114; see also John D. Steinbruner, "Choices and Trade-offs," in *Managing Nuclear Operations*, 535-554.

29. Bracken, *The Command and Control of Nuclear Forces*, 99.

30. See, especially, Ball, *Can Nuclear War Be Controlled*; Bracken, *The Command and Control of Nuclear Forces*; and Carter, "Assessing Command System Vulnerability."

31. Carter, "Sources of Error and Uncertainty," 616-617.

32. Bracken, *The Command and Control of Nuclear Forces*, 118.

33. Ibid., 128.

34. Ibid., 241.

35. Quester, "War Termination and Nuclear Targeting Strategy," 300.

36. Karl Deutsch, quoted in James Thompson, *Psychological Aspects of Nuclear War* (New York: Wiley, 1985), 72.

37. Ball, *Can Nuclear War Be Controlled?* 37.

38. See Ole Holsti, "Crisis Management" in this volume.

39. See Paul Pillar, "Ending Limited War" in this volume.

40. Ball, *Can Nuclear War Be Controlled?*, 36.

Chapter 18

The Effects of Nuclear War on Human Society

ARTHUR M. KATZ

I. Acceptable Damage

The credibility of a nuclear strategy is intimately tied to the perception of its ultimate consequences. Will a nuclear strategy promise an apocalyptic end, impelling both sides to draw back from confrontation? Or will another vision drive one side forward in the belief that it can balance on the brink, while the other falls hopelessly into an abyss of defeat?

Key to the course taken are the underlying, perhaps unconscious, assumptions about the behavior of one nation or the other as they confront the question of whether damage from a nuclear attack can be made "acceptable" to political leaders and the population as a whole. Therefore, measuring the consequences of a strategic attack is central to developing nuclear policies. Even in a rapidly evolving and hopefully less threatening world political situation, these are lessons that should always be heeded.

To provide guideposts for considering what might be acceptable damage, several different levels of survival are described below.[1] In decreasing order of damage these are:

1. Biological Survival of Individuals. Groups of individuals survive, but not necessarily within the organized political, social, and economic structure of a modern society.

2. Regional Survival of Political Structures. Some subnational political units survive but without a functioning central government.

3. Survival of a Central Government. Central control over all pre-attack national territory survives, but the effectiveness of this control may vary over an extremely wide range, depending on the specific nature and pattern of the attack(s). The ability to act independently on world affairs would also be restricted or eliminated.

4. Survival Intact of Basic Societal Structure. Relatively limited social, political, and economic damage to the nation. It remains viable and, while weakened, potentially capable of international independence.

AUTHOR'S NOTE: The author is a currently employed by the U.S. Department of Energy, and the views he expresses here are his own.

Despite occasional speculation that a nation can absorb from tens of millions to more than 100 million casualties, level 4 is really the only "acceptable" outcome of a conventional or nuclear war. Level 3, however, is clearly preferable to alternatives 1 or 2. The kind of entity which would be acceptable in the post-attack world, however, is subject to various interpretations. The USSR, with restive minorities such as fundamentalist Moslems within its border, may have a very different view of what is "acceptable" damage than would a nuclear-armed France.[2] Moreover, one must look at the perception of damage and its political consequences. Vulnerability to long-term radioactive contamination can create a sense of perceived threat and damage that exceed objective reality. Such a perception may give political leaders very little room for maneuvering in deciding whether or not to retaliate against what might be considered a "limited" nuclear attack as described in some nuclear "counterforce" scenarios.

II. Level of Nuclear Attack and Physical Damage

To create an appropriate context for discussing the societal and psychological effects of nuclear war, this section will discuss briefly some of the physical and related consequences of various types of nuclear attacks. In making these assessments we must first address the strategic alternatives which have received the most attention from the United States and look at the assumptions made about possible resulting damage.

The strategy of Mutually Assured Destruction (MAD) seeks to ensure that even after a surprise first-strike attack, both adversaries would retain sufficient nuclear capability to launch countervalue attacks which would inflict totally "unacceptable" damage on the other. Confronted with this inevitable and devastating outcome, an adversary would be deterred from initiating a nuclear war. Counterforce strategies, on the other hand, attempt to make the resort to nuclear weapons more palatable. By directly attacking only strategic military targets such as intercontinental ballistic missiles (ICBMs) and nuclear armed bomber bases rather than population and economic centers, they attempt to avoid the catastrophic population/economic damages that would provoke a MAD type retaliation. Two variants of this strategy can be identified. The "controlled and limited" nuclear war proposed in the early 1970s by then Defense Secretary James Schlesinger assumes an ultimate stalemate with both nations "surviving" a matched and balanced counterforce escalation (essentially tit for tat) which never reaches full-scale war.[3] One rationale for this approach was that the United States would gain flexibility in choosing its response to a first-strike attack, thus avoiding the conundrum of having to choose surrender as its alternative to a full-scale attack. The "war fighting" scenario, which several members of the Reagan administration embraced, foresaw a situation in which one nation could prevail (i.e., achieve an ultimate victory at an acceptable price) without an escalation to a full-scale nuclear war.[4] For both variants, the key premise is that the level of destruction and disruption of either side would never get out of control or surpass the "perceived" limits of "acceptable" damage.

Several recent scenarios provide an opportunity to explore the credibility of these assumptions, revealing the complex response of ecological and social systems to such physical destruction.[5] A base case counterforce scenario, "Limited War" is shown in Table 18.1. It postulates a counterforce attack against the United States which might actually take out a majority of the most accurate U.S. first strike weapons. It assumes that 2,100 warheads consisting of one megaton each, would be groundburst to effectively destroy hardened silos. The resulting potentially lethal radioactivity would extend over the farm belt and Midwest (see Figure 18.1).[6] Such an attack would also target, in all probability, at least 46 Strategic Air Command (SAC) airbases and two submarine bases (140 1 Megaton (MT) weapons), damaging several American cities. Many airfield and command centers are located in close proximity to urban areas and attacks on them would create considerable collateral economic and human destruction. To create further disruption without direct lethal effects a few weapons might be used to produce electromagnetic pulse (EMP), which could destroy or damage key unprotected electrical components in communication, electric power transmission, computer and transportation equipment.[7] As a base estimate we project 7 to 15 million deaths and 10 to 20 million initial injuries – most related to radiation exposure.[8] Similar effects would be expected from the scenarios designated SCOPE-1 and SCOPE-2 in Table 18.2.[9]

The heavy radioactive fallout from such an attack would drive out people from the Midwest and farm belt where about one-third of U.S. manufacturing capacity is located.[10] Even if not directly damaged, the economies of regions near SAC bases are likely to be shut down when their populations flee, fearing further attacks or contamination by radiation. As key industries shut down, the problem of "bottlenecks" will arise, that is, the disruption of many industries as a result of the partial or complete shutdown or loss of one or a small group of pivotal producers of essential goods. Even a two-week evacuation without subsequent nuclear attack was projected by Laurino to disrupt the U.S. economy for one or two years.[11]

Smaller countervalue wars, as shown in Katz (see Table 18.1, A-1 to A-4) would cause extensive industrial destruction and high casualties. The smallest attack, A-4, was projected to destroy 25% to 35% of U.S. industry and kill or wound 25% to 30% of the U.S. population.[12] Economic vulnerability also would be magnified greatly in the countervalue attacks envisaged in scenarios A-1 to A-4 (Table 18.1) where critical industries would be systematically targeted for destruction as an integral element of this strategy.[13] An attack on petroleum refining, for example, directly affects the petrochemical industry, the heating of worker's homes, fuel and electricity to run factories, fuel for operating farm machinery and transporting of goods, and the availability of fertilizer and pesticide for production.[14] Under these circumstances complex social and organizational factors play an increasingly critical role in survival and recovery.[15]

TABLE 18.1: U.S. Vulnerability to Nuclear Attack

Attacks	Casualties: Percentage Total United States[a] (a)	Casualties Percentage Urban Population[a] (b)	Percentage of Total U.S. Industry Destroyed[b] (c)	Percentage of SMSA Industries Destroyed[b] (d)	Total Megaton Equivalents[c] (e)	Total Weapons Required[c] (f)
A-1	35-45	50-65	60-65	80+	544-566	700-800
A-2	30-40	45-60	45-60	75-80+	344-366	500-600
A-3	25-35	40-50	35-45	55-70	244-266	400-500
A-4	20-30	30-45	25-35	45-55	144-166	300-400
Limited War	5-15	—	(30-35)[d]	—	20-40	20-40

Source: Arthur Katz, *Economic and Social Consequences of Nuclear Attacks on the United States*, Committee on Banking, Housing, and Urban Affairs, U.S. Senate (Washington, DC: Government Printing Office, 1979). p. 9.

Notes: Total U.S. population, 203 million; total population urban, 139 million; total population of 71 SMSAs, 110 million. Population based on 1970 Bureau of Census data.

a. Based only on 71 SMSAs attacked by 1 Mt weapons. Since the specific targets for the 100 Kt weapons in the 50 additional SMSAs could not be identified, only the damage estimates for 1 Mt weapons are shown, in order to be conservative. The urban percentage is based on total urban population of 139 million in 1970.

b. Based on manufacturing value added.

c. A 1 Mt attack plus a 100 Kt attack (200 to 300 warheads). A 100 kiloton weapon represents one-tenth the TNT potential of a 1 megaton weapon. A "megaton equivalent" is the weapon yield in megatons raised to the two-thirds power and is a standard measure.

d. Refers to industrial capacity in areas heavily contaminated with radioactive fallout.

331

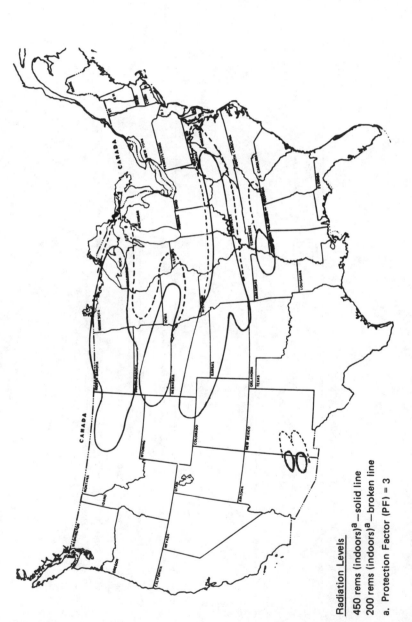

Radiation Levels

450 rems (indoors)[a] — solid line
200 rems (indoors)[a] — broken line

a. Protection Factor (PF) = 3

Figure 18.1. Fallout Patterns for a Typical Winter Day

Source: Subcommittee on Arms Control, International Organizations and Security Agreements, *Analysis of Effects of Limited Nuclear War*, Committee on Foreign Relations, United States Senate (Washington, DC: Government Printing Office, September 1975), p. 52.

TABLE 18.2: SCOPE Study

		Nuclear exchange scenario					
		Aggregate weapons[a]		Military yield		Ind./urban yield[b]	
Phase of the exchange		Yield (Mt)	Number of warheads	Air	(MT) Surface[c]	Air	(MT) Surface[d]
SCOPE-1	Initial counterforce and response	2000	5000	1000	1000	0	0
SCOPE-2	Extended counterforce	4000	8800	1750	1750	0	0
SCOPE-3	Industrial	5000	10,000	2000	2000	750	250
SCOPE-4	Final phase	6000	12,600	2250	2250	1250	250

Source: Scientific Committee on Problems of the Environment (SCOPE-28), International Council of Scientific Unions, Environmental Consequences of Nuclear War (ENUWAR), A. B. Pittock et al., "Vol. I: Physical and Atmospheric Effects," (New York: Wiley, 1985), 31.
Notes: a. Columns accumulate weapons from lower level attacks, e.g. SCOPE-1 and SCOPE-2 shown on SCOPE-2 total.
b. Tactical weapons are not included. These could add 100-500 Mt in the less than 50 kt yield range. The warhead yields and numbers are taken from Table 18.1. It is assumed that the weapons have a fission yield fraction of 0.5.
c. Includes weapons directed at industrial and economic targets as well as weapons.
d. Land surface.
e. Cumulative targets include:
  2500 missile silos and command centers (2 warheads per silo)
  1100 military facilities and airfields throughout NATO and the Warsaw Pack (2 warheads per target)
  100 Naval targets
  500 Mobile missiles (barraged by 1200 warheads)
  1100 miscellaneous military detonations
  3000 military/industrial and energy resource sites worldwide

U.S. food production also would be significantly damaged by fallout from attacks on ICBMs in the West and Midwest: the counterforce attack (Table 18.1) and the SCOPE scenario with military components (Table 18.2).[16] Approximately two-thirds of the U.S. food supply (as measured by calories) is produced in the North Central tier of states from Indiana to Colorado. These states, plus those in the South/Southwest would be most affected by fallout.[17] Many farmers would be killed, injured, or permanently disabled, eliminating the skilled manpower needed to restore productivity quickly. Soil radiation levels would be higher than "acceptable" peacetime levels for growing crops; and residual levels of radiation would endanger remaining workers.[18]

The data from the Chernobyl accident are instructive. In the weeks and months after the accident radiation fears caused several nations—including West Germany, Italy, Poland, and Austria—to restrict or bar the sale of locally produced milk and leafy vegetables.[19] The economic impact was considerable, for example, $250 million in losses for West Germany alone.[20] The European Community barred the importation of a variety of fruit, vegetables, meat, and fish from the

TABLE 19.3: USSR Vulnerability to Nuclear Attack

	Total Population at Risk (millions) (a)	Percentage Urban Population at Risk (b)	Percentage Industrial Capacity at Risk (c)	Total Megaton[a,b] Equivalents 1Mt (d)	50Kt (e)	Total Weapons Attacks 1Mt (f)	50Kt (g)
D-1	15	11	15	26	25	26	181
D-2	21	16	25	90	40	90	300
D-3	46	34	50	144	86	144	631
D-4	74	55	62	303	138	303	1,104

Source: Geoffrey Kemp, "Nuclear Forces for Medium Powers, Parts II and III. Strategic Requirements and Options," Adelphi Papers 107 (London: International Institute for Strategic Studies, 192228882466474).
Notes: a. States requirements in terms of numbers of weapons (warheads and bombs) and "megaton equivalents." Equivalent megatons (EMT) are defined as N (yield) to the two-thirds power. This is a measure of the effectiveness of a given number (N) of nuclear weapons, compared with 1 MT as a standard. Because of the nonlinear effects, weapons with a total megatonnage less than one large-yield weapon could nevertheless have a similar or greater area of destruction than the single large-yield weapon. For example, the destructive area of 4 1-MT weapons is approximately the same as that of a single 8-MT weapon.
b. An adjustment in the weapons requirement is given to account for the possibility of an effective antiballistic missile (ABM) system that is postulated for the Moscow area. The additional weapons required are those that would be necessary to overwhelm such a system, assuming that it is effective against a normal attack. The Moscow ABM system is assumed to have 100 launchers for antiballistic missiles.

USSR and Eastern European countries.[21] Despite extensive effort to decontaminate soil and housing, all or parts of an area 18 miles in radius around the Chernobyl plant was and will continue to be off limits to agriculture and human habitation. Over a wider area, involving up to 75 million Soviet citizens, the food chain will be contaminated with the radioisotope cesium.[22] In northern Sweden (Lapland) 100,000 reindeer contained so much radiation, they had to be killed, endangering the livelihood of 15,000 Lapps, as well as a unique, traditional way of life.[23]

Countervalue attacks, though they may cause fewer food problems related to radiation, will create other problems due to the destruction of petroleum fuel and petroleum-based fertilizers and pesticides production.[24] The food-processing industry is also vulnerable. Almost 90% of the U.S. canning, baking, and packing capability takes place in regions that would be destroyed or severely damaged by the urban attacks shown in Tables 18.1 and 18.2.[25] If countervalue attacks produce enough smoke and soot to create nuclear winter-type effects described in the SCOPE study and elsewhere, crop reductions would become even more profound.[26] Even where less severe short-term general changes in sunlight and cooling are projected, important chronic climatic effects such as late spring and early autumn frost could still disrupt agriculture.[27]

Under either counterforce or countervalue scenarios the results of deprivation would go beyond the possibility of starvation.[28] Food shortages in Japan during World War II resulted in "social conflict, and depression of the will to resist."[29]

Countervalue attacks (see Table 18.2) would create a medical crises of massive proportions. In the United States physicians and hospitals are concentrated in urban targets and would be subject to massive death and destruction.[30] If there were 40 to 90 million casualties (with 20 to 30 million of these being injured), the physicians who survive would have to care for 100 to 600 persons each.[31] Compare this to an ordinary load of about 25 patients a day of whom only 20% have serious problems.[32] Surviving hospitals potentially would have 30 to 40 injured per bed, with hundreds of thousands of burn victims competing for the 10 or so beds in the burn units of the few major hospitals left standing.[33] Good emergency medical practice, which can breakdown even in peacetime emergencies, would be overwhelmed.[34] Physicians in such circumstances are likely to revert to ineffective patterns of treatment, choosing one patient at a time in order of arrival rather than treating those most likely to benefit from the treatment. Many will be reduced to aimlessly "wiping and daubing, wiping and daubing" as an emotional reaction to the magnitude of the carnage.[35]

Public health problems would be staggering. Inadequate food, unsanitary conditions, exposure to animal disease carriers in rural evacuation areas, and the effects of burns as well as radiation exposure in the aftermath of the attack would permit a high incidence of epidemic disease. Pharmaceutical supplies are likely to be badly damaged or destroyed. Estimates project that only 1% of the needed medical supplies would be available after an attack.[36]

For a counterforce attack or combined military/economic attack producing fallout, hundreds of thousands of people would need extraordinary medical assistance merely to assure survival. Overall 10 to 20 million would be injured, most from radiation. A single patient exposed to substantial levels of radiation would require intensive care, bone marrow transplants, blood transfusions, and antibiotics.[37] After the Chernobyl nuclear reaction accident, it took an international medical effort drawing on highly specialized medical resources to perform just 19 bone marrow transplants on the victims, and it was reported that "13,000 doctors, nurses, and laboratory assistants, and 240 first-aid teams participated in the medical operations" which included medical checks for evacuees. Despite the resources and the extraordinary medical efforts, 13 of the 19 victims died within a few weeks. Over a one-month period, 31 died and 203 others were hospitalized with radiation illness.[38] Radiation exposure also weakens individual immunological defenses and seriously reduces the effectiveness of immunization.[39]

Counterforce or countervalue attacks can lead to malnutrition, burn injuries, emotional stress, radiation exposure, and, in the case of countervalue attacks, increased ultraviolet effects from depleted ozone. As the size of the attack increases (as in SCOPE-3 and SCOPE-4 of Table 18.2) there is a growing risk of producing an immunological state similar to that seen in patients with Acquired Immune Deficiency Syndrome (AIDS).[40] The psychological and organizational reactions of the general population to the increased appearance of AIDS-like symptoms or even AIDS (from already infected individuals or contaminated blood) might be very damaging. Increased fear and tension may lead individuals to draw back from suspect social contacts, to demand quarantines, and to engage in scapegoating which would lead to diminished group cohesion.[41]

In short, as a member of one of the Chernobyl medical teams observed, "Adequate medical care would be impossible in a larger nuclear catastrophe . . . I was overwhelmed by the human suffering [of Chernobyl patients]. But . . . the damage and human misery that would be wrought by nuclear weapons would be immeasurably worse."[42]

In addition to the direct losses to the immediate participants in any major nuclear war, the interactive effects would compound the disruption throughout the world. The United States and the USSR and their allies are responsible for about 70% of world trade and 90% of the manufactured goods of the world.[43] The United States alone exports about 50% of the world's grains and holds almost 50% of its reserved stocks.[44] The world's medical supplies are provided by the major powers. The United States and the USSR and their allies, for example, produce about 90% of the world's pharmaceuticals.[45] In developing nations, 75% of the pharmaceuticals and 70% to 100% of the medical equipment used are imported, with approximately 75% of this total coming from the United States and Europe.[46]

Massive destruction of these countries would cause not only a major disruption in world trade, but also lead to critical worldwide shortages of fertilizers, pesticides, and food.[47] Alternative food sources such as Australia and Argentina, even if not directly attacked, could find their food production disrupted through the partial loss of fertilizers and herbicides imported from the United States, Europe, or the USSR.[48] The worldwide food situation would become more critical if attacks against urban targets would produce enough smoke and soot to induce temporary global climate modifications.[49] The SCOPE study concluded these effects could lead to so much damage that the world's population would be at risk of starvation.[50] In sum, many nonparticipant nations would also face severe demands to find a formula to stabilize their societies.

III. Social-Psychological Effects

The preceding sections examined the scope of potential damage of nuclear war. In this section we address directly the psychological and social consequences of responding to these extraordinary events and human demands. It is particularly instructive to look at disasters of the past. As Allen Barton notes in his study, "Communities in Disaster," there is a process that occurs between the cataclysmic event and the return to normal life.[51] After the initial stress of a small-scale disaster, a period of unorganized response ensues. Individuals and groups may help neighbors and nearby survivors who are injured or trapped, or they may withdraw or engage in ritualistic activity (for example, sifting aimlessly through wreckage).

Leaders (mayors, organizational heads, persons with skills relevant to the disaster) are apt to evolve in the situation. But these leaders also are likely to suffer role conflicts. Torn between protecting one's family and the performance of organizational or civic functions, between dealing with personal losses or serving the community, leaders may not provide the direction needed for an effective early disaster response. After the Chernobyl accident, for example, it was reported that local Soviet party officials rushed "their own families out of the area before the general public was alerted."[52]

Early responses to disasters ordinarily involve small-scale rescue operations. In the next stage, a more organized response emerges. Community disaster organizations and other functionally relevant agencies and institutions may be mobilized to meet local needs. Help from a larger community begins to appear—police and medical aid, possibly the army or national guard. The consequences of this movement, however, may not all be positive. Properly directed, these individuals can aid in the disaster relief operations. However, their numbers and sometimes ambiguous motivation (e.g., as voyeurs), can overload disrupted transportation facilities. Some may engage in antisocial activities (looting) and aimless and unproductive work.[53]

At this stage a number of significant functional roles must be fulfilled. Organizing relief efforts into productive channels is the most crucial. Two-way communication is needed so that the leaders can inform and direct the population within and outside of the disaster area and obtain crucial information from the community as to the nature of the casualties suffered as well as the local needs. When these organizational and communication functions are performed well, the supply of food, clothing, shelter, and medical assistance can be effectively distributed. This application of resources forms the bridge between the termination of the immediate, critical post-disaster period and the rebuilding of the community.

The third phase, ideally, is characterized by relative harmony and cooperation within the community itself. An "altruistic" society emerges, focusing on rebuilding normal life. Finally, there is an attenuation of the altruistic society, and a return to normal relationships. The disaster life cycle is complete.

The scenario given above, however, is not likely to be followed after any of the nuclear wars described above. The destruction is apt to be so great that it would overwhelm the indigenous resources, while the potential leaders who survive are likely to be demoralized and capable only of helping those closest to them. The reaction of survivors of the Hiroshima disaster is instructive along these lines. A German Jesuit witness, Father Siemes, reported:

> Among the passersby, there are many who are uninjured. In a purposeless, insensate manner, distraught by the magnitude of the disaster, most of them rush by and none conceives the thought of organizing help on his own initiative. They are concerned only with the welfare of their own families.[54]

Other accounts of the Hiroshima and Nagasaki bombings suggest that the main pattern of behavior of the survivors was to help family members and sometimes neighbors. People would then try to escape from the city of ruins and fires into the countryside, ignoring the plight of strangers.[55]

After any future nuclear attack, responses similar to those occurring at Hiroshima are likely to occur. The spontaneous organization of rescue and relief groups would be difficult. Potential helpers and rescuers would be overwhelmed emotionally by the numbers of victims needing help. But unlike Hiroshima and Nagasaki, survivors would not be able to return to a normal world within a few hours or days of the initial explosions. The organization of outside help would be far less likely to occur. With the information that people now have about radioactivity, the impulse would be for those who have not been exposed to radioactivity to flee, to avoid the contaminated area.[56]

The sudden and extremely destructive nature of nuclear attacks would intensify the emotional responses evident in smaller disasters.[57] At Hiroshima, for example, the survivors experience what Lifton has called a "death immersion."[58] As one man recalled after the attack "the whole world was dying." His body and everything else "seemed black, dark all over. . . ." He thought "the world was ending."[59] The feeling was one of annihilation, loss of continuity, of a total break with prior experience."[60] There was, as Robert Lifton described it, "the replacement of the natural order of living and dying with an unnatural order of death-dominated life."[61] Reality, in short, overpowered the normal human capacity to absorb and integrate an experience in a useful way. Even protective mechanisms such as the psychic numbing and denial were so distorted at times that they became the bases for pathological behavior.[62]

Survival for some would represent personal failure or impotence. Personally unacceptable behavior took the form of running away and the inability or the unwillingness to extend adequate assistance to family, friends, or strangers in need. Shame and guilt often were the legacies of this behavior.[63] Even those who tried to remain and help were unable to cope. The magnitude of the destruction and the number of casualties were physically and psychologically overwhelming. They, too, experienced guilt related to feelings of helplessness, impotence, and shame.

A unique element in the Hiroshima disaster — exposure to radioactive fallout — created great long-term difficulties in adjustment.[64] The slowly evolving recognition of the effects of the radiation irrevocably tied the victims to the event.[65] The "hibakusha," as the survivors were called, were doubly damned. They were gripped by the emerging understanding of radiation effects, and they were shunned as "tainted" by Japanese society. The latter was a devastating rejection in a society that prizes acceptance and continuity.[66]

In any future nuclear war, Kinston and Rosser conclude from their survey of the available literature, it is likely that 75% of survivors would show the disaster syndrome.[67] They would display an absence of emotion, inhibition of activity, docility, indecisiveness, lack of responsiveness, and automatic behavior, together with the psychological manifestations of automatic arousal. Of the remaining survivors, 12% to 25% would exhibit hysterical reactions and psychosis. Another 10% might become so disoriented that they would need immediate direct specific intervention such as physical restraint and removal from the site. Complicating the psychological response, particularly in countervalue urban attacks, may well be fears of nuclear contamination that exceed the objective reality of the threat.[68] Because of the uncertainty and lack of specificity about its effects on individuals, radiation evokes an unusually powerful fear and a sense of foreboding. As a Swedish Lapp explained after Chernobyl: "It's so terrible because you can't see it, you can't smell it — it's just there."[69]

FROM PSYCHOLOGICAL PAIN TO HUMAN BEHAVIOR

While psychological pain is a tragedy, the key issue from the perspective of a surviving society is whether this pain inhibits or distorts behavior effective for recovery. The evidence shows that extreme disaster experiences are disabling. Demoralization is "a common distress response when people find themselves in a serious predicament and can see no way out."[70] It takes the form of feelings of helplessness and depression.[71] After the Three Mile Island (TMI) accident, individuals ordinarily capable of appropriate actions were reduced to feelings of helplessness and dependency. The problem was beyond their realm of experience and no adequate information was available to guide them.[72] Indeed, at the time of the accident, 10% of the household heads (male and female) suffered levels of demoralization similar in severity to clients of community mental health centers.[73] The average level of demoralization in the total population was increased, though these persons returned to normal functioning over time.[74] While psychosomatic problems (loss of appetite, difficulty in sleeping, and irritability) disappeared shortly after the disaster, actual somatic symptoms (e.g., stomach trouble, diarrhea, constipation) continued to affect a small percentage of the population four months later.[75]

After the flood at Buffalo Creek, West Virginia, in 1972 where the death rate was between 2% and 3%, traumatic neurotic reactions of grief, serious shame, rage, and hopelessness were found in 80% of the survivors interviewed.[76] In this case it was the widespread physical destruction — of the community and traditional support systems — which was mainly responsible for the apathy and emotional emptiness which followed.[77]

In extreme situations all the individuals involved may show posttraumatic symptoms. Where soldiers have been exposed to battles in which 75% of their companions were killed, all have been emotionally incapacitated.[78] Reid found similar results in studies of UK bomber pilots.[79] Even when the stress was relieved the emotional effects continued. Studies of World War II survivors have identified many cases of posttraumatic neuroses. One study of traumatic resources indicated almost two-thirds were either unemployed or unstably employed 15 years later.[80]

Where whole societies face these kinds of casualty rates the results may last for decades. "Survivors of the Black Death [which swept Europe from 1348-1350] fell into apathy, leaving ripe wheat uncut and livestock untended . . . no one had any inclination to concern themselves about the future."[81] Indeed, for a century after the Black Death, Europeans were increasingly obsessed with death and foreboding in their philosophic outlook.[82]

With the possible exception of the Black Death, any general nuclear war is likely to produce greater demoralization than the disasters discussed above. Kinston and

Rosser estimate that as compared to normal times, "the incidence of depressive illness in a disaster-struck community could increase by 350 percent and that of unspecified neurotic illness by 1,100 percent."[83]

In a study for the Swedish Academy of Science, Chazov and Vartanion concluded that of the 20% to 25% of the European urban population surviving a major nuclear war, one-third would suffer severe mental and behavioral problems, and 20% of the survivors would be unable to care for themselves.[84] Thompson believes that a 30% casualty rate would seriously impair the normal community support system that carries a bereaved person through the crises of separation and renewal.[85] As at Buffalo Creek, many people would become estranged and apathetic. Destructive behavior similar to that seen in Japan near the end of World War II is likely to emerge. There could be "a drift toward accomplishing personal and private aims rather than those which are national."[86] All these effects would result in widespread and extraordinary demands on the police, organization, and health care functions of society, and on the ability of political leaders to organize and motivate.

An analysis of one survey done for the U.S. Office of Civil Defense about the possible psychological and social effects of a large-scale military and urban/industrial attack (100 million deaths) concluded that "one month after the nuclear attack, less than half the potential labor force could be expected to work without immediately beneficial compensation, and that, of these, one in five would be able to function only at a level greatly degraded from his normal abilities."[87]

Other recent findings point to the further demoralizing effect of radiation fallout. The SCOPE study concluded that for the SCOPE-4 level of attack the radioactivity contamination and world-wide dose from this level of attack would be more serious than previously estimated. Of the land in Europe, the United States, and the USSR, 7% would be contaminated, initially, to lethal levels, and the entire northern hemisphere would be subject to a small radiation dose of 10 to 20 rads.[88] In the Northern hemisphere the death rate due to nuclear radiation would not substantially increase; but the fallout would create lingering feelings of vulnerability. The sense of cultural dislocation and personal bewilderment seen among the Lapps in Sweden when their reindeer were contaminated by radiation from the Chernobyl accident is apt to occur on a much grander scale.[89] In addition to these factors, the failure of communication, transportation, and industrial equipment resulting from EMP effects, and the cold and dark of a nuclear winter should it or some variant occur, would compound the demoralization and sense of helplessness.

Thus, all the elements that make a small disaster tractable—limited damage, modest casualties, surviving leadership, external aid, available skilled workers, material resources, and organizational skills—would be lacking in a nuclear war. The result would be a calamity dramatically different from those suffered on a smaller scale. As Thompson notes, the combination of suddenness, destructive impact, geographical extent, degree of environmental contamination, and disrupted communication would represent qualitatively new "experiences" for the survivors.[90] They would be left struggling to come to terms with this new reality, in a society desperately needing their skills and commitment to reorganize and rebuild seriously disrupted or destroyed economic, food production, and medical systems (see Table 18.4, page 347).

EFFECTS ON FAMILIES

In the aftermath of either a limited counterforce or the "smaller" countervalue (A3 and A4 of Table 18.1) urban/industrial attacks, many families would be torn apart by death, severe injury, disease, evacuation, or military and labor conscription. At the time of the Three Mile Island accident, for example, children were evacuated from schools, dropped off at locked houses, and left to fend for themselves while uninformed parents were left in a panic.[91] This separation of parents and children was viewed by local residents as one of the deficiencies in evacuation plans.[92] During the Chernobyl accident, 250,000 children were evacuated. In some cases they were separated from their parents for weeks.[93] Considerable disruption of the family was also seen even under the comparatively mild conditions of British life in World War II.[94] Evacuations, mobilization of the civilian work force, and the closing of the schools had similar consequences for families in Japan. As one observer noted, the social dislocation was "detrimental to Japanese family structure and the feelings and values that go with it."[95]

Even for those families which remain intact, the ordeal of nuclear attack would place severe stress on adults and children alike. While the emotional needs of children can be expected to increase and require more immediate attention, the ability of surviving parents to supply these needs without adequate external assistance, while facing their own traumas, may seriously diminish. In Great Britain during World War II under mild conditions (compared to those of nuclear war) "some mothers and fathers were less able to, less willing to make the home a place of warm activity."[96] For some adults, the death or injury of spouses and children will rob them of any incentive to care for themselves, much less contribute to the general rebuilding of the nation. Rather than helping out, they will thus impose additional burdens on the recovery effort.

Children who have lost one or both parents also will require special care because of their profound social traumas. In one study 40% of normal preadolescent children who lost fathers during the war in an otherwise stable home situation showed severe maladaptive behavior (e.g., social isolation, soiling, and learning problems more than three years following the death of the father).[97] A review of the current literature on the effects of death in childhood found "early bereavement greatly increases a child's susceptibility to depression, school dysfunction, and delinquency" even years later.[98] Some of the effects of death on children can be mitigated by an effective support system created by parent(s) and the community. Children spent the summer after Chernobyl in camps which had helped to "reassure them and calm them down."[99] However, such care may be limited or nonexistent after either a countervalue or even limited counterforce attack, since attempts to remedy this situation can divert substantial quantities of productive energy from recovery needs. Ironically, the consequence of such limited care may be children lacking the normal motivation and self-esteem needed to become productive adults, disrupting long-term recovery and stability.[100]

Not only the young, but the elderly and handicapped would suffer disproportionately since they depend most on society's material and institutional resources. Thus both the young and elderly showed significant increases in accidental death attributed to neglect in Great Britain during World War II.[101] In general, the elderly experience a much deeper sense of deprivation, after a death, reflecting the unlikely probability of returning to the familiar past.[102]

ISOLATION FROM THE OUTSIDE WORLD: IMPLICATIONS

A connection with a dynamic outside world provides the impetus for rebuilding the damaged society, providing the vitality and competence requisite to rebuilding the social structure destroyed by a disaster. It was the intervention of outsiders with resources and leadership that revitalized Hiroshima and played the dominant role in its later boomtown recovery. "The survivors had to be dragged along [hikizuru] by the outsiders."[103] Outside assistance also had a more subtle symbolic function. Assistance from the outside world gave the victims an emotional, almost mythic, reconnection with a larger, normal world. This reconnection has the essential function of binding together a society, restating a common thread of hope and shared aspirations that are the essence of national life.

In any except the smallest nuclear wars of the future, however, external aid is apt to be lacking, reinforcing widespread feelings of individual vulnerability. To put the problem in a contemporary context, the Mexico City earthquake of 1985 required a truly worldwide response to damage that would greatly pale in comparison to the destruction of a nuclear attack.[104] Even if outside assistance were possible, as Hocking has point out, it has its limits. If stresses "are prolonged, breakdown will become universal."[105] The time to act, to eliminate this barrier of isolation may be critically short — only a few weeks or less.

The sense of isolation could only be intensified if any large urban/industrial nuclear attack resulted in a real or apparent variant of a nuclear winter effect. Abrupt changes, even for a short period, in the weather, the pattern of sunlight and temperature, or other atypical events, could lead to a feeling that the environment was out of control. The result could be a profound sense of foreboding and unease in an already tenuous world.

THE DESIRE TO FLEE: RELOCATION PROBLEMS

When survivors are exposed to large numbers of casualties in circumstances in which they cannot take defensive action, their first impulse is to flee. Ikle made observations along these lines in his study of World War II bombings: "In the event of very large disasters, such as nuclear explosions, where shelters and ordinary precautions may not offer sufficient protection, many urbanites will leave the city. *This exodus [is] probably one of the most important morale effects from nuclear bombing . . ."* (emphasis added).[106] Irving Janis noted similar reactions to the destruction of Hiroshima. "One of the most frequent types of sustained emotional disturbance appears to have been a phobic-like fear of exposure to another traumatic disaster. This reaction consisted in strong feelings of apprehensiveness accompanied by exaggerated efforts to ward off new threats." The severity of the emotional and phobic reactions to the disaster scene, as Janis points out, is proportional to the severity of specific injuries and the manner in which one might die.[107]

A similar response has been widely noted in recent studies of disaster or crisis victims. At the time of the accident at the Three Mile Island plant, an uncontrolled evacuation of nearly 40% of the population took place, simply based on the possibility of a major release of radioactivity. The appearance of an ominous bubble in the reactor, the confusing information released by the officials, and the desire to avoid government controlled evacuation led to this result.[108] Even four months after the nuclear accident at Three Mile Island, residents near the reactor expressed continuing interest in moving away. The perceived threat from radioactivity dominated actual definable damage, indicating the power of the imagery of exposure to radioactivity.[109]

In any future nuclear war (including the lower level attacks noted in Table 18.1), the impulse to escape is likely to be very strong.[110] People in the target areas (e.g., near SAC bases) are likely to leave their homes, possibly in an uncontrolled fashion. Such movements, however, would compromise and complicate the relief and recovery efforts of the government. Political leaders would have to face the fact, as Ikle suggests, that there would be a widespread and deep aversion to returning to rebuild the cities and aid in the recovery efforts. The stress on resources in the nontargeted areas, too, would be severe. Population movements in response to a simple counterforce attack on the United States, for example, could lead to a six-fold increase in people per dwelling unit (from three people to 18) in the areas to which they have fled.[111] That level of crowding would create substantial conflict and stress.[112] The combination of insufficient or unavailable food and shelter and social services for the mass of evacuated people would place enormous demands on the government.[113]

These relocation problems would not be short-term. As a result of the effects of radiation from Chernobyl, for example, 135,000 people were evacuated from an area 18 miles around the plant. The towns will not be habitable, requiring the construction of new cities from scratch, at a huge cost both in resources and human terms.[114] These problems, however, were small compared to what would happen after a 2000 MT counterforce attack against missile sites in the United States. In metropolitan areas escaping direct damage, decisions about who will be evacuated and when could become politically explosive, fraught with fears of one group or another becoming the expendable victims. This is not to mention the problem of deciding when and how to evacuate special populations such as prisoners or patients in acute and chronic care facilities.[115]

INTENSIFICATION OF ETHNIC, REGIONAL, AND OTHER CONFLICTS

As it becomes evident that satisfying even the simplest survival requirements may be very difficult, the post-disaster "altruism" which often follows more ordinary disasters should evaporate into significant interpersonal, intergroup, and interregional conflict. Preexisting ethnic, racial, regional, and economic cleavages could emerge as the focal points for new tensions. New antagonisms are likely to develop, between hosts and refugees.[116] Conflict over value systems and life-styles, and over the possession and use of surviving resources could foster these conflicts.

There is evidence along these lines from the past. During the potato famine of the 1840s, for example, the English saw the Irish as an overwhelming burden and responsibility for them. "Little sympathy was felt for Ireland; her misfortunes were too frequent, too hopeless, too impossible to remedy. . . . In the winter of 1848-49 . . . compassion for Ireland was dead."[117] In Japan during World War II social disorganization increased the hostility between urban and rural people.[118] Each perceived the other as causing their unhappy circumstances. The residents of cities such as Osaka, of regions such as Okinawa and Hokkaido, and ethnic groups such as Koreans also became the targets of hostility.[119] An increase in hostility as a response to long-term stress was also evident after the Black Death.[120]

Similar conflicts are likely in a post-attack U.S. society. According to a study conducted by a panel of military officers, civil defense planners, and scientists engaged in disaster research, any general nuclear war would lead to an increase in conflict between sections of the country, between advocates of varying war policies, between urban and rural populations, and between racial and class groups. Such conflicts, most panelists noted, would necessitate the imposition of martial law or other authoritarian systems in many localities, and the widespread use of troops to maintain order.[121]

IV. The Governmental Response

In any countervalue or combination of counterforce and countervalue attacks with a significant urban component, a substantial proportion of the experienced and competent leadership and the infrastructure that maintains continuity is likely to be lost or seriously damaged. The ability of civil authorities to respond to the emergency will be severely constrained by a drastic reduction in the technicians, professionals, managers, and public leaders, who are heavily concentrated in the cities. The ranks of potential replacement personnel will also be significantly thinned, since the apprentices, management trainees, junior executives, and lower level civil servants are concentrated in these same areas.

Given the likely apathy and disorientation in the populace as a whole, only the central government, or what is left of it, is likely to be able to provide direction to any recovery efforts. The delivery of adequate survival support will be a key to the government's ability to maintain its credibility. Any failure on its part to achieve meaningful progress toward recovery, to explain satisfactorily the causes of the attack, to explain and show mastery over the changed physical world, and to demonstrate a genuine concern for social needs and pre-attack values could lead to widespread disaffection.[122]

After a limited counterforce attack in which other attacks might follow, the demands placed upon the surviving leadership would involve new and onerous elements. The population would expect governmental action to minimize the terrible uncertainty over whether a new attack will occur and to ameliorate their fears of invisible dangers such as fallout. Political pressures to act quickly and terminate the uncertainty of the crisis would develop both domestically and internationally.

The performance of governmental responses in the past, however, is not too reassuring.[123] The U.S. response to the accident at Three Mile Island, according to the NRC study, "strained existing emergency plans at all levels of government."[124] One of the key problems was "inadequate communication networks" between the various levels of government.[125] Initially, the political leadership was unable to explain the nature of the catastrophe. Throughout the whole operation there were numerous instances of poor coordination or confused ad hoc planning. For example, when an area larger than the original five-mile radius around TMI was designated for possible evacuation, the buses that had been lined up for evacuating the communities inside the five-mile zone disappeared, forcing local community officials to begin their planning anew.[126] The result was officials did not know what to do because they did not understand what was going on.

The responses of the Soviet government to the Chernobyl accident were even less encouraging. Information and decisions appeared not to flow effectively either vertically (to Moscow) or horizontally (to nearby officials).[127] Soviet officials claimed workers at the plant did not inform Moscow of the seriousness of the problem and thus they did not appreciate the severity of the accident until they saw the plant themselves.[128] A high-level commission was set up to study the affairs within 12 hours of the accident, but the head of that group stated "I had not supposed the scale of the accident was as great as it actually was."[129]

It took 36 hours before the 25,000 residents in the nearby town of Pripyat were evacuated.[130] The complete evacuation took almost a week as the exclusion area expanded. Moreover, as *Pravda* observed, "Some leaders of the evacuation turned out to be psychologically unprepared for the work in the conditions caused by the Chernobyl accident."[131] There were cases of people "deserting, panicking and trying to pin the blame on others. . . . We have already got rid of a few people, including people in leadership positions," said a Kiev Province party leader.[132]

Most troubling, at both TMI and Chernobyl, responsible officials could not believe at first that something terrible had gone wrong. They kept trying to fix "it," instead of admitting "it" was out of control. Unlike a natural disaster, such as a tornado or hurricane, these nuclear events were perhaps too extraordinary and terrifying, "too outside of reality" to actually be happening.

When governments perform ineffectively in demanding situations, widespread distrust of authority is likely to emerge. After the Black Death outbreaks against authority increased.[133] In Japan near the end of World War II there was a growing confusion about war aims and methods and a deepening crisis of confidence between the population and the Government."[134] The strain of large-scale damage and physical deprivation, coupled with the sense of impending military defeat also led to fissures within the military and between the military and civilian leaders in Japan.[135] Resentment and hostility against the government stemming from the effects of the air war also were evident among the British and Germans during World War II.[136] Populations experiencing bomb damage naturally gave the most evidence of this hostility. In Germany, hostility against the political leadership was also observed by the United States Strategic Bombing Study. The hate and anger the bombings aroused tended to be directed against the Nazi regime, which was blamed for beginning air warfare and for being unable to ward off Allied air attacks.[137]

Distrust of responsible officials was also evident in the more recent TMI and Chernobyl experiences. In the TMI case all authorities came to be suspect — from the federal and state governments to the utility company. The power of the imagery was not limited to residents of the immediate vicinity. A matched group of young mothers with children from the TMI area and from Wilkes-Barre outside the immediate area showed similar negative perceptions.[138] It appears that, to some degree, experiencing this event through the media was as traumatic as experiencing the threat more directly. Other indicators of continuing distrust and uncertainty included persistent negative rumors about events occurring at TMI and an increasingly negative perception of TMI. Only 20% thought the advantage of the plant outweighed its disadvantages after the accident, as contrasted to 50% before it.[139] After five years, TMI-II was still a serious enough symbol that the governor of Pennsylvania opposed the start up of its sister plant, TMI-I.[140]

In the wake of the Chernobyl accident there was a strong negative reaction against the Soviet government from the international community, based on the inadequate information that the government provided during the first days after the accident.[141] Even the governments of France and Germany were criticized by their own people for not adequately informing them about the immediate dangers of the fallout.[142] In West Germany the political party in power went through a difficult period when it lost substantial political support for its pronuclear power position; Yugoslavia and Austria even canceled planned nuclear power plants.[143] In short, the need for the government to organize and motivate its surviving population in response to any of the counterforce and countervalue scenarios will be most critical precisely at a time when it is ironically most likely to make demoralizing mistakes.

TABLE 18.4: Categorization of Disasters by Nature of Their Impact

Estimates are given on a 10 point scale

Example	Frequency	Suddenness of impact	Destructive power	Extent	Contamination	Communication disruption
Plague	1	3	0	9	10	0
Hurricane	3	9	8	4	1	4
Fires	3	8	4	4	0	4
Floods	3	8	4	4	0	4
Earthquake	3	6	5	4	3	4
Conv. War	2	4	2	5	3	4
Nuclear	<1	10	10	9	9	9

Source: James Thompson, "Psychological Consequences of Disaster: Analysis of the Nuclear Case," in *The Medical Implications of Nuclear War*, ed. Frederick Solomon and Robert Q. Marston, Institute of Medicine, National Academy of Sciences (Washington, DC: National Academy Press, 1986), 292-294.

V. Policy Relevance

At the beginning of this discussion four levels of damage were defined in an effort to determine what level of damage to society from a nuclear attack might be "acceptable." Only A-4 (see Table 18.1) might marginally satisfy Level 3 conditions (i.e., the survival of a central government capable of national control). None of the attacks with an urban/industrial component—A1 to A4 (Table 18.1) and SCOPE 2-4 (see Table 18.2)—meet the requirements of Level 4 (i.e., minimum damage and the continued existence of a viable, independent nation). Yet only Level 4 is truly "acceptable." In short, the explosion of only a small portion of current United States and USSR nuclear stock—no more than 400 to 500 weapons with the power of 150-200 megatons against urban-industrial targets—would produce damage that most people would see as quite "unacceptable."

It is unlikely, however, that even the limited strategic military attack envisaged in the scenario discussed above could be maintained at that level. Attacks limited to ICBMs, nuclear bombers and submarine bases would cause radioactive contamination of critical food production and industrial areas and sufficient direct damage to nearby urban areas to generate, in all probability, irresistible pressures to retaliate. Scenarios which assume the maintenance of political control under such extraordinary circumstances are very likely to be unrealistic. As the Chernobyl and TMI accidents suggest, it is extremely difficult for leaders to quickly and easily come to grips with a situation far out of the realm of normal experience. The instinctual reaction is likely to be denial and a failure to cope—a reaction that could be disastrous during the initial stages of nuclear crisis. Further, the leaders of a nation subjected to the first use of nuclear weapons are apt to feel fundamentally betrayed and, with trust destroyed, to see every overture to terminate the conflict as doublespeak, masking the aggressor's desire to bring about complete national surrender. The alternative in such a situation might well be escalation and the eliminating of most, if not all, of the options to control the conflict. The terrible consequences of that alternative have been suggested here, but in this context of confusion and destruction retaliation may not be perceived as either unacceptable or unthinkable.

Possible defenses against nuclear weapons do not fundamentally alter the situation. For advanced defensive technologies to provide real protection, the United States government recognized, "they must, at a minimum, be able to destroy a sufficient portion of an aggressor's attacking forces to deny him confidence in the outcome of an attack or deny an aggressor the ability to destroy a militarily significant portion of the target base he wishes to attack."[144]

There is little evidence that such a defensive capability is possible. An opponent who decides to target many of its weapons on each of the most prized industrial and population targets may overwhelm even a highly efficient defense. Suppose 2% to 5% of 10,000 to 20,000 weapons (i.e., 200 to 1,000 weapons) would reach their targets. Those weapons could destroy approximately 50 to 70 major U.S. cities and possibly 200 to 300 military/industrial targets. In reality, a defense system essentially would have to be perfect (a maximum of 1% to 2% leakage) to be considered even potentially effective in such circumstances. Even then, 1% leakage against urban targets could assure substantial damage.

Theoretically a sophisticated, selective defense might be developed to protect key critical targets against such a targeting strategy. This type of defense, however, requires the resolution of difficult technical questions including how to effectively identify and destroy the incoming weapons which are attacking these targets. To choose the "right" target to protect and decide what level of redundant protection is affordable, requires a highly sophisticated understanding of the societal vulnerabilities and confidence in one's own ability to "manage" the damage that inevitably will occur.

An incomplete or "leaky" system, however, can create strong incentives to strike first at an enemy's offensive weapons. With fewer weapons to defend against, even with retaliation, the defense system could "work" better. This would be particularly likely if the defense system degrades at a certain threshold: that is, the defense lets through only one out of 100 weapons when facing a "small" force of say fewer than 3,000 weapons, while it saturates and breaks down when challenged by more than 5,000 weapons, resulting in the penetration of 5 or 10 out of 100 weapons. Indeed, an aggressor may believe a nation attacked with a strategic military or "limited" nuclear attack, and facing the aggressors incomplete yet viable defense, might think twice before retaliating. Otherwise it faces the possibility that it will suffer additional strikes and further destruction. This might be viewed as an efficient method of inflicting sufficient damage on the other side to cause it to sue for peace. This approach represents the aggressive maximalist strategies discussed by Glad in Chapter 14 of this volume. In contrast, the fragile underlying assumption still must be satisfied that, despite the shock and anger, government leaders who feel betrayed personally and for their nation will somehow behave rationally after seeing unthinkable and unfolding disaster.

One final conclusion: Nuclear war between the superpowers would, as noted, have worldwide economic and political impact. National economies and communications are now interrelated and the possibility of some form of nuclear winter serves to emphasize that interdependence most dramatically. Those nations not attacked directly would likely face a world in which fuel for life-sustaining activities is in short supply. Key industrial products and capital goods exporters and importers will have disappeared, and the agricultural supports are likely to be absent or insufficient.[145]

Unmanageable population movements may begin to occur within days or weeks of any attack, driven by perceived radiation danger, vulnerability to additional attacks, and the simple fear of the unknown. Noncombatant nations would have to deliver goods, fuel, and reassurance in the face of a tenuous future. Their leaders would have to master the vocabulary of economic reorganization and international realignments and know how to control the likely domestic social turmoil caused by concrete changes and perceived vulnerabilities. Nuclear stability, in short, is not just a concern for the superpowers. The whole world has a stake in the avoidance of a major nuclear war.

Notes

1. Arthur M. Katz, *Economic and Social Consequences of Nuclear Attacks on the United States* [Committee on Banking, Housing and Urban Affairs, U.S. Senate] (Washington, DC: Government Printing Office).

2. Hedrick Smith, *The Russians* (New York: Ballantine, 1976), 572-574; "Gorbachev Orchestrates New Variations on Soviet Theme," *New York Times* (21 December 1986), sec. 4, p. 1; "Soviet Press Details Kazakhstan Riot," *Washington Post* (11 January 1987), sec. 1; "In the Deep South of the Soviet Fold, Complaints Rise in Many Tongues," *New York Times* (7 January 1990), sec. 4, p. 2.

3. Subcommittee on Arms Control, International Organizations and Security Agreements, Committee on Foreign Relations United States Senate, *Analyses of Effects of Limited Nuclear Warfare* [94th Cong., 1st sess.] (Washington, DC: Government Printing Office, 1975).

4. M. Getler, "Changes in US Nuclear Strategy," *Washington Post* (14 August 1980), sec. 1, p. 1; C. S. Gray and K. Payne, "Victory Is Possible," *Foreign Policy* (Summer 1980): 14-17.

5. Arthur M. Katz, *Life After Nuclear War* (Cambridge, MA: Ballinger, 1982); Scientific Committee on Problems of the Environment (SCOPE-28), International Council of Scientific Unions, *Environmental Consequences of Nuclear War (ENUWAR)*, A. B. Pittock et al., "Vol. I: Physical and Atmospheric Effects," and M. A. Harwell and T. C. Hutchinson, "Vol. II: Ecological and Agricultural," (New York: Wiley, 1985).

6. The table is from Katz, *Life After Nuclear War*. See also Joseph Rotblat, "Acute Radiation Mortality in Nuclear War," in *The Medical Implications of Nuclear War*, eds. Fredrick Solomon and Robert Q. Marston (Washington, DC: National Academy Press, 1986), 233-250. The total attack would consist of approximately 2,240 megatons (MT) carried by 2,240 warheads targeted upon ICBMs, Strategic Air Command (SAC) airfields and submarine bases.

7. Samuel Glasstone and Philip J. Dolan, *The Effects on Nuclear Weapons*, 3rd ed. (U.S. Department of Defense and Department of Energy, 1977), 514-540.

8. Katz, *Life After Nuclear War*, 45. Casualty estimates for attack scenarios of this type range from 14 to 30 million casualties (7 to 15 million deaths and 7 to 15 million injured) to 25 to 64 million casualties (12 to 34 million deaths and 13 to 30 million injured). See Office of Technology Assessment, *The Effects of Nuclear War* (Washington, DC: Government Printing Office, 1979); William Daugherty, Barbara Levi, and Frank von Hippel "Casualties Due to the Blast, Heat and Radioactive Fallout from Various Hypothetical Nuclear Attacks on the United States," in *The Medical Implications of Nuclear War*, 207-232.

9. The study was done by the Scientific Committee on Problems of the Environment (SCOPE) of the International Council of Scientific Unions to examine global scale agricultural and environmental issues. The four phases of the scope attack, SCOPE-1 to SCOPE-4 in Table 18.2 are intended to simulate the stages of an escalation scenario but were not directly used to develop the detailed damage estimates of the study.

10. Office of Technology Assessment, *The Effects of Nuclear War* (Washington, DC: Government Printing Office, 1979); William Daugherty, Barbara Levi, and Frank von Hippel, "Casualties Due to the Blast, Heat and Radioactive Fallout from Various Hypothetical Nuclear Attacks on the United States," in *The Medical Implications of Nuclear War*, 207-232.

11. R. K. Laurino, F. Trinkel, C. F. Miller, and R. A. Harker, *Economic and Industrial Aspects of Crisis Relocation: An Overview* (Palo Alto, CA: Center for Planning and Research, 1977), DCPA 01-75-c-0279: R. Laurino, F. Trinkel, R. Berry, R. Schnider, and W. MacDougall, *Impacts of Crisis Relocation on US Economic and Industrial Activity* (Palo Alto, CA: Center for Planning and Research, 1978), DCPA 01-76-c-0331.

12. Katz, *Life After Nuclear War*, 100.

13. Richard L. Goen, Richard B. Bothun, and Frank E. Walker, *Potential Vulnerability Affecting National Survival* (Menlo Park, CA: Stanford Research Institute, September 1970). Systematic efforts designed to virtually obliterate several critical industrial sectors such as pharmaceuticals petroleum refining, nonferrous metals, iron, and steel production; and engines and turbines, could assure devastating, long-term disruption of the economies of several nations. Unfortunately, even attempts to defeat this strategy with the industrial civil defense of hardening specific industrial targets, would be useless if specific plants were attacked directly and caught up in massive fires.

14. F. W. Dresch and S. Baum, *Analysis of the U.S. and U.S.S.R. Potential for Economic Recovery Following a Nuclear Attack* (Menlo Park, CA: Stanford Research Institute, Strategic Studies Center, January 1973), 1-16; Jack Sassen and Kenneth Willis, *Data Base and Damage Criteria for Measurement of Arms Limitation Effects on War Supporting Industry*, ACDA/WEC-242 (Alexandria, VA: Metis Corporation, June 1974), 44; Katz, *Life After Nuclear War*, 109-118; Stephen L. Brown and Pamela G. Krusic, *Agricultural Vulnerability: The National Entity Context* (Menlo Park, CA: Stanford Research Institute, July 1970), 12 DAHC-20-69-0186; Stephen L. Brown, H. Lee, J. L. Mackin, and K. D. Moll, *Agricultural Vulnerability to Nuclear War* (Menlo Park, CA: Stanford Research Institute, February 1973), 30 DAHC-20-70-C-0395.

Increasing the likelihood of expanded urban economic collapse, as Postal's projections indicate, are frequent firestorms. They could burn out the central urban core for many targeted cities. If realized, the core area of heavy destruction would extend beyond the range of blast damage normally attributed to a one megaton weapon (i.e., a 10-12 mile radius as compared with 5 miles). See Theodore A. Postal, "Possible Fatalities from Superfires Following Nuclear Attacks in or near Urban Areas," in *The Medical Implications of Nuclear War*, 15-72; Ashley W. Oughterson and Shield Warren, *Medical Effects of the Atomic Bomb in Japan* (New York: McGraw-Hill, 1956), 17; Committee for the Compilation of Materials on Damage, *Hiroshima and Nagasaki* (New York: Basic Books, 1981), 55-66.

15. Soviet prospects (see Table 18.3) would be no more reassuring because their centrally planned economy contains even more intense concentrations of critical industries than does that of the United States. The urban infrastructure in attacked areas — transportation, utilities, sanitation systems — would emerge either badly damaged or of very limited use. It would be difficult for the economy to cope with these losses if superfires or firestorms were a common element of nuclear attacks. See U.S. Arms Control and Disarmament Agency, *An Analysis of Civil Defense in Nuclear War* (Washington, DC: ACDA, December 1978) 3-8; Congressional Budget Office, *Retaliatory Issues for the US Strategic*

Nuclear Forces (Washington, DC: Government Printing Office, June 1978): Central Intelligence Agency, *Soviet Civil Defense*, NI-1003, July 1978; Hal Cochrane and Dennis Mileti, "The Consequences of Nuclear War: An Economic and Social Perspective," in *The Medical Implications of Nuclear War*, 381-412. Also, "Europe Is Bracing for Chernobyl's Grim Legacy," *New York Times* (31 August 1986), sec. 4, p. 1.

16. Stephen L. Brown, and Ulrich F. Pilz, "U.S. Agriculture: Potential Vulnerabilities," Contract no. DAHC-20-67-C-0116, OCD Work Unit 3535A (Menlo Park, CA: Stanford Research Institute, January 1969), 23-28; Katz, *Life After Nuclear War*, 50-62, 143-160.

17. Office of Technology Assessment, *Effects of Nuclear Weapons*, 88-89. (Washington, DC: Government Printing Office, 1979).

18. C. M. Haaland, C. V. Chester, and E. P. Wigner, *Survival of the Relocated Population of the United States after a Nuclear Attack* (Oak Ridge, TN: Oak Ridge National Laboratory, June 1976), 53; Katz, *Life After Nuclear War*, 54; Steve A. Fetter and Kosta Tsipis, "Catastrophic Releases of Radioactivity," *Scientific American* (April 1981), 4145.

19. "Chernobyl Fuels Nuclear Anxiety in Europe," *New York Times* (18 May 1986), sec. 4, p. 1.

20. "England Farmers Count Nuclear Cost," *The Guardian* (13 August 1986), 6.

21. "Chernobyl Fuels Nuclear Anxiety in Europe," *New York Times* (18 May 1986), sec. 4, p. 1.

22. "The Aftermath of Chernobyl," *Science*, 233, 4769 (12 September 1986): 1141-1143.

23. "Europe Is Bracing for Chernobyl's Grim Legacy," *New York Times* (31 August 1986), sec. 4, p. 1; "Chernobyl Shakes Reindeer Culture of Lapps," *New York Times* (14 September 1986), sec. 1, p. 1.

24. Brown and Krusic, *Agricultural Vulnerability*, 12; Brown et al., *Agricultural Vulnerability to Nuclear War*, 30.

25. Katz, *Life After Nuclear War*, 157.

26. SCOPE, *Environmental Consequences of Nuclear War*, Vol. II, 422-423; R. P. Turco et al., "Climate and Smoke: An Appraisal of Nuclear Winter," *Science*, 247 (1990): 166-176.

27. Stakey Thompson and Stephen Schneider, "Nuclear Winter Reappraised," *Foreign Affairs*, 64, 5 (1986): 998.

28. R. J. Hammon, *Food, Vol. I. History of the Second World War*, in United Kingdom Civil Series, ed. W. K. Hancock (London: H. M. Stationery Office, 1957), 156; Ikle, *The Social Impact of Bomb Destruction*, 151; The U.S. Strategic Bombing Survey, *Pacific Report No. 58* (Washington, DC: Government Printing Office, 1946-1947), 166.

29. Alexander Leighton, *Human Relations in a Changing World* (New York: E. P. Dutton, 1949), 61, 71.

30. In the United States, for example, 68% of the physicians are located in the 76 largest urban areas. See *Physician Characteristics and Distribution in the U.S., 1981* (Chicago: American Medical Association, 1982).

31. Katz, *Life After Nuclear War*, 120, 176.

32. National Center for Health Statistics, *National Ambulatory Medical Care Survey, Series 13*, no. 33. (PHS, HEW, 1975); American Medical Association, *Profile of Medical Practice*, 1978.

33. Katz, *Economic and Social Consequences of Nuclear Attacks on the U.S.*, 93; Howard Hiatt, *Journal of the American Medical Association*, 244, 20 (November 1980): 2314. Hiatt was quoted as describing the demands of a single burn patient on a well-equipped hospital; "American Burning," Report of the National Commission on Fire Prevention and Control, in "Caring for Burned Children" by Colman McCarthy, *Washington Post* (22 April 1978).

34. V. Infantes et al., "Psychopathological Observations in the Earthquake Area Aancahs 1970," *Rev. Neurosiquiatr*, 33 (1970): 171; "Miracle Amid the Ruins," *Time* (7 October 1985): 36; "Disaster in Mexico," *Newsweek* (30 September 1986): 16.

35. John Hersey, *Hiroshima* (New York: Bantam, 1947), 33-34.

36. Herbert L. Abrams, "Medical Supply and Demand in a Post-Nuclear War World," in *The Medical Implications of Nuclear War*, 349-380.

37. David H. Greer and Lawrence S. Rifkin, "The Immunological Impact of Nuclear War," in *The Medical Implications of Nuclear War*, 317-328; Gladstone, *The Effects of Nuclear Weapons*, 580-581.

38. "Chernobyl: Six Months Later," *Washington Post* (26 October 1986), sec. A, p. 1; Richard Champlin, "With Chernobyl Victims," *Washington Post* (13 July 1986), sec. B, p. 2.

39. "AIDS and the New Apartheid," *New York Times* (7 October 1985), sec. 1, p. 30; "The AIDS Conflict," *Newsweek* (23 September 1985): 18; "State Permits Closing of Bathhouses to Cut AIDS," *New York Times* (26 October 1985), sec. 1, p. 4; "AIDS: Reasons Clouded by a Plague Mentality," *New York Times* (27 April 1986), sec., p. 28; Barbara Tuchman, *A Distant Mirror* (New York; Alfred A. Knopf, 1987), 96, 109-115; "Epidemic: A Paralyzing Effect," *Newsweek* (23 September 1985), 21.

40. Greer and Rifkin, "The Immunological Impact of Nuclear War,"; Gladstone, *The Effects of Nuclear Weapons*, 580-581.

41. See sources in note 39.

42. "Chernobyl: Six Months Later," *Washington Post* (26 October 1986), sec. A., p. 1; Richard Champlin, "With Chernobyl Victims," *Washington Post* (13 July 1986), sec. B, p. 2.

43. Department of International Economic and Social Affairs, *Yearbook of International Trade Statistics*, Vol. 1 (New York: United Nations, 1982), iviii; Report of the Secretary General, *General and Complete Disarmament, Comprehensive Study on Nuclear Weapons*, United National General Assembly, A/35/392, English Annex (New York: UN General Assembly, September 1980), 87; Department of International Economic and Social Affairs, Statistical Office, *Yearbook of International Trade Statistics, 1981 Vol. I*, Special Table C, "World Trade by Commodity Classes and Regions," (New York: UN General Assembly, United Nations Publication, 1982), 1118-1206; United Nations, *General and Complete Disarmament Comprehensive Study on Nuclear Weapons*, 87.

44. Grains, Foreign Agriculture Circular, *World Grain Situation and Outlook*, U.S. Department of Agriculture, Foreign Agriculture Service, August 1985, FG-11-85.

45. Solomon and Marston, eds., *The Medical Implications of Nuclear War*, 371.

46. Ibid., 372-373.

47. Department of International Economic and Social Affairs, *Statistical Yearbook 1982*, Statistics Office (New York: United Nations, 1985), 691-691; SCOPE, *Environmental Consequences of Nuclear War*, Vol. II, 374-376.

48. SCOPE, *Environmental Consequences of Nuclear War*, Vol. II, 371-374.

49. Paul J. Crutzen, and John W. Birks, "The Atmosphere After a Nuclear War: Twilight at Noon," *Ambio*, 11 (1982): 114-125; R. P. Turco et al., "Nuclear Winter: Global Consequences of Multiple Nuclear Explosions," *Science* 222 (1983): 1283-1292; Thompson and Schneider, *Foreign Affairs*, 981-1005.

50. SCOPE, *Environmental Consequences of Nuclear War*, Vol. II, 422-423; see also R. P. Turco et al., "Climate and Smoke: An Appraisal of Nuclear Winter" *Science*, 247 (1990): 166-67.

51. Allen H. Barton, *Communities in Disaster: A Sociological Analysis of Collective Stress Situations* (Garden City, NY: Doubleday, 1969).

52. "Chernobyl: Six Months Later," *Washington Post* (26 October 1986), sec. A, p. 1; Richard Champlin, "With Chernobyl Victims," *Washington Post* (13 July 1986), sec. B. p. 2.

53. V. Infantes et al., "Psychopathological Observations in the Earthquake Area Aancahs 1970," *Rev. Neurosiquiatr*, 33 (1970): 171; "Miracle Amid the Ruins," *Time* (7 October 1985), 36; "Disaster in Mexico," *Newsweek* (30 September 1986), 16.

54. Father Siemes, "Hiroshima — August 6, 1945," *Bulletin of the Atomic Scientists*, 1, 2 (May 1946): 6.

55. Robert J. Lifton, *Death in Life* (New York: Vantage Books, 1969), 7.

56. "Moscow Says Some at Chernobyl Panicked and Abandoned Posts," *New York Times* (18 May 1986), sec. 1, p. 18.

57. James Thompson, "Psychological Consequences of Disaster: Analysis of the Nuclear Case," in *The Medical Implications of Nuclear War*, 292-294; Lifton, *Death in Life*, 21.

58. Lifton, *Death in Life*, 19-30.

59. Ibid., 22.

60. Ibid., 30, 68.

61. Ibid., 30.

62. Ibid., 37-56.

63. S. Cobb and E. Lindermann, "Neuropsychiatric Observation During the Cocoanut Grove Fire," *Annuals of Surgery*, 117 (1943): 814.

64. Lifton, *Death in Life*, 165-208.

65. Ibid., 165-181.

66. Ruth Benedict, *The Sword and Chrysanthemum* (New York, NY: New American Library, 1974).

67. Warren Kinston and Rachel Rosser, "Disaster: Effects on Mental and Physical State," *Journal of Psychosomatic Research*, 18 (1974): 437-456; see also Anthony F. Wallace, *Tornado in Worcester*, National Academy of Sciences Disaster Study No. 3, Washington DC, 1956.

68. Baruch Fischoff et al., *Acceptable Risk* (New York: Cambridge University Press, 1981); P. Slovic and B. Fischoff, "How Safe Is Safe Enough?" in *Risk and Chance,* eds. J. Dowie and P. Lefrere (Milton Keynes, Open University Press, 1980); P. Slovic, B. Fischoff, and S. Lichtenstein, "Facts Versus Fears: Understanding Perceived Risks," in *Judgment Under Uncertainty: Heuristics and Biases,* eds. D. Kahneman, P. Slovic, and A. Tversky (New York: Cambridge University Press, 1982); Report of the President's Commission on the Accident at Three Mile Island (Washington, DC, October 1979), 35.

69. "Chernobyl Shakes Reindeer Culture of Lapps," *New York Times* (14 September 1986), sec. 1, p. 1.

70. Jerome Frank, *Persuasion and Healing* (Baltimore, MD: Johns Hopkins University Press, 1973).

71. M. Popovic and D. Petrovic, "After the Earthquake," *Lancet,* 2 (1964): 1169.

72. "Technical Staff Analysis Report on Behavioral Effects to President's Commission on the Accident at Three Mile Island," (Washington DC, President's Commission on the Accident at Three Mile Island, October 1979), 26.

73. Katz, *Life After Nuclear War*, 369-371.

74. *Technical Staff Analysis Report on Behavioral Effects to President's Commission on the Accident at Three Mile Island*, 34.

75. Cynthia B. Flynn and James A. Chalmers, *The Social and Economic Effects of the Accident at Three Mile Island: Findings to Date*, NUREG-CR1215 (Washington, DC: Government Printing Office, January 1980), 21.

76. J. L. Tichner and F. T. Kapp, "Family and Character Changes at Buffalo Creek," *American Journal of Psychiatry*, 133 (1976): 295.

77. J. Erikson, "Loss of Communality at Buffalo Creek," *American Journal of Psychiatry*, 133 (1976): 302.

78. R. Swank, "Combat Exhaustion," *Journal of Neurological and Mental Disorders*, 109 (1949): 475.

79. D. D. Reid, "Neurosis on Active Service: Experience Among Air Crew on a Bomber Station," Interallied Conference on War Medicine, *Neuropsychiatry* (1944): 220-233.

80. H. C. D. Archibald, D. M. Long, C. Miller, and R. D. Tuddenham, "Cross Stress Reactions in Combat 15-Year Follow Up," *American Journal of Psychiatry*, 119 (1963): 317.

81. Tuckman, *A Distant Mirror*, 98-99.

82. Anna M. Campbell, *The Black Death and Men of Learning* (New York: Columbia University Press, 1931), 179; W. L. Langer, "The Next Assignment," *American History Review*, 63 (1958): 283; G. Sjoberg, "Disasters and Social Change," in *Man and Society in Disaster*, eds. L. Baker and D. Chapman (New York: Basic Books, 1962).

83. Warren Kinston and Rachel Rosser, "Disaster: Effects on Mental and Physical State," *Journal of Psychosomatic Research* 18 (1974): 437-456.

84. E. I. Chazov and M. E. Vartanian, "Effects on Human Behavior," in *Nuclear War: The Aftermath* (Stockholm Royal Swedish Academy of Sciences/Oxford, Pergamon Press, 1983).

85. James Thompson, "Psychological Consequences of Disaster: Analysis of the Nuclear Case," *Symposium on the Medical Implications of Nuclear War*, Institute of Medicine, National Academy of Sciences (20-22 September 1985), Washington, DC.

86. Leighton, *Human Relations in a Changing World*, 61, 71.

87. Bruce C. Allnut, "A Study of Consensus on Social and Psychological Factors Related to Recovery from Nuclear Attack," HSR-RR-71/3-D1 prepared for the Office of Civil Defense, Department of the Army (McLean, VA: Human Sciences Research, May 1971), S-4.

88. SCOPE, Vol. 1, Executive Summary, p. xxxii-xxxiii.

89. Lifton, *Death in Life*, 30.

90. James Thompson, "Psychological Consequences of Disaster: Analysis of the Nuclear Case," in *The Medical Implications of Nuclear War*, 292-294; Lifton, *Death in Life*, 21.

91. Flynn and Chalmers, *The Social and Economic Effects of the Accident at Three Mile Island: Findings to Date*, 37, 38.

92. Ibid.

93. "Kiev, Its Playgrounds Vacant, Scrubs On," *Washington Post* (9 June 1986), sec. A, p. 1.

94. Richard Titmuss, *Problems of Social Policy* (Westport, CT: Greenwood Press, 1971), 334; see also A. Freud and D. T. Burlington, *War and Children* (Des Plaines, IL: Greenwood Publishing, 1973).

95. Leighton, *Human Relations in a Changing World*, 234.

96. Titmuss, *Problems of Social Policy*, 423.

97. E. Elizur and M. Kaffman, "Children's Bereavement Reactions Following Death of Father: II" *Journal of the American Academy of Child Psychiatry* 21 (1982): 474-480.

98. Marion Osterweis, Frederic Solomon, and Morris Green, eds., *Bereavement: Reaction, Consequences and Care* (Washington, DC: National Academy Press, 1984), 116.

99. "Two Experts Forsee Deaths of 24,000 Tied to Chernobyl," *New York Times* (27 August 1986), sec. 1.

100. Titmuss, *Problems of Social Policy*, 334.

101. Ibid., 134.

102. Warren Kinston and Rachel Rosser, "Disaster: Effects on Mental and Physical State," *Journal of Psychosomatic Research*, 18 (1974): 437-456.

103. Lifton, *Death in Life*, 100-101. "It was the outsiders who had to come in and begin the work. The survivors had to be dragged along (hikizuru) by the outsiders."

104. "Miracles Amid the Ruins," *Time* (7 October 1985), 36; "Disaster in Mexico," *Newsweek* (30 September 1986), 16.

105. F. Hocking, "Human Reactions to Extreme Environmental Stress," *Medical Journal of Australia*, 2 (1965): 477.

106. Ikle, *Social Impact of Bomb Destruction*, 107.

107. Irving Janis, *Air War and Emotional Stress* (New York: McGraw-Hill, 1951), quote on 46, 16-17, 28-29.

108. Flynn, *Social and Economic Effects of Three Mile Island*, 14, 16, 22, 25, also private communication.

109. Cynthia Flynn, *Three Mile Island Telephone Survey, Preliminary Report on Procedure and Findings* (Mountain West Research Inc. with Social Impact Research Inc., NUREG/CR-1093, 24 September 1979), 39.

110. Katz, *Life After Nuclear War*, 39, 70, 223.

111. Haaland, *Survival of Relocated Populations*, 28.

112. Titmuss, *Problems of Social Policy*, 114.

113. Katz, *Life After Nuclear War*, 73-74.

114. "The Aftermath of Chernobyl," *Science*, 233, 4769 (12 September 1986): 1141-1143; "Chernobyl: Six Months Later," *Washington Post* (27 October 1986), sec. A, p. 1. It was reported that the initial estimates of the costs of losses in energy supplies, resettlement, and clean up were $3 billion.

115. Flynn, *The Social and Economic Effects of the Accident at Three Mile Island*, 37-42; Titmuss, *Problems of Social Policy*, 189; Leighton, *Human Relations in a Changing World*, 67; Ikle, *Social Impact of Bomb Destruction*, 119.

116. Leighton, *Human Relations in a Changing World*, 245.

117. C. Woodham-Smith, *The Great Hunger* (New York: Harper & Row, 1962), 381-382.

118. Leighton, *Human Relations in a Changing World*, 66.

119. Ibid., 243-246.

120. Anna M. Campbell, *The Black Death and Men of Learning*, 132.

121. Allnut, *Social Psychological Factors* s-3, s-4.

122. James D. Rudolph, ed., *Nicaragua, A Country Study* (U.S. Government, Secretary of the Army, 1982), 38; Alan Moorehead, *The Russian Revolution* (New York: Harper, 1958).

123. Titmuss, *Problems of Social Policy*, 150, 195, 296-297.

124. Flynn, *Social and Economic Effects of Three Mile Island*, 28.

125. Ibid., 31.

126. Ibid., 34.

127. E. Hoffman, *Nuclear Deception, Soviet Information Policy,"* *Bulletin of Atomic Scientists*, 43, No. 1 (August/September 1986), 34; U. M. Falin, "Der Speigel Interview No Vostirls. Falin on Accident," in *DR*, III, no. 92, J. supp. 93, 13 May 1986, L3-L7.

128. "Chernobyl: Six Months Later," *Washington Post* (27 October 1986), sec. A, p. 1.

129. "Chernobyl: Six Months Later," *Washington Post* (26 October 1986), sec. A, p. 1; Richard Champlin, "With Chernobyl Victims," *Washington Post* (13 July 1986), sec. B, p. 2.

130. "Two Plant Managers at Chernobyl Fired," *Washington Post* (13 May 1986), sec. A. p. 1.

131. E. Hoffman, "Nuclear Deception, Soviet Information Policy," *Bulletin of Atomic Scientists*, 43, no. 1 (August/September 1986), 34; U. M. Falin, "Der Speigel Interview No Vostirls. Falin on Accident," in *DR. III*. no. 92, J. supp. 93 (13 May 1986), L3-L7.

132. "Moscow Says Some at Chernobyl Panicked and Abandoned Posts," *New York Times* (18 May 1986), sec. 1, p. 18.

133. Campbell, *The Black Death and Men of Learning*, 129.

134. Leighton, *Human Relations in a Changing World*, 67-69.

135. Ibid., 248-249.

136. Janis, *Air War and Emotional Stress*, 128.

137. U.S. Strategic Bombing Survey as cited in Janis, *Air War and Emotional Stress*, 129.

138. Katz, *Life After Nuclear War*, 364.

139. Flynn, *Three Mile Island Telephone Survey*, 41.

140. "Three Mile Island Opponents Race for the Court House," *Energy Daily*, 13, 106 (4 June 1985), 1.

141. "Reagan Protests Lack of Details on Soviet Plant," *New York Times* (4 May 1986), sec. 1.

142. "Delayed Warnings Stir Outcry in France Against the Government," *Washington Post* (13 May 1986), sec A, p. 14.

143. "Yugoslavia Cites Chernobyl in Canceling Power Plant," *Washington Post* (13 May 1986), sec. a, p. 14; "The Chernobyl Accident," *Nuclear News* (June 1986): 87-94.

144. *The President's Strategic Defense Initiative*, Office of the President, 1985.

145. SCOPE, Vol. II, Executive Summary.

PART IV

Conclusions

Chapter 19

Implications for the Future

BETTY GLAD

Several observers of the contemporary scene see a new epoch in the making, one in which warfare between the major powers becomes as outdated as dueling and slavery have in the past. Francis Fukuyama has argued, in what may be a purposively provocative statement, that the triumph of Western liberal economic and political ideals over the contending ideologies of fascism and communism has created a new world in which one will see the "growing 'Common Marketization' of international relations."[1] John Mueller, in his *Retreat from Doomsday*, makes a detailed and serious argument that historical factors have made warfare between the major powers obsolete.[2] He argues that in the past war was seen as a romantic and heroic enterprise in which national leaders made the choice for battle on the basis of rational considerations of self-interest. The experiences of World War I and II, however, made it clear that war was no longer a rational option and gradually the older heroic notions of war have been replaced by ideas that it is not an acceptable activity. In the post-World War II period, the revolutionary goals of the Soviet Union were destabilizing and the source of "big power" conflict. With the Soviet renunciation of its revolutionary goals and the clear manifestations of its military weakness, however, whatever residual factors might have led to big power wars have been eliminated.

There are some encouraging trends in contemporary big power political arrangements and the way in which these powers view their relationship that may make wars between them less likely in the future as will be discussed below. But if we look at the contemporary world in terms of the broader historical and psychological perspectives suggested in this volume, these visions of a world without war are far too sanguine. The thaw in the cold war between the United States and the USSR and the complex linkages that are being built across various traditional national boundaries are blurring the old lines which demarcated the conflicts we have lived with since the end of World War II. But particular enemy and alliance systems, historically, have never been permanent. New arrangements lead to new conflicts and new conflicts may lead to the resolution of these conflicts through arms, given the absence of a central system of justice and law and the proclivities of human beings to identify with their own regimes and look down on those that differ from them. The possible transition to a no-war world, then, promises to be much more difficult to obtain than the optimists of the day suggest.

The assumption that the spread of democracy will eliminate war, moreover, is based on a short and atypical history. Popular governments have engaged in wars against each other, as did the United States and Great Britain in the war of 1812. Moreover, as the history of fifth century B.C. Athens, Republican Rome, and Napoleonic France suggest, popularly supported governments can often become imperial republics bent on expansion. The United States has not been a stranger to such ambitions. In the nineteenth century, the goals of manifest destiny led it into wars against Mexico, Spain, and the conquest of the Philippines. More recently, the widespread domestic enthusiasm in the United States for the interventions in Grenada and Panama suggest that even democratic publics are apt to overlook the niceties of international law in the pride of national effort to accomplish a higher purpose through arms.

Democracies, too, may breed demagogic political leaders who can lead their peoples into imperial exploits. Sometimes the leader gains his following through appeals to pride and gain. Alcibiades tapped these kinds of feelings when he convinced Athenians in the winter of 416-415 B.C. that they should undertake their Sicilian campaign. The inhabitants of the Sicilian towns were a "mixed rabble," victory over them would probably make the Athenians master of all Hellas.[3] At other times the demagogue gains his power because democratic leaders are unable to deal with economic, social, and political disorders. Hitler came to power in Germany and Mussolini in Italy, partly, for reasons such as these. Collective disappointments and fear of a world that one does not understand may also provide fertile breeding grounds for demagogic leaders who are only too willing to focus popular frustrations on an external enemy. Thus, in the early years of the cold war, many Americans, disappointed by the failure of the United States to transform the world into friendly democratic territory, were susceptible to Senator Joseph McCarthy's charge that these failures were due to the enemy's infiltration of key American institutions such as the State Department and the Army. Similar reactions could arise in certain kinds of futures. Robert Altemeyer's experimental findings suggest that even in North American democracies today, the threat of domestic disorder, whether created by a challenge from the left or the right, is apt to create a climate in which a people are predisposed to embrace traditional authority and the use of coercive measures to maintain order.[4]

Even the evidence that war does not pay cannot be counted on to completely constrain decision makers. Norman Angell and others at the beginning of this century had argued that contemporary weapons had become so destructive and the world so economically linked together, that major warfare was no longer a real possibility. Yet, as William Mueller has shown, many political leaders on opposite sides of both World Wars assumed that their wars would last only a few weeks or months.[5] The most destructive conventional war since then was based, moreover, on similar miscalculations. Iraq, as Mueller suggests, started the war against Iran "under a 1914-style illusion that the war would be a short, successful blitzkrieg."[6]

Similar mistakes could lead contemporary decision makers into situations which are much worse than anticipated. Nuclear strategists who assume their country could fight a nuclear war in a way that would lead to some positive outcome, whether it be called "winning," or "prevailing," would in all probability soon discover the serious limitations on their ability to control and limit the destructive capacity of these weapons in any meaningful way.

A close look at several conflicts in which the United States and the USSR had direct or indirect interests at stake during the cold war suggest that had certain military and political leaders near the top prevailed, similar mistakes would have been made. During the Korean War, General MacArthur and his political allies in the U.S. Congress wanted to expand the war to the Chinese mainland. Their assurances that the Soviet Union would not respond militarily were as problematical as their earlier assurances that China would not enter the conflict. President Truman resisted these views, as we have seen, but he paid a large political price. During the Cuban missile crisis other military and political leaders pushed the American President to take more provocative stances than he ultimately took. The Joint Chiefs urged Kennedy to undertake a major air strike against the missile bases in Cuba. Indeed on Sunday, October 28, after the Russians had said they would move their offensive missiles from Cuba, Air Force Chief of Staff Curtis Le May wanted to mount the air strike the next day, anyway.[7] Maxwell Taylor, more than 20 years after the event, still thought that a possible air strike would have created no strong Soviet response. If Khrushchev was a rational man he would not counterescalate. If not, his colleagues would "look after him."[8]

The assumption that one's opponent will simply back down when confronted with the threat of a major military response is questionable at best, as Glad and Taber have suggested in this volume. The backdown is most likely in those situations where one power has local military predominance, more central interests at stake, and can permit its adversary to get out with a minimal loss of face. Even then, concessions may be very hard to make, and there is always the possibility that the state challenged may retaliate at some other place in the world where it has the advantage. Had Curtis Le May or the Joint Chiefs of Staff prevailed during the Cuban missile crisis, as President Kennedy was well aware, the Soviet Union might well have retaliated with aggressive moves of their own against Turkey or NATO. Indeed, even in the face of U.S. restraint, the Soviets felt humiliated by their retreat and vowed it would never happen again. The massive buildup in Soviet missile capabilities was sparked by that humiliation and Khrushchev, less than a year later, paid dearly for his perceived failures in that encounter when the other members of the Politburo removed him from office.[9] Earlier, when the Soviet Union had invaded Hungary within their own sphere of influence, President Eisenhower and Secretary of State Dulles had realized that there was nothing the United States could reasonably do, militarily. Yet even in that instance, Robert Amory, the Deputy Director of the Intelligence Directorate of the CIA, suggested that the United States employ nuclear weapons to bomb railroads leading from the Soviet Union to Hungary.[10]

Perhaps the weakest component of these no-war world arguments is their inattention to the kinds of psychological processes delineated in this volume. Mueller's assumption that leaders' "mistakes" as to the length and the costs of the war they undertake are simply the product of ambiguities in the situation[11] overlooks those leaders who have been more perspicacious. The best statesmen as Thucydides suggested, are able to peer into the future, to make sound judgments on the capabilities of their peoples relative to others even in the face of ambiguities.[12] Moreover, the direction of the errors made (i.e., the proclivity to overestimate one's own capabilities and underestimate the lengths and costs of war) suggest that those mistakes are often "motivated" by domestic political concerns and personal interests and emotions. "Men think out an enterprise in desire and hope suggests that fortune will supply the means of its success," Thucydides wrote. That is why they avoid facing "dangers that are plain to see." These factors motivate "states even more than individuals, because they are throwing for the highest stakes, freedom or empire, and because each man, when he has a whole people acting with him, magnifies his own power out of all reason."[13]

The motives of leaders who initiate wars can vary, as we have seen. "Glory-loving youngsters," as Theseus observed in one of Euripides plays, lead their people into war for a variety of motivations!" One of them wants to be a general; Another to seize the power and riot in it; A third is bent on gain."[14] People follow their leaders' into these enterprises, as contemporary social scientists suggest, because of their own needs. Pride in one's own group and the need to diminish others, aggression that is channeled in a socially supported direction, the desire to destroy and renew, fear that an enemy may gain the upper hand, the desire for revenge — all have been important motivators as Berkowitz, Kull, Waite, and Quester have pointed out in their essays in this work. There is even the possibility, as Freud and Mumford have suggested, that advanced civilizations, insofar as they inhibit the direct expression of various kinds of aggression, can create individuals who are quite susceptible to demagogic appeals, thus permitting the expression of these emotions against outside targets, legitimated as the "enemy."

Under the sway of these forces, the possibility of death and the destruction of one's home is not apt to be the deterrent one might think. It is true, as Anthony Kellett has pointed out in this volume, that most people, when they are in the actual battlefield situation, find it very difficult to kill or face the concrete possibility of their own death, and must be sustained in their activities by prior indoctrination, specially trained leaders and peer group pressures. Civilians who become the objects of bombing and other attacks, as Quester and Katz note, suffer and respond in ways that suggest that they clearly do not like war. Anticipation of the fear and pain, however, are not the prevailing emotions when people make the decision to go to war and for those who do not directly suffer the consequences. As the herald noted in Euripides' "The Suppliant Women,"

When the people vote on war, nobody reckons
On his own death; it is too soon; he thinks.
Some other man will meet that wretched fate
But if death faced him when he cast his vote,
Hellas would never perish from battle-madness.[15]

The root of this denial, as Janis and Mann, Lebow, and other contemporary social scientists have suggested, is based on the human need to avoid dissonance and/or anxiety. Buttressing the alternative preferred for the gains it might bring, human beings often refuse to confront the costs of their enterprise.

Crises, as we have seen, are particularly apt to elicit nonrational forces. Individuals have difficulties in making rational choices, as Rapoport notes, in any situation where multiple values are at stake. In such situations, simplistic assumptions that more is better are likely to distort the evaluation process. When one has little time to process crucial information, and the level of stress is very high, these problems are compounded. The result, as Holsti shows in this volume, is the intensification of proclivities toward tunnel vision, rigidity, and the mismanagement of the situation. Fear and/or aggressive feelings that are apt to be elicited in such situations can make the discovery of a peaceful solution to the crises even more difficult to reach.

Decisions to go to war, in short, are not simply rooted in competing national interests and/or the existence of competing ideologies. Because these choices are more deeply rooted in human organizational forms and psychological proclivities, one cannot simply assume that with changes in technology and the disappearance of certain ideological differences a whole new era will be attained.

Yet, the analyses provided in this volume does provide us with grounds for hope that great power wars can be avoided in the foreseeable future and other conflicts diminished in number. There is no instinct for aggression as Berkowitz has noted; and the aggression that does arise, for one reason or another, need not be expressed in the form called war. Various cultures, as we have also suggested, differ in their proclivities to initiate war. Their basic values, their images of their place in the world, and the nature of their political leadership will influence their choices. Thus cultures in which many individuals are polarized around either their destructive impulses or their need to identify with and preserve established structures, as Steven Kull suggests, may be most inclined to embrace violence as a means of transcendence. The values of the few tribal cultures that refuse to go to war suggests other possibilities as Sir Geoffrey Gorer has suggested. Perhaps a greater emphasis on the satisfaction of concrete pleasures and less emphasis on the attainment of heroic masculine roles would diminish the attraction to violence.

The issue of how major moral transformations within a given culture are wrought and whether or not one might do things to bring them about in several cultures simultaneously is one we shall not attempt to deal with here.[16] Yet, even if we assume that most people remain psychologically pretty much the same as they are now, there are two factors at work that could make major power warfare less likely. First, the tendency to buttress a preferred option is not absolute, as we have seen. Cognitive frameworks, as Glad and Taber have shown, may be rooted in interests and needs and resistant to change. Yet strong, countervailing evidence that commitment to those frames will cost one dearly in terms of other needs and interests foregone may lead to alterations in those frames. Some adaptations, as we have seen in "Limited War and Learning," can go beyond mere attempts to avoid pain to analytical adaptations that enable decision makers to anticipate consequences not yet felt. Second, as Kull has suggested in "Perceptions in the Nuclear Arms Race," when people face massive threats, they prefer to think they can take meaningful action to reduce the threat. When leaders offer up illusory programs to meet that need for action, many people will follow them. But it is also true that a leadership offering realistic, step-by-step programs for confronting and managing some of the unique problems these weapons offer could probably win an even more enthusiastic following.

There are already some promising developments along these lines. Nuclear weapons are potentially so much more destructive than traditional weapons of war that the fear of their actual employment has provided a strong motive to reassess traditional military doctrines. The view that arms can be used to pursue honor, power, security, and other goods is countered by a growing body of knowledge suggesting that the employment of these weapons could destroy the national goals sought, possibly even the nation itself. Moreover, as Kull has shown, most people are aware of how damaging these weapons would be.

Contemporary deterrence strategy, as noted in "Dilemmas of Deterrence" in this work, was in its origins a sophisticated straddle between two basic values. One could use nuclear weapons to secure the traditional goals obtained through arms by threatening to use these new weapons, but one would not have to pay the price by actually having to do so. It was a straddle, however, that really never resolved the basic dilemmas. For threats to be credible, one had to make commitments of one sort or another to assure that they would be actually employed should deterrence fail. But deterrence, given the past experience of nations in misreading each other's signals and their problems in managing crises, might very well fail. The result in this instance is that one has in effect made a choice for enormous self-destruction, though the choice has been made at an earlier moment in time when the response was programmed in ways to make it more or less automatic.

The attempt to resolve this difficulty by suggesting that nuclear weapons could be so controlled and limited in their impact that they remain useful weapons of influence ignores recent experiences with limited war, as well as the unique nature of nuclear weapons systems. It is possible of course, as Quester and Sederberg note, that an attack could be limited to a few military targets in geographically circumscribed areas. Yet, as Glad and Rosenberg show in their analysis of the American experience in Korea, domestic political and psychological factors are apt to create pressures on the political leadership to escalate the level of conflict. The political leaders themselves, having committed their energies and reputations to such policies, as Milburn and Christie's study of the Vietnam War suggest, are very likely going to find it difficult to cut their losses when that might appear to be the rational course to take. Nations generally, as Pillar has shown, have great difficulty in making the political and psychological shifts requisite to ending wars that they cannot win. In addition to these problems, as Peter Sederberg shows in this volume, strategic and technical-operational control problems specific to nuclear weapons would compound the control problem. With the use of nuclear weapons, one of the most important remaining markers for limiting a war has been passed (i.e., conventional vs. nuclear). Attacks against the command and control center of the other side would eliminate the possibility of deliberate control by that side. The need for centralized control to prevent "fools" from going off on their own requires a smart and centralized system that is inevitably vulnerable.

Anything beyond a few small demonstration attacks, moreover, would cause more physical and human destruction than any known disaster of the past. Even conservative counterforce attacks, as Arthur Katz suggests, would result in direct physical damage that through synergistic effects would spread throughout agriculture, industry, and the medical and other social systems. Recovery efforts, as the analysis of past disaster studies suggest, would be impeded by the massive social disorganization and the demoralization and apathy of human beings that would result. In short, the nuclear wars most likely to occur, including those counterforce attacks that simply target the weapons of the other side, would issue in costs so severe that they would far outstrip conceivable gains.

The leaders of the major powers, despite their formal plans for employing nuclear weapons in certain contingencies, have shown a certain appreciation of the above probabilities in their reluctance to get involved in direct confrontations with each other. The fear of Russian intervention in the Korean war was a powerful force contributing to American limitation in that engagement, as we have seen. The concern with Chinese intervention played a similar role in the Vietnam war, as Berman has noted.[17] During the Cuban missile crises, as Blight has observed, leaders on both sides backed off from the more confrontational stances recommended by some of their advisors because of an "overpowering fear" that they could get into a process in which things would get out of control, spiraling in a holocaust.[18] At the height of the crisis Robert McNamara led the American decision makers in the ExComm group into the contemplation of what a nuclear war would be like. In that same meeting, President Kennedy, himself, pushed the discussion in the direction of considering what the Russian might do if the United States refused to make any concessions to their concerns.[19] Though we know less about what was going on behind the Kremlin wall, Khrushchev's fears were evident in the long emotional letter he sent Kennedy at the height of the crisis. The forces pulling on each end of the "knot of war" he exhorted must "relax" rather than "tighten" their grip on the catastrophe of thermonuclear war.[20] In short, Robert Jervis has pointed out, "with the penalty for blundering into war so great, even bold and foolish decision makers behave cautiously."[21]

For some political and intellectual leaders these fears have led neither to policy paralysis nor rigid denial. Local conflicts, they realize, must be managed so they do not escalate into big power military encounters. Crises in which the nuclear powers face each other eyeball to eyeball should be avoided altogether. Perhaps the most important insight consists of the understanding that nations must take steps to avoid getting into situations which could spin out of control, that they must make advance preparation for curbing and channeling the political and psychological currents that might otherwise sweep them into war.

Kennedy, for example, came out of the Cuban missile crisis, convinced, as Holsti has pointed out, that "you can't have too many of those." One tangible manifestation of such efforts was the development of the Washington-Moscow "hotline," an idea which, after years of languishing on the agenda in the face of opposition from both capitals, was finally brought to fruition by the 1962 crisis. In Kennedy's subsequent announcement that the United States would unilaterally halt nuclear missile testing in the atmosphere, he initiated a series of cooperative interactions eventuating in the signing of the Test Ban Treaty in August 1963.[22] GRIT was the policy he followed, though he probably opted for that approach out of his own political instincts rather than from any descriptions of how that process might work.[23] Old-fashioned diplomacy also was resorted to from time to time in an effort to limit the arms races between the super powers. The SALT Agreements were one undertaking along these lines. Other efforts were engaged in to neutralize countries previously subjected to big power competition or to permit one side to disengage from an area to which it has been committed without a loss of face. The resolution of the Middle Eastern crisis of 1973, Blechman and Hart have argued, was motivated by such concerns.[24]

The most promising developments, however, have arisen since Mikhail Gorbachev's dramatic entry onto the world political stage. In his "new thinking" he has challenged the very way national political leaders have traditionally thought about the world and their place in it. He has outlined the problems inherent in zero-sum definitions of national security interests and the reliance on coercive diplomacy and threats. He has emphasized the need for diplomacy to deal with the threat nuclear weapons present to both the United States and the USSR and delineated the barriers to progress along these lines presented by established images of the nature of the world (i.e., what he calls "false consciousness") and the proclivity of nations to stereotype the enemy. He has been sensitive to the importance of the changing environment in redefining national interests as well as the importance of understanding human psychology to be successful in adapting to that new environment.

To demonstrate these points, let us look at several of Gorbachev's early statements on these matters. In December 1984, shortly before his ascent to the post of General Secretary of the Communist Party, he argued that a nation cannot build its security "at the cost of causing detriments to the security of others." Soviet goals, he proclaimed, are to promote — through cooperation with others — the settlement of extant conflicts and crises, the prevention of war, a halt to the arms race, and eventual disarmament. To secure these objectives, the USSR he proclaimed, is prepared to go as far toward the Western partners in diplomatic talks "as they will come to meet us."[25] National security, he stated in an interview with the editor of *Pravda*, can no longer be forwarded by measures to secure a military advantage over the other. The only way to attain such ends is through a cooperative effort to secure a "general security." Confrontation between the United States and the USSR is not an "inborn defect" but an "anomaly" and there is nothing "inevitable about its continuation." The Strategic Defense Initiative, however, is not really a "space shield" as its proponents proclaim, but a "space sword."[26] Recent technological developments, he noted in an interview on French television, has led the world to a point where we must embark on a new adventure to keep events from getting "out of control." The major powers, having a responsibility for the "fate of the world," must do something about it. Serious talk is difficult, however, because of the "militarization of political consciousness." People find it disadvantageous to see things as they really are.[27]

Gorbachev delineated the psychological barriers to progress in the arms limitation talks in an interview with American journalists. "Supergladiators," with their attempts to secure through "deft blows" an "extra point" in their "bout" make it difficult to reach any agreement. Abusive words do not help. "Why stage noisy shows and transfer the methods of domestic political struggles to the relations between two nuclear powers?" To end the impasse in the arms negotiations talks, it is necessary to break out of "vicious circles." The statements by some Americans that nuclear war must not be waged and cannot be won provides a basis for hope. Because the world is on the verge of a race in space, substantive talks cannot be delayed. It is "too great a luxury for the leaders of the Soviet Union and the United States to go to Geneva merely to get acquainted and then admire Lake Geneva and the Swiss Alps."[28]

In line with this "new thinking" Gorbachev also has undertaken several diplomatic initiatives. In April 1985, shortly after becoming General Secretary of the Communist Party, he declared a moratorium on the deployment of intermediate range nuclear missiles, suggesting that the United States make a similar gesture of good will. In late July that same year, he announced a unilateral moratorium on nuclear testing for several months, and suggested that the freeze could be extended if the United States were to take similar action. In January 1986, he again extended the freeze in an effort to promote a climate favorable to a comprehensive test ban treaty and a ban on space weapons.[29]

In his subsequent arms limitation proposals, moreover, he made a series of concessions to the American position. His proposal for the reduction of intermediate range missiles in Europe was based on America's zero option offered in 1981. The acceptance of on-site inspection, of the exclusion of British and French nuclear forces from the INF agreement (provided London and Paris agree that they would not expand or modernize their forces), the unrestricted deployment of sea launched cruise missiles — all were major concessions to the United States. Even the Soviet suggestion that defensive systems could be researched was a compromise between their earlier position that all research and development on the weapons should be banned and the Reagan administration's stance that it was committed to building the SDI.[30]

The specific bargaining techniques Gorbachev has employed correspond, in many respects, to the recipes for successful diplomacy forwarded by psychologically oriented bargaining experts such as Roger Fisher, William Ury, and Dean Pruitt. These moves are being delineated in a more detailed study to appear at a later date.[31] Suffice it to say at this point that he has employed new formulas in an effort to break up prior rigid stands. Issues have been separated so that progress on some matters may be achieved. Threats which could have intensified American defensiveness have been avoided for the most part, replaced by straightforward expressions of the measures he sees necessary to protect Soviet interests. In presenting his specific proposals, moreover, he has emphasized the development of objective standards, avoiding for the most part ideological statements and emotionally laden matters which could threaten the self-esteem of American leaders and people.[32]

Initially, many Americans, employing worst-case scenarios interpreted Gorbachev's statements, proposals, and strategic moves as simple propaganda attempts to undercut the American nuclear advantages and drive a wedge between the United States and its European allies.[33] For some time, the U.S. policy response, as Robert McNamara has argued, was not as responsive and creative as it might have been.[34] Nevertheless, Gorbachev's persistence has paid off and the United States, at the time of this writing, has joined with the USSR in various attempts to reduce the possibilities of continued political and nuclear confrontations between them. The INF treaty providing for the elimination of intermediate-range missiles in Europe has been signed and the prospects are good for significant reductions in long-range strategic weapons as well as conventional forces in Europe. After the Soviet Union announced that it would pull its troops out of Afghanistan, the two powers were able to mediate an agreement for the withdrawal of those troops and act as guarantors of a neutral Afghan state. Indeed, as McGeorge Bundy has recently argued, the superpowers for the first time are in open agreement on the futility of nuclear war.[35]

New measures also have been adopted to decrease the likelihood that crises might occur inadvertently and/or accidentally spin out of control. These include steps to facilitate accurate communication during crises. In 1984 the hotline between the two countries had been upgraded to permit the nearly instant transmission of maps, charts, photographs, and other important crises-pertinent information. In 1987 the United States and the Soviet Union agreed to set up Nuclear Risk Reduction Centers in each country, providing a 24-hour diplomatic channel for monitoring information on arms movements, missile launchings, and other such matters. The next year a U.S.-Soviet military group was formed to consider ways of averting undue superpower military confrontation.[36]

Confidence building approaches have been employed by both major powers. American-Soviet scientific and military exchanges have been resumed. Scientists from the two countries, for example, have jointly monitored nuclear tests in an effort to check the relative accuracy of American and Soviet methods for measuring the yield of underground nuclear explosions. Top level military leaders have visited military installations in each country.

More work remains to be done in the future. Offensive systems which create incentives to strike first are destabilizing and should be replaced with systems which enable states to ride out crises.[37] The Soviets have had a legitimate concern about the Strategic Defense Initiative along these lines in that it could be used for offensive purposes (e.g. the destruction of the enemy's information gathering satellites and communication systems). Forward movement, however, is possible even in this direction. The USSR eventually decided to go along with the American insistence on the funding of SDI research in an effort to move forward on other arms control measures. Moreover, the United States at the time of this writing, is quietly dropping any plans for a major deployment program, commiting itself only to a modest development program.[38] In these circumstances, formal agreements to limit a project that has become symbolically important to both sides, albeit in different ways, may not be necessary.

A test ban treaty and a modified freeze, as Admiral Gayler suggests, could further contribute to nuclear stability by checking the race toward new weapons and technologies.[39] Joint pledges not to resort to nuclear weapons in the defense of Europe, as George Kennan, Robert McNamara, McGeorge Bundy, and Gerard Smith suggested in 1982 might be a good idea.[40] The Soviet Union has offered to engage in such a pledge. Though the United States government has rejected such pledges up to the time of this writing, recent advances in conventional arms negotiations and the decline of Soviet power in Eastern Europe may make that proposal more palatable in the future.

The major powers, too, might agree to specific rules for competing in particular regions in the third world. To be effective, as Alexander George has noted, they must reflect the relative interests of each side and offer techniques for compromise, thereby limiting the incentive of the other side to escalate.[41] The Soviet Union, in its renunciation of the Brezhnev doctrine has already contributed to some advances along these lines. The Soviet Union's announcement that it would pull its troops out of Afghanistan and the agreement of the two powers to the creation of a neutral Afghan state is another positive development along these lines.

For the conflicts which remain, it would best to replace confrontational strategies with mixed strategies in which cooperative behavior is rewarded and non-cooperative behavior punished. The tit-for-tat strategy, as Robert Axelrod's work suggests, can provide incentives for parties that do not really trust each other to cooperate in prisoner's dilemma games over a series of encounters. If one player opts for a cooperative strategy when he moves first and responds in kind to every subsequent move by the opponent, incentives are built into the system which maximize the values that both sides can attain.[42] When one party feels that it is dealing with another party not bent on aggression but inclined to worst-case analyses of its own motives, a modification of that approach may be most useful.

Gorbachev, as we have seen, managed to break through American mistrust of Soviet motives because he persisted in a series of cooperative moves, some of which did not bring at the beginning a positive diplomatic response.[43]

Eventually, the "madman problem" must be addressed. There does seem to be some screening process going on in most states which keeps the most destructive individuals out of the top political leadership and the most reckless proposals from being acted upon. To keep madmen from acting on their own, moreover, the control of access to command systems for launching nuclear warheads has been centralized in the major nuclear states. There remains, however, another chilling prospect that we really have not faced. A grandiose leader, as Waite has shown us, convinced that his powers are unlimited and harboring unconscious needs to destroy and be destroyed, can under certain conditions win command of a country and shape it in his own image. Certain kinds of sociopaths, moreover, can hide their insanity under the mask of normalcy and there is still a possibility that such a person could rise to power in some state, somewhere in the world at some time in the future.[44] To avoid the possibility that such an individual will ever have the ability to unleash a nuclear holocaust, the number of nations possessing such systems must be reduced and the destructive capability of any one system must be curtailed. For long-term survival, then, steps should be taken to curtail the spread of nuclear weapons to countries that do not yet have them. For those already possessing such weapons the goal should be a mutual and balanced reduction back to a minimal, retaliatory capability.

Between the United States and the USSR the developments outlined here seem to be issuing in a new moral climate. Cooperative solutions in prisoner's dilemma games, as Deborah Larson has pointed out, often are pursued because both parties think it the proper and morally correct way to respond.[45] If the process persists over time, the United States and the USSR could move to a situation where war between them is seen as highly unlikely, just as it is now in the relations between America and any of the European powers. New political alliances and new political conflicts may come to the fore. But if these two powers remain united in their commitment to a just and peaceful world, they may be able to mediate these new conflicts and prevent new kinds of wars from arising.

In short a clear understanding of what nuclear war would really be like, if combined with a deeper understanding of the human psychological vulnerabilities which can get them on the slippery slope to that war, can provide the incentives for the building of new understandings, new arrangements, new processes, and a political climate that will minimize the possibilities of major power war.[46] People may still strive for glory, revenge, and gain. They may even fantasize that destruction toward others could bring about a better world. But the world we are in makes it clearer than it has often been in the past what the price would be for acting on those inclinations. "All people want to live, nobody wants to die," Gorbachev proclaimed in his interview with American journalists in 1985. He may have overstated the desire for self-preservation somewhat. But he was right when he said that for those so disposed, "it is necessary to muster political courage and stop the developing sinister process."[47]

Notes

1. Francis Fukuyama, "The End of History?" *The National Interest* (Summer 1989).

2. John Mueller, *Retreat From Doomsday: The Obsolescence of Major War* (New York: Basic Books, 1989).

3. Alcibiades also suggested that the Athenians were propelled by a general social law. If a nation does not expand its domain, he proclaimed, it is in danger of becoming the victim of others so inclined. According to Thucydides, Alcibiades, himself, was motivated by a desire to secure a command and through success on the battlefield reclaim his reputation, enhance his glory, and increase his personal wealth. P. A. Brunt, ed., *Thucydides: The Peloponnesian Wars*, trans. by Benjamin Jowett (New York: Twayne, 1963), 196-197.

4. B. Altemeyer, *Enemies of Freedom* (San Francisco; Jossey-Bass, 1988), 308-309.

5. Mueller, *Retreat from Doomsday*, 7, 67, 229.

6. Ibid., 257.

7. Graham T. Allison, *Essence of Decision: Explaining the Cuban Missile Crisis* (Boston: Little, Brown, 1971), 198, 206.

8. J. G. Blight, J. S. Nye, and D. A. Welch, "The Lessons of the Cuban Missile Crisis Twenty Five Years Later," *Foreign Affairs*, 65, 1 (Fall 1987): 170-188.

9. Stephen Ambrose, *Rise to Globalism* 5th ed. (New York: Penguin, 1988), 200-201; Thomas Wolfe, *Soviet Strategy at the Crossroads* (Cambridge, MA: Harvard University Press, 1964).

10. There is no evidence that Amory's recommendations were taken seriously. See Kenneth Kitts and Betty Glad, "Crisis Management: The Eisenhower Administration and the Hungarian Rebellion of 1956," forthcoming. See end of this chapter for discussion of circumstances under which extreme solutions are apt to become policy.

11. Mueller, *Retreat from Doomsday*, 228-229.

12. Themistocles and Pericles were identified as Athenian leaders of this sort. See P. A. Brunt, introduction to *Thucydides: The Peloponnesian Wars*, xxviii. In the unedited text, I: 138; II: 65.

13. Thucydides, *The Peloponessian Wars*, 105.

14. David Grene and Richmond Lattimore, eds., "The Suppliant Women," *The Complete Greek Tragedies: Euripides II*, Vol. 6 (New York: Random House, 1958), 414.

15. Euripides, "The Suppliant Women," 422.

16. For the debate between various psychologists on how they might best influence nuclear policies, see J. G. Blight, "Toward a Policy-Relevant Psychology of Avoiding Nuclear War: Lessons for Psychologists from the Cuban Missile Crisis," *American Psychologist*, 42, 1 (January 1987): 12-29. His argument that psychologists have been too removed from the concerns of policymakers to have impact is critiqued in several short statements by Michael Intriligator, Linden Nelson, Walter B. Earle, Robert Holt, and M. Brewster Smith in the "Comments" section of the *American Psychologist*, 43, 4 (April 1988): 318-326; for Blight's rejoinder in the same issue, see "Must the Psychology of Avoiding Nuclear War Remain Free and Insignificant?" 326-329.

17. Larry Berman, *Planning a Tragedy: The Americanization of the War in Vietnam* (New York: Norton, 1982), 46.

18. Blight, "Must the Psychology of Avoiding Nuclear War Remain Free and Insignificant?" 329.

19. McGeorge Bundy, ed., trans. J. G. Blight, "26 October 1962: Transcripts of the Meetings of the Excom," *International Security*, 12, 3 (Winter 1987-1988), 72-73, 37, 48, 59.

20. Quoted in Mueller, *Retreat from Doomsday*, 153.

21. See Robert Jervis, *The Illogic of American Nuclear Strategy* (Ithaca, NY: Cornell University Press, 1985), 155. For the value of U.S.-Soviet mediation of conflict in the Third World see Alexander

George, ed., *Managing U.S.-Soviet Rivalry: Problems of Crisis Prevention (Boulder, CO: Westview, 1983), 1-15.*

22. Amitai Etzioni, "The Kennedy Experiment," *Western Political Quarterly*, 20, 2 (June 1967): 361-380.

23. See Charles E. Osgood, "The GRIT Strategy," *Bulletin of the Atomic Scientists* (May 1980): 58-60; and his *An Alternative to War or Surrender* (Urbana: University of Illinois Press, 1962).

24. Barry Blechman and Douglas Hart, "The Political Utility of Nuclear Weapons: The 1973 Middle East Crisis," in *Strategy and Nuclear Deterrence*, ed. Steven E. Miller (Princeton, NJ: Princeton University Press, 1984), 273-297. For the value of third party mediation in the resolution of regional disputes, see Jeffery Z. Rubin, "Some Roles and Functions of a Mediator," *Dynamics of Third Party Intervention: Kissinger in the Middle East* (New York: Praeger, 1981), 3-43, 288-292.

25. Speech to the British parliament, published in *Pravda* (19 December 1984): 1st ed., 4. The translations for all the citations to Gorbachev's speech appearing in *Pravda* were provided by Margaret Hermann of Ohio State University.

26. Interview with the editor of *Pravda*, in *Pravda* (8 April 1985): 1st ed., 1.

27. He also noted that Russians live in the European house and that they want to develop communication in that house. Interview on French television. Speech of 30 September 1985, as published in *Pravda* (2 October 1985), 1.

28. Interview with *Time Magazine*, printed in *Pravda* (2 September 1985) 1st ed., 1, 2. For similar critiques of coercive diplomacy by American academics, see Patrick M. Morgan, "Saving Face for the Sake of Deterrence," in *Psychology and Deterrence,* eds. Robert Jervis, Richard Ned Lebow, and Janice Gross Stein (Baltimore, MD: Johns Hopkins University Press, 1985), 125-152.

29. See Matthew Evangelista, "The New Soviet Approach to Security," *World Policy*, 3, 4 (Fall 1986): 561-599.

30. For the extent of the Soviet concessions, ibid.

31. Betty Glad, "Mikhail Gorbachev, "Beyond Grit," forthcoming.

32. For these "recipes," see Roger Fisher and William Ury, *Getting to Yes: How to Negotiate Agreement Without Giving* (Boston: Houghton Mifflin, 1981). Dean G. Pruitt, *Negotiation Behavior* (New York: Academic Press, 1981). Hans J. Morgenthau's earlier recommendations for successful diplomacy anticipates many of the recommendations of the political psychologists. Thus he argues that one should avoid a crusading spirit, distinguish central from marginal interests, see the issues from the opponents' point of view, and allow that opponent to concessions in face-saving ways. See Hans Morgenthau with Kenneth W. Thompson, *Politics Among Nations: The Struggle for Power and Peace*, 6th ed. (New York: Alfred A. Knopf, 1985) 584-594; see also Richard Ned Lebow, "Conclusions," in Jervis et al., *Psychology and Deterrence*, 203-232.

33. For details of this response, see Betty Glad, "Mikhail Gorbachev, Beyond Grit," forthcoming.

34. Robert S. McNamara, "Out of the Cold," *Newsweek* (4 September 1989): 35-41.

35. McGeorge Bundy, "Ending a Common Danger," *New York Times Magazine* (20 August 1989): 54-71, passim.

36. Webster Stone, "Moscow's Still Holding: Twenty-Five Years on the Hot Line," *New York Times Magazine* (18 September 1988): 58ff. The ideas for many of these measures may have come from the academic world. See W. Ury and R. Smoke, *Beyond the Hotline: Controlling a Nuclear Crisis* (Cambridge, MA: Nuclear Negotiation Project, Harvard Law School, 1984). For a review of this literature, see James Thompson, *Psychological Aspects of Nuclear War* (Chichester: British Psychological Society and John Wiley & Sons, 1985), 101-102.

37. See McGeorge Bundy, "Arms Control, Not Competition," *New York Times Magazine* (5 April 1987): 46-47.

38. For the argument that a successful strategic defense program would promote instability in the arms race, see Steven J. Brams, "Deterrence Versus Defense: A Game-Theoretic Model of Star Wars," *International Studies Quarterly*, 32, 1 (March 1988): 3-28. For the argument that the ability to retaliate is a key to the cooperative solution in the deterrence games, but that a probabilistic retaliation may suffice, see Steven J. Brams and D. Marc Kilgour, "The Path to Stable Deterrence," in *Dynamic Models*

of International Conflict, eds. Urs Luterbacher and Michael D. Ward (Boulder, CO: Lynne Rienner, 1985), 11-25.

39. N. Gayler, "How to Break the Momentum of the Nuclear Arms Race," *New York Times Magazine* (25 April 1982), 48-88.

40. McGeorge Bundy, George F. Kennan, Robert S. McNamara, and Gerard Smith, "Nuclear Weapons and the Atlantic Alliance," *Foreign Affairs,* 60, 4 (Spring 1982): 753-768. For a somewhat different proposal to reduce the likelihood of first nuclear use in Europe through a change in force structures and operational plans, see Morton Halperin, *Nuclear Fallacy: Dispelling the Myth of Nuclear Strategy* (Cambridge, MA: Ballinger, 1987), 95-103.

41. Alexander L. George, "Crisis Prevention Reexamined," in Alexander George, ed., *Managing U.S.-Soviet Rivalry,* 365-98.

42. For an analysis showing the nature of such moves in stochastic games see, Robert Axelrod, *The Evolution of Cooperation* (New York: Basic Books, 1984), 20-21.

43. Betty Glad, "Mikhail Gorbachev: Beyond Grit," forthcoming.

44. For this personality type, see Hervey M. Cleckley, *The Mask of Sanity: An Attempt to Clarify Some Issues About the So-Called Psycho-Pattern Personality,* 3rd. ed. (St. Louis, MO: Mosby, 1955).

45. Deborah Welch Larson, "Game Theory and the Psychology of Reciprocity," (mimeograph, Columbia University, 29 October 1986).

46. For studies showing how the major powers can contribute positively to the settlement of disputes in various regions of the world, see William Zartman, "The Strategy of Preventive Diplomacy in Third World Conflicts," in Alexander George, ed., *Managing U.S.-Soviet Rivalry,* 341-63; Jeffrey Z. Rubin, "Some Roles and Functions of a Mediator," *Dynamics of Third Party Intervention: Kissinger in the Middle East* (New York: Praeger, 1981).

47. Interview with *Time Magazine,* published in *Pravda* (2 September 1985): 1st ed., 1, 2.

Index

About the Contributors

LEONARD BERKOWITZ is the Vilas Research Professor in Psychology at the University of Wisconsin-Madison. He has been a Fellow at the Center for Advanced Study in the Behavioral Sciences and received Distinguished Scientist awards from both the American Psychological Association and the Society for Experimental Social Psychology. His special interests are in aggressive and helpful behavior. His books include *Aggression: A Social-Psychological Analysis* (1962). He has been the editor of the multivolume series *Advances in Experimental Social Psychology*, Vols. 1-22 (1964-1989) and *A Survey of Social Psychology* (1980, 1986).

DANIEL J. CHRISTIE is Associate Professor of Psychology and Research Associate of the Mershon Center at Ohio State University. He is principal investigator of a research program supported by the Ohio Department of Mental Health which is designed to evaluate school-based initiatives on conflict management and the reduction of in-group/out-group biases. His research on children, youth, and nuclear issues has appeared in *The Bulletin of the Atomic Scientists, Journal of Psychology*, and in an edited volume on *Children's Stress*. His interest in international relations is reflected in a number of papers he has coauthored with Thomas Milburn, many of which will appear in a volume on "Psychological Means of Improving Relations Between States." They have published their research on the use of positive inducements as a means of inter-nation influence in *Political Psychology*.

BETTY GLAD is Professor of Government and International Affairs at the University of South Carolina, and previously taught at the University of Illinois. She has been a National Endowment for the Humanities Senior Fellow, a guest scholar at the Brookings Institution, President of the Presidency Research Group of the American Political Science Association and Vice President of the International Society for Political Psychology. Her books include *Key Pittman: The Tragedy of a Senate Insider; Jimmy Carter: In Search of the Great White House*; and *Charles Evans Hughes and the Illusions of Innocence: A Study in American Diplomacy*.

OLE R. HOLSTI is the George V. Allen Professor of Political Science at Duke University. He has written numerous articles and books including *Crisis, Escalation, War* (1972), *Enemies in Politics* (1967, with David D. Finlay and Richard R.

Fagan), and *American Leadership in World Affairs: Vietnam and the Breakdown of Consensus* (1984, with James Rosenau). He is Past President of the International Studies Association, and in 1988 he won the Nevitt Sanford Award of the International Society for Political Psychology for "distinguished contributions to political psychology."

ARTHUR M. KATZ is the author of an important book titled *Life After Nuclear War: The Economic and Social Impacts of Nuclear Attacks on the United States*. Earlier he did a major study for the Joint Committee on Defense Production of the U.S. Congress. He is a chemist currently employed by the U.S. Department of Energy.

ANTHONY KELLETT is an analyst with the Directorate of Social and Economic Analysis at National Defence Headquarters in Canada. His works include *Combat Motivation* (1982), the first book written in a number of years dealing with the problems of combat motivation; it was recently translated into Portuguese and published in Brazil. He also has written several chapters and articles dealing with terrorism, and military organization and behavior. He served as a Captain in the Royal Canadian Hussars (Montreal) from 1970 to 1977.

STEVEN KULL is a Senior Research Associate at Global Outlook in Palo Alto, California and author of a recently published book, *Minds at War: Nuclear Reality and the Inner Conflicts of Defense Policymakers*, based on an extensive series of interviews he carried out with defense policymakers in the United States and the Soviet Union. He was trained as a clinical psychologist and practiced for more than 10 years. He has been a Fellow at the Center for International Security at Stanford University and a Social Science Research Council MacArthur Fellow at the Department of Political Science at Stanford University. His articles have appeared in such publications as *Foreign Policy*, the *Los Angles Times*, the *Bulletin of Atomic Scientists*, and *Political Psychology*. He recently received the Erik H. Erikson Award of the International Society of Political Psychology. Currently he is working on a study of Soviet "New Thinking" on international security.

THOMAS W. MILBURN is the Mershon Professor of Psychology and Public Policy at Ohio State University. He is the author of *On the Nature of Threat; A Social Psychological Analysis*, and *A Study of Leader Behavior in the Effective Management of Organizational Crises*, Final Report to the U.S. Army Research Institute for the Behavioral and Social Sciences by the Ohio State University Research Foundation, July 1980. In 1989 he was a Fulbright Scholar at the University of Canterbury at Christchurch, New Zealand, where he conducted a study of perceptions and attitudes of New Zealand academics and officials toward the Cold War.

PAUL R. PILLAR is an analyst for the Central Intelligence Agency and the author of *Negotiating Peace: War Termination as a Bargaining Process*. He received his M.A. and his Ph.D. in Politics from Princeton University, and served as a U.S. Army officer (1971-1973), including Vietnam.

GEORGE H. QUESTER is Professor and Chairman of the Department of Government and Politics at the University of Maryland, and has been a Professor at the National War College, Department of Military Strategy. He has acted as Rapporteur at the Harvard-MIT Arms Control Seminar (1963-1966), Chairman of the Government Department at Cornell University, and has been a Fellow at the Center for Advanced Study on the Behavioral Sciences (1974-1975). He has written numerous articles and books including *American Foreign Policy: The Lost Consensus* (1982); *Offense and Defense in the International System* (1977); *Sea Power in the 1970s* (1975); *The Politics of Nuclear Proliferation* (1973); *Nuclear Diplomacy: The First Twenty-Five Years* (1970); and *Deterrence Before Hiroshima* (1960).

ANATOL RAPOPORT is Professor of Peace and Conflict Studies at the University of Toronto. He is a Fellow of the American Academy of Arts and Sciences. He received the Lenz International Peace Research Prize in 1975 and has authored numerous books and articles including *Strategy and Conscience* (1964) and *Mathematical Models in the Social and Behavioral Sciences* (1983). His other works include *Fights, Games and Debates* (1960); *Two-Person Game Theory* (1966); *N-Person Game Theory* (1970); *The Big Two* (1971); *Conflict in Man-Made Environment* (1974); and *The Origins of Violence* (1989). His most recent work is *Decision Theory and Decision Behaviour* (1989).

J. PHILIPP ROSENBERG is Professor of Political Science at Blackburn College. He has written extensively in the area of the psychological dimension of the American foreign policy-making process. His publications include articles in such journals as the *Journal of Politics*, *Political Psychology*, *Presidential Quarterly*, and *Journal of Social Psychology*.

PETER C. SEDERBERG is Professor in the Department of Government and International Studies, University of South Carolina. His teaching and research interests include nuclear security issues and revolution and political violence. He has published five books and numerous articles and book chapters. His recent publications include *Nuclear Winter, Deterrence and the Prevention of Nuclear War* (1986), of which he was the editor and contributor; and *Terrorist Myths: Illusion, Rhetoric, and Reality* (1989). His current work includes research into alternative security regimes for the United States and the study of political transformation in South Africa.

CHARLES S. TABER received his Ph.D. in 1980 from the University of Illinois at Urbana-Champaign. He is Assistant Professor of Political Science at the State University of New York at Stony Brook. He has written "Power Capability Indexes in the Third World," in *Power in World Politics*, edited by Richard Stoll and Michael D. Ward (1989). Currently, he is working on computational models of U.S. foreign policy belief systems.

ROBERT G. L. WAITE is the Brown Professor of History Emeritus at Williams College. He is currently a Senior Fellow at the Center for the Humanities and the Social Sciences at Williams College. He received a Guggenheim Fellowship and is the author of several books including *Vanguard of Nazism: The Free Corp Movement in Post War Germany, 1918-1923* (1954); *The Psychopathic God: Adolf Hitler* (1978); and a forthcoming study, *The Kaiser and the Führer: A Comparative Study of Personality and Politics*.